# 501

## MUST-TAKE JOURNEYS

# 501
## MUST-TAKE JOURNEYS

**Bounty**
Books

**Publisher:** Polly Manguel

**Project Editor:** Emma Beare

**Publishing Assistant:** Sarah Marling

**Designer:** Ron Callow/Design 23

**Picture Researcher:** Vickie Walters

**Production Manager:** Neil Randles

**Production Assistant:** Gemma Seddon

First published in Great Britain in 2008 by
Bounty Books, a division of Octopus Publishing Group Limited
2-4 Heron Quays, London E14 4JP
www.octopusbooks.co.uk
Reprinted 2010
An Hachette UK Company
www.hachette.co.uk

A CIP catalogue record is available from the British Library

ISBN: 978-0-753715-92-5

Printed and bound in China

**Please note:** We now know that political situations arise very quickly and a city or country that
was quite safe a short time ago can suddenly become a 'no-go' area. Please check with the
relevant authorities before booking tickets and travelling if you think there could be a problem.

Where a journey crosses country borders, it appears in the chapter that relates to its starting point.

# Contents

# Introduction

Journeys – journeys to work, to school or university, to the theatre or cinema, to do the shopping or laundry or pick up the kids – most of us are taking journeys every day. We see the same old sights each time and mostly we let our brains work on automatic, failing to derive any pleasure from the actual trip, because we just don't expect to. Our most ardent wish, if ever expressed, would be for the journey to be over with just a click of the fingers. The destination is all.

Many sun-seeking holiday makers would also much rather reach their seaside holiday destination without the trials of the trip there – the queues at the airport, the flight, the walking, the traffic. Yet in recent years increasing numbers of people, though still not immune to the occasional lazy pleasures of beach life, have become fascinated by the variety of interests and challenges presented by all manner of different journeys. They have realized that to take a journey can enable them to have more unusual experiences, to encounter and interact with local peoples, to observe and explore new places, different cultures, historic landmarks and superb scenery.

There's an eclectic variety of fascinating journeys described in this book – some of them take only an hour or two to complete while others could last up to six months. Most modes of transport are covered: on foot, by bicycle, car, boat, train, plane, horse, mule and even dog sled. There are trips to be taken at different times of year, through mountains and valleys, jungles and pine forests, rivers and seas, from the snowy wastes of the Arctic Circle to the mind-numbing heat of the Sahara Desert. They encompass journeys taken for the extraordinary beauty of the landscape, to reach ancient monuments, to meet people living in remote regions and to see wildlife of all descriptions.

Whether it's canoeing down the Yukon, mountain trekking in Bulgaria, a boat trip up the Norwegian coast, a rail trip in the Himalayas, touring the Chilean vineyards or cycling in Northern Australia – there are journeys here to satisfy even the most jaded of travelling palates.

Some of the journeys – the walk along the Great Wall of China, or driving the famous US Route 66, or a camel trek from

Timbuktu on part of the old Salt Road – are well known classics; others are little known and rarely travelled. Some require feats of endurance and that you are at the very peak of fitness. On others you can relax in the lap of luxury with very little physical exertion: South Africa's famous Blue Train, for example, provides you with 5-star accommodation and haute cuisine as you travel from Cape Town to Pretoria and marvel through the window from the comfort of your carriage at the landscape, the elephants striding across the plains and the herds of giraffes and antelopes grazing peacefully before you. Quite a few of the journeys can be taken more or less on the spur of the moment; other very different types of journey in some distant land could involve months of planning.

There are all sorts of reasons for making a journey. You might want to see mysterious Mayan pyramids, or make a pilgrimage to an important religious site. You might want to feel at one with nature in part of the Canadian wilderness or simply walk an ancient trail beside a lake. Perhaps you are an active person, one whose idea of bliss is to trek through rainforest, or cycle in southern Italy – or you might want to keep the kids happy with a trip inland from a seaside resort. You may have a special interest: bird watching, whale watching, art, the Roman empire, food or wine – whatever your preferences, there is certain to be a journey to take that will fulfil your dream.

Having made your choice of journey, you should take the time to read and research it as thoroughly as possible. You need to be prepared, to take appropriate clothing and footwear, maps, medication, food and water, camping gear – anything you may need en route. While some journeys are easy, and you will never be far from help, others are seriously remote, and what you carry with you is desperately important.

Happily much of the time it's not a question of either the destination or the journey – you can have both! In many cases you have the opportunity to visit your chosen destination and have an exciting and interesting trip as well. The beautiful city of Luang Prabang in Laos is truly a joy to behold, but if you are able to reach there by gently travelling down the Mekong River from Huay Xai, then your whole experience of the visit will be much enhanced.

So have a good look through this book, find a journey that speaks to your soul – and get going.

# Around the World in 80 Days

Undoubtedly the most dramatic journey you can ever undertake – circumnavigating the world in 80 days, following in the footsteps of fiction's Phileas Fogg, created by 19th-century author Jules Verne, and TV globetrotter Michael Palin. This is definitely not a matter of booking long-distance flights that get you back to your starting point in a few days. Instead, you must follow Phileas Fogg's 45,000 km (28,000 mi) route as closely as possible, using only transport methods available in Jules Verne's time.

The journey starts outside the Reform Club in London's Pall Mall. To follow Palin's route, take a train to Folkestone, ferry to France and train to Venice via the Alps, Switzerland, Liechtenstein, and Austria. From there, a boat through the Corinth Canal takes in Greece, Crete and Egypt.

After boat-hopping down the Persian Gulf, visiting Saudi Arabia, Qatar and the United Arab Emirates, a week on a traditional sailing dhow brings you to Mumbai (Bombay), from whence a train across India leads to a sea passage to Singapore and on to Hong Kong. A railway marathon across China to Shanghai is followed by a ferry to Japan, and then a monotonous crossing of the Pacific on a container ship. The journey across the USA is by train. From New York another ship will return you to England and journey's end – Palin made it with a few hours to spare.

There's ample scope for planning an individual itinerary packed with plenty of interesting stops and fascinating sights. Though the basic methods of transport are boat and train, half the fun is finding alternative means of progress. For example, Phileas Fogg travelled by elephant and sledge, whilst Palin rode a camel and took a hot-air balloon trip. Not many have done it, because this really is the epic journey of a lifetime!

*TOP: Venice; MIDDLE: Sailing through the Corinth Canal; RIGHT: The Parthenon at the Acropolis in Athens; FAR RIGHT CLOCKWISE FROM TOP: The Great Pyramid of Giza; India Gate in Mumbai; The skyline of Singapore; A bullet train speeds past Mount Fuji; Hong Kong Harbour; A minaret amongst skyscrapers in Dubai*

**HOW:**
Various!
**WHEN TO GO:**
Any time you can arrange a very long vacation.
**TIME IT TAKES:**
80 days (if you don't fall behind schedule).
**HIGHLIGHTS:**
Venice – use a precious day to explore this special city, once a stop on another great journey – the 8,000-km (5,000-mi) Silk Road linking the Orient with the Mediterranean.
The Great Pyramid of Giza, near Cairo, and the enigmatic Sphinx – the former is the last survivor of Seven Wonders of the Ancient World.
Great Nicobar – this sparsely populated island is India's southernmost point, largely covered by a unique rainforest Biosphere Reserve.
Trying to emulate Michael Palin's big win at Hong Kong's spectacular Happy Valley racecourse.
**YOU SHOULD KNOW:**
Although many people associate travelling by hot-air balloon with *Around the World in Eighty Days*, this method of travel was never actually used by Phileas Fogg and his French valet Passepartout.

# AMERICAS AND THE CARIBBEAN

*A wall of yellow and green trees in front of a cloud-covered Mount Robson*

# Trans-Canada Train Journey

**HOW:**
By train
**DEPART:**
Halifax, NS
**WHEN TO GO:**
Year round, but schedules can be disrupted in winter (November to April)
**TIME IT TAKES:**
Plan your schedule and book tickets in advance. Currently it takes about six days with a long stopover in either Montreal or Toronto. If you want to see a lot of Canada allow two weeks and spend time in Montreal, Toronto, Jasper and Vancouver.
**HIGHLIGHTS:**
The Thousand Islands – the islands that gave you the dressing.
Old Montreal – fabulous, French and funky.
Mount Robson and Pyramid Falls – in the Rockies.
Vancouver – it really is as good as they say: the sea, mountains, excellent affordable eating and really friendly people.
**YOU SHOULD KNOW:**
The combination of harsh weather, 1950s rolling stock and the prevalence of mega-weight goods trains can make this a bumpy ride, but who needs sleep anyway when you're having such a good time?

There is no rule which states that crossing a whole continent will ever be easy and this journey certainly tests the mettle of the traveller. Nevertheless, the sights you see and the people you meet on this epic trip will stay in the memory for the rest of your life. Nearly all those who make the journey from Halifax to Vancouver do so for fun (flying is cheaper and quicker) – and this gives the whole experience a real party feel.

Completing the journey currently comprises three stages. The first from Halifax to Montreal takes you from the extremely picturesque Nova Scotia coast, through New Brunswick. Skirting the Appalachian Mountains, you are then transported to Montreal, the beating heart of French Canada. The second leg allows you to sample the most modern railway Canada has to offer. The Montreal to Toronto link feels strangely normal compared with the rest of the trip. Business people barely look up from their laptops as the train passes along the St Lawrence River, past the Thousand Islands and along the shore of Lake Ontario.

From Toronto, Canada's most modern of cities, you embark on the truly monumental part of the train ride. The seemingly endless forests of Northern Ontario eventually give way to wide open prairies as you cross the Continent's interior – the vastness of it all is quite breathtaking. After two nights on board, the train approaches the Rockies. Waterfalls and sheer rock faces heave in to view one after another and this is the time to grab a seat in the panoramic dome car. After this, Kamloops is the last major stop before arriving in Vancouver and your chance to experience the city often voted the 'World's Best Place to Live'.

# Fraser Discovery Route on the Rocky Mountaineer

**HOW:**
By train
**DEPART:**
Whistler, BC
**WHEN TO GO:**
The service only operates between mid-May and mid-October.
**TIME IT TAKES:**
Two days
**HIGHLIGHTS:**
Mount Robson – the Canadian Rockies may not be as tall as those south of the border, but you are looking at it from near sea level. Mount Robson is the biggest vertical rockface you will find anywhere on Earth.
The Fraser River – which in spring is one of the fastest flowing rivers in the world.
The chance to see bear, wolves and elk – and more – along the way.
Jasper – unspoilt by mass development and well preserved – it's an ideal town to end your journey and tarry for a while.
**YOU SHOULD KNOW:**
The service on board is first class, but it doesn't come cheap. However most people who have made this journey will tell you that there is no better way to spend the kids' inheritance…

If you could design your own railway journey, it would probably look something like this one. Opened in 2006, this latest addition to the Rocky Mountaineer experience offers the best service and the most spectacular scenery Canada has to offer. It even has the added benefit of stopping overnight so that you can get a good sleep and miss nothing that the Rockies have to offer.

Leaving the hustle and bustle of the ski resort of Whistler behind you and with a glass of champagne in hand, you travel eastbound through the rich farmland of the Pemberton Valley. It is time now to climb the stairs to the domed observation car as the train wends its way along the shores of Anderson and Seton Lakes, which are framed by the picturesque mountain scenery. Breathtaking views of the Fraser Canyon feed the eye as you near the improbably high Deep Creek Bridge. The train runs alongside the mighty Fraser River until it reaches the sleepy town of Quesnel where it stops for the night, allowing you to explore one of the Canadian interior's oldest towns and home to the world's largest gold pan.

The next morning your journey continues eastward to the main Canadian Rockies. Entering the Rocky Mountain Trench and the upper reaches of the Fraser River, you are surrounded by mountains on all sides. The route then leaves the Fraser River at Tête Jaune Cache, and climbs past majestic Mount Robson, the highest peak in the Canadian Rockies at 3,954 m (12,972 ft) and the highlight of the journey.

It is now time to put your watches forward one hour as the train crosses the top of the Yellowhead Pass and the border to the province of Alberta. The journey ends as the Rocky Mountaineer descends through Jasper National Park to the perfect little town of Jasper.

*Sunset over the Fraser River*

# The Skeena Train

*Fishing boats docked in Prince Rupert.*

Billed as Canada's best-kept secret, the 1160-km (721-mi) long Skeena Railway is probably the most scenic journey you can take in the whole of North America.

Taking passengers between Jasper National Park and Prince Rupert on the Pacific coast, it is more than just a tourist track. The railroad links many otherwise isolated communities and gives travellers a chance to view hidden Canada at first hand. This region is one of North America's last great wildernesses and it's sprinkled with tantalizing reminders of its rich First Nations history and the spirit of the pioneer.

Soon after leaving Jasper, the train passes Mount Robson and the Pyramid Falls, two of the most stunning sights the Rockies have to offer. The track then heads in a north-westerly direction, skirting the spectacular Columbia Mountains alongside the Fraser River and down to Prince George for an overnight hotel stop.

This sumptuous land of waterfalls, huge rivers, lakes and wilderness is home to bear, elk, wolves and moose and such is the gentle pace of the train that the driver often slows down for people to take photographs. The Story poles (or Totem poles) of the region offer great depictions of the area's fauna and often make good resting points for eagles scouring the landscape for prey.

The last leg of the journey, between the 'two Princes' takes you to ever more remote communities. There is ample opportunity for people-watching at the request stops on the way, recalling a golden era when the railway rolling into town was big news. Following the Skeena River, the train then reaches its final destination – Prince Rupert, gateway to Haida Gwai, northern Vancouver Island and Alaska.

**HOW:**
By train
**DEPART:**
Jasper, AB
**WHEN TO GO:**
The train operates year round, but snow can disrupt services any time between October and May.
**TIME IT TAKES:**
Two days with a compulsory overnight stop in Prince George.
**HIGHLIGHTS:**
The Rockies – the wow factor never goes away.
The chance to glimpse wildlife feeding and grazing on the riverbanks.
Stopping at small communities such as Dorreen (Pop 1) – and wondering if the passenger bought a return ticket...
The abundance of excellent First Nations art and culture.
**YOU SHOULD KNOW:**
It is important to book your hotel in Prince George in advance. It is also a good idea to ask around your fellow travellers to see if you can share a cab to your lodgings. Taxis and rooms are a scarce commodity when the train comes to town.

*Webster's Falls*

# The Bruce Trail

At 800 km (500 mi) the Bruce trail in Ontario is the oldest and longest marked trail in Canada, taking the hiker along the Niagara Escarpment from Niagara to the tip of the Bruce Peninsula. There are also about 300 km (187 mi) of additional side trails that link well with the Bruce. The iconic waterfalls at Niagara are a great place to start and having left with the sound of crashing water in your ears and ozone in your lungs, it is a short hike to the main trail proper.

This well-maintained trail, with its clear markings and efficiently run campgrounds is the most ambitious of projects. The nine chapters of the Bruce Trail Association work hard at protecting this UNESCO World Biosphere Reserve, acquiring new land and opening up this most beautiful, fragile environment for all to see. Hence, it is important to take nothing and leave nothing, except memories and photographs. The fact that the campsites provide all necessary camping gear, to avoid outside contamination, means that you can travel light and cover more ground than you would otherwise.

This ancient escarpment shelters a rare bio-diversity and is home to an array of woodland dwellers, from chipmunks to bear and chickadees to Canada geese. The further north you venture the more isolated the trail becomes and the more likely you are to witness the resident fauna in its natural environment. A good pair of binoculars and a soft step is all you need – enjoy.

# The East Coast Trail

The 540 km (337 mi) East Coast Trail hugs the scenic shores of the Avalon Peninsula of Newfoundland and Labrador. This grand trail is very much a work in progress, with 220 km (138 mi) of the trail well marked. The remainder of it is accessible but un-signposted and provides a greater challenge to the more experienced hiker.

The marked section of the Trail stretches from Fort Amherst, in historic St. John's, to Cappahayden, on the beautiful southern shore. It is equipped with trail signage, maps and supporting trail information to enhance your hiking experience along the coast and through the wilderness. It consists of a series of 18 paths each with a northern and a southern trailhead. Each of these paths can be hiked individually, some are easy strolls, whilst others are longer and more demanding.

As is fitting for a trail of this magnitude there is much to see and explore. This system of what were backcountry routes and hunting trails takes the hiker through provincial parks, national historic sites and ecological reserves. Sustenance and rest can be taken at any one of the charming fishing villages which line the route.

There are currently plans by the volunteer East Coast Trail Association to expand the marked route to Trepassey in the south and Topsoil in the north. The Association should be your first port of call when attempting this epic trail as their encyclopaedic knowledge of the area can prove invaluable to even the most seasoned of hikers.

**HOW:**
On foot
**DEPART:**
Fort Amherst, NL
**WHEN TO GO:**
More navigable from May to October.
**TIME IT TAKES:**
Allow a month to complete the whole trail.
**HIGHLIGHTS:**
The Spout (a wave driven geyser)
The National Historic Sites of Cape Spear, Signal Hill, and Cape Race.
The suspension bridge at the historic abandoned community of La Manche.
Witless Bay Seabird Sanctuary
**YOU SHOULD KNOW:**
The trail is left intentionally unpaved and unspoiled. This means that underfoot conditions can be slippery and several of the walks are close to cliff edges. Therefore, hiking the trail has an inherently greater risk than taking a stroll in an urban park. Risks to a reasonably fit, prepared and cautious hiker are, however, minimal.

*The Cape Spear Lighthouse, Newfoundland, is located on the most easterly point of North America.*

# The Mantario Trail

**HOW:**
On foot, by bike, or on skis in the winter
**DEPART:**
150 km (94 mi) east of Winnipeg, MB
**WHEN TO GO:**
All year round depending on which activity you choose. Hiking is best between May and October.
**TIME IT TAKES:**
Allow a full week to explore the whole trail.
**HIGHLIGHTS:**
Caddy Lake – a gathering point for wildlife and hikers alike.
Camping in the backcountry near Mantario Lake.
The spectacular fall (September/October) colours of this splendidly diverse woodland.
**YOU SHOULD KNOW:**
You need to be reasonably fit to complete the trail. It is probably not suitable for children under 12. Spring (March/April) can bring difficult underfoot conditions as the snows melt, requiring a little ingenuity to cross certain sections.

*Nutimik Lake, Whiteshell Provincial Park*

Located 150 km (94 mi) east of Winnipeg in Manitoba, The Mantario Trail has become a magnet for seasoned hikers, mountain bikers and skiers alike. Running along part of the Canadian Shield, this most inviting of trails offers dramatic views at every turn. The landscape consists of imposing rocky outcrops, marshes, lakes, rivers, beaver dams and forest. The area is also replete with wildlife and muskrat, snapping turtles, black bear, coyote and wolf are common. Look skywards and it is likely that you will see bald eagles or turkey vultures circling.

A large portion of the 63 km (39 mi) trail is a dedicated Wilderness Zone, where hunting and motorized vehicles are forbidden. This gives the whole hiking experience a pedestrian feel in the best sense of the word, with only the sound of the wildlife, the wind through the trees and the sound of your step breaking the silence. Each stage of the hike takes you up and along granite ridges, which offer wonderful panoramic views of lakes and gullies.

Variety is the watchword for this well maintained trail. Spruce, balsam, jack pine and white birch all thrive here, giving the forest a wonderfully diverse feel. Overseen by the Manitoba Naturalists Society, this is a perfect family hike. Campgrounds are plentiful and in good order and the huge variety of outdoor activities should keep all happy. The fact that vehicular access is confined to the north and south trailheads adds to the sense of being alone with nature. Once you have unloaded the car, it is just you, the landscape and the abundant flora and fauna.

# Across Vancouver Island

There are two main ways to cross Vancouver Island, Canada's largest Pacific island. A seaplane ride from Vancouver takes you over the Lions Gate Bridge and across the Georgia Strait giving you a first full glimpse of this most verdant of lands. When reaching the island you fly over the sunshine coast resorts of Parksville and Qualicum, to the north the glaciers of Strathcona stand out, whilst to the south the mountains of Washington State appear magically close on a clear day. But above all the lush ancient forest, specked with the odd lake, feeds the eye. About halfway across, the Alberni Inlet guides the plane along to the Pacific Rim National Park with its long sandy beaches framed by rich temperate rainforest. Then finally you land in the heart of Tofino.

Since the locals will tell you that everything runs in the laid-back 'Tofino time', it is perhaps better to arrive by road. There is a good bus service linking the main ferry terminal at Nanaimo to both Ucluelet and Tofino, but it affords little opportunity for stop-offs; that said the views along the route are spectacular. Leaving Highway 1 from Nanaimo you turn onto Highway 4 and enter Cathedral Grove, an area of 800-year-old majestic Douglas firs, some measuring 9 m (29.5 ft) in circumference. After Port Alberni you come to Sproat Lake with an opportunity to stumble across the abundant wildlife in the area. In spring brown bears, waking from hibernation, come to eat the dandelion heads that grow near the road – don't leave your vehicle but have your camera ready. Finally the road winds its way past Kennedy Lake and then onto the Pacific Rim Highway that runs parallel to the golden sands of Long Beach.

*Surfers at Long Beach near Tofino*

**HOW:**
By seaplane or car and ferry
**WHEN TO GO:**
June to August can get busy, as can the storm-watching season (December to January). Between times (the 'shoulder seasons') are less crowded.
**TIME IT TAKES:**
Vancouver to Tofino by air 1 hour 15 minutes. By road, Nanaimo to Tofino, 3 ½ hrs without stopping.
**HIGHLIGHTS:**
Long Beach – a 16-km (10-mi) long stretch of pristine Pacific sandy beach.
Tofino Botanical Gardens – a wonderfully unconventional garden with boardwalks and paths through sculptures and forest.
The Pacific Rim Whale Festival in early March – where people gather to watch the 20,000 or so grey whales on their migration.
First Nations culture – there are few places in Canada where the native people live and thrive alongside the settler population better than on the west coast of Vancouver Island.
**YOU SHOULD KNOW:**
The road from Nanaimo to Parksville is deceptively good. After that Highway 4 can get tricky in bad weather so check your oil and tyres. The seaplane journey can be very bumpy in bad weather.

# The P'tit Train du Nord

The P'tit Train du Nord is the most innovative of trails and cries out to be used all year round. Running north from St-Jérôme to Mont Laurier it utilizes an old railway line, decommissioned in 1989, and is popular with hikers and cyclists in summer, while the winters are given over to Nordic skiing and other snow-based activities. If most of Canada is the Great Outdoors, then this is the very good outdoors, offering the feeling of seclusion whilst never straying too far from civilization. The dozen or so villages linked by the trail in the Laurentian hills north of Montreal, offer fine-dining and bountiful delicatessens as befits French Canada.

Good use has been made of the defunct stations and many are given over to service areas. As one would expect of a former railway, the gradients are not steep, making it a perfect trail for groups of all ages and abilities. However, it is sometimes surprising how high you can get – and the views of this rolling countryside are quite lovely from the several 'peaks' along the way. The trail is very much a work in progress, with some of the gravel tracks being upgraded to paved roadways making it even more accessible for summer visitors. In winter the area changes markedly and becomes the domain of cross-country skiers, the toughest sportsmen and women to be found anywhere in the world. Gentle inclines become muscle-testing mountains, as the sub-zero temperatures attempt to freeze every inward breath and the need to carry emergency supplies adds to the challenge.

The trail was designed with people in mind. Be it in summer or winter, the thrill of going from station to station and from village to village provides a perfect structure for those wishing to explore this most pleasant corner of Canada.

*A view across the Laurentian hills*

**HOW:**
On foot or by bike
**DEPART:**
St-Jérôme, QC
**WHEN TO GO:**
It is open all year round although most of the amenities operate shorter winter (November to April) opening hours.
**TIME IT TAKES:**
The full 200 km (125 mi) of the trail can easily be cycled in a week. Skiers should probably allow 10 days.
**HIGHLIGHTS:**
The wildflower meadows in spring (April/May).
The fragrant smell of the pine forests from late May to September.
The bucolic charm of the settlements along the way.
Lac-Saguay – a beautiful lake just a short hop from the trail.
**YOU SHOULD KNOW:**
Nordic skiing is not for beginners as it puts a strain on almost every part of the body. Start slowly and then with the aid of gym work, build up to the challenge.

# The Dempster Highway

Head north to the Yukon for the most exciting drive of your life. An engineering miracle, first opened in 1979 to link the mineral wealth of the north with southern Canada, this gravel road has now become a magnet for thrill seekers from around the globe. Those who like their roads even and services regularly spaced should keep away. This is the most challenging journey of them all, through the most magnificent of Arctic landscapes. From the Klondike gold fields to the Mackenzie Delta you cross mountain ranges, traverse valleys and have the chance to view nature red in tooth and claw.

The area is home to all the wildlife you would expect in northern Canada – and more. Both black and grizzly bear can be found as well as a host of caribou, sheep and mountain goats. With such a bountiful supply of food, predators are plentiful, so keep your eyes open for lynx, foxes and above all any patrolling wolves, the most magical of sights.

Each season brings new wonder, from the midnight sun in the summertime to the icy calm of winter, when ferries on the route are replaced by ice bridges, thus obliging you to place your trust in nature even as you marvel at it. Rarely can completing a road journey be greeted with such a sense of achievement, but the 741 km (463 mi) highway is a true test of man (or woman) and machine. Along the way there are abundant opportunities for adventure, so load up your kayak, pack your hiking boots and prepare to explore and enjoy this amazing wilderness.

**HOW:**
By car
**DEPART:**
Dawson City, YT
**WHEN TO GO:**
Year round, although less arduous from June to August.
**TIME IT TAKES:**
Very variable according to conditions, allow a good few days.
**HIGHLIGHTS:**
The sheer magnitude of it all, as you cross rivers and negotiate mountain passes.
The explosion of colour which heralds the short Arctic summer (July-August).
You can't help but notice the trees, which because of the frozen sub-soil, point in all directions to create a unique landscape.
**YOU SHOULD KNOW:**
Be prepared for almost anything. Sudden changing weather can force you to camp overnight at any time of the year. When camping hang your provisions away from the ground.

*The Dempster Highway links Dawson City and Inuvik.*

# The Coquihalla Highway

The Coquihalla Highway (pronounced 'coke-a-hal-a') is a major toll highway that connects the Greater Vancouver region with the interior of British Columbia. It was constructed in the 1980s to shave a couple of hours off travelling times, but it is much more than just a short cut. It is a four-seasons-in-one-day, peddle-to-the-metal, ear-popping, super highway through the magnificent Cascade Mountains. The dramatic changes of environment are always exhilarating, as you go from misty coastal cedars and tall firs to bright sunlight on the high rock faces in the space of half an hour.

The Coq, as it is affectionately known, travels northwards from Hope to Kamloops via Merritt on Highway 5, passing through Monck and Lac Le Jeune Provincial Parks. The road then climbs through the Great Bear Snow Shed to the summit of the Coquihalla Pass, at 1,240 m (4,068 ft), then crosses the top of the Thompson Plateau, with side roads leading off into rolling countryside speckled with fishing lakes. The route is particularly scenic in the early fall (October), when rolling fields and forest foliage take on a golden glow.

The forest around Merritt provides the greatest diversity of flora and fauna. Pine, spruce and Douglas fir can be found at the lower elevations and the extensive grasslands support moose, mule deer, bear and elk. Also keep your eyes peeled for wolves and mountain goat along the ridges to the side of the road. The sheer strain that the many inclines put on vehicles means that there is less commercial traffic than on many of the region's roads, so you are always guaranteed a smooth passage – weather permitting. Buckle up and prepare for the drive of your life.

*Orchards in the Okanagan Valley*

# The Cabot Trail

Located in the Cape Breton National Park in Nova Scotia, the Cabot Trail, which opened in 1939, winds spectacularly along the flanks of the mountains, offering astonishing vistas at every turn.

The 282 km (175 mi) Cabot Trail loop is popular with experienced cyclists, being both arduous and rewarding. The route meanders up ravines and plummets back down towards the coast. One breathtaking view after another unfolds, and the plunging descent from Mount MacKenzie to Pleasant Bay will be one you will never forget.

The park has 27 hiking tracks branching off the Cabot Trail. Many excursions are quite short and have the feel of a relaxed amble rather than a hearty tramp, but those who welcome a challenge will find something to suit. All trails are listed on the reverse side of the map you receive when you pay your entry fee to the park.

If you're looking to leave the crowds behind, the Glasgow Lake Lookoff is a relatively gentle 8 km (5 mi) round-trip hike that takes you through barren and scrub forest to a rocky bald headland overlooking a series of pristine highland lakes, with distant views of the ocean. The trail is alternately swampy and rocky, so strong footwear is advised.

Further along the Cabot Trail, the 0.8 km (0.5 mi) Bog Trail offers a glimpse of the tableland's unique bogs from a dry boardwalk. Lone Shieling is an easy 0.8 km (0.5 mi) loop through a verdant hardwood forest in a lush valley that includes 300-year-old sugar maples (most stunning in fall). A re-creation of a Scottish crofter's hut is featured along this trail.

**HOW:**
On foot or by bike
**DEPART:**
Port Hastings, NS
**WHEN TO GO:**
Popular year round, but the weather is best from late May to September.
**TIME IT TAKES:**
You could drive it in a day if so inclined, cyclists generally allow a week.
**HIGHLIGHTS:**
The almost vertigo-inducing descent to Pleasant Bay (when travelling clockwise).
Cheticamp – an Acadian village famous for fish and fiddle playing.
St Ann's – home to the world-renowned Gaelic College of Celtic Arts and Crafts.
**YOU SHOULD KNOW:**
This is the most undulating of roads on a grand scale, so whatever your mode of transport, check your brakes before starting and be aware of other road users, particularly in summer when inexperienced trailer-home drivers head off for their summer vacation.

*An uphill struggle near Pleasant Bay, Cape Breton Island*

# Icefields Parkway

**HOW:**
By car
**DEPART:**
Lake Louise, AB
**WHEN TO GO:**
May to September offers the best
weather.
**TIME IT TAKES:**
Around four hours without stopping,
but allow a full day for picnic breaks.
**HIGHLIGHTS:**
The Columbia Icefield – a chance to
witness a pristine wilderness.
Lake Louise – with its turquoise lake
and overhanging glacier.
The Crossings – a chance to reflect
and anticipate.
Arriving in Jasper, a rather special
town set on a small plateau
surrounded by a spectacular
panoramic mountain backdrop.
**YOU SHOULD KNOW:**
Even in good weather the sheer
elevation of this highway can mean
that road conditions can change
rapidly, so come prepared for
all eventualities.

The magnificence of the Icefields Parkway (Hwy 93) can scarcely be overstated – a 230 km (144 mi) road from Lake Louise to Jasper through the heart of the Rockies, it ranks as one of the world's ultimate drives. Its seemingly unending succession of enormous peaks, vast glaciers, iridescent lakes, wild-flower meadows, wildlife and forests – capped by the sheer majesty of the Columbia Icefield – is utterly overwhelming.

Fur traders and First Nations peoples dubbed it the Wonder Trail, though the current road owes much to the depression era works programme and it was only opened in 1940 in its present incarnation.

Leaving the iconic image of Lake Louise behind you, the first 40 km (25 mi) of the road climbs steadily north through forest, until you reach the alpine meadow at Bow Summit, the journey's highest point. The next section, which drops down to the Saskatchewan River, offers the best chance to see black bears and moose. The Crossings marks the transition from the jaw-droppingly good to the truly awesome. This 50 km (31 mi) section is

famous the world over for its breathtaking scenery as Mount Athabasca and the Columbia Glacier heave into view.

Mountain goats, bighorn sheep and elk are common along the final 100 km (62 mi) of the Parkway. The road ascends Tangle Ridge, then drops down through forest and follows the Sunwapta and Athabasca Rivers into the charming little town of Jasper. The outstanding features of this final leg of the journey are the Sunwapta and Athabasca Falls and the opportunity to spot grizzly bears and mountain caribou.

Although over a million people make the trip each year to experience this 'window on the wilderness', the sheer vastness of the landscape still means it can rarely seem crowded.

*Sunlit peaks form a stunning backdrop for the still waters of Lake Louise, Banff National Park, Alberta.*

# Canoe down the Yukon River

**HOW:**
By canoe
**DEPART:**
Whitehorse, YT
**WHEN TO GO:**
When the ice has melted – late June to early September.
**TIME IT TAKES:**
Sixteen to 20 days, allowing for delays caused by bad weather.
**HIGHLIGHTS:**
Fort Selkirk – a renovated pioneer and First Nations settlement.
The abandoned settlement at Hottalinqua.
The vibrant colours of the glacial melt waters.
**YOU SHOULD KNOW:**
Whilst bears pose little danger to humans, you should be aware that you are entering their domain. It is important to keep all food tied up above ground and if you see bears leave the area immediately.

*Canoeing along the Yukon River.*

Starting at Whitehorse near the border with northern British Columbia, this 580 km (362 mi) canoe trip down the Yukon should only be undertaken by the most experienced of adventurers. Even the name of the river conjures up images of the frontier, and this journey takes you through early Canadian history as the river propels you on your way. So harsh is this environment that forward planning is a must. Sudden storms can cause long delays and the area is home to around 5,000 grizzly bears, so great care needs to be taken when setting up camp.

Such is the power of the Yukon, which is fed by melting ice, that it is possible to cover great distances in one day. The spectacular Lake Lebarge offers a good target for your first stop. 48 km (30 mi) long and on average 5 km (3.1 mi) wide, the lake offers the most challenging of paddles. Almost benign on a calm day, it can without much warning turn in to a bubbling cauldron and pose great danger to both man and canoe.

Once through the lake, the river gathers pace and takes you past abandoned wood yards and gold-mining settlements – a reminder of the folly of yesteryear, when the lure of potential wealth brought many to the region. Carmacks, some 350 km (219 mi) into the trip, offers the first opportunity to stock up and this cute little town of 500 even has a couple of hotels and restaurants.

The snow-covered mountains, shining in the midnight sun, frame the river as it runs fast towards the Arctic Circle and your final destination, Dawson City.

# The Inside Passage Ferry

The Inside Passage can be travelled as part of a longer cruise between California and Alaska. However it is difficult to beat the intimacy and affordability of the regular ferry service between Port Hardy on Vancouver Island and Prince Rupert in northern British Columbia. This 500-km (312-mi) voyage is one of North America's truly great journeys.

The first two hours of the trip involves crossing the open sea between Vancouver Island and Rivers Inlet and offers a chance to grab a coffee, soak up the atmosphere on board and get to know your fellow passengers. Soon it will be time to climb to the sometimes optimistically named sundeck, as the spectacular Central Coast Archipelago heaves into view. The route north then meanders through a narrow maze of channels, passes and reaches. The mountains soar up majestically from the ocean floor, their peaks covered in snow and ice.

So rugged is most of the coast here that if you were exploring by kayak, you would struggle to find a welcoming landing site. Passengers should keep their eyes peeled for whales or dolphins in Queen Charlotte Sound. With a little luck, you might even see a white-coated Kermode bear on Princess Royal Island's lengthy shoreline. Snow capped peaks delight the eye as the vessel travels through the improbably narrow channel between Pitt and Banks Islands. The open waters of Chatham Sound then await you before Prince Rupert comes in to view. This BC Ferries operation is more than just a tourist route, it forms part of a vital network connecting outlying communities – your co-travellers may therefore be your best interpreters.

**HOW:**
By ferry
**DEPART:**
Port Hardy, BC
**WHEN TO GO:**
Best in the summer months (May to September) when the voyage takes place entirely in daylight.
**TIME IT TAKES:**
15 hours
**HIGHLIGHTS:**
The sight of schools of migrating whales and dolphins.
Campania Island – a perfectly formed rocky island.
The never-ending wonders of the amazing scenery.
Prince Rupert – a cosmopolitan town full of surprises.
**YOU SHOULD KNOW:**
Unless you are travelling on to Haida Gwai or Alaska, the most affordable way back is by ferry, so be prepared for a round-trip. Also you should book your hotel in Prince Rupert well in advance, as rooms are scarce when the ferry pulls in to town.

*A Kermode black bear on Princess Royal Island, in its white colour phase; it is also known as the Spirit Bear.*

*Thousand Islands Park
in the fall*

# Sail up the St Lawrence

**HOW:**
By boat
**DEPART:**
Kingston, ON
**WHEN TO GO:**
Best between the months of May
and October.
**TIME IT TAKES:**
Around one week
**HIGHLIGHTS:**
The Thousand Islands in the fall
(September-October) – featuring a
spectacular array of colours.
The riverfront of Old Montreal.
Historic, majestic Old Quebec City.
The ever-changing scenery, the
sunsets and the vibrancy of the river.
**YOU SHOULD KNOW:**
Most cruise operators dock their
boat in the evening, allowing you to
explore both the cities and villages of
the area. Check the itinerary before
booking to pick the cruise most
suited to you.

The main pleasure of riverboat cruising is in its constant proximity to the land, meaning that almost every moment brings something new to see and learn. The spotlight is always on the river and its environs, rather than the on-board 'entertainments' associated with ocean cruising.

Your boat up the St Lawrence heads eastwards from Kingston, with Lake Ontario behind you, and after it has rounded Wolfe Island you are greeted by one of North America's most fabulous sights, the iconic Thousand Islands. As most of the islands are the exclusive preserve of the rich or reserved for nature, this really is the best way to see them. From your ringside seat you can marvel at such sights as the abandoned Boldt Castle, while other islands are little more than rocky bird sanctuaries.

The St Lawrence Seaway, a triumph of co-operation between the US and Canada, opens up the heart of the Great Lakes to the Eastern Seaboard. Its strategic importance is evidenced by the prevalence of settlements visible on both banks. For the next 100 km (62.5 mi), rolling pastures frame the river on both sides until it widens at Lac St-François and Lac St-Louis. The names of the towns tell you that you are entering French Canada and that grande dame of Canadian cities, Montreal comes quickly in to view. Most notable among all Montreal's wonderful French colonial architecture is the magnificent dome of St Joseph's Oratory, rising magically above the city.

The final leg of the voyage is its most charming. Settlements become more spaced out and the hills of Parc National De La Maurice to your left contrast with the bucolic flatland to the right. The river then widens and the St Lawrence wends its way to Quebec City, the traditional heart of French Canada.

# Nahanni River on a raft

A Nahanni rafting expedition is truly a trip of a lifetime. Over the course of this 94 km (150 mi) journey from Virginia Falls to Blackstone Landing, this fast flowing river drops a heart pumping 396 m (1,300 ft). Each section of this epic voyage takes you through canyons, over rapids and past some of the most stunning scenery on Earth.

Even the names conjure up images of danger and excitement as you tumble through Hell's Gate, pass Headless Creek and camp out in Deadmen Valley. So remote is this region of north-western Canada that the only practical way to arrive is by air. This start to the voyage could not be more spectacular, as you land alongside the towering Virginia Falls.

Fed by the melt waters of the Mackenzie Mountains, the Nahanni River provides the rafter with the most thrilling of rides. From the figure-of-eight rapids of Hell's Gate to the giant waves of George's Riffle, this is a true test of oars, people and raft. The welcome respite of overnight camping could not be in more imposing surroundings, and the 1,200 m (3,900 ft) walls of Third Canyon are the most magnificent of sights to wake up to in the morning.

The rushing noise of the river is constant and reminds you of the challenges that lie ahead. Towards the end of this epic voyage you pass, as if by design, Kraus' Hotsprings where you can soothe your aching limbs, rejoice in nature and congratulate yourself on nearly completing this most exhilarating of journeys. It is then just a short paddle along the braided channels of The Splits where the river finally loses some of its rage.

**HOW:**
By raft
**DEPART:**
Virginia Falls, NWT
**WHEN TO GO:**
June to August, when the ice has melted.
**TIME IT TAKES:**
About one week
**HIGHLIGHTS:**
Virginia Falls – difficult to tear oneself away.
The thrilling run through Painted Canyon.
The view of Tlogotsho Plateau from Deadmen Valley.
The lush steep-sided forest as you near Blackstone Landing.
**YOU SHOULD KNOW:**
The beauty of rafting is that even a relative beginner can tackle the hardest of runs if accompanied by experienced people. You do have to be fit however, as there is a lot of equipment to be carried on trips such as these.

*Virginia Falls in Nahanni National Park Reserve, Northwest Territories, are twice as high as Niagara Falls.*

# The International Selkirk Loop

The International Selkirk Loop is a 450-km (281-mi) scenic drive, which takes you through some of the most remote, undeveloped and spectacular regions of south-eastern British Columbia, northern Idaho and north-eastern Washington. It's an area of forested hillsides, dazzling waterfalls, snow-capped rocky peaks, and charismatic small towns and is popular with cyclists, recreational vehicle owners and bikers alike.

Much of the land within the Loop is protected National Forest. Hundreds of miles of trails are available for all levels of hiking, biking, horseback riding, skiing and snowmobile touring. You can hit the Loop at any point, but there is no better place to start than the sleepy town of Nelson. Tucked away in the interior of British Columbia, this idyllic place has over 350 heritage homes, though its laid-back townsfolk make it feel like somewhere out of the 1960s. Having stocked up, it is a short ride to Balfour to take the longest free ferry ride in the world, across the Kootenay Lake.

Verdant forests and the lake's deep blue water continue to enrich the senses as you head across the American border. Once into Idaho, every few miles seems to herald a new trail with new possibilities and the only difficulty is choosing when to stop. With the majestic Cabinet Mountains behind you, the Loop takes you into Washington State and the most beautiful corner of America.

The main achievement of the Loop is that it connects Americans and Canadians in a historic relationship of living, working and playing in a spectacular setting. The excellent provision of campgrounds and RV parks is married with the need to preserve the region's wildlife. It is home to endangered species such as the woodland caribou, grizzly bear and the white sturgeon deer, in addition to the more commonly found elk and moose.

**HOW:**
By car
**DEPART:**
Nelson, BC
**WHEN TO GO:**
April to October, but most spectacular in the fall (September-October) when the first dustings of snow cover the mountains.
**TIME IT TAKES:**
The compactness of the Loop makes for a good week's vacation.
**HIGHLIGHTS:**
The tree-covered hills around Kootenay Lake.
The area is home to numerous artists, who are only too happy to explain and sell their work. Look out for 'Open Studio' signposts.
The Pend Oreille County Museum – a museum recording pioneer life.
**YOU SHOULD KNOW:**
Good hiking gear is required when tackling the trails that branch off the Loop. However, it is still an enjoyable tour for those less able or those who simply want to enjoy nature from the comfort of their RV.

*Pine trees at Dog Lake, Kootenay National Park, British Columbia.*

# The Great Divide Trail

Created by the Adventure Cycling Association of North America with the goal of staying within 80 km (50 mi) of the Continental Divide, this is the mother and father of all bike rides. Originally confined to the USA, it was recently extended to include southern Canada, making the journey an epic 4,238 km (2,711 mi). It has become customary to ride The Divide from north to south but you are not obliged to do so.

The route begins in the glacial valleys of Banff National Park in the Southern Canadian Rockies. It then passes through the densely forested mountains of Montana and Idaho, wends its way down into the barren high desert lands of Wyoming's Great Basin, rises again up and over several 3,000 m (10,000 ft) passes in Colorado, before switching back through rugged mountainous sections of New Mexico and it finally drops down into the Chihuahuan Desert.

The route's highest point, Indiana Pass in Colorado, is around 3,600 m (11,910 ft) above sea level. The first half of the Albertan section and the segments in Montana and New Mexico are the most rugged and challenging, but such is the magnitude of this journey that difficulties can crop up at any point. Violent thunderstorms are common and can be the biggest obstacle to your progress as they often make the riding surface impassable. Be prepared to stop and take stock at a moment's notice. Carrying good lightweight camping gear is essential.

The sense of achievement is almost overpowering as you near the Mexican border. It is at this point that even a few miles can feel like a marathon. The incentive provided by doing the journey as a sponsored ride can add power to your legs as you near the finishing line. Only then can you take in what you have seen and done.

**HOW:**
By bike
**DEPART:**
Banff, AB
**WHEN TO GO:**
The degree of difficulty is less from April to September, although you always have to tread a fine line between extreme cold and extreme heat.
**TIME IT TAKES:**
Three months at a leisurely pace, two months for a more experienced rider or under 18 days if you want to break the record.
**HIGHLIGHTS:**
The Canadian Rockies – the ride south from Banff is spectacular.
The mountains of Southern Colorado.
The Flatlands of New Mexico – a chance to build up some strength in your legs.
Getting to the end!
**YOU SHOULD KNOW:**
You have to be fit – very fit – to complete this ride within any reasonable timescale. It is best tackled in a group of people of similar ability. Take advice from the people who designed the route, namely the Adventure Cycling Association.

*The Spanish Peaks in Southern Colorado*

# Historic Route 66

With vast distances and a well-developed railroad system, the USA had roads that were little more than local tracks until well into the 20th century. In 1919 the War Department's first Transcontinental Motor Convoy – an expedition that included future World War II Supreme Commander Dwight Eisenhower – took months to cross from east to west. When a Federal highway system was developed, Route 66 – established in 1926, signed in 1927 and fully paved by 1938 – was one of the first.

This iconic road – from Chicago to Los Angeles through eight states and the heart of America, covering some 3,940 km (2,450 mi) – was nicknamed 'The Main Street of America', bringing prosperity to towns along the way and serving as the major route for westward migration during the Great Depression of the 1930s and industrial boom of World War II. Subsequently, Route 66 facilitated tourist development and acquired legendary status, featuring widely in literature (John Steinbeck christened it 'The Mother Road'), films and popular music. But its death warrant was signed in 1956 by the aforementioned Dwight Eisenhower – by then President – when he put his name to the Interstate Highway Act, which led to today's freeway network and made US-66 redundant, though it didn't vanish from maps until 1985.

*One of the Historic Route 66 signs*

Many sections were incorporated into freeways, and it is now impossible to follow the original route, which anyway varied over the years. But happily nostalgia soon set in and much of the old road has been designated – and marked – as Historic Route 66, with new sections constantly being added. These may be found especially in Illinois, New Mexico and Arizona, and with the help of patience and specialist maps, those who warm to the romance of this famous road can still retrace much of its length – or simply drive individual sections for a reminder of the way America once travelled, not so long ago.

# Florida Keys Scenic Drive

*Highway 1 passing over Pigeon Key in the Florida Keys.*

From the tip of Florida, the Overseas Highway (US-1) runs along a chain of subtropical isles where the Atlantic meets the Gulf of Mexico, connected by over 40 bridges. It runs for 203 km (126 mi) through a brilliant tropical landscape of blue sea, reefs and lush vegetation. Mile Marker 126 is just below Florida City on the mainland, starting the countdown to Key West.

The highway crosses the southern edge of the famous Everglades to bustling Key Largo, the largest and northernmost key. It continues through Plantation Key before sweeping across Snake Creek and on to Windley Key. The Middle Keys begin at Islamorada (Purple Isle), where a memorial at Mile 82 commemorates victims of a 1935 hurricane that was one of the most powerful ever recorded in the USA.

US-1 hurries across Long Key Viaduct to tiny Conch Key, then crosses Grassy Key to Marathon, the sprawling commercial heart of the Middle Keys, before taking the spectacular Seven Mile Bridge, one of the world's longest. Now, the keys seem to become more isolated, and wildlife becomes more obvious – like the endangered miniature deer on Big Pine Key (visit their sanctuary) and a profusion of birds such as eagles, red-tailed hawks and falcons.

For the final section, the road crosses a succession of small keys that almost seem to merge, before arriving at the end of the line – Key West, a quirky place that seems to owe more to Caribbean culture than American. It is truly eccentric and unlike anywhere else in the USA, and this is one drive where both journey and destination more than come up to expectations. It is possible to do the return trip in a day, but with plenty of attractions to explore along the way most visitors prefer a leisurely drive that includes an overnight stop.

**HOW:**
By car
**DEPART:**
Florida City, FL
**WHEN TO GO:**
October through March to avoid storms and scorching summers.
**TIME IT TAKES:**
Half a day
**HIGHLIGHTS:**
John Pennekamp Coral Reef State Park – the first underwater state park in the USA, featuring the coral reefs found only in Florida, for diving, snorkelling or reef trips in glass-bottomed boats.
The Theatre of the Sea on Windley Key, featuring performing sharks, dolphins and sealions.
At Crane Point Hummock on Marathon – the combined Museum of Natural History of the Florida Keys and Florida Keys Children's Museum.
The Ernest Hemingway Home and Museum in Whitehead Street, Key West.
**YOU SHOULD KNOW:**
The southernmost house in the continental USA – a wonderful turreted Victorian confection in pink, may be found at 1400 Duval Street in Key West.

**33**

# Coast Starlight Train

**HOW:**
By train
**DEPART:**
Seattle, WA
**WHEN TO GO:**
Any time of year.
**TIME IT TAKES:**
Official journey time is 35 hours, though some travellers stop off to see some of the many sights to be found en route.
**HIGHLIGHTS:**
Before embarking, visit Seattle's popular landmark Space Needle, built for the 1962 World's Fair.
Informative on-board talks by guides from the Klondike Gold Rush National Historical Park between Seattle and Portland, then Klamath Falls and Eugene.
A break in Paso Robles, with dozens of wineries to tour...before relaxing in the rejuvenating waters of natural hot springs.
**YOU SHOULD KNOW:**
The route has sometimes been disrupted by mudslides, so it's wise to check that there are no problems before planning a trip.

Who says the romance of rail travel is dead? It isn't if you save up your pennies and travel on Amtrak's Coast Starlight service, connecting Seattle's King Street Station with Union Station in Los Angeles via Portland, Eugene-Springfield, Klamath Falls, Sacramento, Oakland, the San Francisco Bay area, Salinas and Santa Barbara. Along the 2,216 km (1,377 mi) route, the train passes through some truly spectacular West Coast scenery encompassing virgin forests, snow-capped mountains, lush valleys...and long stretches of fabulous and unspoiled Pacific coastline. No wonder it's rated as one of the world's most beautiful rail journeys. Amtrak gives every passenger a Route Guide that details what to look out for along the way and includes photo symbols indicating the most photogenic spots.

To take full advantage of all that natural beauty, the train uses double-decker Superliner rolling stock, including a Sightseer Lounge car with floor-to-ceiling windows. If you did indeed accumulate those pennies, you can travel in pampered luxury in the first-class Pacific Parlour Lounge car, with sleeping berths, a library, wine tasting, movie theatre and complimentary drinks. For little people, there's a Kiddie car packed with a variety of distractions. There is a Dining Car for full meals and Café Car for those who want their sightseeing with snacks. To complete the unique ensemble, luggage travels in a Heritage Baggage Car and the train is hauled by Amtrak's mighty Genesis series locomotives.

A gentle word of warning – the Coast Starlight has sometimes arrived up to eleven hours late, though timekeeping has recently improved dramatically.

*A vineyard in Paso Robles, California*

# California State Route 1

Often called Highway 1, this classic West Coast road runs for 1,055 km (655 mi) along much of California's beautiful Pacific shoreline. It starts in Orange County to the south and ends in Mendocino County to the north. Different sections have different names, including Pacific Coast Highway, Cabrillo Highway and Shoreline Highway.

Along the way, this rewarding route can be multi-lane highway or two-lane blacktop, and driving its entire length produces extraordinary contrasts between urban sprawl and some of the finest coastal scenery in the USA, plus the opportunity to visit many important heritage sites. Highway 1 has mile markers that help locate any listed feature or attraction, numbered from south to north, each bearing the abbreviated name of the relevant county. Highway 1 is best driven from south to north as the reverse direction ends anti-climactically with Los Angeles smog.

Starting in San Juan Capistra, the road travels through Los Angeles and the Beach cities, Santa Monica, Malibu, Santa Barbara, Lompoc, Santa Maria, San Luis Obispo, Morro Bay, Carmel (former Mayor – Clint Eastwood), Pacific Grove, Monterey, Watsonville, Santa Cruz, Half Moon Day, Pacifica, San Francisco, Mill Valley and Fort Bragg. It terminates at Leggett, where it meets US Highway 101 (with which it actually shares several sections of the coastal route) for the last time. Many of the place names serve as a reminder of California's historical ties with Spain, and there are a number of old Spanish settlements along Highway 1.

Despite some stretches that are inescapably modern freeways, the leisurely traveller best remembers the characteristic feel of a narrow, winding coast road amidst stunning scenery – not for nothing is it said that to drive Highway 1 is to understand the heart and soul of California.

*Pacific coast, Big Sur, California*

**HOW:**
By car
**DEPART:**
San Juan Capistra, CA
**WHEN TO GO:**
Any season – catch this delightful drive when you can!
**TIME IT TAKES:**
It can theoretically be done in an over-long day, but take two or three and enjoy the sights.
**HIGHLIGHTS:**
Unspoiled Big Sur with its rugged cliffs, where the residents are environmentally conscious and not a billboard is to be seen beside the highway.
Half way between Los Angeles and San Francisco – Hearst Castle in San Simeon, the extravagant edifice built by newspaper tycoon William Randolph Hearst, the model for Xanadu in Orson Welles's film *Citizen Kane*.
Piedras Blancas Lighthouse at the northern entrance to San Simeon Bay, first illuminated in 1875 and still used as a navigational aid – but the real attraction is the vast colony of elephant seals.
**YOU SHOULD KNOW:**
Be prepared to duck a couple of hours into the journey – Route 1 passes beneath the busy runways of LA International Airport.

*Yosemite Valley in Yosemite National Park, Sierra Nevada Mountains, California*

**HOW:**
On foot or by bike

**WHEN TO GO:**
The Trail (starting at the Mexican border) is best between March and September.

**TIME IT TAKES:**
To hike the entire trail without pause you should allow between four and six months.

**HIGHLIGHTS:**
The Ansell Adams Wilderness in California's Sierra Nevada, named after the famous 20th century landscape photographer who was inspired by these mountains.
Yosemite National Park, a World Heritage Site that covers a large area on the western slopes of the Sierra Nevada mountain chain.
Crater Lake National Park in Oregon, the most notable feature of which is the eponymous Crater Lake, a volcanic caldera lake famous for its deep-blue colour.
A civilized stop-off at Timberline Lodge, built within Oregon's Mount Hood National Forest as a work-generation project in the Great Depression, now a National Historic Landmark and popular tourist destination.

**YOU SHOULD KNOW:**
It really can be done – some 300 so-called 'thru hikers' start out along the PCT each spring, and around 200 make it all the way.

# Pacific Crest Trail

Also known as the Pacific Crest National Scenic Trail or simply PCT, this long-distance hiking route is only for the super-fit (and mightily determined!), although some make the going easier by taking to the saddle. The Trail stretches from the Mexican border up into Canada, a distance of 4,240 km (2,650 mi), following the high country of the Sierra Nevada and Cascade Range, inland from and parallel to the USA's West Coast. The highest point is Forester Pass in the Sierra Nevada at 4,000 m (13,150 ft), the low point is sea level at the Columbia River on the Oregon Washington borders.

The PCT mostly crosses forests and protected wilderness, avoiding civilization and even roads wherever possible, ensuring that the intrepid hiker sees and enjoys America's wild grandeur at its pristine best. Those who just wish to experience a section of this rugged Trail – or don't have time for more – often opt for the northern section in Washington, which has much to offer. Start at the Bridge of the Gods across the Columbia River; from there on it's uphill most of the way, as the Trail goes through National Forests, skirts Mount Adams and crosses a vast wilderness area. From there, it enters Mount Rainier National Park, and then continues via Chinook, Snoqualmie and Stevens Passes into the Lake Chelan National Recreational Area and North Cascades National Park. If you get there you've missed Stehekin, the last town near the Trail, and must cross into Canada where the PCT ends in British Columbia's EC Manning Provincial Park.

Oh, when you finally rest those blistered feet after hiking the Pacific Crest Trail from start to finish, take a short break then go for the USA's Triple Crown of long-distance hiking – the Appalachian and Continental Divide Trails await!

# Minnesota State Highway 61

Once the northern extremity of US Highway 61, the great pre-freeway route from New Orleans in the Deep South through the American heartlands up into Canada, State Highway 61 was created in 1991 when a new Interstate was built. It is in the northeastern part of Minnesota, running for 243 km (151 mi) from Duluth to the Canadian border.

MS-61 is a designated scenic highway that follows the rocky North Shore of Lake Superior, offering great lake vistas and soaring views of the Sawtooth Range to the northwest. It passes through three counties – St Louis, Lake and Cook – beginning with a four-lane expressway from Duluth to Two Harbours. Those who prefer more traditional progress can take the original road, now designated County/Scenic 61 (generally known as North Shore Scenic Drive). The road then passes through the lakeshore communities of Silver Creek, Castle Danger, Beaver Bay, East Beaver Bay, Silver Bay, Illgen City, Little Marais, Schroeder, Tofte, Lutsen and Grand Marais, before reaching Grand Portage.

The quality of this impressive landscape may be judged by the large number of forests, state parks, landmarks and features to be found along Highway 61. The road passes through Superior National and Grand Portage State Forests. State parks include Gooseberry Falls, Tettegouche alongside Silver Bay, Temperance River, Cascade River and Judge C R Magney State Park. Grand Portage lies within an Indian Reservation, and the landmark Grand Portage National Monument celebrates the Ojibwa, the third-largest group of Native Americans in the USA after Cherokees and Navajos. The Monument also acknowledges the importance of the fur trade in times past, sitting as it does on the historic trade route to the Canadian interior used in pre-industrial times. It's a reminder of how tough the original inhabitants and pioneers must have been to survive in this rugged terrain.

**HOW:**
By car
**DEPART:**
Duluth, MN
**WHEN TO GO:**
Minnesota Highway 61 is best travelled between April and September.
**TIME IT TAKES:**
A day will suffice, but two days would allow some of the natural wonders to be properly explored.
**HIGHLIGHTS:**
Palisade Head, the highest lakeside cliff in Minnesota – right beside the main entrance to Tettegouche State Park at the end of the Baptism River.
Grand Portage National Park – containing Minnesota's highest waterfall at 37 m (120 ft), the obstacle on the Pigeon River that required 'portage' (using a path to carry canoes and stores past the falls).
An outing on Lake Superior from Grand Portage – take either the *Wenonah* or *Voyageur II* and visit the Isle Royale National Park on the lake's largest island.
**YOU SHOULD KNOW:**
Local boy Bob Dylan (born Robert Zimmerman in Duluth) celebrated his local scenic route in the album and song Highway 61 Revisited (1965).

*The lighthouse at Split Rock, Lake Superior, Michigan*

# Lewis & Clark's National Scenic Trail

**HOW:**
By car and boat
**WHEN TO GO:**
Northern winters can be harsh, so it's best to trace the Trail between April and September.
**TIME IT TAKES:**
By car, the entire Trail can be followed inside two weeks without hurrying (careful planning required!).
**HIGHLIGHTS:**
The Lewis and Clark Memorial in a small park on the Kansas City river bluff, overlooking the confluence of the Kansas and Missouri Rivers.
Historic side-wheel dredging vessel *Captain Meriwether Lewis* in the Brownville State Recreation Area, now converted into a floating museum.
South Dakota's Calumet Bluff, where the expedition held council with the Yankton Sioux, now interpreted at Gavins Point Oam Visitor Centre and at nearby Lewis & Clark State Recreation Area.
A boat trip along the Upper Missouri National Wild and Scenic River, a 240-km (150-mi) section from Kipp State Park upstream to Fort Benton – little changed from 1805-06 when the expedition passed through.
**YOU SHOULD KNOW:**
In 1806, starting a tradition that persists in the US hunting field to this day, expedition leader Meriwether Lewis was shot in the leg by a short-sighted companion while hunting elk.

If there's one thing the USA isn't short of, it's long distances. Lewis & Clark's route across North America underlines the point, covering 5,960 km (3,700 mi) from Illinois to the Pacific. Meriwether Lewis and William Clark undertook their two-year saga from 1804 to 1806 at the instigation of President Thomas Jefferson, who dreamed of exploiting unexplored lands to the west, recently acquired via the Louisiana Purchase. The two men – accompanied by 45 men, three boats and (appropriately) a Newfoundland dog – set off to find a viable route to the west coast, with orders to record every detail of the people, places and things they saw, which they did...meticulously.

Nowadays, the trail they blazed is the second longest of the USA's 23 National Scenic and Historic Trails. Starting at Hartford, Illinois, it goes through ten more states – Missouri, Kansas, Iowa, Nebraska, South Dakota, North Dakota, Montana, Idaho, Oregon and Washington. It is not literally possible to follow in their pioneering footsteps – unless you have a couple of years to spare, 45 men, three boats and an Alreadyfoundland dog!

But many retracement opportunities are available, organized by state, local and private interests under the auspices of the National Park Service. Water segments follow parts of the expedition's waterborne route by boat or canoe. Overland hiking and horse-riding sections are being established and there are marked motor routes where roads nearly or precisely follow the original trail. Perhaps the most complete option is to follow the Lewis & Clark Trail Highway established in the 1960s, allowing one of the most significant journeys in American history to be approximated by car along modern roads. Helpful maps and information can be obtained from state and local tourism agencies, historical societies, chambers of commerce and Federal or state agencies managing lands or waters that are part of the Trail.

*The Missouri River from White Rocks*

# Appalachian Trail

Officially known as the Appalachian National Scenic Trail – unofficially the AT – this marked trail in the eastern USA is a magnet for thousands of hikers each year. Some 3,200 km (2,000 mi) long, it runs from Springer Mountain in Georgia to Mount Katahdin in Maine, passing through North Carolina, Tennessee, Virginia, West Virginia, Maryland, Pennsylvania, New Jersey, New York, Connecticut, Massachusetts, Vermont and New Hampshire as it goes. After that, you know you've had a serious stroll – mostly enjoying the solitary splendour of unspoiled wilderness, though a few stretches do traverse towns.

Many attempt the full length in one hit and about a third of these 'thru hikers' make it. Many more are so-called 'sectional hikers' who either complete the AT bit by bit over a number of years, or just choose one or more choice sections to hike and never essay the whole. Thru hikers generally start in Georgia in early spring to take advantage of warm weather moving north. There are numerous simple shelters along the AT, but these get crowded in summer and most hikers carry basic camping gear. Indeed, living rough on the Trail is very much part of the attraction and this is definitely not an adventure for the faint-hearted (or ill-prepared).

The Appalachian Trail is largely owned by the National Park Service and has been fully mapped and marked to assist hikers. The main markers are white blazes on trees, with blue blazes indicating side trails to shelters, viewpoints, parking areas and even (whisper it if you dare!) short cuts.

A word of warning – the Maine section is particularly tough and demanding. And speaking of Maine, don't start along the wrong trail by mistake! The International Appalachian Trail goes north from Maine into New Brunswick and Quebec, with an extension to Newfoundland planned.

**HOW:**
On foot
**WHEN TO GO:**
Best between April and mid-October (after which hiking in Maine is seriously discouraged).
**TIME IT TAKES:**
A complete 'thru hike' takes four to seven months.
**HIGHLIGHTS:**
Flora – the Appalachian Trail passes through spectacular forests that vary enormously, depending on climate and elevation, and there are a number of sub-alpine and alpine sections with interesting plant life.
Fauna – there are numerous animals, birds and reptiles to be seen along the trail, including black bear, deer, elk, moose, smaller mammals, rattlesnakes...and (on the down side) a variety of biting insects.
So-called 'trail magic' – the AT is maintained by dozens of voluntary organizations and individuals, and is renowned for the generous help given to hikers, often anonymously.
The ultimate colour display of New England's trees along the AT in Vermont during the fall.
**YOU SHOULD KNOW:**
For an idea of what lies in store before starting the epic journey, read *A Walk in the Woods* by humorous writer Bill Bryson.

*Mount Katahdin on the Appalachian Trail*

*Rafter in Rogue River Rapids*

# Rogue River Trail

**HOW:**
By boat and on foot
**WHEN TO GO:**
May to October
**TIME IT TAKES:**
Four to five days
**HIGHLIGHTS:**
Whiskey Creek Cabin, just down river
from Grave Creek – a late 19th
century mining cabin that remained
in use until the 1970s.
The Rogue River Ranch, midway
along the Trail – a preserved ranch
house that was once the centre of a
small gold-mining community, now
on the National Register of Historic
Places.
Gold panning – there is still gold to
be found in Rogue River gravel and
panning is allowed...pack a pan and
the trip might show a profit (but
don't bet on it!).
Scenic Mule Creek Canyon, a
highlight of the hike – one of the
most dramatic stretches of the
Rogue River.
**YOU SHOULD KNOW:**
Movie star Ginger Rogers owned a
ranch on the Rogue River for more
than 50 years, living there full time
and greatly enjoying the fishing.

Wild and rugged are adjectives that spring readily to mind when describing the Rogue River's wilderness surroundings and seething white water, so typical of the northwestern USA. The river rises in Oregon's Cascade Range and rushes down to the Pacific Ocean with plenty of Grade IV rapids along the way (they're almost as difficult as rapids can get, whilst remaining runnable). That makes the river hugely popular with rafters, and there are also fascinating jet boat trips along some 160 km (100 mi) of the Rogue's course.

But for those who get seasick, or prefer to enjoy outstanding natural beauty at walking pace, there is an excellent trail for hikers. The 65-km (40-mi) Rogue River National Recreation Trail along the river's north bank offers a splendid way of seeing the impressive Rogue River Canyon. The western trailhead is at Foster Bar, some 50 km (31 mi) inland from the coastal town of Gold Beach. The eastern trailhead is at Grave Creek, the same distance down river from Grants Pass. Both trailheads (and the middle of the trail) can be reached by road. Most people hike in an easterly direction so the sun is on their backs in the afternoon.

The Trail is not too demanding terrain-wise, with a well-constructed trailbed and moderate grades, though it should not be attempted by the inexperienced or unfit. It is necessary to backpack, carrying adequate water and supplies along with camping gear, though it is possible to restock along the way. For those who prefer not to camp, lodge accommodation is available (pre-booking essential) at regular intervals. Potential hazards along the Trail include black bears, rattlesnakes, ticks and poison oak, but those risks are a small price to pay for the pleasure of experiencing an accessible piece of spectacular American wilderness.

# Oregon Coast Trail

The Oregon Coast Trail (OCT) follows the state's Pacific coastline, from Astoria on the Columbia River in the north to the California border near Brookings – a distance of 600 km (360 mi). It clings to the shoreline, with only an occasional short inland detour where the beach is impassable, usually at rocky headlands like Cape Kiwanda. Where the Trail goes through a coastal town, it usually follows the streets closest to the water.

The OCT experience can only be described as breathtaking. This is one of the most beautiful and dramatic coastlines to be found anywhere in the USA (maybe the world!) where the hiker truly feels at one with awesome Nature. Many travel the Trail and camp as they go. Camping is allowed on many beaches and where it is forbidden (within state parks) there are alternative campgrounds. Others prefer the many yurts along the way – conical shelters modelled on the Mongolian original that can be used for a small fee. There are also plenty of bed-and-breakfast establishments that offer walkers a warm welcome and hot showers. Be aware that some sections of the Trail can only be walked at low tide, necessitating a hold-up or sometimes-demanding detour if you arrive at the wrong time.

Oregon's Pacific beaches certainly justify a visit, even if you have no intention of travelling the whole Trail. An excellent way of experiencing this wild and unspoiled coastline is to choose a section of the trail that can be walked in a day – there will almost always be a local bus to return you to your starting point at the end of the leisurely hike. For those who don't 'do' walking, US-101 more or less follows the OCT (and is, indeed, part of the Trail for some of its length).

**HOW:**
On foot
**WHEN TO GO:**
May to September (but hang tough and go out of season, and you'll have the OCT to yourself!)
**TIME IT TAKES:**
From a single day for one short section to a couple of months for the entire Trail.
**HIGHLIGHTS:**
Oregon Dunes National Recreation Area – south from the Siuslaw River in Florence to the Coos River in North Bend, this is 65 km (40 mi) of the most extraordinary sand sculpture in the USA.
The secluded section of the OCT between Port Orford and Brandon – offering four days of pristine wilderness hiking for those willing to camp...and swim a river along the way.
A night in the yurt at Beachside State Park, just south of Waldport – you'll never see a better ocean view.
The most spectacular one-day hike on the OCT – the sea-stack-strewn stretch between Cannon Beach South and Arch Point.
**YOU SHOULD KNOW:**
Access to the entire length of Oregon's coastline is guaranteed by state law – no private beachfronts here!

*Brandon Beach, Oregon*

# Shenandoah Valley

One of the most historic locations in the eastern USA is the Shenandoah Valley, scene of ferocious conflict in the American Civil War when it was known as 'The Breadbasket of the Confederacy'. It lies between the Blue Ridge Mountains to the east and the Allegheny Mountains to the west, stretching for 320 km (200 mi) and consisting of seven counties in Virginia and two in West Virginia. It is a famously productive agricultural area and numerous heritage sites hark back to the efforts of early settlers.

The Shenandoah River runs for much of the valley's length, as does US Highway 11 and the newer Interstate 81. Ignore the Interstate. A journey through the Shenandoah Valley must involve leisurely progress along US-11 – a former turnpike known as 'The Great Valley Road' – from Roanoke in the south to Harpers Ferry in the north, turning off along the way to explore tempting side roads. This trip will allow you to experience traditional 'Mom and Apple pie America' at its very best and provide real insight into the pioneer spirit that made the country great. The people are friendly and there's usually some sort of festival, celebration or re-enactment to be found – history and tradition are important here.

Bounded by inhospitable mountains, the valley was not easily reached. But the relentless westward thrust of the pioneers saw Shenandoah's first settlements in the 1730s. The wooded valley was soon partially cleared, creating today's picture-postcard landscape that combines natural beauty with traditional farmsteads and historic towns with squares of buildings dating back to the 18th and 19th centuries, all testifying to the energy and industry of those early arrivals. It's said that such places are the backbone of America, and driving through the picturesque Shenandoah Valley it's easy to believe that's true.

*Shenandoah Folk Art & Heritage Center*

# Blue Ridge Parkway

How can you ignore the USA's most-visited National Park, which also happens to be the world's longest and narrowest? Of course you can't – this 755-km (469-mi) National Parkway and All-American Road must not be missed, running as it does through the famously scenic Blue Ridge mountain chain, part of the Appalachians. The road was a 1930s job-creation project in the states of Virginia (Milepost 0) and North Carolina (Milepost 469), though not finally completed as a throughway until 1987.

The effort was worthwhile – the scenery is stunning (those mountains really are a study in misty blues!), whilst the road passes through unspoiled lands maintained by the National Park Service and the US Forest Service. There are 26 tunnels along the way, together with six viaducts and 168 bridges that carry the parkway across ravines, rivers and across roads to ensure an uninterrupted journey. The Parkway starts at Rockfish Gap, Virginia, from the terminus of Shenandoah National Park's Skyline Drive (itself a rewarding journey). It ends in the Great Smoky Mountains National Park near Cherokee, North Carolina. Towns where you can stop off include Waynesboro, Roanoke and Galax in Virginia, or Boone and Asheville in North Carolina.

A drive along the Blue Ridge Parkway is a memorable experience, but to make the most of this unique landscape it really is necessary to stop frequently and explore some of the numerous side roads and trails which often lead to stunning vistas that change according to the seasons, with a variety of trees, colourful foliage and flowers to be enjoyed, especially in spring and autumn. There are also plenty of interesting heritage sites to remind the traveller of the simple lives those hardy mountain families once led.

**HOW:**
By car
**DEPART:**
Rockfish Gap, VA
**WHEN TO GO:**
May to October (the road is not maintained in winter and high sections are often closed).
**TIME IT TAKES:**
Two days, if you hurry along, but taking more time will allow you to explore properly.
**HIGHLIGHTS:**
The Mabry Mill by its tranquil pool at Milepost 176.1, where a trail leads to this vintage gristmill, sawmill and blacksmith shop where old-time skills are demonstrated throughout the summer.
The Blue Ridge Music Center at Milepost 213 near Galax, Virginia – a museum and concert centre with a busy summer schedule, mainly of country music.
Mount Mitchell – the highest point in eastern North America, reached via a road off the Parkway at Milepost 355.4...what a view!
The Folk Art Centre at Milepost 382, for sales and exhibitions of traditional and contemporary Appalachian crafts, with three galleries, a library, book store and interpretive programmes.
**YOU SHOULD KNOW:**
Frontiersman Daniel Boone blazed a pioneering trail to the west that crosses the Parkway near Milepost 285 in North Carolina.

*Great Smoky Mountain National Park.*

# Chesapeake Bay Bridge-Tunnel

There's a toll to pay, but it's well worth it for the pleasure of driving along 'The East Coast's Scenic Shortcut' – US Highway 13 across the Chesapeake Bay Bridge-Tunnel (CBBT) from Virginia's Eastern Shore at Cape Charles to the mainland at Virginia Beach near Norfolk (or vice versa!). The CBBT was opened in 1964 and forms part of the East Coast's Ocean Highway from Florida to New York. It is a dramatic 37-km (23-mi) crossing of Chesapeake Bay utilizing bridges and tunnels, the latter requiring artificial islands as portals, that is both a travel convenience and major tourist attraction. The actual water crossing over this ocean strait is some 28 km (17 mi) long and has been described as 'one of the seven engineering wonders of the modern world'.

This four-lane highway crossing has replaced a passenger and vehicle ferry service that ran from the 1930s and was by the 1960s offering around a hundred daily crossings with large ferries.

The CBBT consists of low-level trestle bridges connected by two tunnels beneath shipping lanes, then two high-level bridges over two other navigation channels. The motorist and passengers mainly have a view of the Atlantic seascape during the crossing, but the bridges do curve to give views of other sections of the CBBT and there are usually plenty of ships to be seen, often including US Navy warships. One novel option is making the crossing by night (perhaps a return journey after a daylight trip?), which offers a fascinating light show. And as a bonus, if you do decide to return within 24 hours, the toll is more than halved!

**HOW:**
By car
**WHEN TO GO:**
Any time of year.
**TIME IT TAKES:**
Half an hour one-way (without stops).
**HIGHLIGHTS:**
Fisherman Island at the entrance to the Bay – a barrier island traversed by US-13 that is part of a National Wildlife Refuge, the habitat of varied waterfowl, shorebirds and waterbirds.
The Scenic Overlook on the tip of Virginia's Eastern Shore, for the perfect spot to admire (and photograph) this engineering marvel.
A quick tour of the Atlantic marshes and the unspoiled countryside of Northampton County on the Eastern Shore.
**YOU SHOULD KNOW:**
The reason it's CBBT rather than plain CBB is that the US Navy feared that accident or hostile action would collapse a bridge-only crossing, thus trapping its Atlantic fleet in Norfolk Navy Base.

*Sunset over the Chesapeake
Bay Bridge-Tunnel*

# Lower Manhattan

New Amsterdam, the Dutch colony that grew into New York City, has long disappeared under Lower Manhattan – yet it remains a fascinating part of the great city to explore. But first look from the water – ride the subway to South Ferry and take a free round trip on the Staten Island Ferry (try for one of the older boats with open decks). Those harbour views are to die for, and you can't help but admire New York's iconic skyline.

Back in Manhattan, walk into Battery Park, with its Castle Clinton National Monument and superb waterfront views of the Statue of Liberty and Ellis Island. Head up State Street to the Bowling Green at the foot of Broadway. The city's oldest park offers a fine view of the impressive Alexander Hamilton Customs House. Go down Whitehall Street to the junction with Water Street. Turn left, walk a block east and go left again up Broad Street, then right into Pearl Street. Go up Pearl (pausing for refreshment at the atmospheric Georgian Fraunces Tavern) and turn left into Wall Street, lined with spectacular skyscrapers and noble buildings, including the Stock Exchange, Morgan Guaranty Trust Company and Citibank. Rest awhile in the tranquil graveyard of Trinity Church at the junction with Broadway. Turn north past historic St Paul's Chapel and go on to City Hall Park, overlooked by the fabulous Woolworth Building and home to New York's venerable City Hall.

End the tour by strolling south down partially pedestrianized Nassau and Fulton Streets to the South Street Seaport Historic District, complete with its working Fulton Fish Market, pavement cafés, Victorian shop fronts, trendy boutiques, street entertainers... and tall ships. The old waterfront is the place to spend the rest of the day, enjoying one of frantic Manhattan's most relaxed quarters.

*A statue of George Washington overlooking the New York Stock Exchange.*

**HOW:**
On foot
**WHEN TO GO:**
Avoid mid-winter (December and January) and high summer (July and August).
**TIME IT TAKES:**
A leisurely day.
**HIGHLIGHTS:**
The suitably tiny Peter Minuit Park at the junction of Water Street and Whitehall Street – commemorating the shrewd Dutchman who purchased Manhattan Island for peanuts.
The Parthenon-like Federal Hall National Memorial on Wall Street, at the very spot where George Washington took the Oath of Office to become first President of the USA.
The Fulton Market Building at Fulton and Front Streets – the wet fish is all gone by dawn, leaving the restored building to interesting shops and tempting restaurants.
**YOU SHOULD KNOW:**
Wall Street used to be...a wall (built by the Dutch in 1653 to defend what is now Lower Manhattan from hostile Indians).

# Roosevelt Island Tramway

**HOW:**
Aerial Tram
**WHEN TO GO:**
Any time.
**TIME IT TAKES:**
Four-and-a-half minutes at a dizzying
26 kph (16 mph).
**HIGHLIGHTS:**
A quick tour of Roosevelt Island for a
bargain 25-cent fare on the 'Red Bus'
that meets each tram.
The extraordinary lighthouse on the
north tip of Roosevelt Island, built in
1872 – a great viewpoint overlooking
the river, Manhattan's Upper East
Side and Triborough Bridge.
A night trip – the view of Manhattan,
the East River and Queens is
magnificent.
The mysterious castle-like Renwick
Ruin at the south end of the island,
named after architect James Renwick
who designed this former smallpox
hospital...and St Patrick's Cathedral
on Fifth Avenue.
**YOU SHOULD KNOW:**
Sex symbol Mae West once served
time in the Welfare Island
Penitentiary (closed in 1935), for
putting on a bawdy Broadway show
entitled...*Sex*.

*The Roosevelt Island Tram
above the East River*

Along with the day's other 10,000-odd commuters and rubberneckers, why not fly through the air with the greatest of ease on New York City's amazing Roosevelt Island Tramway? Completed in 1976, this aerial tramway (cableway to Europeans) spans the East River, connecting Manhattan to Roosevelt Island. Each car has a capacity of 125 people and there are 115 trips per day across the 940-m (3,100-ft) distance, the tramway climbing to a maximum height of 76 m (250 ft) during the journey. The Manhattan entrance to the system is at Tram Plaza (60th Street and 2nd Avenue). The closest New York City subway station is the Lexington Avenue/59th Street complex.

The Tramway runs parallel to the Queensboro Bridge, which crosses Roosevelt Island. Until the 1950s, a trolley (the last in New York) ran to the centre of the Queensboro Bridge, where the cars stopped to let passengers descend to Roosevelt Island by lift. This service was discontinued after a bridge from Queens was built, but there was no direct link to Manhattan until the aerial tram arrived. It was intended to be a temporary measure until the island's subway station was built, but when that was finally completed in 1989 the 'Tram' had become so popular it became a permanent fixture. It was grounded after malfunctioning twice, in 2005 and 2006, stranding passengers in mid-air. After refurbishment, the service was reinstated though (just in case) each car now carries blankets, food, water...and a toilet with privacy curtain.

Roosevelt Island had various names over the centuries – Minnahononck, Varckens Island, Manning's Island, Blackwell's Island and Welfare Island – before its final renaming in anticipation of a Presidential monument to Franklin Delano Roosevelt that never got built. In the 19th century hospitals, asylums and prisons were located on the island, it is now subject to intensive residential redevelopment.

# Hudson River Trip

The mighty Hudson River has made an essential contribution to the New York City we know today. The river rises in the Adirondack Mountains and is 507 km (315 mi) from source to sea. It is entirely in New York State, though in the lower reaches serving as the state line between New York and New Jersey. The Hudson is tidal right up to the Federal Dam south of Troy, which separates the Upper and Lower Hudson Valleys.

Looking out at the hustle and bustle of New York Harbour, it's easy to forget that the Hudson River – and indeed much of upstate New York State – also has a traditional character that's at complete odds with the vibrant modern city. The river has great historical significance, reflected in the Hudson Valley's status as a National Heritage Area. It attracted many of the earliest European settlers and a canal connection to the Great Lakes in the 19th century helped to open up the vast interior of this great continent.

A splendid way to appreciate the contrast is to take a Hudson River Cruise, thus enjoying this striking American landscape much as the pioneers first saw it. There are numerous operators offering cruises, from a week-long luxury trip upriver from New York to a wide selection of interesting day trips from locations along the river. Key ports of call are Tarrytown, Nyack, West Haverstraw, Peekskill, Garrison, Cold Spring, West Point, Newburgh, Poughkeepsie, Kingston, Catskill, Hudson, Albany (the state capital) and Troy. Day cruises can be taken from many of these places, most offering informative commentary that adds context to a dramatic journey that will not only include wonderful natural beauty but also historic sights – from splendid old plantation houses through the massive mansions of robber barons to battlefields and George Washington's Revolutionary War headquarters.

**HOW:**
By boat
**WHEN TO GO:**
Cruise season is May to October.
**TIME IT TAKES:**
From two hours to a week, depending on itinerary.
**HIGHLIGHTS:**
Bear Mountain Bridge, a suspension bridge carrying highways and the Appalachian Trail across the river, flanked on the west bank by Bear Mountain State Park in Rockland County.
The United States Military Academy at West Point, alma mater of so many great Americans.
Vanderbilt Mansion National Historic Site and Franklin D Roosevelt Presidential Library & Museum, both in Hyde Park township, Dutchess County.
Philipsburg Manor at Sleepy Hollow, an atmospheric historic house, water mill and trading site where the Hudson and Pocantico Rivers meet.
**YOU SHOULD KNOW:**
The river is named after Henry Hudson, an Englishman who explored it for the Dutch East India Company in 1609.

*Bear Mountain Bridge crosses the Hudson River at West Point.*

# Cape Cod Scenic Route 6A

**HOW:**
By car
**DEPART:**
Bourne, MA
**WHEN TO GO:**
May to September (high season is
June, July and August).
**TIME IT TAKES:**
An unhurried return journey can be
done in a day, if you aren't tempted to
linger (you will be).
**HIGHLIGHTS:**
One or more of the Cape's famous
lighthouses at Woods Hole, Barnstable,
Hyannis Harbour, Chatham, Truro and
Provincetown.
The 18th-century Bangs Hallet House
in Yarmouth Port – one of many
historic attractions to be found along
Route 6A.
Whale watching out of Provincetown,
a former whaling harbour that has
gained a new lease of life as a result
of tourist interest in its former quarry .
The Cape Cod National Seashore –
dunes, cliffs, swimming beaches and
nature trails located at the far end of
the peninsula.
The exhibit centre at Woods Hole
Oceanographic Institution – the
world's largest private, not-for-profit
ocean research, engineering and
educational organization.
**YOU SHOULD KNOW:**
Beware of local hazards – ticks that
carry Lyme's Disease, poison ivy (nasty
rashes) and mosquitoes.

*Wood End Lighthouse,
Provincetown*

The arm-shaped peninsula that forms the easternmost part of Massachusetts is technically an island, following the completion of the Cape Cod Canal in 1914, but few refer to it as such. Bridges connect 'the Cape' to the mainland, and in summer they're busy with holiday traffic rushing to enjoy the wonderful beachfronts and small-town character of this unique part of New England. Vehicles often back up (both ways), and if planning to leave on a Sunday it's wise to do so before noon or in the early evening, to avoid the inevitable jams.

Massachusetts Route 6A is the official title of parts of former US Highway 6 on Cape Cod, generally known as the Old King's Highway, which runs along the north coast that fronts the enclosed Cape Cod Bay. This is considered to be the Cape's most historic and scenic road, and a journey along it (and back) provides a rewarding opportunity to explore an historic maritime landscape and its quaint New England towns. Though signed, Route 6A can be hard to follow in places and it doesn't officially exist in Eastham or Wellfleet (though the modern US-6 does bridge the gap). Route 6A starts at the Sagamore Bridge in Bourne, and travels for 100 km (62 mi) to Provincetown via Sandwich, Barnstable, Yarmouth, Dennis, Brewster, Orleans and Truro.

These delightful towns are all well worth exploring – full of character, antique shops, galleries, craft outlets and seafood restaurants...but also thousands of vacationers in high season. In order to experience the beauty of Cape Cod without fighting through hordes of like-minded visitors, a journey in late spring or early autumn can pay dividends, though the weather may be cool and some attractions will be closed.

# San Juan Skyway

It's a tongue twister – the San Juan Skyway Scenic Byway. And it's quite a journey – consisting of a 380-km (236-mi) loop through the heart of the snow-capped San Juan Mountains in Colorado.

Starting in Durango, the Skyway follows US Highway 160 to Cortez, before taking Colorado State Highway 145 through Dolores into the San Juan National Forest, over Lizard Head Pass on to Uncompahgre National Forest. It descends near the small town of Ophir, where a spur road leads off to the former silver mining camp of Telluride, now a winter sports centre. After following the San Juan River down to Placerville, the Skyway takes CO-62 over the Dallas Divide to Ridgway. Here, it parts company with the Rio Grande Southern Railroad, which it has shadowed from Durango, and turns south on US-550, through the old mining town of Ouray and Uncompahgre Gorge. The Skyway then crosses Bear Creek Falls and enters the valley of Ironton Park, before climbing over Red Mountain Pass, returning to the San Juan National Forest and descending through the Chattanooga Valley (no, not the Chattanooga of 'Choo Choo' fame, which is in Tennessee) to the historic mining town of Silverton, from whence the Skyway returns to its start point at Durango.

Those are the simple facts of this route, that hint at its rugged character. But in reality they can hardly begin to tell the story of an extraordinary journey. The fabulous mountain views, sheer cliffs, rushing rivers, plunging waterfalls, rocky terrain, old mines, ghost towns, historic railroads and Victorian towns make driving the Skyway a unique experience, as it snakes around mountains, twists through valleys and wriggles through canyons. It's no wonder the San Juan Skyway was designated by the US Government as an All-American Road in 1996. This is the highest possible classification, an accolade that's well deserved.

*The Cliff Palace is an ancient Anasazi cultural settlement in Chapin Mesa.*

**HOW:**
By car
**WHEN TO GO:**
Make the journey between April and October – this is a winter sports area known for avalanches!
**TIME IT TAKES:**
Five hours of non-stop driving, or one to two days for the full experience.
**HIGHLIGHTS:**
Before or after the road journey, take a trip on the Durango & Silverton Narrow Gauge Railroad, riding rolling stock dating back to the 1880s and hauled by classic steam locomotives.
Mesa Verde National Park near Durango – a UNESCO World Heritage Site famous for the many ruined houses, villages and cliff dwellings once occupied by the ancient Pueblo people (often referred to as the Anasazi).
Wonderful mountain vistas from the top of Lizard Head Pass – look for the signed El Diente Peak, Wilson Peak, Mount Wilson and Lizard Head Peak.
**YOU SHOULD KNOW:**
The 'Million Dollar Highway' from Ouray to Silverton is not for the nervous – this two-laner clings to the mountainside and has no guardrails.

*The Skywalk that overlooks the Grand Canyon on the Hualapal Indian reservation in Arizona.*

# Grand Circle Road Trip

**HOW:**
By car
**DEPART:**
Las Vegas, NV
**WHEN TO GO:**
April to October
**TIME IT TAKES:**
At least 10 days, to allow for rewarding time spent exploring this magical landscape.
**HIGHLIGHTS:**
Kolob Arch in Zion National Park, thought to be the world's largest free standing arch at 95 m (310 ft) – see it whilst exploring the amazing Zion National Park Byway.
Hell's Backbone Byway, a dramatic stretch of road near Boulder that travels a ridge with a sheer drop on each side.
Looking straight down into the Grand Canyon from one of the new glass-floored observation platforms – scary!
On the last day – a final stop in the Lake Mead National Recreation Area, just before reaching Las Vegas.
**YOU SHOULD KNOW:**
The famous 1939 John Ford movie *Stagecoach*, starring a young Marion Morrison (John Wayne to you), was shot in Monument Valley.

Viva Las Vegas! But having said that, move on for one of the best sight-seeing road journeys in the USA. This drive of some 1,915 km (1,190 mi) will eventually return you to the world's gambling capital, but not before you've seen some extraordinary natural marvels.

From Las Vegas, drive to St George on Highway 15, then turn off right onto US-89 for Springdale. The attraction here is Zion National Park (overnight in St George or Springfield). Take to the road again – and what a road. You'll be travelling Utah Highway Scenic Byway 12, voted one of the top scenic drives in America for good reason. It winds through National Parks, State Parks and endless scenic vistas encompassing sandstone spikes, petrified forest, high desert and snow-capped mountains.

First stop is Bryce Canyon National Park, with colourful rock formations known as 'hoodoos' (overnight in Bryce). Then take the long and winding road to Capitol Reef National Park (overnight at Torrey). Another long stint through stunning desert landscape will bring you to Arches National Park with its wealth of extraordinary rock arches (overnight at Moab). A short distance further down the road is the Canyonlands National Park, full of amazing canyons, spires, buttes, arches and rivers (overnight at Monticello).

Go on to Monument Valley Tribal Park, with some of the most famous scenery in America – huge sandstone towers amidst unspoiled wilderness (overnight at Kayenta). Last but not least, it's time for the South Rim of the Grand Canyon, 1,830 m (6,000 ft) deep and up to 20 km (15 mi) wide (stay at Grand Canyon village). It is possible to see the North Rim, but it's a long dead-end detour (overnight at Williams).

After all that excitement, the last day is spent driving back to the bright lights of Las Vegas, and more worldly distractions.

# Grand Teton National Park

Part of the Rocky Mountains, the snow-dusted Teton Range soars without foothills from the level floor of Jackson Hole, a long, narrow valley in Wyoming. This special place is preserved as Grand Teton National Park, named after the highest peak that rises to an impressive 4,200 m (13,775 ft). With over 320 km (200 mi) of roads and trails, the Park offers wonderful hiking and biking opportunities.

Mountain bikers can ride the Park from end to end, starting at Jackson, 8 km (5 mi) outside the south entrance. Stay on the road until it forks, giving a choice – Teton Park Road goes over the Snake River and up beside Cottonwood Creek to Jenny Lake, then on past Jackson Lake to rejoin the eastern route. The latter is more straightforward, following the Snake River all the way to Jackson Lake Lodge at the junction with the western route. Thereafter, the road continues alongside the water through Colter Bay Village, which has an informative Visitor Centre, to Lizard Creek at the head of Jackson Lake and then up (and up!) to Flagg Ranch Village. Shortly thereafter, the scenic journey is complete. Or is it? In fact, that may not be the end of the saga after all – as you exit Grand Teton National Park, you find yourself at the south entrance to the awesome Yellowstone National Park, so the temptation to peddle on may prove irresistible.

Be aware that cycling within Grand Teton is restricted to paved and unpaved roads, so hiking trails and the backcountry are no-go areas. Some roads are narrow and vehicle traffic can be heavy in high season, so caution is the watchword. There is accommodation within the Park (pre-booking advisable) or campgrounds for those who wish to explore Grand Teton thoroughly on two wheels or four.

**HOW:**
By bike
**WHEN TO GO:**
May to October
**TIME IT TAKES:**
At least two days – there are numerous scenic side roads providing great views of the Tetons.
**HIGHLIGHTS:**
American bison grazing the lowlands, survivors of the great slaughter in the 19th century that nearly drove them to extinction – just the more obvious representatives of the Park's abundant animal and bird life.
Menor's Ferry and the Chapel of Transfiguration, a historic district off Teton Park Road north of Moose dating back to 1894 – an old cabin, country store, chapel and ferry across the Snake River.
A side trip to the top of Signal Mountain via Signal Mountain Road – it's what your mountain bike is for!
**YOU SHOULD KNOW:**
If you haven't brought your own, it's possible to rent a bicycle in Moose, just inside the park.

*American bison in the Grand Teton National Park*

# Arkansas Highway 7

**HOW:**
By car
**WHEN TO GO:**
September or October for
sensational fall foliage.
**TIME IT TAKES:**
At least a day.
**HIGHLIGHTS:**
The terrific Arkansas Museum of
Natural Resources at Smackover –
1920s scene of one of the wildest
mineral booms in North American
history as up through the ground
came that bubbling crude.
A side-trip from Camden that takes
you to Poison Spring State Park, site
of the Battle of Poison Spring in the
American Civil War.
The best view in Arkansas, after a
short hike to the top of Pedestal
Rocks in the Ozark National Forest.
**YOU SHOULD KNOW:**
Mountain sections of Highway 7 are
not for faint-hearted drivers – they
have numerous steep gradients and
hairpin turns.

Arkansas bills itself as 'The Natural State' – and when you drive Highway 7, the first state-designated Scenic Byway, it's easy to see why. This 465-km (290-mi) journey shows you many different faces of Arkansas, starting just north of the Louisiana state line on the West Gulf Coastal Plain, where an oil boom began near El Dorado in 1921. From there, the road continues to Camden and Arkadelphia through rolling country of river valleys and dense forest.

Highway 7 then enters the Ouachita Mountains, famed for producing amazing quartz crystals, and passes De Grey Lake en route to Hot Springs National Park. The road continues through Ouachita National Forest, past Lake Nimrod and enters the level terrain of the Arkansas River Valley at Russellville. But not for long – it soon climbs into the Ozark Mountains, swinging through the Ozark National Forest, the town of Jasper and on to Harrison, the end of the line.

The journey can be done in a day if scenery is your thing, but Highway 7 deserves a more relaxed approach, with many worthwhile attractions (and distractions) to be found along the way. It's almost impossible not to linger in Hot Springs – the top tourist destination in Arkansas with numerous tempting excuses to pause... not least the USA's oldest National Park, pre-dating the much-touted Yellowstone by 40 years (plunging into therapeutic hot springs mandatory!). Lake Ouachita in the State Park of the same name is delightful, as is the Lake Dardanelle State Park near Russellville. Pedestal Rocks and the Great Arch at Alum Cove will encourage you to linger in the Ozark National Forest. Further north, the Buffalo River is one of the few remaining unpolluted and free-flowing rivers in the USA, as it cuts its way through the Ozarks between massive bluffs.

*Whitaker Point, Ozark National Forest, Arkansas*

# North Cascades Scenic Highway

Its formal name is Washington State Route 20, but the popular North Cascades Highway sounds more romantic. SR-20 runs across Washington State from Puget Sound in the west to Idaho in the east, crossing the Cascade Mountains on the way. This provides a long trip for anyone who wants to drive the whole road, a distance of some 700 km (435 mi), so most prefer to focus on the Scenic Highway, a 225-km (130-mi) section that has some of the most dramatic scenery in the northwestern USA – a trip that would not have been possible before 1972, when this spectacular road was finally completed after decades of argument and much expenditure.

The North Cascades Scenic Highway begins at Sedro-Woolley on SR-20 and enters the rugged North Cascade Range through the Skagit Wild and Scenic River Corridor, following the Skagit through Hamilton, Concrete (true!), Rockport and Marblemount, which has the last gas station before journey's end. The road then enters North Cascades National Park and a good stopping point before the demanding challenge that lies ahead is Newhalem, where the Park's Visitor Center provides information on the vast wilderness bisected by the Scenic Highway. The road continues through the National Park, passing dams that create Diablo and Ross Lakes, providers of hydroelectric power for energy-hungry Seattle.

The Scenic Highway then enters its most demanding stretch, climbing into the mountains towards two incredible high points – Rainy Pass and Washington Pass, each with scenic outlooks that take the breath away. From there, it's downhill all the way as the Highway completes the mountain traverse by winding down through Mazama to Winthrop, a 19th-century staging post for gold miners who flooded into the Slate Creek area. The town has retained much of its original American Old West character and charm.

**HOW:**
By car
**DEPART:**
Sedro-Woolley, WA
**WHEN TO GO:**
May to mid-November
**TIME IT TAKES:**
Five hours with irresistible stops
**HIGHLIGHTS:**
Gorge Creek Falls pull-off outside Newhalem, for an easy loop trail offering great views of the Gorge Dam. Diablo Lake Overlook for restrooms, an interesting geology exhibit and a wide-ranging view across the Cascades. Rainy Pass Picnic Area – take lunch and stop here, before taking a post-prandial stroll along an easy loop trail. Stopping off at the summit of Washington Pass, the journey's literal highlight at 1,699 m (5,477 ft) – admire jutting Liberty Bell and Early Winter Spires (amongst others).
**YOU SHOULD KNOW:**
The Highway is closed between Diablo and Mazama in winter, with a huge depth of snow accumulating on the road. It takes four to six weeks to clear ahead of reopening each spring.

*Liberty Bell Mountain*

# Rim of the World Drive

**HOW:**
By car
**WHEN TO GO:**
Any time of year
**TIME IT TAKES:**
Four hours straight, or a day to enjoy
selected attractions along the way.
**HIGHLIGHTS:**
Before starting off, take the short
hike from Mormon Rock Fire Station
to view the eponymous Mormon
Rocks – a striking pink sandstone
formation that stands on the old
Mormon trail to Utah.
Silverwood Lake State Recreation
Area – take one of the side roads
down to the lake itself.
The Big Bear Discovery Center on Big
Bear Lake's North Shore, offering
wide-ranging visitor information and
interpretive exhibits on the San
Bernadino National Forest.
After Big Bear – Barton Flats, a level
forested area with great views of
Mount San Gorgonio, Southern
California's highest peak at 3,505 m
(11,499 ft).
**YOU SHOULD KNOW:**
Cajon Pass handles more railroad
tonnage than any other rail crossing
in the world, and the overlook is
usually crowded with camera-
carrying railway buffs.

*Big Bear Lake, California*

Up, up and away...into the Californian mountains to experience the 172-km (107-mi) Rim of the World Drive. This National Scenic Byway runs along the crest of the San Bernadino Mountains, passing through magnificent scenery as it connects some of the most popular recreational destinations in the Greater Los Angeles area – Crestline, Lake Arrowhead, Running Springs and Big Bear Lake.

Despite serving these and other well-developed areas, now heavily populated by commuters, the Scenic Byway still manages to twist and turn through some of the last unspoiled country left in Southern California, offering great panoramas at almost every turn. It begins at the Mormon Rock Fire Station just west of Interstate-15 north of San Bernadino, then heads east on California State Road 138 towards the San Bernadino National Forest. At Cajon Pass, several historic routes intersect (the Old Spanish Trail, Santa Fe Trail, Santa Fe Railroad and John Brown's Toll Road). From there, the road goes through Horsethief Canyon, which tells its own tale, and climbs to Crestline.

Now you're up, it's time for the away part – SR-138 becomes SR-18 to carry the Scenic Byway along the rim, with great vistas across San Bernadino and the Los Angeles Basin. There are numerous stopping points and tempting side routes to explore. These lead to mountain communities such as Blue Jay, Twin Peaks, Arrowhead Lake, Skyforest and Running Springs. The next major destination is Big Bear Lake, where SR-18 and SR-38 merge. The Scenic Byway takes the North Shore route – necessitating a diversion along the South Shore to visit Big Bear Lake village. SR-38 then loops back on itself through delightful mountain communities to the Mill Creek Ranger Station at the Byway's end, just short of Redlands, back on the edge of the San Bernadino conurbation.

# San Diego Scenic Drive

This beautiful city in Southern California is just across the border from Tijuana, holiday destination of many-a-million Americans. But as they hurry across the border they are missing something, because San Diego is a major destination in its own right. To make full appreciation of this laid-back place easy for visitors, the 95-km (59-mi) San Diego Scenic Drive guides them around the city. It is clearly marked with blue-and-yellow signs, illustrated with a bold white seagull.

A good starting point is on Harbor Drive at the foot of Broadway, on the Embarcadero (waterfront). Follow the signs carefully and no important sights or outstanding attractions will be missed. Amongst too many to list individually, high points along the way include Harbor Island (wonderful views of San Diego Bay), Spanish Landing, Point Loma (historic lighthouse), Cabrillo National Monument (commemorates the first European visitor, Portuguese explorer Juan Rodriguez Cabrillo, in 1542), Sunset Cliffs, Ocean Beach, Mission Bay Aquatic Park (endless beaches), Soledad Mountain Park (best view in town), the University of California and Salk Institute, La Jolla Cove and Cave, Pacific Beach, Mission Beach, Sports Arena, Old Town State Historic Park (former Hispanic town centre), Hillcrest, Balboa Park (museum and cultural focus), the financial district, Seaport Village (a trendy shopping complex) and back to the starting point.

That's not quite it – the route continues on to the historic heart of San Diego, the Gaslamp Quarter – once the home of opium dens, gambling halls and saloons, now a vibrant entertainment district. If you're not sidetracked there, continue to the end of the San Diego Scenic Drive in the ultra-modern Horton Plaza, where you can spend the rest of the day shopping and dining...a fitting end to a rewarding day spent exploring this beguiling Californian city.

**HOW:**
By car
**WHEN TO GO:**
Any time
**TIME IT TAKES:**
A relaxed stop-and-go day
**HIGHLIGHTS:**
One of the world's best collections of historic ships at the Maritime Museum of San Diego, and the nearby aircraft carrier USS *Midway*, now a floating museum.
The SeaWorld Adventure Park – everything from performing orcas and sealions to a variety of thrill rides.
Balboa Park, largest urban cultural park in North America, complete with Spanish revival buildings dating from the Expositions of 1915 and 1935 – find 15 museums, the Old Globe Theatre complex and lush gardens.
Also in Balboa Park – the world-famous San Diego Zoo and Wild Animal Park.
**YOU SHOULD KNOW:**
Be prepared to say 'Hello sailor' – San Diego is the traditional home base of the US Navy's mighty Pacific Fleet.

*The Plaza de Panama fountain in Balboa Park*

# Beartooth Highway

**HOW:**
By car
**WHEN TO GO:**
June to August
**TIME IT TAKES:**
Two hours
**HIGHLIGHTS:**
Red Lodge – a former coal-mining town that retains much of its 19th-century character, with many buildings on the National Register of Historic Places.
A pull-out after a series of switchbacks 32 km (20 mi) from Red Lodge for a fabulous view over the Beartooth Plateau – spot the Hell Roaring and Silver Run areas, Rock Creek and Glacier Lake.
Everyone should boast of having been there – so visit the Top of the World, a store and gas station of that name just after crossing Beartooth Pass.
Clay Butte – a short side-trip along a dirt road to the right, 68 km (42 mi) from Red Lodge, leading to an old fire tower atop the Butte, from where there are amazing views to Pilot Peak and the jagged Index Peak.
**YOU SHOULD KNOW:**
Beartooth Pass was pioneered by General Phillip Sheridan's Yellowstone inspection party in 1882, when an old trapper suggested the route followed by today's Highway, saving a lot of miles on the return journey to Billings, Montana.

*Index Peak reflected in Mud Lake.*

It initially seems incongruous that so many scenic journeys in the USA are routinely described as 'the most beautiful drive in America' – or perhaps equally strange that several dozen are rated as 'one of America's Top 10 scenic drives'. But then the realization sinks in that there is so much wondrous natural beauty in this vast and varied country that it really is hard to choose the best. That said, few would disagree that the Beartooth Highway in Montana and Wyoming comes very close to the top of any list.

It is a section of US Highway 212 between Red Lodge, Montana and Cooke City, Montana – a journey of just 111 km (69 mi), but what a journey. It ascends to the Beartooth Plateau, zigzagging and switchbacking as it crosses the Montana-Wyoming state line, just north of Yellowstone National Park, climbing above the tree line to offer expansive views. To the south – canyons eroded by the Clarks Fork River over millennia. To the north – the Absaroka-Beartooth Wilderness, complete with the sharply etched spike known as Bear's Tooth that gave these massive mountains their name. Then the Highway climbs to the summit of mighty 3,345-m (10,974-ft) Beartooth Pass.

From there, it's a downhill run into lake country. There are over a thousand in the wilderness with Long, Little Bear, Island and Beartooth Lakes alongside the Highway. After passing a turnoff for Wyoming Highway 296 (the Chief Joseph Scenic Highway – take it for a full-day loop drive back to Red Lodge) the Beartooth Highway runs down into the old gold-mining town of Cooke City. This is the northeastern gateway to Yellowstone, and there will be time a-plenty to take a peek...if you're not already suffering from an overdose of memorable scenery.

# Peter Norbeck Scenic Byway

'Take me back to the Black Hills, the Black Hills of Dakota', croons the seductive song. It's certainly a trip worth making and one way of getting the most from a visit is to follow the Peter Norbeck Scenic Byway, named after the early-1900s South Dakota Governor and conservation-minded Senator. This 110-km (68-mi) route loops through the Black Hills National Forest and Custer State Park in southwestern Dakota, an area rather different from the state's classic rolling prairies.

Start at the town of Custer, named after the late, not-so-great General who camped here in 1874 on his first, not-so-fatal expedition to the Black Hills. Head north on Highway 89, to a section called the Needles Highway where the road winds around hillsides and through tunnels, all the while passing the spectacular granite spires that give the road its name. Turning north on Highway 87 takes you past Peter Norbeck Wildlife preserve, onto the aptly named Iron Mountain Road, famous for one-lane tunnels aligned with Mount Rushmore.

From there, take US-16A along to that iconic American monument – Mount Rushmore, where the faces of four great Presidents were carved into the mountain's solid granite by sculptor Gutzon Borglum and his crew between 1927 and 1941. After admiring Washington, Jefferson, Roosevelt and Lincoln, head on (pun intended) past towering Harney Peak on Highway 244 to the edge of the Black Hills National Forest, where Highway 87 and then Highway 89 will return you to the starting point at Custer. Along the way you will have seen the American West at its best – soaring mountains, rugged rock formations, caves, forests, grasslands, canyons, gulches, rushing rivers and lakes, all made accessible to the motor car by amazing roads built with ingenuity and engineering skills of the highest order.

*A model of Sioux Indian Chief Crazy Horse stands in front of Thunderhead Mountain.*

**HOW:**
By car
**DEPART:**
Custer, SD
**WHEN TO GO:**
May to October
**TIME IT TAKES:**
A day, allowing for sightseeing stops.
**HIGHLIGHTS:**
Pigtail bridges on Iron Mountain Road – you'll know why they're called that when you get to the first one.
The Sculptor's Studio at the foot of Mount Rushmore, providing fascinating insight into the creation of this great 20th-century work.
If you're impressed by Mount Rushmore check out nearby Crazy Horse Monument, an ongoing project to create a massive likeness of the mounted chief in solid granite, which will be the world's largest sculpture – alongside the Indian Museum of North America and Native American Cultural Center.
Wind Cave National Park, near Custer
**YOU SHOULD KNOW:**
If the famous Mount Rushmore Presidential heads had bodies, they would stand tall – 150 m (475 ft) tall.

# Old Spanish Trail

This trade route from Santa Fe to Los Angeles was explored by European pioneers in the 1770s and saw extensive use in the second quarter of the 19th century. It is about 2,000 km (1,200 mi) long, though there were several choices for travellers using the loose network of Indian footpaths crossing the Colorado Plateau and Mojave Desert. In its heyday the Trail was renowned for all the less endearing characteristics of the Wild West – rip-roaring frontier towns, naked commercial opportunism, banditry, horse stealing and raids – as mainly Mexican pack trains went from Sante Fe to Los Angeles to trade slaves and woollen goods for horses and mules raised on Californian ranches.

The demanding journey encompassed six modern states – New Mexico, Colorado, Utah, Arizona, Nevada and California, running through high mountains, deserts and canyon country. Today, few traces of the original Trail remain, though it is remembered by many historical markers, road and street names. The only way to retrace its course is by car. The Old Spanish National Historic Trail offers dramatic landscapes and a rich legacy of pioneering spirit, western adventure and American history, and you can plot your own journey or get a special map that does it for you.

Beginning in the plaza at Santa Fe, the Trail's main route follows the Rio Grande Valley, then veers north, crosses the Continental Divide and reaches the San Juan River in Colorado. It continues across Colorado, passes near Mesa Verde and enters Utah east of Monticello. From there it continues past Canyonlands and Arches National Parks before crossing the Colorado and Green Rivers, then cuts across the Great Basin to Mountain Meadows. It crosses the corner of Arizona, reaches Las Vegas and continues across the Mojave Desert to Los Angeles via Cajon Pass.

*The San Juan River winds its way through the Comb Ridge area in Utah.*

# Sante Fe Trail

Santa Fe was pivotal in the development of the American Southwest. This charming adobe city featured on the El Camino Real Trail up from Mexico and was both the starting point of the Old Spanish Trail to California and end-point of the Santa Fe Trail from Missouri through the modern states of Kansas, Oklahoma and New Mexico. The latter was a vital trade route from its inauguration in 1821 to 1880, when the railway's arrival at Santa Fe made it obsolete. Depending on the route, the Trail was around 1,255 km (780 mi) long.

The original Trail took a northern path. This was the Mountain branch, intersecting the historic California and Oregon Trails at Independence, Missouri. Thereafter it reached the Arkansas River at Great Bend and went upstream to Dodge City, Garden City and La Junta, from whence it swung down through the Raton Pass to Watrous and on to Santa Fe via Las Vegas (no gambling then at this one-horse town!), San José and Pecos. The southern route – the Cimarron Cutoff – was shorter but more dangerous, with little water. It went through the Cimarron River Valley to Boise City, Oklahoma and Clayton, New Mexico, before rejoining the northern route at Watrous.

There were many variations, especially of the Mountain Route, but those who wish to follow the Santa Fe National Historic Trail from beginning to end can do so on modern highways that duplicate the general course of both routes, though some sections are inaccessible. The Historic Trail is administered and promoted by the US National Park Service, who offer specialist maps and a wealth of useful information. Those who follow the Trail today (in vehicular comfort!) can only marvel at the courage and determination of those who travelled only on foot, horseback or by wagon.

**HOW:**
By car
**WHEN TO GO:**
Any season
**TIME IT TAKES:**
Five days, allowing some time for exploration.
**HIGHLIGHTS:**
Arrow Rock – a prominent bluff on west bank of the Missouri River, a major landmark, river crossing and staging post on the Trail.
A National Historic Landmark – the longest clearly visible section of the Trail near once-deadly Dodge City, Kansas.
Spotting wagon ruts – the Trail was so well used over time that deep wagon ruts are still visible at many points along both routes, and may be found by looking for historical markers along the Scenic Byways.
The Fort Union National Monument north of Watrous, New Mexico – a preserved fort and remains of another where the two branches of the Santa Fe Trail reunited.
**YOU SHOULD KNOW:**
At its peak, the Santa Fe Trail carried over 5,000 wagons a year, mostly overloaded with manufactured goods to be traded or sold at Santa Fe and points west.

*Remains of the Santa Fe trail's Mountain branch in western Kansas*

*A paddle steamer is docked below a suspension bridge.*

# Mississippi Riverboat Cruise

**HOW:**
By boat
**WHEN TO GO:**
Cruises are available all year round.
**TIME IT TAKES:**
Most cruises are seven nights, but there are shorter and longer options to be found.
**HIGHLIGHTS:**
Hearing (or even playing!) a calliope – these steam-powered organs were, and still are, very much a part of the riverboat scene.
Small-town America at its best (plus 29 locks) on an Upper Mississippi cruise from St Paul down to St Louis (seven nights).
All the charm and elegance of the old Deep South on a Lower Mississippi cruise from New Orleans to Memphis (seven nights).
**YOU SHOULD KNOW:**
Louis Armstrong sure knew what he was talking about when he sang the classic song 'Ol' Man River – he travelled up the river from New Orleans by paddle steamer, stopping at various towns along the way to play.

An enduring image of 19th-century America is the riverboat – a sternwheeler belching wood smoke from tall twin stacks as she dashed up and down the Mississippi, Ohio or Missouri Rivers. There was probably a high-stakes poker game going on within the fancy white superstructure, ending in gunplay when five aces came down in the same hand, whilst Mark Twain watched from the bank, pen in hand. Well, maybe it wasn't quite like that, but these stylish craft certainly played a vital role in developing the central-southern and mid-western USA.

Americans are good at marrying tradition with commerce, so it's still possible to experience the delights of this traditional river transport by taking a paddlesteamer trip. The modestly named Majestic America Line runs a variety of cruises using a couple of late 20th-century steamboats – *American Queen* (the largest river steamboat ever built) and the *Mississippi Queen*. Each is the ultimate in old-fashioned comfort and style, though *American Queen* is something of an impostor – she looks the part and has a sternwheel driven by steam, but her main source of propulsion is diesel-powered propellers. The company's *Delta Queen*, built in 1927, is a National Historic Landmark, but sadly her cruising future is on hold as a result of modern safety regulations.

These steamboats offer both a selection of 'see the river' cruises and theme cruises including the popular Jazz and Civil War itineraries. A cruise won't be cheap, but really is an opportunity to experience the elegant atmosphere and travelling style of a bygone era. Oh, the romance of paddle steamers is infectious. If you don't fancy the Mississippi, sternwheelers are now working Alaska's Inside Passage and the great rivers of the northwestern USA (Columbia, Willamette and Snake) for the first time in a century.

# Death Valley

Here's one for the tough and super fit – a cycle trip through notorious Death Valley in California and Nevada. It's the lowest place in America at 86 m (282 ft) below sea level, and also one of the hottest on earth with temperatures regularly reaching 54°C (130°F) in the day (but sometimes freezing at night). That makes it the ultimate cycling challenge.

Death Valley National Park is a unique environment, offering a wonderfully atmospheric landscape of sand dunes, salt flats, multicoloured rocks, canyons, snow-capped mountains and seemingly endless wilderness. The Park has a number of roads, mostly narrow and twisting, and not even the most dedicated mountain biker can be expected to explore them all.

A good journey follows California Route 190, which crosses the middle of Death Valley (albeit not in a straight line!) from Panamint Springs in the southwestern corner of the Park. From there it's a 29-km (18-mi) run to Emigrant, then another 13 km (8 mi) to Stovepipe Wells Village, which has all the facilities required for a little R&R. You'll need it – the next leg is the 44-km (28-mi) slog along CA-190, which turns sharply south before reaching the Furnace Creek Visitor Center. If you want to see that low point, detour to Badwater Basin, due south of the Visitor Center. If you can't face that 52-km (34-mi) round trip, continue on CA-190 and make the straight run to the Park exit and on to Death Valley Junction, a 45-km (28-mi) ride.

If that's not enough to test your cycling prowess, you can take the State Line Road to Pahrump, Nevada – or even (if you're feeling lucky) cycle on from there to Las Vegas. Wimps can do Death Valley by air-conditioned car – which does give them the opportunity to explore the Park's many wonders more thoroughly.

**HOW:**
By bike
**WHEN TO GO:**
November to March to avoid the worst heat conditions (and traffic).
**TIME IT TAKES:**
A day, if you don't keep stopping off to admire the sights.
**HIGHLIGHTS:**
A literal highlight – Towne Pass, a 1,510-m (4,955-ft) summit that greets you just inside the Park.
Mosaic Canyon near Stovepipe Wells – take the dirt road for sweeping views and extraordinary walls of polished multicoloured rock.
Zabriskie Point – no, not the iconic Antonioni movie, but the real thing, to be found shortly after the Furnace Creek Visitor Center – it's an amazing rock formation.
A long, cold shower and good night's sleep at journey's end, wherever that may be.
**YOU SHOULD KNOW:**
Death Valley is the low point, but the high point in the lower 48 states – Mount Whitney – is just 123 km (76 mi) west of Death Valley. After cycling the Valley, why not go on to climb the mountain?

*Rock formations at Zabriskie Point*

# Sea Islands

**HOW:**
By car
**DEPART:**
Jacksonville, FL
**WHEN TO GO:**
Any time of year
**TIME IT TAKES:**
Two days to explore properly as
you go.
**HIGHLIGHTS:**
One of the main attractions in
northeastern Florida – the
Jacksonville Landing complex on the
north bank of the St Johns River, with
wonderful shopping facilities and a
rolling programme of entertainment.
Savannah's captivating downtown
area – one of the largest National
Historic Districts in the USA.
A side-trip to Georgia's famed Golden
Isles – Jekyll Island, St Simons Island,
Sea Island and Little St Simons Island
(they're well-signed off US-17 in the
Brunswick area).
Rainbow Row in Charleston – historic
merchants' waterfront houses now
painted in a variety of pastel colours.
**YOU SHOULD KNOW:**
During the Civil War white residents
fled the Sea Islands, leaving slaves to
organize their own lives and
effectively become the first in the
Deep South to be emancipated.

*Houses on Rainbow Row
in Charleston*

This chain of barrier islands runs down the USA's Atlantic Coast off South Carolina, Georgia and Florida. The Sea Islands are captivating and with over 100 to choose from it's possible to plan a journey with ample opportunity to explore this delightful coast. One excellent route is from Jacksonville in Florida to Charleston in South Carolina, allowing you to find and visit Sea Islands in all three states.

From Jacksonville, take State Route 10 before cutting left through Atlantic Beach and taking the Mayport ferry. Turn right along the coast road over Fort George Inlet, continuing through the Little Talbot and Big Talbot Island State Parks, across Nassau Sound and onto Amelia Island. Stay with the water until the road becomes State Route 200 and doubles back on itself. Follow SR-200 until the intersection with US Highway 17 past Yulee. Known as the Coast Road, this mainly follows the line of Interstate-95, but is a route that allows you to take interesting side-trips all the way to Charleston.

US-17 cuts inland to Woodbine and Spring Bluff before turning coastwards and running north though Brunswick, parallel with the Sea Islands. A number of roads lead down to the water if you want the sea for yourself, as there are no major resorts in this area. The next port of call is Savannah, and the historic Georgia town merits a long stop, with a wonderful waterfront and access to more islands. Take US-16 north out of Savannah – it turns into US-17 and you're back on track. At Hardeeville, take the loop through Beaufort on Port Royal Island, perhaps going on to Hunting Island State Park before returning on US-21 via Beaufort, following the road past the air station until it rejoins US-17. From there it's a straight run into the elegant southern city of Charleston.

# The Arizona Trail

*Kitt Peak in the Saguaro National Park.*

Ambitious mountain biker? Be one of the first to cycle the newly signed Arizona Trail, designed to provide a physical challenge even as it showcases the widest possible variety of terrain and ecosystems (including lung-busting mountains!), together with Arizona's cultural and historic diversity. The idea is to keep things simple (primitive, even, though there are campgrounds) so this is a rough, tough adventure that will take you through some of the most rugged and spectacular scenery in western America. Ready, steady, pedal...

The Trail begins at the Coronado National Memorial near the Mexican border and goes north through the Huachuca, Santa Rita and Rincon Mountains. Before you can draw breath, you'll be in the Santa Catalina Mountains north of Tucson, then the Mazatzals. But there's more climbing in store, into the San Francisco Peaks. At last, there's easier going – the Coconino Plateau all the way to the Grand Canyon, across the Colorado River and the final Kaibab Plateau stretch to the Arizona-Utah border. Job done!

Actually, it's not that simple, which is good news and bad news. The bad news is that the Arizona Trail is still under development, and only some 1,207 km (750 mi) of the proposed 1,287-km (800-mi) route have been completed, so it isn't yet possible to travel from beginning to end. There are short breaks in Saguaro National Park, Boyce Thompson Arboretum State Park, Kaibab National Forest and approaching the Grand Canyon. The good news is that the Arizona Trail incorporates many established trails, so it is possible to pick and choose rewarding sections without doing the whole thing.

One thing's for sure – you won't see much human habitation. Apart from the tiny town of Patagonia shortly after starting, the only other place on the Trail is Flagstaff, and even there you can take a detour.

**HOW:**
By bike
**WHEN TO GO:**
September to June to avoid the hottest months.
**TIME IT TAKES:**
Allow a month for an attempt on the complete Trail.
**HIGHLIGHTS:**
Kentucky Camp in the Santa Ritas – the Forest Service has turned it into a living history exhibit of early 20th-century mining.
Pusch Ridge Wilderness in the Coronado National Forest – terrific mountain views, abundant wildlife, an impressive variety of flora.
Saguaro National Park in the Rincons – established to protect those wonderful tall cacti with arms that feature along with the tumbleweed in any self-respecting Western.
Crossing the Grand Canyon by the South Kaibab Trail, then up the other side on the North Kaibab Trail – the experience of a lifetime!
**YOU SHOULD KNOW:**
The Coronada National Memorial celebrates the first European expedition to southwestern America, by Francisco Vásquez de Coronado in 1540, so the Trail follows in the hoof prints of conquistadors.

**63**

# The John Muir Trail

This is a terrific hike for those with strong legs and stronger lungs, running for 340 km (211 mi) along California's Sierra Nevada mountain range from the Happy Isles trailhead in Yosemite Valley to Mount Whitney in the south. And that's the direction to go on the John Muir Trail (JMT), allowing the hiker to become acclimatized to the thin atmosphere before tackling the more remote, demanding southern half. The JMT attracts plenty of day hikers, but the true challenge is backpacking the entire Trail. A permit is required to hike, to be obtained from the National Park or Forest where the journey begins.

Be prepared for some heavy breathing. After the initial climb out of Yosemite Valley, the JMT is mostly over 2,440 m (8,000 ft) in elevation, above and beyond the height most people ever experience for extended periods. And that's not all – the journey crosses six passes (Donohue, Muir, Mather, Pinchot, Glen and Forester). The last – Forester – is the highest at a mighty 4,010 m (13,155 ft). After running through Tuolomne Meadows the JMT parallels the main range of the Sierra Nevada thorough Yosemite National Park, Inyo and Sierra National Forests, Devils Postpile National Monument, Kings Canyon National Park and Sequoia National Park. Along the way it passes through some wild country, including the formally designated John Muir and Ansell Adams Wilderness Areas.

Even after gallantly reaching the end of the JMT by climbing to the summit of Mount Whitney, there's a sting in the tail – a further hike to civilization at the nearest trailhead at Whitney Portal, 18 km (11 mi) farther on. The effort is worthwhile. One of the true wonders of the USA is that – for all the country's sprawling and apparently insatiable urban development – it takes such care of (and pride in) pristine wilderness of the sort preserved along the JMT.

**HOW:**
On foot
**WHEN TO GO:**
July to September
**TIME IT TAKES:**
Allow at least two weeks – three to be sure.
**HIGHLIGHTS:**
Yosemite's most famous sight – the impressive granite Half Dome at the eastern end of Yosemite Valley.
The Devils Postpile near Mammoth Mountain – an extraordinary basalt cliff made up of old lava columns, topped by pine trees and standing above a slope of fallen columns.
Soaking those hard-working feet in soothing hot springs to be found within the John Muir Wilderness section of the Trail.
The breathtaking natural beauty of the Kings Canyon National Park – including Rae Lakes, Marie Lake, Upper Basin, Le Conte Canyon, Evolution Valley and McClure Meadow.
**YOU SHOULD KNOW:**
After hiking the John Muir Trail, you can also boast of hiking the much longer Pacific Coast Trail (well, the section it shares with the JMT!).

*Painted Lady in Kings Canyon National Park*

# Huckleberry Mountain Horse Trail

This glorious scenic journey is in the Ozark National Forest of northwest Arkansas, and for a short distance within adjacent Mount Magazine State Park. Anyone who wishes to tackle the Huckleberry Mountain Horse Trail has a choice of steeds – the good old-fashioned horses for which it was designed, the two well-shod feet of Shanks' Pony or the thoroughly modern lightweight alloy wheels of a mountain bike. That's not all. Sadly for the purists, this Trail is one of four within the National Forest that has been designated for use by those noisy and rather irritating All-Terrain Vehicles (ATVs). Take your pick!

The Trail shows the Ozarks at their best, offering a rugged landscape of shady forests and stunning mountain vistas. It consists of two loops, together offering some 55 km (34 mi) of well-marked scenic horseback riding, if that's the delightfully relaxed way you choose to travel. The terrain is varied – deep, winding valleys and creeks are overlooked by mountain bluffs. There are clear mountain streams and numerous trailside ponds for watering the horses.

The Apple Loop is the easy one – 19 km (12 mi) of old logging roads and existing forest tracks marked with orange signposts or horseshoe blazes on trees. The Huckleberry Mountain Loop is likewise marked, but is definitely more demanding. Some of the sections on the 36-km (22-mi) Horse Trail are quite difficult, and there is a shorter 12-km (9-mi) option within the Mountain Loop, covering easier country for those who do not wish to attempt the full circuit. After rain, some of the creeks and streams can become dangerous and should be crossed with extreme care – especially Shoal Creek. It's not difficult to stray off-route, so a Trail map is a wise investment.

**HOW:**
On foot, a horse, a bike or an ATV
**DEPART:**
St Louis, AR
**WHEN TO GO:**
March to September
**TIME IT TAKES:**
One day
**HIGHLIGHTS:**
The view from the top of Mount Magazine, the highest point in Arkansas – breathtaking.
Brightly coloured butterflies – you'll find an absolute profusion of them from April onwards.
For petrolheads in a hurry – guided three- or five-hour ATV tours of the Huckleberry Mountain Trail.
**YOU SHOULD KNOW:**
Parts of the Mountain Loop are closed in April and May for the turkey breeding season.

*The Ozarks and the Arkansas River Valley from the top of Mount Magazine*

# Tahoe Rim Trail

**HOW:**
On foot
**WHEN TO GO:**
Mid-June to October (hot for hiking,
but no remnants of snow).
**TIME IT TAKES:**
Allow at least two weeks.
**HIGHLIGHTS:**
Spooner Lake and Summit above the
east shore – refill the water bottle
whilst soaking up fabulous views
across Lake Tahoe.
The outlook from Relay Peak – far-
reaching panoramic views of the
entire Tahoe Basin, over the Sierras
to Mount Lassen and beyond.
A stunning display of wild flowers (at
their best in the first two weeks of
July) or fall foliage (September
and October).
Any one of the nine trailheads on the
THT – not only because they mark
progress, but for the opportunity to
restock with essential supplies!
**YOU SHOULD KNOW:**
You get to tackle two for the price of
one – the section above the lake's
west shore is shared with the Pacific
Coast Trail.

Stand by for a tall trail – the Tahoe Rim Trail (TRT) that ranges in elevation from a mere 1,900 m (6,240 ft) at the outlet end of Lake Tahoe to an altogether more impressive 3,150 m (10,335 ft) at Relay Peak, though it has been carefully constructed to ensure that the average gradient throughout is no more than 10 per cent. This long-distance hiking and equestrian route circles Lake Tahoe in the Carson and Sierra Nevada mountain ranges of Nevada and California. Mountain biking is allowed along most (but not all) sections of the TRT.

Lake Tahoe is a deep-blue, natural mountain lake, some 35 km (22 mi) long by 19 km (12 mi) wide. It is surrounded by snowcapped mountains, volcanic peaks, granite cliffs, lush forests, jewel-like small lakes, alpine meadows and a rich diversity of flora and fauna. The Tahoe Rim Trail that girdles this natural marvel is 266 km (165 mi) long, going through two states, six counties, one State Park, three National Forests and three Wilderness Areas. It's all demanding terrain that presents a real challenge to the dedicated hiker, who will need to carry all the essentials for survival in a single backpack. The reward for all that physical effort is experiencing the solitude and outstanding natural beauty of one of America's great trails.

The TRT is open to skiers in winter, but is not marked then. A permit is required to enter Desolation Wilderness (the Echo Lake to Barker Pass section of the Trail). There are blue triangular TRT markers at regular intervals, but anyone attempting the entire journey should get a detailed map. Those who don't have the time (or strength) to undertake the entire journey but wish to see something of this magical landscape can access the Trail at many points for a day hike.

*Lake Tahoe with the Sierra Mountains in the background*

# Mason-Dixon Trail

Connecting the Appalachian and Brandywine Trails, the Mason-Dixon Trail (M-DT) is 310 km (193 mi) long and starts in Pennsylvania at Whiskey Springs on the Appalachian Trail. It then goes east to the Susquehanna River, passing through Pinchot State Park along the way. The M-DT continues along the west bank of the Susquehanna south to Havre de Grace in Maryland, crosses the river and continues east through the Elk Neck State Forest into Delaware's Iron Hill Park. From there, the M-DT heads north along the Christina River and White Clay Creek to the White Clay Creek Reserve. It then turns northeast for the last leg to the eastern trailhead at Chadds Ford on the Brandywine River, back in Pennsylvania.

The Trail is well marked by blue blazes, but is no wilderness excursion designed to avoid human habitation. True, it does go through much pleasing open countryside, but in so doing often follows narrow back roads where traffic can be dangerous. It also passes through plenty of small towns and developed areas. That said, it does offer some fine vistas, along with long and scenic stretches of hilly, rolling terrain that is well wooded, plus rocky climbs out of side gorges along the Susquehanna River.

Though essentially designed for hikers, many sections of the M-DT are increasingly being used by mountain bikers. There is an active Trail Association that provides up-to-date maps and is constantly doing maintenance and improvement work on the M-DT, also dealing with the occasional outbreaks of friction between private owners and hikers that can cause the Trail to be slightly re-routed.

**HOW:**
By foot or by bike
**WHEN TO GO:**
April to October (but September tends to be very wet).
**TIME IT TAKES:**
Two weeks
**HIGHLIGHTS:**
Gifford Pinchot State Park – reverting farmlands and wooded hillsides with Pinchot Lake serving as the centrepiece.
Codorus Furnace, located along Codorus Creek – once owned by James Smith, a signatory of the Declaration of Independence, this furnace built in 1765 supplied ammunition to colonists during the American Revolution.
The Holtwood Environmental Preserve on the banks of the lower Susquehanna River, including the Lock 12 Historic Area.
**YOU SHOULD KNOW:**
The M-DT follows in the footsteps of Charles Mason and Jeremiah Dixon, who surveyed the Maryland-Pennsylvania border in 1764, thus establishing the historic dividing line between the USA's North and South.

*Sunrise over Pinchot Lake*

# Wonderland Trail

**HOW:**
On foot
**WHEN TO GO:**
Late July to October (to avoid possible snow coverage).
**TIME IT TAKES:**
Two weeks
**HIGHLIGHTS:**
An original ranger's cabin at Indian Henry's Hunting Ground, dating from the construction of the Wonderland Trail in 1915.
Mowich Lake, a pretty trailhead in the northwestern corner of the National Park that offers basic facilities to the weary hiker.
Longmire Buildings in the Nisqually River Valley – a brief dose of civilization with an inn, museum and Wilderness Information Center.
**YOU SHOULD KNOW:**
Each year, only two to three hundred people manage to complete the entire Wonderland Trail in a single, unbroken hike.

Up and down, up and down – the Wonderland Trail in Washington State is not for the faint-hearted or unfit. This rough-country route shuns roads and human habitation as it journeys around mighty Mount Rainier in the National Park of the same name, arriving back at the starting point after 150 km (93 mi). As to that up-and-down element, the cumulative elevation gain during the circumnavigation is around 6,000 m (20,000 ft), which adds up to a serious physical effort as the Trail crosses ridge after soaring ridge.

But Wonderland it is – the Mount Rainier National Park offers a variety of eco-systems, from lowland forest to sub-alpine meadows, and Mount Rainier itself reveals a series of spectacular glaciers as the journey unfolds. The Trail crosses many rivers, often by simple log bridges, occasionally by more dramatic suspension bridges. Though there are a number of trailheads that will be busy in summer, many stretches of the Trail provide complete solitude amidst natural grandeur. But hikers should be aware that weather conditions can be treacherous, with dangerous storms always a possibility (especially in September). This is definitely not a journey for the inexperienced, but only the hardened wilderness hiker.

There are several campgrounds on the Trail (booking advisable in mid-summer), together with 18 trailside campsites at regular intervals along the way, each with a nearby water source and a bear pole for hanging food safely. A backcountry permit is required to hike the entire Trail, and the challenge is so alluring that early application is advisable (in March), as a ballot is held in April to allocate a limited number of permits, thus ensuring the Wonderland Trail will never be spoiled by over-exploitation.

*Indian Bear shelter, Mount Ranier National Park*

# California Zephyr

No argument – this is one of the world's great train journeys, sheer heaven for the scenically minded. It covers 3,925 km (2,440 mi) from Chicago to the Pacific coast, traversing Illinois, Iowa, Nebraska, Colorado, Utah, Nevada and California. In so doing, it crosses the American Midwest before heading over the Rocky Mountains and Sierra Nevadas to California. This luxury service was inaugurated in 1949 and has gone through various changes since those early days, though things have stabilized since Amtrak initiated the modern Superliner service (choice of roomy coach seats or private sleepers) in 1983.

Heading westwards from Chicago, the California Zephyr (CZ) crosses the Great Plains, that expanse of corn country where once the buffalo roamed. After reaching Denver, the scenery changes dramatically as the train climbs into the amazing Rocky Mountains. It crosses the Continental Divide via the 10-km (6-mi) Moffat Tunnel, and then follows the Colorado River for hours as it turns from white-water channel to wide river. After Grand Junction the CZ parts company with Colorado and enters Utah. There, it travels the Book Cliffs range before entering the Wasatch Mountains on the Rockies' western fringe, crossing at Soldier Summit.

After Salt Lake City the CZ passes along the south shore of the Great Salt Lake, across Bonneville Flats (scene of many a land-speed-record attempt) and into Nevada. It crosses the Pequop Mountains via the Flower Pass Tunnel, before following the Humboldt River across Nevada until it vanishes in the desert. The Truckee River leads to Reno and California's Sierra Nevada, which are finally crested at the forbidding Donner Pass. The CZ descends to the lowlands and runs into Emeryville, a suburb of Oakland, from whence there's a bus transfer for those continuing to San Francisco. Or start at Emeryville and go east, young man!

*Salt Lake City with the snow capped Wasatch Mountains in the background*

**HOW:**
By train
**DEPART:**
Chicago, IL
**WHEN TO GO:**
Any day
**TIME IT TAKES:**
Roughly 51 hours and 20 minutes (give or take!).
**HIGHLIGHTS:**
Plainview above Denver, for a sensational view of the cities of both Denver and Boulder (and the Rocky Flats nuclear arms manufacturing plant!).
Ruby Canyon on the Colorado River, with its towering red sandstone formations – unless you raft in, the only way to see the place is from the Zephyr.
The amazing series of switchback turns the track takes as it descends from Soldier Summit in Utah's Wasatch Mountains.
Cape Horn near Colfax, California – before the CZ crosses a long trestle is Cape Horn, the steepest slope on the entire route (carved out by Chinese labourers lowered in baskets).
**YOU SHOULD KNOW:**
For those who are hooked on the romance of railways, it's possible to revisit the Zephyr's 'golden age' – an evocative collection of classic CZ silver rolling stock plus locomotive at the Western Pacific Railroad Museum in Portola, northeastern California.

# San Francisco Streetcar

Everyone who visits the Bay City should take a journey on one of the famous streetcars, which have a long history. The first streetcars (technically cable cars) capable of handling San Francisco's steep hillsides were introduced in 1873 and were an instant success – to such a degree that several new lines were opened. The boom was short-lived – cheaper electric streetcars arrived and the great earthquake of 1906 damaged many lines. By the 1940s the old streetcars were in terminal decline, as buses were by then capable of handling the acute gradients. Happily, a citizens' revolt saw the retention of three streetcar lines, which remain to this day as a much-loved part of the city's character.

The survivors are the Powell-Mason, Powell-Hide and California Street Lines, now used more by tourists than commuters. A journey on one or more of these splendid old streetcars (preferably hanging onto the outside!) is a mandatory part of the San Francisco experience. Powell-Mason (Line 59) and Powell-Hide (Line 60) serve residential, shopping and tourist districts (Union Square, Chinatown, North Beach, Nob Hill, Aquatic Park and Fisherman's Wharf). They share some track and both use single-ended, partially open cars that have to be rotated on turntables at the end of each run. Line 61 runs entirely on California Street, from a terminus at California and Market Streets, close to the waterfront, steeply through Chinatown up to the summit of Nob Hill, then down to Van Ness Avenue. It uses double-ended cars with open sides and an enclosed middle section.

To maintain the romance, all three lines use cars that are either restored originals or faithful replicas, and the changing views from the moving streetcars are among the best in the city.

*The old tram climbs up*
*Telegraph Hill.*

**HOW:**
By streetcar
**WHEN TO GO:**
Any time of year
**TIME IT TAKES:**
Get a passport and ride all three lines in a day, hopping on and off to explore this vibrant city as the fancy takes you.
**HIGHLIGHTS:**
The Cable Car Museum beneath the car barn at Washington and Jackson Streets, where you can also look at the main power house and descend to a large basement where the thick haulage cables are routed to the street.
The famously laid-back Fisherman's Wharf area, not far from the Taylor and Bay terminus of Line 59.
Grant Street in Chinatown – a feast for the senses with its colourful shops and crowded sidewalks.
The Maritime National Historical Park with its classic ships, adjacent to Ghirardelli Square.

# Mount Washington Cog Railway

In 1858, after climbing Mount Washington ('home of the world's worst weather'), Sylvester Marsh, nicknamed 'Crazy' Marsh, rashly proposed building a railway to the summit, at the dizzy height of 1,917 m (6,288 ft). After the laughing stopped, the New Hampshire State Assembly granted permission for the summit. So guess who had the last laugh? The first loco ran in 1867 and the line was completed in 1869, since which time Sylvester Marsh's quirky creation has carried over five million passengers.

Laid on trestle all the way, this extraordinary engineering feat has a maximum gradient of 37.41 per cent, and custom-built steam engines push carriages up a 4.9-km (3.1-mi) track, belching smoke as they use a ton of coal and a 3,785 litres (1,000 gallons) of water on every journey. Many of the locomotives, each of which has a name, date back to the 19th century (though much rebuilt over the years) and today's passengers enjoy much the same experience as those who were first captivated by the Mount Washington Cog Railway 150 years ago.

The locos look weird on the flat, with forward-tilting boilers that are designed to be level when climbing and descending the mountain. Both engine and coach are pulled up the mountain (and eased back down) by a 19-tooth cog that meshes into the track's central rail. At the same time, reassuring ratchets that prevent backward slippage are engaged on ascents. After a scenic ride that offers majestic mountain vistas, be prepared to avert your eyes as the summit approaches – a trail crosses the tracks, and there's something of a tradition whereby hikers await the train and 'moon'.

In winter there is a limited service (mainly weekends and school holidays) up through the snow to Kroflite Camp at 1,250 m (4,100 ft).

**HOW:**
By train
**DEPART:**
Mount Washington, NH
**WHEN TO GO:**
May to October (limited winter service November-April).
**TIME IT TAKES:**
Three hours for a round trip, including 20 minutes at the summit.
**HIGHLIGHTS:**
Peppersass, named for its likeness to a pepper sauce bottle – the first engine used in the construction of the line from 1867, now on display at the Marshfield Base Station.
Jacob's Ladder, the steepest section of the track – an extraordinary raised trestle that angles round the mountainside.
A wander round the summit, known as 'the city in the clouds', with numerous buildings including the Mount Washington Observatory and Tip Top House (built in 1853) – some days you can see four states, Canada and the Atlantic Ocean, and on other days nothing but swirling cloud!
**YOU SHOULD KNOW:**
The greatest wind speed ever recorded on earth – 372 kph (231 mph) – hammered the summit of Mount Washington in 1934.

*Looks like a train crash, works like a dream.*

# Rio Grande

Big Bend National Park in Texas is like the state itself – larger than life and many countries. This vast area is bounded by the Rio Grande to the south, which forms the border with Mexico, and the Park is a land of extremes – from desert to mountain, majestic rivers to inaccessible wilderness. The variety of plants and wildlife – especially birds – is extraordinary, and the Park's facilities are often stretched during high season (cooler winter months). But there's one way of getting round that problem – taking to the water, to kayak through the Chihuahuan Desert with open views and a dramatic river-scape that includes canyons up to 460 m (1,500 ft) deep.

The Rio Grande runs for 190 km (118 mi) within the Park, and a further 205 km (127 mi) downstream is designated a Wild and Scenic River. There is plenty of calm water, but this is not a journey for beginners as there are periodic encounters with rapids of varying severity, especially when the water is high. Unfortunately, extraction means it often isn't. The preferred option for experienced paddlers is a one- or two-person inflatable kayak, and even then this magnificent river is so remote that most people travel with a guide or organised party. It is possible to use your own equipment or hire locally (though not in the Park). Permits are required for self-organized trips, allowing you to stop off and explore interesting side canyons.

To run the Rio Grande through the Park, start at Lajitas on Texas Highway 170. Be aware that there are few facilities and a limited number of take-outs along the route and plan accordingly. Unless you intend to run the full length of the Wild and Scenic section, you end this unique journey at the Highway 2627 bridge in La Linda. This is a 200-km (125-mi) trip.

**HOW:**
By kayak
**DEPART:**
Lajitas, TX
**WHEN TO GO:**
November to April
**TIME IT TAKES:**
Lajitas to La Linda takes 10-14 days, depending on stops and side-trips.
**HIGHLIGHTS:**
The beautiful journey through popular Santa Elena Canyon – great scenery, serenity...and the excitement of the Rockslide Rapids.
Sunset over Mexico's remote Sierra del Carmen (Carmen Mountains), south of the river.
Marsical Canyon, the most remote in Big Bend National Park – just 16 km (10 mi) long but with varied scenery, towering limestone cliffs, some rapids and ample stop-off points along the canyon bottom.
Rio Grande Village – one of the few places along the river that has all the facilities.
**YOU SHOULD KNOW:**
Always camp on the US bank and carry identity documents – the Border Patrol can show up at any time and needs to know you're not an 'illegal'.

*Sunrise at Santa Elena Canyon, Big Bend National Park, Texas*

# Going-to-the-Sun Road

Named after the mountain of the same name, Going-to-the-Sun Road runs through Glacier National Park in Montana. It was completed in the 1930s after a dozen years of construction, and this ambitious engineering project was one of the first National Park Service projects to be specifically undertaken with automobile-borne tourists in mind.

The massive construction effort was justified – the parkway runs for 85 km (53 mi) through the craggiest of mountain scenery. Strong nerves are required, as the roadway is both narrow and winding, often clinging to the mountainside without guardrails (they have been attempted, but always get swept away by late-winter avalanches). For those who prefer to watch scenery rather than the road, there is a fleet of shuttle buses that allow visitors to explore the route at their leisure, hopping on and off at any one of numerous stops and catching the first bus along when they've finished sightseeing or exploring.

Going-to-the-Sun Road crosses the Continental Divide that separates the watersheds of the Atlantic and Pacific Oceans. The Road's high point is Logan Pass, with a breathless (disembark and try running on the spot if you doubt that) elevation of 2,025 m (6,645 ft). There is a visitor centre near the Pass that has tremendous views, and there are short hiking trails that give access to an abundance of alpine flowers in summer. This is one of the hardest roads in the US National Park system to clear ahead of reopening – snow can be more than 25 m (80 ft) deep at the top of Logan Pass (even deeper on the east side) and the job takes ten weeks. So there's actually quite a short timeframe when this wonderful drive can be undertaken.

**HOW:**
By car or bus
**WHEN TO GO:**
Early June to mid-September
**TIME IT TAKES:**
Two hours without stops
**HIGHLIGHTS:**
St Mary Lake – so scenic that it has featured in at least two major movies – *Forrest Gump* and *The Shining*.
Wildlife – look out for mountain goats, bears and lots more.
Glacier watching – there is a superb view of Jackson Glacier from the purpose-built overlook to the east side of Logan Pass.
Bird Woman Falls, a snowmelt waterfall that plunges 150 m (490 ft) down the mountainside, nicely framed from the parkway by the V-shaped Mount Oberlin.
**YOU SHOULD KNOW:**
The park (and its stopping areas) can get crowded in peak season.

*St Mary Lake, with the cottonwood trees still showing their golden fall colour.*

# Seward Highway

Go north to go south for glory! That's the message to those determined enough to make the journey down from Anchorage to Seward in south central Alaska, the chilly 49th state. The sometimes-moody Seward Highway was completed in 1951 and is 204 km (127 mi) long, though it follows a route used by Russian fur traders in the 1700s and native peoples for thousands of years before that.

*A bull moose swims low in the water to avoid the moose flies that surround his head.*

**HOW:**
By car
**WHEN TO GO:**
Any time of year
**TIME IT TAKES:**
Five hours non-stop, two days to explore properly along the way.
**HIGHLIGHTS:**
A short but interesting side trip from Canyon Creek Bridge to the historic mining town of Hope.
The Tern Lake Overlook near Moose Pass for sensational panoramic views of the unique Alaskan landscape.
Great wildlife viewing along the way – look out for whales, bears, moose, Dall sheep, a variety of birds and salmon galore in season.
At journey's end, the entertaining Alaska Sealife Center in Seward.
**YOU SHOULD KNOW:**
Beware quicksands! The mudflats and beaches along the coast from Anchorage to Portage can be dangerous and should be approached with extreme caution.

This incredible road runs along the Turnagain Arm and across the Kenai Peninsula, whose collective scenic glories have earned a coveted triple classification: All-American-Road, US Forest Service Scenic Byway and Alaska Scenic Byway.

From Anchorage, driving that tough hire car down Alaska Route 1 beside the reflective waters of Turnagain Arm, the first stops are Girdwood and Alyeska Resort, Portage Glacier and Whittier. Next comes the challenging Turnagain Pass followed by the Chugach National Forest, then a climb and descent past Upper and Lower Summit Lakes. At Tern Lake Junction, Alaska 1 heads off through the Kenai Peninsula and the Seward Highway becomes Alaska Route 9. After that it's a shortish run through Moose Pass and Bear Creek into Seward on the shores of Resurrection Bay.

The natural beauty of the Seward Highway is unlike any other to be found in the USA – stunning fjords and crystal-clear lakes, glaciers and waterfalls, ridges and valleys, alpine meadows and a profusion of wild flowers in season. The area has become a magnet for adventurous tourists who, drawn by a plethora of outdoor recreational options, arrive all year round. Salmon season is May to mid-October and (ironically) the Seward Highway stays open all winter where many Scenic Byways in states farther south do not. That said, occasional avalanches do briefly close the road in winter, but the sweepers soon open it up again.

# El Camino Real Historic Trail

For decades before the Mayflower arrived in North America, El Camino Real de Tierra Adentro (Royal Road of the Interior) brought Europeans up from Mexico to Santa Fe in 'New Spain' (now New Mexico). The significance of this migration route has been recognized by classification of the 650-km (404-mi) US section (from El Paso, Texas to San Juan Pueblo, New Mexico) as a National Historic Trail. This status is relatively new, as are efforts to promote the Trail – so travelling it requires some ingenuity.

The Trail runs along today's Interstate-25 corridor, with the modern highway following much of the old route. Before they arrived at what is now the Mexico-US border, settlers had endured a three-month voyage from Spain, a trek across the rugged Sierra Madre Mountains to Mexico City then a gruelling 1,770-km (1,100-mi) wagon journey to the Rio Grande. The last leg through dangerously inhospitable country was still to come, a reality that discourages modern attempts to hike the Trail.

However, it is possible to plan a self-guided car journey that follows the Trail and sees some remaining sites. First visit the new El Camino Real International Heritage Center, midway between Socorro and Truth or Consequences on I-25 (Exit 115). It overlooks the Trail where it crosses the fearsome Jornado del Muerto (Journey of the Dead Man) desert basin, a reminder of the hazards facing early travellers. The Center contains a wealth of Trail information, plus artefacts, and offers helpful suggestions for exploring the Trail. One recommended journey (described in great detail on a three-CD audio guide available from the Heritage Center) involves journeying between the historic plazas of the main towns along the Trail – Santa Fe, Albuquerque, Socorro, Las Cruces and El Paso, stopping off to look at Trail heritage along the way.

**HOW:**
By car
**WHEN TO GO:**
Any time of year
**TIME IT TAKES:**
Five days for the recommended journey, including exploration time.
**HIGHLIGHTS:**
The Museum of New Mexico's Palace of the Governors in Santa Fe – dating from the early 17th century, now the state's history museum.
San Miguel Mission, also in Santa Fe – oldest church in the USA, built at the last major stopover on the Trail in the early 17th century.
Fort Selden near Las Cruces, a mid-19th-century army post designed to protect travellers and towns along the Trail as it became a major trade route.
The historic district in the heart of Socorro, around a plaza that still holds the essence of the Trail.
**YOU SHOULD KNOW:**
The Trail finally fell into disuse when the railroad reached New Mexico in 1880.

*The San Juan Miguel Mission, Socorro, New Mexico*

# The Pan-American Highway

The world's longest drivable road is the Pan-American Highway, a system with a total length of some 48,000 km (30,000 mi). It passes through Canada, the USA, Mexico, Guatemala, El Salvador, Honduras, Nicaragua, Costa Rica, Panama, Colombia, Ecuador, Peru, Chile and Argentina. With various branches the whole system adds up to a vast and rambling network.

The intrepid traveller must drive from Prudhoe Bay in Alaska down to the Panama Canal. Although the Pan-American Highway has no official status in the USA and Canada, the accepted route follows the Alaska Highway. After reaching Canada, the road splits at Edmonton, one route going via the Great Lakes, Minneapolis and Dallas, the other taking in Calgary, Denver and Albuquerque. The two meet at San Antonio in Texas, before reaching the 'official' Pan-American Highway at the Mexican border south of Monterrey. Thereafter it runs through Central America via Mexico City and San Salvador to Panama City. There the road stops, briefly broken by the Darién Gap, a 90-km (55-mi) stretch of rain forest that may be crossed on foot, by bicycle, motorbike or ATV by reckless adventurers willing to brave bandits, swamps and jungle.

Thereafter, the Highway resumes its often spectacular and sometimes dangerous journey, as the road follows the Pacific coast down through Cali, Quito, Antofagasta and Valparaiso, before cutting across to the Atlantic at Buenos Aires. That marks the official end of the Highway, but there are two unofficial branches – one continuing down the west coast from Valparaiso to Quellon, the other from Buenos Aires to Ushuaia at the tip of South America. This latter route is, of course, mandatory for anyone who wishes to be one of the few individuals on the planet to have travelled America from top to toe.

**HOW:**
By car or motorbike
**DEPART:**
Prudhoe Bay, AK
**WHEN TO GO:**
Start between May and August, to travel the Alaskan leg without risking frostbite!
**TIME IT TAKES:**
How long have you got? Allow at least four months.
**HIGHLIGHTS:**
The Alamo in San Antonio, where a gallant band including 'King of the Wild Frontier' Davy Crockett and Jim Bowie of 'knife' fame defied the mighty Mexican army in 1836, before perishing to a man.
Quito – the capital city of Ecuador is a charming, beautiful city that shows urban South America at its very best.
The Tierra del Fuego National Park – not just because it's journey's end, but for the dramatic scenery, waterfalls, mountains, forests and glaciers.
**YOU SHOULD KNOW:**
It's not just the demanding terrain that will slow you down – there are 13 national borders to be crossed.

*San Francisco Church, Quito*

*Right: The Beagle Channel in Tierra del Fuego.*

# The Copper Canyon

Anyone who has marvelled at the Grand Canyon has an even bigger treat in store south of the Mexican border. The awesome Copper Canyon complex in the Sierra Tarahumara consists of six linked canyons, collectively four times larger (and deeper) than their not-insignificant northern neighbour. The Parque Nacional Barranca del Cobre (Copper Canyon National Park) has been established to protect this remote but beautiful area in southwestern Chihuahua State, home to ultra-traditional Tarahumara Indians.

Happily, you don't have to hike this rugged country to experience Copper Canyon's incredible scenery, because you just have to catch a train and much (though not all) will be revealed. El Chepe, as the Chihuahua al Pacifico train is known, runs from the city of Chihuahua to Los Mochis near the Sea of Cortez, a distance of some 650 km (400 mi), traversing the principal canyon of Urique (North America's deepest). The line, completed in 1961, is a magnificent engineering feat, with 37 bridges and 86 tunnels. The quality of the scenery along the route is pretty good too – recognized by El Chepe's classification as 'one of the top ten most spectacular train trips in the world' in 2005. This accolade is justified – the extraordinary diversity of this unique landscape ranges from snow-capped mountains to tropical forests in canyon bottoms.

There are four departures daily – two from each direction, one luxury and one standard – as the line is extensively used both by tourists and locals. But if you don't wish to take the full train journey, it is possible to stop off along the way to hike in and see attractions such Candameñta Canyon's Piedra Volanda Falls (Mexico's highest) and the huge stone monolith known as Peña del Gigante. Guided tours are available to more remote destinations that El Chepe doesn't reach.

*The Copper Canyon complex consists of six linked canyons.*

**HOW:**
By train
**DEPART:**
Chihuahua
**WHEN TO GO:**
Best months: October to December, March and April.
**TIME IT TAKES:**
About 16 hours (one way).
**HIGHLIGHTS:**
Chihuahua itself – a splendid historic city full of colonial treasures and monumental structures.
The view from Divisadero, where the train obligingly stops for 20 minutes, so passengers can enjoy the sensational vista of three canyons (Tararecua, Urique and del Cobre).
**YOU SHOULD KNOW:**
If you should come across one of the frequent Tarahumara Indian celebrations, respect their privacy – they are shy, proud people and it is polite to ask permission before taking photographs.

# Rio Sonora

To follow the Rio Sonora is to journey through Mexican history, experiencing both the harsh natural beauty surrounding this life-giving river and the traditional towns that have grown along its banks since the Jesuits first arrived in the 17th century. Rough terrain and an uncertain water supply have combined to ensure that the river communities retain their rural roots, so this really is a step back in time.

The river – and journey – starts just across from Arizona at Cananea. Highway 118 loosely follows the river all the way down to Mazocahui, where a right turn onto Highway 14 completes the route to Hermosillo for a total distance of some 320 km (200 mi). It's worth exploring along the way, as this is a journey that can offer fascinating insight into Old Mexico, framed by the sweeping vistas of typically arid Sierra Madre scenery.

Sonora is a mining town that's just a century old – and the massive copper mine west of the city is the largest in Mexico. The road next passes through a couple of ranching centres founded around 1650 – Bacoachi and Arizpe – before reaching Banamichi, settled by Jesuits in 1639. The town's Hidalgo Plaza contains the Piedra Historica, an ancient petroglyph thought to be an irrigation map. At Huépac, look inside San Lorenzo, a 17th-century church with a fine interior. The next port of call is Aconchi, where the Agua Caliente Water Park has hot springs said to possess curative powers. Bavicora has a wonderful tree-lined plaza overlooked by the impressive Nuestra Señora de la Concepción Cathedral. Ures was once the state capital of Sonora, and the town's historic roots are very evident in the Plaza Zaragoza and San Miguel Cathedral. Mazocahui is the last sleepy pueblo before you reach the bustling provincial capital of Hermosillo, one of the largest towns in northern Mexico.

**HOW:**
By car
**DEPART:**
Cananea
**WHEN TO GO:**
March-November
**TIME IT TAKES:**
A day or three, depending whether or not you set a sensible Mexican pace.
**HIGHLIGHTS:**
The magnificent 17th-century Nuestra Señora de la Asunción Church in Arizpe, amid period buildings and a fine plaza.
Delightful riverside walks in Bavicora, shaded by sweeping oak, aspen and walnut trees.
Near Bacoachi – the Sierra de los Ajos ecological park, for a close-up encounter with Rio Sonora's flora and fauna.
La Plaza de Armas in Ures, with four wonderful bronze statues.
**YOU SHOULD KNOW:**
If you visit in October and November there will be numerous bullfights and local celebrations accompanying the cane milling, peanut and chilli harvests.

*Cacti in the Sonoran Desert*

# Yucatán

**HOW:**
By car
**DEPART:**
Villahermosa
**WHEN TO GO:**
December to May (avoiding hurricane season).
**TIME IT TAKES:**
The journey can be done in a day, but far better to take a couple and see the sights.
**HIGHLIGHTS:**
A stopover in Ciudad del Carmen, the 'Pearl of the Gulf' – try the seafood for which the town is renowned.
Mérida's central Plaza, with America's oldest Cathedral (1556-1599), Palacio Municipal (1735) and Casa de Montejo (1542), former home of the founding conquistador.
An outing to the evocative Mayan ruins at Chichen-Itza and the nearby Caves of Balankanche.
Progresso – Mérida's busy port, 30 km (18 mi) to the north, for amazing salt flats and extraordinary flocks of flamingoes.

The Yucatán Peninsula in southeastern Mexico separates two great bodies of water – the Caribbean Sea and the Gulf of Mexico. It has been rapidly developed for tourism in recent years, with the once-tiny fishing port of Cancun now a thriving boom town and the Mayan Riviera on the east coast a major resort destination for those seeking sun-sea-and-sand holidays.

For those more interested in the ancestral heartland of the ancient Mayan civilization, the 300-km (185-mi) journey from Villahermosa in the adjacent state of Tabasco to Mérida, Yucatán's 'White City', will be fascinating. Until recently, Yucatán was isolated, looking more to its Mayan roots and out to the Caribbean than inwards to Mexico, so it has a unique atmosphere and culture. You will appreciate this as you drive, perhaps diverting to explore this special land of jungle, thorny scrub, hills, Mayan ruins, haciendas, colonial cities, wildlife preserves and pristine beaches...not to mention engaging with the most welcoming of people.

From Villahermosa, head north on Highway 180 through Frontera, where you reach the Gulf. Keep going, enjoying stunning coastal scenery all the way (especially the amazing bridge crossing of the Laguna De Términos through Zacatal, Ciudad del Carmen and Puerto Real) before continuing to Chapoton and Campeche. From there, stay with 180 as the road cuts inland and heads for Mérida, via Chencoyi, Tenabo and Calkini. Mérida is worth waiting for. Founded by conquistadors on the site of a Mayan city, it is the oldest continually occupied city in the Americas, and displays much of the traditional splendour and charm of colonial Mexico.

A word of warning. Don't assume upon arrival that you can park anywhere. It may look that way, but police can, and sometimes do, impound illegally parked vehicles – a nightmare, especially if yours is a rental.

*The former home of the 16th century Conquistador, Francisco Montejo in Mérida*

# Oaxaca City to Puerto Angel

*One of the many pretty squares in Oaxaca*

What a journey! Driving Highway 175 through the coastal Sierra Madre del Sur Mountains of southwestern Mexico must be one of the most scenic drives in the whole country.

The experience begins in Oaxaca City – but not before you've explored this UNESCO World Heritage Site with its fine colonial architecture and rich cultural traditions. But it's soon time to leave cosmopolitan distractions behind, finding Highway 175 and heading south. It won't be a straightforward trip – in fact just the opposite. This two-lane road twists and turns violently as it winds through the mountains, to the point where motion sickness is a real possibility. What's more, the road surface is rarely the best – rainy season always sees damage to 175, which in true Mexican style barely gets repaired before next rainy season, so there's every chance of coming across a rockslide or collapsed section that slows traffic to a crawl.

That's just fine. There's no point in hurrying. The Sierra Madre del Sur are noted for their biodiversity, and this extraordinary road reveals stunning new vistas at every turn – take a spare memory card for the camera! You will have pictures of cloud forests with pines in the mist and lush tropical forest when the road descends. What's more, the small villages along Highway 175 often have wonderful indigenous crafts on sale, and the variety of colourful birdlife is mesmerising.

But all good things come to an end, and eventually the road runs down out of the mountains towards the Pacific Ocean. At the junction of 175 with the coastal highway (200), cross over and continue to Puerto Angel, an old-fashioned harbour town crouched around an enclosed bay that provides safe haven for its fleet of small fishing craft.

**HOW:**
By car
**WHEN TO GO:**
October to April
**TIME IT TAKES:**
A day - it's a 240km (150 mi) journey
**HIGHLIGHTS:**
Oaxaca's Zócalo, one of the most beautiful central squares in Mexico, and a vibrant hub of city life.
San Pablo Guelatao, the village on Highway 175 that was the birthplace of self-made Mexican President Benito Juárez – take a break beside the lake and admire a statue of the great 19th-century liberal as a     boy shepherd.
Roadside banana sellers – be amazed by how many varieties you'll be offered, and as a bonus you get to see what a freshly gathered cashew nut looks like.
San José del Pacifico, a hillside community about halfway through the trip – a good (maybe the only) place to spend the night if you decide to break the journey.
**YOU SHOULD KNOW:**
Never attempt to drive Highway 175 at night – it's cold, lonely and hard to spot potentially dangerous potholes or other more serious water damaged places in the dark.

*Kayaking near Ensenada Bay.*

# Espiritu Sanctu and Isla Partida

Describe the difference between the Gulf of California, Sea of Cortez and Mar de Cortéz? Of course they're all the same place – that long, narrow body of water separating the Baja California Peninsula from the Mexican mainland. Most maps prefer one of the English versions; most locals naturally use the latter.

Either way, that's where you'll find the enchanting island of Espiritu Sanctu (oh, all right, Holy Spirit Island). It is connected by a narrow isthmus to Isla Partida, and together they are a protected UNESCO biosphere. Both are small. Espiritu Sanctu has an area of 80 sq km (31 sq mi) and Isla Partida is 15 sq km (6 sq mi). But that doesn't prevent them from being a magical destination.

These rocky wilderness islands with their breathtaking coastline lie in the Sea of Cortez north of La Paz on the rugged Baja California Peninsula, a bustling regional capital. The way to explore them is journeying by kayak, camping as you go, enjoying a memorable outdoor adventure. Take along a snorkel and flippers, as the diving is memorable. You can hire kayaks and canoes for a circumnavigation locally, or choose from a number of guided tours. It is possible to paddle out to the islands, though some prefer to be delivered by motorboat to allow the maximum possible time around the islands. Either way, you'll experience a classic sea-kayaking trip.

The Sea of Cortez is home to a fabulous variety of marine life, and being on the water gives you every opportunity to see many species – look especially for humpback whales, California grey whales, whale sharks, leatherback turtles, sea lions, dolphins and giant manta rays – along with a rich variety of colourful fish and a huge number of seabirds.

**HOW:**
By kayak
**WHEN TO GO:**
Any time of year (warm winters, hot summers).
**TIME IT TAKES:**
Four days allows ample time for exploration.
**HIGHLIGHTS:**
Interesting sea caves within walking distance of Isla Partida's south coast.
A mangrove bay on Espiritu Sanctu, providing a welcome mass of greenery that may be explored by kayak.
The Ensenada Grande beach on Isla Partida, voted by a travel magazine as the most beautiful in Mexico and one of the Top 12 beaches in the world...so don't expect to have it to yourself!
The Malecon waterfront promenade around the bay in La Paz, a quintessentially Mexican town that pays only lip service to tourism.
**YOU SHOULD KNOW:**
The famous French underwater explorer and oceanographer Jacques Cousteau described the Sea of Cortez as 'The World's Aquarium'.

# Rio Usumacinta

Ready for a real wilderness adventure? Something ever-so-slightly dangerous? Then a raft trip down Mexico's glorious Rio Usumacinta, the Sacred Monkey River, could be just the thing. But this is border country, where smuggling between Guatemala and southeastern Mexico is rife. Bandits stalk the roads. Zapatista rebels have been active, so the Mexican army is in evidence. But the security situation has improved and – as the only way to make this incredible journey is as part of an organized group with experienced guides – the danger is not acute.

The river is formed in a great natural basin by the merging of two others – the Salinas and Pasión Rivers – and serves as the border between the Mexican state of Chiapas and Guatemala, after which it wanders through the state of Tabasco to the Gulf of Mexico, forming the only physical boundary between the Yucatan Peninsula and the rest of Mexico. Various hydroelectric schemes have been proposed for the upper reaches of the river, but happily these have been shelved as the long-term benefits of eco-tourism become apparent, though other threats to this vast natural jewel remain.

A number of different trips are on offer. All will start with a drive of several hours' duration to the put-in point, which is often the tiny frontier post of Frontera Corozal. From there, a couple of inflatable rafts, carrying all the necessary stores and inflatable kayaks for side trips, will convey up to a dozen adventurers downriver.

The trip will be a voyage of discovery, with overnight camping on river beaches and numerous stops to swim or explore interesting features and historic sites along the banks. The scenery varies from jungle-covered bluffs, cascading waterfalls, through tumbling rapids and canyons to the broader, slower sections towards the take-out point at Tenosique.

**HOW:**
By car and boat
**DEPART:**
Frontera Corozal
**WHEN TO GO:**
Avoid the rainy season (May to November).
**TIME IT TAKES:**
Around 10 days for a 120-km (75-mi) raft journey.
**HIGHLIGHTS:**
Wildlife, from dazzling butterflies to howler monkeys that inhabit treetops all along the river – you can't miss them, because they really are noisy.
The ruined remains of two powerful cities of the ancient Maya civilization, Yaxchilán (just down river from the start point) and Piedras Negras (further down on the Guatemala bank).
Roaring falls where the Busiljá River enters the Usumacinta.
The Canyon of San José – a deep run with sheer rock walls that tower to over 300 m (1,000 ft).
**YOU SHOULD KNOW:**
Though relatively short in length, Usumacinta is the world's seventh-largest river by volume of water.

*Kayaking on Rio Usumacinta*

# La Ruta Maya

It may come as a surprise to the casual observer that La Ruta Maya, far from being a route trodden by the ancients, is a construct of 20th century American travel writing. This often-travelled route links sites which were mysteriously abandoned by the Mayan civilization over a thousand years ago. La Ruta starts in Southern Mexico and takes you down the spine of Central America to Belize. The least visited and perhaps the most mystical part of the route lies within the modern day boundaries of Guatemala.

As much of the route is a network of dirt tracks, good suspension is a prerequisite for any mode of road transport you choose, though as the crowning glory of the area is so remote many tourists decide to approach it by air. Hidden by thick jungle until the 19th century, Tikal is one of the most stunning archaeological sites to be found anywhere in the world. Once one of the largest and most influential cities of the Mayan era, the city disappeared over the centuries, swallowed up by the lush jungle. The scale of the development can be seen by climbing up Temple IV to view distant structures still half hidden in the forest canopy. It is estimated that the 16 sq km (6.2 sq mi) already uncovered is a mere fraction of the entire city.

This is but one of many important Mayan cities, hidden over many centuries and now re-discovered. Some were home to grand palaces; others were of more modest proportions. All however have something to reveal about the fascinating ancient Mayan empire.

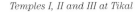

*Temples I, II and III at Tikal*

# Volcano Pacaya

There are times in your life when you have to place total faith in science and the gods – bungee jumping and white-water rafting, to name but two. Walking up the side of an active volcano, as it belches angrily, certainly comes into this category.

Located in the south west coastal region of Guatemala, Pacaya began its most recent active phase in 1965, and since then has offered up a full array of volcanic activity. More often than not, the Pacaya Volcano spews little more than gaseous emissions and relatively small steam eruptions. However, from time to time it can experience more serious explosions that prompt the evacuation of the numerous villages found on its sides. Rising to 2,690 m (8,370 ft) above sea level, the Pacaya volcano is not the tallest in Guatemala, but it is certainly the most climbed. Its constant activity has made it a magnet for vulcanologists from around the globe and predictions of major eruptions such as the one in 2006 have increased in accuracy.

Hikers are charged a small fee that goes towards the maintenance of the trails. Facilities along the way are good, with rest stops and even some primitive washrooms. The main route to the summit takes you from the car park at San Francisco de Sales, up gentle slopes until you reach the rim of the old Cerro Chino crater. This is a chance to catch your breath and admire the stunning views. After this the final steep ascent begins and it is not easy. Loose ash and volcanic rock make walking difficult, while clouds of sulphur can hinder breathing. Hazards aside, when you reach the top the views are astounding, like standing in a lunar landscape.

**HOW:**
On foot
**DEPART:**
San Francisco de Sales
**WHEN TO GO:**
Year round although hottest from June to August.
**TIME IT TAKES:**
Allow a full day.
**HIGHLIGHTS:**
The sight of the volcano from below.
The view of Acatenango, Fuego and Agua volcanoes as you near the Cerro Chino crater.
Being close to something so fundamental to the planet's ecosystem – the sheer power of it is almost overwhelming.
**YOU SHOULD KNOW:**
As a hangover from its recent civil war, Guatemala has a high gun-owning population and armed robberies, whilst falling in number, are still quite common. You are relatively safe within the boundaries of the park, where rangers are employed for security, but it is a good idea to travel in a group and avoid wearing flashy jewellery.

*Hiking on Volcano Pacaya near Antigua.*

*The Rio On storms through Mountain Pine Ridge Forest Reserve.*

# Mountain Pine Ridge Forest Reserve

**HOW:**
On foot
**WHEN TO GO:**
Year round – but expect rain at any time.
**TIME IT TAKES:**
You could do it in a day if really fit, but allow a week or two to soak up the park.
**HIGHLIGHTS:**
Barton Creek Cave – a cave system full of Mayan artefacts.
Green Hills Butterfly Ranch – a host of butterflies flutter by in a jungle setting.
The Hidden Valley Falls – a viewing platform gives a great vantage point to the 460-m (1,500-ft) high waterfalls.
Chiquibul Forest Reserve – home to many endangered species.
**YOU SHOUD KNOW:**
The reserve is recovering from a pine beetle infestation that wiped out as many as 60 per cent of the trees in 2000. This resilient forest is still recovering, but no less beautiful for it.

Pine forests are not the first things that spring to mind when you think of Central America, but the unique Mountain Pine Ridge in Belize has surprises around every corner. This 1020-m (3,400-ft) tall ridge is a natural wonderland of spectacular waterfalls, wild orchids, vibrantly coloured parrots, keel-billed toucans among a myriad of exotic flora and fauna.

Located in the Mountain Pine Ridge Forest Reserve, the trail leads you through thick jungle, past ancient rock formations and most notably to Caracol, the largest Mayan ruins in Belize. Excavation of these relics is still in its infancy – it's fascinating to see the forest slowly giving up its secrets.

All around you the forest invades the senses with ambient noise, colour and smell. Mossy ferns and abundant vegetation form a soft canvas, while exotic birds perch among the treetops and other wildlife plays between the branches. The area is dotted with cool mountain pools to swim in and caves to walk through – if only all life were like this! The tempo of this magnificent walk is perfect. The altitude of the climb takes the edge off the tropical heat and the often-misty summit of the ridge provides a magical backdrop.

It is probable that the forest is the remnant of a volcanic island that collided with the mainland several millennia ago. This would explain the feeling of isolation you get from climbing the trail. This is truly a paradise gained.

# Monteverde Cloud Forest

Bathed in a curtain of life-giving mist, the Monteverde Cloud Forest in the mountains of Costa Rica is a profusion of saturated greenery that stands as an icon of modern day conservation. Originally founded by Quakers fleeing the draft in 1960s America, this privately owned reserve has now been expanded to cover over 10,500 hectares (26,000 acres).

With altitudes ranging between 600 m and 1,800 m (1,970 and 5,900 ft), the Forest Preserve is one of the most flourishing biological sanctuaries in the world. Over 100 species of mammals, 400 species of birds, 120 species of amphibians and reptiles, and 2,500 species of plants, as well as tens of thousands of insect species reside within its borders. In addition, larger animal species including the jaguar, ocelot, resplendent quetzal and baird's tapir inhabit the Preserve's boundaries.

The reserve is best enjoyed at a leisurely pace and a boat trip on the adjacent Lake Arenal is a good way to get your bearings. From there it is possible to join a guided horseback trek around the lake's shores and on to Monteverde. From this vantage point you can marvel at the myriad of colours that surrounds you, whilst the sounds and scents of this most luscious of environments fills every sense. This area is a true haven for wildlife to flourish, protected from humans. It provides scientists with a great natural field station as well as delivering a wonderful, natural utopia for the more casual tourist to enjoy.

**HOW:**
By boat and on horseback
**WHEN TO GO:**
Year-round – though quieter from October to March.
**TIME IT TAKES:**
A combined boat and horseback trip takes around 5 hours.
**HIGHLIGHTS:**
The Butterfly Garden
The Orchid Garden
The World of Insects
The Monteverde Serpentarium
**YOU SHOULD KNOW:**
If travelling with a guide ask for testimonials or get a recommendation from the local tourist authority, as some operators can be less than scrupulous. Make sure that the horses you ride look healthy and that the guide keeps to well-trodden paths.

*Green-crowned Brilliant hummingbird feeding on a ginger flower.*

# Cerro Chirripo

**HOW:**
On foot
**WHEN TO GO:**
Year round, though it's less hot from
November to March.
**TIME IT TAKES:**
Allow two or three days to climb the
mountain or at least a week to enjoy
the surrounding National Park.
**HIGHLIGHTS:**
The sheer thrill of it all – the sounds
of the jungle, the forest scenery and
the panoramic views from the top.
The surrounding National Park – as
close to a pristine jungle as you
could wish to experience.
The descent – climbing the mountain
requires so much energy that it is
sometimes difficult to take in the
amazing jungle location. The descent,
though not easy, affords you that
luxury.
**YOU SHOULD KNOW:**
Do not be tempted to start the climb
without a permit. Sometimes the
rangers say there is a long waiting
list, when in fact there is none.

*The view from Cerro Chirripo*

There can be few more intense fusions of pleasure and pain than the hike up Cerro Chirripo, with its 18-km (11-mi) climb to a 3,000-m (10,000-ft) high summit. If the gradient doesn't slow you down, then the diminishing oxygen at altitude will add extra pressure to the lungs. The rewards, however, for making it to the top are bountiful. On a clear day it's possible to see both the Pacific and the Caribbean by just turning your head!

A permit is needed to make this climb and the monies raised go towards trail maintenance and the employment of park rangers. So with ticket in hand and a rucksack stocked for all eventualities, it is time to breathe in the tropical air and start the climb. Everything from sun block to a sleeping bag is essential, as the hot tropical sun can easily burn you and it has been known to snow near the summit. Thankfully you don't need the added burden of a tent, as there are a couple of dormitory-style huts along the way.

As befits a jungle environment, the slippery trail can make progress hard work. Short of out-and-out mountaineering this is probably the most difficult 18 km (11.25 mi) you will ever travel in your life. Its inaccessibility is what keeps this area special and free from the development and exploitation that blights much of Central America. Besides the challenge of climbing Costa Rica's highest peak, there are numerous trails that wind through more ecological zones than you will find in most entire countries.

# Panama Canal and Lake Gutan

*The Pedro Miguel locks and Centennial Bridge*

For sheer drama it is difficult to top the 77 km (48 mi) passage through the Panama Canal. Built to cut sailing times between the east and west coasts of America, one twentieth of the world's shipping now passes through its locks. It is the perfect marriage of engineering efficiency and Italianate architecture that makes it a true wonder of the modern world.

The locks themselves utilize the waters of the surrounding rainforest to send vessels on their way through improbably narrow passages. The region's rivers and lakes are dammed, and, along with the locks, these dams control the release of 236 million litres (52 million gallons) of freshwater per passing vessel. Where else in the world can you lean over the side of large cruise ship and touch land? When the ship is ready to change locks, it is mesmerising to look down from the stern. With only 10 m (33 ft) between propellers and lock gates the commotion caused by the water is quite incredible.

The canal marks the lowest point at which you can cross the American Continental Divide as you sail through the 13 km (8 mi) of the dramatic Gaillard Cut, where the mountain was literally sliced open to allow passage. Such is the dramatic nature of the scenery that it appears to the eye that you are heading straight towards a cliff as you head through the final lock that takes you into Lake Gutan. Here there is a chance to disembark or simply marvel at the sheer volume of shipping waiting to pass through the canal.

**HOW:**
By ship
**WHEN TO GO:**
The climate is pretty constant all year round.
**TIME IT TAKES:**
Allow a full day for a round trip through the canal and onto the lake.
**HIGHLIGHTS:**
Marvelling at the mechanics of it all.
The evergreen tropical jungle, which adorns both sides of the canal.
The contrast between the bubbling excitement of the canal and the tranquillity of Lake Gatun
Watching passing ships travel close by in the opposite direction on the section between Culebra Cut and Lake Gutan
**YOU SHOULD KNOW:**
The delicate eco-system that surrounds the canal is threatened by deforestation, as a result of illegal logging.

*Clouds drift among the forest trees.*

# Trail to Volcan Baru

**HOW:**
On foot
**WHEN TO GO:**
Year round – it's almost deserted
between November and March.
**TIME IT TAKES:**
Allow a full day – 6 hours up,
4 hours down.
**HIGHLIGHTS:**
The sounds of the jungle.
The misty forest.
El Respingo – a bird-watcher's
paradise, nearby.
The surrounding National Park.
**YOU SHOULD KNOW:**
In 2007 the volcano was the scene of
one of the most astonishing stories of
endurance when the only survivor of a
plane crash, a 12-year-old girl, was
found, injured but alive after spending
two nights alone in the jungle.

Volcan Baru forms the focal point of a sumptuous National Park that shares its name. The highest point in Panama, it has become a Mecca for outdoor adventurers, bird-watchers and nature lovers of all kinds.

It is quite probable that your first view of this 3,474-m (11,398-ft) high iconic symbol of the Central American rainforest will be fleeting, as the summit is usually shrouded in cloud. This is an important consideration when planning a climb and an early morning start is vital in order to maximize your chances of enjoying good views from the top.

When the clouds clear, those who do make this arduous climb are greeted by the most wondrous of sights. A magnificent carpet of green lies before you, framed by the azure waters of both the Pacific Ocean and the Caribbean Sea.

Because of the volcano's height and isolation, this area is considered a bioclimatic island. Its forest is home to distinctive species of orchids and rare flora such as magnolia and giant oak trees, some of which are over 800 years old. You'll also see wild bamboo gardens and gigantic, knotted trees dripping with vines and sprouting prehistoric-looking bromeliads from their stems.

The rainforest also provides a home to over 200 species of bird, the most notable of which is the resplendent quetzal, whose extraordinary beauty puts it in the number-one spot on many bird-watchers' lists. Other rare birds here include the silky flycatcher, the three-wattled bellbird, and the hairy woodpecker.

In higher reaches, an intermittent cloud forest creates an eerie ambience. All said, it is a wonderful place to hike and immerse yourself in untamed beauty, but come prepared, with waterproof outerwear and shoes and a dry change of clothes just in case.

# Railway Trail

Since motor vehicles were given the freedom of Bermuda in 1946, they have become the only real threat to the island's balmy perfection. With 50,000 vehicles for 69,000 residents, clogged roads and noise risk overwhelming Bermuda's extraordinary natural beauty and wealth of history. The Railway Trail traces a traffic-free path through the archipelago – a thoroughfare and playground for walkers, pedal-cyclists and riders. It runs for some 34 km (21 mi) along the roadbed of the narrow-gauge railway torn up in 1948, its continuity broken into seven sections where original trestle bridges no longer exist. Sections are 3 to 6 km (1.75 to 3.75 mi) long, but more than 30 access points make it easy to return to main roads and get a bus if distances prove too much.

The Railway Trail is, in effect, Bermuda's backyard. From Sandys Parish in the west to St George's in the east, it bypasses every town and village, but provides tranquil access to all of them. It is a treasure trove of fascinating sights, unavailable any other way. It winds through sun-dappled countryside, revealing a succession of glorious seascapes. You see beautiful houses with characteristic Bermudan stepped roofs of whitewashed limestone, and skirt magnificent Georgian mansions. You pass pink sandy beaches, marshlands and mangroves. You share the scent of roses with the migrating birds in the upland forest sanctuary of Heydon Trust; and you enjoy the commanding view of the Sound from 19th century Fort Scaur, the smallest drawbridge in the world, and a dozen other wonderful ways to remove yourself from urban Bermuda.

At Store Hill, the Trail becomes more neighbourhood front porch; and the cliffs above Shelly Bay bring you to the Coney Island Road cricket pitch – where you must backtrack a little to take the ferry to St George's, the oldest English-speaking town in the New World, and the beginning of the seventh section.

**HOW:**
On foot or by bike
**WHEN TO GO:**
Year round. From April to September, walking and cycling is more comfortable in the early morning or late afternoon.
**TIME IT TAKES:**
Two to four hours per section
**HIGHLIGHTS:**
The quaint, garage-size old railway stations.
Gibbet Island, seen from the North Shore Road, where witches were burned and felons hanged.
The endemic flora of the farms and plantations of Paget Parish.
The Shelly Bay Nature Reserve.
**YOU SHOULD KNOW:**
In Bermuda, 'cyclists' or 'bikers' means 'motorcyclists': in conversation, and especially if hiring, you must refer to 'pedal-cyclists'.
Mopeds and motorbikes still occasionally abuse the Railway Trail, but local residents, and the police, are getting much tougher.

*Fort Scaur*

# Blue Mountain Downhill

**HOW:**
By bike
**WHEN TO GO:**
Year-round. In the mountains it could rain any time, but very seldom for long; and it doesn't even have to be sunny to enjoy this trip to the full.
**TIME IT TAKES:**
2.5 hours riding time; 6-9 hours including travel from Kingston or Ocho Rios and back, all stops and post-ride swimming in the falls.
**HIGHLIGHTS:**
The demonstration (including much drinking) of Blue Mountain coffee, the most expensive and among the best in the world, at one of the plantations.
The thrill of the steeper descents, especially through elfin forest of stunted soapwood and redwood trees.
Glorious birdlife – there are 200 species in the Blue Mountains, with habitats ranging from the cool, misty upper levels down to brutally-hot sea level jungle.
**YOU SHOULD KNOW:**
The Blue Mountain Downhill is not suitable for children under the age of seven; but they and anyone else who wants to join the group without actually cycling can travel in the support vehicle, which makes the same stops as the cyclists.

*Ride the Blue Mountain Downhill at a leisurely pace!*

It is effortlessly simple. If you want to see the Blue Mountains, have yourself driven to the highest point accessible by vehicle, Hardware Gap (1,707 m/5,600 ft), deep in Holywell National Park and in the immediate shadow of the Blue Mountain peak itself, at 2,257 m (7,402 ft) the highest point in the Caribbean. The forest, Kingston and the sea are spread below you. All you have to do is put on the required helmet and knee pads, mount your bike, and roll gently downhill for 29 km (18 mi).

The actual riding time is about 2.5 hours, but the journey can take all day depending on your starting point. Enthusiasts come from as far as Ocho Rios, adding five hours driving to the ride. In any case, the downhill is punctuated by extremely well chosen photo opportunities and refreshment pauses, culminating in mid-afternoon with a short walk to a forest pool, with creepers and vines dangling from a rock face over which cascades a 30 m (100 ft) waterfall. You'll be ready for the swim. It's a chance to reflect on everything you've seen and everything you've been told about descending through several different ecosystems and the flora and fauna of each.

Because the mountain roads are small, and bikes don't make a lot of noise, you really do get close to some of the blazing colours of Jamaican bird species, and of the clouds of flowers that turn densely packed rainforest trees into floral totems. You can stop and listen any time, or take a better look at plants that catch your eye. But probably you'll be content to drift on down while all your other senses enjoy the feast. Those that want can go as fast as they like but more sensible cyclists ride the Blue Mountain Downhill at a leisurely pace.

# Trek to the Boiling Lake

The Boiling Lake trek is Dominica's ultimate trial of strength. The volcanic island is the most rugged and mountainous in the Caribbean, and its deeply incised valleys attract more rain than anywhere else. The combination of tropical location and active volcanism make it a rainforest paradise of streams and cascades – much of it protected in the wilderness National Park that surrounds its highest peaks, the Morne Trois Pitons. The Boiling Lake lies at its heart, a fittingly dramatic finale to what feels like a mythic adventure into a new world.

The trail starts by the waterfall and pools of the Titou Gorge, and follows the stream through emerald rainforest uphill to the Breakfast River, traditionally the first stop. Then you climb steeply to emerge on the razor edge of 1,020 m (3,168 ft) Morne Nicholls, from which you can touch the clouds and sky. The Valley of Desolation lies below, wreathed in the bubbling sulphur steam of 50 fumaroles and hot springs that colour rocks like stained-glass; and where water may flow black, milky, bright yellow or iron-red. But not even the bizarre formations or the mosses and rare orchids that survive here are preparation for the exhilaration of emerging suddenly, after another hard climb through clouds and steam, at the cliff edge of the Boiling Lake itself.

At 72 m (270 ft) across, the Lake is the second biggest flooded fumarole in the world; and though it can cool to a glassy pale green, it is usually a seething cauldron belching frankly dangerous fumes up its steep, slippery rock sides. Its sheer natural drama – a scorching, unpredictable hotpot 900 m (2,640 ft) up in the clouds – is enhanced by the total lack of visitor facilities. There's nothing to spoil it, and that vision energizes the trek home.

**HOW:**
On foot

**WHEN TO GO:**
Year-round. Outside the rainy season (June to October), the Lake's altitude means you can expect frequent rain squalls at any time, so the trail is usually both wet and muddy in places.

**TIME IT TAKES:**
Six to eight hours return journey

**HIGHLIGHTS:**
The change from the tropical rainforest glades characteristic of Dominica's natural glory, to the wind-battered vegetation of its high peaks, all in just 12 km (7 mi) from the sea.
The 360-degree panorama from Morne Nicholls.
The intensity of effort required for the trek, and proportionate sense of reward afterwards, when you drop into the hot pools of Titou Gorge to soak off the mud and massage weary muscles.

**YOU SHOULD KNOW:**
1. You must go with a guide, because the trail becomes indistinct, especially in the Valley of Desolation. 2. Wear proper footwear (not sneakers) and scruffy clothes – you will get dirty and (probably) wet. 3. Try to go in a group of six to ten, so that there is likely to be someone of similar ability to walk with. 4. The trail includes some relentless climbs, so there is no shame in deciding to stop early.

*Steam rises from the Boiling Lake.*

93

# La Soufrière Summit Hike

**HOW:**
On foot
**WHEN TO GO:**
Year-round. Between June and October, the rainy season and trade winds make extra clothing essential for hiking above 600 m (2,000 ft); and advisable at any other time. Even when it is clear and hot at the foot of the volcano, the summit plateau is often shrouded in fog, chilly and damp. It's worth waiting for the right weather to get the most from the experience.
**TIME IT TAKES:**
Two to three hours return trip, allowing one hour to explore the summit plateau.
**HIGHLIGHTS:**
Above 'Dupuy Pit', just past 'la Dècouverte', the view of the leeward coast of Basse-Terre across the Caribbean to Les Saintes is breathtaking.
The fume-filled mystery of the 'Tarissan Pit' – so deep no-one knows what lies at its bottom.
'Superman Rock' on the 'Col de l'Echelle', an enormous rock fractured into two pieces – and wonderful photo opportunity to pose as Superman splitting it with super-strength.
'Col de l'Echelle' on the descent, littered with huge boulders from the brunt of the 1976 eruption; and with big deposits of sulphur crystals where numerous fumaroles jet out 96ºC (205ºF) vapour.
The flora of the west and northwest slopes, undamaged by the 1976 eruption, and a fascinating comparison with the botanical re-colonization everywhere else.
**YOU SHOULD KNOW:**
1.Take a naturalist guide to explain the significance of the lichens, etc on the summit plateau. 2. Though the hike is only moderately strenuous, wear proper footwear to stay safe on some very slippery rocks.

From Basse-Terre, the capital of Guadeloupe's western 'butterfly-wing', La Soufrière rises to an imposing 1,467 m (4,900 ft) only 13 km (7.5 mi) away. Even much closer, from the trailhead at the car park of Savane à Mulets, 1,142 m (3,800 ft) high at the foot of its summit cone, the dormant volcano reveals none of its secrets. To begin with, you follow the trail that climbs gently round the mountain, scrambling over fissures, and enjoying the mosses, lichens, mountain pineapples and panoramic views over the Caribbean. At the sheer 60 m (100 ft) rock crevice known as the 'Great Fault', you turn right and clamber up some very slippery rocks for ten minutes to reach 'La Dècouverte', the highest point – and enter another world, completely invisible from below.

Instead of a single immense crater, since the massive eruption of 1976 La Soufrière is capped by a cluster of eruptive vents arranged along the fracture zones. The pits and pools form a lunar landscape of damage where the hail of stones and sludge projectiles utterly destroyed previously lush vegetation. Green posts mark the trail through the mist of sulphurous fumes leaking from this wasteland, once so rich in plants it was called 'le jardin Herminier' (in honour of an early 19th century Guadeloupean doctor and botanist), and now known as 'la Porte d'Enfer'. Here you cross the 'Great Fault' by a natural rock bridge and loop right to the multiple fumaroles of 'Piton Napoleon', until you reach the bubbling cauldron of the south crater. Often invisible in fog or hidden by its own thick vapour, you can smell it and feel its radiating heat at some distance. In fact the hellish landscape is a fascinating demonstration of recovery. La Soufrière's summit plateau of bizarre rock formations is covered with the flora of recolonization – a wonderful surprise and a rewarding hike.

*La Soufrière volcano is a very rewarding hike!*

# The Road

Close to St Maarten, the peak of an extinct volcano called Mount Scenery rears out of the Caribbean, the centrepiece of Saba's 13 sq km (5 sq mi) of vertiginous cliffs and lush, forested mountains. So steep are its hills that for centuries the only way to get around was by hiking up long stone stairways, using donkeys to carry produce and household goods: the world's engineers agreed that it was impossible to build a road on Saba's rugged terrain. With the determination of a Joseph Conrad hero, a local man decided otherwise. Guided only by a correspondence course in engineering, between 1938 and 1961 he browbeat the rock into submission using just dedicated local labour and a wheelbarrow. The Road is his testament. It is literally the only road on the island.

The Road defies gravity, common sense, and all the rules of engineering. It's a stomach-churning 14 km (8.75 mi) switchback made of concrete, with no blacktop, edging or markings. It connects the airport on the northeast side and the harbour at Fort Bay on the southwest, twisting and turning through all four of Saba's villages en route. Mango, guava, avocado, lemon and banana trees line it where its narrow ribbon isn't already crowded by the uniform white, red-roofed houses walling its sides. It makes no concessions to fear or vertigo as it careers past sheer drops into the ocean, and plunges up, down and round within the villages. Sabans take it at speed – and wily locals choose laborious hiking trails rather than walk the Road.

Even by taxi, the Road is an adrenaline rush. Given Saba's incomparable flora, the natural beauty of its rainforest, and its reputation as a world-class dive site, it's appropriate that just travelling between its charms should be a unique journey in itself.

**HOW:**
By car

**WHEN TO GO:**
Year-round. Since Saba has no beaches, it doesn't observe seasons like other Caribbean islands. Some adrenaline junkies actually come to drive the Road during the tropical downpours of June to October.

**TIME IT TAKES:**
About 35 minutes end-to-end.

**HIGHLIGHTS:**
The incomparable views that change with every twist and turn, and pass through five of the six distinct ecosystems on the island.
The hairpin ascent up a near vertical slope from the airport to Hell's Gate. Vanishing into cloud on Mt Scenery – at 877 m (2,850 ft) the highest point in the whole of the Netherlands, of which Saba is a part.
The descent from Windwardside, the village where most visitors stay, via The Bottom to Fort Bay, where the dive boats depart. The 15-minute taxi drive combines the thrills of the Road with a temperature rise of 30 degrees at sea level.

**YOU SHOULD KNOW:**
As an hors d'oeuvre for the Road, be sure to arrive by plane – Saba's runway is just 400 m (1,200 ft) long with a sheer drop into the ocean at either end.

*An aerial view of Hell's Gate Village and the Road*

*Riding mules in the pristine wilderness of Pico Duarte.*

# Pico Duarte

**HOW:**
On foot
**WHEN TO GO:**
Year-round – but never without a waterproof coat, winter clothing, a sleeping bag and hiking boots. Traversing distinct climate zones almost guarantees unstable weather at any time of year.
**TIME IT TAKES:**
3 days, 46 km (28 mi) round trip (La Cienaga); 5 days, 90 km (56 mi) (Mata Grande); 6 days, 86 km (53 mi) (Los Corralitos); 6 days, 96 km (59 mi) (Sabaneta); 6 days, 108 km (67 mi) (Las Lagunas).
**HIGHLIGHTS:**
Climbing the highest mountain in North America, east of the Mississippi. The variety and numbers of birds – including trogons, hispaniolan parrots, palm chats, woodpeckers, red-tailed hawks, and zumbador hummingbirds. Riding mules (you can hire as many as you want: the rule of thumb is one guide and one mule for every five hikers).
**YOU SHOULD KNOW:**
With one or two extra mules, even small children can enjoy trekking on and around Pico Duarte. Some have been known to sleep happily while strapped to a mule on a 9-degree gradient.

Pico Duarte (3,087 m/10,128 ft)) is the highest mountain in the Caribbean. More significantly, it is the centrepiece of the huge Cordillera Central Reserve of Bermúdez National Park, and almost untouched by the kind of tourism that threatens to make a Disney World of other parts of the Dominican Republic. The Park is uninhabited, a pristine wilderness of clear mountain rivers, jungle forests alive with the darting colours of hummingbirds and parrots, and the most magnificent landscapes in the Caribbean. Pico Duarte itself is only one of several similar peaks, and incorporates distinct sub-tropical eco-zones ranging from coconut palms and swaying bamboo groves to humid mountain forest, mountain rainforest and cool alpine scrub and pine.

Of the five routes to Pico Duarte, all are strenuous hikes of between 3 to 6 days and 46 to 108 km (28 to 67 mi). The most popular starts 25 km (13 mi) south west of Jarabacoa, from the village of La Cienaga where you have to register for the 46 km (28 mi) round trip, and hire a guide and mule (the mule is all but mandatory – if only as insurance for porterage and safety). Early in the morning, you follow the bubbling rivers up into the wild woodlands, serenaded by Mourning Doves. The dense forest thins, and gaps in the canopy reveal more and more of Hispaniola's fabled, translucent beauty. By nightfall you reach a ramshackle cabin called La Compartición, where the trails meet and hiking parties prepare for the pre-dawn scramble up the last 5 km (3 mi), through scented pines and open meadows, to greet the sunrise from the bare, rocky summit.

On a clear day with the clouds flushed pink below you, with the emerald forest and blue sea sharp contrasts in the distance, Pico Duarte's rugged antiquity fully justifies its mythic status in the Caribbean imagination. A magical trek.

# Tren Frances

Cuba is so big, with so much to see, that sooner or later visitors need to get from one end of the country to the other. The most rewarding method of travel is the train – and the Tren Frances is FC's (Ferrocarriles de Cuba) flagship service. On odd days (1st, 3rd, 5th of the month, etc) it leaves Havana for Santa Clara, Camaguey and Santiago; and on even days (2nd, 4th, 6th, etc) it makes the return journey. It's a stately schedule befitting the air-conditioned, stainless steel rolling stock acquired from France in 2001 after its retirement as a workhorse of the Trans-Europe Express between Paris, Brussels and Amsterdam. With reclining seats, carpets and cafeteria service, the Tren Frances still offers two classes: basic leatherette *especial* (2 + 2 seats across) and *primera especial*, with fabric seats spaciously arranged 2 + 1 across the aisle. It's comfortable, fast and (despite frequent moans from downright unlucky passengers) relatively reliable. It has to be: if it's more than an hour late, you get the fare refunded in full.

But watching the backyard of Cuba's glorious countryside unfurl, punctuated by visions of its colonialist past and the grinding demands of its agro-industrial economic present, you realize quite how extraordinary this train really is in its Cuban context. It's a statement about the country's determined ambition to make do, mend and better itself on its own terms. The Tren Frances really is the best way to see the 'real' Cuba – and the daily evidence is the other passengers. Most are Cuban, keen to talk and share, and (in marked contrast to the grumpy clientele on the 'tourist-only' bus network) thoroughly cheerful about life and its vicissitudes. *Primera especial* may be grubby and worn, but only the Tren Frances provides a first-class insight to match the country you see from its windows.

**HOW:**
By train
**WHEN TO GO:**
Year-round
**TIME IT TAKES:**
Over 12 hours for the one-way journey of 861 km (533 mi)
**HIGHLIGHTS:**
The powerful air-conditioning.
Breaking the ice with fellow-passengers.
In Santiago, the station is opposite the Caney rum factory.
Sub-tropical dusk and dawn.
The sense of intimacy with Cuba you retain, even long after stepping off the train in either Havana or Santiago.
**YOU SHOULD KNOW:**
1. Foreign visitors pay more than Cubans for rail travel; and they pay neither in pesos nor dollars, but in Cuban Convertible dollars (CUC$). 2. It's best to reserve your seat at least 24 hours in advance, and at both Havana and Santiago stations you do so at a special booth (NOT the normal Booking Office). You may be asked to show your passport, and/or to confirm your ticket one hour before scheduled departure, at the same place.

*Cathedral Santiago de Cuba*

# Revolutionary Trail in the Sierra Maestra

**HOW:**
On foot
**WHEN TO GO:**
Year-round. Irrespective of seasons, the Sierra Maestra's super-lush north side has a wet microclimate, but its south side lies in a cacti-studded, semi-desert rain shadow: on Pico Turquino, fickle weather frequently changes from bright sunshine to thunderous rain in minutes.
**TIME IT TAKES:**
One day (La Comandancia); two days (La Comandancia with a visit to the bio-research centre of La Platica for the flora and fauna); two days (summit of Pico Turquino).
**HIGHLIGHTS:**
Listening to revolutionary songs performed by Quinteto Rebelde in Santo Domingo – these are the original performers from 1958, when they wrote these songs and played them in battle (on Radio Rebelde) to confuse Batista's troops. The band re-formed recently, and play regularly in a local hotel.
Getting politically hyped-up by the enthusiasm of fellow hikers along the trails or in the campsites. With history at every turn, the naturalist's paradise of the Sierra Maestra makes this some of the world's most stimulating trekking.
The friendly and informative researchers at the bio-stations.
**YOU SHOULD KNOW:**
You can stay any number of nights at the Park campsites for the price of a guide and a single entry permit, but you need to carry all the food and water you require with you. Remember to tip the guide.

When Fidel Castro led Cuba's successful revolution against the dictator Batista in 1959, he lit a fire that still burns. Whatever anyone thinks about Cuba's progress since, Castro, his brother Raul, Che Guevara and the other 79 young men who landed from the Granma motor yacht west of Santiago on Cuba's southeastern coast in December 1956 are enshrined in a romantic political vision that still enthralls every visitor to the country. The Sierra Maestra is the mountainous jungle stronghold from which Castro fed the tiny flame into a consuming firestorm.

Virtually unchanged since those momentous days, the entire Sierra Maestra region is full of important revolutionary sights – but the Sierra's status as a National Park derives equally from the necessity to preserve some of Cuba's most beautiful landscapes and very best wildlife. Trekking the revolutionary trail is therefore a double whammy for political and ecological heritage. To make the most of your visit, head for the small town of Santo Domingo (itself the site of a key battle) at the north entrance to the Park. From here, you can join tours (the only way to get the necessary permits) to however many sites you have time for. Two are essential. La Comandancia de la Plata was Castro's field headquarters, in a forest clearing on a western spur of Pico Turquino. The wooden huts where Castro lived, and Che (a qualified doctor) ran a tiny hospital, retain their full dramatic potency in their remote, desperate setting up a single tortuous track of mud and rocks. The other is the tough, two-day hike to Pico Turquino's summit, a ritual political pilgrimage for many young Cubans. A famous black-and-white picture shows Castro on the peak, gun in hand, looking imperiously over the country he was to rule for 49 years.

*View of the Sierra Maestra on the jungle trail from Alto del Naranjo to the Comandancia de la Plata. The rangers' hut on the right is where visitors must leave their photographic equipment before continuing the 2km (1.2 mi) to the Comandancia from where Fidel Castro's revolution was originally run.*

# Mariel to Valle de Vinales

Though relatively close to Havana, Cuba's far west has always been isolated from development or tourism by dense forests and rugged mountains. Its remote beauty has been made accessible by the extension of the Circuito Norte – the *autopista* that links Havana east and west along its north coast – to Pinar del Rio, and the paving of access roads close to some of the region's most breathtaking charms. Driving is certainly the most colourful way to see Cuba, and this is one of Cuba's very best scenic routes.

Once you clear the shabby suburbs of Havana, pure pleasure kicks in at Mariel, the fishing port once famous as the departure point for Cubans trying to reach Florida. With the sea sparkling on one side, you drive up into the green hills of the Sierra del Rosario, a protected UNESCO Biosphere Reserve of tropical mountain forests. Cut by numerous rivers and waterfalls, the Reserve is both stunningly beautiful and home to 100 bird species and more than half of Cuba's endemic species of flora and fauna. From the Circuito Norte it's easy to visit Las Terrazas, a woodland eco-community from which you can swim in the forest waterfalls and pools of the San Claudio Cascade, or the orchid gardens at Soroa.

It gets even better. The Valle de Vinales is a UNESCO World Heritage Site, designated as a cultural landscape both for its astonishing beauty, and for its vernacular architecture and traditions. Dramatic panoramas feature huge rocky outcrops called *mogotes*, like islands towering out of a sea of green fields; and huge caves (once the refuge of remnant Taino Indians and runaway slaves) dot surrounding cliff faces. The Valley is Cuba's soul: it is wholly appropriate that such a lovely place is the only source of Cuba's finest tobacco leaves.

**HOW:**
By car
**WHEN TO GO:**
Year-round
**TIME IT TAKES:**
Five hours, excluding detours and stops. The distance is only 170 km (106 mi) but allows for sometimes daunting obstacles (like sleeping cattle in the 'fast' lane) that you may encounter.
**HIGHLIGHTS:**
The short trek through the tropical forest to the falls at San Claudio. Watching cigars being made in the Vuelta Abajo area of Vinales – like the mandatory five grades of leaves, the process is as rigidly traditional, and controlled, as that of making Burgundy's most illustrious Premier Crus.
The single-storey, wooden houses with characteristic porch-balconies that make the town of Vinales feel like a timewarp.
Driving 'Cuban style'.
**YOU SHOULD KNOW:**
This drive reveals Cuba at its loveliest and most fascinating. Even if you don't have time to linger en route, it's well worth doing.

*Countryside and mountains in the glorious Valle de Vinales*

# Highway 901

At the eastern end of Puerto Rico's Ruta Panoramica, in downtown Yabucoa, the major road ends, and a narrow country lane winds straight ahead into the rising hills. Highway 901 is a sideshow, a scenic corniche road that has so far escaped the horrifying urbanization and development of Puerto Rico's fabulous coastline. From Yabucoa it leads straight to the sea at Playa Lucia, a bedraggled but lovely palm-lined beach kept free of crowds by frankly dangerous currents. Highway 901 climbs quickly past the beach, rising to the very cliff edge some 100 m (328 ft) high above the Caribbean, curling round the tail of the Cuchilla de Panduras Mountains as they drop into the sea. From here, you get a glorious view along the top of the cliffs: with a classic white lighthouse drawing your eye to the distance. Driving is hair-raising enough without going fast, because at several points the edge of the road is the edge of the drop. The view is the compensation for frazzled nerves.

The lighthouse is not open to the public, but you can stop outside it to admire the vistas either side of Punta Tuna, on which it stands. Below the rocky promontory, on both sides sandy coves are hemmed in with thick vegetation bursting with colourful flowers, their scent on the air. In crowded Puerto Rico, the breezy solitude is pure balm for the soul: it's usually impossible to resist a scramble down to the beach itself before driving on. Above you, 901 swings back inland to join the roar of traffic at Maunabo, forming the northwestern boundary to the Punta Tuna wetland area of freshwater swamp and three kinds of mangrove. Like Highway 901, the reserve is tiny, beautiful, and a wonderful reminder that Puerto Rico's coast isn't all freeways and billboards.

**HOW:**
By car
**WHEN TO GO:**
November to June
**TIME IT TAKES:**
One hour, although the road is only 15 km (9.3 mi). Everybody stops to admire the view.
**HIGHLIGHTS:**
Leaving the freeway (full of traffic to and from the biggest naval base in the western hemisphere, 30 km/18.75 mi north at Washington Roads).
The Punta Tuna west beach, protected from development so that light pollution does not distract hatching leatherback and hawksbill turtles, for which it is an important site.
The wetlands and mangrove forest, rare in Puerto Rico where backfill practices are common. Here the forest further protects turtles from human encroachment.
The romance of a sub-tropical cornice, the wind and the sun.
**YOU SHOULD KNOW:**
1.The roadside trees chosen for their shade-providing properties are called 'flamboyants'. 2. Puerto Rican authorities are extending the freeway straight through the middle of Highway 901's scenic wonders.

# Ruta de las Nieves

From the coastal jungle around Maracaibo, Venezuela's cordillera rises rapidly to the thriving town of Valera. Now called the Trans-Andean Highway, the road twines upwards into the glories of the Sierra Nevada National Park, passing the Venezuelan Andes' highest peaks and most dramatic landscapes before dropping down to the lovely old colonial city of Mérida. Woven into the snow-capped mountains, the Ruta de las Nieves is an astonishing introduction to the extreme contrasts of Andean eco-systems, culture and way of life. Valley bottoms are a mesh of stone walls and streams enclosing trout fisheries or pasture for horses and cattle – a system as ancient as the carefully-tended terraces (*andenes*) that climb slopes 1,000 m (3,200 ft) high. The Ruta ascends through cloudforest to the high mountain *paramo* of windswept grassland, through 17th century stone villages like Mucuchies or its neighbour San Rafael, Venezuela's highest (3,140 m/10,330 ft) community. It follows the high ridge between Timotes and Apartaderos – said to be the most scenic drive or bike-ride in the country – with vast panoramas of the Sierra Nevada on either side. The greys and whites of the jagged upper peaks shift with pink and pale-gold reflections from banks of scree and snow; and 200 glacial lake surfaces race with the movement of the sky.

Marvellous as it is just to drive, the Ruta de las Nieves also provides access to some of Venezuela's best hiking, mountain-biking, riding, climbing and eco-tourism. In fact, Mérida is the epicentre for these and other sports like hang- or para-gliding, and the place to organize tours, equipment and guides. Locally, the Ruta de las Nieves is shorthand for two to eight day wilderness trips which start from one of its villages on foot, horseback, or bike. It is certainly one of the most dramatic and interesting Main Streets in the world.

**HOW:**
By car
**WHEN TO GO:**
Year-round, according to your preferred activity and level of difficulty. The hiking season is November to April.
**TIME IT TAKES:**
Three hours (by car, 128 km/79 mi Valera-Merida). In practice 4-8 hours to allow for food and fuel stops, and stops to gaze at the scenery and the craft shops along the way and in the villages.
**HIGHLIGHTS:**
The Sierra Nevada backcountry of the *paramo* eco-zone – high grassland full of wildflowers and the endemic, soft-green velvet frailejón, framing the glacial lakes.
Venezuela's highest pass, at 4,108 m/13,146 ft, on the Ruta at Pico del Aguila.
**YOU SHOULD KNOW:**
The Ruta is both an inspirational journey in its own right, and the gateway for some of the best adventures and recreation Venezuela has to offer.

*The Ruta de las Nieves winds upwards into the Sierra Nevada National Park.*

# Teleférico de Mérida

**HOW:**
By cable car
**WHEN TO GO:**
December to February offers the clearest weather, but many visitors prefer July to September when there is more snow on the mountains. Since thick fog often covers the area, choose any clear day, and go early for the best chance of the view.
**TIME IT TAKES:**
Ninety minutes non-stop. Unless you are both very fit and acclimatized to altitude, take a break of 15 to 20 minutes at each stop before joining the next cabin.
**HIGHLIGHTS:**
Standing higher than anywhere in Europe or North America (outside Alaska).
Skiing in the tropics – lots of visitors ski down to the lower stations when conditions allow it.
The astonishing views of Cordillera de la Culata and Quebrada de la Fria, the neighbouring ranges of the Sierra Nevada, from the Aguada-Loma section.
Los Nevados, a fascinating relic of a pre-Hispanic town, six hours on foot, or four hours by mule, from Loma Redonda. From the same station, in one hour you can reach Laguna del Espejo and Laguna de los Anteojos – a terrific way to get used to the altitude and temperature change
**YOU SHOULD KNOW:**
Be cautious, especially on arrival at Pico Espejo: your body will suffer from any quick or sudden movement. Remember that many long treks and climbs end at the Teleférico – so the people you see bounding about are probably experienced mountaineers.

This is the closest you will ever come to flying on a magic carpet. You start in balmy tropical air at 1,625 m (5,330 ft), and in just 90 minutes soar 12.6 km (7.9 mi) to the 4,765-m (15,629-ft) snowcapped Pico Espejo, adjacent to Venezuela's highest Andean peaks. This is the Teleférico de Mérida, the longest and highest cable car in the world.

The ascent is pure drama. Mérida is a lovely 16th century colonial city set like a bowl of flowers wedged into the green slopes of Venezuela's Sierra Nevada National Park. The Teleférico terminal just east of Plaza Bolivar makes a surreal contribution to the antiquity of Mérida's historic heart, and as the city dwindles into pint-sized perfection, most visitors are fixated by the contrast. The focal point changes at the first station, La Montana (2,542 m/8,338 ft). It's a good idea to walk about and breathe deeply, to get accustomed to the sudden increase in altitude – for now the true majesty of the mountains becomes apparent. During the next two sections (La Aguada 3,452 m/11,323 ft, and Loma Redonda 4,050 m/12,263 ft), huge vistas open up of the saw-toothed high peaks stacked behind one another. Reaching into the distance, you can see how Venezuela's cordillera shares the triple spine that characterizes the Andes through Peru, Bolivia and Chile; and

nearer, how apparently insignificant trickles and water cascades have carved mighty canyons and broad river valleys. Finally, the Teleférico climbs into a world of ice, rock, glaciers and still lakes. A marble statue of the Virgin of the Snows marks the place for the finest panoramic views, including nearby Pico Bolivar (5,007 m/16,423 ft), highest of them all. The altitude can induce a state of super-exaltation in some visitors; the statue is a gentle reminder for humility in the face of such natural magnificence.

*The Teleférico 'flies' over the Sierra Nevada National Park.*

# Roraima Tepui Trek

The Gran Sabana of southeast Venezuela's Canaima National Park is a remote wilderness of jungle, tropical savannah, rain and cloud forests, rivers and waterfalls. Over 1,500 million years, erosion studded the region with huge table-mountains, once connected but now isolated into individual colossi whose sheer cliffs rise 1,000 m (3,280 ft) and much more. Roraima is the highest of these *tepuis*, and its 2,810-m (9,217-ft) summit is a geologist's and botanist's paradise. With a microclimate, topography and endemic flora and fauna evolved in virtual isolation, it is a fantastic world of surreal rock formations, fissures, gorges, pools, waterfalls and sandy 'beaches', valleys of sparkling multi-coloured crystals, insectivorous flowers in gaudy red and yellow, and flashing hummingbirds. Minerals in the rock turn streams into liquid rainbows of blue, red and green; and mist, fog, hot sunshine and driving rain make a lottery of the weather.

Getting there starts with a flight (by scheduled Cessna!) to Santa Elena, where you must buy all the food you will need, and then a 4x4 to the Pemon Indian village of Paraitepui, where you (or a tour agency) sort out the Park entrance fee, guides and porters. A full day's trek across rolling grassland, fording the Tek and Kukenan Rivers, brings you to the 1,800 m (5,900 ft) base of Roraima. It takes a further 4 to 5 hour (minimum) diagonal climb up 'the ramp', through cloud forest, waterfalls, and ancient rock formations to the top, where you camp in one of the sandy areas overhung by rock called *hoteles*. Trails lead in all directions to the summit's best sites, like the Valley of Crystals, but you'll need at least two days to explore any but the shorter ones. No matter: from the rim, you understand how Roraima's strange reality beggars imagination, and how it inspired Conan Doyle to believe in a 'Lost World'.

**HOW:**
By plane, 4x4 and on foot

**WHEN TO GO:**
Year-round, but most people prefer the dry season between December and April. At any time, rain can cause rivers to swell, and delay even roped-up crossings.

**TIME IT TAKES:**
Five days (minimum for experienced trekkers); 6-7 days, allowing 1-2 days on the tepui; 8-14 days, allowing a more circuitous approach and lots of time investigating the novelties of the *tepui*.

**HIGHLIGHTS:**
The Valley of Crystals – the river valley of the Arobopo (from its source on the *tepui*, it falls off the sheer rim and eventually reaches the Orinoco), an amphitheatre 'guarded' by weirdly-shaped black stone columns; the river runs over a bed of colourful crystals and crystal fragments.

The 'Kukenan Window' – a 2-hour dawn hike to catch the view of Roraima's eastern wall, with Matawitepui in the distance and the jungle of Guyana below, before the clouds form.

The guacharos (oil birds) in the massive vertical fissures on one section of Roraima's sheer rim: these are thought to be evidence of the break-up of the supercontinent Pangaea.

The swathes of colourful, trumpet- and other-shaped carnivorous plants, humming with greed.

Fording 50-m (164-ft) wide rivers shortly after upcountry rain.

**YOU SHOULD KNOW:**
1. Whatever you take up the *tepui*, you must take back down, including all forms of paper and other refuse.
2. Taking souvenirs – even a single stone or crystal – from the *tepui* is a serious offence; and your baggage is likely to be searched back in Paraitepui. 3. Hooray! There are no mosquitoes on the plateau; but you will need bug repellant for the vicious gnats (*jejenes*) of the sabana.

*Aerial view of the Roraima Tepui*

# Angel Falls

Sixteen times higher than Niagara,
Angel Falls (Salto Angel) has an
uninterrupted drop of 979 m (3,212 ft),
and are the highest in the world. Their
exotic reputation is enhanced both by
their remote location in southeastern
Venezuela, and by the myths they have
attracted. The Falls plunge over the
rim of the largest of the region's
sandstone mesas (sheer-sided
mountains of dense jungle), called
Auyantepui (home of the god of
evil) by the Pemon Indians who
refused to venture onto it; and it was
the direct inspiration for Conan
Doyle's 'Lost World' of mystery,
darkness and dinosaurs.

You might take two, or six or even
ten days to reach Angel Falls by boat.
Starting southeast of Auyantepui, you
can explore the orchid and bird-filled
jungle paradise skirting the mesa,
spending an adventurous week aboard
a motorized *curiara* (dugout canoe)
and sleeping in a hammock. You pause
to swim through canyons (*kavac*) and
frolic underneath waterfalls tumbling
out of tangled flowers and foliage high
in the riverbanks (*toma de agua*).
Eventually, you thread your passage
through mild rapids on the Akanan
River to the Carrao River, where you
will meet other canoe parties heading
for Angel Falls. Some will have flown
direct to Canaima, intending to visit
the Falls in two days: they will miss the pink and orange-coloured river
beaches, the cascades glowing gold in the sunset, the insights into
their river and rainforest world you glean from talking to your Pemon
guides and the villagers at campsites – the richness of 'other world'
experience that makes the breathtaking first sight of Angel Falls a
culmination instead of a tick on a list. Every visitor follows the Churun
River to Devil's Canyon, and Ratoncito Island. A short hike is rewarded
by one of the world's genuinely awesome natural wonders – and just
then, it's a pleasure to share it.

*Angel Falls – the world's
longest drop*

# Rafting the Upano River

On its swift-flowing path from the Andes to the Ecuadorian Amazon, the Upano River becomes a broad jungle waterway spun with thrilling rapids. Occasional clearings in the dense forest on its banks are home to the indigenous Shuar people, whose frail balsa rafts are the only river traffic. The descending river powers through canyons trailed with vines and foliage, then twists into a narrow gorge choked by massive boulders. A dozen waterfalls crash hundreds of feet from the high canyon walls, adding their sparkle to the drenching spume of contorted water. It's spectacular, ecstatic, breathtaking – one of the best whitewater rafting adventures in the whole world.

Everything about the legendary five-day Upano raft trip is perfect. You join the river at the frontier town of Macas, where it runs broad, a flight path for egrets, parrots, raptors, and the darting brightness of songbirds galore. Shuar guides share their knowledge of the forest and of culture in the headwaters of the Amazon. After the Patuca Bridge, the Upano enters a series of rocky gorges, culminating in the Canyon of the Sacred Waterfalls. These are grade IV and V rapids, and all the more exciting because you have been well prepared for them (and the good rafting agencies send a super-stable 'cataraft' down behind you so you never have too far to swim!). Better still, though there are lots of them, they come in groups, so you won't get completely battered or exhausted. By the time you leave the river at Santiago, 104 km (65 mi) downstream,

you feel exhilarated not just by the speed thrills of distance rafting, but by the feeling of having learned a bit about the Shuar and the Amazon rainforest from the amazing side-trips and the evenings in camp. Better than Five Star: this is Wild Thing.

**HOW:**
By raft
**WHEN TO GO:**
November to January is the favourite time; but May to August is also popular. Water levels can fluctuate dramatically according to rainfall at any time, making grade II or III rapids into IV and V. More experienced rafters may prefer heightened thrills.
**TIME IT TAKES:**
Five days, including Put-in and Take-out.
**HIGHLIGHTS:**
The Logrono Caves – a side trip into the jungle, deep into caves of huge stalactites and falling water to the foot of a 23 m (75 ft) cascade. With Wagnerian noise and drama, the torrent crashes from the outside, through a rocky slit of sunlight, into the semi-darkness.
The roiling grade IV & V rafting along Namangosa Gorge.
The wind-whipped beauty of the multiple tributary falls in the Sacred Canyon – some as high as 244 m (800 ft).
Shuar guides and villagers including you in their evening circle of cooking, stories, gossip and speculation. They still use blowpipes for some of their hunting.
**YOU SHOULD KNOW:**
Previous rafting and camping experience is recommended but not compulsory. Rafting agencies permit one backpack (no suitcases) per person. All good agencies are responsible for supplying all rafting and safety equipment.

*One of the many waterfalls of the Upano River*

# La Ruta del Sol

**HOW:**
By car
**WHEN TO GO:**
December to August; from
September to November it is much
colder, and the §coast is often
shrouded in fog.
**TIME IT TAKES:**
Ten to twelve hours driving from
Salinas to Esmeraldas – but then you
wouldn't have time to see how
stupendous it is, or to divert to left or
right.
**HIGHLIGHTS:**
The Pacific Ocean sailing community,
who congregate in the Bahia de
Caraquez, providing a touch of
glamour to the eco-beach idyll.
The Awa and Cayapas Indian culture
still extant in Cotocachi-Cayapas, and
around the estuary of the Cayapas-
Mataje Mangrove Reserve near
Esmeraldas.
Swimming on the equator with a foot
in each hemisphere.
Spending all day in a hammock
beneath swaying palms near Santa
Elena, then partying all night with the
surfers in Montanita.

La Ruta del Sol is Ecuador's Pacific Coast Highway. Officially, the name applies to the southern stretch from Salinas north to Puerto Cayo, but in practice it extends all the way to Esmeraldas. It makes good sense, because La Ruta del Sol is a catch-all for Ecuador's best beaches, reef dive sites, loveliest and wildest coastal landscapes, party-town resorts, and National Parks along the way. But resort development scarcely exists except near the Ruta del Sol's southern end. Great surfing attracts an international crowd to la Punta and the closest town, Montanita; and it's the nearest good beach for Guayaquileños at weekends. The party only stops when you head north. Suddenly, beach follows deserted beach. Apart from small and ancient fishing communities, there are scarcely any buildings. La Ruta leads to a wilderness coastline that gets increasingly pristine the further north you get. The few small towns lining the highway are each of them gateways to delights like the reef at Isla de la Plata or the ecological marvel of the Machalilla National Park, which has both humid and dry tropical forests side by side. Also near Puerto Lopez is the tropical magnificence of Los Frailes beach.

Unfortunately, visiting cruise ships and a local USAF base have recently damaged the charm of Manta, once the source of Panama hat straw; but the best begins at Bahia de Caraquez. Close by are four distinct eco-systems, home to over 350 different bird species. You can go from mangroves to one of the last tropical dry forests in the world, where golden orioles nest in giant ceibo trees, and you can look down on estuarine marsh filled with roseate spoonbills. From June to December you can even watch humpback whales and their young. You can walk, cycle, ride or drive it: the Ruta del Sol seems to include almost everything people want to do for sport, pleasure, or curiosity.

*An empty beach between*
*Chirije and Bahia*
*de Caraquez*

# Devil's Nose Railway

*Tourists 'ride the roof' on the Devil's Nose Railway.*

The Devil's Nose Railway used to connect Quito with Guayaquil. Recently weather-damaged by El Niño, it now operates only between Riobamba and Alausi. It's a spectacular four-hour ride along twisting gorges and high bridges over ravines, and through fertile valley bottoms lined with colourful villages and small towns. But at Alausi, nobody leaves the train, because ahead lies the Devil's Nose itself. One of the world's greatest railway engineering feats, the track switchbacks down an almost perpendicular 1,000-m (3,250-ft) wall of rock to Sibambe. Unable to go any further, the train performs its technological marvel in reverse, and everyone disembarks back at Alausi.

Oh, but it's worth it. The descent from Alausi takes an hour of constant advancing and backing up, zigzagging across the sheer mountain side; and another to re-ascend. Meanwhile you have a matchless view, forever renewed as the train shifts position and height, of the patchwork panorama of fields: yellow, green and grey rectangles moulded to every contour on the hillsides. On most trains you can even sit on the roof for the entire journey, which turns the trip into something of a party. That may be the reason some trains (currently they are single-carriage *autoferros*) no longer allow the practice. In any case, the adrenaline of riding a narrow ledge hacked into andesite volcanic rock, over an Andean precipice inches away, unites even inside travelers in excitement, if not comfort.

The Devil's Nose Railway is enormous fun, and an ideal prelude for travelers intending to trek the Inca Trail to Ingapirca. From Alausi it's only a short drive to the mountain hamlet of Achupallas (3,300 m/10,824 ft) where the Trail begins. Alausi is also en route to the 16th and 17th century colonial splendour blended into the Inca city of Cuenca, the World Heritage Site to the southeast.

**HOW:**
By train
**WHEN TO GO:**
Year-round
**TIME IT TAKES:**
Six hours (Riobamba-Alausi-Sibambe-Alausi, including brief halts)
**HIGHLIGHTS:**
'Riding the Roof' through the indigenous farmland and remote Allot Indian villages of Chimborazo Province, on trains of mixed passenger and freight wagons that run as far as Alausi – locals and travellers make a happy gang crowded on top with their bags.
The sensation, on the Devil's Nose, of being a fly on a wall.
**YOU SHOULD KNOW:**
1. Bring some warm clothes.
2. A trip on the Devil's Nose provides invaluable acclimatization for further Andean adventures.

# Ingapirca Inca Trail

**HOW:**
By car and on foot
**WHEN TO GO:**
Year-round
**TIME IT TAKES:**
Four days (including getting to Achupallas, via either the Valley of Volcanoes or the Devil's Nose Railway).
**HIGHLIGHTS:**
Condors wheeling above the pass at Tres Cruces.
The wilderness beauty of the yellow, green and grey grasslands of the *paramos*, populated only by your fellow-trekkers and pack mules.
The mighty stones that make up the 500 year-old Inca roadway – part of a continuous system that extended further than the Roman Empire's.
Crossing the streams and swampy valley floor before Paredones.
**YOU SHOULD KNOW:**
You must be fully acclimatized to altitude to undertake this moderate to challenging trek, with some previous camping experience.

The Ingapirca Trail is a 35 km (22 mi) remnant of the 5,000 km (3,125 mi) of well-maintained roads that united the Inca Empire from Chile to Ecuador. You reach it by driving southeast of Quito through the Valley of Volcanoes, a spectacular route that passes the snow-capped giants of Cotopaxi (5,897 m/19,342 ft), Illinizas (5,263 m/17,263 ft), and Chimborazo, Ecuador's highest (6,310 m/20,697 ft). Pausing only for provisions at one of the colourful Indian markets at Latacunga or Saquisili, you camp at Achupallas, set 3,300 m (10,824 ft) up in the mountains above Alausi.

At first the Inca road follows the Rio Cadrul across the hills and wild *paramos* (high grasslands) to the lake at Tres Cruces. It's clear that in 500 years, nothing very much can have changed in the spectacular landscape. But above Tres Cruces, at 4,300 m (14,104 ft) on the saddle of the pass and the trek's highest point, the panorama is breathtaking. You can gaze across the high peaks in every direction, and look down on blue gems of lakes in the valley pockets. You camp by one of them, Culebrillas, close both to the Inca ruins of a *tambo* (courier rest-stop) at Paredones, built by the Inca Tupac Yupanqui; and to the quarry where the Incas mined the igneous stone Diorite which they used to build Ingapirca.

Near Ingapirca, the close-set stones show the original Inca roadway to be 7 m (23 ft) wide, a colossal highway through the roof of the world. It's a powerful reminder that the temple to the sun and other buildings at Ingapirca whose walls have been tumbled by wind and grasses, was a mere motel to the culture that built Machu-Picchu. Ingapirca isn't as obviously dramatic as Peru's Inca ruins, but the absence of crowds makes the Inca Trail getting there much more impressive.

*Chimborazo volcano – Ecuador's highest*

# Amazon Journey

The Amazon is navigable for 4,380 km (2,725 mi) from the Atlantic to the foot of the Peruvian Andes. For 3,600 km (2,240 mi) to Iquitos, it's the dramatic highway for people and freight to cross the continent to Colombia, Ecuador and Peru; and boats of all sizes and degrees of comfort make the trip. But although most travellers can enjoy the experience for itself, they have little opportunity to see anything of the rainforest, its indigenous people, or the unique flora and fauna it hides. The main river, for all its apparent emptiness, has too many settlers on its banks. Instead, from Manaus you can explore the pristine wilderness surrounding the confluence of the Amazon and its biggest tributary the Rio Negro. The Negro's waters are crystal clear, and stained dark with dissolved organic matter; unlike the muddy yellow of the main river, they carry no silt. Where the Negro meets the Amazon at Encontra das Aguas, the unified stream flows black and white for more than 32 km (20 mi).

West and north of the confluence the rainforest is almost untouched, and barely inhabited. Over a few days, you can reach deep into all three types – the *igapo*, seasonally flooded with dark water and an orchid-filled, bromeliad-trailing cathedral of fishing-birds; or *terre firme*, where giant trees with buttresses like rocket fins create the high canopy for howlers and other monkeys; and the *varzea*, flooded with rich silts and with a totally distinct flora that attracts large concentrations of birds, mammals and black caiman. You may be able to visit a deep-forest settlement, and learn something of the medicines as well as nourishment provided by the jungle, or stalk birds on aerial walkways 37 m (120 ft) up in the canopy. These are the things that distinguish adventure from a mainstream Amazon journey.

**HOW:**
By boat

**WHEN TO GO:**
In June, the Amazon and Negro reach their flood, which declines until October-November: the *igapo* rainforest, for example, will have depth variations of 12 m (40 ft). You can travel the Amazon year-round, but each year brings a fresh variation on how best to explore its ecology.

**TIME IT TAKES:**
5-7 days Iquitos-Manaus (typical 'line boat'); 8-14 days (tour boat, including excursions into the forest). 5-12 days Manaus-Rio Negro-Amazon round trip (various tour boats). NB. Allow 1-2 days longer upstream from Manaus.

**HIGHLIGHTS:**
Lazing in a hammock in the humid languor of midstream Amazon, overflown by blue and gold macaws. Threading the Anavilhanas Archipelago on the Rio Negro, within constant touching distance of dense unfettered wilderness. The jungle tower at Ariau, providing access to 5 km (3 mi) of aerial walkways within the forest canopy.

**YOU SHOULD KNOW:**
Whatever kind of boat you choose, and wherever your destination along the Amazon, watch out for your baggage in every port.

*The silt-laden waters of the Amazon meet the darker waters of the Rio Negro at Manaus.*

# Serra Verde Express

**HOW:**
By train
**WHEN TO GO:**
Year-round. Curitiba is notorious for its
fickle weather: summer or winter, the
temperature can change from 30 °C to
15 °C (86 °F to 59 °F) in 30 minutes,
and rainfall on the Serra do Mar is
colossal but short-lived in duration.
**TIME IT TAKES:**
3½-4 hours ('Litorina'); 4-6 hours
('Convencional'), to Paranaguá, when
either of them go the full distance.
They often don't, and schedules are
perpetually elastic. Curitiba-Morretes
(the interesting bit) is usually 2-2½
hours; and your ticket will remain valid
if you break the full journey to visit
Marumbi or Morretes.
**HIGHLIGHTS:**
Marumbi – nowhere else can you
access very rare Atlantic rainforest
so easily.
The Sao Joao Bridge, 55 m (180 ft)
above the riverbed, and spanning
113 m (370 ft) in a soaring arch.
The flat-topped Parana pine, or
candelabra tree. It's the symbol of
Parana State – and one of very few
gendered tree species, with male and
female counterparts.
**YOU SHOULD KNOW:**
On the crowded weekend and holiday
trains, vendors will try and sell you
souvenirs through the train window –
when all you really want is food or
drink. Travel with the workers.

*Passengers lean out of the train
windows to take in the view
and keep cool.*

The Serra Verde Express takes you from Curitiba in southeastern
Brazil to Paranaguá on the coast. It's the most spectacular train ride in
Brazil. Forty minutes after you leave the high-rise modernity of
Curitiba and the conventional drab of its suburbs, you emerge from
the first tunnel into the completely unexpected, revelatory world of
the Serra do Mar. Buckled like a concertina into a series of soaring
peaks and precipitous valleys, the Serra do Mar drops 900 m (2,950 ft)
from Curitiba to the delicate old colonial town of Morretes at sea-level.
These mountains form the largest and best-preserved slice of Brazil's
pristine Atlantic rainforest, protected as the UNESCO World Heritage
Site and Biosphere Reserve of Marumbi. The dense forest of banana
trees, palmetto, hard woods, orchids and creeper vines is shot with
rivers and waterfalls, and alive to the colour and movement of toucans
and monkeys. Winding through these steep worlds within worlds, the
train crosses 37 impossibly high girder bridges, and 13 major tunnels
blasted through rock. If you sit on the left side of the carriage, you'll
see the best of the staggering panoramas that change at every turn,
and smell the sweet air that grows balmier as you descend.

There are two kinds of Serra Verde Express. The smart, expensive
version is the weekend-only air-conditioned 'Litorina', which halts in
the mountains for photo opportunities, but does continue to
Paranaguá. It's always crowded. On weekdays, the third-class
'Convencional' chugs as far as Morretes, but stops at Marumbi (Km 59)
for visitors to the Reserve. It's a working train – a passenger equivalent
of the great freight trains that still haul produce out of the mountains
to the sea. There is no on-board service, but at the frequent
unscheduled halts, people offer you coffee, fruit, pastries and bottles
of local banana liqueur through the window.

# Pantanal Fazendas

*Waterways in the Pantanal*

The Pantanal of southwestern Brazil covers 140,000 sq km (87,500 sq mi). Fourteen times bigger than Florida's Everglades, it's the world's largest freshwater marsh. Between October and March every year it floods, and plant life explodes across its vast network of rivers and black waterways, knee-deep floodplains, lush savannahs, ponds, thick forests and lily-covered lagoons. From April the waters recede, returning newly-refreshed pasture and habitat both to the staggering numbers and variety of birds and mammals who make it their home, and to the *fazendas* – the enormous cattle ranches of the region, whose prosperity depends on their ability to adapt to the dramatic annual transformation.

*Fazendas* exist throughout the Pantanal wherever the land remains higher than the surrounding floodwaters. They make it possible for travellers to find good (often deluxe) food and lodgings while exploring the region. They provide horses, canoes or boats, and above all, local knowledge and expertise in finding the best sites and species habitats, which vary from year to year. Some *fazendas* even offer visitors the opportunity to live like Panatanal cowboys, roping, herding and branding specially bred cattle. Horses make the best transport, providing the extra height you need to see down into the shallows, and a commanding view above the vegetation line and through the forest. Their stamina ensures you see much more than you could on foot; and by portaging canoes, or pre-arranging them, you can cross huge areas. You don't even have to retrace your steps – many *fazendas* co-operate so you can travel from one to another enjoying some of the 650 bird species, giant otter families taking breakfast, alligators, anacondas, howler monkeys, piranhas and even jaguars that contribute to giving the Pantanal one of the highest concentrations of wildlife on earth. *Fazendas* are part of the region's ecology and culture: use them to get the most from the Panatanal.

**HOW:**
On horseback or by boat
**WHEN TO GO:**
Year-round. Aquatic species are obviously at their best between November and April; but drought and tropical sunshine dries whole lakes and rivers by October, when land species concentrate close to remaining water sources. Whenever you come, you'll see different aspects of the Pantanal's uniquely abundant ecosystem.
**TIME IT TAKES:**
3-4 days for the barest idea of the Pantanal's character and natural personae; 8-10 days based on 3 or 4 *fazendas* for a glimpse of the range of its ecological variety; 14 days + to get to grips with the region's balancing act between earth and water.
**HIGHLIGHTS:**
The best birdwatching on the planet. Rarities in abundance, of aquatic, shore, field, forest and savannah, and of every size and colour.
Mammals and reptiles in and out of the water, mangroves, forest canopy or on open ground: if you've ever seen them, it was never this closely.
The blissful luxury available overnight at some *fazendas*.
Viewing the rainforest and flooded plains from horseback.
**YOU SHOULD KNOW:**
1.Some *fazendas* insist on previous riding experience – but all of them use horses bred to local conditions.
2. Make sure you choose *fazendas* with good access to whatever features of the Pantanal you want to see most.

111

*A typical house near Canela*

# Rota Romantica

**HOW:**
By car
**WHEN TO GO:**
Year-round. March/April is especially lovely. Come for the December Film Festival in Gramado, the biggest of various events along the Rota throughout the year.
**TIME IT TAKES:**
3-4 hours to drive from end to end. Most people come for 3-8 days.
**HIGHLIGHTS:**
The late 19th century medieval-style half-timbered buildings of Picada Café, along with Novo Petropolis, among the most obviously Germanic towns on the Rota.
The Plateau of Araucarias, part of the National Forest of Ibama, 6km (4 mi) from Canela. The 131m (430 ft) waterfall plunging off the cliff into the dense growth of Canela's Parque de Caracol – a landscape typical of the Serra Gaucha's beauty.
Vale dos Vinhedos, north and west of the Rota, centre of Brazil's best vineyards.
The grandeur of the Itaimbezinho canyon country in Aparados da Serra National Park, north of Gramado, a reminder of what Brazil is really like just beyond the charming Rota.
**YOU SHOULD KNOW:**
The temperature in Gramado, Canela and Novo Petropolis (580 m/1900ft up in the Serra Gaucha) is usually about 5 °C (41°F) lower than in Porto Alegre.

Rota Romantica is Portuguese for 'Romantic Route'. In the mountains of Rio Grande do Sul, Brazil's southernmost state; it's the name for the 184 km (114 mi) scenic road that winds from São Leopoldo to São Francisco de Paula through the Serra Gaucha. It is a fairytale landscape of wooded hills, vineyards, broad rivers, canyons, waterfalls, bluffs and green pastures. It looks almost European, a look enhanced by the predominant German and Italian cultures of its original colonists. Many of the local Brazilians have blond hair and look northern European; and even speak the local Riograndenser Hunsruckish German dialect. The towns are full of black-and-white half-timbered, or Swiss chalet-style, buildings. The shops are full of German and Italian specialities; and Oktoberfest is sacred. Add to this an arcadia worthy of Poussin, in all the moods and colours of four full seasons, and the Rota Romantica is unlike any other Brazilian experience.

For visitors, Gramado and Canela are the hub of the Rota Romantica's attractions, and of the *serra alemana*, the towns with the Rota's typical German flavour. From Gramado it is easy to join the Rota's sister routes, the Italian-influenced Caminhos da Colonia, which runs through the Italian wine-making towns in the parallel *serra italiana*, and the specifically wine-inspired Rota de Uva e o Vinho. Gramado, Canela and the shoemaking and dairy town of Novo Petropolis also form part of the stunning Região de Hortênsias – a shorter road tour through miles of dazzling blue hydrangeas. One of the region's greatest delights is the constant incongruity of its Euro-Brazilian character and the Rota Romantica's popularity thrives on it. It is also the Rota's only drawback: for many northern Brazilians, the emphasis on old-world cultures practised in the Serra Gaucha's communities is a political issue about 'being Brazilian'.

# Corcovado Rack Railway

The 38 m (125 ft) statue of Christ the Redeemer, standing arms outstretched on a mountain, is the symbol of Rio de Janeiro. The mountain is the 709 m (2,326 ft) Corcovado ('Hunchback'), and the Corcovado Rack Railway takes you up – and to the most sublime views of the world's most glittering city. The Rack Railway is itself a treat. Opened in 1884 by the Emperor Dom Pedro II, it runs on the Riggenbach ladder rack system for 3.8 km (2.4 mi) from Cosme Velho Station, climbing the steep, forested hillside to emerge just behind and below the statue. From here, you can choose to climb 222 steps to the statue itself, or take a panoramic elevator all the way.

The rail trip only takes 20 minutes, but there are just four electrically-driven trains with two cars each, so capacity is limited to 360 people an hour. You can wait hours for your turn, but the journey really is worth it. The rack cranks you up Corcovado's granite crags by way of the Tijuca Forest National Park. Originally cleared by early coffee growers, the mountain was replanted with native species between 1855-70 to safeguard the springs that supplied Rio with water. Now the Park is the biggest urban forest in the world, and for visitors to the viewing platform above it, a green frame to the 360 degree panorama of downtown Rio, the Sugarloaf (from its best 'sleeping giant' angle), the Lagoa, Copacabana, Ipanema, Niteroi and several favelas.

For those in the know, a special VIP version of the train is advertised as suitable for business presentations, sofa conversations, and the luxury of onboard cocktails or appropriate snacks. With background music and a tour guide for 20 minutes, it's the best train for the descent.

**HOW:**
By train
**WHEN TO GO:**
Year-round.
**TIME IT TAKES:**
Twenty minutes up and 20 minutes down. Trains leave Cosme Velho Station every half-hour, every day from 8.30 am to 6.30 pm.
**HIGHLIGHTS:**
The vast skies arcing across Rio's bays, beaches, and beautiful grography. The VIP train's 'office' suite – for one of the world's great views Paineira Station – you can leave the train halfway up, take a walk in Tijuca Forest, and re-board with the same ticket (but caution: most of Corcovado is only safe for experienced climbers, not hikers).
**YOU SHOULD KNOW:**
If possible, avoid Christmas and Easter, when group pilgrimages to Christ the Redeemer make the wait for the train even longer.

*The road and railway wind up Corcovado Mountain to the statue of Christ.*

# Lima to Huancayo

**HOW:**
By train
**WHEN TO GO:**
Year-round (according to the often
theoretical schedule), but between
October and March, at least the
Huancayo end of the trip will be
balmier.
**TIME IT TAKES:**
11-12 hours (in daylight: depart Lima
7.00 am, via Ticlio, La Oroya,
Concepcion, arrive Huancayo 6.00-
7.00 pm).
**HIGHLIGHTS:**
The Desamparados railway station in
Lima, built with flourish in 1912.
Coming out of a tunnel, along a cliff-
edge gallery through an arch onto the
Infiernillo Bridge over a deep chasm –
a standout among spectacular thrills
en route.
The Oxygen Matron, whose presence
on the train is required by law; for
which you will be grateful.
**YOU SHOULD KNOW:**
At the railway's highest point, there is
40 per cent less oxygen in the air than
at Lima. People describe feeling
drunk, shell-shocked or nauseous, and
may stagger about or slump gasping.
But help is at hand, and it will pass as
you descend.

*The train soars up into
the Andes*

Second only to the Pan-Himalayan Railway in Tibet which opened in 2005, the Lima-Huancayo line soars 4,829m (15,839 ft) up into the Andes, a masterpiece of engineering and a thrilling ride. It took 38 years to build the 335 km (209 mi) railway, including some 59 bridges, 66 tunnels, and 22 zigzags where the train switchbacks up sheer cliff faces. Its completion in 1908 opened the huge mineral and agricultural wealth of the Andes to market at Lima and the port of Callao. It was, and still is a working train; and that's why it works so well as a visitors' introduction to Peru.

It's a comfortable train, and it needs to be. For six hours you climb steadily from sea level at Lima to the frozen wilderness of the high Andes, feeding your growing altitude headache with coca tea from the trolley. When you stretch your legs at what is still thought to be the world's highest station, Ticlio (4,758m/15,606 ft), you may gasp for air and need the help of the Oxygen Matron who patrols the train. Most people do. The cold is bitter but the scenery is breathtaking. It gets even better as you revive, watching flowing robes and llamas raising dust in the settlements of the altiplano. At La Oroya, you change tracks and direction. Nothing grows around La Oroya. It is the smelting centre for a collection of mining towns nearby, all overhung with the smell of sulphur. After the fantastic mountain panoramas before this section, it's a relief to leave the peaks and treeless tundra behind at Jauja, and descend through the fertile greenery of the Mantaro Valley, one of the greatest of all Andean craft centres. By the time you reach Huancayo, you feel you've travelled through the heart of Peru's economic future as well as its highland geography.

# Cuzco to Machu Picchu

*Tavelling through the Urubamba Valley.*

Three kinds of train run between Cuzco, the Inca capital, and Machu Picchu, the 'Lost City' hidden in the high peaks of the Andes. The 'Backpacker' is the most economical, and usually more crowded. The 'Vistadome' offers the premium service of greater comfort, free onboard refreshments, and mostly-glass observation carriages. Both services leave Cuzco at 6 am for the roughly 4 hour, 112 km (70 mi) long journey, but spend the first half hour climbing steeply up a series of switchbacks called the Zigzag to Poroy, the first stop. The third kind of train starts its journey from Poroy: saving half an hour is the kind of luxury it represents. So is starting at 9 am – so that by the time its passengers arrive at the most glorious Inca ruins in the world, the other visitors will already be leaving. The luxury train is called the Hiram Bingham, and behaves like a 1920s Pullman service, including cocktails and lunch.

The railway runs through typical Andean valley farms, via the Pomatales River Gorge to Ollantaytambo, at the start of the sacred valley of the Urubamba. It passes whole hillsides of broken terracing, dotted with ruined Inca forts, and then follows the river into the Urubamba gorge. It climbs past the ruins of Qente into a valley where the microclimate is fed by a waterfall, and giant hummingbirds are common among the bright flowers of the morning. At Chachabamba, rocky outcrops are overhung with bromeliads and orchids, and tall ceibos crowd the train. Then the view opens as it pulls up at Machu Picchu Town, 2 km (1.25 mi) below the Citadel, and the place where passengers catch the 20-minute bus ride to the top. Anticipation alone makes this a great railway journey.

**HOW:**
By train
**WHEN TO GO:**
Year-round. All three services are more expensive between June and August, the dry season.
**TIME IT TAKES:**
Four hours (San Pedro Station, Cuzco to M Picchu); 3½ hours (Poroy to M Picchu).
**HIGHLIGHTS:**
The comfort, even on the Backpacker, and especially if you've been hiking or trekking.
The Qente waterfall, and the pristine subtropical flora around it.
The view up the Urubamba Valley on the return journey.
**YOU SHOULD KNOW:**
Though much improved, the train from Cuzco to Machu Picchu is notorious for opportunistic thieving. The views and the occasion are so exciting that it's easy to take your eye off the ball.

*A hiker on the trail to the Pisac ruins*

# The Inca Trail

**HOW:**
On foot
**WHEN TO GO:**
June to August is the Andean dry season, and the busiest for visitors, but the Inca Trail is theoretically open year-round, except for February, when it is closed to allow natural regeneration.
**TIME IT TAKES:**
Four days for the 45 km (28 mi) classic Inca Trail. It's a steady hike, made more difficult by the altitude. Most visitors do not give themselves time to acclimatize. Variations on the classic route extend the trek to 6-8 days, making it easier and more comfortable.
**HIGHLIGHTS:**
Acclimatizing at the Inca fortress of Ollantaytambo, and the market and ruins of Pisac – among various Inca sites on the Urubamba River known collectively as the Sacred Valley. The pre-dawn cloud forest hike to reach Intipunku as the sun rises. The Inca paving stones, stairways, tunnel and multiple other ruins. The unexpected orchids among the mosses of the mature cloud forest before Huinay Huayna.
**YOU SHOULD KNOW:**
Restrictions on the number of Trail permits issued annually mean that they sell out months in advance. Trail hikers are also required to hire a Government-licensed guide for every four people in their group.

The trek to Machu Picchu, the Lost City of the Incas, is one of the world's most famous. Even though the route to it is crowded, it's only because of the imaginative appeal of its destination. Crowds don't matter when you first arrive at the Trail's end – the stone portal of Intipunku, the Gateway of the Sun, through which you first see the ruins of Machu Picchu.

The traditional route begins at Cuzco, once the imperial capital of the Incas' Andean Empire. Most visitors choose to acclimatize to the altitude while browsing Cuzco's Inca and Spanish colonial history, architecture and artefacts. The trek leads up the Urubamba River valley from Chilca to the Inca ruins at Llactapata; past the gentle farmland slopes and woods of Wayllabamba to a steep climb through cloud forest to the second campsite at Llulluchapampa. The plants, flowers and birds are completely different in the open terrain before Abra de Huarmihuanasca, the 'Dead Woman's Pass', at 4,200m (13,776 ft) the highest point of the trek; but the hard work of climbing at altitude is worth it for the panorama of the Vilcanota and Vilcabamba mountain ranges. The Trail drops to cross the Pacaymayo River but at the next pass, Runku Raccay, you come to a series of ancient stone steps descending to the Inca town of Sayac Marca, from which a still superbly-paved Inca highway disappears through amazing cloud forest to Phuyupatamarca ('Cloud-Level Town'). This campsite is close to the extensive Inca site of Huinay Huayna, from which the Trail drops through forest until it levels out and climbs to Intipunku itself. No photograph prepares you for the reality of Machu Picchu. The legendary magnificence of the panorama is magnified by the physical investment you make in Inca history and culture on the ascent.

# Cordillera Blanca

The Cordillera Blanca of central Peru is the world's highest tropical mountain range. With 29 summits over 6,000 m (19,680), its landscape of snowcapped peaks, glaciers, lakes, rivers and treeless tundra is among the most dramatic in the Andes. It is a magnet for serious climbers and experienced trekkers, but its paramount beauty can be equally appreciated from the hundreds of old horse trails weaving through its valleys and passes – the highways accessible to mountain bikers. There are few restrictions on biking in the Cordillera, so with a good guide, your choice of routes depends only on energy and the time available.

There's a classic 7-day circuit of the Cordillera that runs past Laguna Querococha, up over the watershed to the extraordinary archaeological ruins of Chavin de Huantar, and along the Conchucos Valley altiplano. The long return ascent brings you to the 4,750-m (15,580-ft) Portachuelo de Llanganuco Pass, and what is considered to be the most beautiful view in South America. With the Andes ranked behind them into the misty distance, you stand in what feels like touching distance of Nevado Huascaran, Chopicalqui, Chacraraju and Huandoy peaks. Then you launch into an incredible flying descent past the Llanganuco lakes to the route's end, at 2,500 m (8,200 ft), Yungay town.

You can acclimatize in and around 3,090 m (10,135 ft) Huaraz, the mountain-biking and trekking hub in the Callejón de Huaylas valley. You can explore the villages descending the Huaripampa Valley; follow the Ulta up to the Punto Olimpica Pass and a long thrilling ride down to San Luis; tour the glacial lakes full of coots and herons; break for a thermal bath set in the Quercos River Gorge; and always against the magnificent backdrop of Peru's loveliest mountains. The Cordillera Blanca makes you feel you reinvented mountain biking.

**HOW:**
By bike
**WHEN TO GO:**
May to September
**TIME IT TAKES:**
Four days (minimum for a short 'circuit'). 7-10 days is usual, to include 2 days acclimatization rides with a guide. It's possible for independent riders to go it alone – but parties of at least 2-4, plus a guide, are usual (and easy to arrange) for security and safety.
**HIGHLIGHTS:**
The Andean panorama, seen from the Llanganuco Pass.
The 'folded mountains' above the lovely Laguna Purhuay – a geological wonder of a mountain of rock apparently melted, like chocolate, and petrified in mid-flow.
The grove of Puya Raimondii cactus spikes, 3 m (10 ft) tall, each rising out of a ball of spiky fronds, near the rim of Laguna Quesquecocha.
Freewheeling through the Quechua farming communities of the temperate Conchucos Valley (adding cultural to the geographical shock!)
**YOU SHOULD KNOW:**
Most of the Cordillera Blanca falls within the Huascaran National Park, but the region is barely regulated or policed. On short or long trips, even on popular routes, you need to keep your wits about you, both on your bike and in camp.

*Puya Raimondii cactus plants tower over this tourist.*

# The Huayhuash Circuit

**HOW:**
On foot
**WHEN TO GO:**
May to September
**TIME IT TAKES:**
Twelve days (minimum for the full Circuit, including two 'rest' days for detour treks). Most travellers need to add at least two days for acclimatization, if not attached to a tour programme that already includes it. It is not at all unusual for trek agencies to propose Circuit treks of 18 to 22 days to allow plenty of time for detours during the trip.
**HIGHLIGHTS:**
The detour trek from the campsite at Laguna Carhuacocha to Laguna Siula, at the foot of Siula Grande itself.
The view from Punta Cayoc – north to the entire Huayhuash group of peaks, south to the Cordillera Raura, and immediately to one side of where you're standing, the glaciers of Puscanturpa.
The campsite at Laguna Jahuacocha – a beautiful lake reflecting Rondoy, Jirishanca, El Toro, Yerupaja, Siula Grande and Sarupo, among other snowy peaks.
Trekking with mules and Quechua muleteers.
**YOU SHOULD KNOW:**
Even highly experienced trekkers can be at risk of altitude sickness. Lack of regulation and policing in the Huayhuash range means that it is better to attempt the Circuit as part of a guided group, for security and safety.

*The infamous Siula Grande*

The Cordillera Huayhuash (pronounced 'why-wash') is isolated, rugged, difficult and dangerous to trek in. The Circuit trek is the most challenging of all its routes. The reward for completing it – available only to experienced and determined travellers – is a mythic sense of communion with seriously high mountains. It is no coincidence that the Huayhuash Circuit goes close to Siula Grande, climbed in 1985 by Joe Simpson and Simon Yates, and the setting for Simpson's epic memoir of courage *Touching The Void*.

The Huayhuash repays adventurers with majestic vistas of some of Peru's highest peaks, high alpine valleys and turquoise lakes. The actual circuit begins in sight of Yerupaja (6,634 m/21,760 ft), Peru's second-highest mountain, at the Quechua town of Chiquian. Accompanied now by mules, you follow the Quero River to the meadows of Mitacocha and up to the wild terrain enclosing Laguna Sacracocha. By the fourth day, you leave the alpaca herds of Cartelhuain below to cross the Continental Divide, zigzagging to the Punta Cacanan pass (4,700 m/15,416 ft). From here, you look down on the idyllic meadow campsite of Laguna Mitacocha, famous for its trout and its birdlife, and the fabulous range of the Huayhuash high peaks, including 6,126 m (20,093 ft) Jirishanka. The panorama ahead improves each day as you follow the green valleys and high passes deeper into the mountains, but on the sixth day the terrain above the Atocshaico lakes becomes a lunar wilderness of boulder-strewn ridges before a steep descent through herds of grazing alpaca and vicuna to Huayhuash Village. Punta Cuyoc (5,050 m/16,564 ft) is the trek's highest point, and from here the Quebrada Huanactapay is the first of a series of valleys, passes, waterfalls, lakes and glaciers that ends after some twelve days at Laguna Jahuacocha, nestled in a huge amphitheatre of the Cordillera's most impressive peaks. This trek creates feelings that should be bottled.

# Headwaters of the Amazon

Chiclayo is the major regional centre for northern Peru, the crossroads between the coast, the highlands, and the jungle. Iquitos lies on the other side of the Andes, a major city that can only be reached by air or by boat along the Amazon and its headwaters. Local businessmen in a hurry claim to make the trip in three full days. Nobody else would dream of taking fewer than seven days, and most opt for two to three weeks for the journey. There are far too many world-class distractions en route.

Scattered around Chiclayo are Peru's most important pre-Hispanic and pre-Inca cultural sites, including the massive citadel complex of Chan Chan, capital of the Chimu people, and Huaca Larga, the greatest adobe building in South America and one of 26 in Tucume's Valley of Pyramids. It's a 10-hour drive up and across the watershed to Chachapoyas, through the wonders of the cloud forest and mountain jungle; but curiosity will divert you to Cajamarca, where the conquistadors imprisoned Inca Atahualpa, or the fortress sites of Sipán and Kuelap. The region's rich history is hand in hand with its astonishing natural beauty. Tarapoto is as famous for the multiple waterfalls in its surrounding forests, and the variety of rare birds and butterflies, as for the Quechua music, art and dancing of local villages, and the 2,500 orchid species in its leafy environs.

The road ends at Yurimaguas, where cargo boats leave for the two-day journey to Iquitos. You watch the river grow – from the Huallaga to the Maranon, the Ucayali and the broad Amazon stream. You get some idea of how the forest people live, and the extraordinary biodiversity of the upper Amazon. Most of all, you feel an urgent desire to stop and explore.

**HOW:**
By bus or car and then by boat
**WHEN TO GO:**
Year-round; but the unpaved highland roads off the main route can be treacherously muddy in the December to March rainy season, and in the Peruvian Amazon lowlands it rains from December to May. Even the shallow Huallaga remains navigable in the 'dry' season of June to August.
**TIME IT TAKES:**
24 hours by bus or car from Chiclayo to Yurimaguas. Then two days minimum by boat to Iquitos. Coming the other way, any number of agencies will allow you to spend weeks or even months on the river system at various jungle reserves, eco-lodges, or Indian villages, before leaving you at Yurimaguas.
**HIGHLIGHTS:**
Swimming below 35 m (115 ft) Aguashiyacu waterfall.
The colossal Pacaya Samiria Reserve, the pristine jungle jewel of northern Peru – accessible only by boat, either from the riverboat stop at Lagunas, or as a side-trip from Iquitos. (NB it can take at least 3 days to get in and out of the Reserve, and with no tourist infrastructure, you need to hire or attach yourself to a guide).
**YOU SHOULD KNOW:**
At its shortest, this journey reveals greater natural, historical and cultural variety than any other in Peru.

*The citadel complex of Chan Chan*

# El Choro

**HOW:**
On foot
**WHEN TO GO:**
May to September
**TIME IT TAKES:**
3 days
**HIGHLIGHTS:**
The dramatic mountain scenery.
Monkeys swinging through the trees.
Giant tropical flowers and butterflies.
Incan remains and indigenous people.
Coroico – the charming and relaxed
main town of Las Yungas, around
which there are some lovely
short hikes.
**YOU SHOULD KNOW:**
Apart from needing a strong pair of
knees, this trek only requires average
fitness. However, you should spend a
few days in La Paz to adjust to the
high altitude and ensure that you
pack sufficient provisions and
insect repellent.
If the idea of a 3-day trek puts you off,
there is a much quicker way to
descend from the Altiplano. You can
cycle down the parallel route, a
narrow strip of dirt road with death-
defying bends and sheer drops of
1 km (0.6 mi) or more. It is known as
'The Most Dangerous Road in the
World' and is regarded as a
rite of passage amongst the
mountain-bike fraternity.

*Hikers on the Chucuro Pass*

Bolivia may be the poorest country in South America but whatever it lacks in the way of material comforts is more than compensated for by an extravagance of cultural heritage and sublime natural scenery. Nowhere is this more evident than on El Choro, the 70-km (40-mi) long, ancient Inca road that connects the high mountains of the Altiplano with the sub-tropical jungle of Las Yungas.

From La Cumbre, near La Paz, you scramble your way up the barren mountainside to the Chucuro Pass, high above the tree line at nearly 5,000 m (16,000 ft). Toss a stone onto the cairn beside the statue of Jesus for good luck, then set off along the paved path, cut into the mountains a thousand years ago, now worn smooth and polished by centuries of human and animal feet. You wind your way down, past gushing waterfalls and torrential rivers, across old wooden bridges, alongside ancient dry stone walls, pre-Columbian ruins and isolated thatched huts. On your journey you will encounter itinerant Aymará Indians in their traditional brightly coloured costumes – traders and alpaca herdsmen, leading pack-llamas loaded with goods to sell in the Altiplano.

Desolate mountain rock gives way to the mysterious twisted and stunted trees of the Challapampa cloud forest – a magical place to stop for the night. The next day, as you continue your rapid descent, the rarified high-altitude air becomes ever more dense and humid, ripe with the smells of the rainforest, and the vegetation starts to grow luxuriantly thick and green. By the third day, you find yourself in a paradise of verdant jungle, with all your senses quickened by the exotic sights and scents and sounds of Las Yungas. You will reach the laid-back hill town of Coroico glowing with a real sense of achievement at having accomplished one of the best treks in South America.

# The Lost World of Huanchaca and the Caparú Plateau

The 600-m (1,968-ft) high Caparú Plateau emerges abruptly out of the midst of the primeval Huanchaca rainforest, a 1.5 million hectare (3.7 million acre) conservation area in northeast Bolivia. The awe-inspiring sight of this 150-km (95-mi) long pre-Cambrian sandstone mesa (table mountain) was first documented by the explorer Colonel Percy Fawcett in 1910 and the description of his journey through the wilderness inspired Arthur Conan Doyle to write his famous novel *The Lost World*.

Flor d'Oro, in the far north of Huanchaca National Park, is only accessible by light aircraft or a long boat journey up the River Iténez, the border with Brazil. On the flight from Santa Cruz, there are spectacular aerial views. The sky is reflected in the land below, an endless patchwork of rainforest, wetlands, and lakes threaded through with huge rivers. Out of this kaleidoscopic swirl of greens, greys and blues, a rust-red wall of cliff suddenly rises to the savannah plain of the Caparú – a complete contrast to the lowland tangle of jungle. From above, you witness the surreal spectacle of rivers tipping over the sheer edge of the plateau in huge cascades.

The region is one of the last virgin areas on the planet, with a diversity of habitats and species unmatched anywhere in the Americas. As you trek from Flor d'Oro to Lago Caiman and then scramble up Caparú, you will pass through four different eco-regions, seeing all sorts of exotic plants, birds and animals. Eventually you clamber up to Mirador de los Monos (Monkey Point) and, as you gaze down from the plateau at the rainforest and wetlands below, it strikes you that you are among the privileged few who have ever adventured this far into the wild.

**HOW:**
By plane or boat and on foot
**WHEN TO GO:**
May to October
**TIME IT TAKES:**
Flight two hours. Hike 10 hours. Allow between four and seven days to make the most of your visit to the region.
**HIGHLIGHTS:**
Aerial view of the plateau, rivers and waterfalls.
Swimming in the pool of El Encanto waterfall.
Sights of rare birds and animals including spider monkeys, jaguars and macaws.
Los Torres rocks.
View from Monkey Point.
**YOU SHOULD KNOW:**
The Huanchaca was renamed the Noel Kempff Mercado National Park after a famous Bolivian biologist. It is a controlled region and you must plan your itinerary with the authorities beforehand. The hike described here is moderately difficult and requires a good level of fitness. You can plan a less arduous route and/or explore by 4x4 or canoe.

*View of the rainforest from the Caparú Plateau*

*Isla del Sol and Lake Titicaca*

# To The Home of the Sun God

**HOW:**
By boat
**WHEN TO GO:**
February to October. (6 August to experience Independence Day celebrations in Copacabana – one of the best fiestas in Bolivia.)
**TIME IT TAKES:**
Two-hour boat journey; 3-7 hours walking. Stay at least one night.
**HIGHLIGHTS:**
The Basilica of Our Lady of Copacabana and the 16th century shrine – containing the most revered image of the Virgin in the whole of Bolivia.
Climb up the Cerro Calvario, near Copacabana – pass the Stations of the Cross to take in the view.
Wander through the Incan remains on the Isla del Sol – the Chincana Ruins and the Titi-ka'ka Sacred Stone, Escalera del Inca, and the Pilko Kaina Palace.
Watch the sunset over Lake Titicaca from the southern tip of Isla del Sol.
**YOU SHOULD KNOW:**
Never attempt to take photographs of local people without asking permission and giving them a tip.
Always remember that the indigenous Indians are extremely poor; don't haggle over ludicrously small amounts of money.

From the picturesque town of Copacabana, on the southwestern shore of Lake Titicaca, it is only a boat ride to the heartland of the Incas. In Incan mythology, the rugged island mountain of Isla del Sol is venerated as the birthplace of civilization. Here the Sun God created the first Incan, Manco Capac, out of the sacred waters of Lake Titicaca. Today, the Aymará Indians still cultivate the same ancient terraces that their ancestors carved into the mountainsides more than a thousand years ago.

The ferry is a small cabin boat into which you are packed like a sardine, or you must perch perilously on the almost equally crowded roof. The underpowered outboard motor splutters, straining to carry its load out into the lake. There is no doubt at all that the boat will capsize; you are entirely at the mercy of the gods. Since you are shortly going to drown, you may as well take a last glimpse at the world. And it is spellbinding. The lake stretches before you – 8,000 sq km (3,120 sq mi) of the bluest water you have ever seen, encircled by the tallest mountains in the western hemisphere.

Your joy at still being alive, as you tread the path along the island ridge, is soon replaced by a sense of wonder. You are in a place untouched by time: *campesinos* patiently till the unyielding soil with wooden hoes, bowler-hatted Aymará women trudge uphill bearing loads larger than themselves, and raggedy urchins scamper along the terraces after their skinny sheep. As you sit in the ruins of an Incan palace watching the sun go down over the lake, the glistening peaks of the Cordillera Real take on an almost mystical hue. It is only too easy to believe that you have reached the origin of the world.

# Torres del Paine 'W' Trail

The 'W' Trail through the Torres del Paine Biosphere Reserve is one of the world's classic treks. The spectacular scenery, shaped by the combined forces of glaciation and fierce Patagonian winds, is an extraordinary dreamlike landscape of spiky mountains, water and ice – a phantasmagoria of colour and form. You camp beside turquoise, aquamarine and green lakes strewn with icebergs, cross tumultuous rivers and waterfalls, walk through wild grasslands and primeval forests, gaze hypnotically at blue-tinted glaciers, and marvel at wondrous rock spires soaring to 3,000 m (9,800 ft).

An initial boat journey northwards across Lake Grey takes you to the trail head. From the boat, you will see great chunks of ice dropping off the face of Glacier Grey and icebergs drifting along the lake. The trail leads along the eastern shore where you can view Glacier Grey from above. This huge fractured river of ice, over 3-km (2-mi) wide, reflects the constantly changing skies, with a mesmerising effect of dancing shapes of light and shade.

The strenuous climb through French Valley – a cirque of spectacular sheer cliffs – leads you to a heart-stopping view over the lakes and another glacier. Walking the 13 km (8 mi) Sendero Paso los Cuernos (Horns Pass Way) along the northern shore of Lake Nordenskjold, you will see guanacos and humueles roaming the grasslands, and condors wheeling gracefully around the horned peaks of the bizarre bi-coloured slate and granite Cuernos mountains, possessing the sky.

The last leg of the trek is a scramble over a steep moraine of boulders to the most dramatic view of all – the Torres. These three stark granite monoliths, from which the Reserve gets its name, loom over the land like sentinels, dwarfing you beneath the power of nature.

**HOW:**
By boat and on foot
**WHEN TO GO:**
High season is from December to March when there is up to 18 hours of daylight.
**TIME IT TAKES:**
Four to six days
**HIGHLIGHTS:**
The lake crossing with views of Grey Glacier.
Mirador Francés
Cuernos del Paine
Torres del Pain
Wildlife sightings.
**YOU SHOULD KNOW:**
This is a moderately strenuous trek, difficult in parts, requiring a good level of physical fitness. There are overnight shelters and camping sites at regular intervals along all the trails. There are also facilities for cycling, horse riding and rafting. Despite its remoteness, the Torres del Paine attracts trekkers from all over the world and, at the peak of the season, can feel crowded.

*Sendero Paso los Cuernos in Torres del Paine National Park*

# Through the Patagonian Channels

**HOW:**
By boat
**WHEN TO GO:**
November to March
**TIME IT TAKES:**
Four days
**HIGHLIGHTS:**
Taitao Peninsula.
Messier Channel – the changing colours of the water from the rivers pouring down from the icefield.
Ultima Esperanza Sound – cascades tumbling over verdant cliffs.
Views of Pius XI and San Rafael Glaciers.
Whale sighting.
**YOU SHOULD KNOW:**
You can make this voyage equally well in either direction by cruise ship as well as the local cargo/passenger ferry described here. You can also go on sea-kayak expeditions through channels off the shipping route for a close-up experience. Anyone sailing their own boat must report to the port authorities twice a day with notice of their whereabouts.

The ferry that travels the wind-lashed west coast of Southern Patagonia takes you through the intricate glacial labyrinth of channels, islands and fjords at the tail end of the Andes Cordillera. It is a wonderful voyage past forest, river and mountain scenery and across a stormy stretch of open sea, accompanied by dolphins, albatross and even the occasional whale.

From the port of Puerto Montt, the ferry weaves through the Gulfs of Ancud and Corcovado, passing by picturesque wooden villages on stilts huddled on the shore of the UNESCO World Heritage Isla de Chiloé and the beautiful thickly forested islets of the Chonos Archipelago, before heading round the Taitao Peninsula, the westernmost promontory of the Chilean coast, and across the wild, windswept waters of the Golfo de Penas (Gulf of Sorrows). It almost defies belief that the Kawesqar Indians, the pre-Hispanic nomadic inhabitants of the Patagonian Channels, habitually crossed this tempestuous sea in their dugout canoes.

At the end of the Messier Channel, one of the deepest fjords in the world, the lush scenery becomes bleaker, and the further south you go, the lower the snowline creeps down the wild, barren mountainsides. The ferry calls in at Puerto Edén, the only settlement along this untamed stretch of coast, home to the last of the Kawésqars. The passage continues through miles of narrows, often scarcely wide enough for the boat to negotiate. It finally enters Ultima Esperanza (Last Hope) Sound, with stunning views of the mountains of the Patagonian Icefield, and journey's end at Puerto Natales, gateway to the iconic granite spires of Torres del Paine National Park. You will look back on your voyage with fond memories – as much for the atmosphere of human camaraderie among the disparate bunch of passengers and motley ship's crew as for the magnificent glacial scenery.

*The Patagonian Andes tower over Ultima Esperanza Bay.*

# Wine Route

*A vineyard in the Colchagua Valley*

The wine region is a fertile basin of eight upland valleys between the Andes and the Pacific extending 950 km (600 mi) southwards from Santiago, Chile's capital city. The conditions are perfect for vine-growing – crumbly loam and volcanic soils, clear unpolluted air, and a balmy frost-free climate of hot sunny days and cold nights with a long dry season, allowing for slow, steady maturation of the fruit to produce wines of superb taste and texture. Vines were first brought to Chile by 16th century Jesuits who, with a weather eye for potential converts, followed closely in the footsteps of the Spanish conquistadors. They zealously set about their missionary task, introducing the indigenous farmers to their sacramental joys and teaching them the art of viticulture.

The 120-km (75-mi) long Colchagua Valley produces the best world-class red wines of all and is Chile's first official Ruta del Vino. The route starts at San Fernando, heart of the country's Hispanic folk-culture, homeland of the rodeo and the *huaso* – the chic Chilean equivalent of a cowboy, kitted out in long leather silver-spurred boots, swirling poncho and broad-brimmed hat.

The Wine Train chugs through the scenic agricultural landscape of fruit orchards, wheat fields and wineries at a gentle 30-40 kph (20-25 mph), its 1920s German-built carriages pulled by a heritage Chilean steam engine. Passengers are treated to wine tastings as the train passes each beautifully tended vineyard. From the window, there are panoramic views of snow-capped Andean volcanoes, oak-forested hills, and *huasos* on horseback riding down country roads lined with slender poplar trees. Arriving at Santa Cruz, you find yourself in a charming traditional country town surrounded by wineries, where you can watch the production process and taste the new vintage direct from the vat.

**HOW:**
By train
**WHEN TO GO:**
November to April
**TIME IT TAKES:**
Train journey of 90 minutes plus a full day sightseeing.
**HIGHLIGHTS:**
Museum of Colchagua – a beautifully curated collection.
Casa Silva – the oldest and most traditional winery in the Colchagua Valley.
Santa Cruz – picturesque rural town surrounded by lakes and vineyards.
*Huasos* – Chilean 'cowboys' in traditional dress.
**YOU SHOULD KNOW:**
Chile is the only wine-producing country in the world free of the dreaded phylloxera pest that wiped out so many European vineyards in the 19th century. This means the vineyards do not have to constantly renew their root stock; some of the vines here are more than 100 years old, producing wines of exceptional character.

*A cyclist on the Carretera Austral road*

# Carretera Austral

**HOW:**
By bike or car and ferry
**WHEN TO GO:**
January or February
**TIME IT TAKES:**
Three to four weeks by bike. Seven to ten days by car.
**HIGHLIGHTS:**
Rio Negro Hornopirén – one of the loveliest villages in Chile, nestling in a bay enclosed by volcanoes.
Pumalín National Park
Queulat National Park – Pedro Aguirre Cerda Lagoon, glaciers, cascades.
Lago General Carrera – Catedrales de Mármol, village of Puerto Bertrand, and Rio Baker.
Caleta Tortel – picturesque coastal village, built on stilts.
**YOU SHOULD KNOW:**
Although only mountain bike aficionados with stamina and determination should attempt the entire route, any properly equipped enthusiastic cyclist can do a stretch without too much difficulty. If you want to go by car, it is advisable to use a 4x4. More sections of the road are being paved every year so no doubt it will not be long before droves of tourist buses are hurtling down it.

Otherwise known as 'Pinochet's Folly', the construction of the 1,200 km (750 mi) Carretera Austral trunk road was part of the Chilean dictator's scheme to open up the impoverished, sparsely populated region of Aisén. Thirty years and millions of dollars later, it is still a work in progress. It wends its tortuous way through the mountainous, fjord-fragmented terrain of North Patagonia, a potholed dirt and gravel track barely wide enough for two vehicles, only paved around the larger towns, with ferry crossings wherever the complex coastal topography bars its path – a nightmare for drivers but a dream come true for mountain bikers. From the port of Puerto Montt to the sleepy southern village of Villa O'Higgins on the edge of the Patagonian Icefield, the road carves a path through phenomenal scenery that makes the senses reel. You travel for miles without seeing a soul, camping by riversides on a journey through one of the world's most remote and rugged regions.

Within minutes of hitting the road you hop on and off a ferry into stunning volcanic scenery of sub-tropical rainforest. At the precipitous cliffs of Hornopirén you face more water – five hours crossing the bay to Caleta Gonzalo. This initial cyclist's frustration is worth enduring for what follows – hundreds of kilometres of fantastic cycling. After a bumpy ride through the glorious forest and fjord country of Pumalin National Park to the fishing town of Chaitén, you cycle 425 km (265 mi) along a switchback of mountain ridges and lush valleys, across tumbling rivers with glaciers and waterfalls to the beautiful turquoise lakes around Coihaique, the regional capital. A final 440 km (275 mi) stretch through the awe-inspiring, isolated mountain terrain around Cochrane and Tamango National Park takes you to road's end – the accomplishment of the 'ultimate' bike ride.

# Across the Patagonian Cordillera

A horse and a guide are prerequisites for a trek into the Cordillera. A packhorse is the only realistic means of travel in this uncharted Andean wilderness, a land that is just as it was 500 years ago when the first pioneers and missionaries made their way across it. There are no roads at all, only ancient Indian paths and drovers' tracks, known only to the *arrieros* (mule drivers) and *vaquearos* (cattle and sheep drovers) handed down from one generation to the next.

From Lago Puelo in Argentina, the Puelo River flows through Lago Inferior on the Chilean side of the border to the Reloncavi estuary on the Pacific Coast. This is the starting point for your ride into the wilds, some 100 km (60 mi) from the city of Puerto Montt.

The tranquil ride from the village of Puelo along the Reloncavi fjord is a scenic treat with the Yate Volcano towering ahead of you. After loading your horse onto the ferry to cross Lago Tagua-Tagua you then take to the narrow trails that lead through verdant rainforest scored with tumbling rivers, dramatic waterfalls and rapids, to high mountain plateaux of wild flower meadows, sparkling streams and azure lakes. Apart from the occasional isolated farmhouse, you really are in the back of beyond, entirely reliant on your guide to pick your way along the valleys and ridges, across the lakes and rivers to Lago Inferior on the border with Argentina.

You re-encounter the 21st century world in the form of the Chilean border police. Here you must say farewell to your horse and take a boat across Lago Inferior to Argentina where you disembark in the steppes of Lago Puelo National Park under the snowy peaks of Tres Picos, at the end of an amazing journey.

**HOW:**
On horseback
**WHEN TO GO:**
November to March
**TIME IT TAKES:**
Eight to ten days
**HIGHLIGHTS:**
Crossing Rio Puelo in a wooden boat with your horse swimming alongside.
La Pasarela del Rio Puelo – spectacular rapids and waterfalls.
Lago las Rocas – a beautiful lake in a glorious setting.
Staying in a traditional Chilean homestead.
**YOU SHOULD KNOW:**
It is easy to hire horses and guides. No previous experience of riding is needed but you should be reasonably physically fit. Treks vary in length; a single day's ride in this beautiful region is well worth doing even if you do not have the time or inclination for the full haul.

*Lago Puelo lies in the National Park of the same name.*

127

# Tren a las Nubes

**HOW:**
By train
**WHEN TO GO:**
April to October
**TIME IT TAKES:**
Seven to eight hours
**HIGHLIGHTS:**
Salta – a beautifully preserved colonial city.
Puerta Tastil – ruins and rock paintings.
The Loop – vertiginous mountain views.
La Polvorilla Viaduct – a masterpiece of engineering, 224 m (735 ft) long and 63 m (206 ft) high.
The condors flying above, and the clouds below.

**YOU SHOULD KNOW:**
The Tren a las Nubes is a once-weekly heritage tourist train with stops en route, guides, viewing cars, and folk music. You can cover the same route on the cargo train that goes from Salta to Chile or in a 4x4 along National Route 51.

Built in the 1940s, the Tren a las Nubes (Train to the Clouds) is the third highest railway in the world. It is worth travelling along for the sheer technical wizardry of the railway line itself, quite apart from the mind-blowing terrain it goes through on its skyward journey. American engineer Richard Fontaine Maury designed the track so that an engine could pull a train up the mountains by its own power alone without needing the conventional mechanism of a cog-and-pinion rackrail. The resulting train journey is a thrilling 220-km (136-mi) zigzag switchback ride crossing some of most complex topography on the planet by means of 13 viaducts, 29 bridges and 21 tunnels. There are two huge loops along the route where the track virtually doubles back on itself in order to gain height and you feel that you have been given a front row circle seat over the world as you gaze down from vertiginous mountain heights.

From the sub-tropical colonial city of Salta, the train travels up the Lerma Valley passing quaint mud-built villages and red-flowering ceibo trees as it heads into the Quebrada del Toro (Bull's Gorge) and across the rocky salt desert canyons of the Andes – the little-known lands of the Diaguita Indians. Awesome rock formations, blasted into grotesque shapes by aeons of erosion, appear in a kaleidoscopic whirl of colour where the earth has been tinted by rich veins of mineral ore – vivid shades of red, yellow, pink, green and orange.

The train stops along the way so that you can wander around in this strange land on your way to the altiplano copper-mining town of San Antonio de los Cobres. Here, standing at 4,230 m (13,900 ft) on the Polvorilla Viaduct among the snow-capped peaks, you will find the clouds really are drifting beneath your feet.

*La Polvorilla Viaduct near San Antonio de los Cobres*

# The End of the World Train

*The End of the World Train*

This is a journey to delight any railway enthusiast. Not only are you travelling on the world's southernmost railway line but you are pulled by one of several heritage steam engines along a narrow gauge track with a fascinating past.

The railway starts 8 km (5 mi) from Ushuaia and runs for some 14 km (9 mi) into Tierra del Fuego National Park, a protected area of 630 sq km (240 sq mi) once inhabited by Yamaha Indians. As the train meanders along the River Pipo valley at a sedate 15 kph (9 mph) you have breathtaking views of the wild glacial landscape of the South Andes Cordillera – steep snow-capped mountains, rivers, waterfalls, woods and lakes interspersed with tundra plateau carpeted in lichens and mosses. The journey ends at Estación del Parque from where you can explore this remote region on foot.

Although today the End of the World Train is a tourist attraction, it was originally built to fulfil an altogether murkier purpose – the transportation of forced labour to the hinterland forest and of felled trees back to the coast. By the end of the 19th century the Argentinian authorities had established a penal colony as far away from civilization as possible, at the tip of South America. From these inauspicious beginnings emerged today's city of Ushuaia, its earliest buildings constructed by convicts using timber from the surrounding sub-polar forests. The prison was transformed into a naval base in 1947 and the railway was decommissioned in 1952 after an earthquake badly damaged the track. The growth of the travel industry led to its re-opening in 1994 as an environmentally-friendly means of conveying tourists to an otherwise inaccessible part of the National Park. Despite the best efforts of tourist brochures, the railway is still commonly known as 'The Prisoners' Train'.

**HOW:**
By train
**WHEN TO GO:**
All year
**TIME IT TAKES:**
One hour
**HIGHLIGHTS:**
Ushuaia Museo del Presidio – Prison Museum.
Cañadón del Toro gorge
Cascada La Macarena waterfall
Tree cemetery
**YOU SHOULD KNOW:**
To fully appreciate the trip it is a good idea to visit the Prison Museum first, where you will get atmospheric impressions of life in the penal colony and find out more about the railway and National Park.

# South Patagonia Ice Cap Trek

Los Glaciares National Park in the Patagonian Icefield is a 4,450 sq km (1,720 sq mi) wonderland – a maze of rivers and glaciers, milky glacial lakes, and mountain spires soaring like cathedrals into the sky. This is a landscape from another planet – unimaginably strange and overwhelmingly beautiful. At the heart of the Park are two huge glacial lakes, Lago Argentino to the south, the largest lake in Argentina, and Lake Viedma to the north, in the shadow of the 'ultimate' granite massifs of Mount Fitz Roy and Cerro Torre.

The starting point for any trek is El Chaltén, an isolated mountain village at the confluence of two rivers north of Lake Viedma. From here, after you have hiked through the romantic lenga beechwoods along the banks of the Rio Eléctrico, you hike up to Paso Marconi for incredible views of Mount Fitz Roy and don your snow shoes for the tough but scenic journey across the icefield, traversing the Viedma and Upsala glaciers through magical ice landscapes, bivouacking in rough shelters along the way.

At last, as you scramble across Upsala's rocky moraine ridge, Lake Argentino comes into view. The boat ride across the lake to the southern edge of the Park, passing the glacier faces, is a fitting grand finale to your trek – both spell-binding and scaring. These relentless rivers of ice make awesome creaking and juddering sounds as the iceface continually fractures and falls. Huge chunks come crashing down into the weird milky-green coloured water and then sail calmly off, littering the lake with icebergs.

You end your ice-journey at El Calafate, a friendly rustic town on the southern shore where nature once again wears a benign expression and you can mull over your unforgettable experience over a traditional meal of Patagonian lamb and home-made bread.

**HOW:**
On foot
**WHEN TO GO:**
December to March
**TIME IT TAKES:**
Seven to nine days
**HIGHLIGHTS:**
Rio Eléctrico – beechwoods, wildlife, rare birds and exotic flowers.
View of Mt Fitz Roy at dawn when the granite spires glow pink.
Snoe-shoeing on the Viedma Glacier.
Lago Argentino boat trip to see Perito Moreno.
Walichu Caves – palaeolithic cave paintings near El Calafate.
**YOU SHOULD KNOW:**
The South Patagonian icefield is the third biggest continuous stretch of ice in the world – only the ice caps of Antarctica and Greenland are larger. This trek is difficult; previous experience of hiking in winter conditions and good physical fitness is required. There are many other walks and hikes to suit all abilities from one day to two weeks.

*Mt Fitz Roy in the Parque Nacional los Glaciares*

# Cycle Across the Andes to the Atacama

The road between San Salvador de Jujuy in north-west Argentina and the Atacama, the world's driest desert, is the highest route in the Americas. It takes you through jaw-dropping World Heritage scenery and over the Paso Jama into Chile at an altitude of nearly 6,000 m (20,000 ft).

This is not a trip for the faint-hearted. It is 400 km (250 mi) of tough mountain road. You start gently enough, pedalling slowly along the ancient Camino Inca, constantly distracted by the incredible multi-coloured rock of the Quebrada de Humahuaca. After about 60 km (40 mi) you turn off to the picturesque mud-built village of Purmamarca, admire the Cerro de Siete Colores (Seven Coloured Mountain) and prepare for some serious cycling.

The Cuesta de Lipan is a hair-raising stretch of fiendish bends through desolate wilderness, spiralling up to 4,000 m (13,000 ft). From the top, you gaze down at a hallucinatory view of blank whiteness – the entrancing salt landscape of the Salinas Grandes. You cycle across in a light-headed haze to make the ascent to the remote border town of Susques, the place to take a break and wander round the ancient ruins.

After the triumph of crossing Paso Jama – Argentina's gateway across the Andes – the road, to your horror, goes uphill again. You stagger on, for what feels like forever. Just when you've decided you must be on the wrong road, you are suddenly there – at the top of the world. The Atacama Desert spreads below you, and beyond, the dream of the Pacific Ocean. The descent to San Pedro is fantastic. You hurtle downhill in a spirit of wild exhilaration to a tourist town chock-full of backpackers – the sort of place you might normally deride. For once, you will be only too grateful for the creature comforts it provides.

**HOW:**
By bike
**WHEN TO GO:**
April to October
**TIME IT TAKES:**
Three to five days (or 12 hours in a 4x4)
**HIGHLIGHTS:**
Quebrada (Gorge) of Humahuaca – UNESCO World Heritage Site
Purmamarca's beautiful 16th-17th century Chapel.
Salinas Grandes
Moon Valley rock formations San Pedro de Atacama.
Flamingoes at Salar de Tara, Atacama.
**YOU SHOULD KNOW:**
You need to be very fit for this difficult journey. You will be travelling through an isolated semi-desert region at an average altitude of 3,000 m (10,000 ft). Be properly equipped and take warm clothing – the temperature drops dramatically at night. To avoid altitude sickness you should spend a day at Purmamarca to acclimatize; don't eat before you travel, and drink maté (herbal tea) to help oxygenate the blood.

*The incredible salt landscape of the Salinas Grandes*

# Explore the Península Valdés

**HOW:**
By car
**WHEN TO GO:**
June to December to see southern
right whales and orcas. Wildlife is at
its peak October-November.
**TIME IT TAKES:**
Although this is only a 200-km
(125-mi) drive, the roads are mainly
unpaved. You should allow 2-3 days
if you want to explore the
peninsula properly.
**HIGHLIGHTS:**
Watch southern right whales from El
Doradillo Beach.
Boat ride out to sea from Puerto
Piràmides to see dolphins
and whales.
The sea lion and seal colonies.
The saltpans of Valdés Peninsula.
Diving from Punta Pardelas beach.
**YOU SHOULD KNOW:**
Península Valdés is a protected
nature reserve and you must pay a
fee to enter. You can also see the
largest Magellan Penguin colony in
the world at Punto Tombo, 110 km
(70 mi) south of Puerto Madryn.

*A southern right whale erupts
out of the water.*

If you are in search of an escape from the mundane, you would be hard put to find anywhere more inspiring than the windswept shores and blue waters of the Patagonian coast. This magical region of multi-coloured pebble beaches, steep cliffs, jagged rocks, and miles of sand flats is one of the most precious wildlife habitats in the world where, amongst a plethora of sea and land creatures, you can see dolphins playing, orcas out on a seal hunt, and the largest southern right whale breeding-grounds in the world.

The drive from Puerto Madryn, on Golfo Nuevo, along the Ameghino Isthmus to the tip of the World Heritage wilderness of Península Valdés, plunges you straight into the savage beauty of the natural world. You can hear the southern right whales calling to each other as you watch them play in the water along the remote shores of El Doradillo beach. You drive along dirt tracks through desolate country of steppe and saltpans where guanacos, rheas, maras and grey foxes roam at will among the sheep. On the mudflats of Puento Norte, while you watch the elephant seals and sea lions, you will see opportunistic orcas lurking offshore ready to pounce on any unprotected pup and drag it into the water. At Valdés Caleta, a long gravel spit, you can observe a colony of Magellan penguins among the thousands of seabirds that congregate here.

At the end of the road, at Punta Delgada lighthouse on the south-eastern tip of the peninsula, as you gaze down from the high cliffs at the huge colony of elephant seals on the beach below and out over the endless spread of the Atlantic Ocean, you feel you have reached the very edge of the earth, far beyond the clutches of the man-made world.

# Ruta de Las Siete Lagos

Imagine a giant-sized, untamed version of Switzerland and you will get some idea of the phenomenal scenic beauty of Argentina's Lake District. The 200-km (125-mi) drive from Bariloche on the southern shore of Lago Nahuel Huapi up to the mountain resort of San Martin takes you through two national parks along a winding road with panoramic views round every bend.

From the beautiful city of Bariloche, a scenic 70-km (40-mi) lakeside drive takes you to the charming resort town of Villa La Angostura, the starting point of the famous Ruta de las Siete Lagos (Road of the Seven Lakes). The road zigzags its tortuous way along the narrow river valleys and ridges of Nahuel Huapi, the oldest of Argentina's national parks. The lower slopes of the rugged Patagonian mountains are swathed in evergreen coigüe forest, lightened by paintbox colours of wild flowers and shrubs – eye-catching daubs of yellow, red, orange and pink. The savage dark rocks and snowy peaks tower above you and, at every turn, just when you think you have seen the view of a lifetime, you are greeted with yet another incredible sight to take your breath away.

The road takes you through Villa Traful, a picturesque Andean village of wood and stone houses overlooking a turquoise lake, past Lago Escondido (Hidden Lake) twinkling behind its forest canopy, the twin lakes, Villarino and Falkner, joined by an isthmus, and the most beautiful of all, Lago Hermoso. At the entrance to Lanín National Park the landscape becomes drier, the thick evergreen forest gives way to southern beech woods, and you soon catch sight of the immaculately still waters of Lago Machonico. The road ends at the tranquil tourist town of San Martin, nestling among the mountains on the shore of Lake Lácar.

*Lake Traful in Patagonia*

**HOW:**
By car or bike
**WHEN TO GO:**
September to April; December for wild flowers in full bloom.
**TIME IT TAKES:**
One day by car. Three days by mountain bike.
**HIGHLIGHTS:**
Valle Encantada – strange rock formations.
Los Arrayanes National Park on peninsula of Lake Nahuel Huapi – forest of rare 300-year old and 20-m (66-ft) high arrayán trees, said to be Disney's source of inspiration for the film *Bambi*.
Lake Traful vantage point
Vullinaco Waterfall
LagoHermoso
**YOU SHOULD KNOW:**
The Lake District is a very popular area for sports activities. Cerro Catedral, near Bariloche, is one of Argentina's main ski resorts. In the summer you can go sailing, rafting and fly-fishing as well as mountain hiking, horse riding, off-road driving and cycling.

*Iguazú Falls*

# The Northern Loop

The eighth largest country in the world, Argentina has an amazing diversity of scenery, climates and cultural influences. This 5,000-km (3,000-mi) road trip enables you to see sights and landscapes that you would not even glimpse from a plane, takes you to four great cities, across the pampas, into the wine lands, up into the Andes, through desert, ending in the sinister rainforest borderland of Brazil and Paraguay, at the heart of South America.

From Buenos Aires, sultry tango capital, you start on the most gruelling stretch of road – 1,000 km (600 mi) cross-country through the stark monotony of the pampas. You are rewarded with an overwhelming buzz of accomplishment when you hit the hills of the wine country and the beautiful green city of Mendoza, gateway to the Andes.

You head north-eastwards through wild green mountains and picturesque hill villages to see the sublime colonial architecture of Córdoba, and continue north to Tucumán, 'the garden of the republic'. You will experience one of the most beautiful drives of your life in the polychrome desert canyons of Cafayate on the way to Salta, a charming sub-tropical colonial city on the edge of the Andes.

Travelling back eastwards through the cactus-dotted plains of the Chaco and the verdant wetlands of Corrientes you reach the historic north-eastern province of Misiones, a rainforest region of deep red ferrous earth and lush green jungle, named after the brutal Jesuit missionaries who converted the Guarani Indians to Christianity by force. The road to the Brazilian border ends at the spectacular Iguazú Falls, one of the greatest natural wonders of the world. The deafening roar of thousands of tons of water cascading down stirs feelings of fear, awe, wonder and respect at the indomitable power of nature. It's a sensational end to an incredible journey.

# The Beagle Channel & Magellan Strait

Short of travelling to Antarctica, the southern hemisphere's most incredible scenery is to be found in the crazy maze of channels, islands and bays that make up the south-western coastline of Tierra del Fuego. The sea passages that connect the Atlantic and Pacific Oceans are notoriously difficult to navigate. Changeable, often tempestuous weather and the narrowness of the straits promise to make the voyage from Ushuaia an unpredictable one. You will see dolphins, Magellan penguins, seals and cormorants, hear the creaking sounds of the glaciers and the thunderous crashes as great chunks of ice break off into the sea, and experience a sub-polar wilderness of forest and mountain.

The Beagle Channel is named after the eponymous surveying ship that the great naturalist Charles Darwin sailed on. His description of the landscape is just as valid today as it was in 1839: 'The lofty mountains on the north side...are covered by a wide mantle of perpetual snow... numerous cascades pour their waters through the woods into the narrow channel below...magnificent glaciers extend from the mountainside to the water's edge. It is scarcely possible to imagine anything more beautiful than the beryl-like blue of these glaciers and especially as contrasted with the dead white of the upper expanse of snow. The fragments which had fallen from the glacier into the water were floating away and the channel with the icebergs presented...a miniature likeness of the Polar Sea'.

You disembark at Punta Arenas, a charming colonial town of red-roofed houses and a lovely tree-lined central square. Here the statue of Ferdinand Magellan, the first explorer to sail from the Atlantic into the Pacific, reminds you of the full historical significance of your journey, adding an extra dimension to the wondrous spectacle of nature you have witnessed.

**HOW:**
By boat
**WHEN TO GO:**
November to March
**TIME IT TAKES:**
Four to five days
**HIGHLIGHTS:**
Cape Horn National Park – stark promontory with sheer 400-m (1,300-ft) cliffs.
Wulaia Bay – spectacularly beautiful Magellanic forest scenery.
Avenida de los Glaciares – stretch of the Beagle Channel lined with hanging glaciers.
Magdalena Island – Magellan penguin colony and lighthouse.
**YOU SHOULD KNOW:**
You can do this journey equally easily the other way round – starting in Punto Arenas, Chile and ending in Ushuaia, Argentina. Either way, the route is weather-dependent. In calm seas, the boat will make a diversion to Cape Horn National Park. There are several cruise companies or, for a truly authentic experience, you can go on a cargo boat if you are prepared to rough it a bit.

*Cormorants in the Beagle Channel*

# Che Guevara's Revolutionary Road

**HOW:**
By motorbike or bus and by boat
**WHEN TO GO:**
Year-round (remembering that in the southern hemisphere, June to August can be very cold; and rainy seasons vary, and are subject to micro-climates along some of the route).
**TIME IT TAKES:**
Che famously took nine months. Recently, two actors took a year, making a film on the way. You can travel the road by bus and boat in roughly a month, but nearer three months is considered the minimum.
**HIGHLIGHTS:**
The Chuquicamata copper mine, biggest open-pit mine in the world, in the Atacama Desert south of Iquique – primary source of Chile's wealth, and Che's indignation that it was US-owned.
The Amazon jungle around the leper colony of San Pablo – with indigenous Indian guides recounting tales and lore of the dense forest.
Cuzco, once capital of the Inca Empire, overprinted with the Hispanic colonial boot – a dangerous but charming city, and base for Machu Picchu.
**YOU SHOULD KNOW:**
1. Outside cities and major tourist attractions, a knowledge of Spanish is invaluable and occasionally vital. 2. Throughout South America, local rules and regulations may not always be those decreed by official federal agency. You must check at the time you want to go. 3. Check, if you plan to enter Colombia via Leticia, how you can proceed either into Colombia or elsewhere in the Amazon basin. It can be notoriously difficult to leave without great expense. Che flew to Bogota.
NB. On this journey, Che never visited Bolivia. But aficionados traveling from Chile to Peru may want to pause and take one of several Bolivian tours based on his later exploits.

Heading south from Buenos Aires in 1952, 23 year-old Che Guevara circled South America on a motorbike, with a friend. His diaries of their epic journey are a tale of high drama, low comedy, disaster and discovery. Retracing his route even approximately may not influence your political philosophy, but it will provide you with a particular insight into the nature of South America as a continent, and to the historical and geographic reasons for collective aspects of its social cultures. Of course, your trip will be much more comfortable: but if the main roads are paved, and you travel in an air-conditioned bus or car or train, you can still find the sleepy, sun and wind-parched villages in the dust of Patagonia or the Atacama desert, the stone hut shelters of the Andean altiplano, and the broiling humid shacks in the Amazon jungle in which Che sought to quantify 'workers' conditions'.

Down Argentina, across the Andes, up Chile to Peru, then from Cuzco through the Amazon headwaters to Iquitos and (via Leticia) Colombia and Venezuela – Che's diaries provide much more than just the inspiration to keep your eyes properly open. His carefree exuberance is infectious, a reminder to take opportunities to share the back of a dusty truck with whoever, or to swim when the ferry needs pushing. His route goes deep into remote backcountry, to borders and regions which can still be dangerous. Seek help where you can from local people – but use the tourist infrastructure where it is useful. Balance some of your curiosity with caution (eg when hitch-hiking, as Che did), but enjoy unexpected adventures when they happen.

Che's journey did not end in Venezuela. Choose to follow him, and nor will yours: you'll share his lifelong respect for the magnificence of South America, and of its peoples' durability.

*Inquisitive young villagers in Iquitos, Peru.*

# AFRICA

# Krom River Trail

**HOW:**
On foot
**WHEN TO GO:**
October to May
**TIME IT TAKES:**
A few hours
**HIGHLIGHTS:**
A plunge into one of the splendidly cooling swimming pools that greet you enticingly at either end of the Krom River Trail.
Views of Du Toits Peak – highest point of the Limietberg Nature Reserve at 1,996 m (6,557 ft).
The animals and birds – including klipspringer, baboon, caracal, an occasional leopard, Cape sugarbird, protea canary and black eagle.
**YOU SHOULD KNOW:**
Be prepared to meet anglers along the Trail – the Krom is a popular trout-fishing river.

Sadly this great river, along with its associated wetlands, is coming under increasing pressure from the development demands of modern South Africa, with consequent degradation. But it is still possible to experience the pristine beauty of the Krom River and environs as it has always been by hiking various marked trails in Limietberg Nature Reserve, which is located in the De Toitskloof Pass between Paar and Worcester in the Western Cape. To hike the Krom River Trail, approach through the Huguenot Tunnel from the Worcester side and park. A permit from Cape Nature is required.

The Trail is 7 km (4.4 mi) long, and can be comfortably walked in half a day. No guide is needed, though sensible pre-hike precautions (appropriate clothing plus a basic supply of food and water) should be taken. The Trail crosses the Molenaars River and ascends along the right-hand slope above the Krom River. It passes through an area of indigenous forest and reaches a waterfall with pool beneath. There is then a hair-raising climb up a chain ladder to a second fall and pool – this waterfall in its lush setting is one of the very best in the whole Western Cape. The Trail then returns by the same route.

There are other rewarding trails in the park – each different, each taking no more than a day. The Rock Hopper Trail from Eerste Tol to Tweede Tol is more adventurous, and involves finding your own way down (or up) an 8-km (5-mi) stretch of the Witte River's boulder-strewn riverbed, using a combination of walking, swimming and rock-scrambling. This Trail requires a drop-off at the beginning and pick-up at the end. The Elands Trail initially involves a steep climb, providing great valley and river views, before descending to Fisherman's Cave with its inviting pool.

# Cape Wine Route

If you are interested in glorious scenery and delicious wines, a trip along Route 62, in South Africa's Western Cape region, is a must. Some 50 years ago, a highway was opened here, and Route 62 became a forgotten road, with little traffic and fewer visitors. Surprisingly, this was a godsend for the area: its fruitful farming communities were left in peace. The result is probably the longest wine route in the world, meandering through some of the most sublime scenery and prolific vineyards you can imagine.

Leaving Cape Town, the road climbs through majestic mountains, over a series of dramatic passes, alongside crystal clear streams, through fertile valleys rich with magnificent vineyards and orchards. The approach to Montagu, the first town en route, is astonishing. Set in a narrow valley, by a mountain stream, with towering ochre cliffs to

*The Franschhoek Valley is one of the leading wine growing regions.*

either side, and peach and apricot trees laden with blossom, this Victorian era town might be in the Garden of Eden. Continuing through the Breede River Valley, the Worcester winelands provide 27 per cent of the country's wine as well as being the main brandy producing area.

Stop at some of the many wineries to taste both white and red wines – the gabled, Cape Dutch architecture, set in gold and green vineyards against a backdrop of mountains, makes a memorable sight. Farther on the road travels through the Klein Karoo region, a huge, khaki coloured, treeless space with flat-topped hills and small towns lying under the vast, cloudless African sky. Here are several small, picturesque towns such as Ladysmith, set at the foot of the Towerkop Mountain. Route 62 ends at Port Elizabeth, South Africa's water sports mecca. The splendid beaches, scuba diving, game fishing and whale watching tours could hardly be more different from the mellow journey you have just completed.

**HOW:**
By car
**WHEN TO GO:**
September to November, late January to April.
**TIME IT TAKES:**
About two days, but take a week to fully enjoy the experience.
**HIGHLIGHTS:**
The Robertson Wine Festival, which takes place over a week every October.
The historic town of Tulbagh, with its Cape Dutch architecture and lovely gardens.
Addo Elephant Park.
**YOU SHOULD KNOW:**
This is the first wine route in the world to produce a Braille wine bottle. A percentage of its sales go directly to the Institute for the Blind.

# Garden Route

**HOW:**
By car
**WHEN TO GO:**
November to May
**TIME IT TAKES:**
It is possible to drive in a day, but to enjoy and appreciate this trip you should spend several days, up to a week.
**HIGHLIGHTS:**
Watch the endangered southern right whales in their calving grounds, November and December.
Go cage diving with great white sharks at Gansbaii.
Cable slide across the rainforest canopy in Tsitsikamma.
Visit an ostrich farm at Oudtshoorn.
**YOU SHOULD KNOW:**
The Garden Route and the Wine Route are sufficiently close together to move easily between the two. If this is your plan, give yourself a few extra days.

South Africa's Garden Route is a spectacular road trip along the coast from Mossel Bay east to Storms River. Sandwiched between the Outeniqua and Tsitsikamma mountains and the Indian Ocean, the road is named not for its floral gardens but because of its lush and varied vegetation, so different from the country's harsh, dry interior.

From Mossel Bay, an old-fashioned seaside town, the N2 links a series of charming towns, with areas of great natural beauty in between. This is part of the Cape Floral Region, named a UNESCO World Heritage Site in 2004. It is famed for its *fynbos*, natural heathland vegetation that includes 9,000 species, 6,200 of which are endemic. Of these, many are flowering and others are fragrant. Rooibos and honeybush are both commercially harvested, and one of the many proteas, *Protea cynaroides*, is South Africa's national flower.

Pass through the Wilderness National Park – its lagoons and wetlands are home to 250 species of bird, including Knysna Lourie, a bright green bird with red wings, and many kingfishers. If you like oysters, you can feast on them here to your heart's content, and of course the local wines are excellent. From Plettenberg Bay, another seaside resort, the road descends sharply, winding through old growth forest until it reaches the finest stretch of untamed coastline in Tsitsikamma National Park, before reaching the journey's end at Storms River.

Along the way there is much to do, hiking, diving, kayaking or even playing golf. Keep an eye open for the very rare Knysna elephants – a handful are said to roam the magnificent yellowwoods between Knysna and Plettenberg. Perhaps you'd like to travel on the last continuously operating steam train on the continent, the steam train Choo Tjoe, currently running only between Mossel Bay and George, after mud slides in 2006 damaged the track.

*The Tsitsikamma Range in Eastern Cape Province.*

# The Blue Train

The Blue Train is one of the world's most prestigious train journeys, luxury on wheels, right up there with the Orient Express. Its origins go back to 1923, when trains were introduced to carry passengers from Johannesburg to Cape Town, where they embarked on the long voyage to England. In 1933, a dining saloon was introduced, and gradually further luxuries were added. After a break for World War II, the service returned, and this time it was named the Blue Train after its blue carriages. Three years after the end of apartheid, in 1997, the service was re-launched in all its present day glory, taking passengers from Cape Town to Pretoria.

Arriving at the station at 7.50 am, passengers are ushered into a splendid check-in lounge, where sparkling wine and delicious nibbles are offered before a butler takes you to your suite, where your luggage is already in situ. This is 5-star accommodation: top quality bed linen, goose down duvets, marble bathroom, a desk set by the window, even a multiple choice entertainment centre. Elsewhere, there are two comfortable lounges and a dining car, where elegant outfits are obligatory for dinner.

This is a fabulous journey – the train glides smoothly through superb scenery. From its windows you'll see tea and citrus estates, vineyards, thick, indigenous forests, cliffs and gorges, and deserts where giraffes, zebras and elephants roam in peace. Enjoy an off-train visit to the privately owned Aquila Game Reserve at Kleinstraat, where you can experience a close encounter with cheetahs. Back on board, wonder at the extravagant sunset as you sip your pre-dinner drink before enjoying a gourmet meal and a great night's sleep. After a leisurely breakfast in the morning, in your suite if you wish, the Blue Train reaches Pretoria, the end of its 1,600-km (1,000-mi) journey.

*The Blue Train has been operating for over a century.*

**HOW:**
By train
**WHEN TO GO:**
Any time of year but November to April is probably best.
**TIME IT TAKES:**
27 hours
**HIGHLIGHTS:**
The views from the top of Cape Town's Table Mountain.
A trip to the infamous, apartheid era prison on Robben Island.
Sitting in the Blue Train's observation car.
A driver's eye view of the unfolding journey ahead, shown both in the club car and on a TV channel in your suite, via a camera mounted on the front of the train.
**YOU SHOULD KNOW:**
There are two Blue Trains. Both travel at 90 kph (58 mph), are 336 m (1,102 ft) long, and consist of 18 carriages, 11 of which are for the use of the passengers. The beds are custom made, and are hidden in the wall during the day, when the suite is a sitting room. Some of the suites even have bathtubs rather than showers, and all bathroom fittings are gold.

*The very Orange River, running through the very orange mountains.*

# Running the Orange River

**HOW:**
By raft, kayak or canoe
**WHEN TO GO:**
March to January
**TIME IT TAKES:**
Four to six days for a typical journey.
**HIGHLIGHTS:**
Rapids like Dead Man's Rapid and Sjambok Rapid – not too dangerous, but definitely enough to get the blood pounding.
Birds – the water and banks are alive with species including cormorants, goliath herons, fish eagles and kingfishers.
Tall tales around the campfire under an amazing African sky at the end of a rewarding day's paddling.
**YOU SHOULD KNOW:**
If a custom journey doesn't appeal, various canoe societies in the Northern Cape organize annual marathons on the Orange River.

For those in search of adventure, running the Orange River in the Richtersveldt National Park on the border of South Africa and Namibia is just the ticket. In this isolated part of the Northern Cape, the Orange River's long journey from the Drakensberg range to the Atlantic Ocean finally ends. Here, this majestic river is a long, green-fringed oasis that offers scenic stretches of serene water as it twists and turns through a striking desert landscape, with occasional fun rapids to spice up the journey.

This is a river run to be undertaken with a guide, either solo or with a group. The Orange River is usually tackled using two-person inflatable rafts, kayaks or canoes, sometimes with the support of a larger raft carrying supplies. A typical trip will be around 80-km (50-mi) long and different guides and organizers use various starting and take-out points. There is usually a base camp at the start where personal belongings may be left, with transport back at the end of the trip. Most expeditions assemble at Vioolsdrift on the Namibian border, just upriver from the Park – and some 350 km (217 mi) from the mouth of the Orange River – from where paddlers are driven to base camp.

The Richtersveldt National Park has recently been made a UNESCO World Heritage Site and it's easy to understand why. The Richtersveldt is one of the most remote and unspoiled areas of South Africa, and one of the best ways to see this barren but extraordinary place is from the river that runs through it – some say the best way. It's a true wilderness experience, in a rocky landscape that one writer has eloquently called 'too beautiful to describe'. Somehow, that says it all – though that means you must see for yourself!

# Chapman's Peak Drive

The journey may not be long – just 9 km (5.6 mi) – but Chapman's Peak Drive on the Atlantic Coast at South Africa's southwestern tip is one of the world's most spectacular marine cliff roads. Starting from the picturesque horseshoe-shaped fishing harbour of Hout Bay, the Drive skirts Chapman's Peak, the southerly extension of Constantia Berg. It winds up towards Chapman's Point, offering views down to sandy coves below, from whence it descends to sea level at Noordhoek. That sounds simple enough, but doesn't begin to hint at the drama that will be enjoyed as this unique toll road unfolds.

It was constructed between 1915 and 1922, and has 114 bends and sections blasted out of sheer rock faces. The effort was worthwhile. The geology is fascinating – the road was cut where base granite meets sedimentary limestone above, creating brilliantly coloured layers of orange, red-yellow silt shot with lines of dark purple manganese. But that's not the main attraction, because Chapman's Peak Drive delivers almost unbelievable views of the Atlantic Ocean meeting and greeting the rocky coastline, as it snakes towards journey's end – a journey that seems far too short.

This is, of course, a two-way road, but those who wish to see the sights without worrying that it's dangerous to drive whilst eye-balling the views can take a bus. These may travel only from the Hout's Bay end in the interests of safety, though short tours that include Chapman's Peak Drive are freely available from various start points. This is the best direction to drive, too, as it makes pulling off into scenic overlooks easier. The Drive may be hiked from either end but not right through – walkers are barred from the central section. It is occasionally closed to all traffic as a result of adverse weather conditions.

**HOW:**
By car or bus
**WHEN TO GO:**
Any time of year
**TIME IT TAKES:**
Just 15 minutes end-to-end (without stopping).
**HIGHLIGHTS:**
Stopping at one or more of the many scenic overlooks above the sea to have a picnic – or simply drink in the staggering seascapes.
Sunset over Hout's Bay, seen from the Chapman's Point lookout.
Parking and hiking the trail to the top of Chapman's Peak for truly amazing views (four to five hours needed, take water).
**YOU SHOULD KNOW:**
The Drive was closed in 1999 after a motorist was killed by falling rocks, but it has since been improved by major works and is now much safer.

*Chapman's Peak Road winds around the cliffs.*

# Drakensberg Traverse

**HOW:**
On foot
**WHEN TO GO:**
March to May
**TIME IT TAKES:**
From one to three weeks depending on Traverse chosen.
**HIGHLIGHTS:**
Photographic opportunities – extraordinary landscapes and up-close animals and birds.
Magnificent sunrises, sunsets and (way above light pollution) starry nights of unbelievable intensity.
The celebratory dinner at a mountain lodge after the Traverse has been completed – job
well done!
**YOU SHOULD KNOW:**
Drakensberg weather can be severe – storms blow up from nowhere and, whilst there are no snowfields, snowfall has been recorded on every day of the year.

Call it Quathlamba or call it Drakensberg, the end result is the same – the rugged mountain range that extends for 1,125 km (700 mi) from Mpumalanga (formerly Eastern Transvaal) to Eastern Cape Province. Traversing the Drakensberg (Dragon Mountains) involves a wilderness adventure, camping out (unless there's a handy cave as night approaches) and backpacking everything needed during the trip. This is a guided expedition, as only extremely experienced wilderness hikers could contemplate going solo. The main challenge is the altitude, with thin mountain air making physical effort more difficult, testing resolve and endurance to the limit. Daily distances of 8 km (5 mi) to 16 km (10 mi) are the norm.

There are lots of routes to choose from, in both northern and southern Drakensberg, usually titled according to length – Mini-Traverse (five days), Classic-Traverse (seven days), Super-Traverse (14 days) or Grand-Traverse (21 days). One option is trekking in the Drakensberg Park, two hours from Durban, with all the magic of these mountains plus ancient cave dwellings with rock paintings – now a UNESCO World Heritage Site.

Traverses begin with an ascent to the escarpment, either by climbing a steep pass or using the local specialty short-cut – metal ladders bolted to the sloping rock – after which each party treks for the set distance and time before descending back to civilization. Although the parameters of each Traverse are loosely established, the sort of flexibility dictated by unknown factors like weather conditions and the party marching at the pace of the slowest will determine final itinerary.

One thing never changes – these mountains always offer an opportunity to experience an enchanting wilderness of peaks and high escarpment, astonishing natural architecture, incredible views...and the sense of achievement that comes from undertaking and making one of the world's greatest hikes.

*A hiker enjoying the beautiful mountain view.*

# Table Mountain Aerial Cableway

*The magnificent views from the cable car include looking down on Cape Town.*

Opened in 1929, and extensively refurbished in 1997 when new cars and double cabling were introduced, the Table Mountain Aerial Cableway has transported more than 16 million people to the top of Table Mountain, a dramatic ride which offers wonderful views of Cape Town and surrounds, both on the way up and from the summit.

This isn't a journey for the faint-hearted (or vertigo sufferers). Some 1,200 m (3,940 ft) of cable link the Lower Cable Station on Tafelberg Road near Kloof Nek with the Upper Cable Station on the westernmost end of the Table Mountain Plateau. In the course of their upward journey, the cars rise steeply from a height of 302 m (990 ft) to 1,067 m (3,500 ft). The latest Rotair cars can each carry 65 passengers, more than doubling the capacity of the old cars.

Once up, there are various pathways leading to stunning views over Cape Town, Table Bay, Robben Island, Cape Flats and the Cape Peninsula. There are three signed walks. Klipspinger Walk follows the plateau edge above Platteklip Gorge. Agama Walk has been designed to give wonderful all-round views of Cape Town. Dassie Walk offers spectacular views to the north, south and west. There are two free, guided plateau tours each day, at 10.00 am and noon.

Directions to the Cableway are found on all major roads into and in Cape Town – follow the brown information boards. There is ample parking near the lower cable station. You can't book in advance, but queuing is rarely necessary. Hours of operation vary according to season, and the service can be suspended at short notice if wind speeds become too severe. Always take a jacket, as it is usually much cooler above than below.

**HOW:**
By cable car
**WHEN TO GO:**
Any time of year
**TIME IT TAKES:**
Ten minutes
**HIGHLIGHTS:**
Seeing a 360° view of Cape Town during the journey, thanks to the cable car's rotating floor.
An extraordinary diversity of plant life on the summit – look especially for the sunshine conebushes in full flower (summer only).
Doing it the hard way – a serious hike from Plattklip Gorge to the Upper Cable Station, returning by cable car (or vice versa if you want gravity on your side).
**YOU SHOULD KNOW:**
The dassie, or rock hyrax – a small, rabbit-like creature likely to be encountered on the flat summit – is surprisingly the elephant's closest living anatomical relative.

*Robben Island with Cape Town and Table Mountain in the background.*

# Robben Island Ferry

**HOW:**
By ferry
**WHEN TO GO:**
Any time of year
**TIME IT TAKES:**
Allowing time for a prison tour and island stroll, the round trip takes three to four hours.
**HIGHLIGHTS:**
Cell number 46664, where Nelson Mandela was incarcerated for 18 years.
The Moturu Kramat, a sacred Muslim pilgrimage site dedicated to the Prince of Madura, a Cape Town imam who was exiled to Robben Island in the mid-1700s and died there.
The Robben Island lighthouse, built at the Island's (rather low) highpoint in 1863 to try and reduce the large number of ships regularly wrecked on the rocky shores.
Observation of the over-active and ever-entertaining penguin colony.
**YOU SHOULD KNOW:**
Have a beady-eyed look along the shoreline – a Dutch treasure ship was wrecked on Robben Island in the 17th century and the occasional gold coin still washes up today.

Cape Town's Victoria & Alfred Waterfront is the departure point for one of the city's essential activities – the 12-km (7.5-mi) ferry trip to Robben Island, for centuries a safe dumping ground for those deemed undesirable by the authorities, from Muslim leaders and Dutch colonial dissenters through lepers to anti-apartheid freedom fighters – among the latter Nelson Mandela, who went on to become a Nobel Peace Prize winner and South Africa's first black President. During the apartheid years the prison on Robben Island (established in 1959) became known for brutality designed to isolate opponents of the regime and crush morale. The harsh regime failed to achieve its objective and Robben Island became known in Africa and throughout the world as a symbol of resistance to tyranny and the triumph of the human spirit over adversity.

Today, Robben Island is a UNESCO World Heritage Site and the prison has become a living museum, where many of the guides are former political prisoners who really do know what they're talking about. After a period of neglect, resources are being devoted to sprucing up the prison in particular and the island in general.

In times past, the ferry journey from the mainland to Robben Island was notoriously unpredictable. Sailings by five ancient ferries were frequently cancelled as a result of mechanical problems, but the launch of a new 300-seater ferry, the Sikhululekile ('We are free'), has restored reliability to the service. Even so, the ferry journey can be an exciting roller-coaster ride – or not take place at all – if one of the sudden storms for which the area is famed blows up. It's a risk worth taking, as there are stunning bay views during the approach to Robben Island, with Table Mountain as the brooding backdrop.

# Trans-Oranje

One of South Africa's great train services is the Trans-Oranje's twice-weekly run between Cape Town and Durban (or vice versa), the longest inter-city train journey in South Africa. The operator is Shosholoza Meyl ('Pleasant journey') and this comfortable train is incredibly good value. The Wednesday tourist-class departure from Cape Town is the one to aim for, as the ticket includes a sleeper bunk, hot shower (bring your own soap and towel) and restaurant car. The Monday train is the much more basic economy class with few facilities, and is mainly used by locals for shorter hops (not recommended for the full journey).

Contrary to popular opinion, the recently refurbished Trans-Oranje is completely safe, with no danger to families or women traveling alone – it is carefully policed by courteous staff who take great pride in their train and the provision of high-level service. Travellers have the choice of an economy Sleeper-6 (formerly Second Class) with six same-sex bunks, Sleeper-4 (formerly First Class) with four same-sex bunks and the two-berth Coupés for couples.

From Cape Town, the multicoloured Trans-Oranje heads out across the arid Karoo Desert. It then passes the famous De Beers diamond mine in Kimberley, crosses the plains of the Orange Free State and continues on into Natal, passing through the mountainous landscapes of Cliffdale, Ntshongweni, Situndu Hills and Marianhill before arriving on the shores of the sparkling Indian Ocean at Durban, that humid city of bananas, sugar cane and fun. Along the way the train stops at names writ large in the annals of South African history, including Kimberley, Bloemfontein and Ladysmith. The ideal journey is a return trip, allowing full appreciation of the varied sights of this extraordinary land of contrasts afforded by a journey on the Trans-Oranje – from ever-changing scenery to shantytowns.

**HOW:**
By train
**WHEN TO GO:**
April to November (no air-conditioning on the train!).
**TIME IT TAKES:**
37 hours and 15 minutes each way (all being well).
**HIGHLIGHTS:**
The Karoo Desert landscape as night falls – the train is timed to allow travellers to enjoy spectacular sunsets.
The biggest man-made hole in the world, on the left just after Kimberley station.
The full 'English Farmhouse Breakfast' that awaits in the restaurant car each morning.
Pietermaritzburg Station, where the future great but humble Indian leader Mahatma Gandhi was thrown off a train in 1893.
**YOU SHOULD KNOW:**
The Trans-Oranje passes the spot where Winston Churchill was taken prisoner in the Boer War, when the armoured train he was on was derailed by insurgents.

*Sunflower fields in Freestate Province*

# Namib Desert

**HOW:**
By car
**WHEN TO GO:**
May to October
**TIME IT TAKES:**
Two days plus
**HIGHLIGHTS:**
Sossusvlei – climb one of the dunes
and look down over the waves of the
Sand Dune Sea.
Escape the crowds at Hidden Vlei, a
low landscape surrounded by
lonely dunes.
Bird watching at Walvis Bay. Huge
numbers of flamingoes visit the
surrounding wetlands.
**YOU SHOULD KNOW:**
Visitors to Sossusvlei need a park
entry permit.
4x4s can drive up to the Pan; other
vehicles use a car park a long, hot
walk away – take water.

The name 'Namib' means 'Vast Dry Plain', and the Namib Desert extends along the Atlantic coast, with vast seas of towering dunes rolling inland towards gravel plains and isolated mountain ranges. This is one of the oldest and driest deserts in the world.

Windhoek, Namibia's capital, is a graceful city set on low hills; the road southwest (C26) crosses lovely countryside and desert hills. South of Solitaire on the C14 a signed road leads south to Sesriem and the Namib Dunes. These are 'dynamic' dunes – they shift and change shape, sculpted by the wind. They are made of quartz sand, and their colours also change, from cream to copper, red to violet. Some of these enormous sandhills are easily accessible, by foot or 4x4.

Sossusvlei, 60 km (37 m) deeper into the desert is the most photographed place in Namibia. It consists of a huge clay pan surrounded by massive red dunes, some as high as 300 m (975 ft). When the Tsauchab River fills and spills into it, this briefly becomes a turquoise lake, flocked by aquatic birds. The park opens at sunrise and closes at sunset; to experience the glorious technicolour effects it is necessary to stay around Sesriem.

The road northwest towards Swakopmund, the C14, runs along the eastern edge of the dunes then through the Gaub Pass and the Kuiseb Pass, turning west to cross the Namib-Naukluft Park, an area of gravel plains and occasional hills. It reaches the coast at Walvis Bay, a busy harbour town. Swakopmund, 30 km (19 mi) north, is an attractive German-colonial seaside resort, and Namibia's most popular holiday destination, with a wide range of adventure sports on offer on land and sea.

*The red dunes of Sossusvlei*

# Skeleton Coast

The Skeleton Coast stretches from Swakopmund to the Angolan border 500 km (300 m) north. This is an inhospitable place, where immense stretches of beach are beaten by breakers, engulfed by fog and cut off by trackless, shifting dunes. Early Portuguese sailors knew it as 'The Sands of Hell', for the crew of a foundering ship was doomed. The skeletons on this coastline are not just human: the bleached bones of innumerable whales, dating from the whaling industry's heyday, as well as the remains of countless ships swept ashore during the mercantile era, dot the sands. Pounded by the sea and blasted by sand the latter have been reduced to scraps of rusty metal, scattered planks and shattered masts, while the wrecks of later vessels, though more intact, are inaccessible.

The narrow strip of dunes was proclaimed a Nature Reserve in 1971. This ancient, untouched wilderness has a fascinating ecosystem – although almost rainless, the desert is moistened by the dense fogs that are brought by the icy Benuela Current and blown inshore. Plants and lichens adapt to the extreme conditions by taking on strange forms. Visits are limited to minimize human impact on this ecologically sensitive area. The coast road runs along the margin of the dunes, but there is no access. The northern section is a private concession, and offers fly-in safaris. However, a sightseeing flight from Swakopmund is a good option – these low-level flights allow a view of the vast graveyard of the shore and the mesmerising changing shapes and colours of the dunes.

*Walvis Bay on the Skeleton Coast*

**HOW:**
By plane
**WHEN TO GO:**
May to October
**TIME IT TAKES:**
About three hours
**HIGHLIGHTS:**
The remote wrecks, including the *Dunedin Star,* which ran aground in 1942.
The Ugab Formations, a moon-landscape whose black ridges contrast with the white desert.
The Clay Castles, fragile mud deposits laid down along the Hoarusib River when the area was a lake.
Sarusa Springs Oasis – a perennial water source.
**YOU SHOULD KNOW:**
The dense coastal fogs occur most mornings and evenings.

*The desert hills and gravel plains of Damaraland Plateau*

# Damaraland

**DEPART:**
Swakopmund
**HOW:**
By bike
**WHEN TO GO:**
May to October
**TIME IT TAKES:**
Five or six days
**HIGHLIGHTS:**
The Damaraland Plateau is well known for its desert-adapted elephants – you may meet some.
The Petrified Forest, composed of fossilized logs, which were once driftwood, is 260 million years old.
Twyfelfontein – more than 2,500 engravings are cut into the huge red rocks.
The strange *Welwitschia mirabilis*, or the living fossil plant, a tree dwarfed by the extremes of the desert, lives for over 1,000 years.
**YOU SHOULD KNOW:**
Any fit cyclist should be able to tackle this safari; a back-up vehicle will carry luggage and over-tired cyclists.

Damaraland occupies the area between the Skeleton Coast and Namibia's central plateau. It was named for the people who still occupy it as subsistence farmers – the Damara are one of the most ancient ethnic groups in the country. Here, desert hills are interspersed with mountains and gravel plains. The rugged landscape is networked by streams which streak the land with green, providing water for the Damara people and their livestock and for many desert-adapted, free-ranging animals including elephants, zebras and the rare black rhino.

This region is rich in geological features – mountains, craters, strange rock formations and the renowned petroglyphs. These paintings and engravings on rock are found near The Brandberg and at Twyfelfontein, a beautiful spot with a perennial spring which has always attracted not only wildlife but also hunter-gatherers. These recorded their rituals – hunting, and religious ceremonies – on stone, leaving a record of life as far back as the Stone Age. Twyfelfontein was made a UNESCO World Heritage Site in 2007.

Here are many quiet roads and tracks, off the main tourist routes, and some companies offer mountain bike safaris. These typically start from Swakopmund, with visits to the Spitzkoppe (the "Matterhorn of Africa") and Namibia's highest mountain, the Brandberg. A night is spent in the remote and beautiful landscape of the Ugab River in a camp run by the Save the Rhino Trust, after which the route climbs the Damara steppe and eventually reaches Twyfelfontein. These safaris use carefully chosen routes to highlight the extraordinary geology of the region.

# Fish River Canyon Trail

The second largest canyon in the world, Fish River Canyon winds and twists (legend suggests it was formed by the frantic writhings of a giant serpent) for over 160 km (100 mi). It is actually formed of two canyons, the outer one up to 27 km (17 mi) wide, and the inner reaching a depth of 550 m (1,787 ft). The figures do not prepare the visitor for its enormous drama and beauty.

Because of flash flooding in the rainy season and the extreme heat of summer, the canyon is open for a limited season to trekkers for the challenging walk down the 85 km (52 mi) trail from Hobas to Ai-Ais near the southern end. From Hobas a gravel road leads to Hikers' Viewpoint, the start of the route, and from here those not braving the walk can enjoy an awe-inspiring panorama. The first part of the walk is the most rugged and exhausting, with the steep descent of the canyon wall and several miles of rough sand and boulders. On the canyon floor there is good, flat, sandy camping by the cool river pools (the river water is drinkable if boiled or sterilized); tents are unnecessary in the warm clear weather. The route follows the serpentine course of the river past sulphur springs, viewpoints and strange rock formations. There are recognized short cuts bypassing the longer bends.

The last section of the walk is relatively easy going, though by the end of the season the river will be dry and water must be carried. At Ai-Ais (the name means 'scalding hot') the weary but triumphant walker will find the Hot Springs Resort with all its welcome facilities.

**HOW:**
On foot
**WHEN TO GO:**
1 May to 30 September
**TIME IT TAKES:**
Five days plus
**HIGHLIGHTS:**
'Palm Springs' at the end of the demanding first section. This spot offers good camping and the bliss of a soak in the hot, bubbling sulphur springs.
The Grave of Lieutenant Thilo von Troths, a German killed in a skirmish with the Nama in 1905.
The amazing experience and sheer beauty of the canyon.
Reaching Ai-Ais, where the mineral rich thermal springs are piped into baths, jacuzzis and an outdoor pool.
**YOU SHOULD KNOW:**
This is a very tough walk and should not be attempted by inexperienced hikers.
A medical certificate is required.
The trek must be booked in advance; numbers are limited.
The rains shift sand and vegetation and the route can change from year to year.

*The descent into Fish River Canyon is not an easy hike.*

# Okavanga Delta

**HOW:**
By *Mokoro* or dugout canoe
**DEPART:**
Maun
**WHEN TO GO:**
July to September
**TIME IT TAKES:**
1, 2 or 3 days
**HIGHLIGHTS:**
Wildlife: you will spot hippos and crocodiles in the waterways, and you may see elephants and antelopes while trekking.
Local knowledge:  as well as identifying wildlife, polers can explain Delta life.
**YOU SHOULD KNOW:**
Wildlife can be dangerous: camp sensibly and never swim without checking with your poler.

The Okavango River rises in Angola, flows south through Namibia and into Botswana; then the river's waters spread, sprawling over the sandy wastes of the Kalahari Desert to form an immense, extraordinary inland delta. This maze of channels, islands, waterlily-covered pools and lagoons covers more than 15,000 sq km (6,000 sq mi). The waters of this, the largest landlocked delta in the world, never reach the sea; trapped in the parched Kalahari (which covers most of Botswana) this watery wilderness is a magnet for wildlife. In the lush forests and along the floodplains, hundreds of species of bird flourish and lions, elephants, hippos and crocodiles, as well as smaller animals, congregate.

Trekking trips and motorboat cruises are based at various lodges on the islands, but the perfect way to experience the beauty and serenity of the Delta is drifting along passageways of papyrus, gliding across the pale golden waters in a shallow-draft dugout canoe, a *mokoro*. Traditionally made from logs of ebony or sausage tree wood, these amazingly stable craft are now often constructed of fibreglass – international conservation groups encourage this to save the slow-growing trees. Generally a *mokoro* carries two passengers, supplies and a poler, who stands at the back with the *ngashi*, a long pole made from the mogonono tree. Day trips start at the town of Maun, which lies to the south of the Delta; two- or three-day trips can also be arranged, overnighting in campsites in the Delta. Trips combine poling and trekking – poling is hard work. Most polers speak some English, and are very knowledgeable about the flora and fauna, though they tend to be rather shy.

*A mokoro moves quietly through the marsh reed of the Delta.*

# Nxai Pan Old Cattle Trek

The Nxai, Sowa and Ntwetwe Pans, once part of a 'superlake' which evaporated leaving only salt, form northeastern Botswana's Makgadikgadi Pans National Park, which covers 12,000 sq km (4,800 sq mi) and protects large tracts of palm forests, grasslands, savannahh and salt pans. The parks complement each other in enabling wildlife migration.

In the heat of August this is a land of dizzying mirages, but with the rains, temporary lakes form in the depressions and the earth greens. Now herd animals, including elephant and zebra, arrive in their thousands and waterbirds, most spectacularly flamingoes, flock to feed on algae and crustaceans.

Nxai Pan lies north of the highway which cuts through the Park area. To visit, a 4 x 4 is essential, since the track to the entrance is loose sand, and the area is 2,578 sq km, (1,031 sq mi), with just three designated campsites, one of which has apparently been trashed by elephants. There are two viewing platforms. The permanent residents of the grassy expanse include lion, giraffe, kudu, impala and ostrich, and during the migration period the huge herds are followed by predators.

Running inside the western boundary is the Old Cattle Trek route, the Pandamatenga Trail. This once linked boreholes along the route – used till 1963, when stock fences were introduced – of cattle drives. It runs to the Zambian border. In a 4x4 it is still possible to follow this trail out of the Park, north-eastwards to Pandamatenga, some 200 km (125 mi) away. However, careful planning is essential: this seldom-used track is indistinct and the tall grasses conceal obstacles.

**HOW:**
By 4x4
**WHEN TO GO:**
All year, but November to April for the animal migration.
**TIME IT TAKES:**
Two days plus
**HIIGHLIGHTS:**
The wildlife
The vegetation – umbrella acacias, Mokolae palms (the nuts are eaten by elephants, the sap makes palm wine and the fronds, baskets). Baines' Baobabs, immortalized by the artist/traveller in 1862 and little changed.
**YOU SHOULD KNOW:**
Visitors must have a campsite reservation.
The nearest fuel supply is 102 km (64 mi) east.

*Baobab trees in Naxi Pan National Park*

*Traditional houses in Malealea*

# Jobo Mountain Adventure Drive

Lesotho – the 'Kingdom of the Sky' – is a small, mountainous country surrounded by South Africa. Though British rule was resented in the 19th century, this British Protectorate (Basutoland) was not included in the Union of South Africa, and the peaceful kingdom avoided the long years of apartheid.

Rural Lesotho is perfect trekking country. Dominated by mountain ranges, this is a land without fences where herd-boys drive their flocks and blanket-wrapped farmers ride. In the south, a relatively small area around the village of Malealea seems to offer all the best features of the highlands. Here are precipitous mountains and gorges, ancient rock paintings, waterfalls and a scattering of remote villages fluttering with bright flags. These flags are colour-coded advertisements for the available comestibles – red and green for meat and vegetables, white and yellow for sorghum or barley beer. Fittingly, this area is reached through the Gates of Paradise Pass.

The lodge here will advise on routes for walkers and drivers of 4x4s and arrange pony treks. Ponies and guides are provided by the villages, and longer treks spend nights in village huts. The Basuto are a nation of horsemen and their small, strong, surefooted ponies are the ideal form of transport. No wild gallops here, though: the ponies pick their way carefully up and down the steep tracks. Very gentle, they are ideal for non-riders.

A trek to Jobo Mountain and village is one of the most rewarding and exciting journeys. The route covers the Sani rock paintings and the Botso'ela Waterfall and the final climb is along a precarious pass between two beautiful, deep gorges. Most 4x4 drivers prefer to walk the last, vertiginous section.

# The Tea Road

One of the smallest African countries, Swaziland, under its king Mswati III, has a strong sense of pride; the King represents and maintains the traditional way of life. This is an absolute monarchy and the power and clan links of the still highly revered King are perhaps the basis of Swaziland's continued stability. Many Swazis wear traditional robes and the high points of the year are the Incwala, the sacred ceremony of kingship and the Umhlanga, performed by the country's maidens.

The superb scenery of this relaxed and friendly country ranges from rainforest and savannah scrub to jagged mountains and high veld. Originally set aside for the royal hunt, several of the excellent game and nature reserves owe their existence to the monarch and this is one of the best areas to see rhinos, despite poaching. Happily, the King is on the side of the conservationists.

The Tea Road makes a good scenic circular tour for travellers with limited time. It is named after a failed project to establish tea plantations. The route runs north from the main road from Mbabane, climbing into the Mzdzimba Range, the burial place of the kings. The ridge provides a panoramic view of the beautiful Royal Valley, Ezulwini. At its centre, the town of Lobamba contains the palace, parliament and the royal kraal, where the King participates in the two magnificent annual ceremonies. A boulder marked gravel road crosses the mountains through Swazi villages and descends to the Malkerne Valley, a lovely area famous for skilled craftwork. North of the country road back towards Mbabne, the mountainous Miliwane Wildlife Sanctuary has a variety of wildlife and good walks.

**HOW:**
By 4x4
**WHEN TO GO:**
May, June and October
**TIME IT TAKES:**
One day
**HIGHLIGHTS:**
The view from Mdzimba includes Sheba's Breasts, twin peaks traditionally the site of King Solomon's Mines.
Even businessmen wear *emahiya*, the traditional dress of Swaziland.
The cultural festivals are an extraordinary spectacle.
**YOU SHOULD KNOW:**
The gravel roads are often very steep and impassable during the rainy season.

*Traditionally dressed Swazi women taking part in a festival.*

# Bazaruto Archipelago

**HOW:**
By dhow
**WHEN TO GO:**
May to November
**TIME IT TAKES:**
One day or three to five days
**HIGHLIGHTS:**
A viable population of the endangered dugong inhabits the waters.
Excellent black marlin fishing can be found around Santa Carolina.
The top of the Bazaruto dunes gives a fine view or three over the archipelago.
The cooking of the dhows' resident chefs is famously good.
**YOU SHOULD KNOW:**
Rock reefs can be razor-sharp. Winds, tides and sandbanks can be hazards for motorized dhows; if you arrange your own trip, check the reliability of your dhow with the tourist office.

Mozambique's attractive holiday resort, Vilankulo is a charming town with a lively market and lovely beaches, and the gateway to the Bazaruto Archipelago. The main islands of the chain, lying between 10 and 25 km (6 and 15 mi) offshore, are Bazaruto, Santa Carolina, Benguerra and Margaruque (which is close enough for a day-trip). The whole area is protected as a conservation area. The sand dunes, tidal flats and saline lakes support a wide variety of seabirds; the coral reefs teem with fish and marine mammals. Once this was a backpackers' dream, with nothing but campsites; now the islands offer luxury accommodation. The most enjoyable way to explore this tropical paradise is by dhow.

With billowing sails and graceful silhouettes, dhows epitomise a romantic dream of travel. In reality traditional, sail-only dhows, fighting wind, wave and current, becalmed or grounded, with nothing but a rudimentary toilet, have their drawbacks. Dhows with auxiliary outboards and more comfortable facilities offer catering and on-board sleeping arrangements and camping options.

Typically a trip will call at Margaruque for snorkelling and the beach and continue to Benguerra. The journey on to Bazaruto, with its high dunes, anchors at Two Mile Reef for diving. The deep waters around Santa Carolina offer good game fishing. All these low-lying islands have white, palm-fringed beaches – wild and wave-beaten on the windward side, calm turquoise waters and glorious sunsets on the leeward.

The diving in these protected reefs is first class. Uncrowded dive-sites have excellent visibility; as well as a rainbow of small fish, dolphins, rays, humpback whales and turtles are widespread.

*Isla Benguerra in the Bazaruto Archipelago*

# Zambezi River Cruise to Victoria Falls

David Livingstone first saw Victoria Falls in 1855. In awe he wrote that 'angels in their flight must have gazed' on such sights. Though he named the falls for his queen, the Kolola name, 'the smoke that thunders', is more evocative. Here, the Zambezi races over a cliff nearly 2 km (1.2 mi) wide and plunges into the Batoka Gorge more than 100 m (325 ft) below. When the river is in flood, the spray can be seen from miles away.

The falls must be seen, felt and heard from close quarters. At the Victoria Falls World Heritage National Monument Site a walk over a narrow footbridge leads to a buttress, the Knife Edge, with a dizzying view of the falls and the sheer drop. A steep track leads down to the river and a whirlpool called the Boiling Pot. There are advantages to visiting in both the wet season – the falls are at awe-inspiring full flow – and the dry when, though the flow is reduced, the size and structure can be seen clearly.

The range of adventure activities on offer around the foot of the falls includes abseiling, bungee jumping and river boarding as well as white water rafting. However, a river cruise is a leisurely and luxurious way to see the falls from the top and, on the stately progress upstream, watch for wildlife in the parks on both sides of the river. Various cruises are on offer, but the double-or triple-decker craft have a certain style. They leave from the Royal Mile, named for George VI, who visited the Falls in 1947. There is a choice of sunrise and sunset, breakfast, lunch and dinner cruises.

**HOW:**
By river cruiser
**DEPART:**
Livingstone
**WHEN TO GO:**
All year
**TIME IT TAKES:**
Most cruises last one to two hours
**HIGHLIGHTS:**
A sunset cruise with cocktails has a touch of colonial elegance.
Livingstone Island is in the middle of the river, right by the falls.
Wildlife – from the river you might be lucky enough to see a rhino as well as elephants and hippos.
The Monument Site Park opens during full moons for the mysterious lunar rainbow.
**YOU SHOULD KNOW:**
Prepare to get soaked while viewing the falls.

*Victoria Falls at the border of Zambia and Zimbabwe*

# The Albertine Escarpment

**HOW:**
By 4x4
**WHEN TO GO:**
December to February and June to
September
**TIME IT TAKES:**
The road can be driven in one
day but a break in the journey
is recommended.
**HIGHLIGHTS:**
The National Parks – large
populations of chimpanzee inhabit
Budongo and Kibale Forest Parks.
Semliki Forest Park is particularly
famous for its birdlife. Rwenzori Park,
home to many species of wildlife,
stretches over the foothills into the
mountains.
Birds of Semliki Forest – of the
hundreds of species, 35 are found
only here, including the Congo
serpent eagle and three types
of hornbill.
Views of the 'Mountains of the
Moon' from Fort Portal are often
misty but always impressive.
**YOU SHOULD KNOW:**
The situation on the northern border
with Sudan and the south-western
border with Congo is volatile.

Described by Winston Churchill as 'the pearl of Africa', Uganda has superb landscapes – mountain ranges, rolling countryside, lakes, rivers and waterfalls. Most of this landlocked country is fertile and the heat is tempered by altitude. Uganda's troubled recent history should not deter tourists.

In the west lie the Rwenzori Mountains (Africa's highest range). Permanently snow-capped, they are called the 'Mountains of the Moon'. Lake Albert stretches about 160 km (100 mi) along the Congo border to the Albert Nile and spectacular Murchison Falls, where the Victoria Nile rushes and tumbles on its way to Lake Albert.

Masindi, five hours west of Kampala, is the gateway to the Falls area. Between Masindi and the Lake lies the Budongo Forest National Park. The road south along the escarpment is not good: little used and often very steep, it can be a difficult drive, but it crosses some of the loveliest country in Uganda and, with a 4x4 and plenty of time, this is a pleasurable journey.

Ringed by eucalyptus trees planted in colonial times, Hoima lies on a plain. In 1862 it became the capital of the King of Banjora, and the throne room of the current Kitari is open by arrangement. South of Hoima the road rises again, passing through mountainous, lushly forested countryside where occasional cultivated areas allow views for miles around. Finally, the road reaches the hilly greenness surrounding Fort Portal.

One of the most attractive towns in Uganda, Fort Portal lies high in the well-watered foothills of the Rwenzie among tea-estates. With an excellent climate, this refreshing and pleasant spot is a good base for exploring the National Parks (Semuliki, Kibale and Rwenzori) that encircle it.

*A young chimpanzee stops playing to pose for the camera.*

# Mount Elgon & Sasa River Trail

A single, massive extinct volcano towering over the plains, Mount Elgon straddles Uganda's border with Kenya. Wagagi, the highest peak of the caldera ring, is, at 4,321 m (14,043 ft), East Africa's fourth highest mountain. It is an important water catchment and a conservation area of astounding richness. The ascent traverses fertile cultivated foothills (coffee and fruit), montane forest, bamboo and low canopy forest, heath and, above 3,800 m (12,350 ft), Afro-alpine moorland, supporting rare plants. The larger animal residents are rarely spotted, though the forest abounds in monkeys and, of the hundreds of bird species, many are restricted to this location.

Mount Elgon is uncrowded and unspoilt, a magnificent and fascinating wilderness of truly spectacular scenery. It rises in a series of quite gentle slopes punctuated by steep cliffs and scrambles, and is a straightforward climb which can be made by non-mountaineers. The Sasa Trail is the most direct route to the summit, though the first day is strenuous, scaling the cliff by the 'ladders', a series of steep steps and muddy passages. The descent can be made by the Piswa/Sipi Trail, ending at the pretty, relaxing resort at Sipi Falls.

Several companies run climbs. If you organize your own, guides, porters, permits and routes should be arranged at Budadiri, easily reached from Mbale. After the 'ladders' the trail leads through forests and open moorlands, affording breathtaking views. Wagagi is reached by way of Jackson's Hole; then the path follows the caldera rim and joins the Piswa Trail. This passes through lovely terrain – streams, waterfalls and gorges. The last leg follows the Sipi Trail down to Kapkwai, upstream from Sipi Falls.

**HOW:**
On foot
**WHEN TO GO:**
June to August and December to March
**TIME IT TAKES:**
Five days plus
**HIGHLIGHTS:**
Flowers – rare species include giant groundsel, giant lobelia, giant heather.
Bird – restricted range birds include Jackson's francolin, tacazze sunbird and the moustached green tinker bird. The endangered lammergeier may also be spotted.
Tutum Cave on Sipi Trail – a spectacular cave and waterfall hidden in the forest.
Sipi Falls is an impressive, three-tiered waterfall; the lowest section drops over a sheer cliff.
**YOU SHOULD KNOW:**
No specialized equipment or skills are needed, but altitude sickness can be a problem.
The area is subject to sudden weather changes.
All tourists must be accompanied by a licensed guide.

*Sipi Falls in the foothills of Mount Elgon*

*Waterbuck at Lake Mzizimia in the Selous Game Reserve*

# Tazara Railway

**HOW:**
By train
**WHEN TO GO:**
June to February
**TIME IT TAKES:**
About 24 hours on the slow train, 19 on the fast (straight through).
**HIGHLIGHTS:**
The Pugu Hills begin just outside Dar; the traveller is plunged straight into green, rural Tanzania.
Selous Game Reserve – in the daylight, elephants, zebras, giraffes, monkeys and birds of all sorts are easily spotted from the train.
**YOU SHOULD KNOW:**
Tickets must be booked in advance; sleeping cars are single sex.

The Tanzania and Zambia Railway Authority runs trains from Dar es Salaam to Mbeya in Tanzania's Southern Highlands and on to Kapiri Mposhi in Zambia. This line was built by the Chinese while Tanzania was more or less communist and some of the poorly maintained rolling stock is still Chinese. This is a notoriously unreliable train service, particularly west to east, and catering can cease completely, though the food is good when the restaurant car is open and food sellers throng the platforms at every stop. Without the railway, however, much of the Southern Highlands is hard to reach and the journey is enjoyable – staff and passengers are friendly and the line runs through some marvellous countryside.

Two fast trains a week leave Dar in late afternoon, and one slow train in the morning. If time is of no concern and landscape is, take the slow train and break the journey at Ifakara, a leafy old trading-station town eight hours southwest of Dar. This means a daylight journey through the lovely, verdant countryside west of Dar and the huge expanse of the Selous Game Reserve where the train crosses woodlands, grasslands and waterways teeming with wildlife.

The fast train reaches Ifakara after midnight and, after some hours of darkness, offers views of the Highlands – the lushly forested slopes of the Udzungu Mountains towering to the north, the ranges, one after another, southwards towards Lake Nyasa. This train arrives in Mbeya at lunchtime. Mbeya, a major trade and transit centre, is set in low hills clothed in tea plantations, coffee, bananas and cocoa. It is surrounded by mountains and the climate is pleasantly cool.

# Lake Manyara National Park

Lake Manyara, a large, shallow, soda lake, is dramatically situated at the foot of the western escarpment of the Rift Valley. The National Park, a UNESCO World Biosphere Reserve, occupies its northwest corner; though one of the smaller parks – the road through it is only about 40 km (25 mi) long – it enjoys diverse vegetation, which provides a variety of habitats.

The wildlife species are not as numerous as in better known parks  (though this is home to the elusive tree-climbing lion), but the birdlife is a huge attraction, particularly flamingoes, which visit the lake in millions during the wet season.

Early morning is the best time to arrive, to catch the game drive. It is very peaceful, with more chance of spotting animals. The safari trips visit in the afternoons, when the Park can be crowded. The road runs the length of the park through marsh, savannah and acacia woodlands and close to the steep escarpment wall, where a variety of trees grow. It passes two sulphur springs, and ends. Tracks and loops off the main road, lead to different habitats – the lake, plains where buffalo, zebra and impala graze, and a pool which is home to hippo and flamingoes.

There are camps inside the Park, and the village of Mto wa Mbu just to the north has accommodation. Travellers who arrive by bus may rent 4x4s from the tourist hotels here.

**HOW:**
By 4x4
**WHEN TO GO:**
June to February (December to April for birding)
**TIME IT TAKES:**
One day plus
**HIGHLIGHTS:**
Elephants – their numbers have decreased, but they are relaxed around vehicles.
Hippos – it is possible to observe them at quite close range.
Flamingoes – during the rains, the lake can look rosy pink from a distance.
Tree-climbing lions are rarely seen; stop in the acacia woodlands and sit very still…
**YOU SHOULD KNOW:**
Walking is not allowed in the Park.

*Elephants on the edge of the Lake*

# Mount Kilimanjaro

Kilimanjaro's iconic snow-capped summit hovers above the lush rainforest and cultivated farmlands of equatorial Tanzania. This is Africa's highest mountain and one of the world's highest volcanoes. Uhuru Peak, one of a jagged group to the east of Kibo, reaches 5896m (19162 ft). Kibo itself appears as a snow-covered dome, but this is a dormant volcano and its caldera conceals a huge crater.

Every year hundreds set out – in theory no specialised expertise or equipment is needed – but a large percentage do not reach the summit. Though the climb can officially be undertaken all year, the rains make the paths slippery and the unpredictability of the weather should never be underestimated. Altitude sickness is a problem which can be alleviated by acclimatisation. What with Park and hut fees, obligatory guides and porters, camping and catering, this is an expensive venture. All treks should be organised through a tour company, but one essential is to allow enough time. Whatever route is chosen, variables such as local conditions and illness must be allowed for in flexible timetabling.

The Machame Route, though not the easiest, is one of the most scenic. It follows steep paths through magnificent forests and over moorland plains, followed by a long track running runs east below the precipitous glaciated cliffs, traversing scree and ridges. This leg importantly gives time to acclimatise at around 4,000 m (13,000 ft). After a night at Bafa Hut, the last day of the ascent involves and early start and a gruelling climb up a bleak and barren section (often snow-covered) to the caldera rim and onwards to Uhuru. The trek down is by the steeper but more direct Mweka Route.

*Reading the signposts on
Mount Kilimanjaro*

*The still-active Ol Doinyo
Lengai volcano*

# Ngorongoro Crater Highlands Trek

Ngorongoro Crater is one of Africa's best known reserves, with its huge, steep-sided crater and an unequalled concentration of wildlife, though here tourists sometimes seem to outnumber animals. But the Crater is just part of the enormous Ngorongoro Conservation Area (a UNESCO World Heritage Site). The beautiful and rugged Crater Highlands, formed from volcanoes and collapsed volcanoes, extend in a chain along the east of the area. Several of the peaks top 3,000 m (9,750 ft), and the collapsed volcanoes have produced the eponymous craters. This remote and little-visited area offers remarkable scenery, plenty of wildlife and very good trekking.

All treks in the Highlands must be accompanied by a guide, and some use donkeys for portage and Maasai warriors as guides, who make up for their lack of English with botanical knowledge and ability to spot wildlife. The area is also home to the Datoga pastoralists and Hadzabae foragers, and guides may be able to negotiate visits to villages. Camping is often in 'cultural Bomas' where visitors can learn about Maasai life. Treks can last up to a week.

There are no designated routes in the Highlands, so the places visited will vary. Deserted Empakaai Crater, with its deep, flamingo-crowded lake, offers dramatic views over the whole area from the caldera rim; wooded Olmoti Crater is the source of the Munge River. The soda lakes of Eyasi and Makat are home to many waterbirds (and their predators) and the deep river gorges provide breeding grounds for raptors and water for the Maasai cattle. The higher peaks include Oldeani with its forested crater, and the still-active Ol Doinyo Lengai (Mountain of God). The acacia forests are rich in wildlife.

**HOW:**
On foot
**WHEN TO GO:**
June to February
**TIME IT TAKES:**
One to seven days
**HIGHLIGHTS:**
Acacia wildlife includes giraffes, impala and elephants.
Empakaai views – the Great Rift Valley, Lake Matron and even snow-capped Kilamanjaro.
Olmoti – the river pours through a notch in the rim in a spectacular waterfall.
Ol Doinyo Lengai – the brave and energetic can scramble up to watch the steaming, bubbling crater.
**YOU SHOULD KNOW:**
Treks into the craters must be with an armed ranger.
Weather in the Highlands can change to fog or rain very quickly; temperatures at night can fall to freezing.
Respect local customs and beliefs and learn a few phrases in Kiswahili from your guide or the villagers themselves.

# Mombasa to Zanzibar Cruise

**HOW:**
By dhow
**WHEN TO GO:**
June to October
**TIME IT TAKES:**
Three or four nights
**HIGHLIGHTS:**
Mombasa's Fort Jesus and its museum are a must for anyone interested in the history of East Africa.
Misali is home to numerous species including flying foxes, rare monkeys and turtles.
Stone Town's alleyways, intricate balconies, coffee sellers and the market, full of colour, scent and noise.
The traditional music of Zanzibar is a vibrant mix of African, Arabic and Indian sounds.
**YOU SHOULD KNOW:**
Both Mombasa and Zanzibar are Muslim cultures; respect the dress code.
Stone Town has a reputation for robberies, so be careful in empty streets.

Some companies now offer holidays that combine the glorious beach life of the Kenyan coast with a short cruise from Mombasa to Zanzibar. These are designed to give a taste of the pleasure of life at sea and a fascinating glimpse of East Africa and the Indian Ocean.

Mombasa has a very long history; Roman, Arabic and East Asian seafarers sheltered in its fine natural harbour. For centuries the Old Town saw bloody battles between the Portuguese and the Omani Arabs following the Portuguese seizure of the city in an attempt to break the Arab monopoly of the lucrative spice trade. Modern Mombasa, despite its turbulent history, is a fine city, and, with its laid-back Swahili culture, a relaxing one.

Simply the name conjures up exotic fairytale images, and Zanzibar in reality is a bewitching place. This fertile tropical island is clothed in spice plantations and ringed by picture-postcard beaches and perfect blue waters. The capital, Stone Town, is steeped in history; it is a maze of narrow winding lanes and hidden courtyards, minarets and mysterious, massive closed doors. Zanzibar, under the rule of the Omani Arabs, who moved their capital from Muscat, was the world's most important clove supplier. Now, though the sultans and slaves have gone, the spices remain.

Most cruises sail from Mombasa in the afternoon and, after a night on board, provide a tour of the island, visiting Stone Town and a clove plantation. The journey back to Mombasa may allow a day on the tiny coral islet of Misali, off the coast of Pemba, Zanzibar's northern neighbour. This is a marine haven, with idyllic beaches and fascinating nature trails.

# The Asmara to Nefasit Steam Train

The narrow gauge, Italian era steam train from Asmara to Nefasit is a joy, not just for steam train buffs but for anyone finding themselves in Eritrea's delightful capital city. Set high on the Kelbessa plateau, 2,350 m (7,755 ft) above sea level in the Eritrean Highlands, Asmara itself is delightful, but take a day out for this trip and you'll be richly rewarded.

The journey is just 25 km (16 mi) long, but from the moment you clamber aboard, you know it will be fun. Built between 1887 and 1938, this track was the brainchild of Mussolini, also responsible for the fabulous Art Deco and Modernist architecture of the city itself. With his demise, it sank into disrepair, but using the expertise of the old railway workers, brought out of retirement, and most of whom are now in their 70s and 80s, it was rehabilitated in the late1990s.

Pulling out of Asmara, the train chuffs and puffs along the track. Great plumes of dirty grey smoke rise into the air and urgent tooting alerts the world as it makes its way down the escarpment. The views are spectacular: dramatic mountains, deep valleys and forest. You'll pass traditional villages with orchards of lemon trees, banana plants and the ubiquitous prickly pears, and now and again you'll stop at a small station.

This was an amazing engineering feat – the downhill gradient is an almost constant 1 in 28, and the train negotiates its way through some 20 tunnels and over 65 bridges during the course of the journey. Some of the track runs along narrow ledges cut into the mountainsides, with a vertiginous drop to the valley below. These scenes are much as they must have been for hundreds of years, and now, thankfully, it is possible to enjoy them again.

**HOW:**
By train
**WHEN TO GO:**
September to March
**TIME IT TAKES:**
About an hour
**HIGHLIGHTS:**
The fabulous Art Deco architecture in Asmara, such as the Fiat building and the Impero Cinema.
TThe neo-Romanesque cathedral, with its plaque commemorating its benefactors – including Benito Mussolini himself.
The evening *passegiata*, where the town turns out to walk and talk.
Debre Bizen, a 14th century monastery set high above Nefasit, with its remarkable collection of medieval manuscripts. But beware – only men may enter!
**YOU SHOULD KNOW:**
The narrow gauge rails are 950 mm, the locomotives are pre-war 440 and 442 Mallets, the shunting tanks are Breda, built between 1927-1937 and the railcars are Art Deco style Fiat Littorinas, built in 1935.

*The old narrow gauge Italian steam train crosses one of the many bridges on the line.*

# The Blue Nile Gorge

The Blue Nile Gorge is one of the world's most spectacular sights, rivalling, if not beating, America's Grand Canyon. The river itself flows south from its source near Lake Tana, and then north-west until it joins the White Nile at Khartoum in Sudan. Then, as the Nile, it flows through Egypt, eventually discharging into the Mediterranean. It is the longest river in the world, and the source of life for millions of people.

There are different methods of arriving at and travelling through some or all of the gorge. From Lake Tana, the road drops sharply for well over 300 m (1,000 ft), to the riverbed, with outstanding views in every direction. The closer you get to the bottom, the hotter and more humid it becomes, but the breathtaking views more than make up for this minor problem. Crossing an Italian era bridge over the river, you may be surprised to be strictly forbidden to take photographs – particularly since you will be approached by people selling postcards of it!

The gorge is glorious, covered in beautiful vegetation including dragon trees and junipers that jostle for space between small, terraced fields of a grain known as *teff*, used in Ethiopian flatbread, which sways and bows in the light breeze. Frankincense trees are grown as part of a project – they can be tapped for resin up to ten times annually. There are small Amharan villages to be seen, the round houses roofed with grass blending naturally into their surroundings. Baboons bound in and out of view, and birds include lammergeyers, bee-eaters and various raptors. The road is carried on Italian viaducts for part of the way – watch out for crocodiles and hippos down in the river beneath. People here are friendly folk, fascinated by foreigners, the women and girls often nonchalantly balancing huge, beautiful pots full of water on their heads. The climb out of the gorge is exhaustingly steep, but walking here is well worth the effort.

*The Tis Issat Falls drain Lake Tana into the Blue Nile near Bahir Dar.*

# Raft the Omo River

The Omo River rises in the Shewan Highlands, and tumbles south for 760 km (475 mi) before emptying into Lake Turkana on the border with northern Kenya. Its total fall is some 2,000 m (6,600 ft), and the only easily navigable stretch is in the far south. The entire river valley is archaeologically important, and after the earliest known fossil fragments of *Homo sapiens* were discovered in the southern reaches, a UNESCO World Heritage Site was declared. This is a truly remote region, not only rich in wildlife and birds, but also in the many unique tribal peoples, hunters and pastoralists, who inhabit the surrounding areas. The river passes through the Omo and Mago National Parks, two of the richest and least visited of East Africa's wildlife sanctuaries.

Starting the trip at the small town of Omorate, your raft carries you along the broad, brown river, which by now has levelled out and become quite placid. There are crocodiles sunning themselves upon the banks, and hippos to be seen as you glide through open forest of tamarind and figs. Colobus monkeys chatter and leap, baboons bark in the distance and the birds are magnificent – you will see goliath herons, kingfishers, turacos, fish eagles and more. The Omo Delta, a maze of islands and marshes, is inhabited by the Dassenach people. Pastoralists who practise flood retreat cultivation, they hunt crocodiles at night, by spearing them from small canoes – a small crocodile makes a large meal.

As Lake Turkana, the world's largest desert lake, is shrinking, so the delta is expanding, having reached 250 km (156 mi) at its widest point and becoming a wetland of international importance. Drifting closer to Lake Turkana, you will notice the silt-laden water gradually changing to the colour that gives the lake its other name – the Jade Sea.

**HOW:**
On a raft
**WHEN TO GO:**
November to January
**TIME IT TAKES:**
Between one and several days, depending on the tour company you are using.
**HIGHLIGHTS:**
Enjoying the sights and sounds of the wildlife and birds.
Visiting Mursi, Karo and Hamer Koke villages and meeting the tribal people.
Continue your journey into Kenya, exploring Lake Turkana and its National Parks, also a UNESCO World Heritage Site.
**YOU SHOULD KNOW:**
During five days in August 2006, the lower reaches of the Omo flooded, resulting in 456 deaths, and leaving 20,000 people stranded. Ethiopia's rivers are losing capacity as they are filling with silt.

*A Karo warrior*

*Looking towards the northern escarpment, near Sankabar*

# The Simien Mountains

**HOW:**
On foot
**WHEN TO GO:**
October to April
**TIME IT TAKES:**
Two to three days
**HIGHLIGHTS:**
Spotting endemic and rare species of mammals, birds and plants.
Axsum, Ethiopia's most ancient city, said to be the hiding place of the Ark of the Covenent and the home of the Queen of Sheba.
Lalibela, and its monolithic, rock hewn churches.
Ascend Rash Dashen, Ethiopia's highest peak at 4,600 m (15,159 ft) and the fourth highest on the African continent.
**YOU SHOULD KNOW:**
The Simien fox is actually a rare, red wolf. On the Internation Union for Conservation of Nature (IUCN) Red List, there are less than 500 individuals of this endangered animal left.

One of Africa's major massifs, and a UNESCO World Heritage Site, the magnificent Simien Mountains have to be seen to be believed. Formed some 40 million years ago by violent seismic activity, erosion produced the dramatic mountain-scapes we can enjoy today – dramatic escarpments, mile-deep gorges, sculpted mountains, plateaux, river valleys and *ambas*, sheer pinnacles of lava, the last remnants of ancient volcanoes. Many of the peaks rise above 4,000 m (13,000 ft), and snow and ice are often to be seen at the highest levels.

Despite the altitude and harsh terrain, villages and terraced fields are dotted about these mountains, linked by rough tracks. Starting the trek to Chennek from Sankabar, the most scenically exciting route takes you down into the Jinbar Wenz Gorge, across the river to Gich village, and up to Gich Camp. Situated at 3,100 m (1,900 ft), this manned park station looks across richly forested valleys and mountains bursting with wildlife, including large groups of the endemic Gelada baboon, also known as the Bleeding Heart baboon for the patch of deep red on the chests of the males. Here too are very rare Walia ibex and Simien fox. Take the opportunity to hike to the superb viewpoint of Imet Gogo, with its tremendous vistas across a vast canyon to the rock spires beyond – looking down you might see a Lammergeyer (Bearded vulture) repeatedly dropping its prey onto the rocks far below – a process designed to access the marrow by pulverizing the bones.

Following a tough, tussocked trail through magnificent Afro-alpine vegetation – giant heather, giant red hot pokers and endemic lobelia, you come at last to Chennek. Situated on a cliff edge, this is one of the world's most spectacular campsites: the dizzying views spreading below make you feel you are at the edge of the world.

# Timbuktu by Boat

Though Timbuktu remains a fabled place in the minds of many, today it is quite possible to reach. In order to do so, you can't beat travelling there by boat, along the mighty Niger, Africa's third longest river. Setting out from Mopti, to the west of Timbuktu, take a *pinasse*, a type of motorized canoe with a domed grass canopy, and enjoy the travelling as much as the arriving.

The flood plains around Mopti provide a wonderful habitat for birds of all sorts, including many migratory species, and the river itself is home to many fish, some of which will no doubt be caught and cooked for you. You may well see hippos, too – their large, irascible presence alerting you to the relative fragility of your craft. The river is full of activity: local boats carry goods and livestock, fast boats speed tourists to Timbuktu. Children shriek '*toubab*' (white man), and wave frantically as you pass, men fish, women wash clothes at the river's edge or pound millet in time-honoured fashion. Occasionally houses here have solar panels, often powering televisions – an unlikely sight indeed.

This journey is fun: from time to time the *pinasse* stops at a village, which you can explore while provisions are bought. Lunch is cooked on board, and at night tents are pitched on the riverbank, and dinner cooked over a fire. Gradually the scenery changes: marshlands give way to grasslands and finally, the desert. The trip ends at Korioume, just 10 km (6 mi) along a paved road from Timbuktu. Just a few decades ago the Niger ran through the town, but the desert has been encroaching. In 2007 a Libyan-built canal and reservoir was opened, joining Timbuktu to the river once again, and bringing a better water supply to this legendary but beleaguered city.

**HOW:**
By boat
**WHEN TO GO:**
November to March
**TIME IT TAKES:**
Two to four days, depending on your boat.
**HIGHLIGHTS:**
Visiting riverside villages, appreciating the Moorish mud brick architecture and meeting tribal people such as Fulani and Bozo.
Spotting birds and other wildlife – you might see a manatee.
Taking a camel trip to a Touareg village from Timbuktu.
The Festival in the Desert, held at Essakane each February, a 'must' for world music fans.
**YOU SHOULD KNOW:**
The late, great, musician, Ali Farka Touré owned a farm near Niafounke, on the banks of the Niger, not far from Timbuktu. Appointed mayor of the area in 2004, he introduced a tree planting scheme and modern irrigation systems and was living there when he died in 2006.

*An adobe village along the Niger River*

171

# The Salt Road from Timbuktu to Taoudenni

Azalai, as the camel caravans travelling from Timbuktu to Taoudenni are known, regularly trek some 800 km (500 mi) across one of the harshest regions of the Sahara desert. They have passed this way for over 1,000 years, ever since salt, which could be traded weight for weight with gold, was discovered in the area.

Join a Touareg caravan leaving from Timbuktu, or take a guide and a 4x4 – whichever way you go it will be the journey of a lifetime. There is austere beauty in the desert, and little sound other than the soft shoe shuffle of camels moving over hard sand and sharp stones. Sleeping under the stars in the immense silence of the desert is a profound experience.

Days begin before sun up, and the caravan travels doggedly until darkness falls. Strong, sweet mint tea is frequently brewed and begins to taste like nectar from the gods. At night, rice and dried meat is cooked and eaten, with a sprinkling of sand thrown in. Reaching the halfway point of Arouane, a tiny settlement en route, feels like a great achievement. From there on in, the desert is empty – no grass, no trees, just sand stretching to the horizon. There is little wildlife – desert rats, lizards, beetles and, perhaps, gazelles, but you may pass camel bones: bleached by the sun they underline the fact that your life is in the hands of your guide.

When the stony desert becomes sand dunes, you know you are within reach of Taoudenni. Here, in a vast basin that was once a sea, a couple of hundred men dig for salt, living in primitive, almost Biblical conditions. However, within 24 hours the camels are all fully loaded with their heavy cargo, and are ready to begin the trek back to Timbuktu and civilization.

*A Touareg caravan travelling along the Salt Road – the salt is transported in large rectangular-shaped slabs.*

# Mount Cameroon Trek

*The trail up to the volcano*

An active volcano (the last eruption was in 2000) rising steeply from the Gulf of Guinea, Mount Cameroon is, at 4,095 m (13,309 ft), the highest mountain in West Africa. It is a 'biodiversity hotspot', a scientifically important area with varied habitats and endemic plant and birdlife. The terrain ranges from farmland and dense rainforest to scrub savannah and a harsh tract of volcanic rock and ash up to the bare summit.

There are several routes up the mountain. The most direct, the Guinness Route, is straight up and down, very steep, and can be completed in a day and a half (the runners in the annual Race of Hope manage it in as little as five hours). But spending longer on the mountain is very rewarding and set hikes of several days, starting at Mann Spring or Buea and descending the northwest face by Elephant Opening allow time to appreciate the diverse vegetation, do some bird-spotting and admire the views.

An eco-tourism organization based at Buea, which works closely with the villages round the mountain, arranges various treks. It employs locals with specialized knowledge as guides and uses some of its profits for community projects. The climb to the summit is demanding: altitude sickness is common – because the mountain starts at sea level, a short climb brings a big change in altitude. The weather is notoriously changeable – even in the dry season trekkers can be engulfed in sudden tropical downpours and, at the summit, the temperature can fall below freezing. There are, however, a number of options for treks of different durations around the lower slopes. These include lava-flow walking, visits to the numerous craters, and bird-watching.

**HOW:**
On foot
**WHEN TO GO:**
November to April
**TIME IT TAKES:**
The ascent: three to five days. Other treks: one to three days.
**HIGHLIGHTS:**
A night on the mountain – the brightness of the stars and sunrise on the slopes.
Birds include the Cameroon pigeon, Purple-throated cuckoo-shrike and the Cameroon francolin.
**YOU SHOULD KNOW:**
The ascent requires a good level of fitness and preferably some climbing experience. The treks can be tailored to the individual's needs and abilities.

*Boats crossing the Gambia River at Basse Santa Su.*

# Cruise the Gambia River

**HOW:**
By boat
**WHEN TO GO:**
November to April
**TIME IT TAKES:**
Four hours or a day or two, depending on whether you go direct or overnight on board or at a lodge.
**HIGHLIGHTS:**
The Baobolong Wetland Reserve
Spotting birds and other wildlife en route
Abuko Nature Reserve
The island of Janjangbureh and its port, Georgetown
Wassu Stone Circles
The beautiful, empty beaches of Kombo South.
**YOU SHOULD KNOW:**
The River Gambia was an important slave trading route. Each year a Roots music festival is held, named after the book by Alex Hayley, whose supposed ancestor lived in a small village near Albreda, until he was captured, enslaved and sent to America.

Continental Africa's smallest country, The Gambia, is shaped like a wedge cut into the middle of Senegal. Dominated by the Gambia River, which runs from the Atlantic coast inland for some 320 km (200 mi), the country consists of the river and the land to either side of it. The river is the country's lifeblood, providing water and food in an otherwise arid region, and for those who like wildlife, and birdlife in particular, a cruise along all or part of this essential waterway is a treat.

Begin your trip at Bintang, a small town some 80 km (50 mi) from the capital, Banjul, and take a pre-arranged boat along the river to Farafenni, passing the renowned Baobolong Wetlands on the north bank. This is The Gambia's first designated RAMSAR site, and the country's largest nature reserve, covering 220 sq km (85 sq mi). It is a maze of small islands with waterways, or *bolongs*, weaving their way between them. Here you will see ancient mangroves, many over 19 m (60 ft) tall, as well as tidal mudflats and savannahh forest. It is home to up to 300 species of bird, including fishing owls, goliath herons, spoonbills, and much more besides. It's not uncommon to spot 60 or 70 species during a three-hour spell.

This is a gentle, pleasant jaunt, puttering along the river in the sunshine, binoculars at the ready, with the sounds of water, birds and chattering monkeys in the background. The river itself is full of life – you may see dolphins and otters, crocodiles and even hippos, and if you want to spend more time away from the tourist resorts of the coast, there are several lodges in which to stay and chill out in an unspoilt natural paradise.

# Ile de Gorée

Dakar, a huge, feverish city, brims with life. Here are all the sights, smells and sounds of Africa – noisy markets, great live music, fabulous street-food and exuberant nightlife. The sprawling city swarms with jet-setters, expats, French military types and the grindingly poor. A mere 20-minute ferry ride away lies the meditative calm of the Ile de Gorée.

Europeans first colonized the easily defensible island in 1444; power shifted between the Portuguese and the Dutch until the French took over in 1677. They stayed, with brief periods of British rule, till Senegalese independence in 1960. The colonial legacy is evident in the island's lovely old mansions, flower wreathed balconies and quiet unpaved lanes (there are no cars on the island).

Gorée became a centre of the West African slave trade – the first Portuguese slave house was established in 1536. The trade continued, officially and unofficially, under the French till 1848. Now the island's main draw is La Maison des Esclaves and its 'doors of no return', with its grim basement 'storage rooms' for slaves, the airy quarters for traders above. It has become a place of pilgrimage for African Americans, though it is debateable whether this was in fact a major shipping point for slaves – Gorée is a tiny island, and the Maison has no good moorings. But this UNESCO World Heritage Site is a universal heritage, which brings slavery's iniquities movingly to life. This is a brief journey, but memories of it will be long.

**HOW:**
Local ferry
**WHEN TO GO:**
January to May, November and December
**TIME IT TAKES:**
One day, or longer
**HIGHLIGHTS:**
Stay on Gorée – in one of the several pleasant hotels – and, outside weekends, enjoy the peace of this beautiful, faded place.
Museum –      as well as the Maison des Esclaves there are some interesting museums and fortifications.
Sit on the mainland wharf at twilight and watch the low, rocky outline of Gorée fade into the night.
**YOU SHOULD KNOW:**
All museums on Gorée close on Mondays.

*Ile de Gorée*

# Mole National Park Safari

Mole, an immense, remote tract of wooded savannah in northeast Ghana, is home to a huge range of animals (over 90 species including elephants, baboons, warthogs and antelope) and birds (300 species recorded, from tiny bee-eaters to vultures and eagles). However, its tourist potential is unrealized – 95 per cent of its area is unvisited even by rangers, which has allowed regular poaching. The game-viewing circuit is limited to a few miles of poor roads around the southeast corner.

The area is best seen on foot and, unusually, most visitors arrive by public transport. The daily bus from Tamale (four to six hours west by dirt road) comes right into the Park. This is a crowded, dusty uncomfortable ride, with frequent breakdowns, but it is regarded as a memorable part of the Mole experience. Mole Motel, where the bus journey ends, is the only place to stay. The buildings are old and basic, the accommodation far from luxurious, the water supply erratic, but its situation, high on a steep escarpment above the savannah, is superb, affording views of the untouched wilderness landscape, the glorious sunsets and of two waterholes and the animals which gather there to drink.

Outside the hotel grounds, walkers must be accompanied by armed rangers (rifles protect against poachers, not big cats – lions have not been observed for some time). The hotel runs 'walking safaris' in the early morning (cooler) and late afternoon, when more animals may be seen. These guided walks allow close-range observation of wildlife and can be tailored to the needs of the group.

*A troop of baboons take a stroll along the trail.*

# Marrakech Express

For the baby-boom generation, the Marrakech Express conjures up the old hippy days of the late 1960s and early 1970s, when everyone seemed to be discovering the wonders of Morocco, a country and culture so fascinatingly different from Europe, yet sitting on its doorstep. Immortalised by the eponymous song, the Marrakech Express remains an iconic journey.

Rabat is Morocco's capital. Less famous than other Moroccan cities, it is a delightful place, with a marvellous fortified Kasbah, and an ancient, walled medina, as well as a French-built new town. It is well worth spending a day or two here before taking the train.

The track follows the coastline south-west to Casablanca, passing the up-market beach resort of Skhirat, as well as Mohammedia, an industrial town but with a huge beach which draws tourists from both Casablanca and Rabat. All Morocco's cities pride themselves on their individuality, and Casablanca is no exception. Built mainly in the 20th century by the French, and boasting some fine Art Deco architecture, this is the country's business and financial hub.

Leaving Casablanca, the track veers inland, through the city's fertile, agricultural hinterland, past orange groves loaded with fruit and fields of crops and vegetables. Gradually the green fields are left behind as the train makes its way across a flat, increasingly barren plain. Scoured by the wind and sun for millennia, the deep red earth and rocky outcrops look bleak and under populated.

As the train approaches its goal, the scenery changes again and the magnificent range of the Atlas Mountains, with their snow-capped peaks, come into view. Finally, the spectacular, ancient, red mudbrick walled, Imperial city of Marrakech is reached. Founded in the 11th century, this tourist mecca and architectural gem demands that you explore its labyrinthine souks and remarkable, secret gardens.

*Marrakech city walls with the Atlas Mountains in the backgroud*

**HOW:**
By train
**WHEN TO GO:**
March to June and September to November. Try to avoid Ramadan.
**TIME IT TAKES:**
About four hours.
**HIGHLIGHTS:**
Marrakech's famous square, Djema el-Fna, crowded with exotic street entertainers and excellent street food.
The 12th century Koutoubia minaret
The Saadien Tombs
The Majorelle Gardens, founded by the artist Jacques Majorelle in 1917, the gardens were restored by Yves Saint Laurent and Pierre Berge who bought the property after Majorelle's death in 1962.
**YOU SHOULD KNOW:**
Trains in Morocco are frequent, efficient and reasonably priced, first class and second class compartments contain six or eight seats respectively, with air conditioning in first class on certain inter-city routes. Plans to build a high-speed link between Tangiers and Marrakech have been agreed, as has the building of a tunnel under the Mediterranean from Paloma, Spain to Tangiers.

177

# Rif Road Trip

**HOW:**
By car
**WHEN TO GO:**
March to June and September to November
**TIME IT TAKES:**
A minimum of two days, but up to a week or more if you want to explore some of the fascinating towns en route.
**HIGHLIGHTS:**
The Medersa Bou Inania, Fes.
The view of Fez from the Merenid Tombs.
The Museum of Moroccan Arts and Crafts in the Dar Batha Palace, Fes.
Friouato Cave, perhaps the deepest and most impressive cave in North Africa, 22 km (14 mi) from Taza.
Sidi Yahia, a lovely oasis and holy place 6 km (4 mi) from Oujda.
**YOU SHOULD KNOW:**
There are alternative routes across the Rif Mountains; the most straightforward takes you through awe-inspiring mountain scenery, via the pleasant, coastal city of Al Hoceima. Whatever you do, make sure you avoid Ketama, the dangerous town at the heart of the drugs trade.

The highly scenic Rif Mountains stretch across northern Morocco, from Tangiers to Oujda on the Algerian border. Entirely separate geologically from the Atlas Mountains, they were originally part of Europe. With the highest of the craggy, limestone peaks rising to some 2,500 m (8,250 ft), this is Morocco's Wild West – untamed country, full of hidden valleys, gullies and streams. The only large towns lie on the foothills; otherwise the mountain settlements are merely extended villages. This is a lawless area, where much of the forest has been cut and the land put to *kif* (cannabis) and hashish production.

Driving from the port city of Tangiers, the road climbs to Tetouan, and then on to Chefchaouen, a beautiful town of blue and white houses, nestling on the edge of the wildflower-strewn mountainside. Continuing to Fez, the road twists and turns for 217 km (135 mi), through steep bends and dramatic scenery. Take a small detour to Ouezzane, a town honoured by Muslims and Jew alike, busy with craftsmen and surrounded by olive groves.

Fes is unique: its old town, one of the great medieval cities of the world, contains some of the most spectacular buildings in the country. The narrow, twisting alleys of the souks are extraordinary and thrilling to explore, your senses swamped by sights, sounds and smells that are both alien and bewitching.

Leaving Fes, the road takes a circuit around Jbel Tazekka, a high altitude national park of cork oaks and cedar forests, before reaching Taza. One of Morocco's oldest towns, Taza lies between the Rif and the Middle Atlas on the edge of a plateau. From here you pass over sparsely populated plains and plateaux, the countryside becoming increasingly green and fertile, until you reach Oujda, the capital of eastern Morocco and the gateway to Algeria.

*The city of Chefchaouen with the Rif Mountains beyond*

# High Atlas Mule Trek

*The Kasbah at Ait Ben Haddou*

Morocco's High Atlas mountain range stretches east from the Atlantic Ocean to the Algerian border. Centuries of erosion have produced rocky peaks that descend to deeply carved, green valleys. Djebel Toubkal, at 4,167 m (13,670 ft), the highest peak in North Africa, dominates the Toubkal National Park. Established in 1942, and situated 60 km (37 mi) south of Marrakech, this remote area is a traditional Berber homeland, and small settlements and villages are scattered throughout, clinging precariously to the mountainsides. Built of *pisé* (rammed earth), they blend perfectly into the environment.

From Tamatert, the highest village at about 2,000 m (6,600 ft), you set out, with mules and a guide, to ascend to the Tamatert Pass, trekking through terraced fields of wheat and barley, orchards of apples, cherries and walnuts, and finally forests of pine and junipers. Walking or riding is the only way to travel and transport goods in this region, and the undulating tracks, though sometimes rocky, are well maintained.

The views from the pass are vast, encompassing two separate valleys: this majestic sight can barely have altered in 1,000 years. The high peaks, including Toubkal itself, are the source of water for the Tamatert valley – a multitude of springs, fed by melting snow and ice, trickle, tumble and cascade downwards, irrigation canals ensuring every inch of fertile land is well watered. The golds and greens of the valley floor turn to purples, reds and browns as you gaze at the barren peaks above. In spring the mountainsides are covered in gorgeously colourful wildflowers, attracting scores of butterflies, some of which are endemic. Birds thrive here: Alpine accentor, chough, booted eagle – altogether about 50 different species can be seen, not to mention Barbary sheep, endangered through over-hunting, and shaggy mountain goats that skip up and down seemingly impossible inclines.

**HOW:**
On foot with mules
**WHEN TO GO:**
All year round, but if you don't want snow, go between April and October.
**TIME IT TAKES:**
There are treks to suit everyone, varying between about four hours and ten days. The latter means camping, but your guides will do all the hard work, including the cooking, and the mules will carry all the essentials leaving you free to enjoy the experience.
**HIGHLIGHTS:**
Climb Djebel Toubkal – you do not have to be a very experienced mountaineer to achieve this.
Trek to the lovely Lake Ifni, and its nearby waterfalls.
Visit traditional Berber villages including Sidi Chamharouch, a place of pilgrimage.
Visit Ait Ben Haddou, a remarkable fortified village and UNESCO World Heritage Site.
Spend a few days in Marrakech, a city unlike any other.
**YOU SHOULD KNOW:**
Even trekking with mules, you'll want to walk some of the time, and as the tracks are rocky and uneven, a walking pole will be a great help.

# From Tozeur to Douz across the Chott el-Djerid

**HOW:**
By car or 4x4
**WHEN TO GO:**
March to May and September to
October, unless you can bear the
heat of July and August when you
will see the Chott at its driest.
**TIME IT TAKES:**
One day
**HIGHLIGHTS:**
Medina of Tozeur – decorative
brickwork and ornamented doors
dating back to 14th century.
Fata Morgana Mirages.
Market day in Douz.
**YOU SHOULD KNOW:**
The Chott el-Djerid was used as a
major location in the blockbuster film
*Star Wars*.

The Chott el-Djerid is the largest saltpan in the Sahara, covering an area of over 5,000 sq km (1,900 sq mi) and separating the steppes of northern Tunisia from the Grand Erg Oriental desert in the south. In the summer, when the Chott is completely dried up, it is a vast gleaming expanse of apparently solid bluish-white crust. In spring and autumn, heavy rains transform it into a salt marsh, which soon evaporates into weird-shaped crystalline masses and pools. Whatever the season, it is incredibly dangerous to walk on. There are terrible local tales of it swallowing whole caravans of camels.

The only way to cross this forsaken land is by using the 250 km (155 mi) causeway that runs from the picturesque town of Tozeur on the northwestern fringes of the Chott, to Douz, on the border of the desert. As you leave Tozeur, the road runs through undulating hills where goats and camels graze. You cannot help but feel a sudden lurch of excitement when the Chott comes into view. The completely straight gypsum causeway plunges you into an eerie otherworld. This is like nothing on earth that you have even begun to imagine. As far as the eye can see, there is literally nothing but salt crusts gleaming in the sun against the straight line of the horizon. By the roadside there are lurid pink-tinted crystalline deposits, wherever you look there are shimmering reflections, and Fata Morgana mirages pop up out of nowhere.

Thoroughly disorientated and with some relief, you finally arrive at Douz, the 'gateway to the Sahara' – a date palm oasis inhabited by the Mrazig, a tribe of nomadic desert shepherds. Here you can do something 'normal' – like take a camel ride out into the dunes – to ground yourself back in reality.

*Tribesmen near Douz*

# Jebel Nafusa Mountain Drive

Once an international pariah but mellowed with age, Colonel Ghadaffi is almost respectable nowadays, entertaining world leaders in his desert tent. They're not the only ones who are welcome, as tourism is developed to supplement Libya's oil wealth. It's a great policy, because this Mediterranean country is full of sights that surprise and delight. A good way of seeing traditional Libya is to journey from Tripoli to the Jebel Nafusa Mountains and on to Nalut at their western extremity, up by the Tunisian border. Don't hurry to hit the road, though – take a day to explore the exotic capital city and see some of its famous sights.

Then head for the mountains. Apart from the narrow coastal trip, Libya is all Sahara Desert, and this 300-km (185-mi) journey is an ideal way to experience something of the unique atmosphere of that silent sea of sand. Head south from Tripoli through scrubby semi-desert for 80 km (50 mi) to Bi'r al Ghanam, where you meet the Jebel Nafusa Mountains, a harsh landscape of rocky escarpments and barren hills broken by fertile patches where olives, figs, apricots and grain are grown. This is the heartland of the Berber people and remains of their civilization dot the landscape, with ancient stone villages overlooking the plain from perches high above.

Follow the road along the northern foothills past Bi'r Ayyad, Qasr al-Hajj, Shakshuk, Tiji and Al Hawamid until – at the westernmost end of the Jebel Nafusa range, up by the Tunisian border – you reach Nalut. Then you'll appreciate the reason for choosing this destination. It's one of the finest Ghurfa (storage chambers) villages in Libya, in a commanding position with sweeping desert views, atmospheric twisting streets and an old town made up of over 400 extraordinary ghurfas.

**HOW:**
By car or 4x4
**WHEN TO GO:**
April to October
**TIME IT TAKES:**
A day
**HIGHLIGHTS:**
In Tripoli – the medina (old market quarter), castle, Jamahiriya Museum (impressive collection of classical statues, mosaics and artefacts), Gurgi Mosque, Roman Arch of Marcus Aurelius and Gazelle Fountain.
Gharyan, on the edge of the Nafusa Mountains – with extraordinary troglodyte dwellings dug straight down into the ground (a detour via Yefren on the return journey).
At Qasr al-Hajj – an extraordinary grain and oil store that is one of the best examples of Berber architecture.
In Nalut – the 300-year-old mud-brick ksar and the even-more-ancient Alal'a Mosque (rebuilt 1312).
**YOU SHOULD KNOW:**
Most Berbers belong to the Khariji sect of Islam, and females should sensibly cover their heads (besides, the sun can be fierce!).

*The Sahara Desert with mountains in the background*

# Follow the Footsteps of Moses up Mount Sinai

Mount Sinai, or Jebel Musa (Mount Moses) is of enormous spiritual significance in the shared Judaeo-Christian and Muslim Old Testament heritage, for it is here that Moses is supposed to have received the Ten Commandments. The local Bedouins have deep reverence for the sanctity of their land and for over 1,500 years pilgrims have journeyed here to make obeisance. Perched on the summit are both a Greek Orthodox chapel and a Muslim shrine. The 6th century St Catherine's Monastery, supposedly built around the Burning Bush, stands at the foot.

There are two routes up the 2,285-m (7,500-ft) high mountain. The Siket Sayidna Musa (Path of Our Lord Moses) – 3,750 Steps of Penitence hewn out of stone by the monks of St Catherine's – lead directly up a steep ravine to the summit. Or you can take a gentler, more winding path, the Siket El Bashait (Camel Path) either on foot or by camel. Most tourists are herded up the latter track, as likely as not having first been cajoled onto the back of a camel by persuasive Bedouins. The ease of this route is the only thing to recommend it. It is much less scenic and far more crowded. The two paths meet at Elijah's Basin, a sandy hollow where visitors can camp overnight before climbing the final 750 steps to the mountain summit.

As you tread the Steps of Penitence, you cannot help but be moved by its mystical connotations. From the summit, the view over Sinai is breathtaking. Wrinkled folds and ridges of red- and green-hued granite extend to the horizon in 'an ocean of petrified waves'. Even for the most sceptical, it is almost enough to stir some sort of faith in the supernatural.

**HOW:**
On foot or on a camel
**WHEN TO GO:**
October to March
**TIME IT TAKES:**
One to three hours, depending on your pace.
**HIGHLIGHTS:**
St. Catherine's Monastery – UNESCO World Heritage site containing the largest collection of early manuscripts outside the Vatican, irreplaceable works of religious art, mosaics and icons.
Shrive (Confession) Gate – stone hewn arch where pilgrims could have their sins forgiven.
Elijah's Basin – a 500-year-old cypress tree marking the spot where Elijah is said to have heard the voice of God.
The view from the summit.
**YOU SHOULD KNOW:**
Wear good hiking shoes and take plenty of water with you. The climb is a long one but is quite easy for anybody reasonably fit. Tourists are usually persuaded to climb Mount Sinai by night in order to greet the sunrise from the summit. Far better to forego the dawn view, which is accompanied by freezing cold and hordes of other trippers, for the sake of seeing all the amazing scenery on the way and having more space to yourself to contemplate the view.

*St Catherine's Monastery dates from the 6th century.*

# Up the Nile

The cruise from Luxor to Aswan takes you through the heartlands of the oldest nation state in the world, the cradle in which the whole of Western Civilization is rooted. The awesome River Nile, the longest waterway in the world, is the sustainer of all life in the desert, depositing the fertile black silt of its floodplain and supplying water for the crops that grow in it. As you sail past the timeless agricultural scenery of the valley, flanked by sheer desert cliffs up to 550 m (1,800 ft) high, five millennia of history unfolds before your eyes.

Luxor, the ancient city of Thebes, is 'the world's greatest open air museum'. Here is the stupendous Karnak Temple, the tombs of the Valley of the Kings and the Colossi of Memnon. At the great lock at Esna, the Nile is transformed into a chaotic water bazaar as garrulous traders in rickety boats besiege the river traffic, proffering scarves, trinkets and souvenirs. The Temple of Horus at Edfu is the best-preserved temple in Egypt, and on the riverbank at Kom Ombu a temple with beautiful relief carving stands as a wondrous reminder of the antiquity of this land.

The charming southern city of Aswan is a riot of new impressions – the vivid colours and smells of the souks, the tall graceful Nubian townspeople, the Nile at its most picturesque – all swaying palm trees, golden dunes and white-sailed feluccas (traditional wooden sailing boats). Here the river is studded with numerous beautiful islands. Elephantine, the largest, is one of the most ancient sites in Egypt. Just upstream is the first of the Nile's six huge cataracts (rapids), the High Dam and Lake Nasser – the boundary of Egypt and the gateway to Africa.

**HOW:**
By boat
**WHEN TO GO:**
November to April
**TIME IT TAKES:**
Five days
**HIGHLIGHTS:**
Karnak Temple – largest temple complex in the world.
Luxor Museum – stunning ancient Egyptian art collection.
Colossi of Memnon – statues more than 17m (50 ft) high.
Temple of Philae and the High Dam at Lake Nasser.
Sunset felucca trip around islands of Aswan.
**YOU SHOULD KNOW:**
You can take one of the numerous cabin cruiser floating hotels that ply the Nile or sail in a felucca – a rather less comfortable but altogether more liberating experience, sightseeing at whim rather than being restricted to a cruise itinerary. Whichever way you travel, you should study your ancient history to get the most out of the countless sights you will pass.

*A felucca on the Nile at Luxor*

# Oases of the Great Sand Sea

**HOW:**
By 4x4
**WHEN TO GO:**
October to March
**TIME IT TAKES:**
One to two weeks
**HIGHLIGHTS:**
Shali Fortress, Siwa
Gebel al-Mawta – Mountain of the Dead, tombs cut into hillside.
Painted houses of Farafra.
Agabat Valley and Crystal Mountain in the White Desert.
Necropolis of Bagawat, Kharga – 2nd century Coptic tombs.
**YOU SHOULD KNOW:**
This journey can only be done in a 4x4 vehicle. You must obtain permission to travel between Siwa and Bahariya. A permit can be obtained on the spot in Siwa.

The Great Sand Sea is an uninhabitable belt of shifting golden dune ridges up to 100 m (330 ft) high, a natural impassable barrier between Egypt and Libya up to 300 km (200 mi) wide and extending for some 600 km (375 mi) north to south. Human habitation is only possible in the five remote oases at its edge, where mineral springs and waterholes enable life. On this 1,000 km (600 mi) road adventure, you will experience the magical stillness of elemental landscapes and wonder at the resilience of communities who have managed to preserve their culture, continuously since antiquity, in the face of such overwhelmingly hostile odds.

Siwa, Egypt's westernmost oasis is the site of the ancient Oracle of Amun, consulted by Alexander the Great. It is an 80 km (50 mi) swathe of date palms, olive trees and salt lakes inhabited by Berbers. The 400 km (250 mi) road along the ancient caravan route to Bahariya, is part rutted sand track, part concrete and part no road at all – just rough driving across the dunes in vaguely the right direction. From Bahariya, you cross the surreal White Desert with dramatic rock formations like giant mushrooms, to reach Farafra, one of the most isolated places in Egypt.

Compared to this tiny oasis, Dakhla seems huge – fourteen villages surrounded by fields of mulberry, citrus, datepalm and fig, overlooked by magnificent pinkish cliffs. It is perhaps the most beautiful stop on your journey and the village of Al-Qasr with its medieval architecture is one of the most significant archaeological sites of Egypt's Western Desert. Your final stop is Kharga on the notorious Forty Days Road, the slave route from the Sudan to Cairo. Once back in the tourist maelstrom of modern Egypt, you will immediately yearn to return to the mystical desert silence.

*White inselbergs dot the lunar-like landscape of the White Desert.*

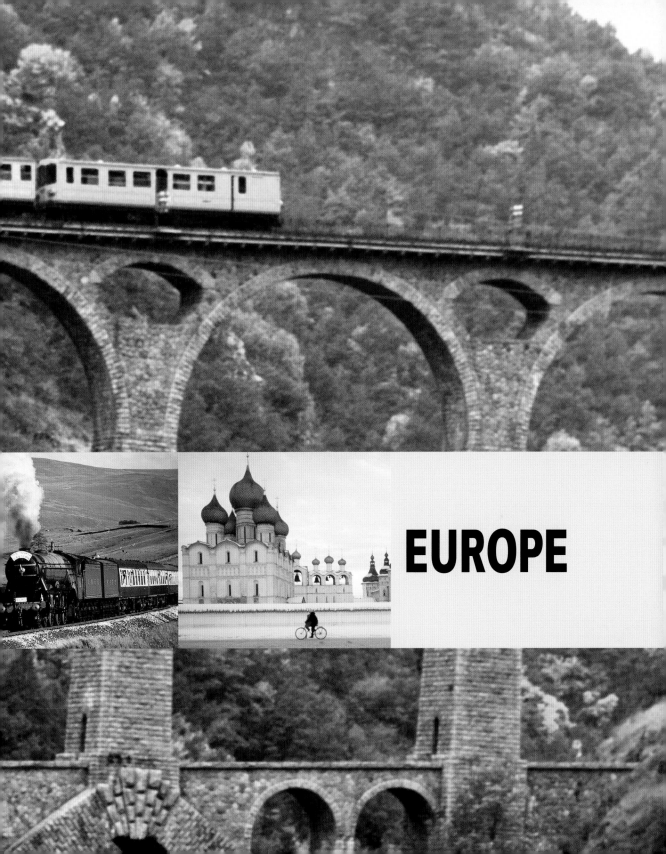

# EUROPE

# Snaefellsnes National Park

**HOW:**
On foot
**WHEN TO GO:**
May to June
**TIME IT TAKES:**
Six to eight hours
**HIGHLIGHTS:**
Bird colonies along the cliffs.
Badstofa Cave, Hellnar.
Mary's Spring – water emerging from
lava, thought to have healing powers.
The Midnight Sun
Spotting orca whales off the coast.
**YOU SHOULD KNOW:**
This walk is quite an easy one. There
are numerous trails and historical
sites in the Snaefellsnes National
Park. From Arnarstapi or Hellnar you
can hike up across the ice cap to the
volcano crater.

A continuously evolving landscape of volcanoes, geysers and lava fields, the whole of Iceland is a geological treasure; and the Snaefellsjokull is the absolute jewel in the crown. A mysterious 1,446 m (4,743 ft) high strato-volcano, with a 200-m (650-ft) deep ice-filled crater, shrouded in a 7 sq km (3 sq mi) ice cap, it has lain dormant for the past 1,800 years; ancient plaits of lava trail down its flanks across the plains of the Snaefellsnes Peninsula to the sea. It is one of the seven most potent 'energy sources' of the planet, the well-spring of Icelandic mythology, looming over a strange land where dwarves still lurk in the crannies, elves hide in the mossy banks and ogres stomp across the ice. Used by Jules Verne as the setting for his novel *Journey to the Centre of the Earth*, the Snaefellsjokull is an enduring source of inspiration for mystics, artists and poets.

From the romantic moonscape wilds of the Budir estuary you walk for 18 km (11 mi) in a surreal fairyland, across a moss-carpeted and rock-strewn lava plain to the picturesque fishing village of Arnarstapi. From here you can walk a further 8 km (5 mi) along a bizarrely beautiful coast of fantastic lava formations and spectacular caves. Fierce Atlantic breakers crash through holes in the rocks, hurling great fountains of spray up into the sky, and the basalt column cliffs are packed with birds – colonies of kittiwakes, fulmars, razorbills and arctic terns. Reaching the sheltered natural harbour by the hamlet of Hellnar you can stand beneath the Snaefellsjokull, only 10 km (6 mi) from the snowline, on the meeting point of the ley lines that supposedly carry currents of transcendental volcanic energy round the planet.

*Snaefellsjokull glacier*

*Vestvagoy island*

# Lofoten Islands

A cycling vacation along the Vestfjord route is a most memorable experience – new, breathtaking sights appear around every bend. Combining ferry trips with cycling, this route serves up almost everything Norway has to offer. White sandy beaches butt up against soaring mountain scenery. Archaeological relics and historical buildings satisfy those who seek more cultural pursuits, whilst for the more active there is ample opportunity to swim, hike or fish.

Idyllic little villages of brightly painted wooden houses line the route as you travel from island to island. It is easy to see why locals describe this area as the real Norway and the archipelago features prominently in Nordic art, film and literature. To cover the full 450 km (281 mi) would be to undertake a journey of epic proportions; however good transport links make it possible to get to almost any part of the trail quickly.

Old market centres such as Løvøy and Grøtøy have been faithfully restored, whilst Steigen is a real hidden gem, teeming with innumerable historical relics. Those who seek more adventure should explore the cave system at Nordskot, whilst those looking for a more sedate outdoor experience can soak up the sun on the wonderful white sandy beaches near Misten. The Vestfjord really does have something for everyone. All you need is a bicycle, good waterproofs, a ferry timetable and a spirit of exploration, and a new adventure awaits you around every corner.

**HOW:**
By bike
**WHEN TO GO:**
May to September provides the best weather.
**TIME IT TAKES:**
Around two weeks for the whole route
**HIGHLIGHTS:**
Tranøy Lighthouse – a fine example and open to visitors.
Steigen Fortidspark – where the past is re-enacted.
Raftsund – a narrow strait between Hinnøya and Austvågøya.
The Stone Age settlements and ruined boathouses on Gimsøya.
**YOU SHOULD KNOW:**
Forward planning is required to make the most of this trip. Although the ferries are reliable, the faster services take you to the most crowded sections. If you wish to leave the beaten track it may require taking two or more of the less frequent services.

*Folda Sound, Bodø*

# Trondheim to Bodø

**HOW:**
By train
**WHEN TO GO:**
Year round; May to August have longer days.
**TIME IT TAKES:**
Around ten hours
**HIGHLIGHTS:**
The journey over three marvellous mountain ranges.
If you are lucky enough or stay long enough – the Northern Lights (September to March).
Bodø Domkirke – a modern Cathedral in Gothic style.
Nordlandmuseet – a museum recording local life.
**YOU SHOULD KNOW:**
If travelling in high summer (June or July) the train can get crowded; also advance booking of a hotel room in Bodø is recommended.

This is an incredibly beautiful journey and, when taken in summer, the light evenings ensure that you miss nothing. The train transports you through pine forests, across foothills and alongside fjords and rivers. This sea of green and blue is broken only by the occasional red wooden farmstead.

It is a curious feeling to head towards something that you will never see, but the Arctic Circle announces itself in many ways. As you head north, the light changes imperceptibly. The snow, which was confined to the mountain tops moves ever nearer, whilst on the track the wooden tunnels, constructed to protect the line from avalanches, grow more numerous.

As the signs of human habitation thin out and the mountains get more rugged, the landscape becomes ever more hypnotic. Thoughts turn to wildlife watching and there is every chance that you will spot a majestic reindeer in its natural surroundings. The Arctic Circle is heralded not only by a hoot of the train's whistle and two cairns on the side of the track, but by curious rituals on the train. A party spirit suddenly erupts; some partake in illicit drinking, while others share food and sometimes kissing breaks out as though it were New Year's Eve. It does feel significant to have crossed 'the line' and it is always interesting to watch the impromptu ceremonies that mark it.

The final steep descent takes you from Arctic tundra towards the blue Atlantic Ocean. This is as far north as the railway goes and as the charming town of Bodø comes into view, you are left with the feeling that you have taken more than just a train journey.

# Spirit of Norway

It is hard to think of a better trip anywhere in the world that can be completed inside a single day. It could be that the Norwegians, ever mindful of their high cost of living, feel that most tourists want to get their money's worth. Several companies operate excursions that whisk you up mountain railways, along precipitous roads and then out to sea, to experience Norway's most famous feature, the iconic Fjords.

The typical journey starts with a ride on Northern Europe's highest-altitude railway line, the Bergen Railway. Exposed to harsh Atlantic weather systems, it is a huge engineering feat just to keep the line open, but you will be glad they do. The mountain views are stunning as the engine hauls you up incredibly steep inclines. From there the rollercoaster ride continues as you transfer to the Flåm Railway, a 20-km (12.5-mi) journey from the hill station of Myrdal, which runs alongside magnificent mountain scenery and tumbling waterfalls.

Beautiful though this all is, you quickly realize that it was merely the hors d'oeuvre. From Flåm the next leg of the excursion is completed by boat. Although the fjords are so obviously a symbol of Norway, one cannot tire of seeing them. These deep-sea gullies, carved by ice, take the breath away and the towering rock faces on both sides make it sometimes hard to believe that you are on water. Legendary, labyrinthine and starkly beautiful, a journey through the fjords leaves you with images that will stay with you for the rest of your life.

The last leg of this most fabulous of days out takes you, by coach, along the amazingly winding mountain road to your final destination of Stalheim. From there it is possible to transfer by train back to Bergen.

**HOW:**
By train and boat
**WHEN TO GO:**
Year round but best under the midnight sun – May to July.
**TIME IT TAKES:**
16 hours – but three days if you choose to stop.
**HIGHLIGHTS:**
The picturesque village of Flåm.
The mountains around Sognefjord.
The improbably narrow Naeroyfjord.
The Folk museum at Stalheim – a celebration of traditional Nordic life.
**YOU SHOULD KNOW:**
Norway can be very expensive – there's no shame in taking your own lunch with you, in fact that is precisely what most locals do.

*The magnificent mountains around Sognefjord*

*The coastal village of Ballstad*

# Bergen to Kirkenes

**HOW:**
By postal boat
**WHEN TO GO:**
Year round
**TIME IT TAKES:**
Six or seven days one-way
**HIGHLIGHTS:**
The Lofoten Islands
The Sor-Varanger Museum
in Kirkenes.
Bergen – full of Hanseatic history.
The lovely town of Bodø.
**YOU SHOULD KNOW:**
Whilst the main purpose of these
vessels is to provide supplies to far-
flung communities, the operators do
cater well for the tourist trade. The
vessels alternate between day-time
and night-time deliveries, so that
anyone taking a round trip will
miss nothing.

Large cruise ships ply the 2,000-km (1,250-mi) voyage between Bergen and Kirkenes, but for sheer intimacy it's difficult to beat the more informal service offered by the 'postal' ships that serve outlying Norwegian coastal communities. This odyssey takes you around Norway's breathtakingly beautiful fjord coastline, stopping over thirty times and showing you a side of Norway inaccessible by any other means of transport.

The journey begins in Bergen, a harbour town founded by the Vikings almost a millennium ago, when it quickly became a vital hub, handling trade between Northern Europe and the British Isles. As you leave the port, the splendid 14th-century gabled buildings of the seafront slowly dwindle to nothing and your eyes are drawn to the wonderfully rugged coastline.

Along the way you will see glorious fjords, precipitous mountains and quaint fishing villages before crossing the Arctic Circle. Here, as you approach the North Cape, you will experience the midnight sun in the summer. Winter offers the chance to see the Northern Lights – the ultimate light show.

For much of the journey all eyes are fixed on the starboard side, where snow-capped mountains and fjords abound. This is until the vessel meanders between the Lofoten Islands whose stark, craggy beauty hits you from both sides. The trip gives you a true appreciation of this beautiful country and how most of its population clings to the coast. When you cross the Arctic Circle the population becomes more thinly spread and the scenery ever more dramatic. The awe-inspiring Laksefjorden and Tanafjorden lie ahead, before the vessel reaches its final destination, the sheltered port of Kirkenes.

# Raumabanen Railway

Now over 80 years old, the Raumabanen Railway has always unashamedly been a tourist track. Aside from a brief period when it was used to ferry around the country's gold reserves, it has operated to cater for the cruise ship trade arriving into Romsdalfjord and Åndalsnes. Whereas other railway journeys take you past wonderful sights as if by coincidence, the Raumabanen has a single purpose – to show off Norway at its finest.

This 114-km (182-mi) long marvel of 1920s engineering starts at Åndalsnes, the northern gateway to the fjords. Right from the start the views are spectacular and as the train climbs steadily, hugging the mountainside, you are treated to breathtaking views of the valley below. The imposing peaks of Romsdalhorn and Trollveggen soon dominate the skyline. You are torn between looking up or looking down as the train crosses Kyllingbrua, a startlingly high stone arched bridge which hangs high above the Rauma River.

It seems scarcely possible to climb any higher, but this is exactly what happens just after you pass Verma, as the train takes you through a corkscrew tunnel under the mountains. This really is a giant fairground ride for grown-ups. As you approach Dombås, the scenery opens up offering panoramic views of this most remarkable of lands. Here you can either continue to Oslo or Trondheim or, better still, go back and do it all again.

**HOW:**
By train
**WHEN TO GO:**
Year round – special steam trains serve the line in summer (June to August).
**TIME IT TAKES:**
Around three hours one-way, although a shorter journey between Åndalsnes and Bjorli is available for those wanting to make a quick round trip.
**HIGHLIGHTS:**
The Brudesløret (the bridal veil) – a spectacular waterfall.
The Kylling turning tunnel – quite a ride.
Lesjaskogsvatnet Lake
The procession of mountain peaks from Trollveggen, Romsdalshorn, Karlskråtind, Mongeura to Vengetindene.
**YOU SHOULD KNOW:**
The railway can get crowded and is more expensive in the high season (June to August). If you can be flexible, September or early October are good times to go and the evenings are still light.

*The stunning scenery of the western fjords*

# Lyse Road

The Lyse Road was constructed as a service route for a hydro-electricity station, but that bland description reveals nothing of the experience the road has to offer. It twists and sweeps, clinging precariously to the side of a mountain that rises out of one of Norway's most beautiful fjords, making it the ultimate challenge to your driving skills and a rush like no other.

Built in the 1980s, the 44-km (27-mi) long Lyse Road stands as the critical test for those who have a zest for driving on mountain roads. All along the route you are book-ended by magnificent mountains on one side and the shimmering darkness of Lysefjord on the other – this really is like a scene from a car advertisement.

Viewed from above it would seem as if someone had thrown a giant sidewinder onto the edge of a mountain. With 27 hairpin bends, the Lyse is the ultimate brake-tester. The views are always amazing, if at times a little disorienting – and the relative shallowness of parts of the fjord produces the most wonderful light.

There are a few places where you can stop and it is advisable to do so, if only for the sake of the driver, who should be concentrating so hard on the road that he/she will have little chance to enjoy the stunning scenery. Consideration for other users of the road must be a priority on this often single lane highway, but this is a top rate scuttle if you get a clear run.

**HOW:**
By car
**WHEN TO GO:**
The road is closed in winter – roughly between November and April.
**TIME IT TAKES:**
One to two hours
**HIGHLIGHTS:**
The hike to Pulpit Rock – with its views high above the fjord.
The view of the road from Øygardsstølen.
Tjodan hydro-electric power station – the reason for the road's existence.
The charming little town of Lysebotn.
**YOU SHOULD KNOW:**
Speed limits are rigorously enforced in Norway, so if you are tempted to speed, don't – this road demands the utmost respect and fines can be as steep as the road itself.

*Sightseers on Prekestolen (Pulpit Rock)*

# High Coast Trail

The Höga Kusten (High Coast) was formed when the region sank under a gigantic mass of ice during the last ice age. When the ice retreated, the land sprang back and it is still rising today. This has left a dynamic landscape of vertical cliffs and craggy outcrops, lined with tranquil sandy coves.

Accessibility and flexibility are the watchwords for the exciting 127-km (80-mi) trail that takes you through this terrain. Divided into thirteen stages, it offers the hiker a wide variety of challenges, whilst each stage is handily reachable by car. There are even organized self-guided tours where you can walk between lodgings, while your luggage is transported for you, allowing you to travel light.

This striking area has been given UNESCO World Heritage Site status and the hike takes you through Sweden's highest coastal area. A rich diversity of rivers, lakes, inlets and hills makes it a good test for hikers of all levels. Each day offers varying terrain as well as beautiful views out over the dark blue seas of the Gulf of Bothnia.

Starting near central Örnsköldsvik the trail presents the hiker with compact challenges. Mountains seem more climbable when you know that old-fashioned Swedish hospitality awaits you at the end of each day. Accommodation ranges from simple huts to guesthouses, but for a genuine Swedish welcome, nothing beats staying in a traditional farmhouse, several of which open their doors to tourists in summer.

**HOW:**
On foot
**WHEN TO GO:**
Fully accessible from May to October
**TIME IT TAKES:**
One to two weeks according to fitness levels
**HIGHLIGHTS:**
The Skuleskogen National Park
The imposing Slåtterdalsskrevan Gorge.
The suspension bridge near Härnösand.
Surströmming (fermented herring) – a local delicacy certain to greet you at the table at some point.
**YOU SHOULD KNOW:**
It is important not to be too ambitious. Don't be fooled by the relatively short distances between designated stops – the ruggedness of the terrain can often slow your progress.

*Slåtterdalsskrevan Gorge in Skuleskogen National Park*

# Gota Canal

**HOW:**
By boat and/or bike
**WHEN TO GO:**
Year round, but it springs fully into life from June to August
**TIME IT TAKES:**
Two to six days by steamer
**HIGHLIGHTS:**
The gorgeous lakes of Vättern and Vänern.
The Trollhätte Canal Museum
De la Gardie Palace – a wonderful Baroque-style building.
Birka Viking settlement on Björkö Island.
**YOU SHOULD KNOW:**
Organised tours, though usually all-inclusive, can be expensive. With a little forward planning, it is possible to enjoy this magnificent waterway for a fraction of the cost.

If you want to see Sweden at play, head straight for the Gota Canal. This marvel of 19th-century engineering stretches 190 km (118 mi) from Sjötorp on Lake Vänern to the Baltic Sea at Mem and is a real crowd-puller. Whether you are travelling on it or cycling alongside it you cannot help but be impressed by its sheer scale. Fifty-eight locks, some of them rising to an incredible 90 m (295 ft) above sea level, carry vessels through a chain of stunning natural lakes, making this one of the most impressive waterways anywhere on the planet.

The canal takes you through the heart of Sweden, passing historic sites, medieval churches, attractive towns and rich green forests along the way. Many steamers ply their trade along it and this gentle form of transport has much to recommend it. You can hop on and hop off these boats and, with the aid of a bicycle, it is possible to explore the wider environs.

For a more intimate experience there is nothing better than hiring a boat on any one of the stunningly beautiful lakes that grace the waterway, stopping only to have a picnic lunch by the shore. Most journeys are about getting somewhere, whereas riding the Gota Canal invites you to stop and marvel at every point. It offers great fishing, kayaking, Nordic walking and a whole host of other activities. Like one big joyful playground, it has become more than the sum of its parts – a wonderful potpourri of outdoor adventure.

*The charming city of Mariestad on Lake Vänern*

# Padjelanta Trail

So remote as to be reachable only by helicopter, the 140-km (88-mi) Padjelanta Trail is nature at its most raw. Padjelanta translates as 'the higher land' and is the summer home to the Sami people who bring vast reindeer herds here to graze. Aside from the mountains of the Sarek National Park, the landscape is relatively flat and open, consisting mainly of rolling hills with a scattering of higher peaks. Located entirely above the Arctic Circle, trees are scarce, though there is a surprising abundance of flora, and there is no finer sight than the flowering of an Arctic meadow.

There are no roads in the area, adding to the feeling of complete isolation, and accommodation is rudimentary. This trek has the motto 'as nature intended' stamped all over it. There is no electricity and water is sourced from fast running streams. Heat comes from wood fires and bathing takes place outdoors. All this helps to keep the Padjelanta a pristine wilderness for the ambitious and rugged hiker to enjoy.

At the centre of Padjelanta lies a succession of four wondrous lakes, the Kutjaure, Sallojaure, Vastenjaure and Virihaure. It is here that the Sami set up their summer camps and invite visitors to sample their unique way of life. You soon get to learn that communal living and interdependence are essential in this starkly beautiful setting. This is a lesson that will stand you in good stead, as you continue on your way through this ever shifting landscape – one of Europe's last great wildernesses.

*Padjelanta National Park –*
*one of Europe's last*
*great wildernesses*

**HOW:**
On foot
**WHEN TO GO:**
June to August
**TIME IT TAKES:**
Four days to one week
**HIGHLIGHTS:**
Sitting out under the midnight sun.
Sleeping in a traditional Sami tent.
The comradely spirit engendered by
the need to share.
The view across the spectacular
Tarra Valley.
**YOU SHOULD KNOW:**
You really are cut off from most
modern amenities on this trek. You
should be fit and have a good
knowledge of first aid and some
basic survival skills. This is by no
stretch of the imagination a 'walk in
the park', there is little signage and
pathways are often not very clear.

# Inlandsbanan

**HOW:**
By train
**WHEN TO GO:**
The train runs only in summer (June to August).
**TIME IT TAKES:**
Two days without stopovers
**HIGHLIGHTS:**
The Jamtli Historieland – a heritage museum in Östersund.
The Inland Railway Museum at Gällivare.
Beaverland – a Sami craft gallery located in Vilhelmina.
Swimming in any one of the surprisingly warm mountain lakes along the way.
**YOU SHOULD KNOW:**
Summer brings out the area's large mosquito population. This should not be a problem if you take precautions. Insect repellent can be effective, but you should also avoid using hairspray or any other highly perfumed products.

The 1,067-km (667-mi) Inlandsbanan (inland railway) carries you along the spine of central northern Sweden. Built to serve the logging industry, it has now diversified to cater for the burgeoning tourist trade. The pace of the train is very laid back. As befits a Swedish operation, you are transported at an average speed of 50 kph (30 mph) through magnificent pine and birch forests.

As the train departs Mora on its northbound journey, all eyes are drawn to the deep forest where yellow wild flowers line the track. This is an ideal habitat for bear, reindeer and moose and the train will conveniently slow down if any are spotted, so be sure to have your camera primed and ready. The train passes many water features on the way but the waterfalls at Strorstupet and Helvetesfallet are the most spectacular.

Whilst it is possible to make this gentle journey inside two days, it is best experienced in separate stages with stopovers between. Aside from the wonderful forest surroundings, there is much to enjoy on the way. The first main stop is at Östersund. More associated with winter sports, it takes on a different life in summer. A picturesque little town, it offers historic walks, a heritage museum and the splendid Lake Storsjön is nearby.

The next stop, Vilhelmina, is most worthy of exploration. Surrounded by invigorating fast flowing streams, it is home to many Sami artisans and has many naturally heated pools and an extensive cycleway.

As the train continues steadfastly towards the Arctic Circle, the forest becomes more untamed and the vista ever more beautiful. The train finally pulls in to Gällivare, a town where people successfully combine modern living with a more traditional way of life.

*A train crosses the steel bridge at Storstupet.*

# Norsjö Cable-Way

*The cable cars 'fly' along the lakeshore.*

Originally built in 1943 to ferry ore buried deep in the mountains, the Norsjö Cable-Way seemed to have had its day by the end of the 20th century. It was then that the locals, some of whom could recall the great sacrifices that were made during its construction, rallied round to save it. At over 13 km (8 mi), it stands as the longest cable car journey in the world and now ferries tourists between Örträsk and Mensträsk, gliding at a majestic 10 kph (6.25 mph) high above the Västerbotten countryside.

Fourteen cabins ply their trade in each direction, offering the chance to enter a fragile woodland environment accessible by no other means. Reindeer and moose are common sights and, unlike other forms of transport, the relative quietness of the cable cars does not seem to disturb them too much. As you pass each concrete mast – there are 73 in all – you can't help but marvel at the amazing feat of engineering that produced this modern wonder.

It is a strange experience to be held aloft for so long and the cable-way provides a wonderful bird's eye view of this splendid environment. After the initial jolt into action, the cable-way provides a real Hansel and Gretel experience, soaring above lakes and forests through a dizzying expanse. All passengers have a window seat and the compact cabins have an intimate feel, each housing just four people. In summer, birdsong provides the perfect soundtrack to your voyage, whilst in winter snow and ice cling to the trees as if they were sculpted that way.

**HOW:**
By cable car
**WHEN TO GO:**
The service operates year round and each season has its own unique feel.
**TIME IT TAKES:**
One hour twenty minutes
**HIGHLIGHTS:**
The Cable-way Museum at Örträsk.
The pretty ski resort of Mensträsk
The film of how the cableway was built – shown in the cinema in Örträsk.
The charming little town of Örträsk.
**YOU SHOULD KNOW:**
Booking in advance is essential for this popular attraction. It should also be noted that currently only ten of the carriages are heated, so if you are travelling in winter check that you are in one of these, or wrap up warmly!

# The East Coast Route

**HOW:**
By bike
**WHEN TO GO:**
Year round
**TIME IT TAKES:**
It makes for a good week's holiday.
**HIGHLIGHTS:**
Grenen Museum of Art in Skagen.
Koldinghus – a beautifully
restored castle.
Moesgård Forhistoriske Museum – a
museum of the people, near Århus.
Sønderborg Castle overlooking the
dramatic Flensborg Fjord.

*The coastline of Skagen, with
the village of Skagen in
the background*

Denmark ranks as one of the most bicycle friendly countries in the world. The Danes simply love cycling and any one of their eleven National Cycle Routes provides the lover of two wheels with an exciting and memorable holiday. At 650 km (406 mi), the East Coast Route is the longest and most spectacular of the lot. Stretching from Skagen to Sønderborg, the route meanders through pretty Danish countryside, taking the rider along fjords, round bays and peninsulas.

The towns that line the route are rich in tradition and culture. Charming fishing villages are to be found along the northern section, while to the south grand castles and sumptuous manor houses grace the rolling landscape. You will always be cycling within easy reach of the sea and the many secluded coves along the way

give you good reason to stop and take a dip.

Of all the towns along the route, Århus must be singled out for special mention. Nowhere in Denmark will you find a greater concentration of artists, museums, musicians and historically significant sites. Denmark's graceful and welcoming second city is a perfect place to make a break in your journey and, having explored it, you will probably want to stay for a day or two.

When you make this journey, you will realize how perfectly designed it is for cyclists. The towns that line the route are remarkably evenly spaced, so as the legs begin to tire, there is always something to stimulate the mind or satisfy the stomach.

**YOU SHOULD KNOW:**
Over 90 per cent of the route is asphalted, making cycling easy and fun. The route should present no problems for a reasonably fit cyclist with a good set of brakes. .

# Hærvejen Oxen Trail

If roads could speak this one would recount tales like few others.  Throughout history this route, which starts just the other side of the German border and runs down the spine of Jutland, has borne the weight of Danish hopes – as well as their livestock. A source of great pride for modern day Denmark, many of its secrets still lie by the roadside, yet to be discovered.  It is probable that the route has been trodden for millennia and an air of historical significance hangs over every part of it.

For much of the way it seems little more than a dirt track, while other sections are more like modern roads. Famous for its magnificent stone bridges, the Hærvejen is ideal for hiking or biking vacations. Whichever mode of transport you choose, you will want to stop and marvel at sights both ancient and modern. Runic stones, burial mounds and monoliths line the route and offer cryptic clues to the regions antediluvian past. More recent history is displayed in the German World War I bunkers and the Froslev Concentration Camp, where Danish Communists were imprisoned during World War II.

The road's elevation of some 92 m (300 ft) in places, gives you excellent wide views of the countryside and the ridge forms the source of Denmark's two longest rivers, the Skjernå and the Gudenå. All in all, this is a journey which can be relished as a trek through the tranquil Jutish countryside, or studied deeply like an ancient text. The choice is yours.

**HOW:**
On foot or by bike
**WHEN TO GO:**
Open all year, but the weather is best from May to September.
**TIME IT TAKES:**
Five days hiking or two days by bike.
**HIGHLIGHTS:**
The historic town of Vejen – the only major settlement on the route.
Roede Kro (the Red Inn) – a resource centre for the region.
Hairulf Stone – a splendid inscribed standing stone.
The stone bridge at Immervad – basic, symmetrical and symbolic.
**YOU SHOULD KNOW:**
Only a small part of the road is paved and much of the rest of it makes for a pretty bumpy bicycle ride. So make sure you have good suspension, or better still make the journey in the manner of the ancients and walk.

# Copenhagen Waterbus

**HOW:**
By boat
**WHEN TO GO:**
The service operates from May
to September
**TIME IT TAKES:**
You can buy one or two day passes
**HIGHLIGHTS:**
Frihedsmuseet – a museum
dedicated to those who resisted the
Nazis in World War II.
Little Mermaid statue – a perfectly
formed landmark.
Trekoner Fortress – an imposing
historical monument.
Christianborg Palace – a former
royal palace, now home to the
Danish government.
**YOU SHOULD KNOW:**
It is not possible to book a seat on
this journey and the boats can get
full, especially during the middle of
the day in July and August. If you do
find you are not able to board a
particular vessel, Copenhagen's
compactness means it is possible to
walk to your next destination.

Copenhagen is one of Europe's truly great cities. With its perfect blend of old and new, it is a city that demands to be explored. While most cities are only slowly waking up to the fact that their waterways are a vital resource for life, as well as for trade, Copenhagen has always known it. Most of its great sights are visible and accessible from the water and there is no better way to travel around it than by waterbus.

This hop-on, hop-off service calls at all of Copenhagen's major tourist attractions, as well as providing an important transport link for those who like to travel at a more relaxed pace. Several operators ply the route and offer up to 16 drop-off points. So with ticket and timetable in hand, it is time to climb aboard and investigate this wonderfully compact city. With forward planning, it's possible to stroll along the world famous Tivoli Gardens before having lunch in Nyhavn, the old sailors' quarter which brims with fabulous cafés. The afternoon can then be spent lapping up the cultural delights of the Frihedsmuseet and the Amalienborg Palace, before visiting the artists' district of Christiania. This can all be rounded off with a visit to the city's renowned Opera House.

The choice is really yours on this most flexible of tours. It is an excellent way to get to know your way around Copenhagen and for those who already know the city well, it affords a new perspective on this most magnificent of urban landscapes.

*Tour boats on the canal at Nyhavn*

# Over the Öresund Bridge

The people of the southern Swedish territory of Skåne have more in common with the Danes than they do with their fellow countrymen in the north. Even the relatively flat rolling landscape is remarkably similar. It is therefore no surprise to learn that these two areas were linked by land some 7,000 years ago. Only two courses of action were available to those who wanted to reunite these lands, one was to wait for another ice age, the other was to build a crossing.

Built in a true spirit of cooperation, what resulted was a wonder of modern construction, to rival that of the Channel Tunnel. Before the bridge was officially opened in 1999, the crossing between Copenhagen and Malmö was a joyless one. Coaches and hovercraft would ferry people who found cheap flights to Sweden via Denmark, and they would mingle with Swedes who were looking for bargains on the other side of the water.

The arrival of the combined rail and road crossing changed all this and it is now possible to make the excursion in comfort and with speed. As you depart Copenhagen, the Öresund has a surprise for you as it starts its life as a tunnel, to avoid interfering with the busy airport. Soon it emerges from the water, as a majestic bridge, providing fantastic views on both sides.

The crossing has really opened up this area of southern Sweden and re-attached it to the mainland. Once across, the opportunities to explore are numerous. Outside of the cities the most popular destination is the area around the Falsterbo Peninsula. With its long sandy beaches it draws hikers and sun-seekers from far and wide and transport links connect well with the bridge.

**HOW:**
By train or car
**WHEN TO GO:**
Year round
**TIME IT TAKES:**
Thirty-five minutes by train from downtown Copenhagen to downtown Malmö.
**HIGHLIGHTS:**
The view of the bridge from either shore.
Copenhagen – a compact city, worth a day or two's exploration.
Malmö – a city of green open spaces and a pretty town centre.
The university town of Lund – the jewel of southern Sweden, with its magnificent cathedral and numerous beautiful gardens.
**YOU SHOULD KNOW:**
A hefty toll is charged to road users who cross the Öresund Bridge. If you are intending to cross several times, period passes are available at a more reasonable rate.

*The Öresund Bridge joins Denmark and Sweden.*

# The King's Road Trail

In it heyday the King's Road was as important to Northern Europe as the Silk Road was to Asia. Linking Bergen in the west to St Petersburg in the east, it provided a strategic link, greatly aiding the flow of people, goods and ideas. The Western King's Road that runs from Helsinki to Pohj, takes you on a 100-km (62.5-mi) journey through an area of great natural beauty as well as offering up a superb blend of old and new architecture.

There are many ways to make this journey and you can use a combination of car, train and even boat. However, cycling fits best with the tempo of the region and there is a well-maintained cycle route with good signage. The traveller is taken through forests of silver birch and fir trees, alongside the shimmering Baltic Sea, through picturesque towns and on towards the Russian border.

The King's Road offers a wonderful insight into traditional Finnish life and the route is filled with history and culture. Finland has always been a buffer between east and west and the influences on people, food and places are displayed fully on this trek. This area has long been a summer playground for Scandinavians and nowhere is this better shown than in Loviisa – with its delightful beaches, framed by subtly coloured wooden buildings, it is a seaside resort with few peers.

This is a journey that serves up great contrasts and gives the traveller a new perspective on Finnish life. It may not be too much of an exaggeration to say that without the King's Road Finland would not be the country it is today.

*The Åland Islands*

# The Hetta-Pallas Winter Ski Trail

The 55-km (34-mi) Hetta-Pallas Winter Trail is the Finnish section of the 800-km (500-mi) pan-Scandinavian Nordkalottleden Trail. The Trail passes through the Pallas-Yllästunturi National Park in Lapland, an area of fast-flowing rivers, turquoise lakes, lush forests and glacier-topped mountains. It is not an overly demanding trail for the experienced cross-country skier, as it follows mostly the lower slopes, apart from one ravine section where it travels above the tree-line. Its very simplicity adds to the hypnotic high, familiar to long distance skiers, and for a sense of true wilderness in all its luminous and silent beauty, it is hard to beat.

As Finland has common access to all its land enshrined in law, the intrepid skier is free to ski in any wilderness or forest area. However, the trail itself is well maintained and well marked and the best advice is to follow the signs. 'Wilderness huts' at manageable intervals are available to travellers. These wood cabins are basic and must be shared, though in winter they are rarely over-used and they're free.

In summer, the Hetta-Pallas Hiking Trail covers roughly the same route, though at higher altitudes, as the winter trails are too wet to be hiked in summer. The Trail goes through a ravishingly beautiful landscape of birch-clothed fell highlands and steep-sided ravines but, while the area is utterly wild, the trek can easily be undertaken by any reasonably fit and eager walker. The same wilderness huts are available in summer, though they can get crowded at the most popular times, so it is always wise to take a tent. In this land of the midnight sun, you can, of course, hike all night and find a place to rest in the morning.

*A snowshoer heads towards a wilderness hut along the Hetta-Pallas Winter Trail.*

**HOW:**
On skis or snowshoes in winter or on foot in the summer months
**WHEN TO GO:**
Winter trail – mid-February to end April; Summer hiking – late June to end September.
**TIME IT TAKES:**
Hiking the trail can be completed in four days; skiing, comfortably, in three days.
**HIGHLIGHTS:**
Fell Lapland Nature Centre. Chance to see the Northern Lights. The husky farm at Muonio, a short side trip from the trail.
**YOU SHOULD KNOW:**
It is probably best to avoid the area in July, as mosquitoes and black fly abound at this time.

*One of the many lakes that surround Tampere*

# Helsinki to Tampere

**HOW:**
By train
**WHEN TO GO:**
Year round
**TIME IT TAKES:**
Ninety minutes
**HIGHLIGHTS:**
The train is the real star, as you view pristine countryside through immaculately clean windows.
Helsinki Station – a green trimmed Art-Deco style masterpiece.
The 200 or so lakes that surround Tampere.
Central Museum of Labour (Tampere) a quirky museum full of interesting things.
**YOU SHOULD KNOW:**
One cannot say this too often: train travel in Finland is fun, affordable and stress-free.

The Finns are right to be proud of their trains. Fast, punctual and meticulously clean, they set a standard that is hard to match. In an age where people are increasingly looking for environmentally friendly holidays, VR Ltd Finnish Railways sets the benchmark, giving you every reason to leave the car at home.

If you can tear yourself away from the cultural and architectural delights of Helsinki, the train journey to Tampere is one of the real gems of European travel. This sparsely populated land is a place of great natural beauty, where the modern sits well with the traditional. Summer brings never-ending daylight, while the winter landscape has an ethereal elegance often lit up by the hauntingly beautiful Northern Lights.

As the majestic red and white train glides through the open countryside, passing lakes fringed by forest, you cannot help but be struck by the serenity of it all. It is hard to think of any other intercity journey in the developed world that passes through landscape of such untamed beauty.

The only complaint one could have is that the journey is over so soon. The memory of sumptuous lakes, verdant forests and grand farmsteads is one that will linger long in the mind. The next time you are on the train to work, you will be tempted to close your eyes and try to imagine that you are back on the Helsinki-Tampere Express.

# The Post Boat Route across the Kvarken

The passage across the Kvarken has always been inextricably linked with taxation. It is a long way around the Gulf of Bothnia and, in the 17th century, King Gustav II bestowed on the residents of Björkö the privilege of conveying goods over the water. In return they were excused military service and given tax breaks. Even up until the late 20th century, these waters were busy with vessels plying the lucrative duty-free trade. All this has now gone and the Kvarken has returned to a quiet normality.

Björkö, at the head of a handsome archipelago, still makes its living from the sea. The relatively shallow waters of the Kvarken are rich with fish and this is reflected in the local diet. Great hiking is to be found on this island group and all paths inevitably lead to the sea; as you gaze over the Kvarken an urge to cross it awakens in you.

It is still possible, by private charter, to make this historic crossing and as you set out, the full beauty of the island chain becomes apparent. Soon you are in open sea and the glimmering waters of the gulf surround you, until the imposing landscape of Sweden's High Coast heaves into view. The traditional landing for this journey is Holmön, an ideal place to end a perfect voyage.

Each year, just after the midsummer festival (late June), these superb waters spring to life. A flotilla of white-sailed boats sets out in a faithful re-enactment of the original post boat run – it's a magnificent spectacle to behold and a wonderful event to participate in.

**HOW:**
By boat
**WHEN TO GO:**
The relatively mild waters of the Kvarken mean that it is navigable nearly all year round. The worst weather is from November to March.
**TIME IT TAKES:**
Two to five hours, depending on the type of vessel and sea conditions.
**HIGHLIGHTS:**
Kvarken Archipelago – the first UNESCO World Heritage Site in Finland.
The picturesque town of Björköby (on Björkö).
Holmön Island – a nature reserve and the sunniest area of Sweden.
**YOU SHOULD KNOW:**
A good level of seamanship is required to undertake this trip. So if you do not have the necessary skills, it is advisable to engage the services of someone who does.

*Post boats sailing across the Kvarken.*

# The Curonian Spit Trail

**HOW:**
By bike or on foot
**WHEN TO GO:**
June to September
**TIME IT TAKES:**
Two days
**HIGHLIGHTS:**
Witches Hill – woodland path with beautifully carved wooden sculptures of mythological figures.
Great Dune of Parnidis 52 m (170 ft) high.
Dead dunes near Parvalka – where a whole village was swallowed up.
Thomas Mann's summerhouse and museum.
Traditional weathervanes – unique to the Curonian Spit.
**YOU SHOULD KNOW:**
Cycling is by far the most convenient way of getting around on the Curonian Spit. The bike paths are kept in good repair, making for easy pedalling.

The Curonian Spit is a 98-km (60-mi) long sand bar, a remarkable natural phenomenon created by the combined power of the sea and the wind in a continual cycle of sedimentation and erosion. It is an extraordinarily insubstantial landscape, continually battered by the howling gales of the Baltic Sea, a natural sea-wall of giant shifting dunes up to 60 m (200 ft) tall, held together by pine and birch forests. On its leeward side, it encloses the Curonian Lagoon, acting as a windbreak to ensure a millpond-like calm, in startling contrast to the open sea. The Spit is less than 4 km (just over 2 mi) across at its widest point and 350 m (0.25 mi) at its narrowest. Only the northern 52 km (33 mi) is in Lithuania; the southern section is Russian territory.

From the old port town of Klaipeda you take a ferry across the narrow channel at the mouth of the Curonian Lagoon to the northern tip of the Spit. From here a bike path runs southwards to Nida, the main town, built along the shore of the lagoon. There are several other picturesque hamlets along the way with old churches and traditional brown- and blue-painted tiled-roofed fishermen's cottages, mostly now inhabited by artists and writers.

You find yourself roaming through an eerily beautiful, remote land, crossing endless white-sand beaches and pine-forested dunes, passing old cemeteries where graves are marked by wooden crosses and outdated road signs for half-remembered villages that have been swallowed by the sand. The only sounds are the wind, the sea and the call of birds. A bike ride or walk along the length of the Spit is a wonderfully life-enhancing experience, giving you a heightened awareness of the power of the elements and the fragility of the environment.

*An aerial view of the Curonian Spit*

# The Baltic to Crimea

*An aerial view of typical Russian architecture in Lviv's Ploshcha Rynok*

For anyone in love with the romance of train travel, a journey by rail across Russia, Belarus, Moldova and Ukraine, through cities that have affected the course of European history for more than a millennium, is an eye-opening experience. This vibrant region of Europe, which for the greater part of the 20th century has been inaccessible, is buzzing with a sense of hard-won freedom and a youthful appetite for the future.

From the fabulous imperial city of St Petersburg, take a train down to Moscow then travel westwards through the eerie haunting beauty of the Belarus steppe to Minsk, an old-style Soviet city that now has a certain nostalgic charm, and then to Brest on the Polish border to visit the stupendous Soviet World War II fortress. Travelling southwards into Ukraine, the largest country in Europe, you cross a timeless land of black-earthed wheat fields, copses of silver birch, flower-strewn pastures, and ancient villages to stop at the wondrous World Heritage City of Lviv. Carry on heading south through the startlingly picturesque but little-visited wine country of Moldova – a landscape of rolling hills, tranquil lakes and whitewashed villages – to Odessa, a magnificent Black Sea city founded by Catherine the Great. Next stop is Yalta, a delightful resort on the beautiful Crimean coast and site of the Livadia Palace where Churchill, Roosevelt and Stalin held their fateful 1945 conference to discuss the post-war shape of Europe. Go to the naval base of Sevastopol, steeped in the history of the Crimean War, and visit Bakhchysaray, the 16th century capital of the Crimean khanate. Finally catch a train northwards to bring your journey to an end in the beautiful ancient city of Kiev in the heart of Ukraine.

**HOW:**
By train
**WHEN TO GO:**
May, when the spring flowers are at their height.
**TIME IT TAKES:**
Two weeks
**HIGHLIGHTS:**
St Petersburg – the Hermitage.
Moscow – the Kremlin and Red Square.
Lviv – Ploshcha Rynok, 16th century market square, a World Heritage Site.
Odessa – Potemkin Steps.
Yalta – Chekhov's house.
**YOU SHOULD KNOW:**
A private tour train, The Crimea Express, takes the above route. The advantage of travelling on it rather than ordinary scheduled services is simply the convenience of having the stops organized for you and luxurious accommodation. If you prefer to travel more spontaneously, planning your own itinerary, train services in Eastern Europe are cheap and reliable, especially in Ukraine.

# Golden Ring Towns

The Golden Ring is one of the best-known tourist routes in Russia, a 700-km (440-mi) circular tour of the ancient provincial towns and cities north-east of Moscow. The trip is a spectacular testament to Russia's past. You will see kremlins (fortresses), castles, monasteries, churches and cathedrals dating from the 12th to the 17th century. The fairytale splendour of the onion-domed architecture is fascinatingly unfamiliar to the western eye, and the depth and grandeur of the country's religious heritage is awe-inspiring. It is remarkable that, despite the turmoil of wars, revolution and years of Soviet governance, so much of Russia's spiritual history is still intact.

The journey makes a refreshing change from the noise and pollution of Moscow. Provincial life is surprisingly un-westernized and you will see a completely different side to Russian culture as you travel from town to town through tranquil countryside of cattle pastures, birch forests, fields and lakes.

There are seven main towns on the route. Nearest to Moscow is Vladimir, 12th century Russian capital. Travel on northwards to the rustic tourist town of Suzdal on the Kamenka River, stuffed with monuments; then to Kostromo on the River Volga, famous for

the 16th century Ipatievsky Monastery. Next is the historic city of Yaroslavl and, heading back towards Moscow, the sleepy little towns of Rostov Velikiy, once known as the 'eternal city', and picturesque Pereslavl-Zalesskiy on Lake Pleshcheveyo. The final Ring-town is Sergiev Posad, the 'Vatican' of the Russian Orthodox Church – a famous pilgrimage centre. The Holy Trinity Cathedral's breathtaking blue and golden domes provide a fitting finale to a journey that casts an entirely new light on the historical fabric underlying this influential corner of Europe.

*The Kremlin in Rostov Velikiy*

**HOW:**
By train or car
**WHEN TO GO:**
April to October
**TIME IT TAKES:**
Two weeks
**HIGHLIGHTS:**
Suzdal – St Euthymius Monastery
and Church of the Annunciation.
Sergiev-Posad – World Heritage Site
of Trinity-St Sergius Laura Monastery
and Necropolis.
Rostov – 17th century kremlin, an
architectural masterpiece.
Pereslavl-Zalesskiy – 17th century
monastic architecture.
Yaroslavl – frescoes and ceramics.
**YOU SHOULD KNOW:**
Suzdal and Pereslavl-Zalesskiy can
only be reached by road. The other
towns are all accessible by train.

# The Trans-Siberian Railway

The legendary Trans-Siberian Railway is the greatest train journey in the world, an epic endurance test of nearly 10,000 km (more than 6,000 mi) across the vast Siberian steppe. The journey has such resonance that we have even invented the notion of 'The Trans-Siberian Express' – a mythical train that exists only in imagination. The Trans-Siberian Railway is in fact the collective name given to three routes between Moscow and the East, branching their separate ways at Ulan-Ude near Lake Baikal: the classic line to Vladivostok and alternative routes to Beijing – the Trans-Manchurian line via Harbin and the Trans-Mongolian line via Ulaanbaatar.

The Trans-Mongolian line across the Gobi Desert to Beijing is the usual tourist route. It is the shortest and most scenic. The classic journey from Moscow to Vladivostok is an entirely different experience. Few people travel the entire length of the line and even fewer are foreigners, so you will find yourself completely reliant on your own resources without the camaraderie of other tourists. However, it gives you an entirely authentic experience of this vast country, and with careful pre-planning you can stop off at places of interest on the way. For those who have the stamina to travel without a break, it is still a relief that the train stops every few hours so you can stretch your legs and stock up on food from the platform vendors.

For the first three days, whichever destination you aim for, you cross kilometre upon kilometre of apparently boundless Siberian steppe broken only by intermittent industrialized cityscapes. Whether you end up in Vladivostok or Beijing, the experience will provide you with lasting memories of an incredible journey. This is an epic trip to be undertaken purely for its own sake – for the joy of travelling rather than the anticipation of arrival.

**HOW:**
By train
**WHEN TO GO:**
All year. May to September is the peak time but the trains are well heated in winter and Siberia under snow is an incredible sight.
**TIME IT TAKES:**
One week
**HIGHLIGHTS:**
Yekaterinburg – Obelisk marking the boundary between Europe and Asia, 1,777 km (1,111 mi) from Moscow.
Views of Lake Baikal.
Ulan-Ude – historic Siberian town.
Khabarovsk Bridge – the longest bridge on the railway, 2,950 m (8,500 ft) across the River Amur.
Vladivostok Station – picturesque mock-17th century architecture and the last milestone of the railway.
**YOU SHOULD KNOW:**
A through train goes all the way from Donetsk in Ukraine to Vladivostok – technically the longest train journey in the world. From Vladivostok you can take a boat to Japan. The crossing takes 36 hours.

*The mock 17th-century train station in Vladivostok*

# The Volga-Baltic Waterway

By far the most memorable way of travelling between Moscow and St Petersburg is to take a river cruise along the Volga-Baltic Waterway, an extraordinarily complex network of canals, rivers and inland seas covering a total distance of 1,125 km (700 mi) and linking the mighty River Volga, the longest river in Europe, to the Baltic Sea.

The Volga-Baltic Waterway was part of Peter the Great's grand design. Having moved his capital to the Baltic, he dreamed of sailing from his new imperial city back to Moscow in the heart of the Empire. Construction began in 1709 and continued throughout the 18th and 19th centuries, making it possible to sail all the way from St Petersburg on the Gulf of Finland to Astrakhan on the Caspian Sea. With the completion of the 128 km (80 mi) Moscow-Volga Canal in 1937, Russia's capital was finally linked to this intricate system of canals and rivers.

You sail the Moscow Canal to the River Volga, through the Rybinsk Reservoir and the Mariinsk canal system, around Lake Onega and onto the River Svir to the southern coast of Lake Lagoda, the largest lake in Europe, finally connecting with the River Neva, having passed through 21 locks on your way. The tourist cruisers take a roundabout scenic route with wonderful natural and historic sights – Yaroslavl, a 'Golden Ring' city on the banks of the Volga; the red, blue and golden-domed churches of Uglich; the 14th century Kirillo-Belozersky monastery; the ancient wooden buildings of Kizhi Pogost; the scenic River Svir and beautiful coastline of Lake Lagoda.

By the time you arrive at St Petersburg, a city of haunting magnificence, you are amazed by the imagination and engineering skill involved in creating such a labyrinthine transport route, as well as the sheer size of this perplexing country.

**HOW:**
By boat
**WHEN TO GO:**
May and June are the best months, when everything is in full bloom but it is not yet too humid.
**TIME IT TAKES:**
Ten to thirteen days
**HIGHLIGHTS:**
Moscow Canal.
Yaroslavl – one of Russia's oldest cities.
Uglich – churches!
Kizhi Pogost – island of World Heritage medieval wooden buildings.
St Petersburg – the imperial city.
**YOU SHOULD KNOW:**
The ambitious traveller can travel by water the entire way along the ancient trade route from St Petersburg to Astrakhan, the ancient capital of the Tatars on the Caspian Sea.

*The Church of the Transfiguration in Kizhi Pogost*

*View of the River Dneiper, Kiev*

# River Dnieper to the Black Sea

**HOW:**
By boat
**WHEN TO GO:**
April to August
**TIME IT TAKES:**
Twelve days
**HIGHLIGHTS:**
Kiev – Monastery of the Caves; 11th century caves and tunnels.
Zaporizhzhya – display of Cossack horsemanship and music.
Seeing the backwaters and fishing villages at the river delta.
Yalta – Livadia Palace, Swallows Nest Castle and Chekhov's house.
Odessa – 18th and 19th century architecture.
**YOU SHOULD KNOW:**
You can take another onward boat from Yalta, Sevastopol or Odessa to Istanbul.

The third longest river in Europe, only outdone by the Volga and the Danube, the Dnieper is the lifeblood of Ukraine: vital water source for a country dependent on agriculture, massive hydro-electric power generator, and – not least – commercial corridor, transporting an endless stream of river traffic for the ten months of the year that it is ice-free. Passenger boats regularly ply this majestic river on an unhurried journey between Kiev, the 'Mother of Cities', and Odessa, the 'Pearl of the Black Sea', cruising through the heart of the largest country in Europe – a country steeped in a turbulent history of war and suffering that has somehow, against all odds, retained its distinctive culture and spirit.

After seeing the sights in the 9th century city of Kiev, voyage southwards past scenic forested ravines to Dnipropetrovsk, an old fortress town set in green hills, now a major commercial centre; cruise past the Dneproges Dam – a tour de force of design, one of the seven modern wonders of the world; and stop off at Zaporizhzhya, home of the Cossacks, the legendary warrior horsemen who dominated the southern steppes for four hundred years.

From the wetlands and backwaters of the river delta around Kherson, the boat strikes out along the glorious Mediterranean-like Black Sea coast of the Crimea to Sevastopol, the historic site of the Charge of the Light Brigade; and Yalta, 19th century haunt of the intelligentsia, where the Tsar had his holiday palace and Tolstoy and Chekhov spent their summers. Backtrack across the Black Sea to end your voyage at Odessa, fabled 19th century city of terraces.

# Settle-Carlisle Railway

This was the last great main rail line to be constructed in England, completed in 1876 by the Midland Railway Company after six years of blood, sweat and tears as the builders overcame major natural obstacles to create 116 km (72 mi) of track frequently described as 'the most scenic rail journey in England'. The romantic Victorians and Edwardians certainly thought so, as they loved taking this picturesque route when heading north for their annual summer holidays – using a through service from London to Scotland that lasted until 1977.

Those skilled 19th-century railway engineers built 14 tunnels and 17 major viaducts to create a route through the magnificent Yorkshire Dales, on through the lush, gently rolling hills of the Eden Valley with its charming villages and traditional market towns to Carlisle, gateway to Scotland. Their work has proved enduring, as the Settle to Carlisle line still has regular scheduled services much used by locals, as well as discerning tourists drawn by the opportunity to view some of the country's finest scenery from the comfort of a train seat.

The full journey actually begins in Leeds, with its connection to the intercity rail network. Also, the so-called 'Lancashire Dales Rail' service runs on many Sundays between the beginning of May and mid-October, offering a through trip from Blackpool via Preston and Blackburn on to Settle and Carlisle. This has associated guided walks and coach trips from certain trains to beautiful parts of the North Pennines and Yorkshire Dales. For those drawn by the romance of bygone travel, charter trains with vintage carriages – pulled by classic steam locomotives – regularly do the Settle to Carlisle run (usually as part of a longer journey). But whichever way you choose to go, it will be an experience to treasure.

**HOW:**
By train
**WHEN TO GO:**
April to October to see the countryside at its best.
**TIME IT TAKES:**
Just under two hours (Settle-Carlisle) or two-and-a-half hours (Leeds-Carlisle).
**HIGHLIGHTS:**
The amazing 24-arch Ribblehead Viaduct between Dent and Ribblehead.
The long tunnel beneath Blea Moor – as the train enters the southern entrance it passes under Force Gill Aqueduct that carries a stream over the line.
Delightful Appleby Station – built by the Midland Railway as one of the major stations on the line – spot the water tower and crane that service steam specials.
The Eden Lacy Viaduct between Langwathby and Lazonby, for as fine an English landscape view as you'll ever see.
**YOU SHOULD KNOW:**
When the Government proposed closing the line in 1988, a petition with the signatures of 32,000 protesters resulted in a change of mind.

*A train crosses the Ribblehead Viaduct.*

# The Ferry to Orkney

**HOW:**
By boat
**WHEN TO GO:**
May to September
**TIME IT TAKES:**
From 40 minutes (John o' Groats-Burwick) to six hours (Aberdeen-Kirkwall).
**HIGHLIGHTS:**
The famous waterside stack known as The Old Man of Hoy (take the Scrabster crossing for a sea view).
Scapa Flow Visitor Centre on Hoy, for fascinating insight into this great haven for the British Navy, where the German World War I High Seas Fleet was scuttled in 1919.
Magnificent St Magnus Cathedral in Kirkwall, begun in 1137 by Earl Rognvald – the most obvious reminder (among many) of Orkney's Norse heritage.
The Heart of Neolithic Orkney – a UNESCO World Heritage Site in West Mainland that includes some of the oldest and best-preserved Neolithic sites in Europe.
**YOU SHOULD KNOW:**
The world's shortest scheduled air service at two minutes is between the islands of Westray and Papa Westray – just a minute if the wind is right!

*The Standing Stones of Stennes, Orkney's oldest stone circle*

Sometimes the journey's the thing, other times it's the destination that counts – but when you sail to Orkney you get the best of both. This group of 67 islands is off Scotland's northeastern tip and 20 are inhabited, with most people living on Mainland, the largest island and home of Kirkwall, the administrative centre. Orkney is well served by air, but the way to go is by ferry for a scenic journey on the ocean wave (which, be warned, can be quite high). There is a choice of services.

From Aberdeen (to Shetland, calling at Kirkwall four days a week) a car ferry follows the coast past Peterhead, the gas terminal at St Fergus, Rattray Head lighthouse, Fraserburgh and Kinnaird Head, before heading out to sea. Land is sighted at Wick on the Caithness coast, before Duncansby Head lighthouse and Orkney – passing South Ronaldsay and East Mainland before docking in the Bay of Kirkwall.

The most scenic is the 90-minute crossing from Scrabster, near Thurso. The large MV *Hamnavoe* starts from the low cliffs near Holborn Head lighthouse, before crossing the Pentland Firth, where the Atlantic meets the North Sea head-on. Landfall is at Rora Head on the island of Hoy, after which the route passes through Hoy Sound with Graemsay to the right and round into Hamnavoe Inlet to dock at the picturesque port of Stromness on West Mainland.

For a cheap 'n' cheerful journey by the shortest, least expensive and most sheltered route, the hour-long car-ferry dash from Gills Bay to St Margaret Hope on South Ronaldsay is the one to choose.

In summer there is a short passenger ferry crossing from John o' Groats to Burwick on South Ronaldsay, usually taken in conjunction with various guided tours of Orkney that are offered as part of the service.

# North Yorkshire Moors Railway

Lovers of steam will be beguiled by this 29-km (18-mi) line, especially if they also appreciate the Yorkshire Moors. For those who just love wonderful landscapes, it is possible to travel the line in a train pulled by a heritage diesel loco – but how much better to take one of the steam trains that not only delivers scenery, but also nostalgic transport back to a bygone era?

The North Yorkshire Moors Railway (NYMR) runs from Pickering to Grosmont, from whence onward travel to Whitby is now available by steam train – a popular extension. The NYMR is a charitable trust, with trains mainly staffed by dedicated volunteers. From Pickering, trains run via Levisham, Newton Dale and Goathland to Grosmont.

Pickering station has been restored to 1937 condition, with wonderful period detail. Levisham is in pretty Newton Dale, two miles from the village it serves, and now represents a small North Eastern Railway station from around 1910. Newton Dale Halt is a remote request stop in splendid countryside, mainly used by walkers. Goathland was built in 1865 and is almost unchanged, now restored as a country station from the 1920s. Grosmont represents the British Rail era of the 1950s, where through travellers change for the charming old fishing port of Whitby.

The NYMR timetable is complex, in that not all trains from Pickering to Grosmont have an onward connection to Whitby. However, special Grosmont Day Rover or Whitby Day Rover tickets allow unlimited travel all day, permitting the journey to be broken by anyone who wishes to explore interesting diversions along the way.

Grosmont is also on the Esk Valley Line from Middlesbrough to Whitby, one of the most scenic rural lines in England, and this journey also offers fabulous scenery – trains are modern, though steam specials are run.

*The nostalgic North Yorkshire Moors steam train*

**HOW:**
By train
**WHEN TO GO:**
April to October (limited weekend service in winter).
**TIME IT TAKES:**
From Pickering to Grosmont takes 65 minutes, plus 20 minutes to Whitby.
**HIGHLIGHTS:**
In the busy market town of Pickering – an ancient castle and the Beck Isle Museum of rural life, also featuring superb old photographs of the town, its people and surroundings.
Goathland Station – recognize it from regular appearances in the TV drama series 'Heartbeat' (Aidensfield) and Harry Potter films (Hogsmeade).
Visiting artist-in-residence Christopher Ware – his studio at Levisham station is open whenever trains are running (and some other times too).
A visit to the engine sheds at Grosmont to see the old locomotives that are being painstakingly restored.
**YOU SHOULD KNOW:**
The Grosmont Tunnel is believed to be the oldest railway tunnel in the world, built in the 1830s when carriages and wagons on the line were horse-drawn.

*Boats moored at Ambleside, on the shore of Windermere*

# Lake Windermere

**HOW:**
By boat
**WHEN TO GO:**
April to October for summer services (winter services are limited).
**TIME IT TAKES:**
Just over an hour for the full length of the lake.
**HIGHLIGHTS:**
Windermere Steamboats Museum at Bowness, with a collection of craft that tell the story of lake cruising from its inception in the 19th century – don't miss Beatrix Potter's rowboat.
The Aquarium of the Lakes, a unique freshwater aquarium on the southern shore of Windermere that recreates lake life around the world.
Brockhole Visitor Centre between Windermere and Ambleside, in a mansion with lovely gardens and lake frontage, designed to showcase the attractions of England's largest National Park.
A Windermere cruise plus a return steam journey on the preserved Lakeside & Haverthwaite Railway along the Leven Valley from the south end of the lake – combined tickets available.
**YOU SHOULD KNOW:**
The Lake was originally Winandermere, but the Victorian railway company thought that was too long, called their new station at Birthwaite 'Windermere'...and the name stuck for both town and lake.

England's largest natural lake, set within Cumbria's Lake District National Park, has been a popular holiday destination since 1847, when a branch of the Kendal and Windermere Railway was opened. This magical lake set amidst spectacular fells beneath a big sky has never lost its appeal, surely attracting more visitors now than ever it did during its Victorian and Edwardian heyday.

Windermere is a ribbon lake, some 17 km (10.5 mi) long and never more than 1.6 km (1 mi) wide, stretching from Newby Bridge in the south to Ambleside in the north. Ambleside is one of two towns on the lake, the other being Bowness-on-Windermere, half way along the east bank. Strangely, the town of Windermere does not itself have lake frontage, though it has effectively merged with Bowness, which does.

Although there is a road along the eastern shore of the lake, the best way to enjoy Windermere and its impressive surrounds is from the water.

There are any number of cruises on offer from three main departure points – Lakeside in the south, Bowness in the middle and Waterhead (Ambleside) in the north. A wide variety of options are offered, including travelling from end to end, a return journey from Lakeside to Bowness, a circular islands cruise from Bowness, a return journey from Waterhead to Bowness or circular lake tour from any departure point. All types of cruise boats operate, from large lake steamers, through mid-sized modern launches to smaller traditional wooden launches...and even the occasional vintage steam launch.

It is certainly a busy stretch of water in summer, but all that marine hustle and bustle – set against the majestic grandeur of the unchanging fells and mountains – seems part of Lake Windermere's timeless charm.

# Glasgow to Mallaig

Scotland's West Highland Line is a mighty fine line, especially for lovers of dramatic scenery. The WHL begins at Glasgow's Queen Street Station and takes a while to get going scenically – trundling through suburbs, Dumbarton and Helensburgh before turning north for Garelochhead. It gets up to landscape speed as it passes along the northwestern shore of Loch Lomond and reaches Crianlarich, where a western branch goes to Oban while the northern branch crosses wild Rannoch Moor before arriving at Fort William.

There beginneth one of the world's great scenic railway journeys, starting near Britain's highest mountain (Ben Nevis), crossing Britain's longest inland waterway (Caledonian Canal), visiting Britain's most westerly mainland station (Arisaig), passing Britain's deepest freshwater loch (Loch Morar), Scotland's whitest beach (Morar) and arriving at Europe's deepest sea loch (Loch Nevis). Nothing done by halves around these parts, then!

The train follows the rugged coastline, passing through many tunnels and small stations before reaching Mallaig, 265 km (165 mi) from Glasgow.

You don't have to stop there – ferries link Mallaig to the Kyle of Lochalsh, Armadale, the Small Isles and the Isle of Skye. It's easy to turn a memorable Highlands journey into an unforgettable Highlands and Islands expedition.

It is also possible to marry the romance of steam with that overdose of magnificent Highland scenery, by taking a trip from Fort William to Mallaig and back on The Jacobite, a special service that runs on weekdays between mid-May and mid-October, with added weekend services in July and August. This not only offers the Highland sights, but also the evocative sound of steam...plus a leisurely stop at Glenfinnan where Bonnie Prince Charlie raised his standard in 1745 and time to explore the thriving fishing community of Mallaig.

**HOW:**
By train
**WHEN TO GO:**
May to October (dour winter weather often obscures the scenery!).
**TIME IT TAKES:**
About five hours (Glasgow-Mallaig), of which the super-scenic Fort William to Mallaig leg takes 80 minutes.
**HIGHLIGHTS:**
Britain's only railway show shed, at Cruach Cutting shortly before the WHL's high point at Corrous Summit on vast Rannoch Moor.
At Banervie, where the WHL meets the Caledonian Canal – the amazing series of canal locks known as Neptune's Staircase.
Crossing the world-famous 21-arch Glenfinnan Viaduct in its truly spectacular setting.
The view from Arisaig Station on a clear day – spot the Small Isles of Rum, Eigg, Muck and Canna, plus the southern tip of Skye.
**YOU SHOULD KNOW:**
Having perversely looped down into Fort William from the northeast, the Glasgow train has to reverse back out of the station the way it came in order to continue the journey to Mallaig.

*Fort William with Ben Nevis in the background*

# London to Edinburgh on The Flying Scotsman

The Flying Scotsman is a rail route, train service and world-famous locomotive, in that chronological order. The route is the 627-km (390-mi) East Coast mainline from London King's Cross to Edinburgh Waverley, created by the combined efforts of three different Victorian railway companies.

*The Flying Scotsman passing magnificent scenery.*

**HOW:**
By train
**WHEN TO GO:**
Any time of year
**TIME IT TAKES:**
Four-and-a-half hours
**HIGHLIGHTS:**
Digswell Viaduct over the River Mimram (also called the Welwyn Viaduct) – a landmark on the East Coast Line between Welwyn Garden City and Digswell.
The long viaduct and splendid view of the magnificent Cathedral from the train window at Durham.
The King Edward VII Bridge crossing over the River Tyne at Newcastle, between the iconic Metro Bridge and Redheugh Bridge.
Arriving at Waverley, the grand (and vast!) Victorian station in the heart of Edinburgh, and going straight out onto the city's premier shopping street, Princes Street.
**YOU SHOULD KNOW:**
The Flying Scotsman locomotive was sold by canny British Rail for £3,000 in 1963 – and bought back by the nation in 2004 for over £2,000,000.

The train service is the modern incarnation of one that began in 1862 as the Special Scotch Express, a daily train each way simultaneously leaving at 10.00. Renamed The Flying Scotsman in 1924, it began a non-stop run between the two capitals in 1928, a journey that reached luxury heights in the 1930s with on-board hairdressing, cocktail bar and a fine restaurant. World War II ended that, but the service survived rail nationalization in 1948, with journey times falling steadily as first diesels and then electric locomotives were introduced. After privatization in 1994, the Flying Scotsman was seen as a flagship asset and it continues running to this day.

The locomotive was built in 1923 and named The Flying Scotsman in 1924, to gain publicity for the newly acquired and recently re-titled service of the same name launched by the London Midland & Scottish Railway. At the end of the steam era it was sold, cashing in on its fame with tours of America and Australia before returning to Britain and ending up in the National Railway Museum in York.

Those wishing to ride a train pulled by this grand old loco will have to wait until completion of a lengthy refurbishment. However, it's still possible to enjoy both the route and the train service by travelling from London to Edinburgh, making a truly historic railway journey via Peterborough, Grantham, Doncaster, York, Darlington, Durham, Newcastle, Berwick-upon-Tweed and Dunbar. Many first-timers take the journey simply to see the magnificent coastal scenery before and after leaving England at Berwick.

# Offa's Dyke Path

Who was Offa, and why his Dyke? The first is easy – Offa was the Anglo-Saxon King of Mercia, the great English kingdom that thrived in the Dark Ages, who ruled from 757 to 796. The next answer is more difficult. We know what Offa's Dyke is – a massive earthwork that roughly follows some of the modern English-Welsh border – but why it was created remains a mystery.

It certainly required effort, being some 103 km (64 mi) long, from Rushock Hill in the south to Llanfynydd in the north – not as once thought stretching from 'sea to sea', completely separating two countries. It consists of a ditch on the Welsh side and rampart on the English side, but patently couldn't be defended like that other great boundary construct, Hadrian's Wall. The best explanation is that the famously belligerent Offa built it because he could, simultaneously – like any top dog – marking his territory. The message to potential enemies was 'look how powerful I am because I can build such a mighty earthwork, so trespass across it at your peril'.

Be that as it may, today Offa's Dyke Path is one of the most attractive National Trails, passing through some of Britain's most beautiful countryside. Although following the full length of Offa's Dyke, it is actually longer than the original, running for 285 km (177 mi) from the Severn Estuary near Chepstow through the tranquil Welsh Marches and on to Prestatyn on Liverpool Bay. Anyone who hikes the Dyke will see high moorland, wide river valleys, lush fields and ancient woodland. Along the way there are historic towns and lonely villages, castles and hill forts, churches and abbeys, together with rich and varied flora and fauna. In short, walking the Path is a wonderful journey of discovery.

**HOW:**
On foot
**WHEN TO GO:**
April to October
**TIME IT TAKES:**
Allow two weeks to hike from end to end, five days for the Offa's Dyke section.
**HIGHLIGHTS:**
The ruined but impressive White Castle on a low hill close to the village of Llantilio..
The ancient settlement of Clun, complete with castle ruins, ancient bridge and medieval houses.
The Offa's Dyke Centre in Knighton, a town that straddles the Dyke and is mainly in Wales but partly in England, for all the information you could want on the Dyke.
Crossing the amazing Pontcysyllte Aqueduct en route to the Welsh coast after Path and Dyke finally part company.
**YOU SHOULD KNOW:**
Much of Offa's ambitious Dyke may have survived for over 1,200 years, but it was historically obsolete early in the 9th century, soon after it was completed.

*Walkers take in the stunning scenery along Offa's Dyke.*

# Wainwright's Coast to Coast Walk

**HOW:**
On foot
**WHEN TO GO:**
May to September to take advantage of the best (if still sometimes unpredictable) upland weather.
**TIME IT TAKES:**
Around two weeks
**HIGHLIGHTS:**
Superb views over Buttermere after the steep climb up Loft Beck.
The Pennine watershed at Nine Standards Rigg – the Nine Standards being nine massive cairns at the summit.
The lovely ridge walk down towards Egton Bridge, ending with a walk along the River Esk and through woods to the pretty village.
Stopping off at Grosmont Station towards the end of the walk – have a refreshing cup of tea and inspect steam engines being restored by the North Yorkshire Moors Railway.
**YOU SHOULD KNOW:**
Wainwright's description is A Coast-to-Coast Walk rather than The Coast-to-Coast Walk, and he encouraged hikers to experiment with diversions of their own devising.

Alfred Wainwright was a great hill walker – and writer on the subject – who devised his most ambitious route in 1973. This 305-km (190-mi) walking trail crosses northern Britain from side to side, from Irish Sea to North Sea. On the way it passes through three National Parks (Lake District, Yorkshire Dales and North Yorkshire Moors) that together offer some of England's finest upland scenery. Thousands hike all or some of this wonderful trail each year, stopping for the night at the friendly bed-and-breakfast establishments to be found in almost every one of the 40-odd hamlets, country villages and small towns along the Walk. Some stay at youth hostels and others with strong backs carry all they need for self-sufficiency and camp as they go.

The Walk is generally undertaken from west to east, starting at the sea cliffs of St Bees on the Cumbrian coast. The first port of call is the Lake District with its incomparable mountain scenery – and plenty of steep paths. After Shap the route crosses undulating farmland until it reaches the Yorkshire Dales at Kirkby Stephen, after which the hilly terrain returns, though the Pennines are not quite so demanding as Lakeland mountains. After Richmond there is another level march across the Vale of Mowbray to Ingleby Cross and from there on to the North Yorkshire Moors. This undulating last stretch over heather-covered hills leads to the North Sea and on to the bustling fishing village of Robin Hood's Bay – journey's end!

Though well recognized, the route is not generally way-marked, so map-reading skills are essential (even with the help of a GPS unit that co-ordinates with Ordnance Survey maps!). It can also be quite demanding in the hillier sections, so the rewarding but energetic Coast to Coast Walk should not be attempted by the unfit.

*Beautiful Lake Buttermere in the Lake District*

# Peddars Way & Norfolk Coast Path

*Windswept salt marshes along the Norfolk Coast Path*

Starting from the delightful little country park of Knettishall Heath near the village of Hopton in North Suffolk, Peddars Way travels through Norfolk for some 74 km (46 mi) to Holme-next-the-Sea, where it meets the Norfolk Coast Path. Together, these two routes form a National Trail that showcases some of East Anglia's most interesting landscapes and striking natural features.

Peddars Way follows the line of an old Roman Road built in AD 61 to help subdue those troublesome Iceni, whose warrior queen Boudicca had been doing a bit too much pillaging. The peaceful way-marked route is a pleasing mix of footpaths, tracks and country lanes that runs through Breckland, a uniquely East Anglian area of forest, heathland and shallow river valleys, before crossing rolling wooded farmland to the sea.

Upon reaching the Norfolk Coast Path there is a choice – left for the western end of the Path at the traditional seaside town of Hunstanton on The Wash, or right for the much longer 80-km (50-mi) stretch to the eastern end at Cromer. Many people choose to check out Hunstanton before retracing their steps, so they walk the whole length of this atmospheric route along North Norfolk's heritage coast, within an Area of Outstanding Natural Beauty.

Here, the sights are low clay cliffs that are under constant assault by the restless sea, abundant wildlife, windswept salt marshes punctuated by gutters and creeks, shifting sand dunes, wide beaches and pretty coastal villages notable for their brick-and-flint buildings, quaint quays and harbours. Finally, at Cromer (famed for crabs and classic pier) the journey ends. Or does it?

In truth, those who can't get enough of East Anglia's distinctive character will find connections to the Weavers Way and Angles Way that continue on through the Norfolk Broads to Great Yarmouth.

**HOW:**
On foot
**WHEN TO GO:**
April to October
**TIME IT TAKES:**
Around eight days
**HIGHLIGHTS:**
Historic Castle Acre with the extensive ruins of a priory and the castle that gives the village its name.
A famous seal colony at Blakeney Point – and the delightful coastal village of the same name.
The magnificent Palladian mansion of Holkham Hall in its parkland setting, plus a fascinating Bygones Museum (mainly summer opening, check times in advance).
The Wells to Morston stretch of the Norfolk Coast Path – one of the most remote and beautiful parts of this distinctive coast, with a wonderful river crossing.
**YOU SHOULD KNOW:**
It is possible to reach the start of Peddars Way by bus from Thetford (to Knettishall Heath) or Bury St Edmunds (to nearby Coney Weston).

# Pembrokeshire Coast Path

If someone said 'I'm off for a stroll from St Dogmaels to Amroth' few people would know what they were talking about – but those who love wild, unspoiled coastline should find out fast. For those places are at opposite ends of one of Britain's best long-distance walks, the 299-km (186-mi) Pembrokeshire Coast Path in West Wales. This splendid National Trail is not only a satisfying walk amidst the rugged beauty of an extraordinary coast, but also a hike through history.

For much of the wilder northern section the Path keeps to clifftops, giving marvellous views of beaches, cliffs and offshore islands, plus abundant seabird life. In spring, there is the added bonus of colourful wildflowers. The section from St Dogmaels to St Davids includes the rocky bay of Witches' Cauldron, Whitesands Bay (from where St Patrick set sail for Ireland), the Norman castle at historic Newport, the old harbour at Lower Fishguard and Porthclais (where St David was baptized).

The middle section to Milford Haven follows the sweeping St Brides Bay that has beautiful beaches, picturesque villages, Marloes Sands with extraordinary multi-coloured cliffs, a little chapel at St Ann's Head and the imposing Victorian fort at Dale Haven.

The southern section is gentler, passing along the shores of Milford Haven's great natural harbour (teeming with birdlife) before reaching some of the finest beaches in Wales – Freshwater West, Broad Haven South, Barafundle Bay and Freshwater East. There's also plenty of commanding cliff scenery, especially numerous stacks and arches on the Castlemartin Peninsula. There is plenty of heritage to enjoy, too, including Pembroke Castle and the village of Angle with its wonderful old church, Fisherman's Chapel, dovecote and medieval tower-house. The charming seaside town of Tenby is a worthy last stop before the Coastal Path ends at Amroth.

**HOW:**
On foot
**WHEN TO GO:**
All year (but winter months are reserved for the hardy!).
**TIME IT TAKES:**
Around two weeks for the complete journey
**HIGHLIGHTS:**
One of the finest Neolithic dolmens (burial chambers) in Wales – Carreg Sampson near the village of Mathry.
The glorious medieval Cathedral and Bishop's Palace at enchanting St Davids – Britain's (and surely the world's) smallest city.
Delightful, unspoiled fishing villages – there are plenty to choose from along the Coast Path, but Solva and Little Haven are two of the prettiest.
The great Norman castle of Manorbier and the Church of St James, in a stunning location near Tenby.
**YOU SHOULD KNOW:**
The last invaders to set foot on British soil were French troops in 1797, who landed at Fishguard Bay but surrendered after two days of drunken looting.

*Broad Haven South on the Pembrokeshire Coast*

# Land's End to John o' Groats

This one is reserved for dedicated charity walkers and bike riders (sponsored or not). It's the longest place-to-place journey in Britain, but there are obviously plenty of dedicated cyclists who seek to join the informal LEJoG Club, as several thousand are thought to undertake this marathon trip – the shortest route is 1,407 km (874 mi) – each year.

The start point at Land's End is the signpost giving the choice of New York or John o' Groats (most people choosing the latter) and the first decision is whether to leave the West Country by using the main A30 road, or choose one of the longer, hillier and scenic routes on minor roads. Such is the nature (and beauty) of this long trip – there is no 'official' route and time available can be balanced against the many sights to be found along the way to provide a customized trip.

After Cornwall and Devon it's into Somerset, through the Cotswolds towards Birmingham and then Staffordshire, where a strategic decision must be made – head due north on the western route, through the Lake District, or tack across to the Peak District and the eastern route through the Yorkshire Dales.

Whichever route is chosen, the intrepid cyclist will cross the line of Hadrian's Wall into the Scottish Lowlands, continue through the scenic Borders and on towards Glasgow (western route) or Edinburgh (eastern route). From there the western route takes in Fort William and the eastern route Aviemore and Inverness (capital of the Highlands) before they converge around Dingwall for the final run up the coast to John o' Groats. There aren't too many alternative roads in the Highlands, but those few are all scenic. John o' Groats is a small village and harbour, and nearby Dunnet Head is actually the most northerly point in mainland Britain.

*Hikers by Ashness bridge in the Lake District*

**HOW:**
By bike or on foot
**WHEN TO GO:**
April to September
**TIME IT TAKES:**
Under three weeks at comfortable cycling speed.
**HIGHLIGHTS:**
The Lake District (western route) or Yorkshire Dales (eastern route). The Grey Cairns of Camster – ancient burial chambers that are remarkably well preserved, but especially stimulating as they're almost at journey's end. Cycling the last 3 km (2 mi) from John o' Groats to Duncansby Head, the true completion of the end-to-end trip at the most northerly point that can be reached by road.
**YOU SHOULD KNOW:**
The record for bicycling from Land's End to John o' Groats is under 45 hours.

*Porthcurno in Cornwall*

# London River Journey

**HOW:**
On foot
**WHEN TO GO:**
Any time (but note that specific tourist services are reduced in winter).
**TIME IT TAKES:**
Around 100 minutes from Putney to Woolwich (end-to-end on the commuter service, including one change).
**HIGHLIGHTS:**
A ride on the riverside London Eye (more correctly the Millennium Wheel) for a bird's-eye view.
The famous clock tower at the Palace of Westminster, housing the world's largest four-face chiming clock – the tower is generally referred to as Big Ben, the name of its main bell.
Tower Bridge, the iconic bascule bridge that is recognized the world over as a symbol of London.
The Tower of London, the beautifully preserved Norman (and later) complex beside the Thames that is one of the world's major tourist attractions.
**YOU SHOULD KNOW:**
The oft-quoted tale of the American entrepreneur who bought London Bridge thinking he was getting Tower Bridge simply isn't true – the reconstructed 1831 original now sits happily at Lake Havasu City, Arizona.

*Big Ben and the Palace of Westminster*

Nearly two million commuters (a number that is rising fast) now travel to work on London's river each year, using stylish catamarans with on-board coffee bars, airline-type seats and bicycle racks for those who pedal on from boat to office. These frequent scheduled services run up the River Thames from Woolwich (which has a free car ferry across the river to North Woolwich) to Waterloo and Embankment in Central London, and downriver from Putney via Chelsea Harbour and Embankment to Blackfriars. Taking both trips will allow the voyager to see the many famous sights along the river.

However, there are some 25 major piers and terminals along the London river, and commuter services are supplemented by a wide variety of tourist boats, most of which offer a running commentary on the sights and history of this vibrant capital city as the Thames weaves its way through the heart of historic London and the chosen journey unfolds. Some of these sightseeing services extend the distances that can be travelled on the river down to the Thames Flood Barrier and up to Kew (for the world-famous Kew Botanical Gardens) and Hampton Court (Henry VIII's wonderful palace).

Most tourist cruises concentrate on the central area, from Westminster Pier (close to the Houses of Parliament and Westminster Abbey), Waterloo Millennium Pier (for the London Eye and South Bank arts complex), Tower Pier (Tower of London) and Greenwich Pier (National Maritime Museum, Queen's House, Old Royal Observatory and former Royal Naval College). It is possible to buy 'hop on, hop off' River Rover tickets that permit travellers to disembark at any pier to explore, before resuming their tour. These are also valid for the Docklands Light Railway, to enhance a day's exploration of the River Thames and its environs.

# London Market Walk

The exhilarating 8-km (5-mi) walk from the shabby chic of Portobello Market to the anarchic hippiedom of Camden Lock by the back way along London's canal paths reveals multifarious aspects of this schizoid metropolis – a city that is all things to all people, where wealth and squalor intermingle in a ferment of styles, cultures and creeds.

After a bit of dawdling among the picturesque antique shops, clobber stalls and costermongers' barrows of Portobello, stroll northwards through Golborne Road flea market, where old London scrap dealers, Portuguese pastry shops and Moroccan food stalls vie for trade, and head towards the Grand Union Canal.

Trellick Tower looms menacingly ahead – a 31-storey award-winning, ferro-concrete monolith, an undisguised homage to 1970s urban nihilism. In a triumph of London spirit over adversity, at its foot are lovingly tended community gardens. Escape onto the canal towpath, a haven of rural calm after the bedlam of the market – the occasional narrow boat chugging past, swans drifting serenely in pairs, a lone resident heron in graceful flight. Walk eastwards and, suddenly, the abandoned concrete cityscape morphs into another world – the graceful Victorian villas, brightly painted narrow boats and weeping-willow trees of Little Venice.

Where the Grand Union ends, at the shiny steel wharves and gleaming commercial buildings of Paddington Basin – icons of post-modern anomie, the Regent's Canal begins. Pick your way across the grimy Edgware Road into dank canal tunnels, under railway bridges, past the ramshackle moorings of motley canal-dwellers to emerge into fairyland: gleaming white stucco Regency palaces, rolling lawns and curtains of greenery trailing into the water. Follow the path to skirt Primrose Hill; cut through London Zoo, and along the backs of elegant early-Victorian terraces. Finally, dive into the sub-culture of Camden Lock – the hippest street market in London – for a shot of revitalizing urban energy.

*Camden Lock Market*

**HOW:**
On foot
**WHEN TO GO:**
Any time
**TIME IT TAKES:**
2 to 3 hours
**HIGHLIGHTS:**
Electric Cinema, Portobello Road – London's oldest working cinema; a listed art deco building opened in 1910.
Canal mural – an intricate collage depicting birds, boats, water and sky made entirely from rubbish dredged from the canal. A triumph of community enterprise.
Browning's Island, Little Venice – Robert Browning habitually rowed his skiff here to compose his poetry under the weeping willow trees.
London Zoo Aviary – designed by Lord Snowdon.
Primrose Hill – panoramic view over London.
**YOU SHOULD KNOW:**
A good alternative to walking the whole way is to catch the waterbus that leaves every half hour from Paddington Basin to Camden Lock – a delightful boat ride through Maida Hill tunnel and past London Zoo.
The Portobello Market operates on Fridays and Saturdays throughout the year.

227

# Ferry Across the Mersey

The short but impressive River Mersey runs for just 113 km (70 mi) from Stockport in Greater Manchester to the sea in Liverpool Bay, for some of its length now merged with the Manchester Ship Canal. It is the historic boundary between the counties of Lancashire and Cheshire and – perhaps more significantly – the river has played a huge part in shaping the character and fortunes of the great northern port city of Liverpool.

Its wide estuary is constricted as the Mersey passes between Liverpool and Birkenhead. There, it may be crossed by two road tunnels and a railway tunnel dating back to 1880 – but by far the most famous way of crossing the river is on the Mersey ferry, which runs from George's Landing Stage at the Pier Head in Liverpool to the terminals of Woodside in Birkenhead (opposite the Pier Head) and Seacombe in Wallasey on the Wirral Peninsula bank. There are triangular River Explorer Cruises with informative commentary that take in all three terminals and some of the river towards New Brighton.

But the real experience is the simple Ferry Cross the Mersey, as immortalized in song by Gerry and the Pacemakers as part of the 1960s explosion of musical creativity in Liverpool known as Merseybeat. There was a hit single, album, film, musical plus several cover versions of this well-known song – and the self-same ferries that inspired it are still running today. The three ferries are *Royal Iris of the Mersey*, *Snowdrop* and *Royal Daffodil* (originally *Mountwood*, *Woodchurch* and *Overchurch* after post-war housing developments in Birkenhead when launched in the late 1950s, all renamed after major refits in the 1990s). Ride one of these on the short river crossing and enjoy a wonderful view of the thing that made Liverpool great – its waterfront.

*The ferry heads
towards Liverpool.*

# London to Birmingham by Grand Union Canal

Once an important commercial artery endlessly travelled by barge families who lived in cramped quarters aboard narrowboats that transported a huge variety of goods between the two great cities, initially pulled by horses and later propelled by chugging engines, the Grand Union Canal fell into disuse as the roads conquered all. In fact, despite the 18th- and early 19th-century origins of its component canals, the Grand Union is a relatively recent creation, formed by canal company mergers in 1929 in an ultimately doomed attempt to remain competitive.

Happily, this great engineering feat, with 166 locks on the main 220-km (137 mi) waterway (there are also various arms) has been revived by modern leisure interest, and it is now possible to make the signed towpath walk from Little Venice near Paddington in London into the heart of Birmingham. This not only offers a tranquil (and level!) hike through some beautiful countryside, but also passes some splendid canal architecture. From London, the Grand Union climbs into the Chiltern Hills, then on past the Northampton arm to Royal Leamington Spa, Warwick and Birmingham.

The same scenic pleasures are, of course, available to those who let a narrowboat do the walking, and make the trip in a manner that most nearly recreates the experiences of those old-time bargees (though accommodation is more spacious nowadays). The self-drive narrowboat is the craft of choice and most end-to-end cruises begin at Brentford, on an arm of the Grand Union that connects to the River Thames. In truth, most canal cruises either do a specific section of the Grand Union, or undertake journeys that include other scenic canals as well, as one thing to remember about canal journeys is that the boat usually has to end up back where it started!

*The Grand Union Canal in Warwickshire*

**HOW:**
On foot or by boat
**WHEN TO GO:**
April to October
**TIME IT TAKES:**
Around a week for the walk, at least five days for an end-to-end cruise.
**HIGHLIGHTS:**
Bull's Bridge Junction near Norwood where the two London arms of the Grand Union join – once the main dockyard of the Grand Union Carrying Company.
A fascinating Canal Museum and the Boat Inn at Stoke Bruerne, an old canal town.
The long tunnels at Blisworth, 2,813 m (1.75 mi), and Braunston, 1,867 m (1.16 mi) – boat only (no towpath).
The fabulous castle and medieval buildings of Warwick – well worth an exploration stop.
**YOU SHOULD KNOW:**
Fenny Stratford Lock near Milton Keynes raises and lowers the canal's water lever by a mere 30 cm (12 in).

229

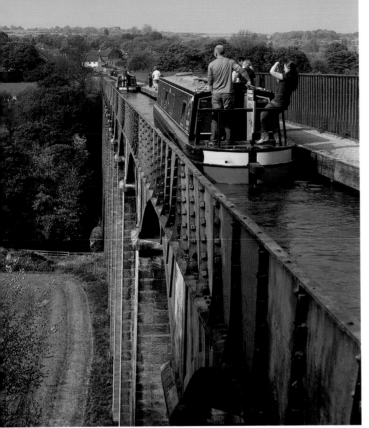

# Llangollen Canal

When canal cruising became popular, the original centre section of the Ellesmere Canal (later part of the Shropshire Union), was renamed the Llangollen Canal – deemed a more appropriate name to underline the wonderful scenery and stunning engineering features of 'Britain's most beautiful canal'. The 66-km (41-mi) route links Llangollen in North Wales to Hurleston in Cheshire, via Ellesmere in Shropshire.

The journey is worth it for two aqueducts alone, though the Canal also passes through wonderful countryside. The amazing 19-arch Pontcysyllte Aqueduct spans the River Dee and 10-arch Chirk Aqueduct crosses the River Ceirog. These were the audacious creations of Thomas Telford and William Jessop in the early years of the 19th century.

Pontcysyllte soars above the Dee Valley to a height of 38 m (125 ft) for a distance of 305 m (1,000 ft). This awe-inspiring engineering marvel certainly deserves its status as a Grade I listed Scheduled Ancient Monument. The water is carried by an iron trough that extends to just 30 cm (1 ft) above the water level, and though there is a towpath on one side, the other is unprotected. When travelling by narrowboat, this leads to the extraordinary sensation of floating through mid-air. The crossing is popular, especially in high summer, with a non-stop procession of boats and walkers experiencing this unique attraction. Chirk Aqueduct is less eye-catching than Pontcysyllte, but an equally clever piece of engineering, with the adjacent tunnel serving as a reminder of the challenges faced by its builders.

From the English end, the Canal passes through lush green countryside with the Welsh hills as a backdrop, then wends its way through foothills and ancient woodland before reaching the final stretch to Llangollen beneath limestone cliffs. Narrowboats are available for hire at Llangollen, Whittington, Trevor and Wrenbury, allowing for a choice of different journeys.

**HOW:**
By boat
**WHEN TO GO:**
April to October
**TIME IT TAKES:**
A week-long round trip along the canal from Llangollen and back involves some 36 hours of actual cruising.
**HIGHLIGHTS:**
Horseshoe Falls – a weir and pumping house on the River Dee near Llangollen built by Telford to supply the canal system with water.
Chirk Castle – a magnificent medieval fortress, the oldest castle built by Edward I that is still inhabited.
Lift bridges – the Llangollen Canal is noted for the number of ingenious lift bridges (operated by the lock key) that often have to be raised before a narrowboat can pass.
**YOU SHOULD KNOW:**
The joints on Pontcysyllte Aqueduct's iron trough are still sealed using the original mixture devised by the builders – a mixture of flannel and lead dipped in liquid sugar.

*The engineering marvel that is Pontcysyllte Aqueduct*

# Three Rivers Ride

This is part of Britain's National Bridle Network, a series of cross-country routes that is being developed for long-distance horse riders. The way-marked 153-km (95-mi) Three Rivers Ride through the glorious Welsh Marches starts at Tidbach near Bromyard in Worcestershire, enters Herefordshire at Wolferlow and crosses the Rivers Lugg and Wye before entering Wales at Hay Bluff and continuing through the Brecon Beacons National Park to the third and final river – the Usk – finally finishing at the Mountain Centre (Brecon Beacons Visitor Centre) near the town of Brecon.

*The Brecon Beacons National Park*

This really is a scenic ride par excellence, with stunning views all the way. It is a journey of two halves. The first section in Worcestershire and Herefordshire offers a peaceful ride past cider orchards and through classic English countryside, across the rapidly flowing River Lugg and along the breathtaking Wye Valley. After crossing the Welsh border the second section runs through a sweeping bank of hills, along the Western flank of the Black Mountains, skirting the picturesque Llangors Lake and crossing the River Usk.

Some riders do the full journey, whilst others prefer to concentrate on the more dramatic mountain scenery of the 56-km (35-mi) Welsh section. The weather in the Brecon Beacons can be unpredictable, and the Path itself is often far from human habitation, so riders are advised to take appropriate all-weather gear and be sure to tell someone their plans before starting out for the day. Don't assume you can rely on a mobile phone to summon assistance if something goes wrong in the remote Welsh hills – there is rarely a signal.

Those who don't have their own horse will find several riding and trekking stables who can provide mounts for the Three Rivers Ride – including sturdy and locally bred Welsh cobs. A selection of bed and breakfast stops for both rider and horse can be found along the route, together with self-catering cottages that have stables.

**HOW:**
On horseback
**WHEN TO GO:**
May to September for the best weather.
**TIME IT TAKES:**
At least a week for the full Ride – more if undertaking side exploration.
**HIGHLIGHTS:**
A bottle of locally brewed farm cider from one of the village shops in Herefordshire – rather stronger than most commercial brews!
Cefn Hill near Hay-on-Wye – for wonderful views of England to one side and of Wales to the other.
Lord Hereford's Knob – a striking hill on the northern edge of the Black Mountains – those who think the name a trifle rude may prefer to use the Welsh *Twmpa*.
**YOU SHOULD KNOW:**
There is a further riding trail at either end of the Three Rivers Ride – the Sabrina Way in England and the Epynt Way in Wales.

# The Ridgeway National Trail

**HOW:**
On foot
**WHEN TO GO:**
April to October
**TIME IT TAKES:**
About a week
**HIGHLIGHTS:**
The White Horse of Uffingham, cut
into the chalk hillside – the oldest
such figure in Britain, dating from
over 3,000 years ago.
Close to the Trail – the private drive
of Chequers in Buckinghamshire,
country home of British Prime
Ministers since 1921.
Getting there – you'll know the walk
is nearly over when you reach the
Boer War Memorial on Coombe Hill.
**YOU SHOULD KNOW:**
Motorcycles and 4 x 4 vehicles can
use stretches of the Ridgeway at the
western end in summer, and tend to
churn up the surface. Horse riders
and cyclists may also use much of
this National Trail.

*Burial mounds on the ancient*
*Ridgeway Trail at Avebury*

This chalk ridge path – a National Trail since 1973 – is known as 'Britain's oldest road', having been in use as part of an ancient trade route from the Dorset coast to The Wash since Neolithic times. Roman, Saxon and Viking armies used the Ridgeway and it became a medieval drovers' road. Following 18th-century Enclosure Acts the Ridgeway – formerly a loose collection of paths heading in the same direction – was consolidated into a single road defined by digging earth banks and planting thorn hedges and trees.

The National Trail runs for 139 km (87 mi) through the counties of Wiltshire, Berkshire, Oxfordshire and Buckinghamshire. It starts at Overton Hill near the prehistoric stone circle at Avebury, within a UNESCO World Heritage Site, then follows the high ground across the open, rolling expanse of the North Wessex Downs to the west of the River Thames. It runs alongside the Thames after crossing at Streatley and continues into the secluded beech woods (carpets of bluebells in spring, spectacular foliage in autumn) and gentle valleys of the Chiltern Hills, ending at the top of Ivinghoe Beacon (from whence the Icknield and Peddars Ways continue on to the North Norfolk coast at Hunstanton).

People have been using the Ridgeway for at least 5,000 years, leaving plenty of evidence of their passing. There are numerous ancient monuments to explore, especially in the western section, including the long barrow of Wayland's Smithy and splendid Iron Age forts such as Segbury Camp, Barbury, Uffington and Liddington Castles. The Ridgeway also follows the Iron Age Grim's Ditch, an 8-km (5-mi) earthwork adjacent to the River Thames. Whilst there will be short sections where the hiker meets other people, travelling the Ridgeway is likely to be a largely solitary experience, with the walker able to enjoy its wonderful landscapes without distraction.

# Isle of Man Steam Railway

Once upon a time there was a considerable network of steam railway lines in the ancient kingdom that is the Isle of Man, but time has taken its toll and only one remains – and that was saved from closure in the 1960s by the Marquis of Aisla, who funded the Southern Steam Railway personally until the Manx Government belatedly took it over as a tourist attraction in the 1970s. A further stretch is currently being restored by enthusiasts, and the Groudle Glen Railway provides a limited summer service along a scenic stretch of line near Douglas.

To travel this delightful line is to step back in history – the journey starts at a classic Victorian Station at the end of North Quay in Douglas, and the trains date back to the 1870s (with rolling stock and seven locomotives maintained in the same local workshops that were always used). Britain's longest narrow-gauge steam railway at 24 km (15 mi) runs from Douglas to Port Erin, via Port Soderick, Santon, Ballasalla, Ronaldsway, Castletown, Ballabeg, Colby, Level and Port St Mary. Several of these stations are request stops and passengers can hop on and off as the fancy takes them.

Each train has an open carriage, plus closed first- and second-class carriages. It's a case of 'first come, first served' when it comes to obtaining seating, with no premium fares. The route passes through pleasant countryside with distant sea views, climbing out of Douglas to a summit at Santon Station, before descending steeply towards Ballasalla with good views of sea-cliffs. The line then runs on across beautiful rolling farmland to the delightful seaside town of Port Erin, which has a Steam Railway Museum adjacent to the station.

*Beyer Peacock steam railway*

**HOW:**
By train
**WHEN TO GO:**
Mid-March to October
**TIME IT TAKES:**
About 45 minutes from end to end
**HIGHLIGHTS:**
The ancient Cistercian Monastery of Rushden Abbey at Ballasalla – recently restored and now with an interpretive visitor centre.
Milner's Tower on Breda Head, overlooking the bay at Port Erin – built in 1871 to represent a lock in honour of local benefactor William Milner, a Liverpool safemaker.
In Castletown – Castle Rushen, probably the finest medieval castle in the British Isles.
Ronaldsway Halt – close to the Isle of Man Airport, making this one of the few places in the world where one can travel from airport to town by steam railway.
**YOU SHOULD KNOW:**
There are other worthwhile railway journeys on the island – the Manx Electric Railway on the east side (Douglas to Ramsey tramway), the Snaefell Mountain Railway and Great Laxey Mine Railway.

# South West Coast Path

**HOW:**
On foot
**WHEN TO GO:**
Any time, though the weather is best between March to October.
**TIME IT TAKES:**
About eight weeks for the entire Path.
**HIGHLIGHTS:**
Somerset and North Devon – the Great Hangman (England's highest cliff), Braunton Burrows (England's largest sand dune system), historic Clovelly (England's most quaint village?).
Cornwall – Tintagel (of King Arthur fame), St Ives, Polperro (a classic fishing village).
South Devon – Slapton Sands (wonderful beach and adjacent freshwater lake), Dartmouth (historic port), Jurassic Coast (fossils in eroded cliff faces).
Dorset – Lyme Regis (the Cobb breakwater featured in *The French Lieutenant's Woman*), Chesil Beach (a long shingle spit).
**YOU SHOULD KNOW:**
As you hike through Westward Ho! you'll be visiting the only place in the British Isles with an exclamation mark in its name.

First trodden by vigilant excisemen who needed to see into every cove and bay in their unrelenting battle with smugglers, the South West Coast Path is a National Trail that hugs some of the most precious coastline in Britain, recognized by the formal status afforded to much if it – the Path goes through World Heritage Sites, National Parks, Areas of Outstanding Natural Beauty, Sites of Special Scientific Interest, a UNESCO Biosphere reserve, past offshore bird reserves... and of course follows a number of designated Heritage Coasts.

This is Britain's longest footpath, stretching for 1,014 km (630 mi) from Minehead in Somerset along the coasts of North Devon, Cornwall, South Devon and Dorset to Poole Harbour. The number attempting the whole path is small, but many hike individual sections or complete the full length in different visits over the years. Those willing to undertake the ultimate challenge must be fit – with all those undulations, walkers who take on the entire path will climb a total of some 27,000 m (88,500 ft) – that's three times the height of Mount Everest – cross 17 large rivers, 300 bridges, 900 styles, skip up 27,000 steps and pass 2,500 way-marks. An epic undertaking indeed!

The West Country is Britain's most popular holiday destination and – whilst there is beautiful countryside and many inland attractions – the real draw is the ocean, the dramatic coastline it sculpted and the heritage created by those who sought to make a living from the sea over countless centuries. Those who walk the length of the South West Coast Path will be rewarded by seeing it all – an extraordinary variety of terrain, dramatic landscapes, seascapes, breathtaking coastal vistas, bustling towns, quaint harbours, delightful villages, beautiful beaches, assorted wildlife and more. It really is the journey of a lifetime.

*An aerial view of Chesil Beach*

# Channel Tunnel by Eurostar

A tunnel linking England and France was first dreamed up around 1800, but Napoleon's rampages and invasion fears put an end to that. In fact, it took nearly two centuries for the dream to become reality, with the opening of the Channel Tunnel in 1994. Known in France as Le Tunnel sous la Manche or simply Le Tunnel, this 50-km (31-mi) double rail tunnel runs from Folkestone to Calais and handles both vehicle shuttle trains plus high-speed passenger services.

The latter are run by Eurostar, offering a fast journey at up to 320 kph (200 mph) between the city centres of London and Paris. With the (somewhat belated) completion of the high-speed line at the English end, it is now possible to take a day trip from one great capital to the other, to do business, shop or just look around.

From London, this stylish journey begins at the excellent new terminal within the magnificent, refurbished Victorian station of St Pancras. There, travellers find everything they need (such as a ticket office, currency exchange, newsagent, cafés and lounges) and some things that are more about setting the mood (like the Champagne Bar). Passengers may carry baggage straight onto the sleek, ultra-modern trains prior to their journey. After speeding through the English countryside via Ebbsfleet International and Ashford Stations, Eurostar shoots through the Tunnel before racing across France via Lille to Paris Gare du Nord. It's a great railway journey that everyone should do at least once.

There are different classes available – Business Premier, Leisure Select and Standard – and Eurostar regularly wins awards for the all-round quality of service it offers. As a result, the service is heavily used and it is advisable to book in advance to be sure of a seat on the train of your choice.

*The Champagne Bar at St Pancras – a fantastic 90 m (295 ft) long*

**HOW:**
By train
**WHEN TO GO:**
Any time of year (but who can resist Paris in the Spring?)
**TIME IT TAKES:**
The fastest London-Paris journey time is two-and-a-quarter hours.
**HIGHLIGHTS:**
A great view of the Dartford Crossing high-level bridge over the River Thames.
The old tunnel-boring machine on display near the English end of the Channel Tunnel.
Crossing beneath the English Channel in just 20 minutes (the ferry on the ocean wave above takes much longer!).
**YOU SHOULD KNOW:**
The American Society of Civil Engineers has included the Channel Tunnel on its prestigious list of Seven Wonders of the Modern World.

# Venice Simplon-Orient-Express

Sadly, one of the great rail journeys of all time – the Orient Express between Paris and Istanbul – ended in 1977 after reaching a peak of perfection in the 1930s when the crème de la crème of society, spies, film stars and the odd femme fatale used this famous service to cross

*One of the beautifully restored carriages*

Europe. The modern Orient Express is less glamorous – a practical, workmanlike sleeper from Strasbourg to Vienna.

Happily, the atmosphere of the original may be recaptured by taking the Venice Simplon-Orient-Express, which offers an old-fashioned leisure experience as it conveys pampered passengers from London to Venice in the lap of luxury. The first leg from London Victoria uses vintage British Pullman carriages, and after a swift trip through the Channel Tunnel the journey to Venice continues using original cars from the old Orient Express, clad in distinctive blue-and-gold livery.

As the train makes its way across France, via Paris, passengers relax in private compartments attended by a personal steward, before cocktails and dinner prepared under the direction of a top French chef. Afterwards, passengers congregate in the bar car, listening to the baby grand piano's tinkling ivories and making new friends. Then it's time to return to a compartment that has been transformed into a bedroom.

Morning sees the train amidst the Swiss Alps as breakfast is served in the compartment. The morning is spent in the bar car drinking coffee and admiring the passing Austrian scenery as Innsbruck comes and goes, before a three-course lunch is served. Then it's back to the bar car as the Italian Dolomites appear, before afternoon tea in the compartment. After crossing the Brenner Pass and passing Verona, just as people are thinking they could get used to travelling like this, the Orient Express crosses the Lagoon and pulls into Venice's Santa Lucia Station.

**HOW:**
By train
**WHEN TO GO:**
March to November
**TIME IT TAKES:**
Two days
**HIGHLIGHTS:**
Eating fine food served in meticulously restored period dining cars where fine linen, silver cutlery and crystal glassware are the norm.
A leisurely visit to the on-board boutique to spend a little pocket money.
Spectacular mountain scenery as the Orient Express passes through the Alps and Dolomites.
**YOU SHOULD KNOW:**
In 1934 fictional detective Hercule Poirot was forced to exercise his little grey cells to solve a murder on the Orient Express (a train which writer Agatha Christie had taken in 1928).

# London to Australia

Since hippies were invented (and gap years became popular), the scenic route from London to Australia has been well trodden by itchy feet. Of course it can be flown in a mere 22 hours, but the scenic overland route is a lot more fun – either going alone or with an organized group.

A classic journey involves travelling from London (by public transport or hitchhiking) through France, Belgium, Germany, the Czech Republic, Austria, Hungary, Romania, Bulgaria, Turkey, Iran, Pakistan, India, Nepal, Myanmar, Thailand, Malaysia, Indonesia, East Timor and (finally!) on to Darwin, Alice Springs, Adelaide and Sydney. The beauty of travelling alone or with a few companions is the fact that there are almost infinite possibilities for varying the route and taking interesting side trips – indeed, an essential part of this rewarding experience is remaining flexible and seeing where the fickle finger of fate points.

However, there are also advantages in joining a pre-arranged bus trip. This choice is good for anyone who has a firm schedule to keep, as arrival is guaranteed after a set period (usually three months), or worries about being on the road alone. It is also ideal for those who enjoy being part of a like-minded group, sharing chores, laughs, companionship and anything else that occurs en route. Also, the itinerary will be planned to provide the maximum number of highlights, including exotic places like the Mount Everest base camp that might not be easy for lone travellers to reach.

The ease of group travel must be set against the loss of freedom to play it by ear and stay or go on as the mood dictates, which many regard as the very essence of this adventurous journey from the top to the bottom of the world. But whichever way you choose it will be the experience of a lifetime.

**HOW:**
By bus/train/boat
**WHEN TO GO:**
Any time
**TIME IT TAKES:**
Three to six months depending on stops along the way.
**HIGHLIGHTS:**
Dracula's Castle in the Transylvanian Mountains of Romania – once the home of fearsome Vlad the Impaler.
Tabriz in the north of Iran – a city of stunning blue mosques and the sort of lively bazaars that are such an essential part of the journey.
World-famous Bagan in Myanmar (formerly Burma) – once capital of the powerful Burmese Empire, featuring literally thousands of amazing temples.
Approaching journey's end – Uluru (formerly Ayers Rock) near Alice Springs in the centre of Australia.
**YOU SHOULD KNOW:**
A certain element of pre-planning is required – many countries require visas that cannot be obtained upon arrival.

*The stunning sight of Uluru as you approach journey's end.*

# Cross the Atlantic on a Cargo Boat

**HOW:**
By ship
**WHEN TO GO:**
April to October
**TIME IT TAKES:**
About two weeks
**HIGHLIGHTS:**
Sunsets at sea.
Being up on the Bridge.
Spotting a whale.
Entering New York Harbor.

In a post-modern age of counting carbon footprints, freighter-travel is about as eco-friendly as it gets, short of a rowing boat. Cargo ships are the life-line of the global economy, transporting containers of goods all over the world. Although they do carry passengers, freighters don't advertise themselves. To book a passage you must be prepared to do plenty of research and be dedicated to the idea of a cryptic adventure into the unknown.

Of all the trade routes, the Trans-atlantic crossing is perhaps the most romantic, harking back to the belle époque, era of the ocean liner. The prospect of crossing the bleak immensity of the Atlantic without any organized on-board entertainment may seem a challenging one, but if you are self-reliant yet

*A container ship enters New York Harbor.*

congenial then a freighter is the ideal way to travel. There is enormous pleasure to be had in wandering between decks, mucking in with the crew, or just sitting outside your cabin reading *Moby Dick*.

On the voyage to New York from Tilbury, London's container port, there comes a point, after the ship has weighed anchor at Rotterdam and Le Havre and there is only ocean ahead, when you may fleetingly feel stir-crazy; until the mesmerizing effect of the sea suddenly makes you aware of your own insignificance in comparison to the immensity of nature and you start to experience a joyful sense of liberation from mundane responsibilities.

After days of nothing but sea and sky, the sight of the Statue of Liberty is both elevating and humbling. As you step down the gangplank into the Land of the Free, you cannot help sparing a thought for the countless numbers who made this crossing before you, at the same time as wondering how anyone could possibly be so foolhardy as to attempt it in a rowing boat.

# Antrim Coast Road

**HOW:**
By car
**WHEN TO GO:**
Any time of year – winter weather tends to be relatively mild, though often wet.
**TIME IT TAKES:**
A mere hour non-stop – but if you don't linger to enjoy some of the many attractions along the way you're not human.
**HIGHLIGHTS:**
Glendun's magnificent viaduct bridge by engineer Charles Lanyon, built in 1832 – a fine example of the engineering genius required to construct the Antrim Coast Road.
Near Ballypatrick – Loghareema, the vanishing lake...after rain it fills to a considerable depth but a few days later is empty again.
A worthwhile detour in Ballypatrick Forest Park – a loop around Carneighaneigh Mountain (don't miss the Megalithic burial chamber).
Culfeightrin Church at Ballyvoy – complete with exotic palm in the graveyard and large standing stone next to the door.
**YOU SHOULD KNOW:**
The Londonderry Arms is a delightful old coaching inn (now a welcoming traditional hotel) at Carnlough once owned by Winston Churchill.

*Red Bay in the Glens of Antrim*

With an end to the Troubles in Northern Ireland – when Protestant and Catholic activists squaring up to each other frightened away outsiders for several decades – the economy has boomed, especially tourism. It's hardly surprising – Ireland is a delightful country, and the North has its share of fabulous scenery. This is especially true of Northern Ireland's rocky coastline, and the best way to appreciate that is to take a leisurely drive along the Antrim Coast Road, unquestionably one of Ireland's most scenic drives.

This is part of the A2 road, which actually begins in Newry in County Down and runs through Belfast and on to Derry City. The two-lane Antrim Coast Road section was constructed in the 19th century to open up the hauntingly beautiful but then-isolated Glens of Antrim, and is quite an engineering feat. It starts at Larne, then follows the coast through Ballygalley, Glenarm, Carnlough, Waterfoot and Cushendun, where it leaves the sea for an inland stretch before rejoining the water at Ballycastle to complete the journey. However, it is possible to stay with the coast by turning off the A2 at Cushendun and finding Torr Road, a very narrow and winding road that will return you to the A2 at Ballyvoy. This detour delivers truly awesome coastal views, though you will miss the enchanting Ballypatrick Forest Park on the main road. Tough choice!

No denying it, the Antrim Coast Road is stunningly beautiful. Not only does it offer ever-changing vistas of this extraordinary coast, but it also passes glacial valleys, sandy beaches, wooded glens, waterfalls, picturesque villages and ancient sites. Taken together, it all adds up to a very special journey that becomes not only a magnificent scenic drive but also a fascinating voyage of discovery.

# Bushmills to Benone

This well-marked coastal cycle journey officially begins at the famous Giant's Causeway, just outside Bushmills in County Londonderry. The North Atlantic Coast section of the National Cycle Network Route 93 then runs beside the sea for some 32 km (20 mi) to Castlerock.

Bushmills is the first town along the way, after following the tracks of Northern Ireland's only heritage steam railway. Beware – before continuing along the cycleway it's very tempting to visit the famous distillery and take a glass or two of the finest Irish whiskey. Providing the hospitality doesn't get out of hand, the resumed ride passes Dunluce Castle, where the limestone cliffs of the White Rocks end in a dark basalt outcrop crowned by this ancient castle joined to the mainland by an arched walkway, beneath which lies Mermaid's Cave.

It's hard not to pause at either Portrush (built out on the peninsula of Ramore Head) or nearby Portstewart (with the wonderful long beach of Portstewart Strand). These two coastal resorts enjoy wonderful natural settings and have a full range of facilities. From Portstewart Route 93 drops down to the large, bustling town of Coleraine at the mouth of the River Bann. There's no avoiding the crowded streets, because this is the first point at which it's possible to cross the impressively wide river, but that's no bad thing – the town has a fine central square.

After Coleraine, the cycleway follows the river to the seaside village of Castlerock. The North Atlantic Coast section actually ends here, as Route 93 turns away from the sea towards Limavady, so many cyclists simply return to their start point along the main A2 coast road. However, before doing that it's worth going on through Downhill to Benone Strand, one of the longest beaches in Northern Ireland.

**HOW:**
By bike
**WHEN TO GO:**
May to September
**TIME IT TAKES:**
A leisurely three hours end to end.
**HIGHLIGHTS:**
The Giant's Causeway itself – the amazing grouping of interlocking basalt columns that are one of Ireland's most famous (and impressive) natural features. Mountsandel Forest near Coleraine, containing the ancient site of Mount Sandel Fort – said to be the oldest site of human habitation in Ireland. The ruined mansion at Downhill built by Frederick Hervey, Earl of Bristol and Bishop of Derry in the 1770s – see also the circular Mussenden Temple, his library.
**YOU SHOULD KNOW:**
Bushmills is the world's oldest legal distillery, founded under licence from King James I in 1608.

*White Rocks near Portrush*

# Carrick-a-Rede Rope Bridge

**HOW:**
On foot
**WHEN TO GO:**
March to October
**TIME IT TAKES:**
At least two minutes
**HIGHLIGHTS:**
Fabulous views from Carrick Island across to Rathin Island and Scotland. Abundant seabird life around the rocky coastline, plus unique geology, flora and fauna to be found within this Site of Special Scientific Interest. A relaxing cup of tea in the tearoom after completing that daring return journey across the bridge.
**YOU SHOULD KNOW:**
There is a small charge for crossing the bridge, levied by the National Trust – though some suggest they should be paid for trying it!

Only those with the strongest head for heights should make the swaying journey across the rope bridge at Carrick-a-Rede near Ballintoy in County Antrim. Mind you, it's not quite as perilous as it was until recent years, when this rope suspension bridge from the mainland across to tiny Carrick Island consisted of widely spaced wooden slats and a single-strand handrail. At least the modern bridge is a little more substantial, having been rebuilt as a Millennium project by local rock climbers.

It is at the end of a short footpath that offers wonderful coastal vistas, and crosses a chasm that is 23 m (75 ft) deep (don't look down!) between the mainland and the small T-shaped island. The bridge itself is around 20 m (65 ft) long with a pronounced dip in the middle. It was traditionally erected by salmon fishermen who laid their nets off Carrick Island but it's now a magnet for visitors – some 140,000 of them every year, drawn by the magnificent scenery and the challenge of crossing the bridge. It can get crowded in high summer, and as only eight people are allowed on the bridge at any one time it is best to go early (it opens at 10 o'clock every morning).

The bridge is now taken down around the end of November and not replaced until the beginning of March, depending on the weather, as attempts to cross during windy winter conditions would be both foolhardy and dangerous. Although there are no reports of anyone actually having fallen from the bridge, it's not always a return journey. Every year a number of people who have made it across to Carrick Island simply can't face a second trip, and have to be taken off by boat.

*Tourists on Carrick-a-Rede Rope Bridge*

*Weathered trees at Ballydowane Cove*

# Copper Coast Drive

This should be in England's West Country, the old centre of tin and copper-mining in the British Isles. But it isn't, because Country Waterford also has its mining heritage – its cliffs were mined for lead, silver and copper in the 18th and 19th centuries. Mining finished in 1880, but the name Copper Coast remains.

The short journey along this magical road from the seaside town of Tramore offers haunting views of the Comeragh Mountains to one side and the wild splendour of cliffs, beaches, coves and caves to the other. The scenery is indeed magnificent, but that's not all there is to enjoy – the road passes through six delightful villages and each has something to offer.

Fenor has peaceful Kilfarrasy Beach, plus forest and lakeside walks and the Bog of Fenor. Annestown is a tiny hillside village, overlooking a scenic valley and wide bay with a sandy beach and rock pools. Dunhill has ancient Stone Age dolmens and a traditional Irish shop and pub that is an ideal refreshment stop, plus a church on the hill – a superb vantage point.

Boatstrand is a picturesque little harbour, with a path to imposing Dunabrattin Head. To the east, beaches and stacks lead towards Sheep Island, whilst to the west successive headlands recede to Helvic Head. Mining Bunmahon's cliffs gave this coast its name, and evidence of this activity may be seen in the cliffs that flank the beach. There is also evidence of an older occupation – the ruined monastery – and a geological garden. The last of these delightful villages is Stadbally, an ancient place with three beaches and a medieval church and tower. The Copper Coast ends at the harbour town of Dungarvan – a journey long to be remembered.

**HOW:**
By car
**WHEN TO GO:**
April to October
**TIME IT TAKES:**
Allow a full day to see the sights.
**HIGHLIGHTS:**
The ruins of Dunhill Castle, destroyed by the hated Oliver Cromwell in 1649.
One of the best coves on the Copper Coast – Ballydowane Cove near Bunmahon.
The cliff-top mining trail at Bunmahon, with the well-preserved remains of a Cornish-style engine house.
Dungarvan Castle, with a shell keep dating from the time of King John, who appointed the first constable in 1215.
**YOU SHOULD KNOW:**
There are 17 designated UNESCO European Geoparks and the only one in the Irish Republic is...the Copper Coast.

# North Mayo Drive

Drama underpins everything about North Mayo, whether it's the rugged landscape or its often-troubled history. Although only a few hours' drive from Dublin or Belfast, it feels light-years removed from them. The area's population is now lower than it was before the potato famine and those who remain are among the hardiest and most welcoming people to be found anywhere.

The 173-km (108-mi) North Mayo Drive takes you in a loop that starts and finishes in the county's largest town, Ballina. A choice of over fifty hostelries awaits you and good simple food is prepared in most of them. The drive, in essence, links ten communities, each with its own distinct feel. In between there is ample opportunity to visit magnificent abbeys or simply wander along any one of many riverside trails.

Driving counter-clockwise, the road hugs the Atlantic coast before turning inland at Belderrig. From there it travels alongside the picturesque Carrowmore Lough, a perfect place to pull over and have a picnic. As the road swings round and you start the journey back towards Ballina, the peaks of the Nephin Beg Range dominate the landscape and the charming town of Bangor Erris demands that you stop and dwell a while. For those wishing to engage in more rugged outdoor pursuits, a well-appointed hiking trail leads off to the mountains.

This drive is a must for anyone who wants to experience the real Ireland. Around every corner there are symbols of martyrdom and sainthood, of suffering and triumph. It is a land of desolate beauty, where the pace is gentle and the *Craic* is at its most genuine.

**YOU SHOULD KNOW:**
Be prepared to be slowed down by agricultural activity on your way – be patient and remember that the gentler pace of life is part of the reason this area is so special.

*A sea stack at Downpatrick Head*

*Heather-covered hills along the Wicklow Way*

# The Wicklow Way

**HOW:**
On foot
**WHEN TO GO:**
Year round; more crowded and better weather from May to September.
**TIME IT TAKES:**
Five to ten days depending on fitness or ambition.
**HIGHLIGHTS:**
The views from Croaghanmoira Mountain.
The boardwalk climb up White Hill.
Byrne's pub in Greenane – traditional Irish hospitality.
Powerscourt Gardens – one of Ireland's treasures
**YOU SHOULD KNOW:**
Ireland's reputation for rainfall is well deserved. A good set of waterproofs is a must. Public transport in the area is pretty infrequent, so forward planning is required. Thankfully most of the hoteliers in the area will offer to take you short distances.

The countryside of Ireland is a collage of many different landscapes, including several mountainous and upland areas. One of the most spectacular of these is in County Wicklow, just south of Dublin. Despite its closeness to the capital, the county contains many large stretches of delightfully unspoilt mountain trails of which the Wicklow Way is the best known. In fact, the Wicklow Way was the first such trail in Ireland, having been formally established in 1980.

The Wicklow Way begins in Dublin's southern community of Rathfarnham and travels in a south-westerly direction across the Dublin and Wicklow uplands, then it goes through the rolling hill country of southwest County Wicklow to finish in the small, County Carlow village of Clonegal some 132 km (82 mi) later.

A mixture of suburban parkland, forest trails, wild and scenic mountain landscape and, finally, gently sloping countryside, the trail offers a wonderfully varied experience for the enthusiastic hill-walker. En route the Wicklow Way passes tarns, ruined buildings, occasional memorials to historic events of past centuries and extensive remains of the early Christian monastic settlement in the stunning Glendalough Valley. The central section is covered by the Wicklow Mountains National Park and its headquarters in Glendalough are well worth a visit.

This is a pleasurable, well-marked trail, with tougher sections of the track graded to prevent erosion. The route occasionally follows the Military Road, constructed by the British in the early 19th century in an attempt to root out rebels hiding in the hills. The only downside of the trail is its reliance on forest paths to avoid walking on private land, which at times limits views. However this does little to detract from the superb scenery, craggy narrow valleys and fabulous hills.

# The Ring of Kerry

The Ring of Kerry is the jewel in the crown of Irish tourism; it is easy to see why visitors return time and again to this 178-km (112-mi) circuit of the Iveragh Peninsula. This is a wild and out-of-the-way region, sparsely populated inland but lined with quaint little towns along the coast. Superb scenery bombards the senses at every turn; rugged mountains, perfectly sculpted by the last ice age 10,000 years ago, frame 120 km (75 mi) of unspoilt beaches.

Several operators offer coach tours, but for those wanting greater flexibility, travelling by bicycle or car is the best option. Starting from Killarney, with the wonderfully named Mcgillycuddy's Reeks (Ireland's highest point) to your left, the first port of call is Killorglin, a town where time has stood still. Replete with traditional Irish fare, it is an excellent place to stock up or simply relax and have a meal. From here on the views get even more spectacular and the road between Glenbeigh and Kells offers the most magnificent coastal scenery.

The area is brimming with history and if you can take your eyes off the natural spectacle, the Ring of Kerry provides fascinating glimpses of the ancient heritage of Ireland – Iron Age forts, Ogham Stones and monasteries abound. The route then hugs the coastal road, offering several chances to cross to the Skellig Islands, a paradise for birdwatchers. The loop takes you through the charming towns of Waterville, Caherdaniel and Castlecove, all of which are worthy of exploration and, if you time it right, the sunsets over the Atlantic can be sensational.

The final stretch runs along the Kenmare River until finally, with the water behind you, the road passes through the wooded Killarney National Park, full of rivers, waterfalls, lakes and wildlife.

**HOW:**
By bike or car
**WHEN TO GO:**
Year round
**TIME IT TAKES:**
It can be done inside a day, but the longer you take the more you see. It is worthy of a least a week of anybody's time.
**HIGHLIGHTS:**
Killorglin – home of the pagan Puck Fair.
The beach at Waterville.
Caherdaniel – Derrynane Estate home of Daniel O'Connell.
The 2,500-year-old Staigue Fort.
Picture-postcard-pretty Kenmare.
**YOU SHOULD KNOW:**
The Ring can get monstrously busy in high season (June to August). Just before and just after these times it is quieter and more rewarding.

*Spectacular scenery in the Ring of Kerry*

# Connemara Coast Trail

**HOW:**
On horseback or on foot
**WHEN TO GO:**
Year round, although horse riding is
generally offered from May
to October.
**TIME IT TAKES:**
Around ten days for the experienced
hiker; horse-riding tours are generally
five to seven days.
**HIGHLIGHTS:**
The ferry ride to Inishbofin Island.
Omey strand – a beach par
excellence.
The views over the Atlantic from
Mace Head.
The smoked salmon – the area
produces some of the finest to be
found anywhere.
**YOU SHOULD KNOW:**
Before setting out you should be
equipped for any weather. Storms
can roll in quickly from the ocean
and disappear just as quickly. Good
waterproofs are therefore a must.

Founded in the late 1980's, the Connemara Coast Trail takes you through a landscape of untamed beauty and serves up the most stunning scenery Ireland has to offer. Refreshed by salty zephyrs from the Atlantic Ocean, the traveller is treated to a wonderful mélange of unspoilt valleys, bogs, shimmering lakes and fabulous mountains. The coast itself is blessed with spectacular rocky inlets and the most magnificent long white sandy beaches.

Connemara translates from Gaelic as 'inlets of the sea' and there are dazzling views that greet you at every twist and turn. The trail presents a good challenge for the experienced rider or hiker and has the added bonus of taking you through the Gaelic heartland of Ireland. Even the smallest of settlements is teeming with Celtic culture and history and whilst you would be hard pushed to find someone who didn't speak any English at all, it is a good idea to have a couple of words of Irish, even if it is only to say hello or order a drink.

At all times the views out to sea and the sight of the brooding Twelve Bens inland both compete for your attention. But even in a place so consistently beautiful, the stretch of the coast between Roundstone and Moyrus stands out. Taking you around the dark recesses of Bertaghboy Bay you are treated to ever changing light as the curving pathway seamlessly changes the view.

The coastal trail and its inland sister trail make up one of the most invigorating outdoor experiences in Ireland. It is home to a community intent on preserving what it has and which takes great pride in showing it off to the rest of the world. Come and enjoy.

*Dawn reflections of the Twelve Bens in Derryclare Lough, Connemara*

# Sligo Yeats Trail

Nothing evokes the spirit of old Ireland better than the sight of horse and rider silhouetted against the setting sun, and there is no better place to ride than the captivating coastline of Sligo, an area steeped in history and blessed with natural beauty.

Many operators cater for those who wish to indulge in what is now called the Yeats Trail. The preferred option for the experienced rider has to be a self guided tour riding between lodgings. A typical tour starts near the exquisite Streedagh Beach, which is your first chance to slacken the reins and experience the gallop of a lifetime along the wonderful long golden sands. If the tides are right it is possible to ride across to the magical Dernish Island, scene of many a shipwreck. A long soak in the bath, a hearty meal and a pint of the black stuff (Guiness) are your rewards at the end of a long day in the saddle.

The new day arrives with the sun rising over the towering rocks of Benbulben. It is time to shake off any saddle-soreness and remount. This stage takes you along small tracks and down country lanes and then on to the magnificent white sands of Trawbawn. It is then but a small climb to the Cullumore cliffs for an amazing view over Sligo Bay.

Having fed and stabled your horse and done the same for yourself, the final leg of the trip takes you towards Ardtarmon Castle, both sumptuous and rich in history. A ride along Lissadell Beach then takes you on the most challenging part of the trip as you climb steadily up the foothills of Benbulben.

**HOW:**
On horseback
**WHEN TO GO:**
Year round, but best in May and June when the wild flowers are in bloom.
**TIME IT TAKES:**
Allow anywhere between a couple of days to a week.
**HIGHLIGHTS:**
The long sandy beaches – the perfect place to ride.
Inishmurray Island – a monastic settlement founded about 500 AD.
Ardtarmon Castle – family home of Countess Markievicz.
Drumcliffe Churchyard – burial place of William Butler Yeats.
**YOU SHOULD KNOW:**
Intermediate to advanced riding skills are required for this trip. Most operators also do not allow children less than 13 years old.

*Galloping along the golden sands.*

*Arran Quay along the Liffey*

# Cruise the Liffey

**HOW:**
By boat
**WHEN TO GO:**
River cruises operate from Easter to September.
**TIME IT TAKES:**
45 minutes on the water but allow a full day to explore the river and its environs.
**HIGHLIGHTS:**
A stroll through Trinity College.
O'Connell Bridge – a world-class structure.
The nearby fish, fruit and vegetable markets – great for people watching.
Dublin Castle – a short walk south from Grattan Bridge.
**YOU SHOULD KNOW:**
The Liffey is subject to high tidal variation. This can affect the route of the river trip and in some instances lead to cancellation, so check before you set out.

No trip to Ireland's resplendent capital is complete without a trip along its iconic river. So much has changed in recent years for this tiger economy of the Eurozone, and nowhere is the transformation better exemplified than along the shores of the Liffey. It was not so long ago that Dubliners referred to their river as 'the slime' and those who walked near it could not help but notice its special aroma. Much effort and money has been put in it to changing this and, as people started to return to living by the water's edge, the river has improved markedly.

Now proud of its river, the city offers cruises through this most magnificent of urban landscapes. Old and new sit side-by-side, offering up a wonderful mix of historical buildings and stunning new architecture. The downstream journey takes you beneath the world famous Ha'penny Bridge while the commentator waxes lyrical on Dublin's past, taking you on a journey through time, from before the Viking invasion to the point where Cromwell first landed through to the present day.

There are great sights to be seen along the way, most notably Trinity College and the Spire in O'Connell Street. However Dublin does not have a waterfront to rival that of London or Paris. To get the full benefit of what the river has to offer, a cruise should form part of a wider walking tour. Using Fleet Street and Abbey Street as your southern and northern boundaries you can cross the Liffey several times and get a most rewarding view of this wonderful city and its fabled river.

# Amsterdam Tram

Unlike their counterparts in many other European cities, citizens of the Dutch capital never lost their trams – but by the end of the 20th century Amsterdam's extensive network was getting tired, with antiquated cars that were constantly out of service for repair. By 2003, a fleet of new Combino trams came into service, with wheelchair-friendly low floors. These sleek blue-and-white trams have become a welcome sight, operating alongside a number of older cars that have been retained.

Riding the trams is an excellent way of seeing Amsterdam for those who don't have time for the water tour, and the Combinos with their large windows provide a great view of 'The Venice of the North'. New trams went hand in hand with a major refurbishment and extension of the network, a work in progress, but the first fruit was the introduction of a new route – Line 26 from Central Station to the new housing developments of IJburg on artificial islands reclaimed from the vast (and equally artificial) IJsselmeer inland sea – the former being yet another example of the Dutch genius for turning water into dry land, and the latter of their ability to turn salt water into fresh.

Line 26 is inevitably known as the IJtram. This 8.5-km (5-mi) route runs mainly through residential areas, rather than amidst heavy city traffic, and includes the 1.5-km (1-mi) Piet Hein Tunnel. Happily for commuters, it is the only tramline in Amsterdam that accepts non-folding bicycles. It also provides an interesting return journey from the city centre, passing the spectacular new Muziekgebouw concert hall, the passenger terminal where cruise ships dock, the Lloyd Hotel and Eastern Docklands, before crossing IJburg's successive islands. This is not a particularly scenic journey, but the opportunity to see the on-going work of redeveloping Amsterdam's waterfront and IJburg should not be missed.

**HOW:**
By tram
**WHEN TO GO:**
March to October to avoid short days and sometimes bitterly cold winter weather.
**TIME IT TAKES:**
The IJtram takes just 18 minutes from Central Station to the Harbour Island terminus in IJburg.
**HIGHLIGHTS:**
The heart of the old city around Central Station, for the scenic Amsterdam of canals and tall houses at its best.
A visitor centre near the Vennepluimstraat stop on Line 26, which explains the ambitious creation of IJburg.
Crossing the impressive Enneus Bridge that carries both the IJtram and the only road to and from IJburg.
**YOU SHOULD KNOW:**
Amsterdam's trams cross more than 1,500 bridges, often after making the sharpest of turns.

*Riding trams is a great way of seeing Amsterdam.*

# Waterway Cruise

**HOW:**
By boat
**WHEN TO GO:**
April to September
**TIME IT TAKES:**
Around a week from Sneek to Loosdrecht, including time for exploration.
**HIGHLIGHTS:**
Fields full of contented black-and-white Friesian cattle that – unlike others the world over – have never moved from their region of origin.
Mooring up right in the centre of Amsterdam – nip ashore to visit the world-famous Rijksmuseum and the Van Gogh Exhibition.
Loosdrecht Broad, full of uninhabited islands and alive with water birds.
Utrecht – cruise from Amsterdam on the River Vecht, via Loosdrecht, and moor at the quay opposite the Cathedral of Saint Martin.
**YOU SHOULD KNOW:**
There is often a small toll to pay at the well-maintained locks and lifting bridges on Dutch waterways.

*The windmills along the canal at Kinderdijk*

The Netherlands is awash with waterways, and one of the very best ways of seeing this distinctive country is by taking a self-drive boat cruise. This is a country where boating is not just a way of spending leisure time but is still very much a part of commercial life, with free mooring everywhere and plenty of shops, bars, cafés and restaurants along the waterside to cater for passing boat traffic. As serene progress is made along rivers, canals and through lakes, the traditional Dutch picture of big skies, windmills (actually they're mostly wind pumps), dykes and other craft of all sorts is constantly repainted – and there will be plenty of interesting towns and villages to see, too.

There is, of course, an almost endless selection of worthwhile routes that may be cruised – and a wide range of hire craft to choose from. But one excellent journey is from Sneek in Friesland to the north, down to Loosdrect south of Amsterdam. Confined only by the length of time for which the cruiser has been booked, the beauty of this trip – and Holland's huge variety of waterways – is that part of the pleasure is planning an interesting individual itinerary with stops and diversions, or simple cruising wherever the mood suggests.

However, the basic route south from Sneek is via Joure (where the world-famous Douwe Egberts trading company was founded in 1753), Ossenzijl (turn off here for the Friesian Lakes), Giethoorn (known as 'Little Venice of the North', with no roads in the old village, which must therefore be explored by water or bicycle), Zwartsluis (home to a fleet of heritage fishing and inland cargo vessels), Strand Horst (a major boating centre), Spakenburg (spot local women wearing traditional costume), Muiden (for Amsterdam side trip, or moor up at nearby Weesp and take the train) and finally Loosdrecht.

# Keukenhof Gardens

*The tulips at Keukenhof Gardens*

There's only a limited opportunity to enjoy the vast 'Kitchen Garden', which opens for a few short weeks each year. Contrary to its name, Keukenhof has some seven million flower bulbs, which provide an amazing display of spring colour (mid-April sees the daffodils, crocus, narcissi, tulips and hyacinths all in bloom), so is perhaps best described by its alternative name, 'The Garden of Europe'. The world's largest flower garden is located near Lisse, in an area southwest of Amsterdam called the Dune & Bulb Region.

Whilst a visit to the Keukenhof Gardens is an experience to savour, it may be combined with a cycle journey through the surrounding fields, which together deliver an equally spectacular collection of flowering bulbs. Taken together, the garden tour and cycle ride go a long way to explaining Holland's preeminence in the world of horticulture in general and bulbs in particular.

The gardens are easily reached by bus from Amsterdam, The Hague, Leiden, Haarlem and Schipol Airport. Cycles are not allowed within the gardens, but may be hired at the main entrance. A number of proven scenic cycle routes are recommended, ranging in distance from 5 km (3 mi) to 25 km (16 mi). Any of these may be combined with a visit to Keukenhof, or the gardens can be a major port of call on a tour of the bulb fields.

One 'must see' on every cycle tour is the Tulipland Panorama in nearby Voorhout. This mural depicts the bulb fields as they were half a century ago. It is a work in progress, but has already attained a size of some 65 m (215 ft) long by 4 m (13 ft) high. There's only one word for this extraordinary artistic effort and the bulb fields themselves...and that's 'amazing'.

**HOW:**
By bus and bike
**WHEN TO GO:**
Last week in March to mid-May for the Keukenhof Gardens (may vary slightly depending on the weather).
**TIME IT TAKES:**
Allow a full day for visiting Keukenhof Gardens plus a cycle journey – half a day for each.
**HIGHLIGHTS:**
Within Keukenhof Gardens – the largest fountain in Europe, plus an unusual 700-tree labyrinth.
Aalsmeer Flower Auction from the viewing gallery – the largest flower auction in the world held in the world's largest commercial building.
Spring Flower Parade – a wonderful day-long carnival procession through the bulb-growing region every April, from Noordwijk to Haarlem via Lisse.
**YOU SHOULD KNOW:**
You won't exactly have Keuchenhof Gardens to yourself – around 750,000 visitors drop by to be dazzled each spring.

# North Holland's Historic Triangle

**HOW:**
By train and boat
**WHEN TO GO:**
April to September
**TIME IT TAKES:**
Hoorn to Medemblik by steam train takes an hour (or 15 minutes more with the intermediate stop at Twisk). Medemblik to Enkhuizen by boat is around 75 minutes.
**HIGHLIGHTS:**
The steam museum in Hoorn – for a splendid collection of vintage locomotives, rolling stock and bygone railway artefacts.
Impressive former Dutch East India Company building in Hoorn and Enkhuizen.
Zuiderzeemuseum in Enkhuizen – reached only by water, this is an atmospheric recreation of a working fishing village from the past.
**YOU SHOULD KNOW:**
Hoorn is just 30 minutes from Amsterdam by thoroughly modern double-decker train.

The 'Historic Triangle' in Noord Holland consists of three small but charming former ports – Hoorn, Medemblik and Enkhuizen. Once fronting the Zuiderzee, since 1932 they have been contained within the freshwater IJsselmeer, the largest lake in western Europe. This area due north of Amsterdam not only offers classic Dutch landscapes of dykes and patchwork fields, but also well-preserved historic towns and villages that grew wealthy in the 17th century as the Dutch East India Company thrived. As always, wealth translated into fine architecture, and there are many splendid buildings from that opulent colonial era to admire.

The classic way of seeing these three is by taking the steam train from Hoorn to Medemblik. With lots of stops and starts for crossings, the preserved 'steam tram' (as the Dutch describe narrow-gauge railways), resplendent in original 1920s livery, chugs and whistles through the countryside, past incurious sheep and cattle and restored stations to Medemblik, complete with period extras that make it perfectly possible to imagine the reality of travelling this delightful line in its heyday.

From there, a steamer takes you on to Enkhuizen from whence the 'Historic Triangle' can be completed by returning to Hoorn by the scheduled train service. It is possible to book combined tickets for the train and steamer legs of the trip, with a 'hop on, hop off' option that allows ample opportunity to explore. But do consult a timetable before attempting to undertake this rewarding journey to be sure you won't be disappointed. The steam train doesn't run between December and February, and there is a limited service only in March, October and November. The train does not always operate on Mondays, so a little pre-planning is required.

*The historic steam train travels through patchwork fields.*

# Luxembourg City Walk

This was one of many tiny fiefdoms that made up the jigsaw of medieval Europe, and the Grand Duchy of Luxembourg has retained its independence to this day. At its heart is the old part of Luxembourg City, once a mighty fortress. Most of the defensive walls were demolished in the 19th century, but the impressive ramparts that remain are now a UNESCO World Heritage Site.

The defensive qualities that made Luxembourg so important in the Middle Ages are based on its location – high above two rocky gorges at the confluence of the Rivers Alzette and Pétrusse. These narrow valleys are up to 70 m (230 ft) deep and spanned by many bridges and viaducts that connect the 24 quarters of this complicated place, which perches atop crags and spills down into the depths. This is also a city of green spaces, at dramatic odds with its bustling streets and squares.

An ideal way to appreciate the unique combination of the city's heritage and natural beauty is to take the well-signed Wenzel Walk – a circular stroll around the oldest areas that is boldly billed as 'a thousand years in a hundred minutes'. This journey through European history focuses on the defensive stronghold at the heart of the old city, beginning at the historic Bock Promontory where Count Siegfried built his castle in the 10th century.

It then visits the Chemin de la Corniche, old city gates, the Wenzel defensive wall, medieval bridges, the Alzette Valley with its medieval waterside buildings and explores extraordinary Spanish and French military works. There are frequent information boards that put the sights along the way into context, or it is possible to take a guided tour. As a bonus, the Wengel Walk not only delivers fascinating insight into Luxembourg's heritage, but also stunning scenic panoramas from commanding vantage points.

**HOW:**
On foot
**WHEN TO GO:**
April to October
**TIME IT TAKES:**
Less than two hours
**HIGHLIGHTS:**
An informative visitor centre in the archaeological crypt beneath Bock Promontory and the Jacob Tower. The red sandstone Castle Bridge, built in 1735 – providing access to the Bock Promontory both on the surface and beneath the ground. The splendidly fortified Rham Plateau with its defensive towers and gates. A warren of underground casements and tunnels hewn into the solid rock by Spanish and French engineers in the 17th and 18th centuries.
**YOU SHOULD KNOW:**
The Wenzel Walk is named after a 14th-century ruler, Duke Wenceslas II, many of whose ambitious fortifications may still be seen.

*Houses on Chemin de la Corniche in the old town*

# Flanders Fields

**HOW:**
By car or bus
**WHEN TO GO:**
May or June for those symbolic poppies – they're still to be seen everywhere.
**TIME IT TAKES:**
At least a day to get some sense of the enormity of what happened in Flanders between 1914 and 1918.
**HIGHLIGHTS:**
The vast Bedford House Commonwealth Cemetery in the grounds of a once-beautiful chateau that remains as war left it...a poignant pile of rubble.
Recently opened Bayernwald trench complex – German trenches later captured by the British, near which a Austrain corporal named Adolf Hitler won his Iron Cross.
The sombre Langemark Cemetery where tens of thousands of German dead lie in a mass grave.
**YOU SHOULD KNOW:**
The war in Flanders was immortalized by the famous poem In Flanders Fields written by the Canadian doctor Lieutenant Colonel John McCrae in 1915, after the death of a friend.

*Tombstones mark the graves of British soldiers killed in the Third Battle of Ypres, Passchendaele.*

Some of World War I's most intensive fighting took place in the 'Fields of Flanders'. Medieval Flanders no longer exists, but loosely corresponds to the Flemish area in southern Belgium. Around 550,000 soldiers were killed there, with countless more wounded. There are still plenty of reminders of those dark days and a tour of Flanders Fields gives some idea of what that awful conflict was like – though it's hard to equate today's peaceful countryside with vast expanses of liquid mud, shattered trees and ruined towns that characterized the hellish battlefields that once were here.

The place to start is Ypres (in Flemish, Ieper), the medieval city that became the centre of fighting in Flanders. It doesn't have one building more than 85 years old, as the place was reduced to rubble during 1915. The In Flanders Field Museum is on the second floor of the rebuilt Cloth Hall and it provides real insight into the nature of the conflict and the lives (and deaths) of the ordinary soldiers who fought hereabouts.

There are guided minibus tours of key locations for those who appreciate informative commentary, but battlefield maps are available and it is possible to make a more reflective journey alone. Sadly, the hardest moments will be in one or more of 200 beautifully maintained cemeteries containing war dead of all nationalities, known and unknown. Passchendaele was the sight of one of World War I's bloodiest battles in 1917, reflected in Tyne Cot Cemetery, where 12,000 lie. The Sanctuary Wood Museum has thousands of artefacts and photographs, plus a preserved section of battlefield. The eerie Hill 60 is another historic battlefield. There are other evocative locations, too – but whatever route you choose, this is sure to be one of the most moving journeys you ever make.

# Gorges du Verdon

Provence in summer is magical, with superb weather that sets off magnificent landscapes and ancient villages to perfection. One of the most dramatic geological features in the region is the Verdon Gorge, a 25-km (15-mi) long ravine that ranges from 6 m (20 ft) to 100 m (330 ft) wide at the base, 200 m (660 ft) to 1,500 m (4,920 ft) across the top and 300 m (990 ft) deep. Carved from limestone by the turquoise Verdon River, this is the world's second-largest gorge – one French name is Grand Canyon du Verdon. It is also, by general agreement, the most beautiful in Europe.

There are hiking routes within the Gorge, but most people prefer to enjoy its unique charms by driving or cycling one of two winding rim roads. The northern route from Castellane follows the D952 road to Moustiers-Sainte-Marie. The south side may be seen to great advantage by leaving Aiguines on the D71, twisting and turning towards the spectacular Corniche Sublime, one of the very best scenic sections overlooking the Gorge.

For a round trip, take the northern route, but before reaching Moustiers-Sainte-Marie turn south on the D957 along the lakeshore and take the D19 to Aiguines. From there, follow the southern route until it leaves the Gorge at Le Petit Saint-Maymes and continue on the D71 to Comps-sur-Artuby. Turn north onto the D995 to rejoin the D952, and return along the Gorge to the start point at Castellane.

These popular cycling routes are not for the faint of heart or weak of leg – they are strenuous rides that should not be attempted by those lacking fitness. That said, the dividend for those who are up to the challenge is considerable, with sensational views all the way to complement that sense of physical achievement.

**HOW:**
By car or boat
**WHEN TO GO:**
April to September
**TIME IT TAKES:**
Two hours by car (round trip), a full day by bicycle (round trip).
**HIGHLIGHTS:**
The section between Castellane and Rougon where the road runs alongside the river, before plunging into the Gorge at the Point Sublime.
The Museum of Prehistory at Quinson – celebrating primitive man's presence in the area, in a thoroughly modern building designed by English architect Norman Foster.
The large reservoir known as Lac de Sainte Croix where the Verdon River emerges from the Gorge.
On the southern route – the Fayet Tunnel with viewports cut into the walls, followed by the striking Chaulière Bridge over the River Artuby.
**YOU SHOULD KNOW:**
Cyclists should carry an ample supply of liquid – dehydration can be a problem on this physically demanding journey and water sources are few and far between.

*The stunning Gorges du Verdon – France's 'Grand Canyon'*

# Aiguille du Midi Cable Car

**HOW:**
By cable car
**WHEN TO GO:**
Any time of year (apart from three weeks in October or November when the cable car is closed for maintenance).
**TIME IT TAKES:**
Around 20 minutes from Chamonix to the summit.
**HIGHLIGHTS:**
An elevator ride up another 42 m (138 ft) at the summit of the Aiguille du Midi – to the top terrace with even better views.
Spotting the distant Matterhorn on a clear day.
Getting as close as is humanly possible to the summit of Mont Blanc without actually climbing.
Another 'up and away' outing from Chamonix – on the old funicular Montenvers Railway (now with electric or diesel locomotion) to the Mer de Glace glacier.
**YOU SHOULD KNOW:**
The literal translation of Aiguille du Midi is 'Midday Needle', as the sun sits directly above the peak at noon when viewed from Chamonix.

*The cable car above the Dent du Geant*

Once, only a very few people could enjoy the sensational views from the top of the Aiguille du Midi, a sharp-topped peak in the Mont Blanc Massif in the French Alps – and they were intrepid Alpine climbers capable of reaching the summit under their own steam. Nowadays, the panorama may be enjoyed by anyone who rides up from the centre of Chamonix by cable car, in two stages, enjoying terrific mountain scenery all the way.

The pre-war Téléphérique fell into disuse but it was rebuilt, extended and reopened in the 1950s, for many years offering the world's most elevated cablecar journey. It has lost that distinction, but still delivers the world's highest vertical ascent, from 1,035 m (3,400 ft) up to 3,842 m (12,608 ft), with the first stage to the Plan de l'Aiguille at 2,300 m (7,500 ft). The second stage traverses the Pelerins Glacier before rising up the mountain's North Face. Once all the way up, it's possible to enjoy those amazing 360° views of the Swiss, French and Italian Alps, have a cup of coffee and check out the gift shop before catching a return car. But in fact there are other options, winter and summer.

The famed Vallée Blanche ski run begins here, and the nearby Cosmiques Refuge is the starting point of a climb to the summit of Mont Blanc. In summer only, there is another cable car – the 5-km (3-mi) Panoramic Mont Blanc route, open from mid-March to September – across the Geant Glacier to Helbronner Point on the Italian side of the massif. From there, another cable car runs to and from the Italian village of La Palud in the Aosta Valley, facilitating one of the world's most unusual border crossings.

# Paris

An excellent way of conserving shoe leather, whilst seeing Paris, is to ride L'autobus 38 from south to north through the centre of this romantic capital city. As the delightful journey unfolds, the traveller will not only see famous sights but also the hustle and bustle of everyday Paris.

The ancient southeastern gate of Paris, Porte d'Orléans, is the starting point of Route 38's green single-deckers. From there, they pass the Church of St Peter of Montrouge and the superb Metro entrance at Mouton Duvernet. Observatoire de Paris, with its lovely gardens, was created at the behest of Sun King Louis XIV, and appropriately the first map of the moon was made there. Note the chic La Closerie des Lilas in passing – a restaurant once frequented by the likes of Verlaine, Lenin and Ernest Hemingway.

Route 38 passes the 17th-century Luxembourg Palace and Gardens, built for a homesick Italian Queen. A short distance away is the Panthéon, where many of France's greatest citizens are interred and the Sorbonne, where most were educated. Break the journey at Saint-Michel – the square and boulevard are famous meeting-points – then wander over the River Seine to the Ile de la Cité, enjoying a wonderful close-up of Notre Dame Cathedral before catching a Route 38 bus in front of the historic Palais de Justice, passing the grand Hôtel de Ville and reaching the terminal at rue de Victoria. Half the buses stop here.

Those that continue go through what Emile Zola described as 'The stomach of Paris' – Les Halles market area (now the Forum shopping centre). Then it's the George Pompidou Centre and the triumphal arch of Porte Saint-Martin before Route 38 nears journey's end, reaching the magnificent Gare de l'Est and terminating at another piece of splendid Victorian railway architecture – the Gare du Nord.

**HOW**:
By bus
**WHEN TO GO:**
Any time
**TIME IT TAKES:**
This is not a bus journey to take in one go – allow at least half a day to get off and explore along the way... or better still make it a day.
**HIGHLIGHTS:**
The unostentatious monastery shop at avenue Denfert Rocherau, opposite rue Cassini, for a wide range of hand-made goods produced throughout France by monks.
The Musée de Cluny in its 15th-century building at Boulevards Saint-Michel and Saint-Germain – a fabulous collection of medieval artefacts and pictures.
The 136 statues of the great and the good from French history on the façade of the Victorian Hôtel de Ville.
Interesting passages (small covered streets) between Boulevard de Strasbourg, rue du faubourg St-Denis and rue du Faubourg St-Martin.
**YOU SHOULD KNOW:**
Route 38 follows in famous footsteps – Porte d'Orléans is where General LeClerc, greeted by ecstatic flag-waving crowds, entered Paris to liberate the city from German occupation in 1944.

*The Hôtel de Ville*

# Route Napoléon

**HOW:**
By car
**WHEN TO GO:**
April to October
**TIME IT TAKES:**
It took Napoléon six days, but he didn't have a car – allow one day, including stops (five hours non-stop).
**HIGHLIGHTS:**
Visiting traditional parfumeries in Grasse to learn the secrets of turning flower petals and jasmine into liquid gold.
Turn off at Castellane for a spectacular detour around France's 'Grand Canyon' – the Gorges du Verdon.
The long climb up the Col du Corobin near Barrême – it has been known to sort out the men from the boys during the Tour de France cycle race.
The quaint old town of Sisteron, crouching beneath Rocher de la Baume, an amazing pointed peak – check out the Citadel and 12th-century Cathédral Notre Dame et Saint Thyrse.
**YOU SHOULD KNOW:**
The N95 was officially designated as Route Napoléon, waymarked and opened in 1932.

You may be forgiven for thinking the 'N' in Route N95 stands for Napoléon, especially when you keep passing gilded imperial eagles on stone plinths bearing the legend ROUTE NAPOLEON. Actually, it stands for National as in Route National, but there is a strong connection with the Great Emperor (or Little Corporal, depending on your point of view).

For this 325-km (200-mi) journey from the French Riviera to Grenoble is the route travelled by Napoléon Bonaparte upon returning from Elban exile in 1815, determined to overthrow Louis XVIII. What followed is history – one hundred days that culminated in the Battle of Waterloo, which finally ended the Napoleonic era. He may have had other things on his mind as he journeyed north, but the comeback kid must surely have appreciated the rugged beauty of the mountainous landscape as he went, using a remote route unlikely to bring him into conflict with hostile Royalists.

Starting from Golfe-Juan, Route Napoléon passes through Cannes, where Napoléon's party spent the first night, and up to Grasse with its sweeping coastal views. From there, the road winds to Séranon, where they slept. They proceeded via Castellane to Barrême through heavy snow on day three. On the fourth day it snowed again but they pressed on, taking lunch at Digne-les-Bains before following the River Bléone to Malijai. On the fifth day they progressed through Sisteron (another mandatory French lunch stop!) and Tallard to Gap. The next day saw them complete the demanding stretch over the Col Bayard to Corps, from whence they proceeded via La Mure to a triumphal entry into Grenoble on the final evening. Today N95 is a scenic through road – but in Napoléon's time it was no more than a series of mule tracks and rough trails through the mountains.

*Sisteron in Provence – the perfect spot for lunch!*

# La Méridienne Scenic Route

France's vast and rugged range known as the Massif Central traditionally made communication difficult and isolated southern France from the more economically advanced north. A railway was built through the mountains in the 19th century, but it was not until the end of the 20th century that a really good road was constructed.

The autoroute A75 runs from Clermont-Ferrand to Pézenas, a distance of 340 km (240 mi) and is a work in progress, with the final short section to Béziers still under construction. For all those who head for the Languedoc each summer (and the rather fewer number that use this spectacular road at other times of the year) this extraordinary constructional feat has proved to be a real blessing, offering an alternative route to the old and slow A6 road which became choked with traffic every summer.

Known officially as La Méridienne Bonne Route, the new A75 not only offers a fast, efficient route to the south, but also delivers a wonderful scenic drive as it snakes through the mountains, for much of its length at a height of 800 m (2,600 ft) or more. Along the way there are five mountain passes, three tunnels and eight major bridges or viaducts. Undoubtedly the most impressive engineering (and design) feat is the Millau Viaduct, designed by Norman Foster and appearing to be impossibly delicate as it crosses the Tarn Valley, reaching a greater height above ground than the Eiffel Tower.

Best of all, those enjoying this rewarding journey through the Massif do not have to pay a toll to use the road, which – unlike many French autoroutes – is free. But there is a small charge for crossing the Millau Viaduct, which seems like a bargain – especially to anyone who ever tried to drive through gridlocked Millau during the holiday season.

*A view across to the Millau Viaduct*

**HOW:**
By car
**WHEN TO GO:**
Any time of year
**TIME IT TAKES:**
Around five hours non-stop from end to end at sightseeing speed.
**HIGHLIGHTS:**
The Aire de Marvejols – a rest area with amazing mountain views that is ideal for a picnic.
South of St Flour – an excellent view of a 19th-century engineering marvel, the soaring Garabit Viaduct, a railway arch bridge built above the Truyère River in the 1880s by the master, Gustave Eiffel. Well worth the effort – a diversion from the autoroute at Exit 45 to visit the exhibition centre and (after a climb) the overview that gives a tremendous view of the Millau Viaduct (follow the signs for Observatory).
**YOU SHOULD KNOW:**
If a bottle of champagne had been accidentally dropped from Millau Viaduct's high point during the opening ceremony in 2004, it would have taken eight seconds to hit the ground.

# Chamonix-Zermatt Haute Route

**HOW:**
On foot or on skis
**WHEN TO GO:**
Any time of year
**TIME IT TAKES:**
No less that 12 days on foot and a week on skis.
**HIGHLIGHTS:**
Spectacular views all the way to the Matterhorn from the top of Col Superior du Tour at a dizzy altitude of 3,288 m (10,787 ft).
A welcome break at the picturesque Alpine village of Champex-Lac, surrounded by woods and with a beautiful lake.
A worthwhile short-cut by cable car from Le Chable up the mountain to Verbier – incredible views as you relax, recharge the batteries and let the winding gear take the strain.
Above the impressively sited Vignettes Hut – the best Alpine views you'll ever see from the Haute Route's high point at the 3,796-m (12,454-ft) Pigne d'Arolla summit.
**YOU SHOULD KNOW:**
Even in high summer the walking route is likely to involve crossing patches of snow, using crampons.

Why go on foot or skis when there's a car or public transport available? Actually, if the journey rather than the destination is the thing it makes perfect sense to give a simple answer – 'because I can'. In the case of the Chamonix-Zermatt Haute Route, that reply really means something – this is one of Europe's ultimate physical challenges, and anyone who successfully undertakes this 180-km (110-mi) traverse through the Alps from Chamonix to Zermatt (bridging the spectacular gap between those two iconic Alpine mountains, Mont Blanc and the Matterhorn) can feel proud indeed – around half fail, especially in winter.

The summer walking route, pioneered by 19th-century English mountaineers, crosses Alpine meadows, passes shining lakes, skirts glaciers, goes through forests and visits picturesque mountain villages. There are variations allowing for a personal itinerary. In the case of a summer hike, the basic choice is between the original 'high' route and a lower-level option that avoids collapsing glaciers that have made the high route even more difficult. Along the original route hikers mostly stay at mountain huts, whilst the lower route involves staying in village accommodation.

The winter route, first skied in 1911, is one of the world's most prestigious ski tours, making a tortuous way through the highest and most dramatic Alpine scenery with skiers staying at high huts that allow them to cover considerable distances each day. To carry off this hazardous enterprise, both snow conditions and weather need to be favourable and again there are route decisions to be made, with a number of established variations to choose from, including a reverse journey from Zermatt to Chamonix. Whatever the route, the rewards are exhilarating skiing amidst breathtaking scenery.

Be warned – the Haute Route should only be attempted by parties of super-fit, highly experienced and well-prepared adventurers.

*The best Alpine views you'll ever see from the Pinge d'Arolla summit.*

# Le Train des Pignes

This 150-km (130-mi) rail line, up through the mountains from Nice to Digne-les-Bains, is a nostalgic reminder of a bygone era of railway travel. It is the sole survivor of the Train des Pignes network built during the late 19th century, once consisting of four narrow-gauge lines. Even with the benefit of modern rolling stock the train bounces and rattles as the track follows rushing rivers through steep-sided mountain valleys, reaching places vehicles cannot and making the journey something of an adventure.

The section from Nice to Plan-du-Var is busy, but once the route follows the Var River into the rugged Vésubie Gorge the landscape improves dramatically. The train continues along the river, stopping at delightful old-fashioned stations until it finally parts company with the Var, climbing more steeply up the beautiful Vaire Valley, going through tunnels and looping back on itself to gain the necessary height to continue into the mountains, passing through a 3.5-km (2-mi) tunnel between Méailles and Thorame. The next stage is along the wide Verdon Valley, before another long tunnel carries the train beneath the Col des Robines and along another lovely valley. The final stretch follows rivers through the mountain park of Trois Asses and curves through gentler terrain to Digne-les-Bains, completing this scenic journey par excellence.

It is possible to buy a 'hop on, hop off' ticket for this route (either one-way or return) that allows passengers to disembark along the way, before re-boarding a later train. Picnic sites and walks are signed from many stations and there are plenty of historic villages to explore. For those with steam tendencies, there is a section of the line (between Puget-Théniers and Annot) where like-minded enthusiasts run a service pulled by old steam locomotives at weekends between May and October.

*The ancient walled village of Entrevaux*

**HOW:**
By train
**WHEN TO GO:**
April to October
**TIME IT TAKES:**
About three-and-a-half hours
**HIGHLIGHTS:**
The pretty station at Villars-sur-Var – now also operating as a restaurant and tempting chocolaterie.
A perfect stop-off – the ancient walled village of Entrevaux, complete with drawbridge, citadel, Gothic church and narrow streets.
The village of Saint-André-les-Alpes, at the head of Lake Castillon – the station has a picnic area shaded by giant sequoia trees.
The thermal baths that put 'les-Bains' into Digne-les-Bains – but don't think you're the first to find them (the Romans were here first).
**YOU SHOULD KNOW:**
The term Train des Pignes comes from the fact that pine cones were used as tinder in the fireboxes of the original steam engines.

# Rhône Cruise

**HOW:**
By boat
**WHEN TO GO:**
April to September
**TIME IT TAKES:**
A typical cruise from Chalons-sur-Saône to the sea, with daily sightseeing trips, will last six days.
**HIGHLIGHTS:**
Exploring the traffic-free narrow streets and alleys of the famous old St Jean Quarter in Lyon.
The famous medieval Pont d'Avignon, as immortalized in song, and the impressive Palais des Papes.
The ruined Crussol Castle near Valence – one of the most impressive sights in the entire Rhône Valley.
A visit to those famous free-roaming bulls and white horses in the Camargue's extensive marshlands.
**YOU SHOULD KNOW:**
Once steam propulsion came in during the 1830s, Rhône steamers cut the journey time from Lyon to Arles to just one day – horse-drawn barges took up to three weeks.

The mighty River Rhône rises in the Swiss mountains, flows through Lake Geneva and on into France. Joined by the River Saône, this fickle river used to be hazardous, with fierce currents, unexpected shallows and sudden spates. It was tamed in the 20th century with the construction of locks and other major works – a process that both improved navigation and created several hydro-electric plants.

A cruise down the Rhône is an excellent way to appreciate the river and some of the special sights to be found close to its banks – most organized cruises stop to offer passengers an opportunity to visit places of interest (of which there are many).

Most end-to-end cruises start at Chalons-sur-Saône, to offer an entrée to wine country in the form off those splendid Beaujolais and Mâconnais vineyards, all within easy reach of Bordeaux. The rivers merge at Lyon. From there the first port of call is Vienne, capital of the Roman province of Viennoise. As the ship heads for Tain l'Hermitage this too, is wine country – the famous vineyard-clad Cotes du Rhône slide by as the cruise passes Valence and Montelimar before reaching the delightful medieval village of Viviers. Below Viviers, the boat traverses the extraordinary Bollène Lock and cruises down to Avignon, home of 14th- and 15th-century Popes and Antipopes. It then continues to Arles, the important Roman city that retains many well-preserved reminders of that era. From there, you have a choice of route as the Rhône splits, its two arms (Grand Rhône and Petit Rhône) forming the fabulous Camargue Delta as they proceed to the Mediterranean.

For those who do not wish to take an extended luxury cruise there is, of course, a huge variety of day cruises and it is also possible to hire self-drive boats.

*Vienne on the banks of the River Rhône*

# Riviera Corniches

The French Riviera may be a playground for the rich and famous, but there's much more to the Côte d'Azur than casinos, exclusive villas and harbours stuffed with billion-dollar yachts. This delightful coast stretches from St Tropez to Menton on the Italian border, with Fréjus, Cannes, Antibes, Nice and Monaco along the way. There couldn't be a better way of appreciating the natural beauty and diverse character of this special place than by driving the three spectacular coast roads known as corniches, with each of these parallel highways delivering a different perspective on the Riviera.

*Eze can be seen from the Middle Corniche.*

The Grand Corniche (La Grande Corniche) is a 31-km (19-mi) cliff-top road, rising to a height of some 450 m (1,475 ft) as it passes above the Principality of Monaco. It was built at the beginning of the 19th century (following the line of the Roman Via Julia Augusta) to facilitate the movement of Napoléon's troops to Italy, and as such does not pass through many interesting places. No matter – the road itself is the star of the show, offering sensational far-reaching views. It is by far the most satisfying way of entering and leaving Nice, and the drive from there to sober Menton is unforgettable.

The 33-km (20-mi) Base Corniche (La Corniche Inférieure) along the shoreline is an altogether different experience – slow-moving and traffic-choked, it was built by a Prince of Monaco and visits each and every place on the Côte d'Azur in turn. This is the way to go if you're interested in the hothouse social and commercial street life of the Riviera.

The Middle Corniche (La Moyenne Corniche) runs between the other two roads, clinging to the escarpment's rocky backbone as it winds through the Mediterranean landscape, offering wonderful views of the coast and the Riviera's towns and villages below.

**HOW:**
By car
**WHEN TO GO:**
Any time
**TIME IT TAKES:**
Allow a day to drive all three in turn, with leisurely stops.
**HIGHLIGHTS:**
La Turbie on the Grand Corniche – the symbolic border between Gaul and Ancient Rome, with an impressive Roman colonnade.
On the Middle Corniche – the view of Cap Ferrat from the elevated Villefranche Neck, and (upon exiting a tunnel) the sudden appearance of the dramatic village of Eze, perched high on its soaring rock.
On the Base Corniche – Cap Ferrat... and of course Monte Carlo, where you definitely won't break the bank.
**YOU SHOULD KNOW:**
Princess Grace of Monaco died when her car mysteriously plunged from the Middle Corniche.

# Vosges Wine Route

**HOW:**
By bike or car
**WHEN TO GO:**
May to October
**TIME IT TAKES:**
Allow four days to cycle the Route du Vin at leisurely speed – or a day to drive it.
**HIGHLIGHTS:**
The red-roofed l'église Sainte Colombe in Hattstatt, begun in the 11th century with a 15th-century Gothic choir and 18th-century furniture.
Colmar – it's packed with tourists in mid-summer, but the well-preserved capital of the wine region is far too good to miss.
The Postal Museum at Riquewihr – actually that's a bonus, because the real attraction is that Riquewihr is one of the finest medieval villages in Alsace (which means it beats lots of competition).
The imposing restored castle of Haut Koenigsbourg above the village of Orschwiller.
**YOU SHOULD KNOW:**
The local dialect is more Germanic than French, and many street signs are bi-lingual.

*Riquewihr is one of the finest medieval villages in Alsace.*

Much of Alsace looks as though it has been created as the backdrop for a Hansel-and-Gretel fairy tale...or maybe a Disney film. The picturesque medieval villages with their brightly painted half-timbered houses vie with each other to put on the best floral display, as they sit in an undulating landscape beneath rocky crags topped with romantic ruined castles, surrounded by terraced vineyards that produce the region's famous white wines.

The 200-km (130-mi) Route du Vin runs through the foothills of the Vosges, following the western edge of the wide Rhine Valley from Marlenheim west of Strasbourg to Thann, near Mulhouse. It winds from north to south and biking is an excellent way of fully appreciating this delightful area, though fitness is required – there are plenty of thigh-sapping hills. For car drivers with a discerning palate, the journey can be a battle against temptation – there are free roadside *dégustations* (wine tastings) at almost every turn, along with endless *caveaux* (commercial wine cellars) imploring you to 'try before you buy'.

Apart from wine and related matters, the glory of this journey is the number of unspoiled Alsatian villages and small towns to be visited, each with its own unique selection of regional food and wine to be sampled. There are nearly 70 such villages and the Route du Vin is loosely divided into four stages: Thann to Wettolsheim; Colmar to Ribeauville; Bergheim to Bernarsdwiller; Obernai to Marlenheim. In summer and autumn there's a wine or food festival almost every weekend at one village or another, with generous wine tasting, a surfeit of local delicacies and hand-made arts and crafts on offer... just follow the unmistakable sound of traditional Alsatian music.

# Echoes of Rimbaud & Verlaine

The names of Jean-Nicholas-Arthur Rimbaud and Paul Verlaine may not mean all that much to today's world citizens, but these 19th-century literary giants are French national heroes. The poet Rimbaud made an enormous impact in his home country, and the older Verlaine was an eminent Symbolist poet who invited Rimbaud to Paris, where the pair soon started living a Bohemian life of hashish- and absinthe-fuelled excess.

*The old mill at Charleville-Mézieres*

Rimbaud was from the Ardennes, the region of rolling hill country and extensive forests that is mainly in Belgium and Luxembourg, but extends into France. He returned there after his relationship with Verlaine ended badly (the drunken Verlaine shot him in the hand), walking endlessly through the countryside and writing poetry. He then travelled extensively, working in many exotic parts of the world, before he died at the age of thirty-seven in Marseilles and was interred in the family vault at Charleville. Ironically, Verlaine also spent time in the Ardennes after Rimbaud had departed, working as a teacher.

Today, it is possible to follow in their footsteps through this beautiful region by taking the Route Rimbaud-Verlaine. This 150-km (95-mi) pilgrimage from the Old Mill in Charleville-Mézières to the Auberge du Lion d'Or in Juniville has been devised as a themed route that includes places where the poets lived, worked and caroused, and has therefore been well mapped and described for the would-be traveller. It is a journey that may be made on foot, bicycle or by car.

Although this is called the Rimbaud-Verlaine Route, and the links with the two poets form an interesting extra dimension, in truth this journey is really about exploring the beautiful and – in tourist terms – largely undiscovered Ardennes countryside and its interesting towns and villages.

**HOW:**
On foot, by car or bike
**WHEN TO GO:**
September or October for the splendid autumn foliage.
**TIME IT TAKES:**
Allow one day by car, two on a bike or around a week to complete the walk.
**HIGHLIGHTS:**
Rimbaud's grave and dedicated museum at the town where he was born – Charleville-Mézières.
Roche, where Rimbaud wrote his famous prose poem *Une Saison en Enfer* (*A Season in Hell*), supposedly in a laundry.
Rethel, where Verlaine taught at the higher education college and Coulommes, where he stayed.
**YOU SHOULD KNOW:**
Don't expect to find a coach tour that lets you do the Rimbaud-Verlaine Route the easy way – some of these tiny country roads are simply not suitable for buses.

# River Charente Cruise

**HOW:**
By boat
**WHEN TO GO:**
April to September
**TIME IT TAKES:**
At least two weeks for an end-to-end sightseeing cruise (a month's better if you can afford it!).
**HIGHLIGHTS:**
At Saintes – a large number of important Roman remains from the time when this was one of the most important towns in Gaul.
A trip on the *gabare* (traditional Charente cargo boat) *La Dame Jeanne* from the Quais du Port in Cognac.
Angoulême – a lovely old town with fine 17th- and 18th-century streets, plus Cathédrale de St Peter with its stunning Romanesque façade, a grand château and cartoon museum.
Tasting fine brandy – visit the famous names in Cognac itself (Hennessy, Martell, Rémy Martin among others) and nearby Jarnac (Courvoisier).
**YOU SHOULD KNOW:**
In the late 16th century King Henri IV of France described the River Charente as 'the most beautiful stream in my kingdom' – his favourite river must have been quite something!

It doesn't take long for a tamed river to revert to the wild, and that's pretty much what happened to the River Charente in western France after commercial traffic ceased in the 1950s. It rises in the Haute-Vienne and flows into the Bay of Biscay near Rochefort, just south of La Rochelle, once forming a major transport artery that brought prosperity to the Cognac region.

Happily, the Charente's fortunes have been restored by the arrival of waterborne tourism, with major works restoring navigability. It is now possible to sail down from Angoulême via delightful towns like Jarnac, Cognac and Saintes to the bustling ship building port of Rochefort. And this process is still new enough to ensure that the Charente isn't solid with boats from bank to bank all summer long.

That said, small (for up to eight people) boats are available for hire at many marinas along the Charente (by the day or for longer) and navigation is easy. The popular choice is a cruise that allows leisurely exploration of the chosen area. For those with deep pockets, an end-to-end trip from Fleac near Angoulême to Rochefort would deliver a dream holiday – along all 170 km (105 mi) of navigable water, passing through 21 locks on the canalized section as this idyllic river meanders through its beautiful valley.

Anyone who undertakes this journey will appreciate why so many put France at the top of their holiday wish list, because such a cruise ticks all the boxes that make the French countryside such a special destination – incomparable pastoral landscapes, a timeless river, ancient villages and towns with traditional markets, vineyards, fine churches and splendid châteaux, history everywhere. Of course the modern world has impinged on that idyllic image of rural France, but somehow that's easy to forget when cruising the Charente.

# The Loire Valley

The Loire Valley is known as 'The Garden of France and Cradle of the French Language'. The lush landscape combines with architectural and cultural heritage to make this an area of outstanding natural and cultural excellence. High on everyone's list of special attractions are the numerous châteaux along the river – around a thousand remain in the Loire Valley out of a total that was once much greater, with some 300 along the river itself. The reason for this over-abundance of great houses is simple – just about every one of the country's serious movers and shakers – from kings on down – built here over the centuries.

The Valley between Chalonnes-sur-Loire and Sully-sur-Loire is classified as a UNESCO World Heritage Site, and this is an ideal section for an extended cycle tour. Starting at Chalonnes and heading east, the route follows the river to Angers, Saumur, Tours, Amboise, Chaumont-sur-Loire, Blois, Beaugency, Orléans, Châteauneuf-sur-Loire and finally Sully. The distance is around 300 km (185 mi). The riding is not too hard, and this is a splendid way to see and appreciate the best that the Loire Valley has to offer – which is very good indeed.

What an experience – the banks of this delightful river are ablaze with sunflowers and home to the finest examples of the castle-builder's art, from imposing medieval fortresses like Angers and Amboise to Renaissance masterpieces like Chambord and Chenonceaux and spectacular gardens like Villandry. This is also the home of great white wines, with the vineyards of great domaines everywhere, so there will be plenty of opportunity to sample fine vintages and enjoy the distinctive local cuisine (river fish a speciality!).

Shops in most of the Loire towns rent bicycles by the day for those who prefer to explore locally rather than make the full journey.

**HOW:**
By bike
**WHEN TO GO:**
April to October
**TIME IT TAKES:**
A week to cycle from Chalonnes to Sully, with ample sightseeing time included.
**HIGHLIGHTS:**
The Royal Abbey at Fontevraud – resting place of the English King Henry II, his wife Eleanor of Aquitaine and their son Richard the Lionheart.
Leonardo da Vinci's manor house at Clos-Lucé near Amboise – now a museum dedicated to the great man and his revolutionary ideas.
The château at Cheverney – see stunning interiors full of original furniture, tapestries and paintings (plus a Tintin museum...this is Captain Haddock's Castle).
A side-trip to see the extraordinary troglodyte dwellings of Les Goupillières near Azay-le-Rideau on the banks of the Indre River – the caves were made by quarrying the limestone used to construct the magnificent château.
**YOU SHOULD KNOW:**
The fairy-tale château of Ussé, begun in the 15th century and re-modelled in the 1600s, provided inspiration for the timeless tale of Sleeping Beauty.

*A bridge crosses the Loire near Château d'Amboise.*

*Mountain bikers enjoy the view of the cliffs of the Gorge de la Jonte.*

# Jonte River Gorge

**HOW:**
By bike

**WHEN TO GO:**
September or October to miss the crowds and enjoy spectacular foliage.

**TIME IT TAKES:**
It's well worth a full day for the round trip.

**HIGHLIGHTS:**
Be sure to stop and enjoy one of the very best viewpoints on the entire route – the Belvédère des Terrasses.
A side-trip to the fabulous limestone cave of Aven Armand between Meyrueis and Saint Enimie.
The 16th-century Château de Roquedols near Meyrueis – a sturdy 15th- and 16th-century castle in the forest that doubles as an information centre for the National Park (castle open July and August only, grounds all year).
The bizarre Le Rozier Museum in a former priory – an extraordinary collection of miniature buildings loving created using tiny blocks of the region's natural stone (open June-September).

**YOU SHOULD KNOW:**
Birdwatchers flock to the Jonte Gorge for the rare opportunity to see three species of vulture circling (Black, griffon and Egyptian vultures).

The Cévennes Mountains are in the southern part of the Massif Central, a place described as 'being between land and sky' – an assessment that's easy to appreciate when standing on high ground beneath a big sky, looking out over wooded hills that roll away into the far distance. This area has been accorded National Park status and is an unspoiled wilderness, but this land of dramatic moors and gorges, rivers and forests, medieval towns and little villages that cling to hillsides is a well-kept secret as far as mass tourism goes.

To get a feel for this special area, cycle the round trip along the short Gorge de la Jonte from Le Rozier to Meyrueis – but be warned that you will have to make a serious physical effort to earn those scenic rewards. The Jonte River rises in the Massif du Mont Aigoual within the Cévennes National Park and runs into the Tarn River at Le Rozier. The Jonte Gorge may not be quite as spectacular as the nearby Tarn Gorge, but it has a romantic charm all of its own.

For a ride to remember, this takes some beating. The outward journey from Le Rozier is the hard part. It's just 19 km (12 mi) long, though this is a demanding climb. But with the help of gravity the run back down from Meyrueis to Le Rozier makes all that effort worthwhile, as the narrow road snakes above the blue river, within the V-shaped Jonte Gorge with its rocky sides rising to the high plateau of the Grandes Causses. This really is a journey through breathtaking scenery – a genuine case of 'seeing is believing'. And if you duly like what you see, over 200 km (125 mi) of dedicated cycle paths await within the National Park...

# Brittany's Emerald Coast

Brittany is a jewel in France's coastal crown, as the soubriquet 'Emerald Coast' suggests. The Breton coast is a wonderland of cliffs and seascapes, magical islands and estuaries, beaches and coves, fishing villages and ports...and a gastronomic delight for lovers of seafood and rich regional cuisine. It's possible to spend a lifetime exploring this endless coastline but an excellent introduction to the sort of delights to be found is provided by a round-trip cycle ride from Saint Malo via Dinan to Dinard and back. This offers excellent seascapes, sandy coves, fishing villages and (as a bonus) some lush Breton countryside.

The easy journey (no steep hills!) starts beside the River Rance at Saint Malo (cycle hire available), setting off in an easterly direction along the D201 coast road that hangs above the sea, through Rothéneuf to Cancale – the picturesque fishing village famed for its delicious oysters. From there, head south to Les Portes Rouges and pick up the D155 – the spectacular Rue du Bord de Mer that hugs the coast to Le-Vivier-sur-Mer. Stay with the D155 as it turns south to Dol-de-Bretagne, then turn onto the D676 and ride to the walled town of Dinan, high above the River Rance. This last stretch provides an opportunity to enjoy rolling Breton countryside, as does the next.

From Dinan, take the D2 through La Hamonais to Ploubalay, where the D786 returns you to the coast at Lancleuc, from whence the road follows the sea to the Belle Epoque resort of Dinard, the 'Cannes of the north', via the charming fishing villages of La Chapelle and Saint-Lunaire. A ferry across the mouth of the Rance completes the scenic circuit to Saint Malo. Appetite whetted, you'll surely be back to see more of the Emerald Coast next year!

**HOW:**
By bike
**WHEN TO GO:**
April to October
**TIME IT TAKES:**
It can be done in a day, if you're not tempted to linger along the way (you will be).
**HIGHLIGHTS:**
Saint Malo – this dramatic walled port city is worth a day of anyone's time, with many splendid sights to see, including Chateau Saint Malo, Cathédral de St Vincent and the Solidor Tower.
Dinan – for historic attractions including the Chateau Dinan, Duchess Anne's Tower, the 13th-century Jacobins Theatre, St Saviour's Basilica and the flamboyant Gothic l'eglise de St Malo.
A side-trip from Dinan to the grand Château de la Bourbansais with its wonderful garden and appealing zoo that nurtures endangered species.
A treacherous skip across from Brittany into Normandy to visit one of France's most famous attractions – the Benedictine abbey and medieval dwellings of Mont St Michel.
**YOU SHOULD KNOW:**
The infamous house above the Bates Motel in Alfred Hitchcock's famous thriller *Psycho* was modelled on a villa near the Ecluse Beach in Dinard, where the great director spent many summers.

*Saint Malo*

# Normandy Beaches

**HOW:**
By car
**WHEN TO GO:**
April to September
**TIME IT TAKES:**
Two hours non-stop by car, or a full
day with exploration stops.
**HIGHLIGHTS:**
One of the best D-Day museums –
the seafront Musée du
Débarquement in the main square of
Arromanches, overlooking the
remains of 'Port Winston' (the
prefabricated Mulberry Harbour).
The immaculate American Cemetery
above Omaha Beach at Colleville-sur-
Mer, putting the invasion's cost into
sharp perspective – here lie over
9,000 fallen US soldiers and the D-
Day Memorial names another 12,557

It's easy to jump into a car and whiz along the Normandy Coast
from the mouth of the River Orne to the Varneville Dunes on the
Cotentin Peninsula. It's a pleasant journey, as the coast road passes
sand dunes with wide expanses of sand beyond and a series of small
seaside towns. For most visitors today, this is the place for relaxed
sun, sand and seafood holidays.

Nothing hints at the drama played out here when Allied troops
stormed ashore on D-Day – 6 June 1944 – to begin a fight to liberate
France that saw 100,000 dead and dozens of Normandy's towns and
villages destroyed. From east to west, the invasion beaches were
codenamed Sword, Juno, Gold, Omaha and Utah. Sword stretches
from Ouistreham to Saint-Aubin-sur-Mer, and here British forces
came ashore. From Saint-Aubin to Courseulles-sur-Mer was Juno,
where Canadians landed. Gold occupied the next 8 km (5 mi), again
attacked by British troops. Omaha Beach was another stretch of

broad sand from Saint-Honorine-des-Pertes to Vierville-sur-Mer, where American troops sustained heavy casualties. By contrast, the Americans found Utah Beach between Pouppeville and La Madelaine to be lightly defended.

Little evidence of the furious battles that raged here survives, though the sheer size of these beaches makes it easy to imagine the enormous scale of operations. Some traces are left – like remains of the astonishing Mulberry Harbour that was towed across the Channel to Arromanches and many German bunkers, notably at Pointe du Hoc on Omaha beach, where cliffs are pitted with shell holes. Also, nearly every town has a D-Day museum and war memorial that helps to bring the reality of the savage fighting that took place along this coast to life, as do numerous Allied and German war cemeteries. It's a drive that's well worth making – a journey of solemn remembrance.

who died but were never identified for burial.

The modern Juno Centre above the beach of the same name, commemorating the Canadian involvement in D-Day. Here also is a memorial to the French Resistance and a preserved German bunker.

A side trip to Bayeux – damaged in the Battle of Normandy, sympathetically rebuilt and home of both the famous Bayeux Tapestry and a magnificent cathedral.

**YOU SHOULD KNOW:**
The first Allied soldier to die in combat on D-Day was Lieutenant Denholm Brotheridge, killed during the British glider-borne night attack on the now-famous Pegasus Bridge over the Caen Canal near Ouistreham.

*Gold Beach at Arromanches*

# Cathar Castle Walk

The Sentier Cathare is a 250-km (155-mi) trek from Port-La-Nouvelle on the Mediterranean near Narbonne, through the breathtaking Languedoc countryside. It is so called because – in crossing the Corbières and Pyrenean foothills of the Aude en route to Foix, in Ariège – the walk passes nine ruined Cathar castles. These 'castles in the sky' are picturesque ruins built high on rocky pinnacles by the Cathars, a Christian religious sect with mystic links to the Holy Grail that emerged in the 11th century, before being crushed as heretical by the Catholic Church in the bloody Albigensian Crusade of the early 1200s that is said to have cost over a million lives.

As a result, France acquired lands that were more Catalan than French, and it is through this wonderful terrain that the Sentier Cathare passes. The trail is way-marked with red-and-yellow signs (combining the colours of Languedoc and Catalonia), and is divided into manageable daily stages of around 20 km (12 mi). The trail is well maintained and – whilst there are some quite steep and rocky sections – it can be safely tackled by anyone who is fit. It might best be described as a challenging hike rather than demanding mountain trek, and there are rest houses and gites d'etape where travellers can bed down at the end of each day.

This exceptional walk combines a tangible sense of history with an exceptional landscape and the clean mountain air that together make it a joy to be afoot (or in the saddle, as the trail is also popular with horse-riders). Staging points on the journey are Durban, Padern, Duilhac, Galamus, Bugerach, Quillan, Puivert, Espezel, Comus, Montségur and Roquefixade. The western end of the Sentier Cathare towards Foix has the best Cathar remains, and also some of the best landscape.

*The remains of Château Peyrepertuse*

# Canal du Midi

In the 17th century boats provided the most efficient way to carry goods – but waterborne commerce between northern and southern France was fraught with danger, as ships had to sail around hostile Spain, running the gauntlet of Barbary pirates on a month-long voyage. Solution? Build a canal that links the Atlantic Ocean to the Mediterranean Sea.

The result was the 235-km (145-mi) Canal du Midi, connecting Toulouse on the Garonne River to the Mediterranean port of Sète. Opened in 1681, it was a monumental engineering achievement with over 300 significant structures, including more than 100 locks, many bridges, several dams and a tunnel. For three centuries this extraordinary waterway served its purpose well, bringing prosperity along its length, and since commercial traffic ceased in 1980 it has become Europe's most popular leisure waterway.

It's easy to understand why. The Canal du Midi goes through stunning countryside and time has been kind, mellowing the canal to the point where it seems like a graceful extension of the landscape as it meanders through Cathar country, passing towns and villages that have preserved their traditional character and charm. Cruising the canal is hugely popular and there are many options for those who wish to experience the delights of this unique waterway, now a UNESCO World Heritage Site.

It is possible to travel from end to end (either way) on cruise boats, which usually offer additional sightseeing opportunities along the way. This journey can also be done by hire craft, though the schedule often demands a hectic pace with little time to stop and explore. Most people prefer to focus on a section of the canal (often one with no locks!) and proceed slowly, opting for one of the many different types of craft on offer from numerous boat-hire establishments and enjoying a truly relaxing holiday in wonderful surroundings.

**HOW:**
By boat
**WHEN TO GO:**
April to October
**TIME IT TAKES:**
At least a week for an end-to-end cruise without sightseeing stops. Boat hire available from one day upwards for custom cruises.
**HIGHLIGHTS:**
The Malpas Tunnel, the world's first-ever canal tunnel, under Ensérune Hill in Herrault – there are now two more tunnels beneath it, a railway tunnel and a drainage adit.
A typical canal-side village – there are dozens to enjoy, but a fine example is Capestang with its fine stone bridge, splendid fortified church and picturesque central square.
Wine – the canal runs through France's most prolific wine-producing region, so there are endless opportunities to stop and taste.
Surrealistic wood sculptures lining the canal at Aiguille, near Puichéric – created by an artist who is also the lock-keeper (or the lock-keeper who is also an artist).
**YOU SHOULD KNOW:**
The Canal du Midi was created by visionary Languedoc tax collector Pierre-Paul Riquet, but the enterprise bankrupted him and debts incurred in building the canal were not paid off for 100 years.

*The Canal at Capestang*

# Le Petit Train Jaune

The Languedoc-Roussillon Region's Little Yellow Train – operated by the French national rail company SNCF – runs from Villefrance-de-Confluent over a 63-km (39-mi) route that climbs steeply to Bolquère in the Catalan Pyrenees – the highest station in France at a giddy 1,593 m (5,225 ft). From there, le Petit Train Jaune crosses the plateau beneath the brooding presence of the Cerdagne Massif to Latour-de-Carol, where it connects with two mainline services – to Barcelona and Toulouse.

In summer, these quirky red-and-yellow narrow-gauge trains are much appreciated by tourists, as they run through dramatic mountain scenery, passing through many tunnels and over viaducts and bridges. In winter (with a snow plough fitted to the front) the reduced twice-daily service carries skiers and acts as a lifeline for the isolated communities along the line.

This service has been running for over a hundred years, and (much to the dismay of purists) the characterful original rolling stock – which is becoming increasingly difficult to service and repair – has now been supplemented by modern units, though heritage trains still run all summer long. Both types are 'multiple units', where electric motors are spread along the length of the train to permit the train to climb (and more importantly descend!) steep inclines safely – until this was developed around 1900, a rack-and-pinion system would have been the only option for le Petit Train Jaune.

Things to watch out for along the way are the mountainside village of Olette (spot the tall houses jutting precariously over the river), the fortified village of Mont Louis and the futuristic 'solar oven' at Fort Romeu...and of course the mountain scenery, which speaks for itself.

**HOW:**
By train
**WHEN TO GO:**
Any time of year
**TIME IT TAKES:**
Around three hours (up) and about 20 minutes less (down).
**HIGHLIGHTS:**
Before starting – a tour of Villefrance-de-Confluent, an unspoiled medieval town within its original walls...don't miss sensational views from Fort Liberia above the town.
Riding at one with nature in one of the train's open-top carriages with bench seats, known by the locals as 'bathtubs'.
The splendid viaduct across a rocky valley at Séjourné – one of around 650 major engineering feats along the line.
**YOU SHOULD KNOW:**
With typical French ingenuity, the line is powered by its own hydro-electric generators on the River Têt.

*The Yellow Train passes over the viaduct at Séjourné.*

# Pyrenean Haute Route

This 800-km (500-mi) trek runs from Hendaye on the Atlantic to Banyuls-sur-Mer on the Mediterranean. It takes the high line along the spine of the mountains, avoiding centres of human activity. Though it rarely strays too far from useful facilities, the Haute Route Pyrénéenne (HRP) from one end of the Pyrenees to the other is not always well marked (good maps are essential) and there is little prospect of rescue in case of difficulty. It is therefore an undertaking reserved for adventurers experienced in demanding back-packing, as the sheer length of the journey precludes professionally guided trips. That said, many people choose to hike shorter sections of this superb mountain route alone or with an organized party.

The HRP is one of Europe's classic hikes and is definitely the highest, most beautiful, dramatic and challenging walk the Pyrenees can offer, as it weaves to and fro across the French-Spanish border. Although not way-marked, the path is generally well defined, and there are a number of refuges along the way that allow the intrepid walker to 'stay high' and rarely descend into the valleys. The true joy of walking the Pyrenees – apart from the rugged mountain scenery – is the fact that this is one of Europe's last great wilderness areas.

There are many variants along the HRP where trekkers can choose alternative paths – for example to avoid the few sections that require the use of crampons and an ice axe. If you are only able to spare a limited amount of time, be sure not to miss the section containing the spectacular Ordesa Gorge and the Cirque de Gavarnie, a breathtaking natural amphitheatre. Other rewarding short-trek options are the major summit ascents (choose from ten, Pico Aneto being the highest).

**HOW:**
On foot
**WHEN TO GO:**
Mid-June to mid-September
**TIME IT TAKES:**
Allow around six weeks for the sea-to-sea journey
**HIGHLIGHTS:**
The Pic du Midi d'Ossau (known as 'the Matterhorn of the Pyrenees'), a striking twin-headed peak.
Aigues Tortes National Park, an area of outstanding natural beauty sprinkled with deep-blue glacial lakes.
The Pic d'Ansabère, with extraordinary fingers of limestone rock that look like organ pipes.
**YOU SHOULD KNOW:**
Emergency rations are essential – one of the main difficulties in walking the HRP is that food supplies cannot be replenished every day.

*Wonderful scenery makes this very arduous trek worthwhile.*

# Corsican Mule Trails

**HOW:**
On foot
**WHEN TO GO:**
May to September
**TIME IT TAKES:**
At least two weeks for the entire GR20 route.
**HIGHLIGHTS:**
Reaching the summit of Mount Alcudina, the high point of the GR20's southern section at 2,134 m (7,001 ft) – see both coasts...and the demanding terrain that lies ahead!
A short detour to the summit of a 'lookout mountain' – Paglia Orba with its stunning panoramic views.
Meeting the shepherds who still take their flocks of sheep and goats to the high pastures in summer.
The lovely glacier lake, Lac de Nino – surrounded by greensward that is likely to be populated by grazing mules, ponies and cattle.
**YOU SHOULD KNOW:**
Napoléon was born in Corsica, and after hiking the GR20 you'll have a pretty good idea why he was such a determined character.

As its rises abruptly from the Mediterranean, with pink granite peaks that soar to a height of over 2,500 m (8,200 ft), Corsica is often described as the 'mountain in the sea'. What's more, many aficionados of the long-distance hike say that Corsica's Haute Route GR20 (GR stands for Grandes Randonnées) from coast to coast is Europe's finest mountain walk. There may be other contenders, but there can be no denying the fact that this is a supreme physical challenge.

Paths are well defined – most are former mule trails – and clearly marked. But they are often rough underfoot with many steep ascents and descents. It is rarely possible to progress for more than 16 km (10 mi) in eight hours of demanding hill walking. From south to north, the GR20 follows the high mountains that divide the island's two regions, starting amongst the soaring pinnacles around Conca.

The path goes through woods and alpine meadows, crossing high ridges, bare granite slopes and deep gorges. It demands fitness and endurance, but the reward is a fantastic experience – sensational scenery, nights spent in refuges or old shepherds' cabins and the opportunity to gain insight into one of the few mountain communities in Europe that still maintains a traditional way of life, barely changed for centuries.

This is not an adventure that can be fully vehicle supported and most people attempting the G20 from end to end do so as part of an organized party with logistical support, so they have to carry no more than the supplies needed for the day's hike. Alternatively, it is possible to arrange for a local guide, who will supply mules that carry everything needed to ensure that this spectacular journey may be made with little recourse to the modern world.

*Montemaggiore and the
Corsican mountains*

# Via de la Plata, Santiago de Compostela Pilgrim Route

*The Cathedral at Santiago de Compostela*

Santiago de Compostela, the 'Jerusalem of the West' was Europe's first tourist destination. Ever since the 9th century, when skeletal relics supposedly belonging to St James (Santiago's namesake) were discovered, people have been flocking here on the premise that the Way of St James pilgrimage cuts in half the time to be spent in purgatory. Walking along one of the many traditional routes that lead here from all over Europe is as popular a journey today as it has ever been.

The Via de la Plata is one of the least-travelled of the Ways of St James – an uplifting 1,000 km (625 mi) physical and spiritual trek for anyone who would prefer to walk in contemplative solitude rather than socialize with the throngs of wayfarers along the much better known Camino Francés. It follows the path of the old Roman Road from the orange groves of Seville to the northern market town of Astorga, where it merges with the Camino Francés east-west route. Much of the path is a reminder of how it must have been two thousand years ago, with Roman bridges and ruins, original paving and ancient milestones. You walk across open country of fields and olive groves, woods and moors, passing through some of Spain's most beautiful cities and stopping off at pilgrim *refugiós*.

The road runs through the hills and plains of the Extremadura taking you to Mérida, one of the richest Roman sites in Spain, and Cáceres, an intact medieval walled city, through the pastures and highlands of Salamanca, along the Duero River to the Romanesque city of Zamora, and into the verdant woodlands of Galicia. The final triumphant step of your pilgrimage is onto the carved scallop shell inscribed into the pavement of Santiago Cathedral, a ritual that supposedly purges you of your sins.

**HOW:**
On foot
**WHEN TO GO:**
April to June or September to October. Avoid July and August when the heat is unbearable.
**TIME IT TAKES:**
Six to seven weeks
**HIGHLIGHTS:**
Mérida – Roman ruins.
Cáceres – city walls.
Zamora – Romanesque churches.
Salamanca – Plaza Mayor.
Santiago de Compostela Cathedral.
**YOU SHOULD KNOW:**
For the most part, the path is undulating but not too taxing. However, after you enter Galicia, there are some very steep climbs and descents that require a reasonable level of fitness. Pilgrims often wear a 'uniform' of cloak and wide-brimmed hat and carry a walking stick, a gourd (for drinking from wells) and a scallop shell (the St James' pilgrim symbol).

*The cathedral and castle in Zamora from the Duero River*

# A Coruña to Madrid

**HOW:**
By train
**WHEN TO GO:**
April to October
**TIME IT TAKES:**
Ten hours minimum
**HIGHLIGHTS:**
Tower of Hercules, A Coruña – the oldest lighthouse in the world, dating from the 2nd century with magnificent views from the top.
Scenic mountain landscape between Ourense and Zamora.
Duero Valley.
Castle of Medina del Campo.
**YOU SHOULD KNOW:**
If you have the time, this journey is interesting to do in stages, stopping off at Ourense and Zamora on your way.

Considering how long Spain has been a major tourist destination, its magnificent hinterland has remained remarkably undiscovered. There is no better way to see the interior of this beautiful country than catching the train from the lovely city of A Coruña, on the Galician coast, to Madrid – a 740-km (460-mi) scenic journey that takes you through a sparsely populated rural backwater of historic hill villages and ancient agricultural landscapes with breathtaking Mediterranean and Alpine views.

Leaving the dramatic coastal cliffs and bays of A Coruña behind, the train travels through the lush valleys and verdant woodlands of Galicia, up to the desolate romantic moorland around the city of Ourense on the banks of the River Miño, and through the virtually uninhabited borderlands of Spain and Portugal towards Zamora, across a mountain wilderness of rugged heath and forest where wolves still roam. Passing through countless tunnels, you cannot help thinking about the forced labour that built this section of the railway – half-starved Republican political prisoners of the 1940s and 50s, hacking their way through the mountain rock in pitch-darkness.

From Zamora, known as a 'museum of Romanesque art' for its 12th and 13th century churches, the railway meanders through the vineyards of the fertile Duero Valley and cuts across the ancient farmlands of the Tierra del Campo. The last leg takes you up past olive and citrus groves, oak and pine forests into the highlands north of Madrid. Finally you descend to the plain of Castilla-La Mancha and arrive at Spain's impressive capital city, by which time your head will be full of splendid scenic impressions and your appetite whetted to explore more deeply into this world away from the usual hackneyed tourist itineraries.

# Green Spain

The railway system that runs across northern Spain is a mere 1m (3 ft) wide, originally designed for transporting coal from the mines of the Cantábrican Mountains. The network runs for 800 km (500 mi) through the exuberant terrain of 'Green Spain', the fertile coastal strip between the stormy seas of the Bay of Biscay and the misty slopes of the Cordillera Cantábrica, from the French border town of Hendaye to the Atlantic port of Ferrol, near the pilgrim city of Santiago de Compostela.

Travelling on the little electric railway lines that weave their way along the coasts of four provinces – the Basque country, Cantabria, Asturias and Galicia – is an enchanting way of seeing the little-known Celtic face of Spain. You pass through magical landscapes of brooding mountain peaks and white-water rivers, verdant estuaries and craggy shorelines, vibrantly green valleys and luxuriant woods. There are more than 250 stops along the way – historic provincial capitals, market towns, fishing villages and remote hamlets in the heart of the countryside – with several changes en route. You are unlikely to encounter many other tourists as the train trundles through the back of beyond. Your travelling companions will be a miscellaneous assortment of commuters – local fishermen, housewives going to market, teenagers off for a day trip in the city, and the odd village priest.

Although the whole journey can be undertaken in one long day, it is far more fulfilling to take your time, seeing the city sights in Bilbao, Santander, Oviedo, Gijón and Avilés, branching off to visit the Gothic city of León and the gorges of the Picos de Europa, and spontaneously stopping at any number of picturesque seaside towns or country villages, spending the night at tourist guesthouses.

**HOW:**
By train
**WHEN TO GO:**
April to October
**TIME IT TAKES:**
Nineteen hours minimum
**HIGHLIGHTS:**
Bilbao – FEVE Railway station, a period masterpiece.
Guggenheim Museum
Santander – Magdalena Palace and period architecture.
Churches and monuments of Oviedo.
**YOU SHOULD KNOW:**
An alternative means of exploring Green Spain is by taking an 8-day rail-cruise on El Transcantabrico, a FEVE Railway luxury tourist train which stops for sightseeing.

*The Santander a Bilbao station
– a period masterpiece*

# Madrid to Barcelona

**HOW:**
By train
**WHEN TO GO:**
Anytime
**TIME IT TAKES:**
2 hours 38 minutes
**HIGHLIGHTS:**
Madrid – Prado Art Gallery
Zaragoza – Cathedral of San Salvador
Barcelona – Parc Güell and Sagrada
Familia Church both designed by
Antoni Gaudi.
Barcelona – Las Ramblas and Barri
Gòtic – old city centre
**YOU SHOULD KNOW:**
Spain is aiming to have more high
speed train lines than anywhere else
in the world by 2010. Travelling by
train creates four times less pollution
than air travel.

The Alt Velocidad Española, better known as the AVE ('bird' in Spanish), is a high-speed train capable of travelling at 350 kph (220 mph) – the Spanish super-equivalent of the French TGV. AVE trains have been running between Madrid and the south of Spain since 1992 but, until recently, it still took more than six hours to get to Barcelona, Spain's second most important city. Although construction of the high-speed line to Barcelona was a priority and started years ago, engineering problems caused by repeated land sinkage kept delaying its completion.

The Madrid-Zaragoza-Barcelona line was finally inaugurated in February 2008 with seventeen trains in each direction per day. It is one of the world's fastest trains covering a distance of 660 km (410 mi) in just 2 hours 38 minutes. This brand-new self-driving, high-speed train may well live up to its acronym and make air travel obsolete. The AVE takes hardly any longer than the plane once you include check-in times and the journey to and from the airport, and is far less hassle and much more comfortable.

Madrid's Atocha Station looks more like an airport terminal than a station, its huge central atrium decked in palm trees. The AVE glides away from the platform and is soon whizzing across the beautiful countryside of Aragon and Catalonia. But it goes so fast, the view from your window is a blur; you are more likely to pass the time reclining in the luxury of your swivel seat, relishing the Michelin-starred food that is served on board, and playing with the audio, video and internet technology at your fingertips. Before you know it, you are at the World Heritage city of Zaragoza and only a little while later pull into Sants Station in the vibrant heart of Barcelona.

*The Tower of St Magdalena and Pilar Basilica in Zaragoza*

# El Greco Walk, Toledo

Known as the 'city of three cultures', the World Heritage city of Toledo was renowned in medieval times for intellectual and religious tolerance. The expression of this can still be seen in the variety of the city's monuments – churches, synagogues, mosques, palaces and battlements built over the centuries in an exuberant blend of Gothic-Mujedar-Sephardic styles. Wandering through the twisting medieval streets and narrow covered passages, you feel as though you have been time-warped into a mysterious fairytale past.

The famous 16th century artist El Greco, born in Crete, settled in Toledo long after its heyday when the city was in the grip of a fervid mystical Christianity, which he translated into extraordinarily vivid visual imagery. Toledo itself, perched on a rocky hill enclosed on three sides by the deep ox-bow gorge of the River Tajo, appears in many guises as a favourite background in his paintings and is the subject of one of his most iconic – and haunting – works ('View of Toledo').

If you cross the 13th century five-arched Puente San Martin to the south bank of the Tajo and walk along the Carretera de Circunvalción, following the bend in the river all the way along the gorge to the restored Roman Puente de Alcántara, you can see the amazing views that were the inspiration for El Greco's Gothic masterpiece. The time-scoured city walls of earth-brown brick emerge from the hill in perfect harmony with the golden landscape, dark green olive groves contrast with the parched hills and the spire of the Cathedral, like a raised sword, stands guard over the land.

Your walk culminates in the magnificent spectacle of the four towers of the Alcazár fortress looming dramatically above you as you re-enter Toledo through the Baroque Gate of the Alcantara Bridge, and your head is filled with visions of this magical city from an entirely different perspective.

*The World Heritage city of Toledo is enclosed on three sides by the River Tajo.*

**HOW:**
On foot
**WHEN TO GO:**
April to October
**TIME IT TAKES:**
One to two hours
**HIGHLIGHTS:**
Toledo Cathedral – one of the largest in the world.
The Alcázar (Castle).
Museum of El Greco – re-creation of the artist's house with exhibits of his work.
Puerta Bisagra – main entrance gate to the Old City.
Iglesia de Santo Tomé – contains the famous El Greco painting *Burial of Count Orgaz.*
**YOU SHOULD KNOW:**
This walk is particularly lovely in the evening light. To even skim the surface of this beautiful historic town, you should aim to spend at least one night here.

# Montserrat Rack Railway

A railway to the legendary monastery of Montserrat was first opened in 1892, built for the ever-increasing number of pilgrims who trudged up the mountain to make obeisance at this centre of Catalan faith and culture, the home of La Moroneta (the Black Madonna). The disruption caused by war, followed by a number of nasty accidents and catastrophic floods resulted in its closure in 1957. Since then many attempts have been made to re-open it, culminating in the present state-of-the-art railway inaugurated in 2003.

From the town of Monistrol de Montserrat, the train makes a brief but thrilling, sometimes near-vertical journey along the original 5 km (3 mi) route through tunnels and across bridges with amazing views of the bizarrely-shaped granite teeth, for which Montserrat is so famous, outlined against the sky. You plunge into the darkness of the recently constructed La Foradada tunnel then across the 480-m (1,574-ft) long Pont del Centenari – an awesome engineering design of steel lattice supported by eight pillars – to arrive at Monistrol Vila Station. Here the rack rail section of the line begins and the cog-wheel kicks in to haul you farther up the mountain. Suspended between mountain and valley you continue your ascent in and out of tunnels to make one final spectacular upward heave to Montserrat Monastery, a gargantuan 19th century complex of buildings, complete with basilica and museum, resting on a broad ledge enclosed by steep cliffs that soar skywards.

After this sensational ride you may need a pause to get your breath back and see the sights before you feel ready to rise to the challenge of further thrills in the form of two funicular cableways, one transporting you to the mountain summit and the other down the sheer cliff-face to the shrine of Santa Cova.

*The Monastery was founded in 1025.*

**HOW:**
By train
**WHEN TO GO:**
April to October
**TIME IT TAKES:**
Fifteen minutes
**HIGHLIGHTS:**
Old Monistrol Vila Station exhibition.
El Rosari Monumental – a series of sculptures by Gaudi and others along the path to the Santa Cova shrine.
Montserrat Nature Centre – panoramic views from the top of the mountain reached by the Sant Joan Funicular from Montserrat Monastery.
Basilica and Black Madonna.
Montserrat Museum.
**YOU SHOULD KNOW:**
Montserrat ("Jagged Mountain") is named after its bizarre spiky rock outcrops, dramatic formations of pink-hued rock that can be seen from miles away. This is a popular day-trip from Barcelona.

# La Pedriza

One of the many wonders of Madrid is its proximity to some astounding natural scenery. Less than an hour's bus ride northwards and you can breathe pure mountain air and escape the crowds in the wilderness of La Pedriza. This 32 sq km (12 sq mi) granite massif, a spur of the Sierra de Guadarrama, is a mind-blowing landscape of golden-pink granite spires and domes, veined with streams. Crazily complex rock formations sprout out of the woods, with names like El Pájaro (the Bird), La Foca (the Seal), and La Tortuga (the Tortoise). Wild goats roam among the granite slabs and falcons and vultures whirl through the sky.

La Pedriza is incredibly popular among Madrileños for the hiking and climbing here but it's not much frequented by tourists. There are numerous romantic legends and anecdotes attached to the area. It is all too easy to lose one's way among the granite cliffs and slabs, making it a haven for 19th century bandits and later a Republican hideout in the Spanish Civil War.

At the foot of La Pedriza lies Manzanares el Real, a faintly bohemian village inhabited by artisans, artists and musicians. From here you can walk along the tranquil tree-lined banks of the River Manzanares, swimming in one of the waterholes on your way up to the shrine of Peña Sacra for a spectacular view; or, for a more testing journey, take the 4-km (2.5-mi) zigzag route to El Yelmo (the Helmet), a high rock dome to the north of the village, perhaps the most famous feature of La Pedriza. Whichever route you take, you cannot fail to be awestruck by the beauty of this unique landscape.

**HOW:**
On foot
**WHEN TO GO:**
April to October
**TIME IT TAKES:**
A daytrip from Madrid with a 2-5 hour walk.
**HIGHLIGHTS:**
Castillo de Manzanares.
16th century Church of Nuestra Señora de las Nieves.
Panoramic view from La Ermita de Nuestra Señora de la Peña Sacra.
**YOU SHOULD KNOW:**
If you want La Pedriza to yourself, go on a weekday. You need to be fit to scramble across the granite slabs in your path. This is a great place for climbers of all levels.

*The Castillo de Manzanares*

# La Rioja

**HOW:**
By bike
**WHEN TO GO:**
April to October
**TIME IT TAKES:**
One week
**HIGHLIGHTS:**
Wine tasting
Romanesque architecture on Camino
de Santiago.
Rio Oja Valley
San Millán de la Cogolla – World
Heritage Site13th Century Yuso and
Suso Monasteries.
San Vicente de Sonsierra – Church of
the True Cross.
**YOU SHOULD KNOW:**
La Rioja is a good place to go for the
inexperienced cyclist, with little
traffic and easy-going terrain.

La Rioja is practically synonymous with wine. The economy of the Alavesa hills around the River Ebro has relied on wine production since Roman times and produces some of the most famous vintages in the world. The region is only 150 km (90 mi) long and 50 km (30 mi) wide, almost completely encircled by mountains, ensuring a perfect micro-climate for grape growing. It is brilliant cycling country – kilometre upon kilometre of quiet country road, sleepy villages, historic monuments and dozens of *bodegas* (wineries) where you can sample the wares on your way.

Laguardia, the heart of Alavesa, is a walled medieval hill-town with 320 cellars dating back to the late 18th century. From here you cycle along the banks of the Ebro, passing the historic towns of El Ciego and San Vicente de la Sonsierra, to Haro, where the 15th century monastery has been converted into a winery. Then, skirting the Ebro, wind your way through vineyards to reach the atmospheric town of Briones, cut almost vertically into the hillside.

Many of Spain's monasteries and convents are hidden in the mountains of the Sierra de Demanda, the south-western boundary of La Rioja. Cycle southwards through the densely wooded hills and verdant grasslands of the Cárdenas Valley to San Millán de la Cogola and see the World Heritage Yuso and Suso Monasteries. Go to Santo Domingo de la Calzada, beautifully situated at the foot of the highest peaks of the Sierra de Demanda, a famous stop on the Camino de Santiago pilgrimage route. Finally, cycle past ancient hamlets up through the meadows of the Oja Valley to the breathtaking evergreen mountains of Ezcaray.

By the end of your journey you will be sated with the combination of historic landscapes and heady wine-tastings, leaving you with many lasting memories.

*Vineyards around the hilltop town of Laguardia*

# Ruta de Califato

Andalucia is a region steeped in history and legend, reflecting centuries of Arab influence. The Moorish occupation of Spain lasted for the best part of 800 years, reaching its zenith under the Caliphate of Cordóba. From the early 10th century Cordóba became the most important city in Europe, a bridge between east and west where new ideas flourished in an atmosphere of intellectual and artistic enlightenment. The Caliphate eventually collapsed through ruinous civil wars, leaving Granada as the last bastion of Moorish rule after the fall of Cordóba in 1031.

Today the remains of this Andalucian golden age are to be seen in the incredible Moorish monuments of the cities and startlingly picturesque architecture of the hill villages. Setting out from Cordóba for Alcala La Real, 125 km (78 mi) away, you drive through the olive groves, vineyards and fields of the Guadalquivir Valley, stopping at whitewashed hill villages bedecked with petunias, and admiring the rugged limestone scenery of the Sierra Subbéticas, clothed with wild olive and oak groves.

From Alcala, an ancient strategic stronghold dominated by its magnificent Moorish castle, you can either take the direct 50 km (30 mi) route to Granada, through the village of Pinos Puente, where Queen Isabella is said to have granted permission for Christopher Colombus to sail the Atlantic, or add a few kilometres to your journey by touring the Vega, frontier territory between the Moors and the Christians, where medieval fortified villages are dramatically perched on craggy outcrops of the Sierra de Huétor, guarding the plains below.

As you approach Granada, the snow-capped peaks of the Sierra Nevada, the highest mountains in Spain, gradually loom into view, a splendid backdrop to this glorious city of the Alhambra Palace, where Moorish culture achieved its spectacular climax.

*Zuheros is one of the 'white villages' of Andalucia.*

**HOW:**
By car or bike
**WHEN TO GO:**
March to June when the flowers are at their best, or September to October.
**TIME IT TAKES:**
Two to three days by car; seven days by bicycle.
**HIGHLIGHTS:**
Cordóba – the Mesquita.
Priego de Cordóba – historic town.
Alcala La Real – picturesque plaza and Moorish castle.
Villages of Subbéticas – Zuheros, Luque, Iznajar.
Granada – the Alhambra Palace.
**YOU SHOULD KNOW:**
Sierra Subbéticas is an area of outstanding natural beauty. There are alternative routes through it and lovely country walks.

# The Rapids of the Noguera Pallaresa River

**HOW:**
By kayak or raft
**WHEN TO GO:**
The best time is May and June when the river is in full flood but you can raft anytime between April and September.
**TIME IT TAKES:**
Four to eight hours
**HIGHLIGHTS:**
The thrill of running the rapids.
Romanesque churches of the Pallars Sobirà.
Castle of Gilareny
Collegats Gorge
Medieval bridge and Abbey of Gerri de La Sal.
**YOU SHOULD KNOW:**
The Pallars Sobirà is a paradise for camping, trekking, climbing and mountain biking holidays and, in winter, skiing and snowshoeing.

The 146-km (90-mi) long Noguera Pallaresa River is the most powerful river in the Pyrenees – a major source of hydro-electric energy. Its turbulent waters pour down from the 2,000-m (6,550-ft) high Val d'Aran in the Pyrenees through the beautiful lake and mountain scenery of the Pallars Sobirà. Over the past forty years, this romantic pastoral region of picturesque mountain villages, ancient stone houses, isolated churches and Roman ruins has become increasingly popular as a Spanish holiday destination for sports, nature and adventure enthusiasts but, so far, has been relatively free from international tourism. The reliable flow and relative safety of the unpolluted white water rapids make the Noguera Pallaresa perfect for rafting and kayaking.

There are charming cobble-stoned villages up- and down-stream, from any of which you can take a dramatic river journey through breathtaking countryside. You can run a 45-km (28-mi) stretch of water from the village of Escaló through Sort, the main sports centre for the area, to the Collegats Gorge. Or, for novices, the 14-km (9-mi) stretch between Llavorsi and Rialp, with eight rapids along the way, is a brilliant introduction to the joys of river navigation and a lot less dangerous than it feels: despite unpredictable rapids and a lot of boat-bumping as you swirl downstream, the worst that can happen is a good soaking. From Sort, you make a jaw-dropping descent down the fastest rapid of the entire river and float through the spectacular rock formations of the Collegats Gorge, an epic climax to a journey of thrills and spills. Whether you decide to test your solo oarsman-ship in a kayak or cling with several others to an inflatable raft, you will experience an exhilarating buzz of adrenaline that makes you want to take another trip as soon as you can.

*The Noguera Pallaresa River*

# Tarragona to Lleida

*Poblet Monastery*

When you have had your fill of the hedonism of the Catalan coast, it is time to head inland, to explore the agricultural heartlands of Catalonia where the villages have their own folklore, culture and customs, local festivals rooted in medieval tradition, and magnificent regional food and wines. The people of this fiercely independent, semi-autonomous province have a strong sense of nationalism. They are Catalan first and Spanish second, their identity clearly visible in their preference for speaking in their native tongue, a language very different from the Castillian Spanish spoken elsewhere.

Inhabited since prehistoric times, Tarragona, on the Costa Dorada, was the base from which the Romans set out to colonize Iberia. It is beautifully situated on a rocky outcrop overlooking the sea with a walled old quarter and impressively intact Roman remains both in and around the town. A 115-km (70-mi) cycling tour of the back roads to the pleasant inland town of Lleida on the River Segre gives you an insight into Catalan rural culture as you meander through the pretty farmlands from village to village, winding along country lanes, passing dry-stonewalled terraces of fruit and olive groves, visiting ancient chapels and monasteries, old farm buildings and windmills along the way.

Although this part of Spain is heavily dependent on tourism, the old quarters of the villages are still devoted entirely to food production, with a co-operative in each village. You pass the vineyards of Montsant and see the olive oil factory at El Soleras at work, the famous olive villages of Les Garrigues and the historic curiosity of the old oil mill at Albatàrrec. You will be able to gorge yourself on wonderful regional dishes as you exercise them off, ending your bike ride glowing with well-being at the gateway to the Pyrenees.

**HOW:**
By bike
**WHEN TO GO:**
October for the olive harvest.
**TIME IT TAKES:**
Two days
**HIGHLIGHTS:**
World Heritage monuments of Tarragona.
Monastery of Poblet.
Stone huts of Ulldemolins.
Seu Vella, Lleida – 12th-15th century Cathedral.
**YOU SHOULD KNOW:**
This is easy cycling over gently undulating or flat terrain.

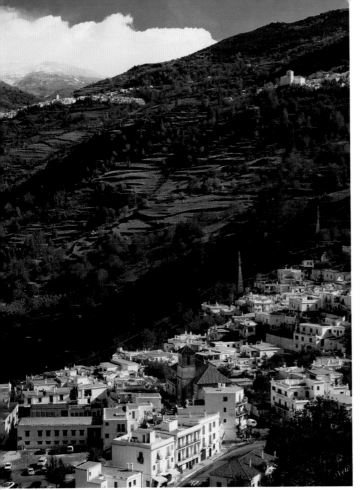

# The White Villages of La Alpujarra in the Sierra Nevada

After the official expulsion of the Moors from Spain in 1492, refugees retreated into La Alpujarra, an inaccessible region of steep valleys in the southern Sierra Nevada, where they survived in isolated pockets for a further 150 years by cultivating the fertile silt washed down from the mountains. Today some 70 'white villages' are testimony to the Moorish cultural roots of the inhabitants. On a hike through this beautiful rugged country the Moroccan Berber influence can be seen all around – in the inimitable terracing of the fields, intricate irrigation techniques and cubic architecture.

The land is so steep that the quaint whitewashed houses with flat roofs and crooked clay chimneys seem to be piled on top of each other, each village an idiosyncratic jumble of narrow streets. The beautifully tended terraces of olive, fig, mulberry and nut trees are constantly watered by melting snow, directed down the mountains along *acequias* (irrigation channels). A network of ancient walled trails and mule paths takes you along ridges dotted with cacti, down into rocky wooded gorges, through almond groves and wildflower meadows, always with breathtaking views of the snowy peaks of the Sierra Nevada.

From Mairena, a typically picturesque white village, you head westwards to the charming village of Yegen, leaning precariously on a narrow ledge. The twisting trail leads through several hamlets up to the pretty village of Mecina Bombaron and then across ridge and river to Bérchules in the high mountain grasslands. A steep descent through pine forest followed by another climb through flower-filled meadows takes you to your destination – the village of Trevélez. Toppling over a frighteningly steep gorge, it is arguably the highest village in Spain. Here you can reward yourself for your long trek with what is indisputably the best-tasting Serrano ham in the country.

*Pampaneira in the Sierra Nevada Mountains*

**HOW:**
On foot
**WHEN TO GO:**
March to May for the wild flowers or September to October for the autumn colour.
**TIME IT TAKES:**
Six to seven days
**HIGHLIGHTS:**
Moorish cubic architecture.
Outstanding natural scenery.
Trevélez – highest town in Spain with a church at 1,476 m (4,840 ft).
Yegen – village made famous in the 1920s and 30s by the Hispanophile English writer Gerald Brenan, a friend of Virginia Woolf who came here to stay with him.
**YOU SHOULD KNOW:**
This is a moderately easy trek for anyone reasonably fit. La Alpujarra is excellent walking country, criss-crossed by trails of varying difficulty, but can equally well be toured by car, bike or horse.

# Cross the Strait of Gibraltar

The ferry ride across the Strait of Gibraltar is a startling journey of contrasts and culture shock. You suddenly realise how incredibly close Europe and Africa really are, which makes the differences between them even more unaccountably stark. The Strait is very narrow indeed – only 13 km (8 mi) at its narrowest point, and 50 km (31 mi) separate Algeciras from Tangier.

Algeciras is not the sort of place that anyone goes to by choice. A sprawling industrialized city on the Bay of Gibraltar, at the bottleneck between the Mediterranean and Atlantic, it is one of the busiest ports in the world. But, for that very reason it is a peculiarly exciting city, with the highly-charged, chaotic atmosphere that invariably pervades a port. Once you start to explore, you will be pleasantly surprised by how attractive the older parts are.

Even before you step on the ferry you feel the presence of North Africa in the groups of djellaba-clad migrants and back-street tea shops. As soon as you are aboard this sensation is heightened. Everyone around you is suddenly speaking Arabic; you are the outsider. As the boat departs, you experience a surge of anticipation then, looking back to catch a last glimpse of the Rock of Gibraltar, a quite extraordinary sense of loss, only to be overwhelmed minutes later by the thrill of sighting the minarets of Tangier in the distance.

Landing in Tangier, your nostrils are assailed by the exotic smells in the air, and there's a sultry atmosphere that befits the city's reputation as a seedy adventurers' haunt. Tangier has a curious, fading grandeur about it and while it's by no means a typical Moroccan city or indeed an African one, it is an exciting and idiosyncratic introduction to an extraordinary continent.

**HOW:**
By boat
**WHEN TO GO:**
Any time
**TIME IT TAKES:**
70 minutes to 2½ hours depending on ferry speed.
**HIGHLIGHTS:**
Algeciras – Mercado de Abastos – main market,
Barrio San Isidro – old quarter of Tangier – Views of the Rock of Gibraltar and
Dar el Makhsen, Tangier – 17th Century sultan's palace housing vast art collection.
Drinking mint tea or coffee at one of the cafés in the Petit Socco in Tangier or having a drink at the (posh) Minzah Hotel or the (unposh) Muniria Hotel, where William Burroughs wrote *The Naked Lunch*.
**YOU SHOULD KNOW:**
You can also get to Tangier by the fast ferry from Tarifa in only thirty minutes – much quicker but far less thrilling.
Cecil Beaton, Tennessee Williams, Truman Capote, William Burroughs, Allen Ginsberg and Jack Kerouac are just some of Tangier's famous past residents and habitués. Though the Tangier of today is a pale shadow of its former self, it still has a certain seductive allure.

*The lighthouse in Algeciras*

# Mountains of Majorca

**HOW:**
By train
**WHEN TO GO:**
April to May or September
**TIME IT TAKES:**
1 hour 20 minutes
**HIGHLIGHTS:**
Palma Cathedral
Mountain views
Picturesque antique railway
carriages
Sóller – Plaça Consitució
**YOU SHOULD KNOW:**
The Serra de Tramuntana is brilliant
walking country with well-marked
trails to suit all levels of ability.

The reality of Majorca belies its reputation as a high-rise hell of commercialized tourism. Apart from the narrow coastal strip along the Bay of Palma and the grim east coast resorts, the island is startlingly beautiful, particularly in the Serra de Tramuntana, the rugged mountains of the north-west. Here are soaring peaks interspersed with valleys of olive and citrus groves, sheer cliffs plunging into the sea, and charming mountain villages tucked away in the hills.

By far the most enjoyable way of travelling to the mountains is to catch the quaint little antique train from Palma to Sóller, originally built for the orange merchants of Sóller who needed a more efficient means of getting to the island capital than the long circuitous haul across the mountains by horse and cart. The train has been running since 1912 and its mahogany panelled, brass-fitted wooden carriages take you a step back in time as you make the 28 km (17.5 mi) journey along a narrow gauge track through staggeringly beautiful countryside. The train winds its way northwards across the plain of Palma and climbs into the mountains across enchanting valleys thick with citrus groves. It stops at villages along the way and there are some astounding views as well as scarily long sections of tunnel that only end after you've begun to think they're never going to.

Sóller is a lovely mountain town, built on a slope around a main square with several cafés and bars. The town has miraculously retained a genuine, un-touristy atmosphere about it and you stroll through sleepy narrow streets of 18th and 19th century stone houses with huge wooden doors and wrought iron *rejas* (screens). It is a brilliant base for hiking expeditions or you can take an old-fashioned tram down to the coast.

*The town of Sóller hides at the foot of the mountains.*

# Peneda-Gerês National Park

Little known, Peneda-Gerês National Park is located in northern Portugal, part of a system of mountain ranges along the border with Spain. It is a glorious, unspoilt region of mountains, valleys, forests, lakes and rivers speckled with small, traditional farming communities linked by ancient footpaths, old paved tracks and even the remains of a Roman road.

Starting at Caldas do Gerês, an old spa village in a lovely, wooded valley, hike over the Serra do Gerês, past Campo do Gerês and on through woodland over Serra Amarela to the picturesque mountain villages of Brufe and Cutelo. Arable land is scarce and maize and grain are staples, grown on ancient terraces; the lush mountain pastures are grazed by the rare, long-horned Barrosao ox. From Ermida, a tiny, remote community not far from the splendid Arado waterfalls, trek through a wonderful valley to Soajo, well accustomed to visitors thanks to its collection of 18th and 19th century *espigueiros* – stone granaries – set on mushroom-shaped granite legs. Finally, make your way to Arcos de Valdavez, a lovely, welcoming, old market town.

The sense of wilderness is strong – tourism is light, and you will often find yourself alone for hours at a time, despite almost always being within easy reach of a village. The dense woodland includes birch, juniper, holly and several species of oak and silver birch at the rivers' edge. Peneda-Gerês is a rare refuge for both golden eagles and wolves, both of which were hunted remorselessly until recently, but there is more chance of seeing roe deer, otters or wild boar. There are birds, too – red kites, falcons and more. Gazing at the magnificent views, with buzzards wheeling in the sky and the ever-present sound of rushing water, the tourist towns and golf courses of the Algarve seem a world away.

**HOW:**
On foot
**WHEN TO GO:**
The Park is open all year and entry is free; hiking is best from May to October.
**TIME IT TAKES:**
About a week
**HIGHLIGHTS:**
Rio Caldo, a village surrounded by mountains with a large reservoir and water sports centre.
The Ethnographic Museum of Vilarinho da Furna, dedicated to the eponymous village that was 'drowned' to make way for a dam in 1972. If the water levels drop dramatically in summer, the village begins to reappear.
The ruined castle at Lindoso.
Soajo Festival, held each August, it features a 'corrida' or race, run on foot, not horseback, where the competitors carry water on their heads.
Arcos de Valdavez Festival, held during the second week of August.
**YOU SHOULD KNOW:**
There are various hiking trails in the Park as well as themed trails. You will need to carry a map and compass and be prepared for a challenging walk. It can be very hot in the uplands, so be careful not to start an accidental fire.

*The Peneda-Gerês National Park seen from the village of Brufe.*

*The train crosses the Tua River.*

# Tua Railway

**HOW:**
By train
**WHEN TO GO:**
May to October
**TIME IT TAKES:**
About two hours
**HIGHLIGHTS:**
The jet-ski championships held at
Mirandela each year.
The narrow gauge Corgo line, from
Peso de Regua to Vila Real.
The Parque Natural do Alvao, the
smallest in the country.
Vila Real, with its Roman site at
Panoias, and 18th century palace of
Solar de Mateus.
**YOU SHOULD KNOW:**
There is an extra 4 km (2.5 mi) of
track open between Mirandela and
Carvalhais, which is also open,
thanks to local enterprise.

The historic, narrow gauge railway line that runs from Tua to Mirandela is thought to be not only the most spectacular train journey in Portugal, but also of the entire Iberian Peninsula. The 54-km (34-mi) track clings to the rocky edge of a gorge as it carries you up into the Trás-os-Montes ('beyond the mountains') region, following the course of the Tua River valley. This major feat of engineering was completed in 1887, after three years of difficult, dangerous work, requiring vast quantities of dynamite to blast a track through these rugged mountains. Today the line is under threat of closure, so this is a journey you should take soon.

From the Douro River at Tua, the lime green and white diesel locomotive quickly leaves the town behind and begins to climb north towards Abreiro, the halfway point. For a while the main Douro line from Porto to Pocinho, of which this is an off-shoot, is visible beneath you, but you rapidly reach the most dramatic part of the journey, which takes you through narrow tunnels and over bridges, with exceptional views across the river on your left, which itself drops further and further away. Sometimes, looking out of the window, there appears to be absolutely nothing between you and a vertiginous drop of hundreds of feet to the water below, tumbling along at speed, over granite boulders, between the rocky walls of the gorge. After Abreiro the incline lessens as the train reaches the Trás-os-Montes plateau and its olive groves, before finally pulling in to Mirandela.

# Lisbon Tram Line 28

Lisbon's Tram Line 28 takes you across four of the seven summits upon which Lisbon stands, in the course of a classic journey through some of the most interesting areas of this historic city. In 1873, a mass public transport company called Carris began operations, gradually introducing electric trams and new routes across the city. Although most lines today use modern, articulated vehicles, Line 28 uses remodelled vintage beauties, which are entered at the front and exited at the rear.

The trams depart every seven minutes or so from Largo Martim Moniz, making their way up the Mouraria hill to Largo da Graca, before trundling down through Alfama, the oldest, most beautiful and best-known part of the city. The next port of call is Baixa, the lower city, which was rebuilt in French neo-classical style after the earthquake of 1755, by the Marques de Pombal. Climbing uphill again, the trams pass through the old city centre, replete with theatres, and on through the traditional nightlife areas, the Bairro Alto and the Bica, haunt of writers and artists. Rattling and clanking their way up and down the hills, through narrow streets, the trams pass many important sites, including handsome churches, the Parliament building and the Cathedral, before finally reaching the Cemitério dos Prazeres – Cemetery of the Pleasures – where members of Lisbon's noblest families are buried.

This trip is great fun. The trams are often crowded – people sometimes even hitchhike by hanging onto the outside as it rattles along. It's noisy with laughter, chitchat and occasional shouts of abuse at cars blocking the way. The bell rings to alert people and traffic to the tram's presence, and there are frequent stops. Your best bet is to buy a pass allowing you multiple journeys, in order to jump on and off whenever you want.

**HOW:**
By tram
**WHEN TO GO:**
All year round, but April to June and September to November are probably the best months.
**TIME IT TAKES:**
45 minutes, theoretically, but usually more like one hour plus.
**HIGHLIGHTS:**
Café A Brasileira – opened in 1905, this is Lisbon's most famous coffee house; a bronze statue of the poet and writer Fernando Pessoa sits outside.
The Basilica da Estrela and the Estrela Gardens.
The English Cemetery, where the author Henry Fielding is buried.
The Castello de Sao Jorge, originally the Moorish Governor's stronghold.
The Gulbenkian Museum, a superb collection of treasures.
**YOU SHOULD KNOW:**
Fado is Portugal's traditional music, and Lisbon is the best place to find it. During June, Fado singers accompany visitors along the route of Tram Line 28.

*The tram crosses the pedestrianized Rua Augusta.*

*Sunset at Cape St Vincent*

# Vicentine Coast

In 1995 a large stretch of Portugal's Atlantic coast was designated The South-West Alentejo and Vicentine Coast Natural Park. Consisting of a remarkably well-preserved landscape of outstanding natural beauty, this region is a remote and unusual area to explore by car or bike, though easily reached from either Lisbon or the Algarve.

Sagres in the south is well known throughout Portugal as it was here, during the 15th century, that Prince Henry the Navigator not only made his home, but also started his school of navigation. All the great Portuguese explorers of the age studied here, including Vasco da Gama and Magellan. From the beach halfway between Sagres and Sao Vicente, newly designed ships set sail into the unknown, thus launching Portugal's colonial empire. The town itself was damaged first by Sir Francis Drake and again during the earthquake in 1755, but it is still dominated by Prince Henry's impressive fortress.

The scenery along this coast is wild and exciting: towering cliffs, secluded, sandy coves, sand dunes, estuaries, rocks and islets provide many different types of coastal habitat. You will find rare, even unique, wildflowers that have adapted to life in sand or rocky crevasses, while inland are orchards of fig, orange and almond. This is a major migration route for birds of prey as well as a multitude of seabirds. You may see Bonelli's eagles, kites and fishing eagles, as well as rock doves and white storks, making their untidy nests on rocky pinnacles by the sea.

En route you'll pass through small villages of gleaming, white houses, where you can stay the night and enjoy delicious seafood, taking walks along tracks through flower-filled fields to the sea. Zambujeira do Mar, a pleasant, seaside village with a splendid beach, makes a convenient conclusion to your tour.

# Walking the Levada do Caldeirao Verde in Madeira

In the early 15th century, Portuguese settlers found an uninhabited, densely forested, mountainous island, which they named Ilha de Madeira, meaning 'Island of wood'. After clearing the mountain slopes for cultivation, they realized that although the north of the island had more water than it needed, the south – the best agricultural land – was dry for much of the year.

This led to the building of *levadas*, a huge system of irrigation channels that divert the excess water from the mountains to the rest of the island. Many were dug into the ground, but many others were hand-hewn into rock or tunnelled through mountains, often by slave labour from Portugal's colonial empire. Today the 2,000-km (1,250-mi) long system is still being expanded, and the footpaths alongside the *levadas*, essential for maintenance, are now a favourite destination for walkers, and a perfect way of exploring the stunning interior of the island.

The *levada* of Caldeirao Verde, (Green Cauldron) built in the 18th century, is a beautiful, steep walk, beginning at Queimadas Forestry Park, at an altitude of 890 m (2,900 ft). The path first takes you up through the forest of laurels, beeches, Japanese cedars and junipers, soon providing spectacular views of the terracotta roof tiles of the villages below. The route winds through four different tunnels, the second of which is 200 m (660 ft) long, each carved by hand, after which you will soon see the Caldeirao on your left – a natural, mossy rock bowl containing a waterfall-fed lake. All along the narrow path, moss, ferns and lichen growing to either side, you will see dramatic mountain scenery, and by the time you reach the Caldeirao you'll be glad to have a rest and, perhaps, a picnic, with just the sounds of splashing water and birdsong for company.

**HOW:**
On foot
**WHEN TO GO:**
April to November
**TIME IT TAKES:**
Two to three hours
**HIGHLIGHTS:**
Levada of 25 Fontes – where you will find 25 springs cascading into a lake.
Ribeiro Frio to Portela, through glorious heather forests.
The UNESCO World Heritage Nature Site (1999) of Madeira's Laurissilva Forest.
The volcanic caves of Sao Vicente.
**YOU SHOULD KNOW:**
Some *levada* walks are much harder than others. For this one, take walking boots and a torch for the tunnels.

*A hiker walks along a* levada.

# Amalfi Coast Road

**HOW:**
By car or bus
**WHEN TO GO:**
April to June or September to November; during the high summer months (July and August) the area suffers from too many visitors and far too much traffic.
**TIME IT TAKES:**
About three hours, but you'll find it far more rewarding to spend two or three nights in different places along the way.
**HIGHLIGHTS:**
Amalfi's Wednesday market.
The Grotta dello Smeraldo, a swimming spot accessible only by boat from Amalfi or Positano.
The gardens of the Villa Cimbrone in Ravello.
The summertime music festival honouring Wagner, which is held in the gardens of the Villa Rufolo in Ravello.
A boat trip from Positano to the Grotta delle Matera, the three Li Galli islands and Capri.
**YOU SHOULD KNOW:**
The Amalfi Coast is a UNESCO World Heritage Site.

Winding its way between Sorrento and Salerno, on the ankle of Italy's boot, is the famous Amalfi Coast Road. This heavily used stretch of tarmac, carved into the mountainsides, is renowned for its stupendous views and extraordinary hairpin bends. The route, along with the charming villages and towns along the way, has been one of Italy's major tourist attractions for decades.

Sorrento, situated on cliff-tops, overlooks the whole of the Bay of Naples. From here you can see Naples itself as well as Vesuvius and the island of Ischia. Steps and lifts drop down 45 m (150 ft) to the sea, where swimming is from wooden jetties rather than a straightforward beach. From here, the road twists around the rocky peninsula to Positano, where pastel hued houses of pink, peach and apricot, enhanced by brightly coloured flowers, seem to cling precariously to the mountainside, up which they scramble from the small beach below.

The road soars and descends, through occasional tunnels, curling round frightening bends where one false move could send you hurtling off into the sparkling blue sea, hundreds of metres below – these spectacular, dizzying views are unparalleled. Visit Amalfi, set at the foot of Monte Cerreto, and admire the magnificent 9th century cathedral, built when the town was a major maritime republic. Make the trip up to the stunning medieval hill town of Ravello, a tranquil gem of a place, boasting palaces, villas, gardens, narrow, cobbled lanes and a view which writer Gore Vidal rated as the most beautiful in the world.

From Amalfi, the road passes through Vietri, known for its ceramic production since the 15th century, and a mere 5 km (3 mi) farther, head into the bustling port area of Salerno, an historic town with a wealth of splendid palaces and churches.

*The Amalfi Coast Road winds its way around the beautiful town of Amalfi.*

# Via Ferrata High Route

The first via ferrate, iron roads, were built in the Dolomites during World War I. These high mountain routes consist of fixed steel cables, ladders and bridges, forming long trails through the mountains that are available to walkers and climbers of varying experience and ability. Originally built to help high altitude troop movements taking place in very harsh, winter conditions, these routes have not only been renewed and restored, but many others have been added, enabling access to much of the high Dolomites.

A great many towns and villages give access to via ferrate, but one of the most popular routes is Alta Via Uno. Beginning at Pragser Wildsee, near Toblach, this 120-km (75-mi) hike, ending at Belluno, takes days to complete and carries you through some of the most unforgettable scenery in the 'Pale Mountains'. The routes are all very well signed, and there are frequent refuges in which to stay, providing simple, inexpensive meals and beds for hikers. It is also possible to take a much shorter, weekend trip that ends at Passo Falzareggo.

These are mountains of exceptional beauty. Tranquil, gentle valleys are interspersed with soaring steeples and pinnacles reaching up to 3,000 m (9,900 ft). The sheer walls, and jagged ridges formed from dolomite rock change colour with the passage of the sun, glowing red, pink, yellow, grey and white. On your way you will see rivers, lakes and forests laid out around you, an endless variety of trees, orchids, edelweiss and thousands of wildflowers in spring. In the highest regions, Alpine chamois and steinbock can be seen – even brown bear have been spotted. Elsewhere there are weasel, marten and the ubiquitous marmot, standing to attention, checking out eagles on the hunt in the sky above.

*Climbing the Via Ferrata.*

**HOW:**
On foot
**WHEN TO GO:**
May to mid-September
**TIME IT TAKES:**
The entire length of Alta Via Uno will take up to two weeks to complete, but there are shorter sections that take only two to three days. Other via ferrate can be completed in a few hours.
**HIGHLIGHTS:**
Skiing and other winter sports in the region.
The spectacular, panoramic views.
Paragliding and hang gliding during the summer.
**YOU SHOULD KNOW:**
The name Dolomites derives from Deodat Gratet Dolomieu, the French mineralogist who first described the type of carbonate rock that forms these mountains.

299

# Great Dolomites Road

**HOW:**
By car
**WHEN TO GO:**
April to September
**TIME IT TAKES:**
About three hours, but you'll see more and have more fun if you spend a night or two en route.
**HIGHLIGHTS:**
The breathtaking views in every direction.
The South Tyrol Archaeological Museum, home to the 5,000-year-old mummy known as 'Otzi the Iceman'.
Bolzano's Gothic cathedral, started in1184 and completed in 1382.
The Tyrolean village of San Genesio, known for its celebrations, where the locals wear traditional Tyrolean costume.
**YOU SHOULD KNOW:**
Cortina d'Ampezzo, which was the host town of the Winter Olympics in 1956, has also hosted many a film crew. The surrounding mountains have been the location of several films, including *The Pink Panther*, *For Your Eyes Only* and *Cliffhanger*.

There is no doubt that the journey along the Great Dolomites Road between Cortina d'Ampezzo and Bolzano is one of Europe's great road trips. It twists and turns, switchbacking around some of the highest peaks in the range, and passing through ski resorts and mountain villages along the way. This astonishing feat of engineering was built between 1895 and 1909, and provides a true feast for the eyes of those who travel along it.

From Cortina d'Ampezzo, a chic, expensive ski resort during the winter months, surrounded by magnificent peaks dotted with cable cars and funicular railways, the road ascends sharply to the high pass of Passo Pordoi. During the winter, when the mountains are covered with thick snow, the road may sometimes be impassable without chains, but in spring and summer the scene is verdant and the slopes are covered with a million wildflowers – buttercups, rhododendrons, Alpine poppies and more. The narrow road twists past the Stella mountain group, which looms above you and there is a superb view of Sassolungo thrown in.

As you descend towards Canazei, an attractive town in its own right and the halfway mark, you find yourself at the base of the area's tallest peak, the mighty Marmolada. At 3,342 m (10,000 ft) the mountain, with its pristine white glacier, is known affectionately as the Queen of the Dolomites. As the road drops down to Bolzano it passes through an amazing canyon, near vertical walls rising on either side. The town itself is enchanting: its historic centre rich with notable buildings, Hapsburg era churches and narrow, cobbled streets ensuring its enduring popularity as a tourist resort.

*The Great Dolomites are the setting for one of Europe's great road trips.*

# Cinque Terre

The Cinque Terre are five little, coastal villages set in steep valleys surrounded by rugged, mountainous terrain. This region remained isolated until roughly 100 years ago, when a railway line was built, but the area's unique landscape and culture has been well preserved, and it's now a UNESCO World Heritage Site.

*Corniglia – one of the pretty villages in the Cinque Terre*

The Cinque Terre region is characterized by a multitude of terraces carved into the hillsides over hundreds of years. Vineyards and olives groves are cultivated here, and the villages are linked via a maze of footpaths. The main, coastal path, or Sentiero Azzuro, is the most direct, but there is another, more difficult ridge path too, and many shorter, ancient tracks up to the village sanctuaries.

Starting in the west, at Monterosso al Mare, the cactus lined trail climbs through terraces to Vernazza. This is the toughest section of the coastal path, but Vernazza is stunning – rose and ochre painted houses nestle at the base of the mountain, jutting out on a promontory beside a natural harbour, with the ruins of an ancient castle high above. Corniglia offers the Gothic-Ligurian style church of San Pietro (1334) while Manarola, situated beside a stream, is known for its wine. The famous 'Lovers Walk' starts here: a paved path through vineyards to Riomaggiore, the most easterly of the five villages. Here a picturesque cascade of pastel houses tumble down to the small dock below.

Whether you decide to walk the coastal path directly, or stay in one or two of the villages on the way, this is a magical place. The air is fragrant with wild herbs, the views inspiring, the wine and food delicious. Take your time, walk and swim, drink local wine in the sunshine, visit some beautiful churches – this is a splendid place for a break.

**HOW:**
On foot
**WHEN TO GO:**
April to November, but avoid July and August if you don't like crowds.
**TIME IT TAKES:**
Five to six hours direct, but so much more pleasurable to stay a night or two along the way.
**HIGHLIGHTS:**
Vernazzo – Santa Margherita di Antiochia
Manarola – San Lorenzo
Riomaggiore – San Giovanni Battista
Riomaggiore – The Sanctuary of Madonna di Montenero
The renowned local pesto – a sauce of basil, garlic, pine nuts, olive oil and pecorino cheese.
**YOU SHOULD KNOW:**
You don't have to walk the whole way. Instead, use the train, or go by boat, for part of the way. A small fee is payable to use some of the most popular trails.

# Sentiero del Viandante

**HOW:**
On foot
**WHEN TO GO:**
Late March to October
**TIME IT TAKES:**
Five to six hours
**HIGHLIGHTS:**
Fiume Latte – the shortest stream in Italy appears in spring from a grotto, white-ish in colour because of its steep descent.
Villa Cipressi – named for its Cyprus trees; now a hotel, its splendid gardens reach right down to the lakeside.
Villa Monastero – another historic building, now an international cultural and scientific centre, with a magnificent garden.
Take the ferry from Varenna to Bellagio and Menaggio.
**YOU SHOULD KNOW:**
In 2007 Lake Como was reported as being too polluted for swimming. Check on the situation before you dive in.

Lake Como, situated in northern Italy close to the Swiss border, has attracted visitors for centuries. Today, the actor George Clooney has a villa here, but wealthy Lombardians and Milanese holidayed here long before the region was 'discovered' during the 19th century, when Europe's writers, artists and composers began to arrive. The lake, shaped like an inverted 'Y', boasts a delightful, sub-tropical climate, and the resulting vegetation, olive and citrus groves, bougainvillea and palm trees, looks remarkable against the backdrop of snow-clad mountains.

The Sentiero del Viandante, or Wayfarer's Trail, is an ancient mule path connecting the villages along the lake, originally used for bringing goods both from Milan, to the south, and the northern plains. Nowadays it is a little piece of hiker heaven, with orange signs marking the route. Starting at Lierna, a lovely, medieval town with two of the lake's best beaches, follow the path up towards Ortanello, through the forest to the 13th century church of St Peter. This is a perfect spot for a picnic. A sunny, grassy space – complete with fountain, tables and even barbecue equipment – spreads out around the church, and by now you'll need a break.

Follow the trail through Ortanello and soon you'll be heading down to Varenna. You are now high over the lake and this is the

trickiest part of the hike, but the views over the sparkling blue lake and the mountains are glorious. Visit the ruins of Vezio Castle – from the top of the tower you can see over the entire lake. Varenna, perhaps the most picturesque town on Lake Como, has steep, narrow lanes that wind down to the harbour, past lovely houses, their balconies a mass of colourful flowers. Here you can finally sit down and sip a glass of cold Prosecco whilst looking over the water.

*Varenna is perhaps the most picturesque town on Lake Como.*

# Rome to Catania

You may well puzzle over the idea of a train running all the way from Rome, in mainland Italy, to Catania in Sicily, but this is a rare journey where the train boards a ship to cross the sea. It may be faster to fly, but you would miss watching the landscape changing from a European aspect to a harsher, almost North African one as it slips by.

Leaving Rome's main station in the morning, the suburbs finally give way to plots of well cultivated land interspersed with small houses, many only half-built, multi-coloured washing flapping on lines in the sunshine. Yellow and white flowers brighten the fields and the trees begin to appear smaller and more gnarled.

After drawing into Naples, its shabby, colourful tenements strung with washing, the line turns to run parallel to the coast. You'll catch a glimpse of the island of Capri and the Sorrentine peninsula, and soon the landscape becomes one of bare, rocky hills, abandoned villages, with an occasional sprinkling of modern houses. The beach too, looks somewhat abandoned: with few people and just the odd fishing boat out to sea. Finally the train pulls into Villa San Giovanni, where the carriages, uncoupled, are rolled onto the ferry, and taken across the Straits of Messina, where they are rolled back onto tracks and re-assembled. During the crossing, passengers either stay in their compartments or climb the stairs to the deck, where they can relish the sight of Sicily and Messina gradually drawing closer.

The journey down Sicily's eastern coast takes you past citrus groves, crumbling castles, prickly pears and cactus. You even get a good enough look at Taormina to want to visit it properly, as well as passing the imposing mass of Mount Etna, before eventually arriving at Catania, the island's second city and seaport.

*Taormina with Mount Etna in the background*

**HOW:**
By train
**WHEN TO GO:**
All year round, but April to November is probably best.
**TIME IT TAKES:**
Ten to thirteen hours, depending on Italian Railways
**HIGHLIGHTS:**
The journey itself – having the time to realize you are travelling and watching southern Italy pass by.
The Vatican City and St Peter's.
Rome's famous ruins, such as the Colosseum, the Forum and the Catacombs.
Exploring Mount Etna.
Catania – the two markets in the historic centre
**YOU SHOULD KNOW:**
The Straits of Messina were described in Homer's *Odyssey* as one of the most treacherous passages on earth, guarded by sirens who tempted sailors to their deaths with songs. Ships had to pass between two monsters, Scylla, who plucked sailors from their ships and ate them alive, and Charybdis, who sucked entire ships into the whirlpool it created.

303

# Via Francigena Pilgrim Trail

**HOW:**
On foot
**WHEN TO GO:**
Late March to June, September to
November. High summer is possible,
but the towns can become over-
crowded.
**TIME IT TAKES:**
About four days, but it depends on
your pace, and how long you spend
in the towns and villages you pass
through.
**HIGHLIGHTS:**
Montaione – San Vivaldo, with its
17 chapels.
The Romanesque church of Santa
Maria a Chianni.
Chianti Montespertoli and Chianti
Colli Fiorentini, two excellent locally
grown wines.
Castelfiorentino – The Baroque
church of Santa Verdiana and
Benozzo Gozzoli's frescoes.
Siena's annual medieval horserace,
the Palio, which takes place in the
Piazza del Campo.
**YOU SHOULD KNOW:**
The recent revival of interest in long
distance walks and pilgrim trails has
prompted the Italian government to
plan to upgrade the route, which is
less well known and less travelled
than the trail to Santiago
de Compostela.

Originally going south to Bari, the launching point for Jerusalem, the Via Francigena is an ancient pilgrim trail stretching all the way from Canterbury to Rome. Much of the trail is relatively undeveloped and the paths are sometimes overgrown – thus allowing walkers to meditate on an enchanted landscape in peace.

One of the loveliest sections of the trail takes you through the Tuscan heartlands. Starting at Castelfiorentino, a fortified town in the Valdesa Valley with a superb Baroque church, the path follows the course of the River Elsa to Certaldo. Like many Tuscan towns, it rests upon a hill, 129 m (426 ft) above sea level, and from its walled, medieval centre you can see the modern section spreading out beneath, surrounded by fecund vineyards. Visible in the distance are the towers of San Gimignano.

The path continues through Poggibonzi: set on a small hill, its crucial position between the old states of Siena, Volterra and Florence provoked centuries of invasions and uprisings. A further 11 km (7 mi) and you reach San Gimignano, an almost perfectly preserved, absolutely gorgeous hilltop town. During the 10th century San Gimignano prospered from pilgrims and traders travelling the Via Francigeno, and art flourished in the many churches and monasteries. The magnificent frescoes in the Duomo are just a taste of the treasures to be found here.

Monteriggioni, the next fortified village en route, boasts almost intact 13th century walls, encompassing fourteen towers that are the largest of their kind in Tuscany. By now you are only some 15 km (9 mi) from Siena, the region's capital. On reaching the Piazza del Campo, one of Italy's most sublime squares, and the Piazza del Duomo, dominated by an astonishing cathedral, you can vividly imagine a medieval pilgrim's awed response to his surroundings. Your own will doubtless be much the same.

*Monteriggioni in the
Elsa Valley*

# Crete Senesi

Cycling through the lovely landscapes of Crete Senesi is possibly the best way to see the part of Tuscany to the south of Siena. Meaning 'Siennese clays', the name refers to the greyish beige colour of the clay soil, which is used in the production of terracotta tiles and splendid, large olive jars.

Leaving the Val d'Orcia, its green, undulating hills occasionally interrupted by eroded gullies, make your way to Montepulciano. Topping a ridge, its superb views stretch out for miles. At the foot of the hill is the Renaissance church of San Biagio. Designed by Antonio da Sangallo, this is an exceptional building. The road from the church up to the town, however, is steep, and you'll need a glass or two of the excellent, local red wine by the time you get there.

Wheel along through vineyards and olive groves on unpaved roads that wind up hill and down vale. Catch glimpses of fortified hilltop villages and ancient farmhouses, and notice the vines giving way to fields of wheat and sunflowers swaying in the welcome breeze, Cyprus trees standing sentinel against the deep blue sky. Arriving in 15th century Pienza, you find a treasure trove of Renaissance architecture, built by order of Pope Pius II, whose birthplace it was. The piazza, with the Pope's family palazzo and a splendid cathedral, is a glorious sight.

Leaving Pienza, you head for Montalcino. Set on a hilltop overlooking the valleys beneath, the town has been settled since Etruscan times, though today it is far better known for its exceptional Brunello wines than for its historic architecture. Make sure you visit the nearby Sant'Antimo Abbey: started in the 9th century, it is a sublime example of monastic architecture. The mellow stone glows in the warm light of the surrounding countryside, forming a perfect, harmonious scene.

*The glorious countryside around Asciano*

**HOW:**
By bike
**WHEN TO GO:**
April to October
**TIME IT TAKES:**
Three days or more, depending on how many places you decide to visit.
**HIGHLIGHTS:**
The Bravio delle Botti, an annual event occurring on the last Sunday in August, when competing teams push large wine casks up the hill.
Asciano, a small walled town in the heart of Crete Senesi, with mixed Romanesque and Gothic architecture.
San Quirico and Bagno Vignoni, popular for their spring water even in Roman times.
The Abbey of Monte Oliveto Maggiore and its famous frescoes.
The glorious landscapes through which you travel and the views from the hill towns.
**YOU SHOULD KNOW:**
The cycling varies from easy to really quite strenuous – bear in mind that this is a hilly region, and mountain bikes are needed.

# Umbria Hill Towns

A tour around the medieval hill towns of Umbria makes for the most pleasant of journeys. Pottering along the small back roads, amidst spreading chestnut trees and luxuriant elms on the hillsides, through valleys and beside clear sparkling streams, you are in a landscape captured by many a master painter. The popularity of nearby Tuscany has allowed Umbria to remain relatively unscathed, although Assisi and Orvieto have always drawn crowds.

*Orvieto's famous cathedral can be seen from miles away.*

**HOW:**
By car
**WHEN TO GO:**
March to May, September to November. High summer is usually pretty busy.
**TIME IT TAKES:**
You should spend at least a week, but three or four would be ideal!
**HIGHLIGHTS:**
Todi, with its ancient city walls.
Civita – an artist's paradise, built on a pinnacle and attached to the wider world by a narrow bridge.
Collevalenza – with its unique Sanctuary, built in 1965.
The church of Santa Maria degli Angeli, outside Assisi, which encloses another tiny church that was the first Franciscan friary.
Orvieto – Tempio Belvedere, the last above-ground Estruscan temple in Italy.
**YOU SHOULD KNOW:**
Not only were both St Benedict and St Francis born in Umbria, but also the painters Raphael and Pietro Perugino had their schools here.

Perugia is both beautiful and lively – home to the University for Foreigners and topped by the 16th century Rocca Paolina, Italy's largest fortress; the July Jazz Festival is colourful and exciting, thousands of people speaking hundreds of languages throng the streets and piazzas, enjoying free concerts late into the night.

Assisi, reconstructed after the shocking earthquake of 1997, is crowded with pilgrims coming to visit the Basilica of St Francis. He was born here in 1181. From the magical castle of Rocco Maggiore look out across the glorious Tiber Valley, which so inspired him. There are treasures to be found everywhere – countryside and town alike: Spello's ancient walls date back 2,000 years, and its 13th century church is illuminated with Pinturicchio's fabulous frescoes. The town itself is peaceful and traffic-free. Tiny Bevagna, for once not a hill town, has Roman remains, lovely churches and a marvellous 19th century theatre.

The road from Todi to Orvieto is particularly scenic, including views of Lake Corbara; Orvieto itself is visible from miles away, its world famous Duomo silhouetted against the deep blue Umbrian sky. The pedestrianized ancient city centre is reached either by funicular railway, or via escalators hewn into the soft, tufa stone cliff. The Piazza del Duomo and the cathedral itself are magnificent, and Orvieto also has an extraordinary labyrinth of underground passages beneath it, begun by the Etruscans and continued during the Middle Ages.

# Itria Valley Trulli

Until recently, Puglia, the easternmost part of the heel of Italy's boot, remained largely unknown, but today things are changing, and the region is recognized as a fascinating place, rich in architecture and lovely to behold. Farming is still the mainstay here – ancient, gnarled olive trees and verdant vines, luscious figs and almond trees emerge from the intense red soil, and deep green pines clothe the low hills.

Begin your journey at Monopli on the coast, with its defensive walls and towers that protect a once important harbour, dominated by an ancient castle. The pedestrianized centre is a charming maze of narrow streets, and there are imposing palaces and a splendid Cathedral to be seen. It's an easy ride from there to Conversano, inhabited since Palaeolithic times. Built by the Normans, part of the megalithic walls form the foundation of the trapezoidal castle, which today houses the town's picture gallery and Paolo Finolglio's 16th century frescoes.

Now ride through the gently undulating landscape of the Itria Valley, with its old fortified farmhouses, *masserie*, standing amidst the cherry trees and olive groves, to the UNESCO World Heritage Site of Alberobello, and its 1,500 14th-century trulli houses. Unique to this area, trulli are small, circular buildings made of limestone blocks, with conical roofs, originally constructed without mortar. The town is, of course, heavily visited, but more trulli are dotted around the countryside.

Finally, make your way back towards the coast to Ostuni, an architectural gem of a place. Known as La Citta Bianca – the White Town – for its brilliant, whitewashed houses, it is built on several levels, approached up steps, through arches and along little alleys. There are balconies and carved entryways everywhere, flowers trail from terracotta pots and from each corner you can see the sea.

**HOW**:
By bike
**WHEN TO GO**:
May to October
**TIME IT TAKES**:
About a week
**HIGHLIGHTS**:
Conversano – San Benedetto, 11th century monastery, with its two bell towers and medieval cloister.
Alberobello – The trullo church of St Anthony and the trulli museum.
Ostuni – 15th century, late Gothic-style cathedral, with its magnificent rose window.
The spectacular caves of Castellana Grotte, near Alberobello.
The 'Processione della Grata, a candlelit procession of up to 6,000 people that takes place on the second Sunday of August, going from the Sanctuary della Grata, outside Ostuni, into the centre of town.
**YOU SHOULD KNOW:**
Lack of water has long been a problem in Puglia – drinking water is brought by aqueduct across the Apennines from Campania.

*Alberobello has been named a World Heritage Site.*

# Selvaggio Blu Trek in Sardinia

**HOW:**
On foot
**WHEN TO GO:**
April to June, September to November – it's too hot during July and August.
**TIME IT TAKES:**
About eight days
**HIGHLIGHTS:**
Swimming at Cala Goloritze, perhaps Sardinia's most beautiful beach. The awesome views of the Orosei Gulf from the top of Punta Salinas. Lying under the night sky, listening to the Mediterranean Sea lapping on the shore.
**YOU SHOULD KNOW:**
Don't try to do this trek on your own – you really won't know where you are and could get into serious difficulties.

Said to be the toughest trek in Italy, as well as one of the most beautiful, Selvaggio Blu is a 45 km (28 mi) hike around the Gulf of Orosei on the east coast of Sardinia, the Mediterranean's second largest island.

In the late 1980s, Peppino Cicalo and Mario Verin, two Tuscans, conceived the idea of finding and linking a network of shepherds' and charcoal burners' paths, long unused, around the Gulf, keeping as close to the sea as possible. These paths are only used by wild pigs and sheep, and are so overgrown with Mediterranean vegetation that they are difficult to recognize – even the blue painted arrows that point the way quickly fade or become hidden, and taking a knowledgeable guide with you is a necessity.

Beginning at Pietra Longa, near Arbatax, the trek to Cala Gonone takes you through a wild, lonely landscape of rock and stone, through ancient forests of oak, canyons, rock gullies and limestone arches. There is no sign of human habitation; in fact you feel you are in an extraordinary space, totally alone, lost between the sky and the sea – your sole point of orientation. In parts you'll need to use ropes to climb or abseil, you'll walk along narrow ledges beside high cliffs, with the sea hundreds of metres beneath you – this is not a trek for the faint-hearted, or indeed for beginners.

Each night you make your way down to a small beach (*cala*) where you sleep under the stars, or perhaps take shelter in a 'sheepfold'. There is no support on this journey, no mountain huts or places to renew your supplies – even drinking water is scarce – but the payback is magnificent panoramas, a complete absence of 'civilization' and the true, unspoilt nature of the Mediterranean wilderness.

*The S'Architeddu Lupiru, one of the rock formations located along the way.*

# Grand Canal

Known as La Serenissima, Queen of the Adriatic and City of Light, Venice is certainly one of the wonders of our world. An archipelago of 118 islands formed by 150 canals within a marshy lagoon on the Adriatic, Venice relies upon her waterways for transport, with the Grand Canal as the principal highway.

Take vaporetto No.1 from Piazzale Roma, the gateway to Venice, and you can travel the whole length of the Grand Canal to St Mark's Basin, with perfect views of some of the finest architecture the city has to offer. Almost 200 remarkable buildings, most of which rise straight from the water, form the 'banks' of the canal in an extraordinary sequence of façades, their reflections rippling below. This was the most expensive and sought-after area in the city, and these fine palazzi were built by aristocrats and wealthy merchants between the 13th and 18th centuries.

The canal winds through the heart of Venice in an inverted 'S' shape, and the vaporetto zigzags across it to stops on either side, passing under three bridges, the 16th century, marble Rialto, the Academia, made of wood (1854) and the stone Scalzi (1858). Today a fourth bridge is being constructed, linking the railway station and the Piazzale Roma.

This is a breathtaking voyage, varied, colourful and surprising. You'll see the postman delivering by boat, gondolas carrying honeymoon couples to their waterfront hotel, and vaporetti that cross from side to side rather than up and down. You'll pass fifteen splendid churches, museums and galleries such as the Guggenheim Collection, housed in the Palazzo Venier dei Leoni. As you head towards San Marco the canal opens out to its widest point, merging with St Mark's Basin and the lagoon in a magnificent expanse of water dominated by the gleaming white façade of Santa Maria della Salute, which guards its mouth.

*The Grand Canal with the domes of Santa Maria della Salute*

**HOW:**
By vaporetto
**WHEN TO GO:**
All year round, though there can be floods from November to March, and June to September can be very crowded.
**TIME IT TAKES:**
Under one hour – but buy a travel card and you can jump on and off at any number of stops to explore.
**HIGHLIGHTS:**
The fish and vegetable markets at the Rialto – go early in the morning.
The Venice Biennale – a major art exhibition every two years.
The Venice Film Festival – the oldest in the world and highly influential; it takes place in late August/early September.
The Carnival – one of the most famous in the world, with fabulously costumed and masked participants, it ends at midnight on Shrove Tuesday every year.
**YOU SHOULD KNOW:**
Venice, with its lagoon, is a UNESCO World Heritage Site. Visit if you possibly can, the entire place is a work of art.

*Sailing along the dramatic Corinth Canal.*

# Venice to Patras

Travelling overland from Italy to Greece is a lengthy and expensive trip. If time is of the essence, take the ferry from Venice to Patras, thereby spoiling yourself with a mini-cruise into the bargain. Even a short stay in Venice can be exhausting, with so much to see, but a couple of days crossing the Adriatic will boost your energy levels.

Many ships leave from Venice port – large cruise liners as well as ferries head off in all directions. There is a frequent service to Patras, indeed some 40 ships ply this route during the summer season. The ferries are large, holding up to 1,600 people and their vehicles. Everyone uses them: locals, holiday-makers and long distance lorry drivers, all chatting in different languages as they explore their 'home' for the next two days.

The ferries are equipped with all mod cons: shops, restaurants, bars, discos, casinos and swimming pools, so there's plenty to keep you occupied if relaxing on a sun deck, gazing out to sea, begins to pall. There is also a choice of cabins, inside, outside, for two passengers or four, with or without shower facilities – and all fully air-conditioned. In fact the cheapest method is to camp on deck, and very pleasant too if the weather is balmy. If not, the campers move inside to corridors and lounges. This is a straightforward journey, stopping twice, once at Corfu and again at Igoumenitsa, the start of a motorway running all the way to Turkey.

Patras itself has a long and distinguished history. Built on the slopes of Mount Panachaikon, its old town is charming, full of neo-classical buildings, churches, monuments, narrow lanes and steps. Greece's third city and second largest port after Piraeus, Patras is large, lively and a good base for exploring.

# Riviera Day Train

The ancient city of Genoa is situated on the Ligurian Sea, on Italy's northern coast, not far from the border with France. Taking the train along the Italian and French Rivieras has been a classic journey ever since the railway arrived in the late 1800s. Prior to that, the coastline was largely unknown to the wider world, but the railway brought an influx of foreign visitors, including European royalty and artists who came for the climate, the lovely scenery and the clear, sharp quality of the light.

To best enjoy the trip, make sure you find a seat on the left side of the train, so your view of the dazzling green-blue sea is uninterrupted. The windows on the right look out mainly at high walls and lines of drying laundry. The train is heavily used, by people going to work, school or college, as well as by day-trippers and more serious travellers, and it stops at every little station along the way. From the windows you will see the gorgeous Mediterranean countryside, decked with flowering shrubs and palm trees swaying in the warm breeze. At Ventimiglia, close to the border, there's an addictive Friday morning market, which many French people come to each week – an easy jaunt as there are no border controls here.

Once in France, the famous towns of the Riviera come thick and fast, in an almost continuous line – gawp at Monte Carlo, home to the famous casino and principal town of the tiny, sovereign state of Monaco, its harbour bursting with millionaires' yachts. The train passes in and out of dark tunnels, making you blink each time you emerge into the golden sunlight. Look out for Eze, perched 400 m (1,300 ft) high above the sea, Beaulieu-sur-Mer, Villefranche and finally, Nice, the undisputed Queen of the Côte d'Azur.

**HOW:**
By train
**WHEN TO GO:**
From September to June to avoid the high season crowds.
**TIME IT TAKES:**
Roughly three hours, but these trains are notoriously late.
**HIGHLIGHTS:**
Genoa – historic centre, the largest in Europe.
The aquarium, the second largest in Europe.
Nice – the Cours Saleya Flower market and the Matisse Museum.
**YOU SHOULD KNOW:**
Genoa boasts many famous sons, including three popes, Christopher Columbus, the composer Niccolo Paganini and the 2002 Nobel Prize winner for Physics, Riccardo Giaccomo.

*Villefranche-sur-mer on the Cote d'Azur*

*The cable car to Schilthorn*

# Lauterbrunnen to Schilthorn

**HOW:**
By cable car
**WHEN TO GO:**
Year-round, the dramatic landscape
has no equal; but from May to
September/October, the wildflowers
and seasonal colours sharpen the
contrasts between mountain
and valley.
**TIME IT TAKES:**
20-25 minutes Lauterbrunnen-
Mürren cog railway (31 minutes via
Stechelberg cable-car station); 31
minutes Stechelberg-Schilthorn
cable car.
**HIGHLIGHTS:**
The incredible 'corkscrew' of the
waterjet of Trummelbach Falls in the
Lauterbrunnen Valley: inside the
mountain, and accessible by lift
installed in the rockface, the
Jungfraujoch meltwater pumps
20,000 litres (4,399 gallons) per
second through twisting, smooth-
bore chutes and curling ravines.
The view opening up as the train
passes Grutschalp.
IIn winter, skiing the black run from
Schilthorn.
**YOU SHOULD KNOW:**
Mürren is the highest, year-round
inhabited village in the Bernese
Oberland, and its peaceful wooden
charms are 700 years old. The slopes
around Mürren were the site of
Switzerland's first competitive skiing
activities – the slalom in 1922, and
the downhill in 1928.

The classic image of Switzerland – dramatic snow-capped peaks, icy
torrents crashing down the sombre grey of sheer cliffs, emerald
meadows studded with the white, gold and pink of wild flowers, and
endless vistas of Uhland-green forests and turquoise lakes beneath a
swollen arc of sky – belongs to Mürren in the Bernese Oberland.
Mürren is a car-free cluster of ancient wooden chalets, an eyrie set on
a ledge 800 m (2,100 ft) straight up (literally) from the
Lauterbrunnen Valley floor. You reach it on a cog railway from
Lauterbrunnen, itself impossibly pretty, and as the train passes
Grutschalp it leaps the valley wall, opening up the best views bar
none of the entire Jungfraujoch. It really is the ultimate: only from
Mürren do you get the slanting range of the Eiger, Monch and
Jungfrau heaving their rocky mass out of the forests and meadows of
their flanking valleys. It's like looking through a cross-section of
natural beauty, of wilderness and domestic pastoral – and it is
especially intoxicating because the view is revealed only as the train
ascends, improving with every metre climbed.

You can ascend much higher than Mürren, on the cable car from
Stechelberg to the dizzy heights of Schilthorn (2,970 m/9,742 ft). If
anything, the panorama – from Bern to Mont Blanc – is even more
magnificent, but from the summit you see an exclusively Alpine world
of peaks and skyscapes. The softer valleys and lakes that from
Mürren balance earth with heaven are lost in this airy empire. On the
other hand, when you regain your powers of speech, you can enjoy a
drink in the revolving restaurant on Schilthorn's summit – made
famous by the James Bond film *On Her Majesty's Secret Service*.
Equally stunning in summer or winter, Lauterbrunnen to Schilthorn is
the best railway journey in Switzerland.

# Bernese Oberland Hike

The Bernese Oberland is famous even among Switzerland's exceptional landscapes. It is home to the great peaks, glaciers, forest valleys, vivid green pastures, rugged gorges and mare's tail waterfalls that form the composite quilt of Switzerland's most potently attractive image. There is a discreet network of trails and paths that enables you to go just about anywhere within its sphere of mythic mountain splendour. You will never be disappointed – but as an introduction to the region, the day's hike from Meiringen to Grindelwald is perfect.

At Meiringen, breakfast on a meringue (invented here) before following the angry Reichenbach torrent up the densely wooded flank of the Haslital to the Falls. Any irritation you may feel about the constant reminders of Sherlock Holmes in the area is quickly subsumed by the sublime beauty of the path ahead. At Kaltenbrunnen you burst out of the trees to get the first, exquisitely framed view of the snowy mountains. Every little valley here is another Shangri-La of flower-strewn meadow, bubbling stream, forest, and soaring cliff-faces; but ahead and behind, the view gradually gets bigger and bigger. Suddenly, you stand on the Grosse Scheidegg Pass itself. From 1,962 m (6,434 ft), with the Wetterhorn to one side close by, you look down across the upper Grindelwald glacier to the wisps of cloud hovering above village and valley. To your left, far along the ridge of snow and rock, the Eiger stands out as a perfect pyramid, blue on the misty horizon. Behind it looms the bulk of the Jungfraujoch; below, Kleine Scheidegg, with the Mannlichen Ridge and the Faulhorn to the right. This is beauty on an epic scale, a breathtaking and worthy partner to the vast arc of the sky; and it is classic Bernese Oberland. Walk down to Grindelwald, where locals understand your shining eyes and eager, wordless happiness.

**HOW:**
On foot
**WHEN TO GO:**
June to September
**TIME IT TAKES:**
Six to seven hours (Meiringen to Grindelwald via Grosse Scheidegg). There are a number of variations on the route, and of alternative means of transport for different parts of it. In a full day, you can hike the route and still enjoy some of the distractions en route as well.
**HIGHLIGHTS:**
The historic cog railway to the Reichenbach Falls – opened in 1899, it runs across cast-iron arched bridges, and the 100-year-old carriages have been rebuilt and two wooden 1899 semi-open cars have been copied from photographs, and re-introduced.
The magical tranquility of the remote and enclosed glen at Rosenlaui, beneath the Wetterhorn.
Riding a sledge or *velogemel* (snow bicycle) at night, in winter, from Grosse Scheidegg to Grindelwald , as fast as you dare down the 7-km (4-mi) ice-covered, snow-banked road.
Drinking in the view behind to Meiringen, and ahead to Grindelwald, from the hotel terrace at Grosse Scheidegg.
**YOU SHOULD KNOW:**
The infinite variety of walks and hikes in the Bernese Oberland means you need never do the same one twice.

*The glorious scenery around Grindelwald*

# Lucerne to Flüelen

**HOW:**
By boat
**WHEN TO GO:**
April to October; but the full
steamship service runs only between
June and late September.
**TIME IT TAKES:**
About three hours by steamer from
Lucerne to Flüelen. The ticket usually
allows you to make excursions from
any of the stops, and continue the
journey on a later sailing, and in either
direction.
**HIGHLIGHTS:**
The panorama across and down the
lake from Lucerne, where the water
is widest.
The needle dam in the Reuss River
outside Lucerne. The dam maintains
the Lake's level at the point where the
river leaves it.
The oldest alpine resort of
Burgenstock, a place of utter calm and
peace set on the low hills of a wooded
peninsula, seemingly set on the water.
William Tell's chapel, near Flüelen.
**YOU SHOULD KNOW:**
Swiss Railways' Flexi-Pass systems
frequently allow you to incorporate all
or part of the steamer journey from
Lucerne to Flüelen in a more
comprehensive travel plan.

*One of the 100 year-old paddle
steamers on Lake Lucerne*

Lake Lucerne is also known as 'Vierwaldstadtsee', the Lake of the
Four Forest Cantons through which it winds. Its complicated shape
contorts through forested mountains that rise steeply from its
shore, opening fresh panoramas of alpine magnificence under the
vast, shifting skies that inspired the British artist Turner and a
dozen other world-class painters. On its southeastern shore lies the
Rutli Meadow, traditional site of the founding of the Swiss
Confederation, and it is lined by many of Switzerland's oldest
communities like Vitznau, Brunnen and Treib. From Lucerne to
Flüelen, at the foot of the Lake's wildest and most remote arm,
these ancient villages and towns are oases of highly picturesque
domesticity set against dramatic peaks that change character with
benign or savage weather.

The unlikely combination is even more impressive when you
enjoy it from one of the fin-de-siècle paddle steamers that turn the
journey to Flüelen into a stylish rite. It's not nostalgia but glamour
that makes the journey such fun: the historic boats seem
appropriate to the grandeur of the waters they patrol. They fit into
a scenario that includes castles on promontories, timber-framed
villages huddled round 12th century stone-quoined ports, waterfalls
cascading down sheer granite cliffs, mountain meadows folded into
rock-filled ravines, and the brooding menace of mountains like Rigi,
forever changing mood, reflected in the sparkling water. Other boats
might reach Flüelen more quickly; the steamers add grace to
breathtaking landscapes that seldom look quite the same twice.

# Alpine Pass Hike

The Alpine Pass route is one of the great European hikes. It crosses Switzerland from Sargans in the east on the Lichtenstein border, to Montreux in the west on Lac Lèman. It crosses sixteen passes along its 354-km (220-mi) length, and completing it involves climbing and descending a total of 19,500 m (63,960 ft), the equivalent of going up and down Mount Everest more than twice! The reward is some of the world's most spectacular mountain scenery, with the additional satisfaction of passing through historically important passes and alpine towns.

The Hike is usually divided into fifteen stages of 9 to 28 km (5.6 to 17.5 mi), but with bad weather and rest days, it's generally regarded as a minimum 19 to 20 day journey. Of course you can undertake any of the stages as shorter excursions: the stages are calculated to connect with a variety of cable cars, chairlifts, funiculars, buses and trains for the weary, footsore and pressed for time. The important thing is to give full vent to the sheer enjoyment of the landscape. You'll pass the Wetterhorn, Eiger, Monch, Jungfrau, Gspaltenhorn, Blumlisalp and Les Diablerets – mountains of consummate grace and charisma. You'll cross huge glaciers in the high wilderness, traverse grassy saddles of alpine meadow, and drop deep into steep valleys of velvet emerald pasture. From the wilder shores of Lake Lucerne at Flüelen, the Bernese Oberland rises in majesty, and the Alpine Pass route weaves over, round and through the best of it. Ancient villages like Meiringen, Grindelwald, Mürren and Kandersteg typify regional variations in decorative architecture, cooking and local tradition – and good planning can make any part of the Hike coincide with the fairs and festivals on local calendars. Best of all: the Alpine Pass Hike needs relatively little preparation to transform it into a genuinely life-enhancing experience.

*The Alpine Pass runs through some of the world's most spectacular mountain scenery.*

**HOW:**
On foot

**WHEN TO GO:**
June to September, when the alpine wild flowers are at their best; every mountain hut and farmstead is welcoming, and good weather prevails.

**TIME IT TAKES:**
About twenty days, including at least fifteen days of actual walking. But with so much to see, and so many brilliant excursions, it's normal to complete the Hike at weekends, over months or even years.

**HIGHLIGHTS:**
The enormous differences between the passes – from the remote needle of Richetli to the spectacular rocky crest of Bunderchrinde or the tourist-thronged Kleine Scheidegg.
Climbing out of the Lauterbrunnen Valley via the Trummelbach Falls.
The changing panorama, familiar but subtly different every day.

**YOU SHOULD KNOW:**
1. Pre-conditioning on similar terrain is valuable if you intend to spend more than 2 days at a time walking; and even in high summer you'll need clothing suitable for the unreliable temperatures.
2. Taking a guide is not mandatory, but highly advisable in the remoter sections like Griesalp-Kandersteg-Adelboden. In any case, guides' intimate knowledge of mountains and folk-lore adds a whole dimension to the hike.

*The beautiful Simmental Valley*

# Golden Pass Panoramic Express

**HOW:**
By train
**WHEN TO GO:**
April to October. The service operates year-round, but many of the excursions that make breaking the journey so exciting do not.
**TIME IT TAKES:**
7 hours 20 minutes (Zurich to Geneva, including 5 hours 18 minutes Lucerne to Montreux). But the onward Golden Pass ticket remains valid however long you take to travel its different sections.
**HIGHLIGHTS:**
The pedestrian suspension bridge over one of Europe's most spectacular gorges near Aareschlucht Ost, Innertkirchen (part of an excursion including the Reichenbach Falls).
The super-privileged view from the very front of the train (beneath the driver's elevated cab), going up the giant horseshoe curve out of the gorgeous Simmental above Gstaad.
The intricate carvings, decorations and paintings on the huge, 113-windowed chalet at Rossiniere, in the distinctive style of the thickly wooded Pays d'Enhaut pre-Alpine region.
The quite stupendous view during the switchback hairpin descent into Montreux – the nearest a railway can get to a mountain road.
**YOU SHOULD KNOW:**
Reservations are necessary for seats in restaurant and 'panoramic' cars; and especially for the 'driver's seats' at the front of the train.

Officially, the Golden Pass links Zurich and Geneva, but its real purpose is to offer travellers a means of exploring the heart of Central Switzerland between Lucerne and Montreux without doubling their tracks. Each of the stops (Lucerne-Interlaken-Zweisimmen-Montreux) is a gateway to a choice of extraordinary excursions and activities in the area. The Golden Pass is designed to make them accessible and heavily discounted when the invitations to linger become irresistible. Otherwise, the scenic beauty and variety of the basic five hour eighteen minute journey is just an exercise in frustration. From Lucerne you can take a paddle steamer across the Lake to the cog railway up Rigi, the artist J.M.W. Turner's 'mountain of infinite mood'; or plunge into the gloomy splendour of the gorges leading to the dramatic Reichenbach Falls. At Interlaken, you can take one of several funiculars or mountain railways into the soul of the Bernese Oberland – even to the top of the Jungfrau itself. The onward journey is always magnificent, past the lakes of Brienz and Thun, through Spiez to the Simmen Valley, guarded at Wimmis by a fairytale 15th-century castle.

At Zweisimmen, you change trains to the special gauge Golden Pass Panoramic train designed by Ferrari's Pininfarina for the best possible views. The train climbs slowly enough to see the intricate and elaborate carvings typical of the region's chalets. These designs change radically from the steep-sided alpine pastoral valleys above Gstaad, to the gentler landscapes of French-speaking Switzerland near Chateau d'Oex (where a perfect sheltered microclimate makes it a world centre for hot-air ballooning). Then, as a visual crescendo of Wagnerian proportions, the train climbs a series of mountains, bridges and viaducts, through the summit tunnel to Les Avants, to emerge with the French Alps spread before you, beyond Montreux and the beckoning sparkle of Lac Lèman below.

# Glacier Express

As befits a service connecting two of the most glamorous resorts in the Alps, Zermatt and St Moritz, the Glacier Express is the last word in panoramic luxury. It needs to be, because in just eight hours it traverses the heart of Switzerland's highest mountain ranges. The journey starts at the foot of the twisted pyramid of the Matterhorn and skirts the Bernese Oberland, following the valley floors (in summer, riotous profusions of wild flowers) where the Rhône and the Rhine begin, and just below the line where glaciers spill out from the high passes. The landscape is a roll call of iconic names. The snow-capped summits of Schilthorn, Jungfrau, Monch and Eiger pass in distant backdrop, and the high peaks close in around the climbing train. Soaring viaducts arch above cloud-filled chasms, carrying it up and over the 2,033 m (6,668 ft) Oberalp Pass. Edging round sheer precipices, across 291 bridges and through 91 tunnels, the Glacier Express brings you so close to the mountains you can actually see the occasional chamois looking outraged at having to share the elemental magnificence of its rocky perch.

In fact, the train is every bit as first-class as the scenery. Though it has both 1st and 2nd class seating, everyone sits (in great comfort) beneath a glass roof, with good services at their disposal. The difference is that 2nd class is more crowded, an indicator of the train's popularity throughout the year. In summer it provides access to some of the finest high alpine walks; in winter it serves three of Switzerland's most justly celebrated skiing areas. But most people take the Glacier Express for the sheer joy of sightseeing in luxury – and then high-stepping off the train in the unadulterated chic of St Moritz or Zermatt.

**HOW:**
By train
**WHEN TO GO:**
Year-round. Seat reservations are mandatory, and lunch on the train should be pre-booked.
**TIME IT TAKES:**
About eight hours (Zermatt to St Moritz, via Visp, Brig, Andermatt and Chur). The unhurried pace of the ascents and descents justifies the route's nickname of 'the Slowest Express Train in the World'.
**HIGHLIGHTS:**
The tunnel at Furka – with its viaduct approaches and staggering ravine views, both a technological and scenic triumph.
The view from the top of the Oberalp Pass, looking along the length of the Alps. On a really clear day you see some 50 peaks in serried ranks leading to Mont Blanc.
The descent from Chur (Switzerland's historic and oldest township) to St Moritz.
**YOU SHOULD KNOW:**
The Glacier Express also has a 'Premium' service available for private parties of a single carriage or even whole trains.

*The Glacier Express travels from Zermatt to St Moritz.*

# Lötschberg

**HOW:**
By train
**WHEN TO GO:**
Year-round. From April to October, the Centovalli (Domodossola – Locarno) Railway operates a service every 30 minutes. Only scheduled Express trains connect with the Lötschberg.
**TIME IT TAKES:**
5 hours (Bern-Lötschberg-Centovalli-Locarno); 1.75 hrs (Domodossola-Locarno, 52 km/32 mi). NB. Though the tourist-oriented Centovalli 'Express' trains pause only at Camedo, Intragna and Ponte Brolla, they are rarely quicker than the stopping service.
**HIGHLIGHTS:**
The beautiful mountain Lake Oeschinen above Kandersteg, and the Lotschen Valley, one of Switzerland's most remote and pristine, in the World Heritage Landscape.
The 2.5 hr walk across the medieval bridge at Intragna, through the meadows up to the old stone hamlet of Rasa. There's no road access, and a tiny cable car whizzes you back over the valley to the next station, Verdasio.
Clanking over the iron viaduct spanning the 75 m (250 ft) deep Isorno River Gorge – the scene of Switzerland's first-ever bungee jump and still a favourite jump site.
**YOU SHOULD KNOW:**
1.The Lötschberg-Centovalli Express crosses international borders. Be sure you have valid documents for both Italy and Switzerland.
2.Unlike other Swiss trains, the Centovalli does not take seat reservations for its 'panoramic' cars, though it does charge a small fare supplement.

Two very different trains combine to make the shortest route between Bern and Lake Maggiore, and one of the greatest scenic journeys anywhere in Europe. The Lötschberg Line connects the UNESCO World Heritage city of Bern with the Jungfrau-Aletsch-Bietschorn, the Alpine world's first UNESCO World Heritage Landscape. It's a grand Euro-train, powering through the Simplon Tunnel to Italy, where Domodossola is effectively a terminus of the Swiss Railway system. Here the Lötschberg transfers its passengers to the delightful blue and white carriages of the narrow-gauge Centovalli Railway, which takes them back into Switzerland at Locarno, at a fraction of the pace but with scenery every bit as magnificent as the Aletsch Glacier north of the mountains. In just five hours, you see some of the very best pre-alpine landscapes – utterly different north and south – either side of the splendours of the Bernese Oberland.

The miniature-scale Centovalli Railway always connects with the Lötschberg, but it runs many more trains on its dedicated section. The route potters for 20 km (12.5 mi) to its highest point at Santa Maria Maggiore (830 m/2,722 ft), before dropping dramatically to Valle Vigezzo and leaving Italy at Ponte Ribellasca. Dense chestnut forests, studded with tranquil, ancient stone-built hamlets fill the web of steep valleys. Slowly inching across deep ravines on seemingly precarious viaducts and bridges, and through 22 short tunnels, the route offers staggering views of Mediterranean Alpine scenery as it cuts across some of the 'hundred valleys' between Camedo and Locarno. The 'panoramic' carriages of the Express are worth the supplement – but the region's incredible beauty is best appreciated if you stop (for lunch, a drink, a short hike or some other local activity) and breathe it in before catching the next train onwards. The Centovalli Railway guarantees you can have your cake and eat it too.

*The iron viaduct over the Isorno River Gorge*

# Andermatt to Grindelwald

*The road to the Furka Pass winds to the right of the Rhône Glacier.*

The yellow livery of the Alpine Postbus Network is a national institution in Switzerland. Punctual and ubiquitous, the buses reach the country's remotest corners, heedlessly coping with the steepest switchback roads and the highest passes. They even have a special, triple-toned horn based on a sequence from Rossini's opera *William Tell*. A series of Express routes covers the most spectacular roads across and between the high passes, and among the best is the 'Romantic Route'. It starts from the rustic village of Andermatt at the foot of the St Gotthard Pass, and climbs a terrifying sequence of hairpins rising 1,000 m (3,280 ft) in 18 km (12 mi). Coming over the Furka Pass, the road down to Gletsch follows the hillside above the awesome Rhône Glacier, before ascending the Grimsel Pass. From here you get one of the best panoramas in the Bernese Oberland, the classic grandeur of the triple-peaked ridge of the Eiger, Monch and Jungfrau (the Ogre, the Monk, and the Virgin).

Most people fall silent as the Postbus weaves past gentle reservoir lakes, dropping over 1,500 m (4,900 ft) to Meiringen on the Reichenbach Valley floor. This is where every dream about the Bernese Oberland is fulfilled. Rugged mountain drama yields to lucid green meadows in their summer glory of wild flowers; and the climb back up to Grosse Scheidegg, on to Grindelwald itself, is a landscape of the kind of beauty that robs you of speech. Every hamlet, farm, cow and cowbell seems in its proper firmament – and that's why the journey is called 'Romantic'. In fact, there's a lot of romance about: the route is so popular that double-decker Postbuses are used. If even that's not good enough, historic Postbuses are available for private charter.

*The road to the Furka Pass winds to the right of the Rhône Glacier.*

**HOW:**
By postbus

**WHEN TO GO:**
June to September, to include the wild flower finery of the valleys.

**TIME IT TAKES:**
Five hours (driving time); up to seven hours (travel time, depending on frequency and duration of stops of certain services).

**HIGHLIGHTS:**
The Rhône Glacier, already an image of nature at its grandest, here at the mighty river's source.
The melodious tinkle of big cowbells, answered by the frequent triple horn of the bus – the sound of alpine Switzerland.
Stopping for a meringue at Meiringen, where it was invented.
The north face of the Eiger seen from near Grindelwald.

**YOU SHOULD KNOW:**
Despite modern interpretations, the 'Romantic' Bernese Oberland got its nickname from the Romantic aesthetic popularized by Goethe, Mendelssohn and Lord Byron, all of whom were entranced by the landscape of the Jungfrau region.

# Jungfraujoch Cog Railway

**HOW:**
By train
**WHEN TO GO:**
Year-round; but many of the services and adventure attractions based in Jungfraujoch 'village' are only open from June to September.
**TIME IT TAKES:**
4 hours 45 minutes round trip from Interlaken (2 hours 25 minutes Interlaken-Lauterbrunnen-Jungfraujoch; 2 hours 25 minutes Jungfraujoch-Grindelwald-Interlaken).
**HIGHLIGHTS:**
Using the big permanent telescopes at Kleine Scheidegg to watch climbers on the North Face of the Eiger, towering above you.
Posting a letter at Europe's highest post office, next to Jungfraujoch Station.
The close-up of the Aletsch Glacier from the Sphinx Observation Platform, accessible by lift, and the highest point of Jungfraujoch.
**YOU SHOULD KNOW:**
The Jungfraujoch Railway ascends so high, so relatively quickly, that many people are troubled by the thin air. If you are affected, tell the nearest official; he/she will arrange immediate help.

*The Jungfraubahn on the way up from Kleine Scheidegg.*

The Jungfrau Railway leads to the highest railway station in Europe, at 3,454 m (11,333 ft). It is literally the zenith of a circular route from Interlaken round the heart of the Bernese Oberland, connecting its most famous resorts and providing access to the very best of the region's incomparable scenery and topographical splendour. The train engages its sturdy cog-wheels at Lauterbrunnen, ready to climb parallel to the fabled Lauberhorn Downhill World Cup course past pretty Wengen to Kleine Scheidegg, 2,061 m (6,762 ft) up at the foot of the fateful North Wall of the Eiger. Then it doglegs up to Eigergletscher, famous for its polar dog kennels (it is also the start of a difficult ski run called 'Oh, Hell!'), before hauling through the 7.3-km (4.6-mi) Eiger Tunnel to Eigerwand and Eismeer Stations. At each, it pauses for five minutes for travellers to gasp at the view unfolding through the giant windows hacked through the rock – but then it reaches the top at Jungfraujoch Station, a haven in the middle of glaciers and still-higher peaks of perpetual snow. In every direction, mountains pierce the clouds in the valleys far below, and in the intense blue clarity of the sky you can see as far as the Vosges Mountains in France, and the Black Forest in Germany. Here on the Jungfraujoch – the saddle connecting the Eiger, Monch and Jungfrau peaks among others – the Aletsch Glacier begins, the longest (22 km/14 mi) river of ice in the Alps.

In summer, there are husky-drawn sleigh rides at Jungfraujoch, as well as glacier skiing and a snowboard park; and it's the jump-off for some of Europe's best hiking and climbing. But winter or summer, it's the sensation of standing on the top of Europe that keeps firing the imagination.

# Val Tremola

If no longer the most famous, the St Gotthard is certainly the most historic of all Alpine passes. It opened to regular foot traffic in about 1200, and the first vehicle crossed in 1775. Its importance to both Switzerland and Italy is demonstrated both by the autoroute and rail tunnels underneath it, and the recent building of a new road over it. Take it if you're in a hurry to reach Bellinzona and Milan. But better by far is the much quieter old cobbled road that branches off just after Andermatt. You get a taste of how spectacular (and how worryingly lonely) Alpine travel must have been – until you reach the wild and windy top of the Pass, where you meet the new road, and where a new hotel and the old St Gotthard Hospice building (now a museum) sit by a small lake surrounded by picnicking families. From here the buses and nearly all the traffic follow the new road down to Airolo. Instead, find the old road which restarts behind the hotel. Now virtually deserted after centuries, it switchbacks in broad hairpins down the Val Tremola (the 'Trembling Valley'). The slick cobbles, hammered and rutted with use, cling to the steep green hillside, with some of its 38 bends propped up by precarious retaining walls. Drivers will be delighted. Passengers will be absorbed in the astounding vistas first, down into the heart of the valley; then along the length of the Ticino Valley (here called the Val Leventina) as it opens up below, descending in a blue haze to distant Bellinzona.

You pass wild gorges and waterfalls as the Alps give way to chestnuts and walnut trees – but the core of the journey is the Val Tremola. For centuries, all Europe passed this way.

*Bridge at the St Gotthard Pass*

**HOW:**
By car
**WHEN TO GO:**
May to October. The roads over the St Gotthard are not always open during winter.
**TIME IT TAKES:**
One to three hours, depending on how awestruck you are.
**HIGHLIGHTS:**
Finding yourself alone on the old road, able to pause when you want.
The engaging Museo Nazionale del San Gottardo (formerly the St Gotthard Hospice) at the summit of the Pass.
The natural rock arches of the Stretto di Stalvedro, at the mouth of the wild Val Canaria, between Airolo and Biasca.
The three castles of the World Heritage Site of Bellinzona, including 14th century Castelgrande, built on a Roman castle/palace, and now a museum of archaeology and arts.
**YOU SHOULD KNOW:**
Beware the Val Tremola in wet weather – not because of the rain itself, but because some motorcyclists view driving the wet cobbled bends as a desirable challenge to be attempted at speed.

# The Spree and Havel Rivers

The Spree River joins the larger Havel at Spandau. It flows from the huge, car-free network of broadleaf woods and *fliesse* (waterways) comprising the benign wilderness of the Spreewald Biosphere Reserve southeast of Berlin. It brings Berlin most of its water – and the opportunity to float through the heart of Germany's capital on practically any kind of boat, and in any kind of style that you choose. The Havel continues to the palaces and pleasure grounds of Potsdam, Germany's former royal capital, and onwards west and north. It bulges with lakes, leading eventually to the forested seclusion of the Shorfeide-Chorin UNESCO Biosphere, but it shares its enchanting natural wonders with evidence of Germany's most illustrious history. The Elector's Castle at Oranienburg, and Brandenburg an der Havel, the medieval town set on three islands in mid-river, are just two of hundreds of jaw-dropping surprises.

Most importantly, the Spree and the Havel form Berlin's alternative transport system. Using the Landwehrkanal linking the Upper and Lower Spree (at Schlesisches Tor and Charlottenburg) you can visit the Reichstag and the very centre of the reunited city. But you can also see the 19th-century elegance of lovely Nikolaiviertel, and the thirty historic ships still working at Berlin's oldest quarter, the old harbour of Fischerinsel in Kreuzberg. Berlin is veined with waterways based on its two rivers, and the options are endless. Wannsee is Berlin's main water playground, and the site of festivals like 'Wannsee in Flames', a September parade of boats with music, dance and spectacular fireworks. Potsdam's gardens, lakes and parks match its peerless architectural magnificence: like Berlin in its variety of historic and modern moods, these treasures acquire a completely novel perspective, seen from the water. Short or long, a cruise on the Spree and Havel will forever change the way you think about Germany.

*With the Cathedral in the background, the tourist boats glide along the Spree River.*

# Berlin Wall Bike Trail

*The heavily illustrated segment of the Berlin Wall*

It appeared in 1961 without warning, and disappeared just as suddenly in 1989. Now, the very few fragments of the original Berlin Wall still in situ are themselves protected by fencing from souvenir hunters. Once an embarrassment, the Wall is now regarded as the defining icon of the reunited, reconstructed and re-born capital of Germany. Recently, Berliners completed a bike trail that follows its path for a meandering 106 km (66 mi) across the city and its suburbs. Where railway lines or reconnected streets forced long detours, tunnels and bridges now link the obstructed sections; and as nature has reclaimed the open spaces originally cleared to make a 'killing ground' along its length, the Wall is now represented by a ribbon of green in a grey urban landscape. This chilling 'death strip' was 5 to 100 m (16 to 330 ft) wide – big enough to get lost in the sprouting birch trees and thick underbrush if you miss one of the grey 'Mauerweg' ('Wall Trail') signs at intersections.

The Trail provides a privileged green access corridor to the heart of Berlin and the best of its sights and amenities. But every inch of it is also a confrontation with some of the city's – and Germany's – worst historical nightmares. Bravely, modern Berliners embrace the past as inevitable. They've rescued one piece of their history, the Brandenburg Gate, from isolated sterility in former no-man's-land, but kept the flaking concrete pillbox watchtower column behind it, from which guards sniped at and killed dozens who made their pitiful dash for freedom. The Trail helps explain how optimism triumphed over the institutionalized violence implicit in the Wall's graffiti-ed concrete and its associated artefacts. It is gut-wrenchingly successful, and a brilliant introduction to modern Berlin.

**HOW:**
By bike
**WHEN TO GO:**
Year-round. Berlin Wall Bike Trail guided tours are only scheduled from May-September, but can be arranged with most tour agents throughout the year. So can the information packs, bike rentals and anything else you need for a self-guided tour.
**TIME IT TAKES:**
Four to five hours (scheduled tour), but with or without a guide, you could easily spend days or weeks refining your explorations.
**HIGHLIGHTS:**
Just think – you're riding the path used by heavily-armed DDR Customs, Police and Army patrols 24/7 throughout the Wall's existence. About 3,200 people were arrested trying to cross it; and 270 died trying to get over, under or through it.
The wackiness of having this parkland 'highway' through a major capital city – in it, and very much of it, but still utterly distinct from it.
**YOU SHOULD KNOW:**
Endlessly fascinating, this is one of the great bike trails in the world, combining the exercise with the highest standard of visual, cultural and historical interest. What it reveals about the Cold War remains a work in progress, of relevance to all of us.

# Bridges Cycle Route

The web of rivers, lakes and canals spread across the flatlands of Germany's northwest corner is cycling heaven. Easy riding leaves you plenty of energy to enjoy the succession of nature reserves, moors and wetlands that stud the rich loam of Lower Saxony's northern farmland. Isolated now, the region's small villages and towns once stood on some of Europe's busiest trade routes. The Bridges Cycle Route follows one of them, from Osnabrück to Bremen. Both cities rose to prominence under Charlemagne at the turn of the 8th/9th centuries, but the region had been prized long before by the Romans (whose ubiquitous relics of defeat are a matter of great local pride). Osnabrück's market place and old town comprise one of the most beautiful survivals of urban medieval architecture anywhere (and the treaty of Westphalia was signed here in 1648, ending the Thirty Years War); while still evident behind Bremen's bustling modernity is the equally ancient city of Roland, who held the pass at Roncesvalles for his King, Charlemagne.

Between them the cycling is mostly asphalt, with some forest, farm and gravel tracks in the nature reserves along the way. Dummer Lake is home to every kind of watery recreation, besides providing sanctuary to a huge variety of waterfowl and bird species. Goldenstedt has an ingenious tunnel to introduce you to moorland ecology; and the historic wonders of Diepholz, Löhne and Vechta are matched by the megalithic tombs and historical monuments of the Wildeshauser Geest. You pick your way across water and wetness on every kind of imaginable bridge: plank, wooden arch, Roman (Bohmte/Hunteburg), medieval stone, moated drawbridge, sculpted Baroque or railway viaduct. The final bridge takes you across the River Weser straight to Bremen's Schlachte, the promenade of restaurants in the heart of the city. Cyclists can even park there.

*The Rathaus (town hall) in Bremen*

**HOW:**
By bike

**WHEN TO GO:**
April to October, but experienced bikers may also enjoy the vast skies and misty, diffused light of winter, when icy roads are not recommended for novices.

**TIME IT TAKES:**
Four to five days

**HIGHLIGHTS:**
The ancient battle site of Kalkriese (aka. 'Varus battle'), near Bramsche, where Roman legions suffered a devastating rout in 9 AD at the hands of Germanic tribes, and never got this far again. The museum has original artefacts of the battle, and colourful re-enactments.
The moated castle at Diepholz.
The citadel and armoury museum at Vechta.

**YOU SHOULD KNOW:**
The defeat by Arminius of the Roman legions under Varus has been the subject of centuries of myth, disbelief, and speculation. Only in 1987/88 did anyone find sufficient evidence (thousands of coins, weapons, and many other relevant objects) to show that the battle really did take place on the scale lauded in German poetry.

# The Romantic Road

Beloved by Germans as one of their favourite holiday routes, the Romantic Road starts by the River Main at the Prince-Bishopric fortress town of Wurzburg. Picking its way through rural backwaters of stunning beauty, it seeks out some of Germany's least-famous but most magnificent castles, palaces, old towns and topographical curiosities; crosses the Danube at Donauwörth, and follows the bubbling torrent of the alpine Lech River all the way to King Ludwig II's 19th century fairytale extravaganzas of Neuschwanstein and Hohenschwangau. Finally, it crosses the Alps in a flourish of jagged peaks to the Austrian Tyrolean city of Innsbruck. It's a route that is archetypically German, a visual poem of misty, chivalrous romance.

Across Francony, Swabia and western Bavaria you pass through the topography of feudalism in all its degrees. Commanding each valley, river junction, or broad plain, a huge castle-palace proclaims the regional duke of yore; a cathedral lends him spiritual authority; in nearby towns, lesser towers and imposing manors announce his fiefs; and his borders are marked and guarded by gigantic fortresses. In each city, town and village, this hierarchy is repeated on a half-timbered domestic scale of wonderful subtlety, their buildings and services ranked according to the medieval or Renaissance priorities when they were built.

The discovery makes the journey entrancing. The system may repeat itself, but even within short distances, the landscapes and styles change completely. Vagaries of history mean you encounter Baroque, medieval, Renaissance and Gothic styles at random, just as you cross ranges of hills, river gorges, and meadow plains before the journey's dramatic finale among Alpine peaks. Tranquil, vivacious, and tempestuous by turn, the Romantic Road generates both cause and effect.

**HOW:**
By bike or car
**WHEN TO GO:**
April-October
**TIME IT TAKES:**
12-14 days (by bike, 576 km/360 mi)
**HIGHLIGHTS:**
Making the rounds with the night watchman in the walled Gothic town of Rothenburg.
The oddity of Nördlingen, an ancient town with the only completely preserved medieval walls in Germany, sitting in the middle of a huge, 15-million year old meteorite crater.
The medieval city centre of Landsberg, set romantically in the wild river bed of the Lech.
Neuschwanstein Castle – especially the Music Room, a great hall on the top floor, its ceiling painted the dark blue of night, set with a thousand stars.
The magnificent mountain landscapes on the Austrian side, near Imst.
**YOU SHOULD KNOW:**
If you take your time, this journey can be just as romantic by car.

*The gloriously romantic Neuschwanstein Castle*

# Middle Rhine Valley

**HOW:**
By car, train, bike or boat
**WHEN TO GO:**
April to October
**TIME IT TAKES:**
About 4 hours (by boat, Bingen-Koblenz ); 2-8 days (by boat, Strasbourg-Koblenz, depending on excursions en route like Heidelberg or Worms); 1 day (by car, Strasbourg-Koblenz, following the river); 6-9 days (by bike, Strasbourg-Koblenz). Try to arrange your trip to coincide with one of many local festivals like the Ritterspiele (Knights' Festival) at St Goar in the shadow of the Lorelei Rock.
**HIGHLIGHTS:**
Listening to German composers like Beethoven, Brahms, Mendelssohn and even Wagner, while contemplating the same dramatic inspiration of precipitous cliffs, ruined castles and half-timbered villages.
Life in the Middle Ages, through the prism of stupendous Marksburg Castle (not a ruin), near Braubach.
The cobbled prettiness of Bacharach, especially Castle Stahleck, and Castle Pfalz, imposing and complete on its island in mid-river.
The constantly recurring thought that in the Rhine Valley, Man and Nature occasionally produce a highly acceptable partnership.
**YOU SHOULD KNOW:**
The attractions of the Middle Rhine Valley deserve more than a fleeting glimpse: the 'Rheinsteg Trail' is a recent addition to the select list of long-distance German walks, and is reckoned at 14-21 days from Strasbourg to Koblenz.

The Middle Rhine Valley from Strasbourg to Koblenz is a slow crescendo culminating in Germany's most iconic geographical feature. By car, train, bicycle or boat, your path runs between the Black Forest and the more rugged Pfälzerwald to the west. The river broadens and unwinds lazily into the wetland sanctuaries downstream around Worms and Mainz. Gaining momentum with the added mass of the river Main, it fusses its way to Bingen before unleashing itself into the 65 km (43 mi) gorge twisting north to Koblenz. Celebrated in painting, poetry, music and the grandest of opera, the Rhine Gorge here is a byword for wild, dramatic beauty – but in fact it is a cultural landscape fashioned not by Nature but by Man.

UNESCO designated its World Heritage status by citing 'the continuous evolutionary nature of the cultural environment'. Meaning that with a railway and two roads (upper and lower) on each vineyard-terraced bank, the Rhine's importance as a highway for commerce and tourism is undiminished in 2,000 years – and we visitors are participants in the continuing process. The Middle Rhine Valley is the gateway to central Europe. The castles, towns and villages perched on its jagged rocks, unable to expand and unwilling to modernize the genuinely historical 'look' that helps to stimulate the mythic notions called 'Rhine Romanticism', have become their own industry. By boat, there are no tollgates but your fare contributes to the river. In a car or on a bike, you tap more directly into the symbiosis of trade and beauty that remains so attractive; but you can only see things on the other bank, where they are unreachable. However you travel, the Middle Rhine Valley is a cultural mirror of venerable age and insight, and should be respected as much as admired.

*Marksburg Castle sits above the town of Braubach.*

# Hell Valley Railway

Höllental (Hell Valley) is a 'V'-shaped gash 9 km (5.4 mi) long in the rocks of the Black Forest in southwest Germany. Its imposing slopes are 600 m (1,970 ft) high, pulled into a gorge so narrow that at one point, a bronze statue high on a crag commemorates a stag that famously escaped its hunters with one gigantic bound right across it. The Valley was typical of the dense impenetrable forest of legend until just 150 years ago, when the only mule track became a narrow road, inspiring the Railway of 1889-1901 that connects Freiburg with Donaueschingen. The Railway's engineering is as awesomely dramatic as the views to which it gives access. It is 25.4 km (15.8 mi) long, rising from 278 m (912 ft) in Freiburg to 885 m (2,903 ft) at Hinterzarten (Donaueschingen); built as a cog railway, its 5.5 per cent average gradient provoked the development of ordinary trains powerful enough to keep traction on the ascent. The new technology improved railways everywhere.

Now, the locomotives are still stubby, but sleeker. They pull double-decker carriages to cope with the large number of travellers seeking the thrill of one of western Germany's most dramatic mountain routes. Even if you're saturated with lovely Freiburg, the trip is a beautiful surprise. The 'Hirschsprungfelsen' is one of several rock formations that make whole mountains look sculpted, but the natural landscapes are enhanced by nine tunnels and a series of impossible viaducts – like the Ravennaschlucht, 222 m (728 ft) long and 42 m (138 ft) high – that carry you up to Doeggingen. Without overt fuss, in the middle of a 535 m (1,755 ft) tunnel, the line crosses Europe's principal watershed, and drops you, blinking in the bright light, in the beautiful high woods where the River Danube springs forth.

*The imposing Hell Valley*

**HOW:**
By train
**WHEN TO GO:**
Year-round
**TIME IT TAKES:**
Forty to fifty minutes
**HIGHLIGHTS:**
Lake Titisee/Neustadt – set into the hills and fringed with woods, and a magnet for sailing and canoeing.
Hiking in the Wutach Gorge: the viaduct at Kappel Gutachbrucke crosses the foaming Wutach at the very head of its beautiful gorge. A 13-km (8-mi) trail traces its wildest corners across rocks and wet, slippery, plank footbridges. A Nature Reserve of maple, oak, lime and mulberry trees, it's home to 1,200 rare species, 30 orchids, 100 species of birds (including kestrels, kites and kingfishers) and butterflies, and a vanishing river.
The ceremonial coach and other treasures of the Furstenberg family, at their 1723 *Schloss* in Donaueschingen. In 1806, everything passed to Baden-Wurttemberg, so the coach looks particularly forlorn.
The 'Donauquelle' – the actual spring, in the *Schlosspark*, of the Danube, on its way to the Black Sea.
**YOU SHOULD KNOW:**
In 1770, the Höllental region of the Black Forest belonged to Austria, so when Marie-Antoinette, daughter of the Austrian Emperor, came to meet her future bridegroom, Louis XVI, she rested here. Being (technically) still in Austria, she was fed Vienna roast a la Black Forest.

# The Alpine Road

**HOW:**
By car or bike
**WHEN TO GO:**
May to October. It can be driven in winter, but some of the Alpine passes close in bad weather. The warmer months are a succession of local festivals and fairs, especially at the Lake Constance end.
**TIME IT TAKES:**
3-6 days (by car, allowing for a number of stops and/or off-route sightseeing); 7-14 days (by bike, a varied cycling distance of 102-396 km/64-248 mi, with no rest days or side-trips); 18-28 days (on foot – though not really on the Alpine Road. The predominantly very difficult hiking route crosses the high peaks more or less congruous to the Road; it's shorter at 320 km (200 mi), and called the Maximiliansweg).
**HIGHLIGHTS:**
The classic quality of the hairpin sections of the highway – if you've ever enjoyed driving, this is the thrill you've always imagined (and with a safety margin on the road's width to take the edge off fear).
The sophisticated liqueurs and brandies produced since 1330 by the Benedictine monastery at Ettal. Mittenwald – old, intricately painted and decorated according to the most ancient, but still living traditions; full of charm and stunningly beautiful. Konigsee, the long, narrow lake near Berchtesgaden, darkened by steep forested banks and one of Germany's most dramatic and romantic natural landscapes.
**YOU SHOULD KNOW:**
To avoid emotional confusion in deciding whether to enjoy the journey, be assured that the Alpine Road was not Hitler's idea, but he did encourage its execution.

The German Alpine Road belongs to the heyday of motorcar 'Touring', when Bugatti battled with Daimler-Benz on road rallies like Italy's Mille Miglia. The Alpine Road was built in the 1930s to stimulate the new mobility, but Hitler, ambitious to impress, annexed the project. Germany's Alpine Road was to be altogether more grand, more sweeping and more beautiful than anyone else's – and 26,000 labourers were to build 105 bridges, 15 tunnels, and ten viaducts to make it so, joining Lindau on Lake Constance with Berchtesgaden in the heartland of the Bavarian Alps. In fact, it was only completed in 2002. Now it carves boldly through some 450 km (281 mi) of Germany's loveliest mountain scenery. Through the Allgau and up into the Alps it winds past 21 turquoise and lapis lakes, 25 castles including the inspired fantasy of Neuschwanstein, and brooding dark green forests cut with secret valleys, where ancient moss soaks emerald in angry waterfalls. Imperiously the Alpine Road swings back and forth, cresting precipices and swaying round the long corniches. It's designed to be driven for fun, and fun it is.

Stunning though it is for people who love their machines, the road owes its sublime pleasures to its fundamental natural magnificence. From the grand, Italianate, gabled houses of medieval Lindau, prettily reflected in the lake, the landscapes are composed of drama and varied history, and each little town has a facet to add to its regional culture. Lakeside Bregenz, woodcarving Oberammergau, Mittenwald where violins are made in one of Bavaria's most evocative villages, Füssen and the high alpine market towns make the perfect domestic foil for the rugged wilderness of their settings. With obvious draws like Schwangau, the Bavarian Rococo ten-sided church of Kloster Ettal near Garmisch, and charming Berchtesgaden itself, the Alpine Road is like a handsome, dashing charmer who will never be out of style.

*The road winds through one of Germany's most dramatic and romantic natural landscapes.*

# Rennsteig Trail

Although the term 'rennsteig' ('racing steep') has been applied to many of Germany's ancient trade routes, 'The Rennsteig' refers exclusively to the famous high altitude trail through the Thuringian Forest. For 168 km (106 mi) it follows a ridge connecting the highest peaks between Blankenstein on the Upper Saal River, and Horschel near Eisenach. The path has served as a geographical and political border as well as a highway for over 1,000 years, but it has been relatively inaccessible until recently. That has helped revive its natural ecology, and the region has become a wildlife haven despite its popularity with summer crowds.

Known as the 'green heart' of Germany, an upland corridor of emerald forest some 20 km (12 mi) broad stretches 60 km (37 mi) northwest, (roughly) from Greiz to Eisenach. This highland plateau includes the Thuringian Forest's most dramatic, unspoilt and beautiful natural scenery. Its hills are bounded by fault lines, rising in steep scarps from the spruce and broadleaf woods whose canopy is broken only by a few open pastures close to the smallholdings of ancient hamlets. Within the forest, the highest peaks are only about 985 m (3,230 ft), but they are geological marvels of gneiss, porphyry and granite. The Rennsteig weaves between them, taking in the best vistas of its pastoral idyll, and occasionally opening up superb panoramas on either side to one of the peaceful, romantic villages folded into the hollows.

Access to the Rennsteig is well supplied by public transport: before reunification some of its sections were the favourite destinations of East German campers and schoolchildren. It also has any number of places to rest and shelter – some recalling the ridge-way's illustrious history as an Imperial messenger route, when it passed through a dozen different states and principalities. The Rennsteig's history is almost a match.

**HOW:**
On foot

**WHEN TO GO:**
April to October. It can be just as wonderful in winter, but fewer facilities make it advisable to walk only short sections at a time.

**TIME IT TAKES:**
8-14 days, depending on walkers' age and experience. None of the stages are difficult, but there are some lengthy ascents when endurance will be at a premium.

**HIGHLIGHTS:**
The satisfaction of the first day, walking far above Blankenstein, looking back across the Saal and its lakes spread below.
The highest section of the ridge, Beerberg (982m/3,221 ft), part of the astonishingly lovely view from Schmucke.
The summer toboggan run at Brotterode – just off the Rennsteig, but worth the detour for its 12 steep curves to the racing kilometer, taken full pelt.

**YOU SHOULD KNOW:**
The Rennsteig is so nearly perfect that some walkers get irritated by the presence of others using it. It can happen to anyone – but truly the landscapes are wonderful enough to share in peace.

*Hikers on the Rennsteig Trail in the Thuringian Forest*

*Burghausen and the Salzach River*

**HOW:**
By bike
**WHEN TO GO:**
April to September (with guide; and self-guided with practical assistance from a tour agent). Come for one of the big festivals or annual religious parades.
**TIME IT TAKES:**
7-8 days (216-272 km/135-170 mi, starting anywhere on the circular Trail, and allowing for diversionary sight-seeing). Emotional logic suggests starting from the Pope's 1927 birthplace in what used to be (1798) the Prince-Electors' Customs House in the dreamy riverside village of Marktl; scenic sense insists you travel clockwise, so your ride culminates in the glories of Altötting, the epicentre of Bavaria's cult of the Black Madonna, and site of the Pope's First Communion.
**HIGHLIGHTS:**
The Baroque church (1698), Cistercian Abbey (1146) and medieval houses clustered below the colossal 15th century castle at Burghausen, built by the Dukes of Landshut (notably George 'The Rich'!) to house their treasure.
The stunning location of the medieval trading centre of Wasserburg, encircled on three sides by the River Inn.
The untouched antiquity of the fishermen's cottages, the mid-8th century Convent, Carolingean-era Abbey and every other building on Fraueninsel, one of the islands on Lake Chiemsee. The other one is famous for Ludwig II's extraordinary version of Versailles, Herrenchiemsee Palace.
**YOU SHOULD KNOW:**
The lime tree on the path outside the Chapel of Grace at Altötting was planted in 1980 by Pope John-Paul II as a votive offering to the Black Madonna, Bavaria's 'national shrine'. Since Pius VI in 1782, five other Popes have made a pilgrimage to Altötting.

# The Benedict Trail

The Benedict Trail is a six-day biographical bike tour round the heart of rural Upper Bavaria. It's a circular route 'in the footsteps' of Pope Benedict XVI. Joseph Ratzinger was born, raised, educated, and found his vocation in the region. He still has family here, and it remains very close to his heart. After his clerical studies, he (and his brother) celebrated their 'Primiz' – the first Mass of a newly-consecrated priest – in Traunstein; and at his Papal inauguration in the Vatican he was handed a special memento of the 'Black Madonna' of Altötting, to whom he had proclaimed devotion as a boy. She has been venerated for 500 years as special to Bavaria, and is one of Germany's greatest centres of pilgrimage. It is as much a compliment to this most devout region of ultra-Catholic Bavaria, where Benedictine educational tenets have been entrenched for centuries, as to the Saint, that the Pope chose Benedict's name for himself. The Trail opens a window into that culture.

The scenic marvels – rivers, forests, ancient hamlets still toting their manorial loyalties on banners and chivalric regalia, massive fortresses, needle-spired churches and capitals of forgotten dukedoms by lakes – unfold forgivingly on the eye. These are landscapes familiar from 15th-17th century oil paintings, and not a lot has changed on the Trail's constantly stimulating historic byways. Pope apart, it's as good as a week's cycling can get. But the Papal associations (domestic and spiritual) are potent enough to re-route the imagination. His life inspires a rare intimacy between visitor and place, bringing the region's history, living, into the present. Piety in this part of Bavaria built and maintains these religious establishments in the context of a community and culture. It nurtured a Pope.

# Rasende Roland

Rugen, the Baltic island close to Germany's northeast border with Poland, has been a popular holiday resort for generations of visitors. Rasende Roland has been one of its greatest attractions for over 100 years. It's a vintage, steam-puffing, narrow gauge train service that connects Putbus with Rugen's southeast resorts of Binz, Sellin and Göhren. Its track is only 750mm (2 ft 6 in) wide and 24 km (15 mi) long, and its immaculately maintained engines and carriages – to the same scale – reinforce its appearance as an overgrown children's toy. In fact, Rasende ('Racing' or 'Runaway') Roland is a year-round scheduled service, and its significance is that only its miniature size permits it to run wholly within the boundaries of the UNESCO Biosphere Reserve that fills Rugen's southeast corner.

It's a region of peninsulas, small islands, hooked spits and sand bars; and it includes the Granitz Forest, the Mönchgut peninsula, and Vilm – a small island whose oak and beech forest has remained untouched for whole centuries, and whose unique flora can only be visited by appointment. Dogged and unobtrusive, Rasende Roland runs just inside the Reserve's edge. Thirteen stations provide access to the many natural wonders and variety of sights and entertainments. Roland is happy to be a bus. At Sellin, you can take a little funicular to the beach and pier below. Get off at Baabe for biking round leafy lanes and blueberry woods, or Göhren, to cycle through the coastal forest to Thiessow, where you can sit near a small café to watch the waders and waterfowl in the marshy lagoons. From Göhren you can also cycle back to Binz by way of long strands of white beach, ice creams and swimming.

Rasende Roland is so right for Rugen. Steam rail enthusiasts swear by its technical brilliance in miniature. The rest of us just enjoy it.

**HOW:**
By train
**WHEN TO GO:**
Year-round (Putbus-Göhren). From May to September, the number of trains between Binz and Göhren is doubled; and the line is extended from Putbus to Lauterbach, the harbour where Roland connects with the boat to and from Vilm.
**TIME IT TAKES:**
About 1.25 hours (Putbus-Göhren); about 4.5 hours (Putbus-Lauterbach-boat to Vilm-Putbus).
**HIGHLIGHTS:**
Rasende Roland's vintage engines – their steaming, hissing tubes and polished brasses are irresistible and glamorous, and each has a special character.
Jagdschloss Granitz Castle, near Binz – rosy pink crenellated towers and an astounding collection of shooting trophies in its 19th century luxurious interior.
Walking through the woods between Binz and Sellin (the train stops at both). Very Grimm!
**YOU SHOULD KNOW:**
Dreams can come true. You can take a 10-day course on how to drive a steam locomotive, supervised by a regular driver with whom you will work during his normal shift. It's the real thing, and you get a certificate as an 'Honorary Engine Driver' of Rasende Roland.

*Rugen's little steam train*

# The Eagle's Nest

The 'Eagle's Nest' is the nickname given by the American occupying forces of 1945 to Hitler's lodge on the 1,834 m (6,017 ft) peak of Mount Kehlstein, pressed against the Bavarian Alps' border with Austria. It commands a 360 degree panoramic view across the mountains, fulfilling the intentions of Martin Bormann and Hitler's innermost circle, who conceived the lodge as a 50th birthday present that would symbolize the singular height and endurance of Hitler's authority. Inevitably, the hubris of that intention makes the Eagle's Nest one of Bavaria and Germany's biggest tourist magnets. Be warned: it is a stunningly beautiful place, but despite local people's most fervent wish it is tainted by history, and no euphemism can change that.

Even so, getting there is a unique journey. There is only one way. You must take the bus from Obersalzberg, because the road (closed to normal traffic) is like no other in the world. From Obersalzberg to the top, it is designed so that in a 700-m (2,296-ft) vertical ascent over 6.5 km (4 mi), there is only one bend, and you cross the steep northwest face of the Kehlstein twice. Your ears pop and you might not look if your eyes weren't glued wide-open. At the upper car park, you are directed into an imposing, marble-lined tunnel that cuts 124 m (406 ft) straight into the mountain, where an ornate, brass-frilled and ornamented lift whisks you up to the inside of the Eagle's Nest buildings in just 41 seconds. The walls are a metre thick, and the place is a fortress. The conference and domestic rooms and the terraces would be mundane except that imagination is in full flow, reconciling extraordinary location and engineering with all the rest. You set out joking, excited. You come back speechless.

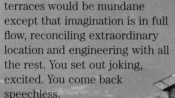

# Southern Wine Road

A towering stone archway called the Weintor ('Wine Gate') marks the beginning of Germany's Southern Wine Road, at the French/German border town of Schweigen in the Pfalz (Palatinate). From here, the Road curls through the small river valleys carved out of the foothills of the Pfälzerwald, a huge UNESCO Biosphere Reserve of upland forest, moors and sandstone crags; then emerges into the broad reaches of the Rhine, where an almost Mediterranean climate makes the low hills ideal for viticulture (the Romans introduced the vines, along with the almond trees, figs, lemons and kiwis which grow here). It is scenic, gentle countryside, set with small castles on promontories and little villages of intricately carved, half-timbered antiquity. Only Neustadt a.d.Weinstrasse, the regional centre, reveals the industrial aspects of the massive wine industry, but its giant silver tanks offer more promise than offence.

The Southern Wine Road continues north as far as Durkheim, September site of the world's biggest wine festival (held around the world's biggest wine-barrel). Durkheim is the centre of a marvellous loop hike through especially picturesque and historic villages, but the Road to Neustadt and Landau is in any case a sybarite hiker's dream – wonderful landscapes, welcoming towns and villages and festivals of some sort in every one. The trip is more intense in the hills between Landau, Bergzabern and Schweigen. Each valley is more isolated and each tiny town more distinct. Filled with flowers and vines trailing across narrow streets and ancient buildings, hamlets like Dörrenbach, Gleiszellen-Gleisorbach or Oberotterbach nevertheless have characters as different from each other as their wines. Dramatically placed between steep terraces of vines, or huddled under cliff-faces (so the higher ground is free for vineyards) they demand that you sit and drink in what makes them special.

*The church and vineyards at Siebeldingen near Landau*

**HOW:**
On foot
**WHEN TO GO:**
April-October. Even from March, there are countless festivals, including Mandelblutenfest (Almond Blossom Festival) in Gimmeldingen (March), Erlebnistag Weinstrasse (Wine Road Day) everywhere (last Sunday in August); and Neustadt's October Deutsches Weinlesefest (Wine Harvest Festival), when the German Wine Queen is crowned.
**TIME IT TAKES:**
6-8 days (Bad Durkheim-Neustadt-Bergzabern-Schweigen, 110-130 km (69-81 mi) allowing for a very short day at least once, following a night's inevitable celebrating en route).
**HIGHLIGHTS:**
Federweisser (featherwhite) wine – 'a cloudy, sweet, bubbly almost-wine' still in the process of fermenting, and much more potent that it tastes. Walking from Deidesheim across the 'Pfalz balcony', with the hills rising on one side and stunning vistas across the Rhine plain, full of ancient and beautiful wine estates.
**YOU SHOULD KNOW:**
A new route opened in 2008 called the Pfälzer Mandelpfad (Almond Trail). It's a 50-km (31-mi) hiking trail through vineyards and long rows of almond trees, from Maikammer to Bergzabern.

# Castle Road

Travelling on Castle Road across Germany to the Czech Republic feels like leafing through a storybook. One day might be a chivalric adventure of knights-at-arms. The next, a Renaissance romance of courtly manners, or a poetic extravaganza of Baroque magnificence, or the military reminiscences of a Roman soldier. There are more than sixty notable castles and palaces between Mannheim and Prague, each one with a 500 to 1,000 year-old history written into its fabric. Individually fascinating benchmarks of power, strength, wealth and pleasure during many eras, they tell an even more absorbing collective tale of German cultural evolution and of its contribution to a shared European heritage.

Castle Road is roughly 1,000 km (625 mi) long, with Nuremberg approximately halfway. Its byways wind through local, provincial and regional capitals from the Neckar Valley to the magic sylvan tranquility along the course of the Jagst and Tauber rivers. It crosses the green, picture-perfect range of Franconian Switzerland and the Main River into the crags of Francony's huge forest and the Fichtelgebirger, with Bohemia beyond. Like the natural landscapes, the castles and great houses range in style and setting from the graceful, gentle and elegant, to the sophisticated, imposing and grand. Some swagger with brooding magnificence. Others inspire frightful awe. After Bamberg (a UNESCO World Heritage Site of breathtaking historical magnitude), the terrain is wilder, and huge fortresses at Coburg and Kronach, along with a dozen medieval masterpieces farther on, show how might was usually found to be sufficiently right. Castle Road passes through whole medieval towns, like Rothenburg, Schwabisch Hall, or Kirchberg on the Jagst, where town and castle clearly show the Rennaissance and Baroque additions on their medieval origins. Castle Road's real achievement is to combine the roll call of towns and the disparate virtues of their unique structures into a single fanfare for Germany's richest history.

*Horneck Castle in Gundelsheim*

# The Route of Emperors and Kings

*The Danube in Budapest*

For more than 1,000 years, the Danube has been the principal highway for the exercise of power in central Europe. It connects major capital cities east and west. Between Regensburg and Budapest especially, its banks are studded with the towns, abbeys, fortresses, palaces and cathedrals built to demonstrate the temporal power of bishops, princelings, dukes and oligarchs whose shifting allegiances raised Kings and lowered Emperors. The gorges of the Danube still echo hallowed names – Charlemagne, Attila, Wittelsbach, Hohenzollern, Hapsburg, Esterhazy – whose assaults and confrontations have left their stamp. Journeying along it now from Germany to Austria, Slovakia and Hungary you could feel that little has changed in centuries – except that modern travellers do so in much greater comfort.

Most go by boat, which certainly offers a unique visual perspective on the Danube's natural wonders as well as its sights. Rounding a curve to your first sight of the Benedictine Abbey at Melk, in the UNESCO World Heritage Cultural and Natural Heritage Site of leafy Wachau Valley, is just one of the princely landscapes you can't see any other way. Even so, lots of people choose to travel the Danube by bike. You can speed or tarry at will, and because the special bike route follows the old towpath, the going is flat the whole way. If you're prepared to use an agent to smooth your path, you can combine bike and boat, either for excursions in Passau, Linz, Durnstein, Vienna and Budapest, or as alternative transport  through the woods, terraced vineyards, orchards and meadows between stops like the venerable towns of Aggspach, Spitz and Weissenkirchen.

Like the emperors and kings who have preceded you, allow plenty of time, however you travel. The wealth of history, culture and giddy-making surprises is too rich, and the Danube too beautiful, to rush.

**HOW:**
By boat and/or bike

**WHEN TO GO:**
April to November. Winter boat services are infrequent, and at the mercy of heavy rains/river levels.

**TIME IT TAKES:**
6-7 days by boat (Regensburg-Passau-Durnstein-Vienna-Bratislava-Esztergom-Budapest); 14-16 days by bike (including 2 rest/excursion days); 19-21 days (bike and boat, with many short excursions and including rest days).

**HIGHLIGHTS:**
Discovering Regensburg to be one of Germany's most complete medieval cities.
Tulln – with its baroque old town.
Brooding medieval magnificence and baroque exuberance – the hallmarks of the Danube's royal cities and towns.

**YOU SHOULD KNOW:**
1. By bike, travel the Danube from west to east – there's an overall incline in your favour, and both the prevailing wind and afternoon sun will be on your back. 2. If you start your journey mid-week, you'll avoid the large numbers who set out at weekends. 3. Follow the route by car only if you have no other option – you'll miss so much

# 'Limes' Route

The longest heritage route in Germany immerses you in the oldest period of German history. From Bad Honningen near Koblenz to Kelheim outside Regensburg, the 550-km (344-mi) route – all of it a UNESCO World Heritage Site – marks the line of forts, watchtowers, earthen palisades and stone walls which 2,000 years ago formed the border between the Roman Empire and the Germanic tribes Romans called 'barbarians'. 'Limes' is the Latin for 'border defences': this route is part of Roman 'limes' stretching over 6,000 km (3,750 mi) round the Middle East, North Africa, Spain and France, at the moment of the Empire's greatest expansion in circa 150. The Upper German and Rhaetian 'Limes' meet at Aalen on the upper reaches of the Kocher River. In fact, for a short way the trail is shared with the 330-km (206-mi) Kocher-Jagst Cycle Route, a delightful circular riverside ramble through the meadowlands of the Kocher and Jagst – but evidently not topographically attractive to Roman commanders.

Working its way from the Rhine-Westerwald nature reserve to the solid walls of Regensburg's Porta Praetoria ('Guardian Gate') in Bavaria, the route is a constant scenic surprise. The Lahn Valley, Nassauer region, Upper Taunus nature reserve, the Wetterau, Main Valley, Odenwald and Franconian forests, Swabian Alb and fabulous Altmuhl Valley nature reserve proffer a selection of the best German landscapes. Woven into them, in addition to original Roman remains, there are any number of reconstructions, restorations and excavations that help illustrate military and domestic life at that time – and many of them offer a range of recreational possibilities to entertain families as well as antiquarians. The German 'Limes' is a route to tackle in short stages.

**HOW:**
By bike

**WHEN TO GO:**
April to October. There are many Roman-themed guided tours, activities, festivals and re-enactments along the route. The Aalen Roman Festival takes place every even-numbered year and is especially worthwhile.

**TIME IT TAKES:**
10-14 days (by bike, and by car too, if you actually want to stop to look at some of the route's attractions and wonders).

**HIGHLIGHTS:**
The reconstructed Roman fort at Saalburg, near Bad Homburg.
The archaeology park, fort and Roman baths, and the 'Limes' museum at Aalen.
The Roman museum and 'Limes' information centre at Weissenburg.
Miltenberg's special, 19-km (12-mi) 'Roman Route' for cyclists and hardy walkers.
The reconstructed Pompeii-style villa, and ruins of the Roman Baths at Aschaffenburg.

**YOU SHOULD KNOW:**
Julius Caesar's history 'The Conquest of Gaul' tells many stories of repelling ferocious 'Alemanni' and other Germanic tribes of 'barbarians' – but the German 'Limes' were never so much a fortress defence as a line of demarcation to demonstrate Rome's authority.

*The reconstructed Roman fort*
*at Saalburg*

# German Avenues: North to South

Germany's longest scenic route picks its way from the dazzling wall of pure white cliffs at Cape Arkona on the Baltic island of Rugen, to the flowered gardens of Reichenau, the island gem in the temperate beauty of Lake Constance. For 2,500 km (1,562 mi) between Poland in the extreme north and the southern borders with France and Switzerland, it wends through central Germany's most vivid scenery. It's a leisurely road, but it is not random. Its path is determined by the avenues of trees that line what used to be trade routes and super-highways, and are now forgotten byways. The trees were planted centuries ago as windbreaks, and to provide summer shade. Now, they provide an almost unbroken, leafy canopy of continuous charm that crosses eight of Germany's federal states – a magical path that brings travellers close to some of the country's finest cities and landmarks, without ever losing its own transcendental quality of peacefulness.

After the rivers, lakes and shimmering water-worlds of Mecklenburg and Brandenburg, the Avenues Route splits at Rheinsberg. One branch continues into Saxony-Anhalt on its way to Goslar (one of dozens of UNESCO World Heritage Sites and Biosphere Reserves in transit) before turning south above Göttingen; the other leads to Dresden and the extraordinary pristine landscapes of the Erzegebirge mountains along the Czech border, then twists along the river gorges and remote forested hills of Thuringia. Linden trees, oaks, maples, chestnuts and poplars alter the road's character with the seasons. Framing castles and palaces, fields of yellow rapeseed and open tracts dotted with red poppies and blue cornflowers, the promise of the Avenues is renewed and fulfilled down the Lahn Valley and above the Rhine gorge, to the Black Forest and up into the Alps. It's one of Germany's very best surprises.

**HOW:**
By motorbike or car
**WHEN TO GO:**
May to October
**TIME IT TAKES:**
7-10 days by motorbike or car, but motorbike clubs recommend allowing at least 14 days.
**HIGHLIGHTS:**
Meissen's porcelain, the Bauhaus at Dessau, Dresden's Zwinger Palace, Saalfeld's fairy grottoes, Bad Kreuznach's medieval bridge-houses, castles at Rheinsberg, Koblenz and 100 other stunning sites.
The 'secret corridor' – if you don't actually visit any of the cities on the Route, you could believe from the Avenues that Germany was to a large extent a vast nature park.
The UNESCO World Heritage site of Reichenau – Germany's oldest monastery complex, and repository of its historic Benedictine soul.
**YOU SHOULD KNOW:**
It's a miracle the Avenues Route still exists. Under an EU ruling, France has been forced to cut down swathes of its own trees along its famous poplar-lined highways because of the 'risk' of 'strobe-effect' when you drive down them very fast in sunshine.

*The Romanesque church of Saint Peter and Paul on Reichenau Island.*

# Zillertalbahn

**HOW:**
By train
**WHEN TO GO:**
All year except April and December
**TIME IT TAKES:**
Half an hour
**HIGHLIGHTS:**
Classic steam engine and antique railway carriages.
Beautiful mountain views.
Hintertux Glacier – for year-round skiing.
Zell am Ziller – once a gold-mining town.
**YOU SHOULD KNOW:**
The steam train runs twice daily in the summer and once weekly in the winter. There is a regular diesel service as well which, although not as much fun, still takes you through the same beautiful countryside.

The little steam train that chugs up the Zillertal (Ziller Valley) in the heart of the Tirol runs on a track only 760 mm (2 ft 6 in) wide. It is the most famous narrow gauge railway in Austria; as well as being a means of transport it's a visible reminder of the valley's history.

The railway was built in 1901-2, in the days when the local inhabitants depended on agriculture, mining and forestry for their living. They desperately needed a freight line to transport timber and minerals down the valley, to replace a thoroughly inadequate road – a tortuous track that was only negotiable by mule. Although the railway's prime purpose was to ensure that the existing economy prospered, it had the secondary unforeseen benefit of opening up the valley to tourism. Throughout the 20th century the Zillertal grew in popularity, attracting skiers, climbers and walkers with the allure of its unspoilt natural surroundings. The picturesque agricultural villages along the railway are now charming little resorts.

The Zillertal inclines gently southwards towards the Zillertaler Alps, enclosed by the Kitzbüheler Alps to the east and the Tuxer Mountains to the west. It is not only the largest valley branching from the Inntal but also the loveliest – a scenic delight of alpine pastures and forests surrounded by mountain peaks. The railway runs for 32 km (20 mi) between Jenbach, on the River Inn, and Mayrhofen, under the Hintertux Glacier, with 14 stops on the way. The train is pulled by a heritage steam engine at a maximum speed of 35 kph (22 mph). It takes you on a romantic journey back in time, in a classic passenger car, listening to the soothing repetitive clickety-clack of the wheels and the intermittent hissings and puffings of the engine, while you admire the unspoilt pastoral beauty of the valley all around you.

*The Zillertalbahn near Mayrhofen*

# The Arnoweg

Hotels in the 19th century spa town of Bad Gastein

In 1998, the 1,200-km (750-mi) Arnoweg long-distance hiking trail was established to celebrate 1,200 years of history, dating from the Vatican's decision in 798 to raise the status of the city of Salzburg by creating an archbishopric. The trail is named after Archbishop Arno, a friend of the Emperor Charlemagne, who was the first appointee to the post. The route combines several well-established alpine trails in a circuitous tour around Salzburgerland with 60 signposted stages and alpine huts along the way. It cuts through three national parks, climbs to heights of over 3,000 m (9,800 ft) and passes innumerable sites of cultural significance.

The Arnoweg is a challenging hike through some of the most beautiful scenery in the world. You feel as though you have stepped straight into the film set of *The Sound of Music* – a land of soaring mountains, precipitous gorges, flower-filled pastures, sparkling streams, medieval castles and picturesque towns.

You hike along mountain ridges, past the medieval town of Hallein to the Hohenwerfen fortress for a spectacular view over the Salzach Valley, then into the lush valleys and glaciated peaks of the Hohe Tauern National Park where eagles and bearded vultures circle the skies. Visit the 16th century gold-mining town of Rauris and the famous 19th century spa town of Bad Gastein, and see the medieval Mauterndorf fortress – hunting castle of the Archbishop. Stroll through the gently contoured landscape of the Grasberge and Nockberge seeing marmots, mountain hares and herds of chamois, and scramble up scree crags in the Niedere Tauern. Hike across gentle hills in the lower Alps to reach the last leg of the trail through the lakes region to the historic city of Salzburg – and return to the real world exhausted but fulfilled.

**HOW:**
On foot
**WHEN TO GO:**
June to September
**TIME IT TAKES:**
Six to nine weeks to do the whole route. Many people just do one or two sections.
**HIGHLIGHTS:**
Hohensalzburg Fortress – the largest medieval fortress in Europe.
Krimml Falls – the largest waterfall in Europe.
Grossglockner – the highest mountain in Austria at 3,798 m (12,460 ft).
Neukirchen – a beautifully situated village.
Dürrnberg Salt Mine – the oldest in the world.
**YOU SHOULD KNOW:**
This hike is not to be undertaken lightly. Some sections merely require stamina and sure-footedness but others demand previous alpine experience and the use of crampons, ice-pick and harness. You should make sure you are properly equipped and always carry a whistle to blow a distress call in an emergency.

# Grossglockner Hochalpenstrasse

**HOW:**
By car or bike
**WHEN TO GO:**
May to October
**TIME IT TAKES:**
Though it takes less than an hour by car/motorbike or 3 hours by bike, it's worth allowing a full day, making stops along the way to walk around and admire the views.
**HIGHLIGHTS:**
Hochmais – a 1,850-m (6,068-ft) viewing point over the impressive glaciers of the beautiful Feirleiten Valley.
Edelweissspitze – take a side road up to panoramic views from a height of 2,571m (8,433 ft).
Fuscher Törll viewing point, at an altitude of 2,428 m (7,964 ft).
Fuscher Lacke, a picturesque mountain lake.
Pasterze Glacier.
**YOU SHOULD KNOW:**
The Grossglockner is a toll road open only in daylight hours and in the summer months. There are plenty of parking spaces at the scenic spots along the way.

The Grossglockner High Alpine Road is one of the most spectacular scenic routes in Europe. It was first opened in 1935, specifically constructed as a tourist attraction – 48 km (27 mi) of death-defying hairpin bends winding far above the snowline with breathtaking views over the idyllic pastoral landscapes of the Hohe Tauern National Park.

The road runs across the highest pass in the Austrian Alps, between the village of Bruck on the edge of the Hohe Tauern and Heilgenblut at the foot of the Grossglockner, climbing through pastures and forests to craggy snow-covered mountain peaks. The landscape is especially striking in early summer when fingers of un-melted snow from the previous winter still reach down into the green valleys.

From Bruck the road heads southwards towards a 10 per cent incline. Make a detour up the steep little side road leading to Edelweissspitze for a mind-blowing panoramic view over the pass before heading up to Fuscher Törll, from where you get your first sighting of Grossglockner, the highest mountain of the Austrian Alps at 3,798 m (12,457 ft). From Hochtor, the highest point of the road at 2,504 m (8,213 ft), descend to Kaiser-Franz-Josef-Hohe, the most dramatic lookout point of all – Grossglockner towers directly in front of you with an incredible view of the Pasterze, the longest glacier in the Eastern Alps. The road winds downwards from the snowline through alpine meadows into the valley below, where the unbelievably quaint village of Heiligenblut sits peacefully at the foot of the Grossglockner.

Although the Hochalpenstrasse is as touristy as it gets, with signage at every bend and information points along the way, nothing can detract from the unbelievable beauty of the dramatic scenery and the thrill of the zigzagging road. This is an absolutely unmissable trip.

*The Grossglockner High Alpine Road*

# Semmering Railway

The 160-year-old World Heritage Semmering Railway is the most scenic route in Austria, running for 41 km (26 mi) across the Semmering Pass in the mountains between Vienna and Graz. Built between 1848 and 1845 in the pioneering days of railway construction, it became the prototype for all high-mountain railways. It is an inspired feat of engineering with sixteen viaducts, fifteen tunnels, and a gradient five times greater than anything that had been built before.

In 1842 Austrian State Railways commissioned Carlo di Ghega, a Venetian engineer, to design a line that would not detract from the beauty of the natural surroundings. It was the last link in the Südbahn line, to create a continuous track between Vienna and Trieste on the Adriatic Sea. The resulting section of railway is a work of art that led to Semmering becoming a fashionable fin de siècle tourist resort, attracting visitors as much for the train journey as for the destination.

The line runs from the country town of Gloggnitz in the Schwarza Valley up to Semmering, a charming 19th century ski resort that today has a distinctly quaint feel about it. The highest point of the railway is 898 m (2,945 ft). It then descends the southern slopes of the mountains to Mürzzuschlag, a small provincial town where Johannes Brahms composed his Fourth Symphony.

The dramatic landscape of sheer gorges, craggy mountains and forest makes for a hair-raising ride – winding round sheer rock faces, shooting into tunnels and crossing precipitous ravines. Despite the progress in engineering techniques since the line was built, you cannot fail to admire the harmonious design. If you only do one train journey in Austria, make it this one.

**HOW:**
By train
**WHEN TO GO:**
Any time of year
**TIME IT TAKES:**
40 minutes
**HIGHLIGHTS:**
Gloggnitz Castle, originally an 11th
Century Benedictine monastery.
Incredible mountain views.
Kalt Rinne Viaduct
Südbahn Kulturbahnhoff – Railway
museum at Mürzzuschlag.
**YOU SHOULD KNOW:**
There is a hiking track over
Semmerling Pass following the route
of the railway line.

*Cattle graze the alpine meadows.*

# Gerlos Alpenstrasse

**HOW:**
By car or bike
**WHEN TO GO:**
Any time
**TIME IT TAKES:**
1-2 hours by car; 4-5 hours by
mountain bike.
**HIGHLIGHTS:**
Zell am Ziller – picturesque
tourist town.
Piesendorf, Neukirchen – quaint
villages.
Krimml Falls – highest waterfall in
Europe, and one of the top eight in
the world.
Zell am See – Scenic views of the
Ziller and Pinzgau Mountains.
13th century Church of St Hippolyte
**YOU SHOULD KNOW:**
This is a toll road, open all
year round.

The main road from the old gold-mining town of Zell am Ziller in the Tirol to the lakeside town of Zell am See in the province of Salzburg is a favourite amongst cyclists and motor-bikers. It is a winding route along a panoramic stretch of road, crossing the Gerlos Pass at an altitude of 1,530 m (5,020 ft) and descending through enchanting mountain countryside, with an amazing view of the famous Krimml Falls, the longest waterfall in Europe.

The history of the road goes back to the 17th century, when gold was discovered in the Ziller Valley. Rather than risk transporting the precious metal through what were then the foreign states of Bavaria and Tirol, the prospectors widened the mule track over the Gerlos Pass so that cartloads of gold could be carried into the safe territory of Salzburg for smelting. After the gold rush, the road fell into disrepair and the Salzach and Ziller Valleys were once again cut off from each other. Amidst much bureaucratic bickering, plans were finally drawn up for a proper highway in 1949 but the road was not completed until 1962.

The present road zigzags its way up from Zel am Ziller in the Ziller Valley to the high moorland at the top of the pass, then descends through the Salzach Valley alongside the innaccessible narrow wooded valleys and fissured gorges of the Pinzgau Mountains, along the edge of the Hohe Tauern National Park. The Krimml Ache River flows through just such a valley, making a sudden plunging drop of 380 m (1,250 ft). Tons of water thunder down in three great cascades, sending clouds of mist into the air – a truly awesome force of nature that will impress itself on your memory.

# The Brine Trail

The Salzkammergut, the old salt-mining region of Austria, is one of those rare parts of the world where mankind has managed to leave its mark without blighting the natural environment. Now designated as a World Heritage Cultural Landscape, the region is not only scenically breathtaking but also architecturally beautiful. Historic palatial buildings and picturesque villages nestle around clear-watered lakes under the silver crags and green forested slopes of the Dachstein Mountains as though they belonged naturally as an integral part of the landscape.

Of all the many charming villages, the old salt-mining town of Hallstatt is the most enchanting – a cobble-stoned lakeside town straight out of the pages of a picture book. Its fairytale 16th and 17th Century houses are squeezed into every square inch of space on a precipitous mountainside, expanding upwards on terraces and outwards into Lake Hallstätter, on piles driven into the lakebed.

The 10-km (6-mi) walk from Hallstatt to the quaint market town of Bad Goisern follows the course of a historic pipeline used for transporting brine from the salt-mine to the trading town of Ebensee on Lake Traunsee, 40 km (25 mi) away. The path, known as the Soleweg (Brine Trail), is cut into the rock face 200 m (650 ft) above the western bank of the lake. As you amble through romantic countryside of woods and pastures, spotting wildlife and breathing pure mountain air, you are accompanied by a heart-stopping view of the opposite shore – the towering crags of the Sarstein Ridge mirrored in the water. The beauty of the pastoral surroundings induces a sensation of mild euphoria and by the time you reach Bad Goisern you will be completely smitten with this glorious part of Austria.

**HOW:**
On foot
**WHEN TO GO:**
June to September
**TIME IT TAKES:**
Three hours
**HIGHLIGHTS:**
A tour of Hallstätt salt mine.
Gosauzwang Bridge – impressive 38-m (125-ft) bridge built on enormous stone piles over the rushing torrent of the Gosau River.
Breathtaking views of the Dachstein Mountains.
**YOU SHOULD KNOW:**
This is a straightforward family walk for young and old. The Salzkammergut is wonderful hiking and cycling country. There are hundreds of trails of all lengths and levels of difficulty leading around and between the lakes and up into the Dachstein Mountains.

*Evening falls over Lake Hallstätter.*

*St Gilgen on Wolfgangsee*

# Mozart Cycle Path

**HOW:**
By bike
**WHEN TO GO:**
June to September
**TIME IT TAKES:**
Seven to eight days
**HIGHLIGHTS:**
Salzburg – Mozart's birthplace and UNESCO World Heritage City.
Herrenchiemsee – island in the Chiemsee with fairytale castle.
Waging am See – picturesque lakeside town.
Wasserburg – historic Bavarian salt-trading town on the River Inn.
Mattsee Abbey,
**YOU SHOULD KNOW:**
This route is easy or moderate cycling, much of it on cycle paths. The route is well signposted with hotels and guesthouses where cyclists are welcome and there are bike repair shops in almost every town.

This 450-km (280-mi) cycling route in the borderlands of Austria and Bavaria is a wonderfully relaxing way to unwind, dawdling along through enchanting pastoral scenery of rolling fields, mirror-like lakes and alpine meadows with the snowy peaks of the mountains always in the background. The region was once the centre of the European salt trade, which brought in huge amounts of money. Its legacy can be seen in the architecture of the old market towns and picturesque villages that you pass – quaint period buildings, beautiful churches and magnificent castles.

From Salzburg you cycle north to Oberndorf, the site of the 'Silent Night Chapel', where the world's best-loved Christmas carol was first sung in 1818, and into the Chiemgau region of Bavaria. Pass the Waginger See, a pretty oxbow lake set in rolling farmland, and cycle along the shore of Bavaria's largest lake, the Chiemsee or 'Bavarian Sea'. The route continues past the Seeon Benedictine Monastery to the lovely old market town of Wasserburg, sited picturesquely on a bend of the River Inn, and follows the course of the river before heading back eastwards through the historic salt-mining towns of Bad Reichenhall and Berchtesgaden to the

Königssee, a beautiful fjord-like lake set in the mountains of Berchtesgaden National Park. The first circle of your journey completed, you head back into Austria through St Gilgen on Wolfgangsee, the village where Mozart's mother was born, along the shore of Wallersee to the final lake of your tour, the charming Mattsee, surrounded by hills and woods, only a few kilometres north of Salzburg. By the end of your journey you will have a marvellous sense of physical tiredness and mental well-being – your legs may ache but your head will be full of the wonderful landscapes you have seen.

# Wild Waters Hike to the Reisach Waterfall

Squeezed between the glaciated peaks of the Hohe Tauern and the limestone spires of the Dachstein, the landscape of the Niedere Tauern is a gorgeous district of lakes and tarns set in rounded mountains and plateaux veined with rivers and streams, reminiscent of Scotland. The Hochgolling, a great stone giant of a mountain, juts out at the end of the range at a height of 2,863 m (9,390 ft), towering over the mountains around the old Styrian mining town of Schladming in the Upper Enns Valley.

Better known as a cross-country ski resort, Schladming is also a great place to come in the summer. Surrounded by nature reserves, it is superb walking country – pastoral mountain scenery of rivers, pastures and woods with tumbling streams and a network of over 500 km (300 mi) of hiking trails.

The 12-km (7.5-mi) Wild Waters Trail leads from the town up through the steep Untertal valley, passing a quaint old mill and through a nature reserve, alongside a river that flows in intermittent bursts of rippling cascades. It is fed by two creeks: the Steinriesenbach, from the direction of Hockgolling, and the Reisachbach. Following the course of the Reisachbach, the valley gets ever steeper and narrower until you reach the Reisach, the longest waterfall in Styria – a violent avalanche of water that pounds down through a cleft in the rocks and drops a distance of 140 m (460 ft) over two steps. After watching this dramatic spectacle, it is worth summoning the energy to continue climbing. Carry on up the steps of Höll, a steep mountain path, and across a perilous suspension bridge to the Reisachsee, a tranquil alpine lake where you can sit and relax, admiring the silver peaks of the Dachstein Mountains in the distance.

**HOW:**
On foot
**WHEN TO GO:**
May to June – to see the waterfall at its most dramatic.
**TIME IT TAKES:**
Four to five hours
**HIGHLIGHTS:**
Hochgolling Mountain.
Views of the Dachstein Mountains.
Reisach Waterfall.
Höll Suspension Bridge.
Reisachsee – alpine lake.
**YOU SHOULD KNOW:**
This is quite a strenuous but not too difficult walk for anybody reasonably fit, including children.

# Carnic Peace Trail – Via Alpina

*The Carnic Alps with Wolayer Lake and the Eduard-Pichi Hutte on the right.*

The Via Alpina is a network of trails traversing the Alps all the way from Trieste on the Adriatic to Monaco on the Mediterranean. It was established in 2005 to create a single cohesive route out of the countless existing trans-Alpine paths. The main artery, known as the Red Trail, is some 2,400 km (1,500 mi) long, broken down into 161 manageable stages as it weaves its way back and forth across the borders of all the Alpine countries.

The summit trail along the ridge of the Carnic Alps in eastern Austria has been integrated into the Red Trail. It was the front-line between the Austrians and Italians in World War I and, in the 1970s, the supply paths used by the troops were linked up and given the symbolic name of the 'Carnic Peace Trail' in remembrance of the devastating loss of life here – as many soldiers died from the freezing weather conditions as were killed by the enemy.

Easily as beautiful as anywhere else in the Alps, the Carnic Peace Trail is one of the less touristy sections of the Via Alpina. You enter a timeless country of traditional villages and flower-strewn pastures, make hair-raising 750 m (2,500 ft) ascents and scramble across valleys, wash in sparkling mountain water and wake each morning in a different mountain hut but to the same inevitable tinkling of cowbells and chorus of moos.

A hike through the Austrian Alps really is the perfect way of getting away from it all – walking through some of the world's most beautiful scenery, spending the night in the shelter of spartan but adequate mountain huts, and living on the staple alpine diet of cured ham and un-pasteurised cheese, you cannot fail to be satisfied.

**HOW:**
On foot
**WHEN TO GO:**
June to September
**TIME IT TAKES:**
A week (four months for the whole Via Alpina).
**HIGHLIGHTS:**
Lienz – beautiful historic town.
Traces of trenches, battery positions and bivouacs from World War I.
Medieval villages.
Outstanding natural scenery.
**YOU SHOULD KNOW:**
The Carnic Peace Path is not technically difficult and requires no climbing equipment, merely sure-footedness and a good level of fitness. In July and August you will be hard put to find yourself walking completely alone. Hordes of trekkers flock to the Alps at this time of year.

# Vrsic Pass Road

**HOW:**
By car, bike or on foot
**WHEN TO GO:**
May to October. Cyclists come for the first Sunday in September, when over 1,000 of them race the 12 steep and winding km to Vrsic Pass.
**TIME IT TAKES:**
1.5-2 hrs (by car, Bovec to Kranjska Gora); 1-2 days (by bicycle); 3-4 days (hiking). Cyclists may prefer to make the round trip of Kranjska Gora-Bled-Bohinj-Tolmin-Bovec-Vrsic-Kransjka Gora, a 5-6 day tour for the experienced
**HIGHLIGHTS:**
The Valley of the Triglav Lakes.
The view from Vrsic to the awesome Martuljek mountain triangle.
The glorious concentration of rarities in the Juliana Alpine Garden, set at 800 m (2624 ft) at the southern foot of Vrsic Pass, in the valley where the mild Mediterranean climate still has influence.
The Russian Chapel at the northern foot of Vrsic Pass. Just one of many moving memorials along this road, this one commemorates the death of more than 300 Russian PoWs in an avalanche in 1916.
**YOU SHOULD KNOW:**
The Vrsic Pass is part of the arena where the young Ernest Hemingway witnessed the daily horror and bitter experience that inspired *A Farewell To Arms*.

Triglav National Park fills the northwest pocket of Slovenia, where it meets both Austria and Italy. It protects Slovenia's Julian Alps, returned to their pristine remoteness since their mutilation during some of the bloodiest and longest battles of World War I. Untouched since, what little development had taken place has now been reversed. Only one road remains across it from which to gauge the stunning landscape of winding glacial valleys, torrent-filled gorges, forested ridges and stark mountains. It follows two of the most beautiful valleys of all. From Bovec, on the Park's southern edge, it traces the milky turquoise Soca River up the last of the narrowing Upper Trenta Valley to the alpine watershed of the Vrsic Pass. The road seems to end before a towering ridge of forest that rises high beyond the tree line to the snowy peaks of Jalovec (2,645 m/8,676 ft) on one side, and Slovenia's highest mountain, Triglav (2,864 m/9,394 ft) on the other; but it twists its way steeply to Vrsic itself, Slovenia's highest pass at 1,611 m (5,284 ft). A short walk to one side leads you to the Soca's source – a cave from which, in spate, a torrent jets out into a series of falls and descending ravines.

From the top of Vrsic, the hairpin descent is dizzying. So is the panorama, of one the most picturesque of all alpine valleys. Zgornjesavska is a Hollywood dream Alpine set of meadow, mountain, snow, stream and forest; and its fame is global thanks to the World Cup skiing venue of Kranjska Gora on its far side (just outside the Park). It's hard to believe that the bitter events of World War I could take place in the face of such beauty – but there is a stream of small monuments and memorials among the rare alpine flora on either side of the road.

*Lake Bohinj in northwest Slovenia*

# Rafting down the Drava River

Born as a mountain torrent in the Julian Alps in Austria, the River Drava is significantly broad and deep by the time it flows through Dravograd into Slovenia, through which it runs for 102 of its total 720 km (450 mi). Since Roman times it has been the region's sole highway – not just for ordinary trade, but also for the lumber industry in the surrounding heavily forested mountains. Rafting lumber became the most important economic activity, and towns and villages grew up along the Drava's banks on the profits. The trade centred on the ancient city of Maribor, where the development of an enormous raft harbour (the 'Lentstatt') attracted the parallel growth of riverside facilities and entertainments. Today, the Lent district is still Maribor's most beautiful, authentically old and cobbled, and lively. Only the Drava has been tamed. Hydro-electric dams slowed its legendary boiling currents to a broad, placid stream; and it's become a watery theatre for Slovenians to re-enact their cultural traditions for visitors.

Which means there are two ways to go rafting on the Drava. If you're determined and lucky, you can raft from Dravograd all the way to Maribor or even Ptuj, passing through the most beautiful section of the entire river's course, camping or sleeping in hotels as your own pace dictates. Otherwise, you join a raft at Koblarjevzaliv (an artificially-wide but very pretty section of river near Maribor) with anything from five to forty others. Unfortunately, each raft promises to send '2 rafters plus a rafter's girl' with you, and their function is not just to steer, but to sing you their selection of hearty Slovenian folk songs, and stuff you full of (quite good) wine.

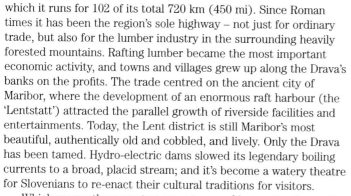

*Ptuj on the banks of the Drava River*

**HOW:**
By raft

**WHEN TO GO:**
May to October/November (depending on the weather). Come for the Lent Festival, when throughout June Maribor's left bank district celebrates its oldest traditions.

**TIME IT TAKES:**
1 hour is the standard Maribor rafting experience, but you can arrange as long a trip as you want. Rafting from Dravograd to Maribor usually takes 2-3 days, but there are many good wildlife, landscape and history reasons along the Drava that could tempt you to spend much longer.

**HIGHLIGHTS:**
The early mists and high summer noon, and water so still you can hear the scurried 'rustle…plop!' of a water-vole.
The lack of river traffic (until very recently, all navigation was banned), which may not last, as jetfoils have now been allowed access.

**YOU SHOULD KNOW:**
If the Slovenian equivalent of Caribbean 'pirate cruises' is what it takes to raft the Drava, it's still worth it. It's fun, too.

# The Bohinj Railway

**HOW:**
By train
**WHEN TO GO:**
April to early November. If you ride the train only part of the way, you can link the journey to one of the spring or summer festivals that abound in the region, or to one of many natural attractions in the Triglav National Park.
**TIME IT TAKES:**
3-3.5 hours (Jesenice to Gorizia, with a stopover before the return of about 4 hours, in either direction).
**HIGHLIGHTS:**
The steam engines – you don't have to be a train enthusiast to appreciate the various engines, borrowed from the Railway Museum at Ljubljana.
The very curious, double Savica Waterfall, near Ukanc village – one of many splendours on Bohinj Lake, it appears to thread itself through two sinkholes, re-emerging lower down.
A ride on a 'Lucija' riverboat – a paddlewheel – on the emerald water of the Soca River at Most na Soci.
The waft of Mediterranean mountain scents as you descend closer to the Friuli.
**YOU SHOULD KNOW:**
All the way along the Bohinj Railway, not one inch of landscape is less than sensational.

The Bohinj Railway is an authentic classic steam train trip on a historic line through some of Europe's loveliest mountain scenery. It runs between Jesenice, just inside Slovenia's border with Austria, to Gorizia in Italy, along what used to be the Austro-Hungarian 'Transalpina' railway from Vienna to Trieste, inaugurated in 1906. Although the service is scheduled (at roughly fortnightly intervals), it's definitely an excursion train. You can get on or off at any of the stops, and rejoin it after your own sightseeing, but the full trip incorporates a bus tour to the Friuli vineyards, staff in period uniforms, tour guides for railway enthusiasts, and entertainment staff to make sure travellers match Slovenian standards of enthusiastic merrymaking.

Partying aside, the Bohinj Railway takes you through countryside so beautiful it will twang your heartstrings. From Jesenice, you steam along the Sava River past the alpine dreamscape lake at Bled (where, if you started your journey in Italy, the medieval castle will be your vineyard-equivalent lunchtime goal). After Bohinj itself, the jewel of Slovenia's alpine crown, a 6.33-km (3.93-mi) tunnel cuts through the Bohinj Mountains to the southern side of the Julian Alps, and skirts the Triglav National Park until it turns southwest along the Soca Valley at Most na Soci. The bridges, viaducts and gradients must have represented extraordinary engineering at the time they were built, and they are still spectacular. The most famous bridge of all is at the Gorizia end of the line. The Solkanski Most features the longest (220 m/721 ft) stone railway arch in the world, with 4,533 chunks of limestone in the principal arch. Bohinj Railway staff have been known to tease travellers by testing their memory for these important facts – after the vineyard visit. The fun is deemed essential to the journey.

*Lake Bled*

# The Amber Trail

*Orava Castle in the Orava River Valley*

For 1,000 years, amber has been traded between the Baltic and Hungary. All along this route you will find amber for sale and as decoration. Exploring the route by bicycle brings you into first-hand contact with people whose lives and culture have been shaped by the rich, golden-brown fossil resin. If you travel with a guide, he or she will be one of them; and an invaluable mentor of the fine details in the rich historical quilt ahead of you. The daily stages of the bicycle tour read like a catalogue of 2,000 years of violent cultural collisions. Between Budapest and Kracow you pass six UNESCO World Heritage Sites, and numerous castles of varying beauty, puissance and repair, attesting conflicts of Roman, Barbarian, Lithuanian, Polish, Ostrogoth, Turkish, Austro-Hungarian, Hapsburg, Nazi German, Soviet Russian, and (most recently) economic origin. Soaring pinnacles on cathedrals, palaces, and public buildings reveal the complex bargains of Church and State at Esztergom, Banska Bystrica, Orava and Kracow. Evidence of more humble aspirations and compromises – at Banska Stiavnica, Vikolinec, Liptovsky Mikulas, Lanckorona, Kalwaria Zebrzydowska and the Wieliczka salt mine – adds an equally stunning perspective of daily lives under feudalism and communism.

The revived Amber Trail is now an outstanding example of central European co-operation: three countries (Hungary, Poland and Slovakia) reserving a corridor across some of their loveliest hills, rivers, and plains for international enjoyment. The Danube Valley and the Great Bend, the Fatra and Tatra sections of the Carpathian Mountains, and the Northern Plain in Poland, include magical landscapes of every variety; and the Trail route follows the smallest back roads. There are wetland meadows as well as mountain beech forests and river gorges. Tranquility has returned to this newly pristine countryside, enfolding former turbulence into exquisite villages happy to extend their welcome to passing travellers.

**HOW:**
By bike
**WHEN TO GO:**
May to October
**TIME IT TAKES:**
Ten days (Budapest to Kracow, 330 km/206 mi by Amber Trail, cycling 40-50 km /25-32 mi in 4-5 hours on 8 days, with one rest day). Guided groups have a back-up vehicle for transfers in case of unspeakable weather or weariness.
**HIGHLIGHTS:**
Riding the length of Szentendre Island in the middle of the Danube as it reaches the Great Bend at Esztergom (and the view of the Bend from Visigrad Castle when you get there).
The UNESCO-cited historic old centre of Banska Stiavnica.
The wooden church at Lestiny, built without a single nail; and the wooden rugmaking looms in Malatina. Both villages are typical of the Chocsky and Oravsky Hills.
The huge Gothic fortress of Orava Castle commanding its world from high above the river at Oravsky Podzamok – you're afraid to imagine what its history signifies.
**YOU SHOULD KNOW:**
With a guide and backup transport options, which can include boats or an enchanting miniature train (near Kremnica and its beautiful 7 peaks), the Amber Trail is suitable for anyone reasonably fit. The route has surprises and entertainments en route to keep the most demanding travellers of any age group riveted and eager for more.

351

*The horses await you.*

# Hortobagy Great Plains

**HOW:**
On horseback
**WHEN TO GO:**
April to November
**TIME IT TAKES:**
7-14 days for a number of scheduled tours; but most are of negotiable length and direction if the right numbers (4-12 usually) want to make the trip.
**HIGHLIGHTS:**
The Kisber horses, mainly chestnuts with some greys, trained to standards of responsiveness and endurance that make you aspire to be a better rider (but be prepared to let them have their eager heads on the canters).
Miles and miles of gently rolling, poppy-filled, long-grass pastures at Hortobagy.
The 'Puszta Otos'('Great Plains Five') – when a *csiko* (horse-herder) stands with one foot on each of two horses, while driving three (or even more) others, unyoked, before him, at a full gallop. Circuses perform a yoked version at a trot. At full pelt, screaming in the Puszta wilderness, it's an elemental glory. Ask, and you may receive.
**YOU SHOULD KNOW:**
Your back recovers.

Unless they are actually cowboys, even experienced riders like their comfort on a long journey, so the most popular way to ride Hungary's 'Puszta' (Great Plains) is to ride from place to place, but to stay in hotels rather than camp. It's possible, but difficult, to do it any other way. And you do need to be experienced for a journey across northern Hungary's vast grasslands to its greatest vineyards at Eger and Tokaj. Depending on your choices, you could take seven to fourteen days, riding steadily with long canters, for five or six hours. There's scarcely a fence or manmade obstacle to bar the way through hundreds of kilometres of woods, shrub-studded hills and a horizon of stirrup-high grasslands. You get to feel the Puszta intimately; and the only people you're likely to see will be herders, practicing inbred equine traditions going back 600 years. If you're lucky, they might show you some of their astounding accomplishments with horses.

After the exhilaration of each day's riding, it's equally stimulating to arrive at places emblematic of Hungary's history and culture. If you start from a stud farm for the Kisber horses you will be riding, you might visit the UNESCO World Heritage village of Holloko, gallop through the beech forests of the wild Bükk Hills to a stud farm for Lipizzaners, spend a day in the beautiful Baroque city of Eger with its 1,000 year-old history, and another week in and beyond Hortobagy, before reaching Tokaj, home to Hungary's most princely history and vines. You arrange your own route and timescale in conjunction with others wanting to go a similar direction – but like most keen riders, after a couple of days you'll be so enthralled by the willing intelligence of your Kisber transport, you'll just want to stay in the saddle forever.

# Poznan to Warsaw Scenic Road

The drive between the two major Polish cities of Poznan and Warsaw can, of course, be made on a multi-lane highway. It's much better though, if you have the time, to take the scenic route, a lovely trip through the Weilkopolska lakelands, passing small towns, old churches, castles and palaces.

Poznan itself is a historically significant city on the Warta River. At one time the capital of Greater Poland, it contains the oldest cathedral in the country, built in the 10th century. Today it is the region's administrative capital, and a commercial and industrial centre. Just a few miles to the south, and a slight detour off your route to the village of Kornik, lies the Weilkopolska National Park, a peaceful area of forests and lakes, cut with a few, well-signed trails. Set on a lake, Kornik boasts a splendid, moated castle, with a landscaped arboretum that includes trees and shrubs from around the world. At Rogalin, not far away, stands a beautiful 18th century palace, with 3 protected oak trees in the grounds that are over 1,000 years old.

The journey takes you to several more castles and palaces before reaching the city of Kalisz, generally considered Poland's oldest city as it was mentioned as being a trading post by Ptolemy in 200 BC. Avoiding heavily industrial Lodz, travel south to Piotrkow, site of the first Jewish ghetto in the country, built in 1939. Outside the town is the infamous Rakow Forest, where memorials stand testament to the 600 Jews massacred here in 1942, and to the 7,000 Polish and Russian prisoners also killed here. Now you are about an hour's drive from Warsaw, Poland's lively capital city. Remarkably, brilliantly rebuilt after World War II, its historic old town is inscribed on the UNESCO World Heritage List.

**HOW:**
By car
**WHEN TO GO:**
May to September
**TIME IT TAKES:**
Can be done in a day, but you may well want to stay en route, perhaps in a restored palace or an eco-farm.
**HIGHLIGHTS:**
The annual Classical Music Festival in Poznan.
Smielow Palace, late 18th century, it is set in a large nature park.
Goluchow Castle, where you can see Polish bison in the grounds.
**YOU SHOULD KNOW:**
The Gothic Cathedral of St Peter and Paul, built on an island in the river at Poznan, contains the tomb of Mieszko 1, the founder of Poland, and of his son Boleslaus the Brave, the first King, crowned in 1025.

*The old town hall in Poznan*

353

# Galician Carpathians

**HOW:**
On foot
**WHEN TO GO:**
All year round, but April to October is probably best.
**TIME IT TAKES:**
The hike to the top of Mount Tarnica can easily be done in a day.
**HIGHLIGHTS:**
Wolosate village, where there is a breeding station for Hucul mountain horses – you can hire these horses in nearby villages and ride in the Park.
Sanok Historical Museum, which contains the largest collection of 14th-18th century icons outside Moscow.
Sanok's Museum of Folk Architecture, a superb collection of wooden buildings, including 3 churches, from all over Poland.
Lesko – the Spanish influenced Renaissance synagogue and historic Jewish cemetery.
**YOU SHOULD KNOW:**
During the 1960s enormous efforts were made to exterminate the wolf population in the area. This resulted in an explosion of the deer population and increasing damage to saplings and crops. Since 1995 wolves have been protected and there are about 100 individuals living in the park today.

Tucked away in the far south-eastern corner of Poland is the Bieszczady National Park. Located in the Carpathian Mountains, which rise in Slovakia and stretch through Poland, Ukraine and into Romania, the Park protects the Bieszczady Mountains, in the eastern section. It has been enlarged four times since its creation in 1973, when this unique region became the world's first tripartite International Biosphere Reserve, encompassing areas lying in Slovakia and Ukraine.

The mountains comprise three zones: foothills forested with willow, ash, sycamore and grey alder, ancient beech forests interspersed with firs and maples at about 900 m (3,000 ft) and high pastures, known as *poloniny*, from 1,050 m (3,500 ft). This gorgeous, Alpine-type grassland includes scree and rocks covered with rare lichen and mosses. Elsewhere, endemic wildflowers as well as Alpine and sub-Alpine species carpet the mountain meadows. Bieszczady National Park has 132 km (83 mi) of marked trails, providing hikes of relative ease. One of the best is the hike to the top of Mount Tarnica, at 1,364 m (4,500 ft) the Park's highest peak.

Starting at Ustrzyki Gorne walkers can follow the red path through the forest, which probably looks at its best when decked in glowing autumnal colour. If you start early enough you may see deer, but these forests are rich with flora and fauna, including wolves, bears, elk, lynx, wildcats, wild boar and beavers, which have been successfully introduced into the creeks and streams. As the trail leaves the forest for the *poloniny*, the landscape opens out around you, the wind ruffles through the grasses, and an extraordinary range of raptors can be seen – honey buzzards, goshawks, sparrow hawks, perhaps even a golden eagle. On reaching the top of Mount Tarnica, the 360-degree views over the whole Park are quite something to behold.

*Bieszczady National Park*

# Dunajec Gorge

Way down in the south of Poland, on the border with Slovakia, is the little-known Pieniny National Park, through which the Dunajec River flows. An important tributary of the Vistula, the river cuts through the narrow Pieniny Mountain range, and over the centuries its waters have gouged a splendid gorge through the limestone crags. For 18 km (11 mi) the river forms the border with Slovakia, and since both countries joined the European Community in 2004, rafting downstream has become a popular jaunt for tourists from many destinations.

*Rafting down the river.*

The Flisaki raftsmen have been active on the Dunajec for centuries, transporting goods, fishing for the salmon that were once plentiful here, and steering log-booms. In 1832 tourism began on the river, and just over 100 years later, the Flisaki registered as an organization. Today some 500 men work about 250 wooden rafts, each carrying ten passengers, and accompanied by two raftsmen, wearing traditional round-brimmed, black felt hats, usually decorated with white cowry shells or embroidery.

Starting from the marina in Sromowce-Katy, the rafts set out on their voyage, bobbing down through rapids which give onto more placid stretches of water, and finding their way around seven loops in the river, changing direction by more than 90 degrees many times over the whole course. On the way they pass through wonderful limestone scenery – 500 m (1,600 ft) cliffs, partially tree-clad, forests and fields, even two formidable castles, one on either side, built as strategic fortresses during the 13th and 14th centuries.

The Flisaki are knowledgeable guides as well as being very experienced raftsmen, and they delight in educating their passengers about the mountains and their folklore. The trip ends in Szczawnica, a charming mountain resort in the Grajcarek Valley, with vistas towards the highest peaks of the Pieniny range.

**HOW:**
By raft
**WHEN TO GO:**
April to October, but late May to mid-September is probably the best time.
**TIME IT TAKES:**
About 2 hours 15 minutes
**HIGHLIGHTS:**
Czorsztyn Castle, a partially restored ruin.
Niedzica Castle, beautifully maintained this is a hotel as well as housing an interesting museum.
Walk the new, 90-m (295-ft) bridge from Poland's Sromowce Nizne, at the foot of the Three Crowns mountains, to the picturesque village of Cerveny Clastor (Red Monastery) in Slovakia.
**YOU SHOULD KNOW:**
You can raft the river every day during the season except for two religious holidays – Corpus Christi and the first day of Easter.

*A view of the beautiful city of Prague*

# Vltava River Cruise

**HOW:**
By boat

**WHEN TO GO:**
Ferries run April to October. Some cruises operate all year.

**TIME IT TAKES:**
Cruises ½ to 3 hours; ferry south, a day trip, north 1 ½ hours each way.

**HIGHLIGHTS:**
The Charles Bridge is an impressive medieval engineering feat; at each end stand fine towers; Baroque statues line the walkway.

Tancici Dum (the Dancing House) in Nove Mesto. This remarkable modern building of two irregular linked towers by Frank Gehry and Vlado Milunic is also known as 'Fred and Ginger'.

Troja – Baroque Troya Chateau in its formal gardens, and the pleasant Prague Zoo.

Vysehrad, the legendary 'birthplace' of Prague. Little is left of the old fortress but the rocky brick-red walls high above the river are impressive.

Since the advent of cheap flights the ancient and magnificently beautiful city of Prague has become a popular destination for short and long breaks and at times it can seem uncomfortably crowded. The river, always an important part of the life of the city, offers a breathing space. Sightseeing cruises of various durations are available and in summer a regular ferry runs north to the suburb of Troja and south, through lovely countryside, to Slapy Dam.

Prague Castle, the best-known image of the city, occupies the heights of the Left Bank. The long, almost blank palace façade is crowned by the irregular Gothic spires and pinnacles of the St Vitus Cathedral. Below are the narrow, hilly streets, steep roofs, towers and cupolas and terraced gardens of Mala Strana, 'Little Quarter'. To the south rises the big, wooded hill of Petrin with its funicular railway.

On the Right Bank, several of the imposing buildings of Stare Mesto, 'Old Town', can be seen, including the Smetana Museum and the National Theatre with its gold-topped roof. From here down to Vysehrad, 'High Castle', with the dominating spires of the neo-gothic St Peter and St Paul, the river side of Nove Mesto – 'New Town' – is lined with fine mansions and commercial buildings, including the Art Nouveau House of the Hlahol Choir.

Boat trips offer good views of some of the city's many bridges and of the islands. On Slovansky Ostrov stands the Baroque Sitka Tower; Kampo, near the weir built in the 19th century to help navigation, has peaceful gardens and an old mill, now an art gallery.

# Gustav Mahler Cycle Trail

This cycle trail, one of a number of well-planned and mapped tours in the Czech Republic, runs from Jihlava in the heart of the Bohemian-Moravian highlands northwards to Kutna Hora in Central Bohemia, west of Prague. The trail covers about 83 km (52 mi) of track, with short country road sections, through wooded, rolling hills, river valleys, villages, and two charming towns with Mahler connections.

In medieval times this was a wealthy and important silver-mining region. Jihlava was founded by King Wenceslas in the 13th century and prospered. However, it never recovered from the ravages of the Thirty Years' War, though it still has many fine medieval and renaissance buildings. In 1865 the Mahler family moved here; Gustav attended the grammar school and learnt music; his love of Czech folk tunes was life-long. His parents are buried in the Jewish cemetery.

Humpolec is another old town with a history of silver mining, though it became better known as a centre for the cloth trade. The art nouveau Town Hall houses a museum with a Gustav Mahler gallery. The hilltop village of Kaliste, with its lovely views over the countryside, was Mahler's birthplace. The tiny cottage has been reconstructed and is visited by music lovers from all over the world.

For a change from Mahler, a restored castle above the Sazava River bridge at Ledec nad Sazavou offers a collection of handicrafts, weapons and coins.

Beautiful Kutná Hora became the favourite residence of several Bohemian kings and rivalled Prague economically, culturally and politically, though after years of warfare and the flooding of the silver mines it fell into decline. Now, with its wealth of Gothic and Baroque buildings, this delightful town is a UNESCO World Heritage Site.

**HOW:**
By bike
**WHEN TO GO:**
May, June, September and October
**TIME IT TAKES:**
2 or 3 days
**HIGHLIGHTS:**
Kutná Hora holds a splendid Gothic pageant every June.
The Gothic Cathedral of St Barbara is spectacular with a 5-aisled nave and a roof of 3 tent-like towers.
In the ossuary at Sedlec is a chandelier constructed from bones.
**YOU SHOULD KNOW:**
This scenic, rural touring cycle route should pose no problems.

*The Cathedral of St Barbara in beautiful Kutná Hora*

# Island hop along the Dalmatian Coast

**HOW:**
By boat
**WHEN TO GO:**
May, June, early July, September
and October
**TIME IT TAKES:**
At least a week
**HIGHLIGHTS:**
Split – Diocletian's Palace. Built for
the Emperor's retirement, the walls
of this UNESCO World Heritage Site
enclose Roman buildings converted
over the centuries.
Brac – the Supetar town cemetery is
a dreamlike conglomeration of
monuments by Ivan Rendic, one of
Croatia's leading sculptors.
Lopud, Kolocep and Sipan – the only
inhabited islands in the Elaphite
chain. Beautiful and unspoiled they
are a day trip from Dubrovnik.
Dubrovnik's city walls: the circuit of
the battlements gives splendid views
of the roofs, towers and domes and
the grid plan of the town.
**YOU SHOULD KNOW:**
The island routes will present no
difficulties for regular cyclists.
Ferry tickets must be purchased
before the journey.

Dalmatia's dramatically beautiful coastline is fringed by hundreds of small, enticing islands. Those south of Split are easily reached and, despite their popularity, peaceful. They offer fine cycling – quiet roads through fertile, hilly, well-wooded countryside, tiny coves, pretty villages, and no long distances. Combined yacht and cycle trips are becoming popular, but bike rental is available in many places and the bike fares on the car ferries are modest. Split is a big, hectic, vibrant city centred on an old town built around and into the massive remains of Diocletian's Palace. The regular ferry connecting Split and Dubrovnik calls at Brac, Hvar, Korcula and Mljet. Wooded Solta and rugged, remote Vis are easily reached from Split but not by the connecting route.

Brac produces good wine and its lustrous white building stone is prized worldwide. The south coast has several seaside villages, including Bol, famous for its lovely beach and for its windsurfing.

Ancient little harbour towns nestle in the deep bays of Hvar's green, indented coastline, but, with its harbour and fortress, Renaissance square and Gothic palaces, Hvar Town is the main attraction.

Popular Korcula, a perfect miniature medieval city, perches on a steep headland. Marco Polo was born here during the long Venetian rule that shaped the glorious architecture of the town. The island is thick with orchards and vineyards and ringed by fishing villages.

Mljet, with its fertile farmland, untouched forest and salt-water lakes, quiet villages and fine monastic buildings, is seductively tranquil. Much of the island is a National Park.

Dubrovnik, a medieval city reshaped by the Baroque and now carefully reconstructed after its infamous shelling in 1991-2 is, with its pearly marble streets, rich history and culture, and setting of lushly wooded mountains and breezy blue waters, enchanting.

*Korcula old town*

# Budva Riviera

The beautiful Budva Riviera, with its azure water, background of mountains and string of bays, coves and fine sand beaches, runs only about 35 km (23 mi) from Budva to Petrovac. Some of the settlements that punctuate the coast date back to Roman, Greek and even Phoenician times, though little archaeological evidence remains. A walk along the Riviera, either on the beaches, by the coast road or on the peaceful hillside path parallel with the old road, allows breaks or overnight stays at irresistible beaches and exploration of the inland villages and old, frescoed monasteries.

Budva is a delightful place. The old town was built on a headland and is surrounded by 15th century walls. This busy tourist town offers old buildings, churches and museums, festivals and a lively nightlife. Southwards, a promenade walk follows the bay round to Becici beach. Milocer, once a royal holiday spot is, with its two beaches – King's and Queen's – and lush parkland setting, a fashionable resort. Sveti Stefan is reached by a causeway; built on a tiny island as a fishermen's village in the 15th century, it is now an exclusive and beautiful hotel complex.

Between here and Petrovac are several small, secluded beaches and an interesting inland area, the peach and pomegranate clad Pastrovici Hills. This was once a semi-autonomous Dukedom with its own language and traditions.

Petrovac, with its spectacular setting and red sand, is an attractive and very popular town. It retains charm and intimacy, but is threatened by the density of recent construction. A walk south to Lucice beach, or on to the relatively undeveloped Buljarica beach escapes the crowds.

*The island of Sveti Stefan on the Adriatic*

**HOW:**
On foot
**WHEN TO GO:**
May, June and September
**TIME IT TAKES:**
Three days plus, depending on stops
**HIGHLIGHTS:**
Views from the battlements over the whole of Budva, Saint Nikola Island and Sveti Stefan.
The little port village of Przno (before it is over-developed) for a sunset drink on the waterfront.
**YOU SHOULD KNOW:**
Accommodation can be over-subscribed and expensive.

# Dajti Express Cable Car

Tirana, the capital of Albania, has its own eccentric charm – hospitable natives, orange trees in the streets, some old Ottoman buildings and a glorious street market. From the chaotic jumble of poverty, hastily erected buildings and traffic which is the city centre, the dark bulk of Mount Dajti, 25 km (15 mi) to the east can, smog permitting, be seen.

This spacious and easily accessible National Park is a favourite excursion and escape for city-dwellers. It has been inhabited from early times and the name could be linked with the ancient cult of Diktynna, a mother goddess venerated around the Mediterranean. Its relatively low altitude – 1,610 m (5,232 ft) – allows forest cover and pleasant shady walking in the summer.

Until 2005 the only approach was by road, passing through the city outskirts and fashionable new housing, winding along the contours of the mountain. Inside the Park, low-key tourist developments are built around restaurants and the road finishes at a large, green area which is used for picnics and barbecues. This is also the terminus for the Dajti Express Cable Car, an Austrian-built enterprise which runs from the edge of town. The 4-km (2.5-mi) ride up to 1,230 m (3,998 ft) takes just fifteen minutes. The views over the mountain range, the sprawl of Tirana and the eastern lowlands are excellent. From the Dajta Field, paths lead through attractive beech woods and areas of pine and fir. These quiet wooded slopes are home to many flower and plant species and to small mammals including red squirrels and beech martens.

The woods are cool and peaceful, a perfect respite from the city.

*Views over the mountains from the Dajti Cable Car*

# The Albanian Coast from Corfu

The southern Albanian coast is very close to Corfu and, since the 7th century BC when Greece established colonies in what was then Illyria, strong trade and cultural links have existed. Now regular short ferry and hydrofoil crossings from Corfu make it easy to reach Saranda and the remarkable UNESCO World Heritage Site at Butrint. It is just possible to make a day-trip of it.

Sunny Saranda is an attractively situated port and seaside town, a pleasant place to stay. An ancient city, it has Roman and Byzantine remains, though little archaeological work has been undertaken. On the Butrint road south lie the interesting ruins of the Byzantine Monastery of Shen Gjergi, a lovely spot with views of the Adriatic and good bird watching in the marshes. Further south, the pleasant beach-resort of Kasmili makes an alternative base.

Butrint is one of the most exciting sites in the Balkan Peninsula. Set against a background of hills and largely bounded by water (ancient Butrint was effectively an island), this extensive and complex site has remains dating from periods covering 2,500 years. The excellent guide to Butrint by Neritan Ceka is essential for serious exploration. The massive perimeter walls, some dating from the 5th century BC, shelter Roman baths, a Venetian tower, a Greek lustral well, fragments of early Christian buildings and a large complex known as the Tri-conch Palace. Finely carved gates pierce the walls, two opening onto the lakeshore, where the ancient harbour lay. The inner fortress contains temples and baths, a gymnasium, a Roman house, Greek theatre and acropolis and an early Christian baptistery. Many of these have fine mosaic floors.

*The Basilica at Butrint near Saranda*

**HOW:**
By boat and car
**WHEN TO GO:**
Late April to October
**TIME IT TAKES:**
It's possible to complete the trip in 1 day, but much better to make it a jaunt of at least 3 days.
**HIGHLIGHTS:**
The enormous baptistery is a building of great beauty and tranquillity.
Kasmili has an idyllic beach, clean, clear blue water and good fish restaurants.
Sunset on Saranda's waterfront, when Corfu seems to drift in a haze.
**YOU SHOULD KNOW:**
Get hold of the guidebook to Butrint before your visit as it's rarely available on site.
The mosaics at Butrint are usually sand-covered for protection.

*A view from the ferry bus as it crosses Lake Komani*

# Crossing Lake Komani

Lake Komani was formed when the River Drin was dammed in 1970 as part of a huge hydroelectric scheme. It winds, fjord-like, from the huge Vau i Dejax dam near Shkodra to the Fierza Dam. The memorable ferry ride is the best way to reach the remote and spectacular Tropoja region – the road is dreadful. From Tirana a minibus leaves to link with the RORO ferry and continues to Bajram Curri from Bregluna at the Fierza end; the return trip leaves early next day.

Another ferry plying the waters is the local waterbus, a ramshackle-looking craft created by welding an old bus onto a hull. This takes about four hours – twice as long as the car ferry – but it provides links for the remote dwellings of the lake and offers a unique insight into the life of the area. A night in Shkodra (old Scutari) makes catching this early ferry bus possible. This interesting old city was, under Ottoman rule, the largest town in Albania; it is still predominantly Muslim, and very traditional. The road to the ferry station – about 35 km (22 mi) follows the river valley and passes through a narrow tunnel. The ferry journey is superb, following the twists and turns of the lake whose deep, still, jade-green waters reflect the precipitous tree-clad gorges. In places the deciduous woods have been cleared, the ground terraced to allow those whose homes are clustered high above the lake to scratch a living.

Bajram Curri is a windy, ugly little town set in magnificent scenery. Named after a key figure in the liberation of Albania from Ottoman rule, it is a good base for exploring the huge lakes and towering mountains of this otherwise inaccessible area.

# Dracula's Transylvanian Tour

Transylvania, part of Hungary and then of the Ottoman Empire, became Romanian in 1918. The name now is synonymous with spiky mountains and castles, dark forests, werewolves and Dracula the Vampire Count. For Romanians and historians, Vlad Tepes, the Impaler, son of Vlad Dracul, was a fierce fighter and ruthless ruler. Though rumoured to be in league with the devil, he was not known as a vampire. Vampirism is an accepted part of folklore. Bram Stoker, after much research but no visits, set his tale in Transylvania and invented Count Dracula. History and fantasy meet in a 'Dracula tour'.

The inhabited, fortified citadel Sighisoara was the birthplace of Vlad Tepes; with its jagged skyline of battlements and spires, it looks the part. If time allows, a visit to the northern town of Bistrita and the Bargau Valley with its saw-tooth peaks and lonely hamlets reveals Stoker's well-described locations. The tour-bus magnet though is Bran, south of Brasov. 'Dracula's Castle', perched on a crag and bristling with turrets, may have inspired Stoker, but was never inhabited by Vlad. The sprawling hilltop castle in nearby Rasnov is more atmospheric and the countryside around both is wild and untouched. Vlad was a Wallachian prince; he spent his boyhood in the Princely Court in Targoviste. A monastery on a tiny island in Lake Snagov is probably his burial place.

This north-south journey ends in Bucharest, but a westward loop back to Sighisoura passes the brooding, little-visited Poenari Castle where the Impaler spent years in refuge before escaping the Turks aided by the villagers of Arefu. The fine Saxon city of Sibiu was briefly his home, and the cathedral contains the tomb of his son, Mihnea the Bad.

**HOW:**
By car or organized coach tour
**WHEN TO GO:**
June to September
**TIME IT TAKES:**
At least a week
**HIGHLIGHTS:**
Lively Baroque Brasov makes a good base to explore the old towns, fortresses and villages.
The road north to Sibiu: cross the mountains by Red Tower Pass or (summer months only) by the breathtaking Transfagarasun Highway.
Vlad Dracul House in Sighisoara houses a medieval-themed restaurant.
**YOU SHOULD KNOW:**
Poienari Castle is reached by climbing 1,400 steps.

*The multi-turreted Bran Castle*

# The Danube Gorge

**HOW:**
By bike and boat
**WHEN TO GO:**
April to June, September and October
**TIME IT TAKES:**
Two or three days
**HIGHLIGHTS:**
Nine massive towers, the remains of
a medieval fort, stand on the Serbian
bank of Golubac Gorge.
The Tabula Traiana (a carved stone
with Roman inscriptions) was laid in
AD 103 to mark the start of
construction of the road and of
Trajan's famous bridge, the first
across the Danube and the largest in
the Roman world.
On the Romanian side, a 40 m (130
ft) face of Decebal, the Dacian chief,
is carved into the rock.
A boat trip with lunch is a good way
to relax and see the gorges from a
different angle.
**YOU SHOULD KNOW:**
The route is not hilly and the wind
usually blows from the west.
Most of the road is quiet though it
becomes busy after Orsova.

*The Tabula Traiana along
the Danube*

The Iron Gate, Portile de Fier, now refers to the 117 km (73 mi) stretch of the Danube from Moldova Veche to the huge dam upstream of Drobeta-Turnu Severin. This joint Romanian and (then) Yugoslavian hydroelectric project was completed in 1972. As well as taming a notoriously dangerous river, this raised the water level by over 30 m (97 ft) and changed the whole character of the landscape.

This popular section of the Danube Bike Trail passes through four gorges. Bazias, where the river enters Romania, was once a busy freight station; it is a convenient point to join the route. At the little port of Moldova Veche the waters divide around an island and flow into the Golubac Gorge. Though the town here was submerged, some castle ruins remain. The second gorge, Gospodin Vir, is, like Golubac, about 15 km (10 mi) long and as little as 220 m (715 ft) wide. Kazan Gorge remains spectacular; here the cliffs tower to 700 m (2,300 ft) and the twisting chasm narrows to just 150 m (492 ft). The Romans built an extraordinary planked road here, inserting supporting beams into the rocks. Upstream from Orsova on the Serbian side a plaque commemorates this road and Trajan's Bridge.

Downstream to the dam with its twin power stations is the true Iron Gates gorge, once the most perilous stretch for shipping and now effectively a reservoir. Beneath the calm deep waters lies Ada Kaleh, an island famous for its independent Turkish community and the site of a Hapsburg fortress (now rebuilt downstream). Local companies run boat trips through the dam's navigational canal and up to the Kazan Gorges.

# Kom Emine Trail

*The Central Balkan National Park*

Between Mount Kom on the Serbian border and Cape Emine on the Black Sea coast stretches the Stara Planina (Old Mountain) range along which runs the Kon Emine Trail, part of the trans-European E3 trek. The whole walk – about 700 km (438 mi) will take about a month. The railway and road which follow the southern contours permit breaks in interesting, historical towns and villages where, as well as rest and provisions, information and advice on routes and day walks can be obtained.

The western and central sections of the range contain the highest peaks – many over 2,000 m (6,500 ft) – and the most demanding terrain. From the ridge the views are superb – south over green undulating foothills, north over sheer rock walls and deep gorges. Large areas are National Parks, rich in birds and wildlife. The weather is fickle; spring is particularly wet.

The trail begins at Berkovitsa, in the northwest – a lovely area of deep wooded valleys and remote monasteries; it can also be reached from Sofia in the south. The Troyan Pass (a link between provinces in Roman times) gives road access, as does the Shipka Pass. Here, the road south leads to Kazanlak, the 'capital' of the rose-growing region and the 'Valley of the Thracian Kings', with many burial mounds. The pleasant town of Slivan is the start of shorter walking trails.

Sleepy, attractive Kotel is a good starting point for the Eastern section where the range is still a dominating north/south barrier. Near the ancient village of Emona on the forested southern slopes, high cliffs run to where Cape Emine juts into the Black Sea. South lie sandy beaches and rolling farmland.

**HOW:**
On foot
**WHEN TO GO:**
July to September
**TIME IT TAKES:**
A month plus for the whole walk; at least a week for road travel combined with walks.
**HIGHLIGHTS:**
Access from Sofia passes the spectacular Iskar Gorge and an impressive waterfall.
Brown bears and wolves are still found in the Stara Planina, which is home to many rare birds including golden eagles.
The road to Emona gives glorious and welcome views of the sea.
The Shipka Pass allows sweeping panoramas north and south; here too is the impressive Shipka Monument to Freedom.
**YOU SHOULD KNOW:**
This is a strenuous trail; hikers who attempt it should be fit and experienced. Day walks offer an easier way into the mountains.

# Attic Coast Road

**HOW:**
By car or bus
**WHEN TO GO:**
All year; but avoid weekends and
high season (July/August)
**TIME IT TAKES:**
One day
**HIGHLIGHTS:**
Sunset at the Cape may be clichéd,
but the views over the islands and
sea are sensational.
Vouliagmeni Lake – the warm
sulphurous water has brought relief
to rheumatism sufferers for years.
Anavysos – a lively little town, with
fish sold from the boats in the
harbour and a colourful market.
**YOU SHOULD KNOW:**
Highway 91, with its sharp curves
and unheeded speed limits, is a
dangerous road.

*A small church on Lake
Vouliagmeni*

Cape Sounion is the windy southern tip of Attica, 69 km (43 mi) from
Athens. Here on a rocky cliff-top spur high above the Aegean stands a
Doric temple to Poseidon, god of the sea. It was built in 444 BC, the
same time as the Parthenon, and its brilliant white columns have been
a welcome landmark to seafarers ever since. The marble, quarried at
nearby Agrileza, contains no iron and retains its whiteness over
centuries. Of the original 34 slender columns, 15 survive; Lord Byron
set an unfortunate precedent in 1819 when he carved his name on one
of them. The sacred site was sealed by massive walls; these can be
followed down to the bay and the remains of ancient boathouses,
which later became a pirates' lair.

The coast road along the Attic Riviera passes many busy and
commercialized beaches and resorts. South of Vouliagmeni and Varkiza
with their marinas and luxury clubs, the road is lined with quieter
coves and tavernas and exclusive villas. There are regular buses from
Athens to Sounion, and it is a popular outing – an early morning visit
avoids some of the crowds. It is possible to drive back round the Cape
and a little north to the rather desolate town of Lavrio. The
Mineralogical Museum is a reminder of its wealthy past as a silver-
mining centre. A loop inland rejoins the coast road at Anavysos.

# Samarian Gorge Hike

The Samarian Gorge now seems to be an essential part of a Cretan holiday. It is a long – 16 km (10 mi) plus 3 km (2 mi) to the coast – and gruelling walk. Wardens, donkeys and helicopters are on hand – every year injured walkers are rescued – and flash floods are not uncommon early and late in the season – weather warnings must be heeded. But this is an exciting trek, with magnificent scenery and remarkable flora and fauna. The Gorge is home to hundreds of bird species and to the shy and elusive kri-kri, the Cretan ibex. Herbs scent the air, and Cretan dittany, used medicinally since ancient times, grows on the rocks.

Organized trips usually arrive early (the Gorge opens at 6.00 am), with boats from the bottom of the gorge to the waiting coaches at Hora Sfakion. This can be done independently, by public bus. A south to north walk is quieter, but uphill, and against the tide of trekkers coming down.

The precipitous early stages of the Gorge, a spectacular gash in the Omalos Plateau, are fitted with wooden rails. At the bottom, ancient cypresses surround a chapel; from here the path follows the stream to Samaria, a village abandoned when the Gorge was made a Park in 1962. The Gorge deepens and narrows, the stream filling its bed and the track crosses it by stepping-stones and wooden walkways. At the short stretch known as the Iron Gates, the walls close in to little more than 3.5 m (11 ft) and soar sheer to almost 300 m (1,000 ft). At the end of the Gorge itself lies the old deserted village of Ayia Roumeli, and a half hour's hot walk over a stony wilderness to the sea. Here the new village provides weary hikers with cold drinks, swimming, ferries and accommodation.

*The stunning Samarian Gorge*

**HOW:**
On foot
**WHEN TO GO:**
1 May to 31 October
**TIME IT TAKES:**
4-7 hours
**HIGHLIGHTS:**
The first view of the Gorge with its startlingly sudden plunge can be enjoyed by non-walkers.
In spring, the Gorge is brilliant with wild flowers including anemones, irises and orchids.
Bird watching: owls, falcons and eagles are frequently seen; the endangered lammergeier (bearded vulture) may be spotted.
Frescoes in the 14th century church in Samaria.
**YOU SHOULD KNOW:**
Walkers should be fit and accustomed to long walks over rough terrain.
Beware of falling rocks.
Obey the Park Rules (these include no smoking and no singing!)

367

*The town of Ermoupoli*

# The Piraeus to Santorini Ferry

Sailing the Aegean between the Isles of Greece may be a dream, but the ferry journey from Piraeus to Santorini is a pleasant reality. Several shipping lines operate but the daily, early ferry via Syros, Paros, Naxos and Ios allows a day of sea travel with glimpses of interesting islands.

The ship leaves the chaotic sprawl of Piraeus, heading south east, and sails round either the rocky north or the greener south of Syros, into the handsome port of Ermoupoli. This, the largest town in the Cyclades, was, in the 19th century, Athens' main port. Its opera house is based on La Scala! On two hills behind the harbour are a medieval quarter and a fine domed church.

The ferry runs south to Paros whose single central peak is ringed by fishing villages, beaches and little bays. The busy harbour at Parikia is the hub of inter-island transport, but behind it, ranks of tightly packed square white houses rise gently to an old kastro. Just an hour west, Naxos is big, beautiful and, unusually, very fertile. Fishing boats and restaurants crowd the harbour and narrow, ancient alleyways climb through stone archways to the fine mansions of the fortified Venetian town. Midway between Naxos and Santorini, the little 'party island', Ios, has one of the prettiest harbours in the Aegean: linked by a stepped path to the port at Yialos, hilltop Hora has snowy houses, blue domed churches and a windmill, all flanked by palm trees.

Santorini (Thira) was part of the Minoan civilization till (probably around 1640 BC) a cataclysmic eruption when its high centre sank to form a deep lagoon around which the island – actually the partial rim of the crater – curves. Above black sand beaches and tiny fishing villages tower darkly striated pumice cliffs; hundreds of feet up, the brilliantly white settlements of Ia and the capital, Fira, cling to the caldera ring.

**HOW:**
By ferry
**WHEN TO GO:**
May, June, September and October
**TIME IT TAKES:**
Ten to twelve hours
**HIGHLIGHTS:**
The traveller entering Naxos harbour has been greeted for 2,500 years by the colossal marble portal of an unfinished temple to Apollo.
While the ferry is moving slowly, dolphins may swim alongside and play for a while.
Indigo sea, sunshine, the misty outlines of the clustered Cyclades, the joy of 'island hopping' for a day.
The extraordinary thrill of entering the great bay of Santorini.
**YOU SHOULD KNOW:**
Buy ferry tickets on the day – weather can cause disruption to schedules.
The last major earthquake on Santorini was in 1956.

# Patras to Messolonghi

A short ride east by back roads from Patras, the attractive port village Rio is the southern entry point for the Charilaos Trikoupis Bridge. Named after the 19th century statesman who first suggested a bridge here, it was opened in 2004 at the time of the Olympic Games. The overall length is 2,880 m (9,449 ft) and its cable-stayed suspended deck is the longest in the world. Designed to improve road communications between mainland Greece and the Peloponnese it has, in addition to toll-paying traffic lanes, a designated bicycle/pedestrian lane which offers, for those with a head for heights, a spectacular crossing of the Gulf of Corinth.

A ferry still runs between Rio and Antirio – both villages still have the forts which guarded this, the 'Little Dardanelles', the narrowest point in the Gulf. On both sides, fertile coastal plains, backed by mountains, are dotted with small seaside resorts. Just east of Antirio is Nafpaktos, ancient Lepanto, where in 1571 the sea battle that ended Turkish domination of the Mediterranean took place. To the west the road passes through coastal villages and over flat swampland to the serene area of salt marsh, reeds and calm waters (a protected biodiversity zone) of Kolsova Lagoon. On its banks lies Messalonghi, once a collection of stilted fishermen's huts, now a lively modern town, usually visited for historical reasons. Lord Byron came here to join battle in the struggle for independence, but died of fever in 1824. His death brought the war to international attention, and he became a national hero. In 1826 after a bitter siege the townspeople abandoned their fallen city by the Gate of Exodus, which still stands. Most were recaptured and killed. The town was awarded the honorary title of Hiera Polis (Sacred City) for its heroic part in the War of Independence.

**HOW:**
By bike
**WHEN TO GO:**
May, June, September and October
**TIME IT TAKES:**
One or two days
**HIGHLIGHTS:**
The fine Castle of Morea, the moated fortress at Rio.
The view from the bridge – lush hillsides, towering mountains and the water, busy with shipping, far below.
The statue of Lord Byron in the Garden of the Heroes in Messalonghi; beneath it is buried his heart.
Bird watching in the wetlands (Greece's largest); many winter migrants visit, and rare species breed.
**YOU SHOULD KNOW:**
Much of the ride is fairly level. The roads between Antirio and Messolonghi can be busy.

*The Rio-Antirio Bridge offers a spectacular crossing of the Gulf of Corinth.*

# Vouraikos Gorge Railway

**HOW:**
By train
**WHEN TO GO:**
May to early July, September and October (avoiding weekends)
**TIME IT TAKES:**
At least two days
**HIGHLIGHTS:**
The lovely landscapes of the Gorge.
The two original steam engines are displayed, one at each end of the line.
Kalavryta Museum is a dignified, undramatized and moving memorial to the 1,436 men who died.
**YOU SHOULD KNOW:**
It is worth buying a first class ticket, as this allows seating in the front and back of the train.
It is a very small train; buy tickets early.

Diakofto is a peaceful village on the Gulf of Corinth. It has a small beach and a background of steep mountains, olive groves and citrus orchards and it is the end of the remarkable Vouraikos Gorge Railway. This was built between 1889 and 1896 to transport ore from the Kalavryta region to the coast. The short – 22.5 km (14 mi) – journey is memorable and enjoyable; the track climbs 700 m (2,275 ft) using a rack-and-pinion system for traction over the steep gradients. The best view of the mechanism is from the front of the train; the very back gives wonderful views of the scenery.

After a gentle ascent through the lush landscape of the valley, the line criss-crosses the river; the gorge narrows and the train enters the first of fourteen tunnels, then runs along a ledge above the river. The only stop is at the picturesque, unspoilt settlement of Zahlorov – there is accommodation and good walking here. The journey continues beside the river in the shade of plane trees, and over open country to Kalavryta.

This is a delightful spot. At 756 m (2,457 ft), with fresh air, bubbling springs and tree-shaded *plateia* (town square), it is a favourite with At henians for weekends. Some miles south of the village the deep Cave of the Lakes has fine stalactites and a chain of deep stone basins which run with water in the spring. Little Kalavryta is famous nationwide – the War of Independence started officially here in 1821, and in 1943 it saw one of the worst atrocities of World War II when the Nazis executed all the men of the area.

*Great views of the Gorge can be enjoyed from the train.*

# Nestos Valley

The Nestos River, which forms the boundary between Macedonia and Thrace, rises in the lofty Rodopi range in Bulgaria. It flows south through craggy mountains, gorges and deep forests to spreading fertile plains and a wetland delta fed by dozens of tributaries. The valley makes a glorious mountain bike ride; some of it is tough going, some uses well-marked donkey tracks, old roads, or paths alongside the railway line.

*The Nestos River*

The mountain road from Drama to Xanthi crosses the valley at the village of Paranesti, from where it is possible to cycle a 'there and back' loop into the remote mountains, a region of hidden waterfalls, thick flower-scattered woodland, a refuge for many animals and birds. From Paranesti downstream the river runs through forested foothills and fields of sunflowers, past isolated villages. Stavroupolis is the only place with facilities for tourists. Here, as well as accommodation, information on cycling, organised hikes and kayaking is available.

South, the thick beech woods are full of birdlife. Now the river flows into The Narrows, a remarkable protected landscape of seven successive hairpin bends. The railway and the track cut along above the river and allow views of the tight meanders and the lush, undisturbed – there's no road access – wildlife habitat.

From Toxotes, the route crosses a huge area of corn and tobacco at the apex of the delta and then the river threads through a protected region of wetland – salt marshes, freshwater lakes and extensive riparian forest. Here, in the green shady tree tunnels, the only sounds are the calls of thousands of birds.

**HOW:**
By bike
**WHEN TO GO:**
May to early July and September
**TIME IT TAKES:**
At least four days
**HIGHLIGHTS:**
Bird watching: forest and river woodland species include peregrines, golden orioles and flycatchers; the delta is home to large numbers of storks, herons and egrets.
Wildlife: bears are occasionally spotted in the mountains. The residents of the Narrows include otters and wildcats.
Stavroupolis is a lovely village with traditional stone houses and a tree-shaded square.
**YOU SHOULD KNOW:**
Sections of this route are very demanding.
Stavroupolis is an ideal place to break the journey, but there is little accommodation and it may be necessary to go by road to Xanthi.

# Ioaninna to Méteora Road

Ioaninna, a lively and attractive town on the shores of Lake Pamvotis, is the capital of Epirus. During Ottoman rule the city prospered; it was at this time that the famous Crafts Guilds of Epirus were started by those driven by poor land to practise skills from silversmithing to baking. The old, walled Turkish town is built on a headland and the despot, Ali Pasha, made it his capital. Now the town has several interesting museums.

The scenic road northeast climbs steadily to the Katara Pass through the Pindus Mountains. This massive range, snow-capped from October till May, stretches to the Albanian border. Below the pass lies Metsova, still the 'capital' of the Vlachs, mountain-dwelling shepherds who speak a dialect of Latin. Metsovo also flourished under Turkish rule and later those who grew rich elsewhere re-invested in their home-town. Here, stone lanes wind between fine old houses and many of the traditional crafts survive.

Méteora – 'suspended in air' is, with its monastery-crowned pinnacles of rock, an astonishing sight. From the 11th century, solitary hermits occupied the caves; Turkish raids in the 14th century drove monks to live here, between heaven and earth, and by the 16th there were twenty-four monasteries. These were built with materials hauled up ladders and winched up in nets, and this means of access allowed the monks to seal themselves off from the world. Steps were cut in the 20th century, and now just six monasteries are occupied and open to visitors. The village of Kastraki at the foot of the rocks off the main road is a good base for exploring Méteora.

*Roussanou Monastery is perched precariously on its rock pinnacle.*

# Prespa Lakes from Kastoria

Set on a promontory in Lake Orestiada and surrounded by mountains, Kastoria in western Macedonia is one of Greece's loveliest towns. Its name means 'place of beavers' and it has long been a centre of the fur trade. After the beavers became extinct in the 19th century, the trade continued with imported fur. The town is architecturally outstanding. Many of the 17th and 18th century merchants' mansions survive and there are 54 Byzantine and medieval churches. Some, tiny and hidden away, were built as private chapels; these are often closed but their exteriors are interesting, with frescoes and geometric masonry. Panaghia Koumbelidhiki has an unusual tall, drum-shaped dome; 10th century Aghia Anarhyri overlooks the lake.

A side road 36 km (22 mi) north leads through fertile meadows to the Prespa Basin where Greece's borders with Albania and the Republic of Macedonia run through the two Prespa Lakes. This was a politically sensitive, little visited place, but now the Prespa Lakes National Park is a Transnational Park and though still remote this beautiful and serene area is more accessible. The huge Megali Prespa has steep, rocky shores interspersed with lush wetlands; Mikri Prespa and its encircling reed-beds is a protected area – among the many birds breeding there is the endangered Dalmatian pelican.

The region has several villages. Agios Germanos is an attractive agricultural settlement with the excellent Prespa Information Centre, which can arrange guided bird-watching tours of the Park. It has two frescoed Byzantine churches, and the hills outside the village give panoramic views over the lakes. The only Greek village on Megali Prespa is Psarades, a lovely traditional fishing village. Fishermen sometimes offer trips to see the lake and the scattered churches on its shores. A floating footbridge leads to the islet of Ayios Ahillios with two ruined Byzantine churches.

**HOW:**
By car
**WHEN TO GO:**
May to early July, September
**TIME IT TAKES:**
At least three days
**HIGHLIGHTS:**
The Folk Museum in Kastoria is housed in an old, sumptuously furnished fur-trader's mansion.
Birdwatching: storks, egrets, herons and white pelicans are among the water birds frequently seen around the lakes.
Boat trips visit painted cave-shrines, old monasteries and the 15th century Panayia Eleoussas, a rock church deep in a chasm.
Tavernas on Psarades waterfront serve fish straight from the lakes.
**YOU SHOULD KNOW:**
Be careful not to wander into the protected reed beds of Mikri Prespa.

*The 15th century rock church Panayia Eleoussas*

*The Temple of Tholos in the sanctuary of Athena in Delphi*

# Sacred Way

The Sanctuary of Apollo at Delphi took shape from the 8th to the 7th century BC, centred on a temple guarding the centre of the world, the Omphalos (Navel), the chasm of the Oracle. Here Pythia, the priestess, perched above the void and spoke the words of the god; a priest interpreted the often-ambiguous pronouncements to the waiting supplicants. From the 6th to the 4th century BC, Delphi was the spiritual centre of the ancient world and an international political centre, for warriors and kings joined the worshippers. Great wealth and power were amassed – in addition to ritual cleansing and sacrifice, those seeking advice paid tribute. Individuals and cities erected dedications to Apollo – statues and small buildings (treasuries) and the Sanctuary grew. Under Roman rule, the power of the Oracle declined, and in the Christian 4th century it was declared defunct.

Delphi spreads over a natural amphitheatre of rocks and cliffs in the foothills of Mount Parnassus. The Sanctuary – the Sacred Precinct – is part of a larger complex that includes a gymnasium, stadium and sanctuary to Athena. The entrance is through the Roman agora; the Sacred Way, a paved path, zigzags up the terraces and slopes. The lower section is flanked by plinths and niches, which once held more than 3,000 votive statues, and the remains of the treasuries. Above these, the Spring of Gaia and the Rock of the Sibyl pre-date the building of the temple. The Athenian Stoa acts as a gateway to the Temple, which now consists of foundations and a re-erected line of Doric columns. The Sacred Way ends at the 5,000-seat rock-cut theatre, which still has remarkable acoustics.

# Mani Peninsula

The middle of three rocky fingers extending from the Peloponnese, the Mani is a mountainous, harsh region. Outer Mani, south of Kalamata, is watered by streams from the thickly forested Taiyetos Range. Inner, or Deep Mani, is barren, rock-strewn, starkly dramatic – blank tawny hills bristling with tower-villages, scattered with tiny churches, tangled with prickly pear. Until Greek independence in 1832, Maniots lived in chieftain-led clans, in villages of almost windowless towers, defence against invasion and blood feuds. Until recently no roads penetrated the mountains; now the little ports, then so vital, are ghost towns. Christianity was not accepted till the 9th century, and then zealously; many of the tiny Byzantine chapels and churches are strikingly frescoed and carved.

Areopolis, named for the god of war, is the chief town of the Inner Mani. From here to Cape Matapan, southernmost point of mainland Greece, about 36 km (22 mi) of very scenic road follows the western 'shadowed' coast, linked by a network of unmetalled roads and stone tracks to villages and churches in the foothills of the mountainous spine and the coves and bays of the jagged rocky coast. From Pyrgos Dirou, where a track leds to the famous Diros Caves, the road runs south to Gerolimenas, a sheltered harbour and fishing village with accommodation. The road onwards crosses the coastal plain to Alika, climbs steeply past Vathia, hugs the cliff edge and turns east to Porto Kayio. This village in a sheltered bay was once a fortified harbour; now it offers rooms and a walk on good tracks south to Cape Matapan, or Tenaron. Tenaron, the legendary entrance to the underworld, is a cave in Asomati Bay just north of the Cape.

**HOW:**
On foot
**WHEN TO GO:**
Late April to June, September to early October
**TIME IT TAKES:**
At least three days
**HIGHLIGHTS:**
Areopolis – several of the churches in have been restored; the frescoes are superb.
Vathia – the most spectacular of the tower villages; the narrow towers cluster in a maze of cobbled streets. It is almost deserted.
Asomati Bay – as well as the rather dull 'entrance to the underworld', there are scattered remains of an ancient settlement and temple to Poseidon.
Relaxed Porto Kayio has good harbour-side fish restaurants.

*Vathia is the best preserved Mani village.*

EASTERN
MEDITERRANEAN
& MIDDLE EAST

# Blue Voyage

Cevat Sakir Kabaagac, a Bodrum writer, recounted his travels by boat around the Carian and Lycian coasts and now the title of his book *Blue Voyage*, describes cruises in these Turkish waters. With rocky coastlines backed by dramatic forested mountains and waters of heavenly peacock hues, this is an idyllic region for a leisurely sea-voyage.

Gulets are the graceful traditional Turkish motor-yachts, still constructed locally of the red pine that covers the hillsides. Most are now built for the tourist business and

they're comfortable and well equipped. They may be chartered by groups, or a cruise can be an alternative 'package' holiday.

A typical Blue Voyage will sail from Bodrum to Marmaris by way of pretty Gökova, mooring here or at one of the neighbouring fishing villages or coves, and along the north of the narrow Datça Peninsula, doubling back to Datça, with its busy harbour and waterfront. Fjord-like Keci Buku Bay provides anchorage on the journey east to Marmaris, at the traditional fishing village of Selimye, or Bozburun, renowned for its boat building. Just short of huge, hectic Marmaris lie the more tranquil bays of Turunc and Kumlubük.

The gulet will be at sea for several hours each day – possibly under sail – anchoring for swimming, visiting fishing villages or, for those with an interest in history, archaeological sites. The captain will establish his passengers' preferences. Scattered around the Gulf of Gökova are the remains of several ancient towns; at the tip of the Datça Peninsula the ancient city of Cnidos, and on a promontory south of Bozburun, are the ruins of Loryma, with its sheltered harbour.

**HOW:**
By gulet
**WHEN TO GO:**
Late April to June, September and October
**TIME IT TAKES:**
One week
**HIGHLIGHTS:**
The Crusader castle of Saint Peter dominates Bodrum Harbour; it contains the fascinating Museum of Underwater Archaeology.
Cnidos is an important site in a wild and beautiful location. A steep street flanked by the remains of houses, a temple and theatre, overlooks ancient twin harbours.
Swimming from the gulet in deep, transparent, cool, blue sea.
At anchor in a quiet bay – watching shooting stars and listening to the lullaby of gently lapping waves.
**YOU SHOULD KNOW:**
Children under 12 are not usually allowed on gulet cruises.

# The Lycian Way

**HOW:**
On foot
**WHEN TO GO:**
Late March to early June, late September to November
**TIME IT TAKES:**
The whole walk takes about a month, sections from one day or more.
**HIGHLIGHTS:**
Patara has a village, the extensive site of a Hellenistic city, and miles of undeveloped (protected) sandy beach.
The Lycians of Olympos worshipped a god of fire manifested in the Chimaera where inextinguishable flames still leap from crevices in the rocks. Best seen at night.
The wildlife – wild boar are found in the mountains; tortoises are frequently seen. Stretches of the coast are turtle nesting sites. The many bird species include winter and summer migrants.
**YOU SHOULD KNOW:**
Anything more than one of the day-walks requires good fitness.
Walking in summer months is unwise; the heat is extreme, and the water sources dry up.

The Lycians settled the wide peninsula between Telmessos (present-day Fethiye) and Antalya around 1400 BC. Their legacy includes a partly deciphered script and many archaeological remains, including the unique rock-tombs which dot the whole area.

The 500-km (300-mi) Lycian Way, a way-marked footpath (with signed detours to places of interest) was inaugurated in 2000. The walk roughly follows the Turquoise Coast, sometimes cutting inland. The terrain is varied – rocky cliff-tops, steep scrambles down to isolated beaches, open stony hillsides, dense forest and shady valleys. You pass many archaeological sites and cross wonderfully unspoiled countryside – wreathed with flowers in spring, in autumn purple with crocuses and heather. The views over the sea to the misty outlines of the Greek islands, or down towards the brilliant water, are stunning. In some places, villages or resorts are accessible, in others, free camping is permitted. An excellent detailed guide to the walk is available.

This is a long and, in many places, demanding path. Many walkers opt for sections of the Lycian Way; others find a base and walk for separate days. Between Fethiye and Patara, along the western stretch, are the Lycian sites of Tlos, Pinara, Letoon and Xanthos and the Ottoman Greek ghost town, Kayakoy. South-coast Kas has a beautifully sited theatre, and Lycian tombs; the path east twists inland before descending to Ucagiz and a cluster of historical sites along the shore and on Kekova Island. At Demre, a church is dedicated to St Nicholas, who was bishop here, and impressive ancient Myra lies nearby. Below Mount Olympos (on the south-east coast) lie traces of the eponymous city and on its slopes, the mysterious Chimaera. Near Tekirova, the picturesque ruins of Phaselis are grouped around three small bays.

*A Lycian necropolis*

# Georgian Valleys

The mountainous region north of Erzurum towards Artvin was part of the medieval kingdom of Georgia, which embraced Christianity early, remained autonomous under the Seljuks and was partitioned between the Ottomans and the Persians after the Mongol invasion. Most Georgians had converted to Islam by the 17th century, but the people here are racially distinct and the Georgian language survives in some remote parts of the far northeast. The area is known unofficially as Turkish Georgia.

This is an area of green valleys, waterfalls and orchards; the high forests are home to wild boar and ibex, the slopes are planted with fruit and vegetables, cotton and tea. Relics of Christian Georgia are the churches in the scattered villages. Some have been converted to mosques, and are well preserved; others are in ruins.Most are built in the Armenian style, with drum and cone domes.

Erzurum, always a transport and military centre, is the largest city on the high plateau of Eastern Anatolia. The road northeast crosses a bleak, sparse landscape and drops into the valley of the Tortum, passing Tortum Lake. The river joins the Çoruh at the alpine town of Yusufeli; in places, the Çoruh Valley narrows to a gorge whose reddish cliffs tower above the rushing river. Local lads have always enjoyed spinning down the race on home made rafts; now this is a popular location for white water rafting, which can be organised in Yusufeli, which also makes a good base for exploring the countryside. Further north, the pleasant little town of Artvin clings to the mountainside and is surrounded by dramatically situated villages, churches and monasteries, with ruined castles and citadels perched on the crags.

**HOW:**
By 4x4 and on a raft
**WHEN TO GO:**
May and June, after the snow has melted, for the best rafting; May to September for exploring.
**TIME IT TAKES:**
Four days plus
**HIGHLIGHTS:**
A popular traditional festival, Kafkasor Yaylasi, held near Artvin in late June, includes dance, music, acrobats, etc; the main attraction is (bloodless) bull wrestling.
The churches are fascinating; for example, Haho Church (10th century) has carved reliefs of biblical scenes such as Jonah and the Whale; massive, elaborate Osk Vank has fine frescoes.
In June, the cherry and apricot orchards are in bloom.
**YOU SHOULD KNOW:**
Some of the white-water runs are very challenging.
Many of the villages can only be reached by 4x4.
Accommodation in this little-visited area is basic.

*One of the fascinating churches in the Georgian Valleys*

# Kackar Mountains

**HOW:**
On foot
**WHEN TO GO:**
July to September
**TIME IT TAKES:**
One to seven days or longer
**HIGHLIGHTS:**
The Hemsinlis – the people of the lovely, verdant valleys spend summers in the mountains with their flocks and herds. They live in pastoral dwellings, *yaylas*, moving upwards as the snows recede.
Wildlife – the slopes are full of flowers – rare orchids as well as lilies, primula and delphiniums; the mountains are a good place to spot birds of prey, including the lammergeier.
**YOU SHOULD KNOW:**
There are no good large-scale maps of the region.
Place names can be confusing; they may be Turkish, or Georgian/Armenian.

The Kackar Mountains are part of the Pontic Alps, the formidable range running along the Black Sea coast, which for centuries provided defence against invasion and a refuge for minorities. The coast enjoys a damp climate and the lower slopes of the mountains are clothed in tea plantations, beech and chestnuts, with dense pine and 'rainforest' higher up; the southern slopes are alpine, with steep high summer pasture.

The Kackars cover a relatively small area, but their close-packed snow-clad peaks, many of which are well over 3,000 m (9,750 ft), block paths from the valleys.

The mountains are increasingly popular with trekkers, and this is a lovely and rewarding area, rich in wildlife, dotted with small lakes and home, in the summer, to flocks and herdsmen. On the Black Sea sections, Ayder and Cat are good bases; both are reached via the beautiful Hemsin Valleys. On the southern side, above the Coruh and reachable from the Western Georgian valleys, Barhal, Hevek, Meretet and Tekkule are good starting points. The hikes are more gruelling from the south, but the weather is much better; the gentler northern slopes are covered in dense, damp cloud most afternoons. The villages have accommodation, and it is possible to hire guides or join an organised trek of anything from a day to a week. The highest mountain is Kackar Dagi – 3,932 m (12,779 ft) – and there are several others almost as high; climbing the peaks requires full kit and some experience, but there are some glorious one- and two-day walks below the highest sections.

*Trekking in the Kackar Mountains.*

# Bosphorus Ferry Trip

Istanbul, capital of mighty Christian and Islamic empires, was always a bridge between east and west; now Europe and Asia are linked by road, but ferries remain essential to life in this great city. Tour companies run Bosphorus Cruises with fast boats, but a leisurely zigzagging trip on a regular ferry from the centre of Istanbul to a village close to the Black Sea is a good antidote to sightseeing fatigue.

The Bosphorus, the 30-km (19-mi) strait linking the Black Sea with the Mediterranean, remains an important trade route; in the past, it was also a defence and a summer escape from the heat and disease of the city. Along both banks are royal residences (including the splendid Beylerbeyi Palace), villas, fashionable suburbs, boatyards, fortresses and working villages. Not many of the beautiful wooden *yalis*, the summerhouses of the wealthy, survive – many burned down, or were demolished before preservation laws came into force.

The waterfronts are punctuated by mosques, including the distinctive Ortaköy Mosque, just below the Atatürk Bridge. South of soaring Fatih Bridge, the twin castles – small Anadolu Hisar and the massive Rumeli Hisar, the Fortress of Europe – could effectively 'lock' the Bosphorus. Inland from the fashionable settlements on the European shore is Belgrade Forest, once a hunting preserve for the Sultans. The last ferry stop is at Anadolu Kavagi, on the Asian shore. Here there is time to explore and have a meal, or plan a return journey by bus, dolmus, and short ferry hops, visiting some of the places glimpsed on the journey.

*The Galata Tower watches over the Bosphorus.*

**HOW:**
By ferry
**WHEN TO GO:**
The ferry runs all year
**TIME IT TAKES:**
About 1 hour 30 minutes each way
**HIGHLIGHTS:**
Kucuksu Kasri, near Anadolu Hisari. The shady site was long a royal favourite for picnics; in the 19th century, the wooden kiosk was replaced with an exquisite tiny Rococo palace.
Sariyer – a fish market and good restaurants, and the private Sadberk Hanim Museum, which displays a fascinating collection in a *yali*, with rooms arranged in the Ottoman style.
Anadolu Kavagi – a lovely village, with old wooden houses and waterfront fish restaurants. From the top of the huge ruined castle there is a panoramic view to the Black Sea. The Istanbul skyline from the water, especially at dusk, is spellbinding.
**YOU SHOULD KNOW:**
There is a reduced ferry service out of season – check timetables.

# Istanbul to Aleppo on the Toros Express

The original Istanbul to Baghdad railway was largely planned and financed by Germany, but the Toros Express (named for the mountain range it crosses) was inaugurated in 1930 by the Compagnie Internationale des Wagons-Lits, to extend its Orient Express service. Though trains no longer continue to Iraq, and the opulence has vanished (along with Belgian detectives), the Toros Express now runs from Istanbul to Aleppo once a week. Haydarpasa Station, on the waterfront south of Usküdur, is reached by ferry from Galata. This grandiose building, with its wood panelling and fine stained-glass, was presented to the Sultan by Kaiser Wilhelm in 1908.

The Syrian sleeping car, with its two-bed compartments and friendly, tea-making steward, is attached to a Turkish train. It heads out of Istanbul by the Sea of Marmara, and then eastwards along a broad valley. Then the line climbs southwards, and continues (past Afyon, where an ancient citadel crowns a dark crag) to the empty, arid plateau, where views expand – tawny plains, distant peaks, isolated villages and minarets. It is late by the time the train arrives in Konya (home to fine carpets and whirling Dervishes); overnight it runs, by way of innumerable tunnels and bridges, through the huge Toros range. In the early morning the train descends the southern slopes towards Adana. Then the line runs east through fertile plains to Febsipasa, where the sleeping car is uncoupled and joined to another train. At the border, after the normal delays, the train is coupled to a Syrian locomotive, and the journey continues through rocky hills and olive groves to the beautiful Syrian city of Aleppo.

**HOW:**
By train
**WHEN TO GO:**
March to November
**TIME IT TAKES:**
About 30 hours
**HIGHLIGHTS:**
The sheer romance of a journey like this – heading into the huge, changing landscape of Turkey and on into Asia Minor.
Descending the Toros at dawn: distant views from the craggy mountains of the green plain below, glimpses of the distant Mediterranean as first light touches it.
Finally arriving in Aleppo: a beautiful, exciting but easy-going city.
**YOU SHOULD KNOW:**
Tea-making is the only catering for the sleeping car. Take ample provisions and liquids. Also take toilet paper.

*Al Khosrowiyya Mosque in Aleppo*

# Cappadocia Cross-Country Ride

This part of Central Anatolia is famous for bizarre scenery, underground settlements and frescoed churches. The weird 'fairy chimneys' – toadstools, cones and pleated domes – were formed by erosion of the soft, volcanic tufa; unusually – most volcanic rock is black or grey – here the colours are soft golds and reds. These easily worked rocks have always provided refuge from raids and persecution; the underground towns were probably dug in Hittite times – 1900-1200 BC – and used, extended and elaborated over the centuries. St Paul brought Christianity to Cappadocia, though most of the cave churches are Byzantine. Caves are still used for stabling, storage and to keep pigeons; cultivation has also been continuous – the Hittites made wine, and grapes are still grown; the fertile soil also produces fruit.

Many of the tourists who throng a few popular areas are day-trippers, but Cappadocia repays a longer stay. An excellent escape from the crowds into the extraordinary landscape is on horseback; several ranches offer anything from short sunset rides to cross-country trips of a week or more.  These combine riding – through fertile valleys, narrow gorges, along winding tracks among the fairy chimneys and over the high volcanic *mesas* with visits to villages and sites of interest. Time is usually allowed in Göreme, where villagers are still troglodytic, to explore the Göreme National Park, an open- air museum of many exceptional churches.

**HOW:**
On horseback
**WHEN TO GO:**
April to November
**TIME IT TAKES:**
Seven days plus
**HIGHLIGHTS:**
Enjoyable riding – the small, nimble horses are happy picking their way over rocky mule tracks or cantering along sandy valleys.
The plain exteriors of most of the rock-cut churches give no clue to the glorious interiors with Byzantine carving and superb frescoes.
The underground settlements (some home to as many as 20,000): complex warrens descending many levels, with deep ventilation shafts, wells, escape routes and sealable doors.
**YOU SHOULD KNOW:**
Riding standard is intermediate; riders should be fit – most days entail 5 or 6 hours in the saddle.

*The Zelve Valley in Cappadocia*

# St Paul Trail

**HOW:**
On foot
**WHEN TO GO:**
May, June, September and October
**TIME IT TAKES:**
Organized treks last about a week,
the whole trail, four to five weeks.
**HIGHLIGHTS:**
Adada – some well-preserved
buildings and tumbled stones in a
lovely hillside setting – the Greco-
Roman road, made of huge stone
slabs, can be followed from
the south.
Wildlife – the beautiful forests are
rich in birds and flowers. The
Volcanic Oak is unique to Kasnak
Forest, south of Egirdir.
Egirdir – superbly sited on the huge
lake, backed by mountains, is a good
place to relax, swim and eat fresh
lake fish.
Following ancient travellers who
walked the King's Way from Ephesus
to Bablyon, and St Paul along roads
he actually trod.
**YOU SHOULD KNOW:**
The demanding trail requires a good
level of fitness.

*Egirdir Lake*

St Paul, a native of Tarsus in south-east Turkey, was, as an educated man and a citizen of the Roman Empire, able to travel and communicate freely. He spent about twenty years spreading Christianity and part of his first journey in AD 46 was from Perge near the Mediterranean coast to Antioch in Pisidia, a Roman colonial town north of Lake Egirdir.

Researched and established, like the Lycian Way, by Kate Clow, the St Paul Trail opened in 2004. The walk starts from Perge, skirting the Yazili Canyon, or from Aspendos, via the Koprolou Canyon. The routes into the wild hills of the Toros range meet at Adada, a little-visited site north of Sutculer, then pass Egirdir, crossing the lush agricultural western lakeshore to the attractive village of Barla. After a boat crossing comes a long climb to the Anatolian plateau and Antioch in Pisidia. Though little is left of the Church of St Paul, the extensive site is impressive.

The way-marked tracks – in all around 500 km (300 mi) – sometimes follow Roman roads or stretches of the Ancient 'King's Way', often lead through beautiful mixed forests of oak, juniper and cedar or chestnut, or by narrow stony tracks over ridges, skirting and scaling gorges, waterfalls and lakes. The trail passes isolated villages and, in summer, the tented settlements of the Yoruk people on the hillsides with their flocks. For the historian, there are sites to visit, for the naturalist flora and fauna and for the climber, some high peaks. There is an excellent guidebook. Some of the villages now offer accommodation, while Egirdir, Sütçüler or Barla make good bases for day-treks, or sections of the route. Several companies offer guided walks.

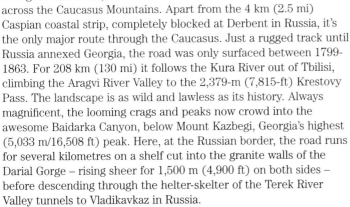

# The Georgian Military Road

Its name seems to encapsulate everything modern, so the first great surprise is that the Georgian Military Road is the historic name for the 2,000 year-old route linking Georgia with Russia, across the Caucasus Mountains. Apart from the 4 km (2.5 mi) Caspian coastal strip, completely blocked at Derbent in Russia, it's the only major route through the Caucasus. Just a rugged track until Russia annexed Georgia, the road was only surfaced between 1799-1863. For 208 km (130 mi) it follows the Kura River out of Tbilisi, climbing the Aragvi River Valley to the 2,379-m (7,815-ft) Krestovy Pass. The landscape is as wild and lawless as its history. Always magnificent, the looming crags and peaks now crowd into the awesome Baidarka Canyon, below Mount Kazbegi, Georgia's highest (5,033 m/16,508 ft) peak. Here, at the Russian border, the road runs for several kilometres on a shelf cut into the granite walls of the Darial Gorge – rising sheer for 1,500 m (4,900 ft) on both sides – before descending through the helter-skelter of the Terek River Valley tunnels to Vladikavkaz in Russia.

Its treacherous hairpins and precipitous drops can still be genuinely frightening – but the road's natural drama is magnified by the accrued wealth of history along its length. At the UNESCO World Heritage city of Mtskheta, cathedrals, monasteries and palaces still guard Georgia's religious soul as they have since the 3rd century, 500 years before Christianity ever reached Russia or Germany. Church and state again combine at the medieval fortress of Ananuri, with two beautiful churches within its crenellated walls; and at the Church of the Trinity, the landmark on the skyline of Mount Kazbegi. The ruins of castles and forts dating to the 3rd century BC are testament to an even older sequence of invasions, tribal migrations, and trade incursions.

*Djvari Monastery overlooks the Aragvi River.*

**HOW:**
By car or bus

**WHEN TO GO:**
June-September. The road can usually be driven year-round, even though there can be deep snow at the pass in May. Georgia's ski resort at Gudauri is always accessible.

**TIME IT TAKES:**
5-9 hrs (by car/bus, direct); 2-4 days (by car/bus, stopping briefly at some of the major sites of man and nature).

**HIGHLIGHTS:**
Svetitskhoveli Cathedral at Mtskheta, architectural symbol of Georgia's religious philosophy and the country's most sacred site. One of the world's greatest cathedrals.
Tamara's Castle, at the southern entrance to the, vertiginous, gloomy magnificence of the Darial Gorge.
The tetraconch plan – prototype for the whole of the south Caucasus – of the Great Church of the 6th century Djvari Monastery.
The contrast between the Georgian and Russian sides of the mountains, like summer and winter.

**YOU SHOULD KNOW:**
1. Delays at the border are frequent, especially on the Russian side. 2. The Georgian Military Road is part of Georgia's national psyche, embodying the drama of its landscape and history. Its romantic imaginative appeal has inspired writers including Pushkin, Tolstoy, Dumas, Gorky, Lermontov and the hero/saint of Georgian nationalism, Ilya Chavchavadze.

387

# Monasteries Hike

**HOW:**
On foot
**WHEN TO GO:**
Late May to early July, September
**TIME IT TAKES:**
Two days plus
**HIGHLIGHTS:**
Debed Canyon is richly green, well watered and densely wooded; it is a lovely place to walk, either along the shady riverbed or the canyon rim.
Sanahin Monastery – the mossy complex of church, shadowy chapels, ancient graves open archways and scattered *khatchkars* is bewitching.
Haghpat Monastery – the extensive walled complex, built in the 12th century, includes bell tower, library, refectory and chapel as well as the fine main church. The views over the canyon are superb.
**YOU SHOULD KNOW:**
Some of the walking can be muddy.

*Haghpat Monastery and bell tower*

Armenia became Christian in 301 AD (around 90 per cent of Armenians are members of the Armenian Apostolic Church) and the lovely countryside is scattered with old churches and monasteries and elaborately carved stone crosses, *khatchkars*. Beautiful, green Lori province has a concentration of medieval monasteries along the spectacular Debed Canyon. Both the railway and the road north to Georgia follow the line of the Canyon, but if time is not pressing this makes an excellent walk. Distances are small, several of the villages have accommodation and climbs are not demanding.

From Tumanyan, the ruined 13th-century convent and the hamlet of Kobayr are visible. Stone steps from the railway line lead up the hill. The roofless church still has some frescoes. The large village of Odzun sits on a shelf over a steep drop to the Debed River; in the centre of the village, the sturdy church is 17th century, with an arcaded cloister once used as a school. On the edge of the cliff is another church and the remains of Horomayri Monastery cling to the slopes a little to the south.

Alaverdi is a quiet town lying in a bend of the canyon. There is a 12th century hump-backed stone bridge over the river, but this is mainly a modern copper-mining town. The cable car (which runs to the shift timetable at the mine) provides an easy way up to the canyon edge, and the villages of Sadahart and Sanahin. Sanahin Monastery is a UNESCO Word Heritage Site. The oldest building dates to 928; this was the seat of an archbishop and there is a funeral chapel for the royal Zakarian family.

Another UNESCO World Heritage Site, Haghpat Monastery, founded in 976, perches on the edge of the canyon and combines superb architecture with a tremendous location.

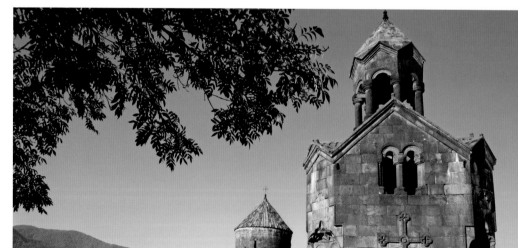

# Lake Sevan to Vayots Dzor

*Lake Sevan*

This huge mountain lake, lying at just less than 2,000 m (6,500 ft) and covering nearly 1,000 sq km (400 sq mi), is famous for its glorious blueness, changing from duck-egg to turquoise to ultramarine with the weather. The fresh air and the white sand beaches make this a popular summer destination for city-dwellers; the 'Armenian Riviera' gets very busy.

Sevanank peninsula – an island till the water level dropped following irrigation/hydroelectric projects – is crowned by two early monastery churches; the climb to the hilltop gives views over the lake to a jagged skyline of surrounding volcanic peaks. South of Sevan town, well preserved Hayravank Monastery stands on a promontory, and the lovely old village of Noratus has a fine church, ruined basilica, enormous cemetery, and access to a quiet beach. At the medieval/modern cemetery the traveller may come across a Karasoonk marking the 40th day after a death – family, friends and musicians gather at the graveside before retiring for food, drink and storytelling.

From Martuni on the southern shore the newly repaired road runs through the Selim Pass to Yeghegnadzor, the main town of the remote region of Vayots Dzor. Small country roads lead off to hidden valleys and architectural delights.

Yeghegnadzor is set in an agricultural river valley. The road west leads to the wild and mountainous Arpa Valley, near the Azerbaijan border. This is a quality-wine producing area. Areni, and several of the nearby villages, have wineries and accommodation.

**HOW:**
By car or 4x4
**WHEN TO GO:**
Late May, June and September
**TIME IT TAKES:**
Two days plus
**HIGHLIGHTS:**
Noratus – the largest *khatchkar* cemetery in Armenia, bristles with the intricately carved upright stone slab crosses dating from the 9th-15th century. Modern memorials often carry etched portraits of the deceased.
The Selim Caravanserai is the best preserved in Armenia. Built in 1332 of basalt blocks, it housed travellers and animals on the Silk Route. Take a torch.
Vayots Dzor has many exceptional early churches; the Veghegis Valley and the areas around Yeghegnadzor and Vayk are particularly rewarding.
**YOU SHOULD KNOW:**
The condition of country roads is often very poor; it is worth hiring a car – preferably a 4x4 – with driver.

**389**

# Rub'al Khali – The Empty Quarter

Covering most of Saudi Arabia and slices of Yemen, Oman and the UAE, Rub'al Khali, the world's largest sand desert, occupies nearly a quarter of the Arabian Peninsula.Wilfred Thesiger crossed this harsh land with companions from the Bait Kathir tribe of southern Oman and his famous book *Arabian Sands* describes its hardships and its spell.

Oman is a peaceable country, politically stable, with a calm, tolerant populace who are in no rush to sacrifice their national identity to tourism. Here, half a day's drive allows a visit to the great desert, and a night or two in the sands, independently or on an organized trip.

The road from Salalah, a colourful south-coast port city with good beaches, crosses the fertile rolling plains and the Jebel Gara Mountains. This area enjoys monsoon rains, and is popular with Arabian visitors during the 'winds of plenty'. The landscape changes to dark gravel hills and narrow wadis – the home of the strange, gnarled frankincense tree. Thumrait, a stopping point for the ancient caravan routes, has a camel racetrack. Sisr, to the north, enjoys year round water; nearby Ubur is the site either of the 'Atlantis of the Sands', a lost Koranic city, or one of the caravanserai. Several towers, a waterhole and thousands of artefacts have been excavated.

The margins of the Empty Quarter are sparsely inhabited by lizards, hawks, small mammals and Bedouin tribes, but off the Desert Highway the traveller enters a world of towering sand dunes, shimmering mirages and colours that shift, red, orange, violet, with the light. On the edge of this fabled wilderness, the emptiness is awe-inspiring.

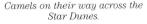
*Camels on their way across the Star Dunes.*

*The city of Sana'a*

# The Incense Road

The wealth of the ancient kingdoms of Yemen depended on trade in frankincense and myrrh, highly valued throughout the civilised world. Part of the overland Incense Road, which stretched through Arabia to the Mediterranean, passes through several historically important places in Yemen, which owed their power to taxes from the enormous camel caravans. Before making this journey now, check with the authorities – access to some areas of Yemen is restricted or prohibited.

Yemen's capital, Sana'a (a UNESCO World Heritage Site) has one of the oldest intact medinas in the Arab world, a jumble of mosques, markets and unique tower houses. From Sana'a the road climbs through the mountains and descends to the eastern desert where, in the 8th century BC, a huge dam was built in what became known as Wadi as-Sudd (Wadi of the Dam) and the city of Ma'rib became capital of the Kingdom of Saba. The kingdom fell, the incense trade declined, the dam collapsed. Temples sunk in the desert and the empty mud brick towers of Old Ma'rib are all that survive, though a new dam and oil finds offer new prosperity.

The old city of Shabwa lies across the Ramlat as Sab'atayn desert. From the hill, where its remains are engulfed by sand and salt, a dramatic panorama covers the eastern end of the mighty Wadi Hadramawt, the largest wadi in the Middle East, named for the ancient people who first inhabited it. The fertile main valley extends 160 km (100 mi) westward; its main town Sayun is an ancient caravan-route market town, with beautiful mosques, fine mud-brick buildings – and an airport. At the Wadi's heart lies Shibam, another UNESCO World Heritage Site, a compact walled city tightly packed with hundreds of five to seven storey medieval mud brick tower houses.

**HOW:**
By car
**WHEN TO GO:**
March to June, October and November
**TIME IT TAKES:**
3 days plus
**HIGHLIGHTS:**
Sana'a's towers have lower storeys of dark basalt, upper of reddish brick; the top floors are mud-plastered, often whitewashed, the facades decorated with white patterns.
The 'Palace' hotels in Sana'a – these converted tower houses have traditional interiors and views over the city, including the hidden network of walled gardens.
A day or two spent exploring the Wadi Hadramawt and the pretty villages, mosques, tombs and historical sites scattered over its tributaries.
The first sight of Shibam, the 'Manhattan of the desert', rising from the valley.
**YOU SHOULD KNOW:**
Check government guidelines on travel in Yemen.

*The cliff–top village of Shahara in the Haraz Mountains*

# Haraz Mountain Trek

**HOW:**
On foot
**WHEN TO GO:**
April, May, September and October
**TIME IT TAKES:**
Three days plus
**HIGHLIGHTS:**
The breathtaking, peaceful countryside, and the uncommercialized villages.
Some of the narrow terraces are the width of just one row of crops – from a distance they look like giant ladders.
The ubiquitous Yemeni tower houses in the villages are stone; the decoration often consists of ornate windows of coloured glass.
**YOU SHOULD KNOW:**
Most of the villages in the Haraz lie at around 2,000 m (6,500 ft) – climbing even the higher peaks (just under 3,000 m/9,750 ft) is fairly straightforward.
Sudden bursts of heavy rain can reduce temperatures and send large boulders rolling down the slopes.

The Haraz Mountains, west of Sana'a, is an area of step hillsides, high peaks and lovely stone villages. From the 12th century, the mountains served as refuge for descendents of the Ismaili Sulayhids, and many of the villages date from this period. During Ottoman occupation this was a strategic area where cannons guarded mountain passes. Farming is intensive – even the steepest slopes have been terraced, and monsoon rain is gathered for irrigation. A large proportion of Yemen's scarce arable land lies in these mountains and a wide variety of crops are grown.

Trekking in Yemen is not organized, with no maps or marked trails, but the Manakha area is perfect for day-treks. Two of the villages, Manakha and Al Hajjara, have facilities for visitors and make good bases. Hostel accommodation offers packed lunches and evening entertainment of local music and dance, and can arrange guides and camping equipment for longer treks. Manakha is the market town for the surrounding region; Al Hajira, to the west, is a lovely fortified hilltop village.

There are many enjoyable circular day-walks using the network of paths between villages – south to Al-Khutayb, an Ismaili pilgrimage site, west to Jabal Masar and a scattering of historic hamlets, or Jabal Shibam, the highest peak in the region. Longer treks to the edge of the mountains, where peaceful villages look down over steep escarpments, or north and south out of the Manakha region can be arranged. Guides will arrange camping outside villages.

# Petra Monastery Hike

Visitors to Petra may choose to escape the crowds and see Little Petra, a few miles north. This was an important suburb of Petra, a re-supply post for travellers and traders. Its Arab name is Siq Barid, 'The Cold' – it is entered by a slit in the rocks so narrow the sun scarcely filters through. The 400-m (1,300-ft) siq opens up into wider areas where the rock walls are crowded with houses, temples and triclinia, linked by rock-cut stairways in the cliff face. Floods have eroded lower facades but some of the higher ones are well preserved. As well as the dining rooms, there are a number of water channels and cisterns. A set of stairs at the bottom of the siq leads to a hidden canyon with views of the surrounding countryside.

A little south are the ruins of Al Beidah, a Neolithic village and one of the oldest sites in the Middle East. The remains are unremarkable, but some of the items found, dating to around 7000 BC, bear witness to early experiments in settled agriculture.

The path drops to a wadi and from here a fairly easy hour's walk reaches the Monastery of Al Dier. Following small wadis through the rocks cuts out some of the hundreds of steps up to this inspiring monument. Near the top views open up over the mountains and valleys. The Monastery was actually a single chamber temple dedicated to a Nabatean king, probably used later as a church. The flat plaza to the front was levelled for ceremonials; the massive façade – nearly 50 m (162 ft) square – is carved into the mountainside; the doorway is bigger than a house.

**HOW:**
On foot
**WHEN TO GO:**
March to May, September and October
**TIME IT TAKES:**
One day
**HIGHLIGHTS:**
The tranquillity of Siq Barid, a beautiful, remote and mysterious place.
The Painted House in Little Petra has the remains of frescoed ceilings dating to the 1st century AD.
The Qattar ad-Dayr on the way up to the Monastery: a green, mossy, silent grotto with year-round water and Nabatean carvings.
The café in the cave opposite the Monastery allows rest, refreshment and views of the façade.
**YOU SHOULD KNOW:**
It is wise to hire a guide for the walk from Little Petra.

*Siq Barid in Petra*

# Lawrence of Arabia Camel Trek

**HOW:**
On a camel
**WHEN TO GO:**
March to May, October and November
**TIME IT TAKES:**
Five days
**HIGHLIGHTS:**
The spectacular landscape and the sheer scale of Wadi Rum.
'Lawrence's Spring', Ain ash-Shallaleh, is a peaceful, ferny spot, the head of a Nabatean rock-cut aqueduct.
The camel-mounted Desert Patrol Corps can be a stirring sight, robed and armed to the teeth.
Bedouin hospitality and nights in the desert: shared food, glorious sunsets, myriad stars, the jangling of a camel-harness accentuating the silence.
**YOU SHOULD KNOW:**
Wear suitable clothes for camel riding; the traditional head wrapping keeps out sun and sand.
Desert nights can be very chilly.

*Wadi Rum at sunset*

In 1917, with Emir Faisal and the Arab warriors (and the support of General Allenby), T. E. Lawrence took Aqaba; he also attacked the Hejaz Railway on several occasions. The railway was originally built to transport pilgrims to Medina, but was used by the Turks as a vital supply line. Now a few trains run from Damascus, but only as far as Amman.

Lawrence had a deep love for the Arab world and the Bedouin, and he spent some time in the Wadi Rum, one of a huge network of valleys in the sandy southern desert. His lyrical descriptions of the great stone jebels rising sheer from the desert floor, weathered into domes and ridges, which appear almost liquid, ring true today. Parts of *Lawrence of Arabia* were filmed here. The area around the main Bedouin settlement, Rum, is very busy, but even on foot it's possible to escape the crowds of day-trippers, exploring red sand corridors through ravines and valleys.

The ideal way to explore the desert is on a camel, with nights in Bedouin encampments. Basic camel riding can be quickly learned and most riders become fond of their silent mounts, despite their grumpy expressions. Long treks include the journey to Mudawarra on the Saudi border, where a railway carriage blown up by Lawrence in 1917 (he made the trip in three days on a racing camel) still lies by the disused track.

After the daunting red cliffs of the Wadi Rum, the trek threads it way south east through small wadis and hidden valleys to flatter terrain and darker rocks. Wadi Mhask is suddenly green (it lies above a huge underground water source); the jagged rocky cliffs near Mudawarra conceal canyons, home to wildlife including ibex and wolves.

# Jerusalem: The Via Dolorosa

Ancient Jerusalem has many sites of immense spiritual importance; for Judaism, the massive Western Wall is all that remains of the Great Temple; the majestic Dome of the Rock is, for Islam, more shrine than mosque. For Christianity, the Church of the Holy Sepulchre enshrines the last resting place of Christ, while the Via Dolorosa marks His final journey from trial to crucifixion.

The Roman Empire adopted Christianity in the 4th century and since then believers have retraced this walk. The route has changed over the centuries, though the destination is the same. Pilgrims from all over medieval Europe came to share Jesus' suffering at the Stations of the Cross and the ritual was adopted universally.

The location of Calvary is undisputed, but Pilate probably lived in what is now the Citadel, not the Antonia Fortress (now a Muslim Madrasah) where the 'Way of Sorrows' begins. The 'Stations' of the Via Dolorosa, which runs east-west through the narrow streets of the Muslim Quarter, are marked with oratories and chapels (modest by comparison with the Gothic and Baroque splendours of Europe), plaques, crosses, and Roman columns. In the Christian Quarter, commerce and spirituality join in the 'pilgrim trade' shops lining the road to Calvary. A jumble of churches and hospices surrounds the huge Church of the Holy Sepulchre (originally built by Constantine at the request of his mother, St Helena), where the tenth to fourteenth Stations are located.

For Christian visitors, joining the Franciscan friars' Friday walk, pausing for devotion at each 'Station', is a very powerful experience. For others, just to walk and reflect can be moving.

**HOW:**
On foot
**WHEN TO GO:**
March to May, September and October
**TIME IT TAKES:**
One hour plus
**HIGHLIGHTS:**
Christ's Tomb – A 19th century rotunda houses the Holy Sepulchre; here a marble slab covers the place where Christ's body is believed to have been laid.
Golgotha – part of the Church where the Greek Orthodox altar is built on the rock of the Crucifixion, and the Catholic chapel has a bronze and silver altar given by Ferdinand de Medici.
In the Convent of the Sisters of Sion, near the start of the walk, is part of the 'Ecce Homo Arch', an ancient rock-cut cistern, and the lithostrotos, a stone-slab pavement where incised gaming boards for dice games recall the soldiers casting lots.
**YOU SHOULD KNOW:**
Unless visiting Jerusalem specifically for a festival, the city is best avoided during Christian and Jewish holidays, when it becomes impossibly crowded.

*The Church of the Holy Sepulchre*

*The ruins of the Arab castle of Qalaat Jaber*

# Along the Euphrates

**HOW:**
By car, bus or train
**WHEN TO GO:**
March to May, September and October
**TIME IT TAKES:**
Four days plus
**HIGHLIGHTS:**
Resafe is a fascinating site in the middle of nowhere. The great walls contain (among much else) extensive remains of a very early basilica and the massive cisterns of the ancient city.
The Archaeological Museum in Deir ez-Zur is outstanding, with excellent well-labelled sections on Dura Europos and Mari.
The first sight of the walls of Dura Europos, standing high above the river, across the parched desert.
Mari was founded in 2900 BC and destroyed in 1759 BC; the foundations of the Royal Palace, with more than 300 rooms, give an idea of its scale. At present, it is the only easily accessible Mesopotamian site.
**YOU SHOULD KNOW:**
Because of the Iraqi border's proximity, police checks are frequent on the road to Mari. Carry documents.
The desert sites can be extremely hot and dusty.

The mighty green Euphrates rises in the mountains of eastern Anatolia and cuts a fertile swathe for 2,700 km (1,700 mi) through the deserts of Syria and Iraq; this was home to great civilisations and city-states. Control of the flow of water has always been contentious; following massive hydroelectric and irrigation projects by Syria and more recently by Turkey, tension has grown.

Along the Euphrates lie some fine archaeological sites. Travel is straightforward – roads with good bus links, and there's a railway line as far as Deir ez-Zur. East of Aleppo, Lake Assad is the huge reservoir formed by damming the Euphrates. From Ath Thawra (purpose built for construction workers and displaced villagers) a road runs over the dam to Qalaat Jaber castle, once high above a river crossing, now on the lakeshore.

Though little is left of busy Raqqa's former glory, a short detour south leads to Resafe, a remarkable ancient walled city in the desert. Downstream, twin Roman forts stand on either side of the river: Halebiye – built by Palmyra's rebel queen Zenobia – still has extensive walls; Zalebiye is fragmentary. Both have great views over the valley and desert.

Deir ez-Zur, a pleasant desert town, is a good base for visiting the southern sites (Abu Kamal is too close to the sensitive Iraqi border). Here, an elegant pedestrian suspension bridge crosses the wide, shallow river.

Dura Europos, an extensive, mainly Roman, garrison town is famous for finds which have been removed – notably the remarkable frescoed synagogue, now in a purpose built wing of the Damascus Museum. Little remains of the mud-brick Mesopotamian city, Mari, but this is an archaeological site of great significance.

# Isfahan River Bridges Walk

Isfahan is one of the most beautiful cities in the Islamic world. In the 16th and 17th centuries under the Safayids (particularly the inspirational Shah Abbas I), it was a city of exquisitely tiled mosques and palaces, paradise gardens, teahouses, fine carpets, and was a centre for the arts. Today, the old city remains a treasure house – squares, domes, minarets, courtyards, and an ancient covered bazaar. The Zayandeh River crosses the city just south of the centre – five of its eleven bridges are old and its banks make a fine walk. The teahouses built under or on the bridges make excellent refreshment stops.

From the bustle of Engelab-e Eslami Square, a path leads southeast to the river and a view of the Si-o-Seh Pol – The Bridge of 33 Arches – a very recognizable landmark, built in 1602. Walking east, the Chubi Bridge, designed to irrigate the gardens, was once joined to a canal system.

Khaju Bridge, built by Shah Abbas II, is two-layered; the bottom section, with locks incorporated into the arches, regulated the flow of the river. Stairs lead to the upper storey. A quiet walk east – 3.5 km (2.2 mi) – leads to the oldest bridge, Sharestan; a mostly stone and brick structure dating from the 12th century. The pleasantly shady south bank is popular with Isfahani picnickers.

South west of the Si-o-Seh Bridge is Jolfa, the Armenian quarter established by Shah Abbas I, whose residents still worship in the many medieval churches. The last Safayid bridge is the short Marnan Bridge, west of the centre.

**HOW:**
On foot
**WHEN TO GO:**
March to May, September and October
**TIME IT TAKES:**
One day
**HIGHLIGHTS:**
The pretty teahouse in the centre of Chubi Bridge is considered one of the best in the city.
The upper story of Khaju Bridge, with niched seats, remains of frescoes and an octagonal pavilion built for the Shah, was a place for meeting and talking.
Vank Cathedral in Jolfa is richly decorated inside with Islamic tiles and magnificent frescoes. There is a small museum.
Sunset and early evening at Si-o-Seh Pol when the light softens on the river and the distant mountains, and the bridges are illuminated.
**YOU SHOULD KNOW:**
The black, tent-like *chador* is issued for mosque visits, but even on the riverbank women must cover heads, arms, legs and general outline; colours are acceptable but never wear red.

*The Khaju Bridge over the River Zayandeh*

*The mountain village of Masuleh*

# Chalus Scenic Road

Tehran lies in the relatively temperate foothills of the Alborz Mountains that run the length of the Caspian Sea coast. The road from Tehran runs west, then north through the mountains. This marvellously unspoilt forested region of high peaks – several are over 4,000 m (13,000 ft) – is sadly threatened by plans for the Tehran-Somal Highway, which seem to be going ahead despite environmental objections. The road down allows panoramic views of the blue Caspian (rich in caviar and salmon) and the bright green coastal plains, where rice, cotton and citrus orchards thrive in the humid climate.

The development of the coast has been piecemeal – the previously charming twin villages of Chalus and Nosahar are now sprawling towns, though east of leafy Nosahar are some pleasant, undeveloped beaches. West of Chalus at Namak Abrud the popular cable car ascends the wooded slopes of Mt Medvin. Ramsar, where the coastal plain narrows and the mountains are a dramatic backdrop, is one of Iran's most pleasant seaside resorts. This is a relaxed, attractive place with good accommodation. In the little town of Lahijun, which still has some traditional Caspian architecture, is a museum of tea history – tea has been grown successfully in the Alborz foothills since about 1900.

The large city of Rasht (the wettest place in Iran) is popular with Tehranis; it has an airport, and makes a good base for exploring the area. The road to the beautiful mountain village of Masuleh passes Fuman, whose wide streets are lined with date palms and plastercast statues.

# Baku to Sheki Scenic Road

Until independence in 1991, Azerbaijan was ruled by great powers including Persia, Mongolia and Russia. Now this beautiful, hospitable little country is a Muslim state with a relaxed attitude to women's dress, alcohol and other faiths, and it's become an exciting tourist destination.

Nineteenth century Baku was a major oil exporter, and international investment has once again made the big, cosmopolitan capital an oil-boom town. The old city seems unaffected by the turbulent 20th century: within its walls, amid cobbled lanes, colourful markets and medieval mosques, stands the massive Maiden's Tower (assumed to be defensive, but possibly an ancient Zoroastrian temple) and the medieval seat of Azerbaijan's ruling dynasty. Among several interesting museums is an excellent Carpet Museum. Along the bustling waterfront, the Caspian is turquoise, but thick with oil.

Outside Baku are bleak reminders of the Soviet petrochemical industry, with views over the desolate coastal town of Sumquayit. Westward, the road hugs the foothills of the Caucasus. Shemaka lies in rolling countryside luxuriant with fruit, vegetables and vineyards; little remains of the ancient city but the hilltop ruins of Gulistan Castle. From Ismayilli, a scenic cliff top road leads to Lahic, a beautiful mountain village whose skilled carpet makers claim descent from the Persians. Near the pleasant market town of Qabala is the site of one of the oldest towns in Azerbaijan, dating from around the 3rd century BC.

Sheki, in its glorious mountain setting, was a major staging post on the Silk Road – in its heyday there were five caravanserai – and its silk weaving industry continues, though now restricted to small workshops. This lovely town has museums, a royal palace and an attractive old town by the stream beneath a fortress.

**HOW:**
By car or bus
**WHEN TO GO:**
June, early July and September
**TIME IT TAKES:**
Three days plus
**HIGHLIGHTS:**
The recently restored Palace of the Shirvan Shahs in Baku is a complex, fascinating site – a fine example of Shirvan architecture.
In the mountain village of Pirquli near Shamaka, the Observatory, an important Soviet space research centre, is open to visitors.
The Khan's Palace, Sheki, is beautifully decorated with tiles and carvings; the interior has murals of flowers and birds, battles and hunting scenes.
One of Sheki's caravanserai has been converted into a fascinating hotel.
**YOU SHOULD KNOW:**
Driving can be hazardous – hire a driver, take a tour or use public transport.
Azerbaijan suffers from pollution and environmental degradation.

*The courtyard of the Caravanserai Hotel in Sheki*

ASIA

*The River Lena is one of the ten longest rivers in the world.*

# River Lena Cruise

**HOW:**
By boat
**WHEN TO GO:**
June to September
**TIME IT TAKES:**
Six days
**HIGHLIGHTS:**
Yakutsk – coldest city on earth.
Confluence of Vilui River – pastoral scenery for forest walks and swimming.
Zhigansk – first settlement beyond the Arctic Circle, founded in the 17th century.
Kyusyur – regional cultural centre inhabited by native hunters and reindeer farmers.
Delta wetlands.
Tiksi – strategic Arctic Ocean settlement, only accessible by boat.
**YOU SHOULD KNOW:**
Cruises start from Yakutsk, from where you can go northwards to the Arctic or southwards towards Baikal. Each voyage is equally interesting in its own way.

A voyage along the River Lena is an eye-opening cultural and ecological adventure, taking you to the shores of the Arctic Ocean through a vast tract of virgin territory, only recently opened to tourists. From its source in the Baikal Mountains of Central Asia, the Lena flows for 4,400 km (2,800 mi) through Siberia. It is among the ten longest rivers in the world, a huge waterway, up to 25 km (15 mi) wide, that is an indispensable transport route through the inaccessible Sakha Republic (Yakutia).

This sparsely populated region of northeastern Siberia contains the largest area of permafrost in the world – where deep-frozen woolly mammoths have been uncovered, perfectly preserved. For most of the year it is a silent frozen land wrapped in snow and darkness, but come spring, a magical transformation takes place – the ice thaws, the river flows and the tundra suddenly bursts into life with an exuberance of leaf, blossom and birdsong.

In the 17th century, the first Cossack adventurers to sail along the Lena discovered a wilderness inhabited by semi-nomadic horsemen, cattle breeders and reindeer herdsmen. Today, little has changed. You voyage through a timeless land of desolate beauty and awesome space, completely forgotten by the march of mankind; disembarking at picturesque riverside villages, you will observe the fascinating world of a self-contained shamanic folk culture.

As you approach the Arctic Ocean, the huge river starts to break up into an increasingly complex labyrinth of channels, islands and streams as it gradually spreads into a 400-km (250-mi) wide delta – a 60,000 sq km (37,500 sq mi) lush summer wetland, the largest nature reserve in the Russian Federation. This unique habitat is a vital breeding ground and safe haven for millions of birds, fish and sea mammals – an ecological paradise.

# The Amur Highway

The Trans-Siberian Highway has to be one of the world's ultimate road trips, along an 11,000 km (7,000 mi) network of roads all the way from St Petersburg to Vladivostok. The Amur Highway, still under construction, is by far the most challenging section – an epic adventure in itself.

This infamous 2,200 km (1,375 mi) stretch of road runs between Chita, historic city of revolutionary exiles, and the picturesque city of Khabarovsk on the River Amur, carving its way through the inhospitable, sparsely populated swamplands of eastern Siberia and the impenetrable taiga forests of Russia's Far East, closely following the route of the Trans-Siberian Railway. It is a prestigious engineering project, bulldozing its way across savage terrain regardless of the natural obstacles in its path. Construction continues relentlessly 24 hours a day, seven days a week, but even so, much of the road is still potholed and rock-riddled gravel or dirt track that all too easily turns into a mud bath whenever it rains. Despite its incomplete state, the road was officially opened by Vladimir Putin in 2004, in a triumph of illusory hope over harsh reality; it is due to be fully asphalted by the end of 2008 but nobody believes this date to be anything other than an official fantasy.

When the Amur Highway is finally completed, it will be a far tamer trip than the one you make today. Gradually, the road is evolving into a four-lane superhighway that will present little challenge other than distance. As yet it is still one of the world's great adventure drives through a vast, untamed wilderness where you stop at isolated villages, camp by the wayside, negotiate with road gangs and test your vehicle's, and your own, stamina to its limits.

**HOW:**
By car, motorbike or bike
**WHEN TO GO:**
Mid-June to mid-August unless you are prepared to brave sub-zero temperatures and ice roads.
**TIME IT TAKES:**
3-4 days by motorbike or car, 9-12 days by bike.
**HIGHLIGHTS:**
Khabarovsk – picturesque city.
River Amur – 9th longest river in the world.
Taiga scenery.
Mikhailo-Arkhangelskaya Museum, Chita – 18th century wooden church now a museum dedicated to the Decembrist anti-tsarist revolutionaries.
**YOU SHOULD KNOW:**
This is a trip through wilderness for which you should be well prepared before you set out. Fuel is sold by the roadside, but there are few places to stay or buy supplies between Khabarovsk and Chita.

*The River Amur flows through the forest near Khabarovsk.*

# Trekking in the Golden Mountains of Altai

**HOW:**
On foot or on horseback
**WHEN TO GO:**
July to August
**TIME IT TAKES:**
12 to 18 days
**HIGHLIGHTS:**
Mount Belukha
Crossing the Karatyrek Pass.
Kucherla Valley
Sighting a snow leopard.
**YOU SHOULD KNOW:**
You must travel with a guide or on
an escorted trip. Organized treks vary
in length and difficulty but you need
a good level of fitness in order to
cope with altitudes above 3,000 m
(10,000 ft) and long days of walking
or riding. If you go on a riding trek
some previous horse-riding
experience is desirable.

Straddling the borders of China, Mongolia, Kazakhstan and Siberia, the Altai ('golden') is a rugged World Heritage wilderness, a remote land of snow-capped mountains, torrential rivers, glaciers, lakes and waterfalls where wild animals roam in the pastures and forests, and humans are few and far between. This was once the heartland of the Turkik tribes, the savage hordes of Ghengis Khan who swept down from the mountains into the plains of Central Asia. Their descendants are peaceful nomads who live traditional pastoral lives scattered through the mountains with their herds. There are no towns, no villages and no roads – just a vast expanse of soul-stirring nature.

The Altai is not easy to reach. A four-hour flight from Moscow gets you to the pleasant provincial city of Barnaul, then you spend another two days on a bumpy bus ride through the steppe. At last you reach Tyungur, a small village at the edge of the mountains where you equip yourself with supplies, and a packhorse to carry them, for a trek into the back of beyond.

Taking ancient herdsmen's trails, you tramp through sweet-scented pine forest and climb across jagged ridges above the tree line, scrambling over moraine and rambling through remote valleys full of wild flowers. Pick luscious clusters of wild currants, camp by clear mountain streams, and wonder at primeval stone mounds that mark the hill-tops as you get closer to Mount Belukha. This sacred twin-peaked mountain towers 4,506 m (14,780 ft) into the sky, clothed in snow and half-hidden behind its veil of clouds. According to shamanistic tradition, you are in Shambhala – the mythical kingdom of Tibetan scripture that holds the secrets of the Earth. The mountain radiates a mysterious silence, overwhelming in its intensity, giving you a strange feeling that the shamans could very well be right.

*The highest mountain in Siberia – Mount Belukha*

# Circum-Baikal Railway

A journey along the Circum-Baikal Railway line is an incomparable cultural, historical, technical and scenic experience. It is one of the most complex railway lines in the world, running for 89 km (56 mi) along a narrow mountain shelf, going through 56 tunnels and galleries and over 248 bridges and viaducts, and passing more than 170 architectural and natural monuments.

Lake Baikal, the world's deepest lake, lies directly in the path of the Trans-Siberian Railway and, before the Circum-Baikal was built, trains had to be uncoupled and transported across the lake by ferry. The Russo-Japanese War of 1904 made it imperative that this final link in the Trans-Siberian line was completed to carry troops and supplies. Huge sums of money and the forced labour of thousands of convicts were thrown at the problem of constructing a railway along the vertical granite mountainsides of the lake's southern coast. In terrible conditions, constantly threatened by landslides and mudflows, the prison work-gangs hacked out ledges and tunnels using only chisel and sledge hammer. The line became operational in 1905 and, in reference to its massive cost, rapidly acquired the sobriquet 'the golden buckle in the steel belt'.

The Circum-Baikal became redundant in the 1950s when a hydroelectric project necessitated flooding a section of line and building a by-pass. Today it is a quiet back-route, serviced by excursion trains that trundle along at 25-30 kph (15-20 mph), stopping every so often for passengers to look at the incredible engineering – all the more incredible for having been built without the aid of machines. The railway runs through a region of outstanding natural beauty with breathtaking views of Lake Baikal's astounding scenery. It is a spectacular testament to Russian skill in engineering and design, quite unlike any other railway journey in the world.

*The train hugs the shores of Lake Baikal.*

**HOW:**
By train
**WHEN TO GO:**
May to October
**TIME IT TAKES:**
4 hours and 40 minutes
**HIGHLIGHTS:**
Ulanovo – see the remains of the original railway sleepers and tunnels.
Local culture in villages along the route.
Beautiful scenery.
Belaya Valemka (White Cutting) – marble outcrop, rare combination of minerals of outstanding geological significance.
Polovinnaya and Shabartuysky Bridges – ferro-concrete arched viaducts.
**YOU SHOULD KNOW:**
You can also explore the railway line on foot, going through disused tunnels and over viaducts as you hike along the lakeshore.

# Kamchatka Ring of Fire Trek

**HOW:**
On foot
**WHEN TO GO:**
June to September
**TIME IT TAKES:**
Two weeks
**HIGHLIGHTS:**
Climbing Mutnovsky 2,323 m
(7,620 ft) high – glaciated caldera.
Ash cones, geysers, fumaroles and
mud pools.
Zhirovskye and Viluchinskye hot
springs.
Kurilskoye Lake – see brown bears
and sea eagles.
Klyuchevskaya Volcano – largest
active volcano in Eurasia.
**YOU SHOULD KNOW:**
Much of the Kamchatka is still
uncharted wilderness and there is no
tourist infrastructure. You need to be
extremely physically fit, adventurous
and prepared to rough it. As well as
adventure eco-trekking, you can also
go on birdwatching, fishing and
rafting expeditions and coastal
cruises.

*Mud face packs for these two
soaking in the hot spring.*

A remote peninsula at the far edge of Russia's Far East, Kamchatka is more or less the same size as Britain, and on the same latitude. But it could not be more different. Barely touched by man, with only a single rough road, it is one of the world's greatest ecological treasures – a rugged wilderness in a constant state of geothermal flux containing some of the world's most spectacular volcanoes. With more than 400 glaciers and 160 volcanoes, it is one of the most active regions in the Ring of Fire volcanic belt that girdles the Pacific.

A journey into Kamatchka is like entering a dreamland – a surreal world of elfin cedar trees and giant savannah grasses; boiling mud pots and blue-algae lakes; blackened lava desert and dense primeval forests; steaming sulphur springs and swirling icy rivers. Brown bears roam in the woods, the rivers are stuffed with salmon and the surrounding seas are rich fishing grounds where whales, sea-lions and sea otters flourish. In the autumn, the swathes of luxuriant green forest turn to fiery shades of brilliant reds, yellows, pinks, purple and gold, transforming the landscape into a dazzling rainbow of colour before the leaves fall and the long dark arctic winter sets in.

You trek through highlands and lowlands, scrambling down steep ravines and wading through rivers, wandering through the woods and along the seashore, camping by clear-watered streams, bathing in hot springs and climbing to the summits of snow-capped volcanoes. At the rim of the Mutnovsky Volcano, you peer down into the caldera through a sulphurous veil of fumaroles to glimpse a sparkling wall of ice crystals – an incredible climax to an awesome eco-adventure at the very edge of the world.

# Lake Issyk-Kul Trek

*Lake Issyk-Kul – one of the world's highest lakes*

Lake Issyk-Kul, the 'Pearl of the Tien Shan Mountains' in northern Kyrgyzstan, is one of the world's highest (1,610 m/5,280 ft) lakes. Yet despite being fed by the icy water of 118 rivers and streams, and the melt-water of the soaring peaks that surround it, it never freezes, because of the slightly saline springs bubbling up in its centre. This quirk, combined with Issyk-Kul's huge size (its shore is 700 km/437 mi long), has resulted in a microclimate that has transformed the adjacent mountains. They should be barren, rugged, windswept and bitterly cold. Instead, below a snowline consistently higher than 4,000 m (13,000 ft), the Tien Shan Mountains here are a hiker's paradise of thick forests, small lakes of vivid colours in rolling alpine pastures, waterfalls and torrents gurgling along valley floors. The lake itself is edged with sandy beaches and the most unlikely of all, flower-filled meadows – and the water's temperature is 24 °C (75 °F) from June to September.

Issyk-Kul's extraordinary climate has made it a favourite resort for visitors from Bishkek and Alma-Ata – but only the north shore has been heavily developed. The best trekking routes are based on Karakol (formerly known, and still often referred to as, Przheval'sk, after the Russian explorer), at the lake's eastern end. Typically, seven to fourteen day treks cherry-pick the region's best two to three day hikes, driving up to 150 km (95 mi) between the most scenic landscapes. From the Dzhetyoguz Valley you cross the Tilety Pass and clamber up the Karakol and Keldyke gorges to beautiful Ala-Kul Lake, from which you can look along the magnificent 5,000 m (16,400 ft) plus peaks of the Terskei Ala-Too range. More remote, and lovelier in all its variety is the Sarydzhaz river valley to Mertsbakher Lake trek. Provided you stay largely on the southern shore, Issyk-Kul offers a pristine wilderness of gentler terrain than you expect in the heart of central Asia.

**HOW:**
On foot
**WHEN TO GO:**
June to October
**TIME IT TAKES:**
7-21 days (including one day's travel each way from Bishkek/Alma-Ata to Przheval'sk).
**HIGHLIGHTS:**
Staying in a yurt, the traditional collapsible and portable nomadic dwelling, made of felt stretched over a birch lattice framework, with a hole (*tunduk*) in the top for ventilation.
The view from Djuuku Pass of Ara-Bel Valley, Djuuku Gorge and Djashyk-Kyol (Green Lake).
Drinking *Kymyz* (mare's milk) in a yurt camp, listening to the guide/shepherd's stories about the beautiful red rocks known as 'Seven Bulls' and 'Broken Heart' in the Sarydzhaz Valley.
Sunbathing on a sandy beach 1,524 m (5,000 ft) up in Central Asia.
**YOU SHOULD KNOW:**
1. Make sure your papers are in perfect order, especially if you are coming from Kazakhstan.
2. Difficult access to health and transport facilities on the south side of Issyk-Kul make trekking inadvisable for children under twelve.

**407**

# The Fergana Valley

**HOW:**
By bike or car
**WHEN TO GO:**
May to June and September
to October
**TIME IT TAKES:**
Ten days by mountain bike or three
to four days by car
**HIGHLIGHTS:**
Khujand medieval citadel.
Kokand – Palace of Khudayar Khan.
Visit the silk factory of Margilan.
Rishtan – small town 50 km (30 mi)
from Fergana, famous for its blue
ceramics.
Shakhimardan – a beautiful Uzbek
mountain village in Kyrgyzstan.
**YOU SHOULD KNOW:**
This is a moderately demanding bike
journey for which you need an open
mind, adventurous spirit and good
level of fitness. The mountains
around the Fergana are wonderful
trekking country. The region has only
recently become politically stable
after years of turmoil and as yet has
little tourist infrastructure.

Known as the 'Golden Valley', the Fergana is a 22,000-sq km (8,500-sq mi) wedge of rich arable land enclosed by the Tien Shan and Pamir Mountains. The 300-km (190-mi) long valley is a picturesque ethnic melting-pot with a distinguished history. In 329 BC Alexander the Great founded the city of Khujand and, some 200 years later, the inhabitants of the valley began trading with China – the origins of the Silk Road. The 7th to 8th century Arab Empire introduced Islam from the west; and Babur, 16th century descendant of Ghengis Khan, spread the splendours of Fergana's Moghul culture into South Asia. In the 1920s Stalin carved up this prosperous province between Tajikistan, Uzbekistan and Kyrgyzstan, creating today's crazily illogical borders.

As you travel up the valley from Khujand, an important Tajik city on the Syr Darya River, you will find yourself drawn into an intriguing cultural adventure. The diversity of customs, costumes and language is fascinating and you may often be surprised by the contradictions between ancient and modern, Islamic and communist ideals. Head northeast through cotton and wheat fields, orchards and vineyards into Uzbekistan, to the historic capital of Kokand; and Margilan, a market town famous for its silks. Admire the faded 19th century grandeur of the elegant tree-lined streets in Fergana town, and visit Andijan, the city where Babur was born. Cross into Kyrgyzstan, a remote mountainous country of breathtaking natural beauty, ending your travels in fairytale surroundings of sparkling alpine lakes, wild walnut orchards and snow-capped mountain peaks.

On your journey, you will see countless historic monuments, haggle in colourful bazaars, relax under the ornately painted roofs of wayside *chaikhanas* (traditional tea houses); and find yourself welcomed into people's homes with a heartfelt hospitality that transcends cultural barriers, leaving you with many fond memories of this remarkable part of the world.

*Fergana Valley with the Tien Shan Mountains in the background*

# The Pamir Highway

The Pamir Highway is one of the highest, most thrilling, least-travelled routes in the world. Here, at the meeting point of the Tien Shan, Hindu Kush and Karakoram mountain ranges, is some of the most extraordinary and beautiful terrain on the planet, an eerie empty land of parched ochre rock, hot springs and turquoise glacial lakes set amongst the magnificent snow-capped peaks of the world's highest mountains.

Built by the Russians as a Soviet supply road, the Highway runs for some 1,250 km (780 mi) from Dushanbe to Osh along an ancient Silk Road route across the Pamir Plateau. Subject to erosion, earthquakes and landslides, the road is in a constant state of disrepair, making for a journey full of sudden unforeseen hazards. There is almost no traffic and, apart from shepherds herding their flocks, scarcely a soul to be seen. You will, however, stumble upon plenty of monuments – petroglyphs, ancient temples, Buddhist stupas and ruined fortresses, charting several millennia of history.

The Highway runs eastwards from Dushanbe across the plains, winding steeply upwards through rugged mountains to Khalaikum. You pass rusting hulks of abandoned Russian tanks and lurid signs warning of minefields as you manoeuvre your way through old landslips and uncontained streams sloshing across the road. The air grows colder and howling winds blow through an increasingly desolate landscape as you climb over the Koi-Tezek Pass at 4,200 m (13,775 ft) and set out across the Pamir Plateau towards China. At the frontier, the road turns northwards along the Chinese border up to Ak-Baital Pass at 4,655 m (15,270 ft) before descending to the hauntingly beautiful Lake Kara-Kul, through the lush pastures and dramatic gorges of the Alai Valley in Kyrgyzstan, to end this epic road trip at the colourful city of Osh.

*The highway slices through the Karakoram Mountains.*

**HOW:**
By 4x4 or bike
**WHEN TO GO:**
July to September
**TIME IT TAKES:**
Five to seven days by 4x4, three weeks by mountain bike
**HIGHLIGHTS:**
Yamchun – 12th century fort with spectacular view.
Bathing in the Garm-Chashma and Bibi Fatima hot springs.
Lake Karak-Kul – salt lake formed by meteorite impact millions of years ago.
Views from the Ak-Baital Pass, 4,655 m (15,270 ft).
**YOU SHOULD KNOW:**
This is a demanding journey whether you travel by jeep or bike. You will be travelling at very high altitudes so must be physically fit. You can shorten the journey by taking a plane part of the way, from Dushanbe to Khorugh – a spectacular scenic flight through the mountains that is an experience in itself.

**409**

*The new bridge over the River Oxus*

# Follow the Footsteps of Alexander across the Oxus

**HOW:**
By car, motorbike or bike
**WHEN TO GO:**
April to June or September to October
**TIME IT TAKES:**
Two to three days by car/motorbike; four to six by mountain bike.
**HIGHLIGHTS:**
Tajikistan – 18th century Hissor Fort.
Ajina-Teppa – 7th century Buddhist monastery complex.
Spectacular view from top of Nurek Dam, one of the tallest dams in the world.
Afghanistan – Blue Mosque of Mazar-i-Sharif.
Balkh – medieval ruins and early Islamic monuments.
**YOU SHOULD KNOW:**
Most governments advise against any unnecessary travel in Afghanistan but, depending on local conditions at the time of travel, the north is not unduly hazardous. Never travel without a knowledgeable local guide and make thorough enquiries beforehand. Afghan visas can be obtained in Dushanbe.

Crossing the Oxus into Afghanistan, one of the most wonderful countries in the world, is a lot easier now than it was two millennia ago when Alexander the Great's armies floated across the fast-flowing river by clinging onto their leather tents converted into makeshift rafts. In 2007, an imposing 670-m (2,200-ft) long bridge was opened, a vital link in a 21st century 'Silk Road' that aims to connect landlocked Central Asia to the Indian Ocean port of Karachi.

The legendary River Oxus (nowadays known as the Amu Dariya) separates Tajikistan and Afghanistan. The people on either side share the same ethnic bonds but for decades they have been divided by political turmoil and the barrier of the river itself, which was crossable only by an intermittent ferry service. The bridge will eventually help regenerate a remote area that is still suffering the aftermath of thirty years of war. Right now it enables the intrepid traveller to undertake a fascinating trip at the cutting edge of adventure tourism.

The spanking new bridge seems utterly incongruous in comparison to its surroundings. As soon as you cross it, you are hurled back through time into a biblical landscape – a startling contrast to southern Tajikistan where the intensively farmed fields and ancient remains of the historic Hissor and Vakhsh Valleys all testify to millennia of civilization.

It may take a while to see beyond the poverty but persevere along the dusty road to Mazar-i-Sharif, the cultural capital of northern Afghanistan, and you will soon be filled with respect for the dignified bearing and beautiful manners of this resilient people; and you will be completely overawed by the staggering beauty of the Blue Mosque – a cogent reminder of the sophisticated civilization in Afghanistan at a time when the West was stuck in the Dark Ages.

# Orkhon Valley

Mongolia is the most sparsely populated country in the world, a vast untamed expanse of mountain, forest, desert and plateau. In this nomadic land where more than thirty per cent of the population are still herdsmen and there are scarcely any roads, riding is the normal means of getting around. Mongolians have an almost symbiotic relationship with their horses – calm, surefooted ponies that easily handle the rough terrain unshod.

An expedition by horse to the Orkhon Valley will open your eyes to a way of life that is utterly unfamiliar. The Orkhon is the cradle of Central Asian nomadic societies, a World Heritage Cultural Landscape where the inhabitants live in harmony with nature, continuing pastoral traditions and shamanic religious practices that have remained unchanged for some two millenia.

As you ride through the wildflower pastures by the River Orkhon, the only signs of human life are the scattered *gers* (yurt tents) of nomad families. A camping trek of some 200 km (125 mi) along the river valley and up into the Khangai Mountains, through verdant, volcanic plains and forested gorges to the dramatic cascade of the Orkhon waterfall is a liberating escape from the complexities of the post-modern age. Here there is just you, your horse and nature in the raw.

Incredible as it may seem, you are travelling through the heart of the largest empire in the history of the world. At its height in the 13th century, the Mongol Empire stretched across Central Asia from Beijing to the borders of Hungary. Ghengis Khan held sway over more than a 100 million people from his capital city of Kharkhorum in the Orkhon Valley. The remnants can be seen today – ruins standing as testaments that this remote valley was once the centre of the world.

**HOW:**
On horseback
**WHEN TO GO:**
May to October
**TIME IT TAKES:**
Ten days
**HIGHLIGHTS:**
Galloping across the steppe.
Staying in a traditional *ger* camp.
Ruins of Kharakhorum – Ghengis Khan's capital.
Erdene Zuu Monastery – most ancient Buddhist monastery in Mongolia.
Drinking fermented mare's milk.
**YOU SHOULD KNOW:**
You should be a reasonably competent horse rider to go on this trek. Alternative means of transport are yak cart, mountain bike or 4x4.

*The Orkhon Valley*

# Gobi Desert Trek

**HOW:**
On a camel or by 4x4
**WHEN TO GO:**
May to October
**TIME IT TAKES:**
Eight to nine days
**HIGHLIGHTS:**
Bayan Zag flaming cliffs
Hongor Sands
Yol Valley glacier
Staying with local herdsmen in a
ger village.
Seeing rare wildlife.
**YOU SHOULD KNOW:**
According to National Geographic
*Adventure Magazine,* the Gobi is one
of the top six trekking destinations.
The Gobi is a wild and remote region
with no roads and dangerously
powerful winds. You should not
attempt to explore it without a guide.

The Gobi is one of the strangest places on the planet. The largest desert in Asia and the fourth largest in the world, it is a cold desert of high plateau and mountain where it is not uncommon to see frost. It stretches some 1,600 km (1,000 mi) east to west, covering the whole of southern Mongolia and extending into northern China, gradually expanding southwards all the time. Although at first sight it looks totally barren, the Gobi supports many unusual mammals and more than 200 species of bird as well as endemic plants.

From Dalandzadgad, a town 540 km (336 mi) south of Ulaanbaatar, you can ride either by camel or jeep through the stunning landscapes of Gurvansaikhan National Park where three mountain ridges rise up to 2,600 metres (8,500 ft). The dramatic scenery is extraordinarily varied – rocky and sandy desert, precipitous cliffs and ravines, oases and saltpans. You can climb to the top of Hongor Sands, a giant 180-km (110-mi) long 300-m (1,000-ft) high sand dune, explore the glaciated Yol Valley, and wander in the other-worldly terrain of the Bayan Zag 'flaming cliffs' – a vast red sandstone amphitheatre of weirdly eroded pillars, rock canyons and ridges, where in 1923 Roy Chapman Andrews famously discovered dinosaur remains and fossilized eggs.

The surreal empty landscapes and the insubstantial beauty of the dunes give you a strangely comforting sense of your own insignificance. You are surrounded by silence, only the singing of the wind; and at night, the only light is a twinkling sky thick with stars. A trek into the Gobi is a life-changing experience that leads one to re-assess man's place on the planet.

*A camel caravan crosses Hongor Sands, the biggest dune in the Gobi Desert.*

# Into the Khentii Mountains

*Terelj National Park*

Mongolia is generally associated with endless empty desert, but a trip through Terelj National Park into the lower Khentii Mountains soon puts paid to any such pre-conceptions. From a lush marshland veined with rivers and streams, where bizarrely shaped granite outcrops rise dramatically from meadows strewn with wild flowers, you clamber through a glorious mountainous landscape of wooded hills and valleys. Apart from the odd nomad camp, the wilderness stretches out before you all the way to Siberia, a paradise for the numerous animals and birds that thrive here.

As you climb from the meadows into the mountains you can watch birds of prey patrolling the huge skies, see wild horses, red elk, moose, wolves and even spot a brown bear. Walk along the banks of clear-watered rivers, catch fish in Khagiin Khar, a 20-m (66-ft) deep glacial lake, and dip a toe in the Yestii hot water springs. Climb to the top of Altan Ulgii, at 2,646 m (8,680 ft) the highest mountain of the Khentii, for wonderful panoramic views and wander round the spooky Gunjin Sum Monastery, deep in the larch forest. Only the outer walls are intact but many old tales are attached to it that will send a shiver down your spine.

Only 80 km (50 mi) from the capital, Ulaanbaatar, and easily accessible by one of the few roads in this vast country, the Terelj National Park and Khentii Mountains cover an area of some 2,864 sq km (1,100 sq mi) with some of the most beautiful scenery in Mongolia. Miles from any signs of civilization, dependent on your own resources, this is a trip for the nature lover in search of a genuine backwoods experience and a complete release from the pressures of urban life.

**HOW:**
On foot
**WHEN TO GO:**
May to October
**TIME IT TAKES:**
Ten days
**HIGHLIGHTS:**
Ulaanbaatar – Gandan Monastery, a functioning Buddhist monastery.
Seeing wildlife.
Weird rock formations
Ruins of the Gunjin Monastery
Altan Ulgii – highest mountain of the Khentii
**YOU SHOULD KNOW:**
Most of the trek is relatively easy-going, although it's steep in parts so you need to be reasonably fit. The Terelj National Park is beginning to cater for tourists at its edges and you can take much shorter trips from Ulaanbaatar to go rock-climbing, rafting, mountain biking and horse riding.

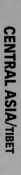

*The road runs parallel to the
Yarlung Tsangpo River.*

# Lhasa-Gyantse-Xigatse Scenic Drive

**HOW:**
By car or 4x4
**WHEN TO GO:**
May to June or September to
October
**TIME IT TAKES:**
Two to three days
**HIGHLIGHTS:**
Lhasa – Jokhang Temple, the holiest
shrine in Tibet.
Yamdrok Lake
Karola Glacier
Khumbum Pagoda
Tashilhunpo Monastery
**YOU SHOULD KNOW:**
Foreigners require entry and travel
permits. The whole of Tibet is at very
high altitude so it is best not to fly in
from a low altitude country but
acclimatize yourself gradually by
travelling through increasingly high
altitude zones on your way here.

Tibet, for so long closed to outsiders, is the world's largest and highest plateau, a land of snow-clad mountains, turquoise lakes, rolling pastures and cobalt skies – the Shangri-La of western imaginings, an ancient spiritual culture that is being slowly crushed by the inexorable march of progress.

Lhasa is not at all the 'Place of the Gods' that you expect. The ancient city has long since been engulfed by concrete and commerce. You have to look hard to find the prayer wheels, exotic temples and cymbal-clashing saffron-robed monks that you pictured. You must leave the city to discover Tibet – an enchanting pastoral world of nomad tents and yaks, wild plateau horsemen, brightly costumed women leading pack-mules, and everywhere pervaded by the mysteries of an ancient shamanic Buddhism.

The road southward from Lhasa crosses the Yarlung Tsangpo (Brahmaputra) River and climbs through the scenic Kyi Chu Valley to the 4,794-m (15,725-ft) Ganba Pass, where prayer flags flutter in the wind. Below you is the sacred Yamdrok Lake – a truly breathtaking sight. You carry on through a ravine up across the Karo Pass, more than 5,000 m (16,500 ft) high, seeing lakes and glaciers, and descend to Gyantse, a charming traditional market town in a fertile valley 265 km (165 mi) southwest of Lhasa. Here you will find the Palkhor Monastery and the staggering 32-m (105-ft) tall Khumbum Stupa, one of the most magnificent buildings in Tibet.

Carry on to Xigatse, ancient seat of the Panchen Lamas and visit the temples and monasteries round about. The Tashilhunpo Monastery is a breathtaking complex of golden-roofed buildings where you can see the incredible 35-m (115-ft) high Thangka Wall, built by the first Dalai Lama in 1468. This is the glorious Tibet that you imagined.

# Mount Kailash Kora

A massive peak, more than 6,600 m (21,700 ft) high in the remote Gangdisé Shan mountain range, Kailash is not only revered in the shamanistic Bön religion of Tibet but equally among Buddhists, Hindus and Jains. It is believed to be the sacred centre of the world and, among Hindus, the home of Lord Shiva.

Pilgrims travel for days through the wilds of western Tibet to make a *kora* (ritual circumambulation) of Mount Kailash in the hope of a better life. The more circuits that are completed, the more auspicious it is. Thirteen is considered especially lucky, while 108 rewards you with instant nirvana. Exceptionally devout believers prostrate their way around the circuit – flinging their entire body flat out on the ground with every step.

The 52-km (32-mi) circular walk starts and finishes at Darchen, a nondescript mud brick village in a tranquil plain of grazing yaks. It is a mortal sin to set foot on the mountain itself. The pilgrim trail leads round the edge through green valleys and narrow gorges to the Drolma Pass at 5,600 m (18,370 ft). This is the high point of the *kora* where celebrating pilgrims chant, prostrate themselves at stone *chortens* (stupas) and tie their prayer flags, adding to the myriad of multi-coloured tattered cloths torn into shreds by the howling wind. As you descend round the other side, the view of the striated north face of the mountain is dazzlingly perfect – alternate lines of black rock and shimmering ice, rising to an unsullied glistening cone of snow outlined by the deep blue of the Tibetan sky.

There is something extraordinarily uplifting about walking with pilgrims. The intensity of their faith creates an inspirational atmosphere and joyful spirit of shared endeavour as you make your personal *kora*.

**HOW:**
On foot and 4x4
**WHEN TO GO:**
May to June or September to October
**TIME IT TAKES:**
Seven days – four days 4x4 journey from Lhasa and three days walking.
**HIGHLIGHTS:**
La Chu glacial valley
Gori Kund frozen lake
Milarepa's Cave
Lake Manosarovar
**YOU SHOULD KNOW:**
Be sure that you are acclimatized to the altitude before setting out. It is the height rather than the terrain that makes the Kailash circuit a demanding walk. Apart from one or two steep rocky parts that require good shoes, it is fairly easy trekking.

*Buddhist prayer stones at the sky burial site above Tarboche in La Chu glacial valley*

# Roof of the World Express

The world's highest railway line, the 'Roof of the World Express' was opened in 2006. It runs for 1,142 km (710 mi) between Lhasa, capital of Tibet and Xining in China, crossing the Tibetan Plateau more than 5 km (3 mi) above sea level. It reaches its highest point at the Tanggula Pass (5,231m/17,158 ft) and goes through the Fenghuoshan, the highest tunnel in the world at 4,905 m (16,093 ft). There are 675 bridges and 45 stations along the line, and more than half the track is laid on permafrost in a miracle of engineering.

The railway is the fulfilment of China's long-term ambition to join its western province with the rest of the country, to promote economic progress and cultural unity. The Tibetans view it rather differently – as yet another threat to their ancient indigenous culture; and environmentalists are concerned about the disruption to the region's delicate ecology. Whatever the rights and wrongs, it cannot be denied that it is both an incredible journey and an inevitability in a globalized economy.

Most of the journey is at an altitude of over 4,000 m (13,000 ft). The carriage windows are tinted to block out harmful ultra-violet rays and every berth has a personal oxygen canister in addition to the oxygenated air that is pumped round the train. As you cross the desolate treeless Tibetan plateau – the 'Rooftop of the World' – you enjoy a spectacular moving picture of the surreal scenery. You pass the highest lake in the world, see yak, wild antelope and donkeys grazing and watch golden eagles cruising through the sky. Puffy white clouds hang in the cobalt blue Tibetan sky above a vast moonscape of yellows, ochres and browns, and a skyline of sharply etched snow-capped peaks glows golden in the sun. This is the train-ride of a lifetime.

*The Qingzang/Qinghai-Xizang train approaching Lhasa.*

**HOW:**
By train
**WHEN TO GO:**
May to June or September to October
**TIME IT TAKES:**
14 hours
**HIGHLIGHTS:**
Lhasa – Johkang Temple
Tanggula Pass.
Qinghai Lake – largest lake in China.
Xining – Kumbum Monastery, one of the most important Buddhist sites in China.
**YOU SHOULD KNOW:**
You can now travel all the way across China on a single train journey between Lhasa and Beijing in three days.

# Sacred Valleys Trek

By anybody's reckoning Bhutan is a most extraordinary country. Tucked away in the folds of the eastern Himalayas, and surrounded by China and India, this remote, mountain kingdom is the last place in the Himalayas where Mahayana Buddhist culture survives intact, informing every aspect of life here. First opened to the world in 1974, the present King's policy has been tailored to keep Bhutan's traditional culture and pristine environment untouched by outside influences and so far, so good.

Bumthang is a complex of four, beautiful valleys, lying at about 2,600 m (8,500 ft). Buckwheat, barley, potatoes and apples grow in profusion, and this tranquil landscape is Bhutan's sacred heart, containing many of its most revered temples. Trek alongside the Chamkhar River, famed for its trout, visit Thamshing Lhakang Temple, built in the 7th century, and Membar Tsho (Burning Lake) where Guru Rimpoche, who brought Buddhism here from Tibet, hid some sacred scriptures.

Walk through traditional villages of unique architecture, meet delightful local people, marvel at gorgeous handicrafts, climb up to Phephela Pass through serene forests of miniature bamboo, rhododendrons and pine. Follow the course of the river up to the base camp of Gangkhar Puensum. Bhutan's highest mountain at 7,570 m (24,000 ft) is the world's highest, unclimbed mountain. Various attempts to climb it have failed, and mountaineering has been forbidden since 2003 because of local religious beliefs.

Flora and fauna flourish in this environment of respect for all living things, and over 600 bird species can be found, including ten that are endangered. There are 165 different mammals including red panda, Himalayan black bear and tiger. Takin, the national animal, can be seen grazing in alpine meadows, also home to some of the country's remarkable flora. What with temples and fortresses, natural beauty and charming people, trekking Bhutan's Sacred Valleys is a magical experience.

**HOW:**
On foot
**WHEN TO GO:**
March to June, September to November
**TIME IT TAKES:**
Up to two weeks
**HIGHLIGHTS:**
The colourful festivals that take place in the valleys during spring and autumn.
Thanbi Temple, founded in 1470.
Thimpu, Bhutan's capital city.
**YOU SHOULD KNOW:**
Bhutan, (known by its people as 'the Land of the Thunder Dragon') accords great respect to the mountain Gangkhar Puensum. According to folklore it is the source of three major Bhutanese rivers, the Kuru, Chamkhar and Mangde. When they first appeared, the rivers proposed a race, but Chamkhar said she would rather take her time and enjoy the views. This is why the Trongsa and Lhuntse valleys are narrow and steep, while Bumthang valley is wide and lush.

*The beautiful and remote mountain kingdom of Bhutan*

# Barsey (Vershay) Rhododendron Sanctuary Trek

**HOW:**
On foot
**WHEN TO GO:**
March and April for the
rhododendrons
**TIME IT TAKES:**
About one week
**HIGHLIGHTS:**
Watching the sunrise over
Kanchenjunga.
The amazing sight of miles and miles
of flowering rhododendrons.
Kechopalri Lake, revered by Buddhist
and Hindu alike for its miraculous,
healing properties.
**YOU SHOULD KNOW:**
Sikkim is the least populated state in
India, and its official language
is…English.

*Rhododendrons in bloom at the
Barsey Rhododendron Sanctuary*

The landlocked state of Sikkim is small, but due to its position tucked into the Himalayas, its climate, flora and fauna is very varied, with elevations that range from 280 m (900 ft) to the summit of Kanchenjunga, the world's third highest mountain standing at an impressive 8,598 m (28,208 ft).

One of the loveliest treks here takes you through the Vershay Rhododendron Sanctuary. Starting from Rinchenpong, a small market village, climb through well-cultivated land, past fruit orchards and plots of rice, maize, millet and vegetables, to Hi Barmoik. This attractive village of wood and stone houses is spread across the wooded mountainside at an altitude of 2,200 m (7,000 ft).

Climbing higher, the trek takes you through mixed forest to Barsey, where the altitude goes up to 4,100 m (13,500 ft), producing habitats that support everything from bamboo to Alpine wildflowers. This is a wonderful area for birds – over 200 species have been recorded here, and mammals include leopard, marten, civet, barking deer and red panda. Barsey lies on a huge ridge, covered with silver fir, hemlock, magnolia, orchid and, of course, rhododendrons. In spring, the sheer quantity of millions of brilliantly coloured rhododendron flowers, (from thirty different species), is overwhelming, and the clear air is redolent with their fragrance.

There are wonderful views too, of the high peaks. At Phoktay Dara there is a superb, panoramic viewing point, where you can see the magnificent snow-capped mountains, including both Kanchenjunga and Mount Everest in all their glory. Passing through flower-filled meadows, and across clear streams you descend to the Khalej Valley before visiting Pamayangtse Monastery, one of the oldest and most revered Buddhist monasteries in Sikkim. Situated on a hill at about 2,000 m (6,500 ft), it commands another spectacular view of the Himalayas and Kanchenjunga. Inside, you can marvel over ancient carvings, frescoes, and a marvellous, seven-tiered wooden sculpture of Heaven.

# Annapurna Circuit Trek

The Annapurna circuit, stretching for 300 km (187 mi), is one of the classic Nepal Himalayan trails – a gruelling, exhilarating, life-enhancing trek through some of the most spectacular mountain scenery the world has to offer. The trail is mostly well maintained, but some snow and ice will almost certainly be encountered, particularly when crossing the high pass of Thorong La, at 5,416 m (17,800 ft.).

*A trekker looking out over the old fortified village of Jharkot along the Annapurna circuit.*

From Besisahar, at about 500 m (1,600 ft), you ascend gently through brilliant, green rice paddies and numerous small streams. As you climb higher, you'll see marijuana fields, goats at pasture, apple and apricot orchards and barley, as well as small villages scattered amongst the terraced farmland. After a few days the trail becomes steeper and you find yourself passing through temperate and coniferous forests, alpine meadows, finally climbing beyond the tree line.

Sometimes you'll spend two nights in one place in order to acclimatize your body – the air is thin up here and altitude sickness can be a problem – but by now you are living in a different world, where the sound of rushing water from streams and waterfalls replaces that of cars and machinery. The villages become more Tibetan the higher you go, and Buddhism takes over from Hinduism. People here seem genuinely friendly and welcoming, and there are many lodges in which to stay.

By the time you reach Thorong La pass and make the descent to Muktinath, an important religious site, you will have seen the most extraordinary, panoramic views of the snow-laden Annapurnas, crossed high suspension bridges, waded through rivers, and eaten masses of dal and vegetable curry. At Tatopani, relax in the welcome hot springs. Watch the sunrise from Poon Hill in Ghorepani, or gaze at the amazing, high altitude lake at Tilicho before descending to the 'real' world once again.

**HOW:**
On foot
**WHEN TO GO:**
Late September to December
**TIME IT TAKES:**
About three weeks
**HIGHLIGHTS:**
The beautiful, terraced valley of Marsyangdi.
The walk between Chame and Manang via Upper Pisang with its stupendous, inspirational views.
The Hindu and Buddhist temples at Muktinath.
**YOU SHOULD KNOW:**
This trek is strenuous – you'll be walking for up to 7 hours per day, carrying a light rucksack. It is also very cold, especially above 3,000 m (10,000 ft). Rent rather than buy everything you need for the trek, and pay the entrance fee to the Annapurna region in Kathmandu or Pokhara.

*Mount Kanchenjunga*

# Kanchenjunga Trek

**HOW:**
On foot
**WHEN TO GO:**
March to May and late September to end November
**TIME IT TAKES:**
Two to four weeks
**HIGHLIGHTS:**
The rhododendron forests in bloom. The Limbus' famous – and welcome – alcoholic drink *tongba*. Made from fermented millet seeds, it is served in a tall, wooden pot, and drunk through bamboo straws.
The outstanding mountain views and the glorious scenery.
**YOU SHOULD KNOW:**
To the locals, Kanchenjunga is the home of the gods. The name means Five Great Treasuries of the Snow, and the avalanches that occur are said to be the largest in the world. This area is also said to be the home of the yeti – perhaps you'll even see one…

In remote, north-eastern Nepal, on the borders of Sikkim and Tibet, the magnificent mountain Kanchenjunga rises to the sky. At 8,598 m (28,300 ft), this is the world's third highest peak, now part of a conservation area. First climbed in 1955, the region was opened to group trekkers 20 years ago. A climate of high rainfall, humidity, frost and snow together with isolation, has created a region of unique mountain ecosystems, supporting snow leopards, Himalayan black bears, goral, blue sheep, yak, serow and red panda.

The long, arduous trek takes you from from the village of Taplejung, gradually ascending through fertile, cultivated hillsides – rice and cardomom – before entering forests of oak, Himalayan larch, rhododendron and pine. There are 69 varieties of orchid to be found amongst the 1,200 species of flowering plants, and the numerous waterfalls are testament to the heavy monsoon rains.

For the first few days you will camp in villages, mostly populated by Limbu people, recognizable by their *topi* hats, which are larger and more colourful than those worn by most Nepalis. The Limbus, along with the Rais, make up the famous Gurkhas of the British and Indian armies. As you climb higher, you'll camp in ever more remote locations, in the midst of magnificent mountain scenery.

Climbing ever more steeply, the forest gives way to high Alpine meadows where yaks graze beside the moraine. You'll pass lakes, some frozen, ford streams, traverse many high passes and cross the Yalung Ri glacier, shortly after which you'll suddenly see the immense, southern wall of Kanchenjunga and its three major summits, in particular Jannu and its glaciers. Crossing the Mirgin Pass another spectacle awaits you – the extraordinary sight of Everest, Lhotse, Chamalang, Maluku and Gyankung Kang on the horizon, and mighty Jannu so close you feel you could touch it.

# Fly over the Himalayas

The Himalayan Mountains are the highest in the world. Of the thirty one summits over 7,600 m (25,000 ft), 22 rise in Nepal, including Everest and seven other great giants that are over 8,000 m (26,000 ft). If you have limited time here but still wish to see some of the highest peaks and do a little trekking, one option is to take the mountain flight from Pokhara to Jomson, where you can take a short trek into the Annapurnas.

Pokhara is the second largest tourist centre after Kathmandu, beautifully situated beside Lake Phewa, and several flights leave here every morning for Jomson. Within 30 km (19 mi) of the town, the elevation changes drastically from 900 m (3,000 ft) to 8,000 m (26,000 ft), and as the small plane takes off it rises sharply, giving you a view of the white, hilltop World Peace Stupa at the edge of town.

The flight is short but spectacular, passing through a narrow corridor between Dhaulagiri, 8,167 m (27,000 ft), and Annapurna, 8,019 m (26,500 ft). You also have wonderful views of Manasulu, Nilgiri and of Machapuchere, with its instantly recognizable fishtail peak. These mountains are seen at eye level, and on a clear day you can see folds and ravines in the rock face as well as a perfect view of the snowline. Sometimes it can be cloudy, but even then you'll suddenly see a towering snow-capped, glacier-draped pinnacle looming majestically beside you.

On sunny days the plane's shadow races along the bare, brown rock face beneath you. Scattered mountain villages, paths and rivers snaking through deep valleys are clearly visible. Suddenly the plane dives steeply into a valley, making alarmingly tight turns as it aligns itself to the runway. Don't worry - moments later you'll be breathing the pure, crisp air of the high Himalayas.

**HOW:**
By plane
**WHEN TO GO:**
March to May and late September to end November
**TIME IT TAKES:**
About 30 minutes
**HIGHLIGHTS:**
The superb views of some of the Himalayas' most majestic mountains. Trekking in the Annapurnas. The fortress town of Kagbeni. Muktinath, a place of pilgrimage and a major religious site.
**YOU SHOULD KNOW:**
The Nepalese word 'himal' means 'snow covered mountain'. The Himalayan glaciers, the source of Asia's largest rivers, are at risk. A UN climate report states that global warming could melt them all by 2035, causing flooding followed by drought in Nepal, India, China, Pakistan and Burma.

*Flying above the clouds, alongside the Himalayas.*

# Swat Valley

**HOW:**
By Suzuki jeep
**WHEN TO GO:**
April to June and September to
October
**TIME IT TAKES:**
Two to three days from Peshawar
to Kalam
**HIGHLIGHTS:**
Buddhist remains.
Mingora – market town on
River Swat.
Madyan – picturesque riverside
village.
Forest walk from Kalam to the
Ushu glacier.
**YOU SHOULD KNOW:**
Swat has long been a wonderful
tourist destination but it has been
badly affected by post 9/11 politics
and at the time of writing it is
dangerous for foreigners. You should
take heed of your government's
advice as to when it is safe to travel
here again.

Although the country of Pakistan was only created in 1947, it was born from a culture that goes back thousands of years, as is evident from the ancient remains, historic monuments, beautiful architecture and the dignified demeanour of its people.

Swat, the 'Switzerland of Asia', was an independent princely state ruled by the Wali of Swat until 1969, when he ceded his authority to the central government. People have lived here for more than 2,000 years and there are plentiful remains from the Gandhara Buddhist civilization (and plenty of people claiming to be descendants of Alexander the Great). Situated in the foothills of the Hindu Kush, it is a spectacularly beautiful region where snow-capped mountains enclose small enchanting valleys, each a magical self-contained world of lakes, forests and waterfalls.

Battered Suzuki jeeps ply the main valley, piled high with passengers hanging onto the tailgate, and they career along in a cavalier fashion that, at first, is frankly terrifying. But, have faith – your driver knows every twist, turn, bump and pothole of the narrow road. Only an attitude of oriental fatalism will enable you to appreciate the captivating scenery as your vehicle whizzes alongside the River Swat taking you from the charming main town of Mingora to the villages of the upper valleys. As the road winds upward, the mountains start to close in and the river becomes increasingly turbulent. Steep verdant slopes, terraced with fruit orchards and poppy fields, reach up to deep green forest and a skyline of glistening icy peaks. The mountain village of Kalam is secreted 100 km (60 mi) up the valley, in the depths of the forest beside a tumultuous river swollen with glacial water. The comparison with Switzerland is belittling. This is an altogether greater, wilder and more mysterious land – a sort of savage Paradise.

*River crossing near Mingora in the Swat Valley*

# Travelling the Grand Trunk Road

According to Rudyard Kipling, the Grand Trunk Road was 'such a river of life as exists nowhere else in the world', the lifeblood of the Indian sub-continent along which the ideas that have shaped its culture have flowed for more than 2,000 years. The Buddhist, Hindu, Jain and Sikh religions sprang up around it, Alexander the Great marched his army across the Indus on it and the Mughals spread the might of their empire along it. Known to 17th century British travellers as the 'Long Walk', the Grand Trunk Road runs for 2,400 km (1,500 mi) between Kabul and Kolkata, passing through the historic cities of Peshawar, Islamabad, Rawalpindi, Lahore, Amritsar, Delhi, Agra and Varanasi.

*Not just red buses in Lahore!*

From the romantic Mughal city of Lahore, the heart of Pakistan, whether you travel northwards toward the Afghan border or south into India, you get swept up in the life of the road. The stream of traffic moves at a cracking pace as motley bullock carts, bicycles, auto-rickshaws and battered 1950s cars play chicken with the psychedelic trucks and buses. These dazzling works of art on wheels are practically a national symbol of Pakistan, each exquisitely painted carriage-work a unique story, telling of the owner's region, ethnic origin, interests and personality in emblematic form of brilliant colour and calligraphy.

In the shade of the wayside trees are street vendors and caravanserais (truckstops), men lolling on charpoys (string beds), children playing in the dust, loose livestock wandering into the traffic, graffiti and garish advertisements on every inch of wall. It feels as though the entire world is on the move. As you cross the Jehlum River, where Alexander defeated the armies of Porus in an epic battle of 326 BC, you are exultantly aware of your own small part in this endless sea of humanity.

**HOW:**
By car or bus
**WHEN TO GO:**
September to April
**TIME IT TAKES:**
As long as you like
**HIGHLIGHTS:**
Qissa Khawani bazaar (Bazaar of the Storytellers) in Peshawar
Badshahi Mosque in Lahore
Bazaars of Rawalpindi
Wah Garden at Hasan Abdal
Greco-Buddhist ruins in Taxila
**YOU SHOULD KNOW:**
At the time of writing, the political situation in Pakistan is very dynamic and most governments advise against all non-essential travel.

423

*The Biafo Glacier*

# Snow Lake Trek

Said to be the 'Most Beautiful Place in the World', Snow Lake is certainly one of the most remote. This is the land of the yeti, an icy mountain wonderland, a week's trek from the nearest human habitation – itself a far-flung outpost in the mountain wilds of Baltistan.

Snow Lake belies its name – it is not a lake at all but a huge ice-basin, 16 km (10 mi) wide and thought to be around 1.6 km (1 mi) thick, enclosed by the stupendous 6,000-m (20,000-ft) peaks of the Karakoram Mountains. It lies at the head of the Biafo and Hispar glaciers, which spread down from the 5,151-m (16,895-ft) high Hispar Pass to form the longest glacier system outside the polar regions, a massive ice highway connecting the ancient mountain kingdoms of Baltistan and Hunza.

From Skardu, capital of Baltistan, a jeep takes you on a white-knuckle ride through the Braldu Gorge where hairpin bends are too tight to take in one go and the wheels constantly threaten to slip over the edge of sheer precipice. Thrilled to be alive, you reach Askole, gateway to the highest mountains in the world – a medieval village in the middle of nowhere. Over the next fortnight, you will trek 120 km (75 mi) through an enchanted land of blue ice pinnacles, deep glacial caves, gorges, crevasses and hanging glaciers – up the Biafo Glacier to Snow Lake and across the pass to descend the Hispar Glacier into Hunza. Climbing 300 m (1,000 ft) a day, camping in remote valleys, scrambling over rocky moraine and using ropes to cross crevasses, you test your stamina to the limit – to collapse, exhausted but elated, amid the terraced orchards and lush wildflower meadows of the Hunza Valley.

# The Karakoram Highway

The Karakoram Highway is perhaps the 'ultimate' road. A marvel of civil engineering, long considered impossible, it was a joint construction project between Pakistan and China across the highest international pass in the world in a region of hazardous weather and high tectonic activity, with constant risk of landslides. By the time of its completion in 1986, it had taken twenty years and the lives of almost 900 workers. The decrepit concrete huts by the wayside are poignant reminders of the road gangs' harsh working conditions.

The Highway covers a distance of some 1,300 km (800 mi) connecting Islamabad to Kashgar in China – a daunting but thrilling scenic drive by way of the Karakoram and Pamir Mountains. You roller-coaster up the Indus Valley through barren foothills until quite suddenly, without any apparent gradation, you are enclosed by craggy, ice-covered peaks. A mellow stretch through the beautiful scenery of the Hunza Valley, with wonderful views of terraced slopes covered in fruit trees and isolated villages clinging to rugged cliffs, takes you up to one of the highest altitude national parks in the world – an icebound wilderness that is the hideout of the elusive snow leopard.

Wind your way up treacherous hairpin bends, passing spectacular glaciers that practically drop into the road, to the Khunjerab Pass at 4,730 m (15,500 ft) and across 120 km (75 mi) of desolate no-man's land into China.

The road surface improves dramatically this side of the border and the landscape is transformed from the savage glacial peaks of the Karakorams to rounded ochre Pamir hills. You descend to the Taxkorgan Valley, pass Karakul, a surreal lake on the Pamir plateau at the edge of the Taklimakan desert sands to finally arrive at the ancient Silk Road oasis of Kashgar with a triumphant sense of mission accomplished.

**HOW:**
By car or bus
**WHEN TO GO:**
June to September
**TIME IT TAKES:**
Four days to three weeks, depending on stops and means of transport.
**HIGHLIGHTS:**
Balti Fort and picturesque Hunza Valley market town of Karimabad.
Khunjerab Pass.
Lake Karakul and Muztag Ata Mountain.
Kashgar – Id Kah Mosque
**YOU SHOULD KNOW:**
The Khunjerab Pass is closed between October and May because the road is blocked by snow. You drive on the left in Pakistan so remember to change sides of the road when you enter China. (At the time of writing Pakistan is politically volatile and most governments have issued travel warnings, but you can still get to the top of the Khunjerab Pass from Kashgar in China).

*The beautiful Hunza Valley*

# The Palace on Wheels

**HOW:**
By train
**WHEN TO GO:**
Year round
**TIME IT TAKES:**
Seven days for this tour – there are
other tours lasting up to ten days
**HIGHLIGHTS:**
Ram Ganj Bazaar in Jaipur.
The Taj Mahal – even more majestic
during a full moon.
The 'Lake City' of Udaipur
The Train – it really is the star of this
journey; from the food to the service
to the décor – everything about it is
first class.
**YOU SHOULD KNOW:**
Despite the high cost, demand for
this journey greatly outstrips supply.
You therefore need to book a couple
of years in advance or find a travel
agent who has block bookings. If you
can be flexible, it's possible to be put
on a reserve list and hope
for cancellations.

The Palace on Wheels train, which runs from Delhi through Rajasthan, is perhaps the most audacious feat of recycling in transport history. In 1981, the former royal train was faithfully restored with the aim of bringing a regal experience to a much wider audience. Although replaced with a newer model some ten years later, it still provides a feast of luxury living for those who travel on it. With its bars, restaurants, personal attendants and even a library, the Palace on Wheels pampers the traveller like no other train journey.

The journey starts and ends at Delhi's Safdarjung Railway Station and takes you to some of the finest sights that there are in this northwest corner of India. The first stop on the week-long excursion is the magnificent 'Pink City' of Jaipur, offering a chance to stretch your legs whilst marvelling at the astonishing architecture of Rajasthan's capital city. The many bazaars within the city give the traveller a real feel of the tastes, colours and smells of India.

The train then continues on its way, allowing you to sample the delights of Jodhpur, the 'Sun City', and Udaipur, the 'Venice of the East'. More colours feast the eye as the train heads back towards Delhi and the vibrant red city of Fatehpur Sikri awaits you. This is a journey that leaves the best to last, as if compensating you for soon having to give up such luxury. The contrast between the heavily industrialized city of Agra and its world famous monument – the Taj Mahal – could not be greater. Though the 'Taj' is one of the most photographed buildings in the world, nothing can match the breathtaking splendour of seeing it up close.

The short journey back into Delhi gives you one last chance to relax and enjoy the opulence of the train.

*The opulent Palace on Wheels*

*The wonderfully preserved steam train*

# Darjeeling Himalayan Railway

The Darjeeling Himalayan Railway is the most fascinating of all the 'toy train' routes in India. With a 610 mm (2 ft) gauge, it's the narrowest to be found on the subcontinent and it has the unique attraction for a mountain railway of having no tunnels – thus allowing passengers an uninterrupted view of the beautiful Himalayan landscape.

Starting from New Jalpaiguri, this wonderfully preserved steam train meanders its way along an 86 km (54 mi) route, making a dozen or so stops along the way before journeying through picturesque tea plantations, and finally reaching the charming hill station of Darjeeling. Aside from the marvellous views, the climb itself is something to behold. Starting at an altitude of 100 m (330 ft), the train reaches an elevation of 2,000 m (6,600 ft) by the time it arrives at its destination. Several hair-raising bends greet you along the way, as the train seems to cling to the hill face like a mountain goat. At the aptly named 'Agony Point', the tightest bend on the line, the train seems to change direction completely in the blink of an eye.

Whilst this journey can be taken in one go, there are several places along the route that are worth exploring. Most notable are the village of Tindharia, which houses a railway workshop, and Ghum, the highest station in India and home to a railway museum.

Having taken this amazing trip, it's easy to see why railway enthusiasts often list it in the world's top ten journeys. This diminutive railway was declared a UNESCO World Heritage Site in 1999, and while many stations are little more than wooden shacks, the sheer effort that has gone into keeping the line open is evident in its well maintained track, burnished engines and comfortably upholstered seats.

**HOW:**
By train
**TIME IT TAKES:**
Around eight hours one-way
**WHEN TO GO:**
Avoid the monsoon season (June to September). Otherwise the climate is good year round.
**HIGHLIGHTS:**
The views of Khanchenjunga – the third highest peak in the world.
The Happy Valley Tea Estate – well worth a visit to see how they produce what some regard as the best tea in the world.
Giddapahar Mandir – a temple dedicated to Lord Shiva, just outside Kurseong.
The Buddhist Monastery at Ghum – home to ancient texts and beautiful murals.
**YOU SHOULD KNOW:**
The area around Darjeeling is subject to periods of unrest, which can cause the line to be closed. You should always check the situation before travelling and take advice from your embassy.

*Rice fields in the valley*

# Kullu Valley Trek

**HOW:**
On foot
**WHEN TO GO:**
Best from April to June or September and October
**TIME IT TAKES:**
Allow three weeks to explore the whole valley
**HIGHLIGHTS:**
The Dhoongri Temple – a magnificent wooden structure near Manali.
The charming little village of Jagatsukh – a perfect place to stop for a while.
Old Manali, with its stone and timber buildings.
The hot sulphur springs at the scenic village of Vashisht.
The views from the Rohtang Pass at 3,915 m (12,845 ft).
**YOU SHOULD KNOW:**
A reasonable degree of fitness is required to attempt the higher passes of the Kullu Valley. Weather conditions can deteriorate rapidly, so allow extra time when tackling the more difficult stretches of the trek.

The Kullu Valley in the northern state of Himachal Pradesh is far removed from the stereotype of India as a country of heat and dust. For many Westerners the valley is merely part of the hippy trail, but to Indians it is a highly productive agricultural area. Freshened by the glacial waters of the Beas River, the valley is home to a major apple-growing industry and is flanked by paddy fields during the monsoon season and wheat fields for the remainder of the year. With conifers and rhododendrons lining the upper slopes, the Kullu Valley is one of the most sumptuous parts of India.

Several operators offer guided tours tailored to meet all requirements and abilities, but a better experience may be gained by hiring a cook and a guide in Manali and venturing out in a smaller group. Engaging locals ensures that you will see the best the area has to offer. Since travelling in nearby Kashmir has become too dangerous, more people are choosing the Kullu Valley as a safer option. However it is still possible to escape the crowds at higher elevations, where you can enjoy the fresh pine forests and the stunning mountain scenery.

Walking over mountain passes and between remote villages, you cannot help but be struck by the beauty of the area. At the higher altitudes craggy outcrops replace the lush vegetation and the snow-capped peaks of the Himalayas frame every scene. There are hot springs to warm you and mountain streams to cool you down. The area is also a hive of outdoor activity, including rock climbing, skiing, rafting and paragliding.

# Manali to Leh

It is difficult to comprehend the sheer magnitude of the Himalayas – while most of the world's great mountain ranges can be traversed inside a day or two, the Himalayas seem to go on forever. They fill the horizon like a giant cumulous cloud – indomitable, magnificent and often impenetrable.

The 3,900-m (12,800-ft) high Rohtang Pass, closed to traffic for most of the year, springs to life when the thaw arrives. It provides a vital lifeline for remote communities, as well as the most memorable of bus journeys. On leaving Manali, the road starts its long ascent towards the pass; beneath you are forests and mountain pasture, whilst ahead lies the permanent snow of Solang Nala. A temple sits at the crown of an escarpment, and the bus usually stops here to allow passengers to gain sustenance and acclimatize to the thin air. From this vantage point the panoramic views over the Beas Valley are simply stunning.

The next couple of hours provide the most spectacular scenery of the entire journey. As the bus negotiates its way along the inclines of the valley, you see soaring peaks and suspended glaciers. You are now well above the tree line and surrounded by the most amazing green and red scree, as the bus continues ever upwards. After an overnight stop at Sarchu Serai and an early start, the bus ascends to a head-spinning 5,328 m (17,475 ft) and the brilliant white of the snow-capped peaks surrounds you. Patches of green return, in land fed by the Indus River, as you gradually make the descent into the beautifully tranquil town of Leh, once the capital of the Himalayan kingdom of Ladakh.

**HOW:**
By bus
**TIME IT TAKES:**
24 hours with an overnight stop
**WHEN TO GO:**
The Rohtang Pass is only open from May to early November, weather permitting.
**HIGHLIGHTS:**
The Buddhist monasteries between Upshi and Leh.
The views over the Bhaga Valley.
Moray Plains – an astonishing plateau, surrounded by white peaks.
The palace at Leh – a Tibetan-style ruin and the focal point of the town.
**YOU SHOULD KNOW:**
Such is the altitude of Rohtang La that disruption can happen even in summer, so be prepared for unscheduled stops. It is recommended that you stay in Leh for a few days to acclimatize to the thin air at this altitude.

*Leh is dominated by the ruins of the Royal Palace.*

429

# The Matheran Hill Railway

Opened in 1907, this narrow-gauge railway is a charming and rather eccentric example of early 20th century engineering enterprise. Traversing difficult mountainous terrain, the train chugs along a track that has over 200 sharp bends and crosses 120 bridges. With a sometimes-cramped capacity of 100, it links the foothill town of Narel to the beautiful little hill station town of Matheran, covering a distance of 30 km (18.6 mi) at an average speed of 15 kph (9.3 mph).

The atmosphere on board is at times one of barely organized chaos, as food vendors and rhesus monkeys climb on board and vie for your attention. The former try to sell you pastries and the latter immediately try to steal them – you can't help but admire the symmetry of the situation.

As it's the only motorized form of transport that is allowed to enter Matheran, the train enjoys a privileged position, but at times the pace is so sedentary that walking would be a quicker option. Matheran translates as 'jungle at the top' and this becomes ever more real to you as the train struggles to climb the very steep tropical terrain.

The views from the train are incredible, with wide-open valleys to one side and steep, mountain faces to the other. The ozone produced by the numerous waterfalls is refreshing even on the sultriest of days. When the train finally pulls into Matheran you realize that the relaxed pace of the journey was entirely appropriate. The town is all about taking it easy, and there's a peaceful, unhurried air about the place. There is no finer feeling than relaxing with your evening tipple on the verandah of your hotel while marvelling at the sunset over the densely forested hills.

**HOW:**
By train
**WHEN TO GO:**
September to June
**TIME IT TAKES:**
2 hours
**HIGHLIGHTS:**
The Lookout Points – short walks take you to 38 observation points to view the stunning valley below.
Charlotte Lake – an area of tranquillity near Matheran
The Bazaar (in Matheran) - a local market specializing in leather goods
The general buzz on the train.
**YOU SHOULD KNOW:**
Whilst monkeys stealing your food may be a source of amusement, losing your camera or even your handbag is much more serious. You need to take great care of your possessions.

*A train winds its way down into the valley.*

# Kalka to Shimla on the 'Toy Train'

*The Kalka to Shimla 'Toy Train'*

An air of excitement builds audibly as the train pulls in to Kalka Station. Railway enthusiasts crowd round to examine the powerful little engine, as street food sellers jostle for your attention. A piercing whistle announces that it's time to board the train and head towards the 'Queen of the Hill Stations' – Shimla. This important rail link was built in 1924 and its 'toy trains' still do a roaring trade running on an improbably small 760 mm (2 ft 6 in) narrow gauge set of rails. The construction was an incredible feat of engineering – the track passes through more than 100 tunnels and over 960 bridges, up into the stunning mountain scenery of the Himalayan foothills.

Immaculately maintained stations line the route and the arrival of the train elicits intense interest from locals at every stop along the way. You are carried along the crests of rich green valleys, climbing inexorably at a sedate 25 kph (16 mph). The charming station at Solan marks the halfway point on this stately excursion, and it is from here that you catch the first sight of Shimla high in the distance. The snow-capped peaks of the Himalayas appear in all their majestic beauty as the forest thins to reveal ever more spectacular vistas.

When the train draws serenely in to Shimla at an altitude of 2,420 m (7,940 ft), it becomes immediately apparent why the British chose the town as their summer capital. While Delhi swelters in the summer sun, Shimla delights in a near perfect 20 °C (68 °F). The town itself is worthy of a day or two's exploration – with its striking Victorian architecture surrounded by magnificent mountain scenery.

**HOW:**
By train
**WHEN TO GO:**
May to July and September to November (July and August are the rainy season)
**TIME IT TAKES:**
Around six hours
**HIGHLIGHTS:**
The Gurkha Castle at Solan – a reminder of the area's former rulers.
Shimla State Museum – a great place to learn about the often-turbulent history of the region.
Shri Sankat Mochan Temple – a beautiful Hindu temple located 5 km (3 mi) outside Shimla.
Dyer-Meakin Brewery – a beer producer founded by Germans in Solan.
**YOU SHOULD KNOW:**
The railway is very popular in high season, particularly during June and July, and advance booking is recommended. There are also many interesting places to see along the way, so breaking your journey is well worth considering.

*Sandstone cenotaphs, built to honour past rulers, lie just outside Orchha.*

# Temple City Journey

**HOW:**
By local bus
**TIME IT TAKES:**
It can be done in three days, but allow a week or two to explore the area fully.
**WHEN TO GO:**
Avoid the monsoon season between June and September when it can be very wet and stiflingly hot. October to March sees the most temperate weather.
**HIGHLIGHTS:**
Gwalior Fort – sitting high above the town with its 3-km (2-mi) long and 10-m (33-ft) high walls.
Man Mandir Palace – A 15th century palace in Gwalior, with an extraordinary network of chambers and dungeons.
The 14 sandstone cenotaphs, built to honour past rulers – just outside Orchha.
The 1,100-year-old granite Brahma Temple in Khajuraho.
The Museum of Man – a wonderful museum of anthropology with an open-air exhibition of the region's history.

It is possible to book this tour on the Internet, travel in air-conditioned coaches and even have your bags carried from hotel to vehicle for you. However for an up-close-and-personal view of this most holy of trails, a far better option is to place yourself in the hands of one of the local tourist bus operators. Sometimes infuriating but always interesting, the buses seem to run to no known schedule. But if you have the time and the inclination these trips offer up a real India from which luxury travel detaches you.

Starting in Gwalior, with its imposing hilltop fort, you enter a region rich in history and legend. This lively city has changed hands countless times over the centuries and its history is etched in the buildings and the faces of the people. The Tuscan and Corinthian style architecture, mixed with more traditional Hindu Mogul temples, makes Gwalior worthy of thorough exploration. From here it is a 120-km (75-mi) journey to Orchha, founded in the 16th century by Hindu rulers. Located on the banks of the meandering Betwa River, this once great city's population has dwindled over the years. It is now eerily quiet with no defined centre, but it's a great place simply to wander around and stumble upon treasures.

After a further 160 km (100 mi) you reach Khajuraho, the 10th century religious capital of the Chandela dynasty and a town now so rural and isolated that it's hard to imagine that it was once a thriving metropolis. Of the 80 or so temples built there, 22 remain and bear testimony to the city's cosmopolitan, multi-faith past. Temples mirror the peaks of the nearby Himalayas, and Jain and Hindu gods sit side by side. Famed for its erotic statues and the extraordinary regularity of its temples, Khajuraho is a place to marvel at.

**YOU SHOULD KNOW:**
How and where to buy tickets for buses in India can be confusing, so ask advice at your hotel. Also, if you board a near-empty bus be prepared for a long wait, as they rarely leave until they're full.

# Saputara Scenic Road

Saputara's location, 1,000 m (3,280 ft) up on the edge of a plateau, coupled with its congenial climate, pure air and breathtaking views of beautiful scenery, has resulted in some modern luxuries being brought to this picturesque hill station. For more than a century Saputara has offered an increasing number of visitors a respite from the often-oppressive heat of Mumbai and it now boasts first class accommodation and several tourist attractions.

Buses to Saputara run from the main metropolitan centres of western India, but a journey undertaken by car or motorbike allows you to create your own unique experience of this lovely area. The 50-km (30-mi) journey from Waghai is short but rewarding, and there is much to distract the curious tourist with time on their hands. You can stop to breathe in the ozone by one of the many waterfalls or linger at a particularly enchanting lookout spot. The whole area is home to many traditional Gujarati villages, whose masked dances and handicrafts are renowned throughout India.

Ancient mixed forests start to crowd in as you near Saputara. Barely touched by human intervention, the forests provide a wonderful habitat for a wide range of wildlife. The dense growth makes a good home for tigers, leopards, pangolins, pythons and four-horned antelope as well as for a great variety of birdlife. The deep forest is also reputed to offer refuge to higher beings – legend has it that the Hindu deity Lord Rama spent 11 years of his exile here.

Whether you start your journey in Mumbai, 265 km (166 mi) away, or from Waghai, the area has such a magnetic quality that you are always left with the feeling that there was so much more to see.

**HOW:**
By car, motorbike or bus
**TIME IT TAKES:**
Two hours driving without stopping (from Waghai), but allow at least a week to explore the area.
**WHEN TO GO:**
The area has a good climate all year round. It is best experienced during the monsoons from March to November when the waterfalls are at their best.
**HIGHLIGHTS:**
Pushpak Ropeway – India's longest cableway, offering a 10-minute ride across the valley.
Sunrise Point – there are great views from here at any time of day, but, as its name implies, they're even better in the morning.
Vansda National Park – a small but thriving wildlife park (entry permit required).
The spectacular Gira Falls – 1 km (0.6 mi) off the Waghai-Saputara road.
Unnai Mata Temple (near Waghai) – a fabulous temple with hot springs.
**YOU SHOULD KNOW:**
While the Saputara-Waghai road itself is in relatively good shape, if you want to make detours to see any of the neighbouring attractions it is advisable to hire a car suitable for off-road driving.

433

*The morning wash on Ganga Ghat*

# The Source of The Ganges

**HOW:**
On foot and by car
**TIME IT TAKES:**
seven to ten days
**WHEN TO GO:**
April to July
**HIGHLIGHTS:**
The sight of the breathtakingly beautiful azure Gangotri Glacier.
The temple at Mukteshwar Mahadeva – a shrine to the goddess Ganga.
Dashashwamedh Ghat adjacent to the Vishwanath Temple in Varanasi.
The Golden Temple – a focal point in Varanasi.
The shopping area of Vishwanath Lane in Varanasi.
**YOU SHOULD KNOW:**
To Hindus this journey is a pilgrimage of huge religious significance. Be mindful of the fact that there are restrictions on footwear, photography and even the presence of women in certain buildings. If you are not of the Hindu faith then it is always advisable to ask whether you can enter temples and shrines.

There are times while making the climb towards the source of the Ganges when you wonder whether the two-day trek to Gaumukh from Gangothri is really worth it. As you climb up the steep hills, your mind is more focused on the ascent than on the astounding mountain scenery. But the Ganges is no ordinary river and to view its source is to witness the birth of the earthly manifestation of a god. It is said that the goddess Ganga was sent down to earth after a heavenly feud, that her descent was broken by Lord Shiva's matted locks and that she finally reached earth as seven streams.

The forbiddingly beautiful Shivling Mountain hangs 6,543 m (21,470 ft) above the blue-green Gangotri Glacier, which marks the emergence of this great river. When looking at the Ganges here in its purest state it's hard to imagine how mighty and muddy this holiest of rivers will become downstream. To journey down it is not only to follow the path of a geographical feature, but also to look deep into the heart and soul of India. Millions come to her to wash their bodies and to wash away their sins. Rivers are central to Hindu culture and they play pivotal roles in life and death; this trip takes you through some of India's most significant holy places.

After journeying back to Gangotri you can travel by road to the hallowed cities of Rishikesh, Haridwar, Garh-Mukteswar and Prayag, before finally arriving at the most sacred city in India – Varanasi. Once there, the true significance of this great river becomes apparent, as worshippers line its steps and magnificent temples, forming a procession along the riverbanks. Few rivers, if any, are granted such high status and the sheer power of the Ganges to draw you and thousands of others towards it is awe-inspiring.

# Kolkata Heritage City Walk

To the outsider, Kolkata (formerly Calcutta) may conjure up images of Mother Theresa nursing the poor, and to the casual visitor it often seems to be an amorphous urban sprawl with poor signage. Thankfully an organization was set up in the early 1990s to change these perceptions. A small group of mainly young volunteers run Cruta (Conservation and Research of Urban Traditional Architecture) and offer walking tours through the meandering streets of this great city. All the proceeds from these tours go to maintaining Kolkata's architectural splendour.

There are two main tours; the first is a short affair focusing on the city centre. Starting at Dalhousie Square, the visitor is taken around fifteen or so historical buildings, including the impressive Writers Building, the Town Hall, St John's Churchyard and the celebrated Metcalfe Hall. But for a taste of the 'real' Kolkata, the North Calcutta Walking Tour is a must. With the aid of a local guide it is possible to venture into areas otherwise inaccessible to most visitors. There are slums and shantytowns and the streets do seem to be totally covered in litter in some places, but there are hidden gems to be found. Several wonderful secluded courtyards as well as the House of Rabindranath Tagore and the Marble Palace stand out in this old mercantile quarter.

Combined, these tours show the visitor both sides of this truly amazing city. Change is happening fast and at times it seems to have left some behind, but at least the members of Cruta are preserving Kolkata's amazing heritage whilst providing employment to local people.

**HOW:**
On foot
**TIME IT TAKES:**
A full day for both tours
**WHEN TO GO:**
The best time to visit Kolkata is from the end of October through to the middle of March, when the weather is pleasant. During the monsoon season (June to September) the rains can cause severe flooding.
**HIGHLIGHTS:**
New Market – a market of over 2,000 stalls specializing in silk and silver.
Eden Gardens – a nice park and home to the test cricket stadium.
Saint Paul's Cathedral
Paresnath Jain Temple
**YOU SHOULD KNOW:**
It is inadvisable to venture into North Kolkata alone. It is easy to get lost as most of the street signs are in Bengali, where they exist at all. It is also not advisable to display your wealth in the form of jewellery or cameras whilst walking through the shanty towns.

*Paresnath Jain Temple*

# Cycle in the Cardamom Hills

**HOW:**
By bike
**WHEN TO GO:**
December to February sees low
rainfall and lower temperatures.
February to May is dry and hot. May to
September is the monsoon season.
**TIME IT TAKES:**
Allow 2 weeks for a thorough
exploration of the hills.
**HIGHLIGHTS:**
The tea plantations at Munnar.
Mangaladevi Temple near Kumily.
Sri Ayappan forest shrine at
Sabarimala – off the beaten track but
worth the effort.
**YOU SHOULD KNOW:**
A reasonable level of fitness and good
suspension are needed to enjoy this
cycling tour. Several companies offer
all-in deals with food and lodgings
provided. However for the more
adventurous it is possible to hire bikes
locally and go it alone.

India is a country of such vastness and complexity that it can be tempting to do too much in too little time. A day in Agra, another in Kolkata and one in Chennai (Madras) – soon the images of red forts can merge into one and you are left with a muddle of memories. A cycling tour in the Cardamom Hills reveals India at its simple best. The slow pace of travel through these fabulously pretty hills on two wheels provides a vacation filled with exploration and discovery of an India that, through increased industrialization, is fast disappearing.

The Cardamom Hills form a long narrow chain at the southern end of the Indian sub-continent. Their ridge acts as the boundary between the states of Tamil Nadu and Kerala, extending from the Palghat Gap in the north and running 280 km (175 mi) to Cape Comorin in the south. Aside from the crop from which they take their name, the hills are renowned for tea production, and the plethora of the other spices produced in the area provides a wonderful gift for your sense of smell.

The region is also home to a wide variety of wildlife, most notably elephants and some big cats and it is very likely that you will encounter the former. Cats however are shy of human contact, so the best chance of seeing them is in one of the local nature parks. The freedom gained by cycling, whilst allowing you to cover ground quickly, fits well with the surroundings. Life here is conducted at a slower pace than in much of the rest of India, and while the Himalayas may have more to offer in the way of spectacular scenery, the Cardamom Hills are more accessible and have their own unique charm.

*Tea pickers in Kerala*

# Houseboat Cruise through the Kerala Backwaters

There can be few more relaxing journeys than floating along the waters of Kerala in a traditional houseboat. The backwaters of Kerala are a labyrinthine network of lakes, canals, and the estuaries and deltas of the 44 rivers that drain into the Arabian Sea. It's a wonderful ecosystem teeming with life – over a quarter of India's plant species are found here. There is such an abundance of flora and fauna, nourished by the tropical sun and generous rainfall, that it's easy to understand why Kerala is sometimes called 'God's Own Country'.

The houseboats, known as kettuvallam, are magnificent creations that blend in perfectly with their environment. They are made with only the locally grown renewable resources of bamboo and coconut fibre – no nails are used in their construction. They were originally designed to carry crops to outlying communities, but since that trade has now sadly all but ceased, many of them have been converted into luxury houseboats for the tourist trade.

With nearly 1,000 km (625 mi) of navigable waterways at your disposal, you are spoiled for choice when it comes to thinking about what route to take, but wherever you go you will see a traditional India, not visible from any other means of transport. It's a tranquil world of ancient fishing methods, huge water lilies, verdant paddy fields, and villages with thatched roof houses and rustic shrines. Gliding sedately along, with the songs of birds as your soundtrack and towering coconut palms sheltering you from the beating sun, there is surely no better place on Earth.

**HOW:**
Houseboat
**WHEN TO GO:**
October to February; avoid the monsoon season – June to August.
**TIME IT TAKES:**
Two weeks is fine but a month would be even better.
**HIGHLIGHTS:**
Periyar Wildlife Sanctuary
Rajamala National Park
The Dutch Palace at Cochin
Kerala is home to Ayurvedic massage – a real therapeutic treat.
**YOU SHOULD KNOW:**
Don't be afraid to haggle over price, especially if you are planning an extended journey. If you haven't booked in advance and are reliant on a local tourist office, take a step back. Those who approach may have paid for the privilege of being there, while just a few hundred metres away there could be a houseboat owner who would offer you the same trip for a fraction of the price.

*A houseboat awaits
your arrival.*

# Nilgiri Mountain Railway

If trains have personalities, and there are some people who think they do, the engines that ply the Nilgiri Mountain Railway are redoubtable little fighters. Now over 100 years old, this 'toy train' route is an engineering achievement that almost defies gravity. So steep is the gradient that a system of racks and pinions was developed to stop the train sliding back down the track, making it unique in all of India.

The line never really paid its way as a carrier of goods, but thankfully it has been kept open and it's now one of India's most spectacular tourist railway trips. For reasons of safety, the train travels at an average speed of less than 10 kph (6.25 mph), making it the slowest train in India. Linking Mettupalayam near Coimbatose with the celebrated hill station of Udagamandalam (Ooty) in Tamil Nadu, the mountain railway was recently declared a UNESCO World Heritage Site.

The train's sedate tempo allows travellers to take in the captivating beauty of these seemingly endless hills. At every point on its steadfast journey, you are surrounded by lush mountain vegetation, as the train meanders its way around spine-tingling curves, through tunnels and alongside deep ravines. An added charm is that it is often possible to get off the train and walk beside it, without any fear of being left behind – such is the serene pace of this journey.

**HOW:**
By train
**TIME IT TAKES:**
Three to four hours each way
**WHEN TO GO:**
Year round
**HIGHLIGHTS:**
Udagamandalam (Ooty) – the 'Queen of Hill Stations'.
The Nilgiri Hills – literally the 'Blue Mountains'.
Idugampalayam Aanjineyar Temple at Mettupalayam.
The Rose Garden at Udagamandalam (Ooty).
**YOU SHOULD KNOW:**
The railway is very popular all year round and it is advisable to book well in advance. Also be prepared for a noisy journey, created by the effort required to climb such steep hills.

*The narrow gauge rack train*

# The Beaches of Goa

Goa has long been India's good-time Riviera, renowned for its sun-kissed beaches, vibrant markets and an energetic nightlife unrivalled anywhere on the subcontinent. This tiny state is blessed with almost year-round sunshine and a coastline graced with long sandy beaches. Each of these many beaches has its own character – some are crowded, others are almost deserted; some have white sands, others are dark brown. Each beach is worthy of exploration if you want to enjoy the total Goan experience.

Several operators offer packages that take you to different beaches each day, but for a more rewarding hike it is hard to beat a self-guided tour. The 120-km (75-mi) coastline is interrupted only by the seven rivers that flow into the Arabian Sea. With judicious use of taxis and local fishermen, who run unofficial ferry services, it is possible to sample all that this amazing coast has to offer.

Starting at the ruggedly beautiful Harmal Beach in the north and journeying to the wonderfully secluded Palolem Beach in the south, you are taken on an odyssey of high contrast. Near the capital, Panaji, the noise of the water gives way to the hubbub of people, as the town seems to spill over into the sea. Venturing south again takes you to Colva, the most popular beach in southern Goa, and it is easy to see why. Golden sands are lapped by the azure sea, while traders, fishermen and visitors give the whole area a wonderful market feel.

The crowds thin out once again as you head towards the silver sands of Palolem Beach. Also known as Paradise Beach, it is framed by the hills of the Western Ghats and lined with cute bamboo huts. It is a perfect spot to unwind.

**HOW:**
On foot
**WHEN TO GO:**
Anytime except the rainy season, which usually lasts from June to August.
**TIME IT TAKES:**
Five to seven days
**HIGHLIGHTS:**
Canacona Island – a ferry ride from Palolem Beach.
The view over the Arabian Sea from Harmal Beach.
Chapora Fort – a 500-year-old Portuguese fort, near Varca Beach.
Albuquerque Mansion – near Anjuna Beach.
**YOU SHOULD KNOW:**
The coast of Goa can get maddeningly busy at times. If it all gets too much for you, remember that the further you go from Panaji, the quieter it will be.

*Anjuna Beach*

# Hill Country Scenic Train Ride – Colombo Fort to Badulla

Most travellers to Sri Lanka fly into Colombo, the capital city, and base themselves either there or at the beaches just to the north. If you have only limited time, but would like to see something different, take the train to Badulla for some of the loveliest landscapes the island has to offer.

Starting at crack of dawn from Colombo Fort, the train sets out towards the hills, running alongside the Muthurajawela Marshland, a protected area teeming with birds. Before long you enter the first of the journey's 46 tunnels and begin the ascent, through lush hardwood forests, to Kandy, the spiritual and cultural centre of the Sinhalese.

As the native forest gives way to pines and eucalyptus, you'll notice that the temperature is cooler and more pleasant. Glossy green tea plantations cover the hillsides, and brightly dressed Tamil women pick the leaves into baskets carried on their backs. From time to time you'll see splendid waterfalls and, as the train climbs slowly up towards Nanu Oya, the dramatic, triangular point of Adam's Peak, 2,243 m (7,400 ft), can be seen to the south. Higher still, tea gives way first to vegetable gardens and then more forest before reaching Pattipola, the highest station in the country. Now you are on a fascinating piece of line, known as the 'Lizard's Spine' where, between tunnels, you can see both north and, more spectacularly, south – way down to the coast.

The train descends through wonderful countryside, crossing an amazing nine-arch bridge connecting two mountains instead of spanning a river. One last treat, particularly for train buffs, comes at Demodara, where the line loops around a steep hill with two stations, one 27 m (90 ft) above the other. After a few more miles of magnificent views, you reach your destination, Badulla.

*Tea plantations cover the hillsides.*

# Sri Pada (Adam's Peak) Pilgrim's Route

*The shadow of Adam's Peak on the clouds*

While Adam's Peak, at 2,243 m (7,400 ft), is not Sri Lanka's highest mountain, its sharply triangular silhouette and religious importance makes it the country's most famous landmark. A place of pilgrimage for over 1,000 years, the mountain resonates in four major religions and, as a result, the thousands of pilgrims who make their way to the top each year are an eclectic mix of nationalities and ages.

The purpose of the pilgrimage is not just to see the Sacred Footprint at the summit, but also to see the dawn break over the mountain. Moments later, the sun produces a unique phenomenon called *irasevaya*, throwing a perfect shadow of the cone onto the clouds. As the sun rises, this shadow retreats down and across the valley below, before disappearing at the base of the peak.

Leaving Dalhousie before dawn for the 7-km (4-mi) climb – the shorter of the two main routes – you join many pilgrims walking beneath the stone arch that marks the start. Soon you reach steps – over 5,000 of them must be climbed – making this a hard slog. Helpfully, there are rest stops and teahouses en route, and the trail is strung with lights that snake ahead of you up the mountain. The eclectic mix of people – fathers carrying babies, bare footed women, children, elderly folk and tourists make this pilgrimage a remarkably friendly one.

Reaching the small, summit temple produces such feelings of euphoria that the fact the 'real' footprint is apparently beneath the cast you can see, detracts not at all. As dawn breaks pink and gold, you'll see the Hill Country rising to the east, while to the west you look all the way down to Colombo and the coast. Catching the awesome shadow on the clouds is the icing on the cake.

**HOW:**
On foot
**WHEN TO GO:**
December to April
**TIME IT TAKES:**
Allow four hours
**HIGHLIGHTS:**
The spectacle of dawn breaking from the top of Adam's Peak.
Visiting nearby tea estates.
Kandy and the Temple of the Sacred Tooth.
The camaraderie en route.
Reaching the 5,000th step!
**YOU SHOULD KNOW:**
The Sri Pada or 'sacred footprint' is a revered site for Buddhists, Hindus, Christians and Islamists alike, but long before the development of these religions, the mountain was worshipped by the aboriginal inhabitants of Sri Lanka, the Veddas.
Their name for the peak was 'Samanala Kanda'; Saman being one of the four guardian deities of the island.

441

# Ngong Ping 360

*No vertigo sufferers wanted on this voyage!*

Ngong Ping is a concept experience for tourists. Like a Disneyland, it is a shopping and recreational opportunity disguised as a theme park, reflecting the 'cultural and spiritual integrity' of its locale on Ngong Ping plateau, high above Hong Kong's Lantau Island. The inspiration for it however, and still Ngong Ping's greatest attraction, is Ngong Ping 360, the amazing cable car ride that gets you there.

From Tung Chung, on Lantau's waterfront, Ngong Ping 360's bi-cable gondola lift system crosses the bay to Hong Kong's new Airport Island, turns a 60-degree angle without stopping and heads up hill and over dale for 5.7 km (3.6 mi) to the plateau village. The 25-minute ride is certainly spectacular – and beautiful when fingers of sea mist thread the rolling grasslands of North Lantau Country Park below. The 360-degree panoramas from the gondolas make the most of the islands scattering the South China Sea to Macau; of the techno-sprawl of Chek Lap Kok's airport complex; of Lantau's own mountain crags (rising to 934 m/3,064 ft); and finally of Po Lin Monastery and the 250-ton, 34-m (112-ft) giant Buddha outside it.

The Tian Tan Buddha motivates many visitors to come here – but neither it nor the monastery is historic or even venerable, and what sincerity exists is brought and taken away by individual visitors. The palpably commercial atmosphere is at odds with Ngong Ping's claim to be the centre of Buddhist interest in Hong Kong, and only your wallet will feel enlightened.

Despite the overly commercial flavour of much of the whole Ngong Ping project, a trip on the Ngong Ping 360, the biggest cableway in Asia, is certainly a once in a lifetime experience.

# Maclehose Trail

*Kowloon from Lion Rock Peak*

The Maclehose Trail is an eye-opening 100-km (62-mi) hike across Hong Kong's New Territories behind Kowloon. Most visitors to Hong Kong – and even a number of habitués – have no idea that huge tracts of beautiful hills and rugged wilderness exist so close to the compressed bustle of one of China's most dynamic cities.

The Maclehose, named after Hong Kong's longest-serving Governor during the colonial era, begins in Pak Tam Chung, among the coves and rocky inlets of the Sai Kung peninsula where, despite the millions living nearby, the green hills drop to totally empty, curving white sand beaches like Tai Long Wan ('Big Wave Bay'). Most of Sai Kung's natural beauty is protected by Country Parks, but their rural isolation is real. No towns ever existed here, and as the terrain grows more rugged it becomes barely inhabited. By the fifth of its ten stages, the Trail runs through woodland to the vast rock bulwark of Lion Rock, an abrupt cliff with Kowloon spread in miniature below. From there to Tuen Mun, the Trail is a series of glorious upland hikes round the slopes of Tai Mo Shan, Hong Kong's highest peak. There are streams and waterfalls in deep ravines full of subtropical birds and dense foliage, grassy moorlands, forests, and ancient hamlets and farms. Near Tai Po Road monkeys may mob you, demanding tolls of bananas or nuts, but wildlife isn't predominant. The Maclehose is an adventure in Chinese landscapes, and every stage provides new surprises.

Once a year, four-person teams compete to race the Maclehose Trail against the clock for charity. Normal hikers reckon on 35-37 hours of actual walking. Star winning teams take a little over 14 hours. But the record is held by four soldiers of the Gurkha Regiment – an incredible 11 hours 56 minutes.

**HOW:**
On foot
**WHEN TO GO:**
Year-round
**TIME IT TAKES:**
35-37 hours of actual hiking; with only two difficult stages, most hikers allow seven days.
**HIGHLIGHTS:**
Post-hike rest & recreation – Hong Kong Central (Wan Chai) is never more than an hour away.
The secret coves of Sai Kung – either deserted or with just a local bar.
Pak Sha O – a wonderfully preserved village on the Sai Kung peninsula.
Ng Tung Chai, on the northern slopes of Tai Mo Shan – a completely secluded series of high waterfalls in a really lush ravine of mosses, ferns and trees growing out of the water-washed boulders.
**YOU SHOULD KNOW:**
Tai Mo Shan means 'Big Hat Mountain'.

# Walking the Great Wall

The Great Wall of China is over 7,200 km (4,500 mi) long, and so familiar that it can seem to be universal property. In fact it was built over 2,000 years and consists of a network of structures reflecting China's expansion west and north. Its magnificence owes much to a breathtaking assumption about where civilization begins (or ends). Archaeologists and historians might choose the most remote earthworks, huge sections of which are still being revealed as far away as Gansu province, even if most people's choice of which section to walk is limited to the best preserved, if not best restored, and to the distance of those sections from major tourist hubs. Nothing could connect you to the past more than the Han Dynasty (206 BC – 220 AD) Wall of concrete-hard reeds and mud, austere and magnificent in the wind-whipped wilderness of the Gobi Desert. Shorn of any outer brick casing, the two gateways of Yumenguan and Yangguan, near Dunhuang still bear majestic witness to imperial power as the two western gateways into 1st century China.

Far fewer people walk the Wall east of Beijing. From Simatai you can follow one of the steepest and most dramatic sections through Huangyaguan, across razor-sharp mountain ridges with a watchtower on every one, to Jinshanling. But to appreciate the culture underwriting the Wall, you need to walk the long western stretches around Datong, beyond the Beijing crowds, but crammed with rich evidence of the Ming, Han, Qin and Wei Dynasties. In fact, for anything less than fourteen days, use a car or bus to cherry-pick the Wall's greatest features from Hongcibao, Motianling, Qidun, Kouzishang and Huashijian, staying in local farmers' houses alongside the Wall itself. Here, the Wall is no theme park. It feels more disused than ruined, and its threatening majesty retains all its power to shock. Sublime hiking.

*The Wall at Badaling*

**HOW:**
On foot

**WHEN TO GO:**
Year-round – especially close to Beijing, sections of the Wall are always open to visitors. Further afield, schedules vary; but the most remote sections have no controls at all.

**TIME IT TAKES:**
1-35 days (of which up to seven might be by car/bus, bypassing less interesting sections to walk) to get any real impression of the Wall's architectural and cultural complexity.

**HIGHLIGHTS:**
The fortified stairways, cannon platforms and other Ming Dynasty (circa 1350) military detailing close to Jinshanling (northeast of Beijing). The only surviving wooden city gate in China, at Deshengbao (west of Beijing). The watchtowers of Xusi and Jinpai. The huge fort and establishment at Yanmenguan Pass near Shuozhou – one of the most strategic sites and the scene of many famous battles.

**YOU SHOULD KNOW:**
Fortresses along the Wall had a social hierarchy reflecting the rest of society. The preserved ruins of the biggest garrisons include still-existing villages or small towns that were originally established as markets for nomad traders from the other side.

# Huangshan Trek

Huangshan means 'Yellow Mountain'. It's in Anhui province, south of the Yangtse flood plains and vast rice paddies, and it is China's most famous mountain. In fact, along with the Great Wall, its image is an iconic representation of China itself; and its grandeur and beauty are acknowledged by its listing as a UNESCO World Natural and Cultural Heritage Site.

*The terrifying path up Huangshan*

The region includes dozens of peaks over 1,000 m (3,280 ft) and three ('Lotus', 'Brightness Apex' and 'Celestial Capital') over 1,800m (6,000 ft). The steep stone steps and chainlink rail to the summit of 'Celestial Capital' are typical of the often hair-raising paths and approaches to Huangshan's finest panoramas – but there are hundreds of beauty spots (with a directory of exotic names like 'Two Immortals Playing Chess', 'Grasping Beautiful Scenes Bridge', 'Beginning to Believe Peak', or 'Monkey Gazing at the Sea') which identify every rock, pine tree, cloud or hot spring. Huangshan is said to combine these four essences of aesthetic pleasure in perfect balance and harmony. Nobody would argue otherwise, but it has a lot more besides. Its terrain and microclimate engenders distinct frigid, temperate and subtropical zones of flora and fauna; and 2,000 years of unabashed tourism means its vegetation is that of ancient China.

There are centuries-old pines, gingkoes, sweet gums, camphor and magua trees; 300 kinds of medicinal herbs; goddess-flowers, crepe myrtles, lilies and orchids. Pine Valley has a 1,100-m (3,609-ft) descent of 6,500 steps to the Emerald Pool's double (reflected) image of mountains and sky; and Huangshan has any number of dramatic waterfalls, curiously-shaped formations, hot springs and cool streams.

The mountain is especially significant to honeymooners and couples, who fasten padlocks even on the remotest trees and rocks to symbolize their union. In Huangshan, you walk in beauty, among people's most cherished dreams.

**HOW:**
On foot
**WHEN TO GO:**
Year-round
**TIME IT TAKES:**
One to ten days, much longer if you open up to the authentic poetic pulling power of this mountain.
**HIGHLIGHTS:**
The beautiful calligraphy inscribed on rocks at beauty spots. You may need someone to tell you just how good the poetry really is, but it looks terrific and many examples are by some of China's greatest poets and emperors.
The inexhaustible magic of pine trees silhouetted against mist curling round precipitous crags and steep forests – like Huangshan's 'Pine Greeting a Guest', or 'Unity', named for its 56 branches matching the exact number of China's ethnic minorities.
Tunxi Ancient Street – astonishingly well-preserved trade centre of the ancient Southern Song Dynasty.
**YOU SHOULD KNOW:**
There may be some truth in the assertion by Chinese poets and artists that once you've been to Huangshan, it is pointless ever to visit another mountain.

# Jiuhuashan Trek

**WHEN TO GO:**
Year-round. Each season has its adherents – for example the Taoyan Waterfall, seen through the trees and tall bamboo of the Ganlusi ('Sweet Dew') Temple on Jiuhuashan's north side, is at its best after seasonal rain, when the river's force creates an all-pervading misty haze.

**TIME IT TAKES:**
2-4 days (to get any real sense of it), though a number of agencies bring visitors for a day's excursion.

**HIGHLIGHTS:**
The Precious Hall of the Bodhisattva Incarnate, on Shenguang Ridge near the Huachengsi Monastery – a scarlet, 7-storey wooden pagoda with over 100 'incarnation'statues of Kim Kiao Kak, the Korean monk who achieved nirvana and brought fame to Jiuhuashan as incarnation of the Hell-King.
People gambling (dice, pool, poker etc) and dancing in special dance houses attached to monasteries or in Jiuhua village: these are ways to attract the benign influence of Ksitigarbha.
The Sea of Bamboo at Minyuan – in a breeze, 405 hectares (1,000 acres) of tall bamboo 'sings' to the gurgling springs and bubbling streams beside the mountain path.
The Phoenix Pine, aka. 'No.1 Pine in the Land Under Heaven' – planted 1,400 years ago, the flat crown of its foliage resembles a green phoenix craning its neck towards Tiantai ('Heavenly Terrace'), at 1,325 m (4,346 ft), one of Jiuhuashan's most important peaks.

**YOU SHOULD KNOW:**
Long ago, Jiuhuashan became known as 'Fairy City of Buddhist Kingdom'. The great Tang Dynasty poet, Li Bai (701-762), described Jiuhuashan's peaks appearing above hanging mist as 'nine lovely hibiscus blooms winging up, out of blue water in the far-off sky'. Tradition says he then became intoxicated on his own words.

Of China's four Buddhist sacred mountains, Jiuhuashan represents the South. Its temples are dedicated to Bodhisatva Ksitigarbha, lord of the earth and underworld. It rises on the northern edge of the Yangtze flood plains in Anhui Province, west of Shanghai. Above the glassy terraces of rice paddy, the road climbs into ragged pine forests, twisting deep into a landscape of forest-capped cliffs, cascades and massive, bizarre rock formations. In the mist creeping up from the valleys, shapes form in the washed-out colours of ancient Chinese paintings, and you feel a déja-vu familiarity. Though there are tea and vegetable plantations among the blossoming azaleas, these are cultivated by the monks and nuns of some 80 temples and sacred institutions, and they don't impinge on the otherwise authentic wilderness. But more than 1,500 years of sanctity means that Jiuhuashan's nine principal peaks, and every cave, stream, path, promontory, pool, waterfall, cliff, temple, pagoda and even the 'Ten Perfect Views', have names of meditational significance (like 'Celestial Presence at the Heavenly Pillar') – which transforms hiking on the mountain into an involuntary pilgrimage whenever genuine pilgrims pause on the often narrow path.

It's no hardship. The goodwill you encounter trekking on Jiuhuashan enhances what is already an exceptionally lovely region. There is no development other than the stunning temple complexes, all of them integrated into the dramatic landscape according to the principles of the Tang, Ming and Qing dynasties in which they were built. You choose temple guesthouses over campsites, and seek out some of their 1,500 Buddha statues and thousands of important cultural relics – because rapidly you realize how their existence gives meaning to every rock and tree that you might hike past. With wafting incense, temple bells and a shrine on every corner, this is not normal hiking – but Jiuhuashan's natural magnificence and spiritual integrity make it abnormally rewarding.

*The temples of Jiuhuashan are integrated into the dramatic landscape.*

# Shanghai's Maglev Train

A ride on Shanghai's Maglev (magnetic levitation) Train is a journey into the future of transport. The Maglev rail system might be only 30.5 km (19 mi) long, but that's enough to demonstrate its potential to transform national and international economies by bringing the most remote areas within reach of trade and tourism.

Although Maglev was created and developed in Germany, Shanghai is the first place in the world to use it successfully in a scheduled service, or indeed in any commercial venture at all, and the statistics are amazing. The train can reach 350 kph (220 mph) in two minutes, and is designed for normal operation with a maximum speed of 431 kph (268 mph). But during tests, the train reached a top speed of 501 kph (311 mph), an indication of what it holds in reserve. With no conventional engine, and on a (necessarily) dedicated track of electromagnetic power and guidance coils, the impetus of acceleration is spread throughout the train. The ride is as smooth as an airborne aircraft, without even the spine-pinning surge of 'take-off'. Looking ahead from the Maglev, you see how the swooping concrete curves of the track are banked; inside, you barely feel it. Once on board, a flickering display charts even the slightest variation in speed, and you can't help sharing the thrill of streaking past the fastest cars on the adjacent expressway.

So far, the Shanghai Maglev only connects Pudong International Airport and Longyang Road, a suburb of the business district, and a long way from downtown. Despite some legitimate misgivings yet to be resolved, plans to extend the line to 160 km (99 mi) between downtown Shanghai and Hangzhou are going ahead. Then you will be able to transfer the 55 km (34 mi) between Shanghai's two airports in 15 minutes – like flying at zero altitude.

**HOW:**
By train
**WHEN TO GO:**
Year-round. Initially, you could only travel on the Maglev as part of an organized tour. Now that it is integrated into the regular transport system, you can ride it at any time.
**TIME IT TAKES:**
Usually 7 minutes 20 seconds (the taxi ride over the same route takes at least 1 hour).
**HIGHLIGHTS:**
No fossil fuel! (The Maglev may not be environmentally perfect, but it's in the right direction.)
Seeing the driver of a Ferrari on the expressway shaking his fist at the Maglev speeding past.
Floating on a magnetic cushion – a thought worthy of both Confucius and China's most imaginative poets.
The exhilaration of pure speed intensified the first time by just a twinge of apprehension, and on subsequent occasions by excited anticipation.
**YOU SHOULD KNOW:**
This technology is going to happen all over the world, and you don't need to know anything about science to share the thrill of it.

*The Maglev train pulls into the station at Longyang Lu.*

*The Grand Canal, Suzhou*

# Suzhou to Hangzhou on the Grand Canal

**HOW:**
By boat
**WHEN TO GO:**
Year-round. Hangzhou has four distinct seasons, but its subtropical, monsoon climate makes it neither too hot not too cold.
**TIME IT TAKES:**
Three hours (Suzhou-Wuxi); 14-16 hours (Suzhou-Hangzhou, overnight); 2-4 days (Grand Canal Cruise on special 'hotel boats', stopping for sight-seeing and excursions).
**HIGHLIGHTS:**
The 18 bridges, reflecting the styles of different dynasties, and ten richly-decorated and colourful land and water city gates opening onto the Grand Canal at Suzhou.
The Lingering Garden and the Garden of the Master of the Nets – ingenious, beautiful, and consummately Confucian.
The Six Harmonies Pagoda at West Lake, octagonal and with 13 curling roofs, representing the six fundamental precepts of Buddhism.
Qing He Fang Street in Hangzhou, much of which survives from the Southern Song Dynasty (1127-1279), and where the shops still sell silks, brocades, parasols, Hangzhou's speciality fans, and the exquisite teas for which the region is revered.

China's Grand Canal is 2,000 years old, 1,764 km (1,103 mi) long, and dwarfs any other man-made waterway on earth. Running south from Beijing, it connects all China's major, east-west running rivers, and thus most of its major cities, in a single, gigantic system. No longer significant to modern transport, communications or defence, the Grand Canal remains as a unique guardian of Chinese history and culture – and nowhere on its length is that more evident than its southernmost stretch from Suzhou to its terminal at Hangzhou. The beauty of both cities is legendary, and the Grand Canal between them passes ancient water towns and villages, lakes and hanging gardens draped in antiquity, and the wood and stone infrastructure of generations of Chinese lives. It is a privileged view of history, and China's greatest poets and artists have recognized and celebrated it since the Sui Dynasty 1,500 years ago: even at its inception, this section of the Grand Canal was imbued with an aesthetic to please.

From Suzhou's gardens, waterways and pagodas, you cruise past a traditional China from the 13th or 14th centuries to Wuxi, the 'Radiant Pear' of Taihu, a lake dotted with islands and gorgeous temples. There you can take a painted dragon-boat across the lake to Tongli, a medieval town split into seven parts by the fifteen river courses flowing through it. Living history just keeps coming for 147 km (92 mi), through Zhenjiang (girlhood home of American writer Pearl S. Buck), to the incomparable natural beauties of Hangzhou itself. The canal passes by ancient stone farmhouses where silk production became famous in the 6th century, but West Lake is Hangzhou's masterpiece, praised by Su Dongpo and Marco Polo, and a major reason for the Grand Canal's citation as a UNESCO World Cultural Heritage Site.

# Pearl River Twilight Cruise

*The port city of Guangzhou*

The Pearl River Delta has been China's southern gateway for nearly 2,000 years, and the city of Guangzhou has been its significant port since the Tang dynasty (618 to 917). Formerly known as Canton, it accommodated first the Portuguese, then the British as predominant trade partners. Today, it is still one of China's fastest-growing cities, and just as devoted to international trade; but its success has been achieved at the cost of pretty well anything that speaks of its history or ancient culture. Instead, Guangzhou is a testament to China's perception of modernity. Concrete confections stretch for blank miles along the Pearl River's broad stream, and river mists turn brown along the banks where they mix with traffic fumes. This is 'Metropolis', and even its residents criticize its lack of redeeming features. Guangzhou's (self-assessed) greatest attraction is to flee the fumes by boat – if only to cruise a short distance up and down the endless concrete shore. Then night falls, and the gorgeous butterfly of the Pearl River takes wing.

Where the Pearl River runs through the city, at night Guanghzou celebrates its industrial heritage and future in a blaze of lurid yellow, red and orange illuminations. Tombstone slabs of daytime grey become canvases for flashing, spinning, flickering sequences of neon. Hotels, shopping malls and high-rise office blocks on both banks create what look like rainbows arcing across the shimmering water. Some co-ordinate lighting sequences, creating themed patterns with names like 'Night Moon Over Goose Pool' and 'Red Heart of the Pearl River'. Multicoloured stroboscopic displays bounce reflections off every ripple, suggesting the hidden pulse of this endlessly energetic city. At any other time of day, a cruise on the Pearl River is merely dull. In the gloaming, the conspiracy of colour in frantic motion reminds you of Guangzhou's ancient, subtle, colourful Chinese soul.

**HOW:**
By boat
**WHEN TO GO:**
Year-round
**TIME IT TAKES:**
1.5-2.5 hours (a leisurely loop between the Guangzhou Bridge in the east, Bai Hedong ('White Crane') Bridge in the south, and the west side of the Shamian district. Duration depends on the size of the cruise ship and the degree of luxury.
**HIGHLIGHTS:**
The Great Bridge of the People – in the heart of the city, it looks its futuristic best by artificial light (or moonlight on its own).
The old colonial villas and cobbled, tree-lined avenues of the Foreign Enclave in Shamian district.
The '13 Hongs' – the line of warehouses along the Shamian waterfront where 19th century foreign traders were allowed to do business. For a long time, these *hongs* were the front line of the opium and silk trades, profits from which flowed to the safety of Hong Kong.
The co-ordinated light shows – even the advertisements look terrific.
**YOU SHOULD KNOW:**
Different cruise companies operate from different wharves. Tianzi Wharf, centrally located near Haizhou Square, is most frequently touted; but many cruises leave from White Goose Wharf in Shamian, usually much more convenient for visitors.

**449**

# Tiger Leaping Gorge

**HOW:**
On foot

**WHEN TO GO:**
Year-round

**TIME IT TAKES:**
1-2 days (sightseeing, or actually hiking the Gorge); 8-14 days (seeing the Gorge, and rafting the Great Bend, staying at 1,000 year-old Naxi villages and including side trips to some of the best attractions on either bank).

**HIGHLIGHTS:**
Lijiang, built in the late Song and early Yuan Dynasties, a UNESCO World Heritage Site where the traditional daily cultures of the Naxi and Dongba peoples are almost untouched.
The view of the 'First Bend' from Shigu Township, upstream of Hutiao, where the River forms a broad V-shape turning from south to north, the site of both Kublai Khan's 'Crossing the River on Leather Rafts', and the 1936 Red Army's Long March.
The trail cut into the sheer limestone cliffs down to the river at Tiger Leaping Rock – where the water flows are 5 to 10 times that of the USA's Grand Canyon.

**YOU SHOULD KNOW:**
Although it is the same river, above Chongqing the Yangtze is called 'Jinsha' ('Golden Sands').

*The calm section of Tiger Leaping Gorge*

Where the Yangtze, Mekong and Salween Rivers rush side-by-side out of Tibet and south along China's border with Burma, the towering ridge of Yulong Xueshan (Jade Dragon Snow Mountain) forces the Yangtze into an abrupt change of direction known as The Great Bend. It turns north, the mountains close in, and the river enters Hutiao (Tiger Leaping) Gorge, one of the world's deepest.

It is narrowest at its start, where a large rock in the middle defies the ferocity of the torrent in a chasm only 30 m (100 ft) wide. This is where a tiger once leaped across it – but its legendary name derives not from tigers' agility, but from their unpredictable savagery. Entering its middle section, the water drops another 100 m (328 ft) without warning. Now at racing speed, whole blocks of water thunder and crash onto sharp outcrops of rock, and you can hear the greedy sucking of deep whirlpools pulling at the air. The third section of Hutiao's 15 km (9 mi) is even more dangerous and spectacular. The steeply-angled (70 to 90 degree) cliffs rise a sheer 18 to 2,400 m (6 to 8,000 ft) from the water, twisting and turning in a surge of high waves and filling the canyon in a haze of frothing spew. Just looking at it is one of the glories of nature, and you can hike along it in two days (rafting it is suicidal!). Beyond the gorge itself, the Great Bend continues for about 190 km (120 mi), turning south and east. For experienced rafters, the prolonged wave-trains and grade IV rapids are one of the world's greatest six to eight day expeditions. For everyone, the proximity of the Gorge to Lijiang, cradle of China's traditional Naxi and Dongba cultures, justifies including this journey in any top-three wish list.

# Rafting Nine Bends River

Wuyi Shan, in northern Fujian province, is southeast China's most remote mountain region. Its incomparable scenic beauty was recognized 4,000 years ago by the Yue people, and it became a site of pilgrimage for Taoism, Buddhism and Confucianism. Already a protected area for 1,500 years before gaining the UNESCO grand slam of World Biosphere and World Natural, Cultural and Historical Heritage Site, Wuyi is the ultimate Chinese expression of the potential for harmony between nature and man. Its heart-stirring landscapes are littered with the temples, palaces and pavilions created in tribute to the aesthetics of Confucian philosophy, whose greatest spear-carrier, the 10th century neo-Confucian Zhu Xi, lived and taught here for fifty years.

Jiuqu (Nine Bends) Gorge, a 10-km (6-mi) section of the 63-km (39-mi) Jiuqu River, is the geographical heart of this summation of Chinese history and culture – and the water element in the formula for harmony. So when you raft the Jiuqu Gorge, you embrace a welter of Chinese philosophy which dictates significance in every rock, every mist of spray, the towering cliffs and solitary, jungle-topped stacks wreathed in cloud; and in the deep placid green pools, the wind-dashed waterfalls and squabbling, rock-strewn rapids of the watercourse. The rafting itself needs no crash-helmet commando training: you sit on bamboo chairs set on six, lashed-together bamboo poles, and swirl gently down stream.

It really is worth reading about Wuyi before you raft the Nine Bends. Each bend reveals a new set of surprises, a geography saturated with sophisticated meaning:  with just an inkling of the nature of the reverence in which the Nine Bends are held, you get a four-dimensional view of what are otherwise merely world-class panoramas. On the water, with visual stimuli at maximum pleasure, this is one of the few places you can go 'holistic' rafting.

**HOW:**
On a raft
**WHEN TO GO:**
Year-round.
**TIME IT TAKES:**
1.5-2 hours (Xingcun – Wuyi Town, through the Nine Bends); one to two days (starting further upriver enables you to reflect in peace on the extent of the region's natural beauty, and renders you immune to the noisy crowds of rafters along the Nine Bends stretch when you get there).
**HIGHLIGHTS:**
The Palace complex and other Minyue remains at Xingcun – the most extensive and best preserved of all South China's Han Dynasty sites, over 2,000 years old.
The Wuyi Nature Reserve (of which the Nine Bends is part) – 95 per cent intact sub-tropical forest.
The green triangles of small terraces backed up in the gullies along the river bank – source of China's rarest and most precious Rock teas, like Dahongpao ('Grand Red Robe').
The 'fairy boats' – the boat-coffins dating back 4,000 years, stuffed into caves and fissures all along the soaring rock walls of the gorge, representing the philosophical and mystical unities of dozens of contrasting dynasties and regimes.
**YOU SHOULD KNOW:**
You can save a lot of time and anxiety at the raft pier by pre-booking through a tour agent.

*Tourists on rafts in the
Jiuqu Gorge*

*The entrance to Qutang Gorge*

# Three Gorges: cruising the Yangtze

**HOW:**
By boat
**WHEN TO GO:**
Year-round. With the Three Gorges Dam now operating, navigation is much less dangerous, and unlikely to be cancelled even when rains swell the Yangtze, which with its huge catchment area can happen at any time of year.
**TIME IT TAKES:**
24-28 hours (Yichang or Zhongbao, the granite island on which the dam is based, to Baidicheng, including an overnight stop at Fengjie, whose massive towering gates face the Yangtze at the division between Wu and Qutang Gorges); 8-14 days (Shanghai-Chongqing).
**HIGHLIGHTS:**
Xiling 100-li Art Gallery – the high cliffs of Yellow Ox, Light Shadow and Yellow Cat gorges, filled with mist and mystery, and said to be like travelling through a painting.
The 12 Peaks of the Wushan Mountains, spread along both shores of the Wu Gorge.

From east to west, Xiling, Wu and Qutang Gorges stretch for192 km (120 mi), compressing China's mighty Yangtze River into an angry torrent between Hubei and Sichuan Provinces. For millennia, the gorges have been celebrated for their uniquely dramatic scenic splendour, and as one of the most important focal points of Chinese history and culture. You could spend a lifetime of fascinating study among the temples, castles, cities, shrines and man-made treasures lining their banks; and the same again, lost in wonder at the natural formations of caves, grotesque rock formations, juddering whirlpools and soaring cliffs that represent so much of China's folk memory – its mythology and legend writ in stone (and in many cases, on it as well: China's most famous poets and artists have left long testaments inscribed on the rock walls).

The Three Gorges may be the highlight of any journey along the Yangtze, but since the building of the new dam, there are only two ways to experience them. Either you can take a short, local cruise from the dam site to Baidicheng ('White Emperor Town'), at the western end of Qutang's north shore and a breathtaking sight of 2,000 year-old vermilion walls and flying eaves; or you must cruise from Shanghai all the way to Chongqing on one of the new 'tourist boats' which are now the only ones to be allowed to use the dam's five locks above Yichang, the eastern gateway to the gorges. You can no longer cruise just from Wuhan to Chongqing. Hopefully, visitors in the future may be allowed to travel on the Chinese commercial boats that lack any comfort, but stop everywhere, enabling you to handpick sites along the gorges, and still enjoy their context – as treasures along the much greater highway of the whole Yangtze River.

# Dalian Coastal Drive

At the southern tip of northeast China's Liaodong Peninsula, Dalian is northern China's biggest port and a former colony of both Russia and Japan. Set between the hills of its own sub-peninsula, the city is unusual in China, because it is full of parks, woods, and green spaces that make the most of the beaches along its twisting shoreline. Dalian's deep-water industrial port is miles away – and the same meteorological quirk that keeps it ice-free makes Dalian a major domestic tourist resort. Since 1955, when the city became exclusively Chinese, its authorities have sought to retain some of the European ideas brought by the Russians – of wide boulevards, and, especially, the wonderful corniche called the Binhai Road.

The Binhai Road runs for 42.5 km (26.6 mi) to Heishijiao, following every cove and promontory around the west and south of the city. It perches between the golden beaches (including 2 of China's designated top ten judged by colour, curve, breadth and fineness of sand) and the coastal hills of the nature park that fills most of the sub-peninsula. Visually, you could be near Sorrento or Cannes above the Mediterranean; but the thicker weight of the air and the sea mists are unmistakably oceanic. Dalian's city fathers proudly refer to their 'dancing silk ribbon', which begins at Asia's biggest plaza, Xinghai Square, and curls out and away among the woods and flower-filled cliff-sides. It's extremely pretty, but the Binhai Road is the centrepiece of a resort region, and nature has been tamed to comply. At regular intervals, close to the beaches, formal entertainment facilities and attractions remind you of how crowded it gets in the summer. There are scenic spots like Wooden-Club Island, the Black Rock Reefs and the novelty sculptures of Donghai Park; and at Tiger Beach, rides like the Jurassic Riptide Adventure and Viking Village...

**HOW:**
By car or on foot
**WHEN TO GO:**
June to October. Come in April only for the blossoming of 3,000 cherry trees (planted by the Japanese in the 1920s) at nearby Long Wangtang.
**TIME IT TAKES:**
1-2 hours (by car); 8-9 hours (steady hiking)
**HIGHLIGHTS:**
Russian Street in central Dalian – the best concentration of buildings among several pockets of architectural history.
Fujiazhuang Beach – the most popular and by far the most fun (but with a steep drop-off 100 m (328 ft) offshore).
The 'Strange Slope' of part of the road called '18-Hairpin Bend' at Donghai Park – a genuinely disturbing optical illusion where your car appears to roll away uphill.
Yanwoling ('Swallow Nest Mountain') – one of Binhai Road's loveliest stretches.
**YOU SHOULD KNOW:**
At Tiger Beach's Ocean Park, the 'Pirate Village' attraction simulates boats in a violent storm at sea, and offers visitors 'an experience of being robbed'.

# The Silk Road

**HOW:**
Various!
**WHEN TO GO:**
Year-round, according to which section you want to travel. A French team recently demonstrated that with meticulous planning, and travelling on horseback, you can travel the entire distance at the optimum season for each region.
**TIME IT TAKES:**
Many agencies offer tours of one or more sections of the Silk Road, ranging from 10-23 days, and including short treks on foot and by camel. Typically, 12-14 days for sections within Turkmenistan, Uzbekistan, Kyrgyzstan and Tajikistan; 14-23 days for sections within China (Kashgar, Xi'an, the Great Wall West Gate at Jiahuagan and Beijing); 15 months (Venice-Beijing, by horse). Most agencies will help you personalize their advertised tours.

*The walled fort city of Jiahuagan lies at the western terminus of the Great Wall in China.*

The wayposts of the Silk Road are a litany of adventure and romance crossing half the world. Already ancient when Marco Polo set out from 13th century Venice, the 13,900-km (8,700-mi) route to Kublai Khan's capital of Beijing is still fraught with the same historic dangers. War, pestilence, religious confrontation and plain banditry continue to influence travellers' choices – and are the reason why the Silk Road is not one, but a series of fragmented routes which tell a collective history.

Created by trade, the Silk Road has always been even more important as a conduit for ideas. The exchange of science and technology, of philosophy, religion and artistic culture has scored a trail of monumental magnificence across two continents. Venice, Istanbul, Bukhara, Samarkand, Tashkent, Kashgar, Urumqi, Dunhuang, Lanzhou and Xi'an stand out, but the mountain ranges, deserts, steppes, rivers and other natural obstacles between them hide a thousand treasures ranging from whole medieval cities to the most exquisite Islamic and oriental objets d'art. There are only two rules for travellers who want to make the most of the Silk Road: always expect the unexpected, and embrace cultural differences to the best of your diplomatic ability.

In many ways, the present Silk Road is the legacy of Kublai Khan. From Turkey to the China Sea he established the 'Ulak' system of caravanserais, where travellers could rest, and his

couriers could change horses (he could send a message from Beijing to Damascus and get a reply in six weeks). You find them, a Byzantine arch or a quintuple-tiered pagoda, on the horizon of mountains and deserts – and just as welcome whether you arrive on foot, by camel train or truck. Kublai Khan's 'Big Idea' always was communication between peoples – and there's no better way on earth than to chase it down the Silk Road.

*The blue domes of the Registan in Samarkand, Uzbekistan*

**HIGHLIGHTS:**
Riding in a camel train on the southern edge of the Taklamakan Desert.
The very rare 'Singing Sand Dune' of Moon Lake.
The maze of markets and alleyways in Kashgar, where colourful traditional dress and a myriad range of Kyrgyz, Uighur, Tajik, Kazakh and Chinese faces demonstrate its historic importance as a melting pot for trade and culture. The Sunday market draws 100,000 people.
Wherever you are on it, just the idea of being 'on the Silk Road' is totally exhilarating – even when things aren't especially comfortable or easy to handle.

**YOU SHOULD KNOW:**
The title of 'Silk Road' was invented by the 19th century German historian and geographer, Ferdinand von Richtofen, father of the 'Red Baron', the World War I Luftwaffe flying ace.

*Donkeys carry bales of hay at the Sunday market in Kashgar.*

455

# Xinjiang to Tibet Highway

**WHEN TO GO:**
May to October – though heavy snow can block sections of the Highway at any time, and in the rainy season of July and August it is often awash.

**TIME IT TAKES:**
9-16 days (by rugged vehicle; and to complete it within 9 days means very long hours of bone-shaking discomfort). Irregular buses operate on various sections of the Highway – and you pay half-price if your height is less than 1.3 m!

**HIGHLIGHTS:**
Travelling the north slopes of the Himalayas – it feels like being on the dark side of the moon.
The monastery at Sagya – an oasis of human generosity, full of welcoming monks in a place of palpable antiquity.
The Potala Palace at Lhasa – approaching it slowly, all the way across Tibet from Xinjiang, makes its magnificence and symbolic potency all the greater when you finally arrive.

**YOU SHOULD KNOW:**
1.World politics directly affects even remotest Tibet, most often in the form of bureaucratic demands. Make sure your passport, visas, and regional travel passes are in perfect order.
2. Be self-sufficient with food, water, warm clothes and basic medical supplies – the region is far too remote to rely on help being nearby.

Getting into Tibet isn't always easy unless you fly direct to Lhasa. Of the five overland routes, the highest and most remote is the Xinjiang to Tibet Highway, so desolate a road that despite a regular military presence it offers travellers blessedly little bureaucratic interference. The Highway begins at Yecheng (Kargilik) in Chinese Turkestan, and climbs straight up the eastern edge of the Karakoram to Dahongliutan, at 4,900 m (16,000 ft) only just higher than the average altitude of the entire Highway. You need to be prepared, either with time to acclimatize, or ancillary oxygen. The 2,743-km (1,714-mi) journey takes from 9 to 16 days on largely unpaved road; and the very few villages and truck stops may be unable to offer you bed, food or even water. That said, usually you find that truckers will happily share their steaming pot of noodles, and every day you'll find some sort of establishment with hot food and a roof.

The rewards of entering Tibet this way are enormous. Over the Kunlun Mountains you skirt the western Tibetan plateau. Instead of people there are birds thronging the small lakes, and wildlife in extraordinary numbers. Mountain peaks form blue on vast horizons of grassland and rocky scrub. There will be a moment when you feel chastened by the biblical immensity of sky and earth and loneliness; and grateful for a human voice. Along the north slopes of the Himalayas into the desert terrain between Gerze and Nyima, only herds of antelope and wild yak disturb the ghosts at the ancient rock paintings at Rutog, among the ruins of the Guge Kingdom. It's a relief to joke with living monks at Tuolin, Sagya, and Tashilunpo monasteries. The contrast makes you realize how this brilliant wilderness journey is also a subtle, cultural introduction to Tibet.

*The Highway near Xinjiang*

# The Romantic Road

One of the loveliest but least known of Japan's scenic routes is the Romantic Road through the mountain heartland of central Honshu. It begins in the historic city of Ueda, once the feudal castle citadel of the Sanada family, and picks its way along the quietest backroads through the mountains of Gunma Prefecture to Utsunomiya. The only logic to its weaving route is to connect landscapes of transcendent beauty, from the cherry blossom of spring pastures to the full-throated blaze of autumn in the mountain forests. It leads to the double waterfalls of Fukiware, the rugged splendour of Lake Chuzenji and the natural glory of Nikko National Park; and to countless shrines, pagodas, castles, hot springs of all shapes, size and location, and ancient towns and villages that reveal some of old Japan's most enduring characteristics.

For some 50km (31 mi) of its 350 km (219 mi) length, the Romantic Road follows the base of Mount Asama, an active volcano. Old and new Japan accommodates itself to nature's dangerous beauty first, with a 1,000 year-old, three-storied pagoda of inspired grace, built at Miyota as protection against eruption; and second, with a miniature version of Tokyo's Ginza shopping district at the upmarket mountain resort of Karuizawa, farther along the road. Both are charming. In the same way, the route passes by traditional and modern hot springs. The old style is for traditional architecture, and a beautifully composed natural setting; some of the newer springs like Kusatsu are factories of hydrotherapy.

You need a car to follow Japan's Romantic Road. It would be worth it even if you stopped only at the ultimate jewel – the World Heritage Sites of Nikko, home to Japan's most lavishly decorated shrine complex, and set in outstanding natural magnificence.

*Toshogu shrine pagoda in Nikko*

**HOW:**
By car
**WHEN TO GO:**
May to October
**TIME IT TAKES:**
Two to five days
**HIGHLIGHTS:**
The impressive view of Mount Asama from the sylvan beauty of Onioshidashi Park, formed round a stream of solidified lava from a previous eruption.
The completely traditional, small hot spring resort of Shima Onsen, in the northern mountains of Gunma.
The glorious twin cascades of Ryuzu Falls, tumbling through the gold and red of autumn forests.
The Yomeimon at the Toshogu shrine complex of the spectacular Tokugawa Mausoleum, just one of Nikko's stunning historical and religious sites.
**YOU SHOULD KNOW:**
For sheer romance, time your visit for the annual historical festival in August in the rural paradise of Numata, nestled at the foot of the Tamahara Highlands.

# Walking the Nakasendo

Developed from the 7th century onwards, the Nakasendo was formalized at the beginning of the Tokugawa Shogunate (1600-1868) as one of the five official roads for the use of the shogun and government dignitaries in ruling their territory. The Nakasendo was one of two highways connecting Edo (Tokyo) and Kyoto, and it runs through the forested heart of Japan across the mountains of Honshu and along its misty, green river valleys. There were 69 post towns and smaller stations established along its 534 km (332 mi) length – and long stretches, especially in the mountainous areas, remain now almost exactly as they were in the 17th century. Despite inevitable modernizing, it's still possible to hike the entire Nakasendo – but most visitors choose to spend one to twelve days on its pristine central section from Ena to Narai.

Between these beautifully preserved Edo towns lies the fabulous Kiso Valley, a living vision of ancient, rural Japan. Huge stretches of the road are paved with their original *ishidatami* cobbles, curling through pedestrianized villages of traditional wooden houses, and stepped to follow the steep gradients of the forest hillsides. With volcanic Mount Ontake as a backdrop, the road reaches its zenith as custodian of Japanese rural cultural tradition between the villages of Tsumago and Magome. Achingly picturesque combinations of rocky hillsides, rivers, waterfalls and forests confound touristic cynicism with their enduring natural beauty. So much so that you appreciate the fact that even the postmen here wear full Edo-period costume. From Magome, some of the Nakasendo's loveliest landscapes unfurl on the steep climb to the Torii Pass, and culminate in the 17th to 19th century treasures of Narai.

One terrific feature of the Nakasendo is the chance to stay in traditional *minshuku* – family-run inns where everyone eats and talks together. It's a rare opportunity for visitors to meet local people – it illuminates the journey.

*The highway weaves its way through villages like Magome.*

**HOW:**
On foot
**WHEN TO GO:**
April to October. Each season creates a new version of the Nakasendo's magic.
**TIME IT TAKES:**
1-12 days. The most popular stretch, Tsumago-Magome, is a 3-4 hour slow ramble, usually as part of a 1-day excursion. Ena-Narai is an easy to moderate 12-day hike of up to 20 km (12 mi) a day, with 2 rest days.
**HIGHLIGHTS:**
The hilarity of composing haiku, partly in sign language, for the Japanese families who run the *minshuku,* where all activities like eating and bathing are communal.
The historical integrity of the road – the restoration along the Ena-Narai section far transcends the usual 'theme-park' approach. This is all genuine and surprisingly moving.
The early morning mists, reinforcing the most powerful aesthetic in the predominant image of old Japan.
**YOU SHOULD KNOW:**
Among the *minshuku* along the Nakasendo's central section are some of Japan's oldest and most famous inns – astonishingly, unwilling to capitalize on their fame and therefore still accessible to all travellers. That really is a cultural shock!

# Shinkansen – the Bullet Train from Osaka to Hiroshima

The high-speed Shinkansen is the pride of Japan Rail, and the core of its entire railway system. Even so, it has its own hierarchy. Though it serves all Japan's major cities, its newest, sleekest, fastest version is reserved for the Tokaido/Sanyo Shinkansen. Powered by the 300-km/188-mph Nozomi Super-Express, it's the Tokyo-Kyoto-Osaka-Hiroshima-Hakata service, connecting the capital with the beautiful coastal region of Sanyo, the southern half of Honshu Island's panhandle, facing the Inland Sea. The Sanyo Shinkansen runs extra services on its section of the route, between Osaka and Hiroshima. The region is a mixture of fruit trees and pasture, backed by wooded hills full of craggy ravines and tumbling streams, but with a fretwork of bays, promontories, coves and offshore islands to further embellish its popularity.

The Shinkansen runs on a route parallel to the much older Sanyo Railway, celebrated for over 100 years as one of Japan's most scenic routes. Much like a dragon on old porcelain, the silver starship of the Shinkansen snakes through the traditional Japanese landscape of ancient, historic towns and villages, and of woods, water and arched bridges. It's a mighty metaphor for Japan's ability to synthesize the future with the past.

As metaphors go, both Osaka and Hiroshima are equally powerful – Osaka, because its history is that of Japan's greatest internal dynastic struggle between the Toyotomi and the Tokugawa; and Hiroshima because of its importance as a symbol of resurrected humanity. In Osaka, the huge castle is a colossus of war, though beautiful and compelling; in Hiroshima, even Peace Park and the Torii Gate on Miyajima reinforce visitors' confrontation with desolation – if only of the mind and common memory. On the Shinkansen between the two cities, you have time for these thoughts.

**HOW:**
By train
**WHEN TO GO:**
Year-round.
**TIME IT TAKES:**
Around two hours (Shin-Osaka to Hiroshima Station)
**HIGHLIGHTS:**
The 16th century Ujo ('Raven') Castle, of Okayama.
The 17th century Koraku-en Garden – one of the three Major Gardens of Japan, it took 14 years to build.
Peace Park in Hiroshima.
Miyajima ('shrine island'), about 40 minutes by local train and ferry from Hiroshima – a profoundly moving memorial of consummate Japanese style.
**YOU SHOULD KNOW:**
Talking on mobile phones is forbidden on all Japanese trains, except in the entrance sections of Shinkansen carriages.

*The Shinkansen speeds through Tokyo.*

# The 88 Temples of the Shikoku Pilgrim Route

**HOW:**
On foot or by bus
**TIME TO GO:**
April to October. It is feasible (for the ascetic) in winter, but some of the more isolated temples are unable to offer winter travellers food or shelter they could otherwise expect.
**TIME IT TAKES:**
60-80 days (on foot); 10-12 days (by pilgrim bus); 6 days (in a fast car). The pilgrimage formally begins and ends with a visit to Mt Koya, the HQ of the Shingon sect of Buddhism, on Honshu. Mt Koya has its own 21-km (13-mi) pilgrim trail, but it's not one of the '88', so even determined hikers usually take the bus. In any case, these visits add 2 days to the total.
**HIGHLIGHTS:**
Every time you hear the phrase *'Gokurosama-deshita'* ('Thank you for your trouble'), which is what tour-bus pilgrims and bystanders throughout Shikoku say when they understand you are walking the entire route. You never get used to this goodwill.
Bathing at Japan's oldest hot spring, Dogo Onsen, near Matsuyama.
Early 17th century Matsuyama Castle, repository of Japanese history.
The stunning natural beauty of south and western Shikoku, where there are far fewer modern interruptions to the ancient footpath and mountain trails.
**YOU SHOULD KNOW:**
The *tsue* (walking stick or staff) is even more important equipment for this hike than the white *henro* coat. Inscribed with the characters *Dogyo Inin* ('we two will walk together'), it is a symbolic replacement for Kobo Daishi. It may seem far-fetched to be walking with the saint, but many pilgrims admit 'thanking' their *tsue* when the staff has saved them from a nasty tumble.

In Shikoku, ancient Japan is no ghost. The smallest of Japan's four main islands, it remains isolated by the Inland Sea despite the increasing development of its north coast cities in the wake of recently improved access to Honshu and Kyushu. Away from this densely populated ribbon of conurbation, Shikoku remains the loveliest and most bucolic region in the country. The south, especially, fits a traditional image of Japan – of fabulous mountain scenery, samurai castles, craft workshops, farming villages where oxen pull creaky wagons, and of small terraces of vegetable or orange trees cut into the hillsides of dense woodland.

This warming, humane landscape is the backdrop to Japan's oldest pilgrim circuit – the 1,450-km (906-mi) journey to 88 shrines established by the 9th century Buddhist priest Kobo Daishi. Every year, more than 100,000 of his followers – called *henro* – complete the rite. Most, devout and determined but subject to modern pressures, do so by bus or car. A small proportion travel on foot, fulfilling the 'walk of life' that Kobo Daishi proposed as an opportunity for self-examination by confrontation with the unexpected and unknown.

And you do confront it: even those who set out merely to enjoy the hiking discover that as a *henro*, they are drawn into a quite novel experience. Pilgrims wear white to show their status. Throughout Shikoku, they find they are the recipient of 1,000 small charities or gifts of food or money. These they must accept in humility as *o-settai*, gifts to help them on their way from people who cannot make the journey themselves. The constant exchange of moral responsibilities and actual goods adds a revelatory dimension to the usual introspections of a long, long hike. However, 1,000 years of pilgrims' comments indicate that the 88 temples hike benefits much more than just leg muscles or lungs.

*A statue stands guard over one of the temples.*

# The Pearl Road

*The pearl farms of Ago Bay*

The Pearl Road is a skyline drive across the coastal edge of the Ise-Shima National Park on the Kii Peninsula in Mie Prefecture east of Nagoya and Nara. It overlooks the saw-tooth ria formations of deep indented bays and complicated fjords facing the Pacific, notably Ago-wan (Ago Bay), south of Toba city, where in 1893 Mikimoto Kokichi produced the first cultured pearl; and which is still the main centre of Japanese pearl production. In fact the Pearl Road begins at Mikimoto Pearl Island, where in addition to memorial statues and pearl museums, you can see the pearl *ama* – the highly trained, women pearl free-divers – at work. But Toba city is principally a resort centre, full of theme parks and huge groups looking for cheap excursion fun, and the Pearl Road provides an escape route to the tranquility of the lovely hills behind the otherwise gorgeous coastline.

It's fair to point out that the unbridled coastal development at Toba and elsewhere in the vicinity (all made misty by distance when you look down from the Pearl Road Observatory) owes its tacky existence to its proximity to one of Japan's most sacred Shinto shrines at Ise City. With so many visitors to the double shrines of Geku and Naiku, it's no wonder developers moved in to cater for them. From the Pearl Road, one side looks down on the shrine precincts. The stylized, traditional wooden buildings are set in ancient forests of sugi (giant cryptomaeria trees), with lakes, ponds and large stone formations of unfathomable symbolism all around. Established in the 3rd and 5th centuries, it's the image of the shrines and not the touristy horrors that you take away with you. They will outlast any modern development – and so will the Pearl Road's naturally beautiful marine landscapes.

**HOW:**
By car or bus
**WHEN TO GO:**
Year-round, it's a lovely region in which to unwind – and easily accessible.
**TIME IT TAKES:**
One hour
**HIGHLIGHTS:**
The Isa Grand Shrines – Naiku houses the sacred mirror of the Emperor – one of the three essential pieces of regalia of the Imperial family.
The isolated, but perfect white sand of Goza Shirahama beach.
A boat trip among the coves and islets of Ago Bay, a marine landscape that changes dramatically with the weather, but always enhanced by the sight of the *ama* (female divers) diving for pearls.
**YOU SHOULD KNOW:**
In the historic city of Matsukaka, below the walls of the magnificent castle there is a row of 19 houses dating back to 1603. Six of them are still occupied by descendants of their original samurai owners.

# The Tokaido Highway

The Tokaido was designated Japan's most important thoroughfare at its creation in 1603. It was to be the Number One highway from the shogun's capital in Edo (Tokyo) to the imperial capital in Kyoto: the coastal route was easier than the alternative mountain route (the Nakasendo). In 1619, it was extended to Osaka, and the 57 official post houses between the Nihonbashi Bridge in Tokyo and Umeda in Osaka defined the heart of Japan's political, economic and social structure. Goods, people, and most of all information passed up and down the Tokaido's length, strictly regulated and efficiently serviced.

They still do, only now they travel on Japan National Route 1 or the Shinkansen, both of which parallel the old road. But the modern highway and express train both cut through hills and shave awkward angles in the name of passenger comfort; and their ribbons of steel and asphalt are anyway hemmed in by buildings and advertising. Almost forgotten, alongside but very much intact, the Tokaido remains, some of it accessible by car, and in some areas like Mie Prefecture, it is 95 per cent intact. Even where the new road is literally on top of the old, the Tokaido is signalled by the shrines, temples and official buildings of its former official status; and one section, in the lovely mountain region between Hakone and Machi has been officially 'preserved' – each November a Daimyo Gyoretsu ('feudal procession') of about 200 people acting as servants, porters, palanquin-carriers and spear-carrying guards re-enacts typical history. Of the rest – the majority – it is astonishing how much survives of the original road fabric. You could use the 1830 pictorial guide of the Tokaido's stages, and still recognize most of it. It is one of Japan's most exciting surprises that you can get so close to its social history.

*The busy Satta Pass, shared by the JR Tokaido Line, the Japan National Highway 1 and the Tomei Expressway.*

# Tokyo Water Cruise

Partly because nobody thinks of Tokyo as a waterfront city, a ride in a *suijo basu* (river bus) provides a completely novel perspective on one of the world's most densely-packed, urban maelstroms. From Hinode Pier green-glassed, sleek double-decker boats like rocket-ships make a futuristic statement for the Sumida River ferry, a service that started in 1885. Now, the ferry carries far more Japanese tourists and visitors than commuters on the 40-minute ride from the mouth of the Sumida River on Tokyo Bay upstream to Asakusa.

The frenzy of the city recedes on the water, and you get an unexpected, 'back-door' view of its working heart. You pass Tsukiji's colossal Wholesale Market for fish and produce; the tidal duck ponds of the moated Hama-Rikyu Tei-En ('Detached Palace Garden'); old lumberyards and warehouses; the landmark green roof of the Kokugikan, housing the arena, museum and HQ of Japanese Sumo Wrestling; and, at Asakusa itself, the giant red lantern of Sensoji Temple, much loved by elderly Japanese.

Four other *suijo* lines start from Hinode, in various guises. The Harbor Cruise Line is a stern paddle-wheeler with a stovepipe stack – take it at dusk as the lights start to twinkle along the shore and across the Rainbow Bridge. Two more serve Odaiba, the massive artificial island in Tokyo Bay. The Odaiba Line goes to Seaside Park, where city folk come to frolic on the shipped-in beach and to practise romance on the boardwalk; the Tokyo Big Sight Line serves the monolithic convention centre and its asphalt grid of office blocks, and the Palette Town shopping malls. Other lines thread the network of manmade islands to the aquarium or the Kasai Sealife Park in Chiba. Travelling by river bus, you get a chance to reflect on what makes Tokyo's energy so exciting.

**HOW:**
By river bus
**WHEN TO GO:**
Year-round (but the illuminations on the Rainbow Bridge and Odaiba shore are revamped for a spectacular evening show throughout August, each year).
**TIME IT TAKES:**
40 minutes (Sumida Line, Hinode-Asakusa); 50 mins (Harbor Cruise Line); 30 minutes (Odaiba Line, Hinode-Seaside Park); 35 minutes (Tokyo Big Sight Line, Hinode-Palette Town); 1 hour (Kasai Sealife Park Line, Hinode-Kasai Rinken Koen/Chiba); 50 minutes (Canal Cruise Line, Hinode-Shinagawa Aquarium).
**HIGHLIGHTS:**
Venus Fort, one of the giant shopping malls in Odaiba.
Plum Grove, at the eastern tip of the 62-acre Hama-Rikyu Gardens – an oasis of sylvan beauty and tranquility, right next to the *suijo* landing stage.
The Museum of Maritime Science on Odaiba: six stories high, shaped like a full-sized ocean liner.
Watching fugu-fish being dissected at the Central Market – only licensed experts are trusted to remove the lethal poisonous bits of one of Japan's most famous delicacies.

*A Tokyo river bus–more like a rocket-ship!*

# Enoshima Electric Railway

**HOW:**
By train
**WHEN TO GO:**
Year-round
**TIME IT TAKES:**
34 minutes (Fujisawa-Kamakura)
**HIGHLIGHTS:**
The woods and flower displays at Inamuragasaki Park, from which you get a wonderful view down the coastline from Shichirigahama to Enoshima, with the Izu islands and Mt Fuji in the misty distance.
The flower temples of Kamakura – like Kaizuoji, Eishoji and Jyoukoumyouji.
Taking an escalator through the woods to the highest point of Enoshima Island – where among the trees is the lovely Enoshima Benzaiten Shrine, a triple Shinto Shrine to the three sister goddesses of the sea.
**YOU SHOULD KNOW:**
The Tokeiji Temple in Kitakamakura (a short walk from the Railway terminus) is particularly famous as a place to break off personal relationships.

It looks like a train, but the Enoshima Electric Railway has the soul of the much-appreciated local tram it used to be. It runs from Fujisawa, 51 km (32 mi) southwest of Tokyo, to the popular seaside resort of Enoshima and on to Kamakura, once capital of Japan and still the religious and historic hub of the Shonan region. The Railway has 15 stations on its 10 km (6 mi) length, with eclectic attractions in the vicinity of each, and there are special tourist tickets available to ensure you miss none of them.

Not even new rolling stock can disguise the Railway's alter ego of Tram. It follows the original tramlines laid out before 1910, at slow speeds determined by the sharp curves between the older buildings. Only near Enoshima Station does it run along the street. Otherwise its narrow-gauge track squeezes between the backs of residential blocks and houses, bursting free of the inelegant tangle of wires and backyard detritus that makes all train journeys fascinating to reveal a procession of sights of extraordinary variety and interest. Most are partly visible from the train itself – like the unusual lighthouse at Enoshima Island, and some of the many shrines and temples for which Hase and Kamakura are famous. Flowers of every colour adorn everything (Meigetsun Temple is actually dedicated to hydrangeas), confirming the region's reputation.

The Enoshima Electric Railway is a humble vehicle, but it takes you to some magical places. Get off at Hase for the 700 year-old brass Great Buddha at Kotoku-in Temple; or Kamakura, with 65 Buddhist temples, 19 Shinto shrines, and historic buildings going back to the city's foundation in 1192. Enoshima Island, a short walk away, offers amazing views of Mount Fuji in the distance, and a restful panorama of the beaches below. It's a marvellous little train.

*The train arrives in the popular seaside resort of Enoshima, with Enoshima Island in the background.*

# The Winding Paths of Soraksan

*Pine trees above the Chonbuldong Valley*

Soraksan (*san* means 'mountain') Nature Reserve sits on the east coast of the central Korean peninsula, behind the South Korean resort city of Sokch'o. The region is a tumbling mass of cracked granite and gneiss peaks, many over 1,200 m (3,936 ft), spread around the highest point, the 1,708 m (5,602 ft) Tae-ch'ongbong.

Threaded with plunging ravines of thick forest, streams and waterfalls, Sorak is full of hidden valleys and unexpected panoramas that take your breath away. A lattice of pathways and hiking trails leads into its remotest depths, but near the Reserve's entrance (just a 15-minute drive from Sokch'o's lovely beaches and resort razzmatazz) you understand what it means to be one of South Korea's most popular recreation sites. Even so, Soraksan has the grandeur to awe the biggest crowds, especially in autumn when its deciduous forests blaze with colour.

Its popularity as a natural wonder is combined with its cultural significance: several of South Korea's most famous temples can be found here. One, Allak-am, is placed above the Yukfam and Piryong waterfalls, celebrating their visual pleasure as an act of worship. Others, ancient structures like Shinhungsa and Anyang-am, are part Buddhist shrine, part working monastery (you may not actually enter the buildings), and part contemplative platform for some of the fantastic rock formations like Biseondae, a platform in the middle of a rushing torrent, or Heundeulbawi, a 5 m (16ft) spherical stone monster on a flat ledge. For centuries, pilgrims and visitors have tried to move it. It rocks but never rolls.

Deep within the Reserve, the hiking paths are rocky, narrow and steep – but effort is rewarded with constant surprise at Soraksan's variety of natural magnificence. In fact, the longer you stay, the more it's clear that Soraksan's paths demonstrate as much of Korea's soul as of its landscapes.

**HOW:**
On foot
**WHEN TO GO:**
Year-round. You can ski in winter, and Sorak's waterways and valleys respond to every shift of season and daily weather – but the reds and golds of autumn are glorious.
**TIME IT TAKES:**
1-14 days. Soraksan's legendary beauty is seductive, and it has many repeat visitors who stay longer each time.
**HIGHLIGHTS:**
The Sorak Cable Car to the Kwongumsong mountain. One way looks out to Sokch'o and the East Sea (NB in Korea you never refer to the Sea of Japan); the other to the immense mysteries – and invitations - of Soraksan's interior.
Trying to move Heundeulbawi.
The tributary streams and valleys of the Chonbuldong Valley – the main route into the heart of Soraksan.
**YOU SHOULD KNOW:**
Throughout Saroksan, especially near the temples, you'll find *ajimas* (temporary stands) selling snacks. One of the local favourites is boiled silkworms, which you recognize by the disgusting smell.

# A Trip to Anak Krakatao

Anak is the offsping of the vanished volcanic island of Krakatao (sometimes incorrectly called Krakatoa). Located in the Sunda Strait between Java and Sumatra, the parent island famously blew apart in the great eruption of 1883, with ensuing tsunamis killing tens of thousands after a 'big bang' that was heard 5,000 km (3,000 mi) away. Starting in 1929, the new island of Anak Krakatao emerged from the sea as the centre point of three encircling islands – the remains of the original Krakatao.

It is an active volcano that is growing steadily. It lies within the remote Ujung Kulon National Park in West Java, created by the Dutch in the late 19th century, and it is possible to find a good selection of cruises that include Anak Krakatao on an itinerary designed to explore this fascinating refuge, which comprises the western tip of Java. This is both

rewarding and the easy way to go – Ujung Kulon is an extraordinary wilderness with no tourist infrastructure, so a do-it-yourself journey to this magical place is a real backpacking adventure.

Even so, those who are interested only in vulcanology can make a dedicated journey to Anak Krakatao. Depending on current volcanic activity, it is possible to land and camp on the vegetated eastern shore of this young volcano before scrambling to the cone's summit – a demanding hike up a steep slope covered in lightweight ejecta (pumice-like rocks) that will take around two hours. But this is not a simple enterprise – the jump-off point is the port of Carita, a 120-km (75-mi) drive from Jakarta that alone takes the best part of half a day. From there, it is possible to hire a dilapidated fishing boat out to the Krakatao Islands, for the unique pleasure of exploring the world's most violent volcano.

# Gunung Agung Volcano Scenic Route

**HOW:**
By car or bike
**WHEN TO GO:**
Any time of year
**TIME IT TAKES:**
Make the journey by car in 90 minutes, at the gentle pace demanded by the not-always-perfect road surface. Cycle it in half a day.
**HIGHLIGHTS:**
Sideman, off the road between Selat and Duda, for stunning views down a valley of traditional rice terraces, over South Bali to the sea.
Sampling delicious *salak* (a curious local fruit with a covering that looks like snakeskin) – available from roadside stalls as you go.
Near Sibetan – a short side trip north to Jungutan to see the Tirta Telaga Tista pool and garden complex built for the Rajah of Karangasem.
Superb metalwork available at Bebandem and surrounding villages, home of the island's iron- and silver-working craftsmen.
**YOU SHOULD KNOW:**
Rendang is both the start point of the scenic drive and the name given to the classic Indonesian spicy meat dish served on ceremonial occasions and to honour guests.

*Rice fields below Mount Gunung Agung*

The island of Bali is Indonesia's top tourist destination and – with stunning sandy beaches in white (to the south) or black (to the north) – it's easy to understand why so many people flock to this tropical paradise. And the island has a warm heart – the active volcano of Gunung Agung in East Bali's traditional Karangasem region, where local culture survives largely intact. This impressive peak rises above the mountains that form Bali's spine, towering to a height of 3,142 m (10,308 ft), and it is the site of Pura Besakih, Bali's sacred mother temple. The peak appears conical, but this fact actually conceals a massive summit crater. Strangely, Gunung Agung is covered in lush vegetation on the western side, whilst the eastern flank is barren.

The best way to appreciate the brooding presence of this mighty volcano is to drive (or cycle) the scenic route along Gunung Agung's southern side from Rendang to the village of Bebandem near Amlapura (there is no public transport to speak of). This delightful road runs through exceptional countryside with water flowing everywhere, descending gradually as it proceeds in an easterly direction.

Reached via an attractive minor road from Bangli, Rendang is a pretty little town. From there, the winding road passes through the village of Muncan, set amidst some of the most attractive rice country on the island. The next ports of call are Selat and Pura Pasa Agung – starting point for the easier southern hiking route up Gunung Agung (the northern route is tougher, and the two are entirely separate). The road continues through Duda, and Sibetan to Bebandem. From there, it's a short step to the bustling centre of Amlapura – this old royal town is still the capital of East Bali, though somewhat reduced in importance after being isolated for three years following Gunung Agung's last major eruption, in 1963.

# Jakarta to Bandung

One striking landmark in the centre of Jakarta in West Java is Gambir Station, with its lime green ceramic façade. Built by the Dutch colonial authorities in the 1930s and recently renovated, this is the main starting point for long-distance trains to other major cities in the south and east – including one of Indonesia's most scenic railway journeys, the 180-km (110-mi) trip from Jakarta to Bandung.

The trains to choose between are the fully air-conditioned Argo Gede executive express and the Parahyangan executive and business class express (no air-con in the latter category, a feature which anyone who wilts in tropical heat will definitely miss!). These trains travel in daylight hours to ensure that visitors can appreciate the passing countryside. This is a rewarding exercise, as the route goes through some fabulous scenery. The Argo Gede is more expensive and faster, the Parahyangan slightly cheaper and slower.

To be sure of securing an A seat that delivers the best views on the outward journey (from the left side of the train) it is wise to book in advance. As the train begins its journey south from Jakarta, the outlook seems pleasant enough if rather ordinary – but don't demand your money back, as the most impressive landscapes will appear during the latter part of the trip, after the line starts climbing into the tranquil highlands. Along the way it passes through tunnels, also crossing spectacular viaducts, huge bridges and steel trestles constructed more than a century ago by Dutch engineers. The lush scenery has – to a degree – been shaped by man, with endless terraced rice paddies against a mountain backdrop.

Bustling Bandung is located in the highlands – a factor that made it a classic hill station in colonial times, where the Dutch could retreat to obtain cool relief from the sweltering lowlands.

*Crossing a high trestle-bridge near Bandung.*

**HOW:**
By train

**WHEN TO GO:**
Any time of year

**TIME IT TAKES:**
Just under three hours (by Argo Gede), three-and-a-half hours (by Parahyangan)

**HIGHLIGHTS:**
The Cibodas Botanical Garden at Cianjur – this fabulous garden at the foot of Mount Gede near Jakarta displays the tropical and highland flora of western Indonesia.
Factory shop outlets – find them everywhere in Indonesia (but especially Jakarta and Bandung).
The extraordinary Pasupati Bridge in Bandung, opened in 2005, boldly crosses above residential areas.
Bandung's wealth of fine colonial-era buildings erected by the Dutch, many in the splendid tropical Art Deco style.

**YOU SHOULD KNOW:**
Beware aggressive Madurese ticket touts at Gambir Station – use only the special offices that sell tickets for the luxury trains.

# Gunung Rinjani Trek

**HOW:**
On foot
**WHEN TO GO:**
April to November (to avoid the rainy season)
**TIME IT TAKES:**
Four days
**HIGHLIGHTS:**
Forest life – a huge variety of birds, butterflies and (if you're lucky) a glimpse of a rare black ebony leaf monkey.
Bathing away the aches and pains of a hard day's trekking in the hot springs of the crater lake.
Sunrise at the summit – the final climb is always done before dawn, so trekkers can enjoy the truly awe-inspiring sunrise.
**YOU SHOULD KNOW:**
The name 'Gunung Rinjani' comes from an old Chinese word meaning 'the place where a child was born' – and indeed a new caldera is rising within the summit lake.

One of the most spectacular volcanoes in Indonesia is Gunung Rinjani on the island of Lombok. The forested sides of the country's third-tallest mountain rise to a height of 3,726 m (12,224 ft) and the spectacular summit crater contains the vast, sacred lake of Segara Anak. Despite frequent eruptions, the lower slopes are intensely cultivated.

There are many well-used routes up Gunung Rinjani from surrounding villages, as locals believe the volcano is the abode of deities and make regular pilgrimages to the lake, where they leave offerings and try to bathe away illness in the hot springs. The most usual start point for a climb to the summit is Sembalun Lawang to the east.

For those who want more than a simple ascent, one of the best short expeditions in Southeast Asia is the Rinjani Trek from Senaru in the north, over the summit and down to Sembalun Lawang. Gunung Rinjani is a National Park, and this rewarding trek is a model for eco-tourism. The Rinjani Trek Centre in Senaru embodies a partnership between the National Park, local people and the tourist industry, which should ensure that – whilst this special place can be enjoyed by those prepared to make the effort – it will never be spoiled.

And effort is required, though any reasonably fit participant can undertake the tough challenge. This is a guided trek that involves overnight camping on the mountain. It begins with a steep ascent through tropical forest and alpine meadows to the Senaru crater rim. The route traverses the spectacular rim ridge and descends to the emerald crater lake, before climbing back up the steep crater to the Sembalun rim. From there it's a hard climb to the summit, before the final descent to Sembalun Lawang to complete a memorable adventure.

*The still active volcano rumbles on.*

# Puerto Princesa Subterranean River Trip

*Entering the cave at Sabang Beach.*

If you want to visit a UNESCO World Heritage Site like no other, the Puerto Princesa (sometimes Saint Paul's) Subterranean River National Park offers a unique experience. Located in the Saint Paul Mountains 50 km (30 mi) north of the city of Puerto Princesa on the island of Palawan, the Park consists of a dramatic limestone karst landscape with a full mountain-to-sea ecosystem that includes important forests.

But the star feature is undoubtedly the navigable underground river that winds through a cave before discharging directly into an aquamarine lagoon on the South China Sea, a fact that makes the lower reaches of the river tidal. Access is from Sabang Beach – but be warned: the last part of the journey there will rattle your teeth, as the unmade road is awful. Once at Sabang, a permit to travel the river is obtainable from the National Park office. A 30-minute boat ride with great landscape views takes you to the river entrance. Alternatively, this can be a pleasant 90-minute hike along the Monkey Trail that takes in a great swimming beach along the way (no swimming is permitted near the river mouth).

From there, the journey continues in an outrigger canoe, a single lamp illuminating the extraordinary geological formations of the lofty cavern within. The knowledgeable guide will be a mine of information on life within this wondrous place – including fish, bats and the swiftlets whose nests are coveted for soup – as he quietly paddles around showing you the best stalactites and stalagmites. Although 8 km (5 mi) of this hauntingly beautiful underground river has been mapped, only 4 km (2.5 mi) is deemed navigable. A special permit is required to explore the full navigable stretch, as the regular tour covers just 1.5 km (1 mi).

**HOW:**
By boat
**WHEN TO GO:**
Any time of year
**TIME IT TAKES:**
Around an hour for the basic river tour.
**HIGHLIGHTS:**
The leisurely 20-hour ship crossing from Manila's South Harbour to Palawan – a worthwhile journey in its own right.
Exploring the amazing forests and limestone formations to be found above ground in the National Park.
Getting up close to the extraordinary (and fearless) monitor lizards that frequent the forest and shoreline.
**YOU SHOULD KNOW:**
If you have a picnic in the National Park don't look away for a second – the long-tailed macaque monkeys are grand masters of food-theft strategy.

*Rice fields at Banaue*

# Banaue to Sagada By Road

Asia's cities are mostly dirty, crowded places full of frenetic activity, but the very opposite is true of vast swathes of the continent's unspoiled countryside, where life often seems to go on pretty much as it has for centuries. Nowhere is this contrast more obvious than on the island of Luzon. To the south is the sprawling metropolis of Manila complete with 14 million people, while to the north is the sparsely populated Cordillera mountain range that forms the island's spine.

Enjoying the unspoiled delights of the latter is no mean feat – by definition there is little tourist infrastructure and – far from the heavy hand of central government – the local Igorot people seem to be inclined to make sure that it stays that way. The two villages that must be seen are Banaue and Sagada. Reaching Banaue is a fairly major undertaking, with the usual method being jeep rental (with or without driver) in Manila, followed by an all-day drive. Be sure to make an early start, as Banaue shuts down for the night in the early evening.

The drive from Banaue to Sagada is awesome. The mountain scenery alone is breathtaking, with countless rushing streams and hilltops rolling away to the distant Mount Pulog, Luzon's highest point. But the bonus is the display of extraordinary rice terraces, created on the hillsides by Igorots over millennia. The road winds down into Bontoc Valley, and then makes the steep climb back up to Sagada, dramatically presented against a backdrop of limestone cliffs and pine forests.

It's more than tempting to make a full day of it, stopping to explore rice paddies, caves, forests and waterfalls, with a leisurely pause for a lunch of smoked meat, red rice and corn washed down with a glass (or two) of the local wine.

# Rice Terrace Hike

Once you've braved the difficulties of reaching the Cordilleras of northern Luzon, it's imperative to make the most of a very special place. The most striking feature of these mountains is provided by serried ranks of narrow rice terraces that climb the hillsides – now collectively listed as a UNESCO World Heritage Site. After allowing the high-maintenance terraced paddies to decline somewhat, the local Igorot people have found a new pride in their heritage following the UNESCO listing and a profitable trickle of tourists.

The way to appreciate fully the endeavour that went into creating and maintaining these extraordinary two-thousand-year-old man-made ledges is to get up close and personal by taking a hike. The paddies, with their high earthen walls, green pools and constantly trickling water, are often divided by bright red chongla plants. They are criss-crossed with paths and steps and there are numerous farms and dwellings that often look identical. It's easy to get disorientated, but local children are happy to act as guides for a few pesos and this is a worthwhile investment.

Having reached bustling Banaue, an onward trek to the less busy village of Batad shows the rice terraces at their very best. It is necessary to drive from Banaue to the Batad junction, and from there up to the Saddle, which is the jumping-off point for the hike. There is ample casual accommodation in the village, and it is best to stay overnight rather than make it a day trip – the return journey to the Saddle up the steep mountain path is strenuous and can take two hours or more. The village sits at the bottom of a natural amphitheatre formed by the curving, terraced hillsides, and the opportunity to stay for a while and do some exploring should not be missed.

**HOW:**
On foot
**WHEN TO GO:**
April or May when the swaying expanses of rice are at their pre-harvest best.
**TIME IT TAKES:**
About 90 minutes (by car) to the Saddle, then another 90 minutes from there down to Batad.
**HIGHLIGHTS:**
Extending the hike to the fabulous Tappiya Falls beyond Batad, where the superb outlook and a cooling swim will be a great reward for the climb.
A 15-minute side trip down steep steps from the Banaue-Sagada road to the unspoiled and traditional farming village of Bangaan amidst its own rice terraces.
Whilst in the Banaue area – a visit to Poitan, a village noted for artisan weaving and wood carving.
**YOU SHOULD KNOW:**
The rainy season (June to August) often makes roads and tracks in the area impassable.

*The rice terraces of Bangaan*

# Death Railway and the Bridge over the River Kwai

**HOW:**
By train
**WHEN TO GO:**
October to April
**TIME IT TAKES:**
Two days to see it all – over-nighting at Kanchanaburi.
**HIGHLIGHTS:**
Kanchanaburi POW Cemetery.
Chung Kai POW Cemetery.
The Thailand-Burma Railway Museum.
JEATH War Museum.
The Sound and Light show at the Bridge, commemorating the Allied bombing attack in 1945 – held annually, during the first week of December.
**YOU SHOULD KNOW:**
Two bridges were built here simultaneously: a wooden one was completed a couple of months before the steel bridge still used today. The river itself was originally named the Mae Khlung, but after the book and film, which erroneously called it the River Kwai, so many people came to the area that the practically-minded Thais decided to re-name it.

*Bridge over the River Kwai*

The journey along the infamous Death Railway and across the Kwai River Bridge is one of Thailand's best-known journeys, taken by thousands of people each year. Some simply want to experience the place, but others come to visit the spot where family members lost their lives.

In 1942, the Japanese needed an alternative supply route for their forces in Burma other than the dangerous sea voyage where they were under attack. They decided on a railway that had to be cut through difficult terrain of remote, jungle-clad hills. Tragically, there was an unlimited workforce to hand – 61,000 Allied prisoners of war, of whom 16,000 died here, and an enslaved population of some 200,000 Burmese, Thais, Malaysians and Indonesians, of whom 80,000 lost their lives.

Trains leave from Bangkok's Thonburi station, along the Death Railway line itself, reaching Kanchanaburi, before crossing the bridge. You can descend at the station just south of the Bridge and walk across the wooden planks, or just stay on board and rattle over at 10 km (6 mi) per hour. If you continue to the terminus at Nam Tok you will pass over the Wampo Viaduct, also POW-built. Looking at the lush vegetation and the tranquil river views it seems unimaginable that some of the worst horrors of war took place here less than 70 years ago.

About 80 km (50 mi) north of Kanchanaburi, on a section of line that has long been disused, is Hellfire Pass. Here the Australian Government, in collaboration with the Thais, has founded a museum and cleared a 7-km (4-mi) piece of track along which are memorial plaques to the fallen. Walkers leave mementos such as flowers, letters, even jars of vegemite: a sight that almost moves you to tears even if you have no direct involvement.

# Cheow Lan Lake and Nam Talu Cave

Located in Thailand's southern province of Surat Thani, roughly halfway between the country's two coastlines, is the wonderful Khao Sak National Park. Covering an area of 739 sq km (285 sq mi), the park comprises the largest area of ancient rainforest in southern Thailand, complete with stunning karst topography – the highest formation is 960 m (3,200 ft). There are several different trails within the park, but one of the most exciting is to explore Cheow Lan Lake and Nam Talu Cave.

Cheow Lan was formed when the Ratchaprapha Dam was built in 1982. Some 169 sq km (65 sq mi), it is surrounded by rainforest and limestone crags, and contains over 100 islands. Basing yourself at one of the simple, bamboo floating bungalow operations, you can enjoy a few days of swimming and exploring the lake by kayak or canoe,

This is the best way of viewing the wealth of wildlife in the surrounding forests, and admiring the multitudes of birds, in particular, hornbills – Helmeted, Great and Wreathed hornbills live here, along with kingfishers, parrots, flycatchers, herons and many more. Sitting quietly in a small cove, you'll see gibbons and macaques in the trees nearby, apparently totally unconcerned by the presence of humans.

Your local guide will take you through the rainforest to Nam Talu cave. After beaching the kayak, you walk for a couple of kilometres looking out for tree snakes, orchids and otters, which inhabit the stream that winds its way through the jungle, to the 30-m (99-ft) entrance, inside which you will see stalactites, stalagmites and eroded stone formations. Thousands of bats inhabit this cave, which takes 90 minutes to walk through, but be warned: a stream runs through it, waist deep in parts, which has to be waded through.

*Canoe and raft house on Cheow Lan Lake*

**HOW:**
On foot and by kayak
**WHEN TO GO:**
December to April
**TIME IT TAKES:**
1 to 3 days or more
**HIGHLIGHTS:**
The extraordinarily diverse rainforest – tall trees, bamboo, ferns, lianas, etc.
The rich and varied wildlife, including wild Asian elephants.
Rafflesia kerri – the second largest flower in the world.
The reflections of the islands and surrounding limestone peaks in the calm, green water of the lake.
**YOU SHOULD KNOW:**
The region receives a great deal of rain, so bring good walking shoes, insect repellent, sunscreen, and a change of clothing in case you get soaked. In 2007 six tourists and two guides were drowned in a flash flood in Nam Talu Cave – take advice and use your own common sense before going there.

**REGENT HOUSE**

**HOW:**
By train
**WHEN TO GO:**
All year round, but best between October and April
**TIME IT TAKES:**
About one hour from end to end
**HIGHLIGHTS:**
The views over Bangkok from the elevated trains.
The welcome respite from the heat.
Nipping up to Mo Chit station on the Sukhumvit line to visit Chatuchak Weekend Market.
Saphan Taksin Station where you can join an express boat and take a trip on the river.
Siam station, where you can change lines or jump out and walk to one of the many shopping malls for some retail therapy.
**YOU SHOULD KNOW:**
Bangkok now has a super modern metro that covers different areas to the Skytrain. There are currently three interchanges with Skytrain, and the metro does go to Hua Lamphong, the main train station.

# Bangkok Skytrain

The Skytrain has changed the face of travel in Bangkok. It used to be a nightmare of a city where one could easily spend two hours travelling a distance of about 5 km (3 mi) because the weight of traffic was bringing the whole place to a grinding halt. All this changed on 5 December 1999, King Bhumibol's birthday, when the Skytrain opened.

Approached by stairs and escalators, the ultra-modern elevated stations are airy, spacious, clean and safe. The platforms are marked to show where the carriage doors will open and, at rush hour, passengers queue up behind one another at these entry points, rather than filling the whole space. Inside there is plenty of sitting and standing room, and air-conditioning ensures a pleasant temperature even when it is sweltering outside.

After a slow start, the Skytrain has really taken off, carrying passengers throughout the day, from 6.00 am to midnight. Apart from the miracle of being able to get around speedily, the train is fun to be on. Passengers get a fascinating, bird's eye view of the city. Not only is one amazed by the vast quantity of skyscrapers, a symphony of chrome, steel, glass and concrete but, in amongst the hyper-modernity are glimpses of ancient temples, their sweeping roofs glittering red and gold in the sunlight, housing stock that varies from villas with flower-decked gardens to slums whose grimy windows are cheek by jowl with the track, advertising hoardings, monuments, traffic circulating and Thais going about their business.

Several of the stations are linked to 'skywalks', elevated walkways leading to nearby shopping malls and other amenities such as the National Stadium, the Chao Praya River and the wonderful Chatuchak Weekend Market. The Skytrain, due to be extended, will eventually cross the river to Thonburi, and run out to Bangkok's new airport.

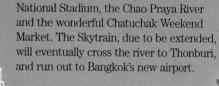

# Maeklong Railway – Bangkok to Samut Songkhram

**HOW:**
By train
**WHEN TO GO:**
Any time, but October to April is
probably best
**TIME IT TAKES:**
It should only take about an hour, but
the two trains don't connect
properly, making the trip more like
half a day.
**HIGHLIGHTS:**
Damnoen Saduak Floating Market.
Wat Sratthatham, a temple built of
golden teak and inlaid with
mother-of-pearl.
The sandbar of Don Hoi Lot, famous
for its endemic
crustacean population.
Ban Maeo Thai Boran – where
genuine Siamese cats are bred
and conserved.
**YOU SHOULD KNOW:**
In 1811 the Siamese twins Chang
and Eng were born in Samut
Songkhram. Joined at the chest, the
twins were taken to the UK and the
USA and shown to the public,
bringing Siam, as Thailand was then
known, to the attention of the world.
The twins lived to the age of 63.

*The Damnoen Saduak
Floating Market*

Built privately around the turn of the last century, the Maeklong Railway brought seafood from the fishing ports of Samut Sakhon and Samut Songkram to Bangkok – a distance of about 75 km (47 mi). The line was never connected to the main rail system, no longer carries freight, and is one of the capital's better-kept secrets.

Leaving from Bangkok's west bank Wong Wian Yai station, take the train to Mahachai. Trundling along a single narrow track, you soon leave the city behind and find yourself in a fertile landscape of coconut palms, banana plants, lychee, guava and white pomelo orchards, interspersed with canals. There are numerous tiny stations along the way – blink and you'll miss them – and the train slows as it approaches barrier-free road crossings, so the driver can check that there is no approaching traffic.

Mahachai, confusingly, is the station for Samut Sakhon. Renowned for its fish, it has a fabulous fresh seafood market and a multitude of restaurants. It is also where you leave the train to take a small ferry across the Tha Chin River to the station on the other side. Here you take another train to Samut Songkhram's Maeklong terminus. This second section of line passes through an area of salt production and prawn farms. Sitting on the left side, you see fields full of shallow, saltwater ponds. When drained, the salt is raked into piles, bagged up and sent off by road.

All too soon the journey comes to an end – but this is almost the best bit, as the line goes through the middle of a large, colourful market. Stallholders clear awnings and goods from the track as the train approaches, putting them all back together again the moment it has passed, like the sea closing behind the wake of a ship.

# Scenic Route to Chiang Dao Caves

The lovely northern city of Chiang Mai makes an excellent base for many different explorations. For this journey you'll need your own transport, to enable you to enjoy a roundabout journey to the Chiang Dao Caves, taking in some unusual, and un-touristy places en route.

Travelling north from Chiang Mai, take Route 107 – you'll soon see a sign to your left pointing to the Hill Tribe Museum. Set in Rama IX Lanna Park, which also contains a golf course, shooting range, fishing lake and the city's racecourse, this interesting little museum contains a wealth of information about Thailand's six main hill tribes as well as other, minor tribal groups. Continuing north you will find the Model Centre of Learning, a project where young Thais learn various handicrafts, and where visitors can see how raw cotton and silk are turned into beautiful lengths of fabric.

The next stop on your journey is the Dara Pirom Palace, former home of Princess Dara Rasamee and an absolute gem of a place, full of fascinating personal effects and objects that give an insight into the royal lifestyle as it was lived about 100 years ago. Further north still and you turn off onto the small Route 3010, winding through the forest to the much-revered Four Buddhas' Temple. Redeveloped over the years, it stands in a tranquil forest setting, little visited by foreigners.

Finally, return to the main road, and head to Chiang Dao. You'll pass an elephant training camp on the way – well worth a visit if you have time. The cave complex is well signed and much visited: there are 100 named caves here, stretching over 10 km (6 mi) into the mountain. Currently only five can be explored, and you'll need to take a guide with a lantern for three of them.

*Elephant camp near Chiang Dao*

**HOW:**
By car
**WHEN TO GO:**
Any time but October to April is probably best.
**TIME IT TAKES:**
This is a day trip
**HIGHLIGHTS:**
Doi Suthep, Chiang Mai's 1676-m (5,500-ft) peak, with its sacred temple, winter palace and delightful National Park.
Trekking in the mountains north of Chiang Mai.
Rafting on the Kok River from Fang.
Pai – this is some peoples idea of heaven.
**YOU SHOULD KNOW:**
North east of Chiang Mai is the area known as the Golden Triangle, where Thailand, Burma and Laos meet, and where many of the world's opium poppies are grown. These days you'll notice the tourists rather than the opium dens, but it is still exciting to stand in one country and see two more across the river.

*The red roofs of Lang Co village*

# Hue to Hoi An on Highway 1

**HOW:**
By car
**WHEN TO GO:**
January to April
**TIME IT TAKES:**
4 – 5 hours
**HIGHLIGHTS:**
The Cham Museum, founded in 1915,
with its wonderful selection of ethnic
sculpture and carving dating from
the 7th to 15th centuries.
The Bach Ma National Park, 40 km
(25 mi) south of Hue – a mountain
nature reserve with waterfalls, lush
vegetation and superb coastal views.
A stop at the fabulous Lang Co
beach south of Hue, with the great
backdrop of the Rang Cua
Mountains.
The thousand stone-carving
craftsmen of Non Nuoc village at the
foot of the Marble Mountains near
Da Nang.
**YOU SHOULD KNOW:**
Take a half-empty suitcase and buy
some custom-made 'designer'
clothes in Hoi An – the many skilled
local tailors can copy anything (from
a magazine picture) at bargain prices.

The Hue, Da Nang and Hoi An coastal strip is one of the most-visited areas in Vietnam, with a great deal to offer. It is close to the former DMZ (Demilitarized Zone) between the old North and South, which were divided by the Ben Hai River. Much of the fighting in the 1960s Vietnam War took place thereabouts, and many interesting relics of that traumatic time remain to this day.

The Vietnamese Imperial City of Hue suffered serious damage in the conflict, but this UNESCO World Heritage Site remains a fascinating place that merits exploration. Hue is also the starting point for the drive south along Highway 1 via Da Nang to Hoi An. This magnificent coastal route is in much better shape than many roads in Vietnam, twisting and turning above the sea and rising to a dramatic high point at the Hai Van Pass (though a tunnel is under construction) where the panoramic view is sensational.

After crossing the pass, it's worth stopping at Da Nang to relax for a while on the splendid China Beach – though in fact there are other, rather more cultural side trips to consider here. These include the World Heritage Site of My Son, centre of the ancient kingdom of Cham and the extraordinary Marble Mountains, which are sculpted limestone hills containing pagodas, temples and grottos dedicated to Buddhist, Taoist and Confucian divinities.

Upon completing the scenic journey to Hoi An, the first thing to do is to explore the quaint old town, yet another World Heritage Site – be sure not to miss the Hoi An Museum, Phuc Kien Communal House, the Japanese Covered Bridge and the ancient Vietnamese houses. Another worthwhile outing is up the Thu Bon River to see traditional boatbuilding, woodworking and pottery-making villages like Kim Bong and Thanh Ha.

# Heaven's Gate Pass

Fancy going to Heaven...on a bicycle? It can be arranged in Vietnam's Northern Highlands, also known as the Tonkinese Alps, where one of the most scenic bike rides in South-east Asia can be experienced. The Heaven's Gate Pass (Tram Tom in local parlance) is the literal high point, but for those who want more it's possible to plan a longer guided trip that will tour through hill country along the Chinese border – a place populated by tribes with a distinctive culture that wear beautiful local dress and have definitely not been turned into hustlers by the few tourist dollars that have come their way.

To undertake this marvelous cycle ride, first take the overnight train from Hanoi across the Red River and on to Lao Cai. From there, a minibus will convey you and your trusty steed up through an impressive landscape of rice terraces to the picturesque village of Sa Pa, below Heaven's Gate. The onward climb from Sa Pa is steep, but the effort is worthwhile – after a refreshing pause at the Silver Waterfall, 3 km (2 mi) from the summit, more physical effort gets you to the top of the world...and the considerable rewards for Herculean pedal-pushing.

You've reached the summit of the highest pass in Indochina, and the views of mountains and the Hoang Lien Valley below are breathtaking (assuming you've got any breath left to take). Having made it to the top, it's possible to turn around and let gravity hurry you back down to Lao Cai. Alternatively, you can coast down the far side into a land of precipitous rice paddies, remote traditional villages, rickety suspension bridges, stilt houses and ox carts. For those who love wild and unspoiled places, that is indeed a heavenly journey.

**HOW:**
By bike
**WHEN TO GO:**
March to May or September to November
**TIME IT TAKES:**
4-5 hours of hard pedaling from Sa Pa to the summit of Heaven's Gate Pass.
**HIGHLIGHTS:**
Sa Pa's Bac Ha bustling market for a slice of local life at its most authentic...and colourful.
Village-made tamarind candy – washed down with a slug of cassava, the local firewater.
A trip to Hoang Lien National Park near Sa Pa, where one of the most diverse landscapes and ecosystems in Indochina is being preserved.
The wonderful view of the lofty Fansipan peak from the summit of Heaven's Gate (assuming it isn't shrouded in mist!).
**YOU SHOULD KNOW:**
Don't be surprised if you get smiles from the locals that cause you to do a double take – the women of the local Lu tribe dye their teeth black.

*The terraced farmland around Sa Pa*

481

# Hanoi Unification Express

This is a train journey that time forgot. The term 'express' is used loosely, as in averaging around 50 kph (30 mph) as opposed to the 15 kph (10 mph) achieved by local trains on the single track connecting Ho Chi Minh City (formerly Saigon) to Hanoi in the north. This amazing 1,725-km (1,100-mi) railroad was built by the French along Vietnam's coastal spine a century ago and passes through wonderful countryside, though in truth the real reason for riding the Unification Express is to experience a railway journey like no other. There are four trains a day in each direction, ranging from the slow to the very slow. For all that, the service is reliable and does get there eventually.

Rolling stock is old-fashioned (with crude toilets amongst other drawbacks) and the train will be hot and crowded. There is a choice of seat (hard or not-very-soft) and sleeper (yes, hard or not-very-soft). Possessions left unwatched for a second will vanish like smoke in the wind. There will be frequent stops on sidings to allow trains to pass in the opposite direction and hordes of hustlers selling everything from food and drink to fake designer goods will appear at every stop. But this is a fascinating and worthwhile journey that will not only convey you through beautiful scenery, but also provide the opportunity to meet the people and experience the reality of Vietnamese life.

For those who don't want to experience the rough-and-tumble of an end-to-end journey on the Unification Express, there are organized guided tours that make use of the train with plenty of stop-offs and side trips to see selected sights along the way. In any event it is possible to break the journey without penalty for a little self-chosen exploration.

*All aboard!*

*A Dragon Boat on the Perfume River*

# Perfume River Dragon Boat Trip

Though not yet described as 'The Venice of the East', the imperial city of Hue – former capital of Vietnam's Nguyen Dynasty – is divided by the Perfume River and has numerous canals. So taking to the water is a great way to see the city's sights, and the famed Hue Dragon Boats – the local motorized equivalent of Venetian gondolas – are the way to travel. These long-tailed, brightly painted boats ply the Perfume River, and most do indeed have some resemblance to those fearsome if mythical fire-breathers, though tending to be of rather haphazard construction.

It's possible to enjoy the Dragon Boat experience by taking one as though it were a water taxi. Any trip around town will have the added dimension of revealing the sights and sounds of Hue's busy river life, with houseboats everywhere, laden sampans heading for market or undertaking another important mission like sand dredging...and of course there are more of those in-your-face Dragon Boats at every turn. This in itself is a worthwhile outing.

But the Hue area has many fascinating monuments and historical sights, and a Dragon Boat journey up river through lush countryside is a splendid way of visiting some of the best. There are many options to choose from, but a typical tour will include the Linh Mu (Thien Mu) Pagoda, Hon Chen Temple, Tu Duc Tomb, Emperor Minh Mang's Tomb amidst tranquil gardens and lakes and Khai Dinh Tomb. Some require a moto-taxi from the bank and the stops (usually 30 to 45 minutes) are not long enough to allow proper exploration, as these tombs are often large complexes. However, the Dragon Boat trip is an experience in its own right, and it's always possible to return on another day and spend more time at particular sights.

**HOW:**
By boat
**WHEN TO GO:**
Any time (January to April is best; from June to August it sometimes rains very hard).
**TIME IT TAKES:**
Around eight hours for a typical day tour by Dragon Boat.
**HIGHLIGHTS:**
A Dragon Boat ride to Thuan An Beach for a bit of typical tropical sun-sea-and-sand relaxation.
Sunset over the Perfume River – take a stroll beside the river as night falls for a wonderfully romantic light show.
A side trip to the Imperial Citadel of the Nguyen Dynasty, damaged by American bombing during the Tet Offensive of 1968 but partially restored and still mightily impressive.
**YOU SHOULD KNOW:**
The Perfume River is so named from the traditional ritual of scattering flower petals on the water.

# Saigon to Angkor Wat

**HOW:**
By bike
**WHEN TO GO:**
November to February
**TIME IT TAKES:**
Allow at least 10 days, with a day each in Phnom Penh and Angkor Wat.
**HIGHLIGHTS:**
A visit to the extraordinary Caodai Great Temple at Tay Ninh, headquarters of Caodaism, one of Vietnam's most interesting religions.
A tour of Phnom Penh, 'The Pearl of Asia' – Cambodia's capital with its wonderful Khmer temples and classic colonial architecture.
Taking a side trip into the beautiful Kiriom National Park with its pine forests, orchids, waterfalls and the Cham Bok Pagoda.
The temples of Angkor Wat, abandoned for centuries, rediscovered in the 1800s and justifiably regarded as one of the wonders of the world.
**YOU SHOULD KNOW:**
If cycling isn't your thing, the Saigon-Angkor Wat journey can be done on water, cruising up the mighty Mekong and along the Tonlé Sap River.

*Cyclists at sunrise, with Angkor Wat in the background*

Don't be afraid to refer to Ho Chi Minh City as Saigon – most of the local people still do. And it's from Saigon that one of Indochina's great cycling expeditions begins, taking the adventurous pedal-pusher from the former capital of South Vietnam through the Mekong Delta and on to the drier country and contrasting sights of Cambodia, ending at the ancient city of Angkor Wat. This fabulous testament to the Khmer civilization was built between the 9th and 12th centuries and is now a stunning UNESCO World Heritage Site.

With proper planning this can be a solo journey, though it does involve travelling light, buying provisions and finding accommodation as you go. It is also possible to find organized groups who are undertaking this marathon ride, where kit can be sent on ahead to pre-booked overnight stops – these are often sponsored trips arranged by charities. There are endless choices of route to follow, but one well tried and proven journey is from Saigon via My Tho, Tra Vinh, Can Tho, Long Xuyen, Chau Doc, Nha Bang (on the Cambodian border), Takeo, Phnom Penh, Tang Krasang and Phumi Loveay to Siem Riep (from whence to Angkor Wat).

This scenic route is not physically demanding, as the countryside is fairly flat. It weaves through rubber plantations, crosses rivers and passes through the paddy fields and lush countryside of the Mekong Delta before crossing into Cambodia – a land of traditional villages, busy markets, ancient temples and colourful pagodas. The locals do not see many foreigners, and those who venture into remote country areas on uncrowded back roads are invariably the subjects of great curiosity, especially to children. But the interesting passers-by from another world are invariably received with warmth and hospitality in these rural backwaters.

# Ho Chi Minh Trail

The Ho Chi Minh Trail began in North Vietnam, cut through the mountains and wound its way hundreds of miles south through both Laos and Cambodia and the various mountain passes along the way enabled access to South Vietnam. It was not simply a single road, but a maze of up to 19,000 km (12,000 mi) of trails passing through triple canopy jungle, karst mountains and open grassland.

This remarkable route enabled troops, arms and supplies to be moved south towards Saigon. As much of it was invisible from the air, the USA began a massive, secret campaign of bombing and defoliation, particularly in Laos, a country with which they were not at war. Between 1964 and 1973, over two million tonnes of bombs were dropped on Laos, making it the most heavily bombed country in history. Absolutely no reparations were offered subsequently, leaving eastern parts of Laos littered with UXO (unexploded ordnance) that kills and maims people to this day.

It is possible to travel on parts of the trail in Laos, by mountain bike, motorbike or 4x4, but you must take a guide, and follow the route faithfully – exploring here could be fatal. Starting from Xepon, you can go as far north as the Mu Gia Pass, travelling through beautiful, mountainous rainforest, across rickety log bridges over rivers, past tribal villages where, for a small contribution, you may be able to stay the night. Along the way you will see the debris of war – burnt out tanks, heavy artillery, scattered UXO and bomb craters. You will also see flowers planted in bomb casings, fences made from war detritus, tank treads used as bridges, and you will meet some amazing people, most of whom, remarkably, seem to hold no grudge.

**HOW:**
By bike, motorbike or 4x4
**WHEN TO GO:**
November to March
**TIME IT TAKES:**
Anywhere between one day and two weeks depending on how far you want to go.
**HIGHLIGHTS:**
Visit the UXO office in Xepon, view the collection of disabled ordnance here and talk to the experts who are clearing this deadly inheritance.
See the enormous Australian/Lao goldmine outside Xepon.
Visit the village of Ban Dong, on the Laos/Vietnam border, site of a major battle.
Enjoy the fabulous journey through the forest, the birds, butterflies and tropical flowers you will see, and thank your lucky stars bombs are not raining down on your head.
**YOU SHOULD KNOW:**
The Ho Chi Minh trail was so named by Americans, after the North Vietnamese president, who came to be known as Uncle Ho. He oversaw the end of the French Indo-Chinese Empire, but died in Hanoi in 1969 without seeing America defeated and Vietnam re-united.

*Rice fields amid the bomb craters in Khammouane along the Ho Chi Minh Trail*

485

*Tourist boats line up outside Pak Ou Cave.*

# Mekong River Voyage – Huay Xai to Luang Prabang

**HOW:**
By boat
**WHEN TO GO:**
November to March
**TIME IT TAKES:**
Two days and one night
**HIGHLIGHTS:**
The Bokeo gem mines near Houay Xai.
The views over the river from the slow boat.
The Pak Ou Buddha Caves, 25 km (16 mi) up-river from Luang Prabang.
The exquisite temple complex of Wat Xiang Thong, possibly the most beautiful in the whole of Laos.
**YOU SHOULD KNOW:**
Apart from slow boats and speedboats (very uncomfortable and rather dangerous), there is at least one other more expensive and more comfortable cruise boat you can book. Right down in southern Laos, there are other Mekong River journeys to be taken, from Pakse down to Si Phan Don.

Since Laos re-opened its borders to westerners in the late 1980s, the Mekong River voyage from Houay Xai to Luang Prabang has become an absolute classic. Crossing the river from Thailand takes a matter of minutes, and you will soon find the 'slow boats' that will carry you downstream.

These are either cargo boats with enclosed sides, or riverboats that have a roof but are open-sided – the better choice. The luggage is stored at one end, and passengers sit on narrow, wooden benches that get less comfortable the longer you sit on them – take a cushion or something to sit on if at all possible. Bring your own food and drink – you can buy drinks on board but of course they are more expensive than they should be.

Discomfort notwithstanding, it is perfectly lovely to be on the Mekong. Most of the passengers are young backpackers, and the atmosphere is sociable. You pass few villages en route, but you'll see fishermen on the river and people on the sandy beaches – tiny glimpses of local life – as well as lovely, riverside scenery. Arriving at the village of Pak Ben, your overnight stop, there seem to be more foreigners in Pak Ben than there are locals – all the slow boats stop here – and it's crammed with guesthouses, small shops and eateries.

In the morning, off you go again on this peaceful voyage: the sound of the water slipping past is hypnotic, though occasionally broken by noisy speedboats that complete the trip in a few hours. As you reach your destination, more villages and fantastic vegetable plots at the river's edge can be seen. The Mekong is wide and beautiful at Luang Prabang, with temples visible on each bank, and you'll be glad to reach dry land once more.

# Siem Reap to Battambang

In the northwestern rice-growing region, Battambang is Cambodia's second largest town, an interesting place with an old-fashioned provincial atmosphere as yet unaffected by the invasion of mass tourism. The architecture is a mixture of traditional Cambodian and French colonial, with streets shared by motorcycles, cars and horse-drawn vehicles. And for those who wish to see unspoiled rural Cambodia there couldn't be a better starting point – within a short distance of the town is a timeless land of small villages, rice paddies and farmland. There also may be found Angkorian ruins, pagodas, waterfalls and caves.

Interesting though Battambang may be, the real attraction is getting to the place by boat from Siem Reap – a trip generally considered to be Cambodia's most scenic river journey. A ferry leaves at 7 o'clock every morning, following a picturesque route across the northern tip of Tonlé Sap and up the Sangker River.

The Tonlé Sap becomes Asia's largest lake when it quadruples in size during the rainy season. It is a huge expanse of water that makes a vital contribution to the Cambodian economy, and the banks are lined with fishing communities. From there, the ferry enters the winding Sangker River and follows it for 40 km (25 mi) upstream to Battambang, through fields and forest, passing numerous villages before the boat moors at the first of three bridges in the town.

Apart from passing through splendid scenery, this fascinating journey is part of everyday Cambodian life. The Sangker (unlike the Mekong River) has no tourist boats and the ferry is a genuine local service. Water is the lifeblood of the local communities, and at every turn there will be something new to see along the bank – and there will be frequent stops for sampans that have urgent business with the crowded ferry.

**HOW:**
By boat
**WHEN TO GO:**
March to October to avoid the rainy season (though it makes the boat trip longer and less predictable).
**TIME IT TAKES:**
4-8 hours by boat from Siem Reap to Battambang, depending on water conditions.
**HIGHLIGHTS:**
Riding a Bamboo Train – with typical creative flair, these bamboo carts powered by a motorcycle engine chug along the regular rail tracks transporting people, animals and cargo, before being whipped off the line when a proper train comes along.
The intriguing floating village of Prek Tol, outside Battambang – actually, most of the houses are on tall stilts.
A side trip to the fabled temples of Angkor Wat from Siem Reap.
**YOU SHOULD KNOW:**
The boats from Siem Reap are rickety (expect frequent breakdowns) but the risk is worth taking – this is indeed a memorable journey.

*The floating village of Chong Kneas on Tonlé Sap Lake*

# Selangor River Cruise

**HOW:**
By boat
**WHEN TO GO:**
April to October
**TIME IT TAKES:**
The 'Firefly Cruise'
usually lasts for
around 45 minutes.
**HIGHLIGHTS:**
Touring the twin forts of Kuala Selangor,
originally built to guard the mouth of
the Selangor River in the early 16th
century and subsequently expanded.
The village of Tanjung Keramat with its
picturesque lake and the fast vanishing
ruins of another major fort.
A visit to the Kuala Selangor Nature
Park, home to a huge variety of wildlife
including numerous species of resident
and migratory birds.
Wonderful local seafood – eat lunch or
dinner (or buy at the market) at the
fishing village of Pasir Penambang at
the mouth of the Selangor River.
**YOU SHOULD KNOW:**
Fireflies are lit up by the rare chemical
luciferin, which scientists have
synthesized for use in important
medical research.

Despite intensive exploitation of Malaysia's abundant natural resources, many of this fascinating country's estuaries, rivers and jungles remain unspoiled – for now, so perhaps it's a case of 'catch them while you can'. One of Malaysia's natural wonders that you can't catch – but can definitely see – is the display put on as night falls by the fireflies (kelip kelip) that feed on the nectar of mangrove trees (berembang) near the mouth of the Selangor River. Colonies gather in individual trees and flash rapidly in unison as the insects seek mates.

A new dam upriver has disturbed the habitat and numbers are dwindling. Even so, this is still an amazing light show. Proceed to Kuala Selangor, northwest of Kuala Lumpur. This once-sleepy town has started to show signs of tourist exploitation, but there is tasteful accommodation to be found on the riverbank for those who wish to stay over and explore the area's other attractions. But the main event is undoubtedly staged by the fireflies, which are actually small Lampyridae beetles.

Starting points for river cruises are the villages of Kampung Kuantan and Bukit Belimbing, where it is possible to embark on a small rowboat (tongkang) after 7.30 pm (though in the way of these things some cruises are now propelled by silent electric outboard motors). Most of the 'flashers' have found a mate and switched off by late evening but in the meantime the synchronised, rhythmic (three flashes a second) display of blinking green lights puts the average Christmas tree to shame. No flash photography, noise or torchlight is permitted during the cruise, to ensure that the habitat of the fireflies is not unduly disturbed. For the most impressive display, it is wise to avoid rainy evenings and those when the moon is near full.

*The Selangor River*

# Taman Negara Expedition

One of the finest jewels in Malaysia's somewhat tarnished ecological crown is the vast and ancient (it's 130 million years old) rainforest within the Taman Negara National Park, in the formidable Titiwangsa Mountains of Pahang State. The Park has been protected for seventy years and remains a treasure trove of Mother Nature's riches – with undisturbed habitats and wonderful flora and fauna that have evolved undisturbed over countless millennia. This magical place may be reached by bus from Kuala Lumpur, with the final leg by boat from Kuala Tembeling Jetty. Once in the Park, it is possible to stay in an eco-friendly lodge, of which there are several.

The high point (literally) of any visit to Taman Negara is a journey along the extraordinary Canopy Walkway. This apparently flimsy ropewalk looks as though it's been there for generations, but is of fairly recent construction and is entirely safe. At 510 m (1,675 ft) it's the world's longest, weaving through the very tops of the trees at a height of 45 m (150 ft) to give a unique view of a sunlit jungle world that can only be guessed at from ground level.

But that's not all Taman Negara has to offer. There is a great variety of animal life within the Park – including headline species like elephants, tigers, leopards, sun bears and Sumatran rhino – but these are shy and rarely seen. However, long-tailed macaque monkeys are a common sight and there is plenty of visible bird life (over 300 species recorded), plus reptiles aplenty. The adventurous visitor can undertake guided jungle treks by day or night, stroll along marked nature trails or even shoot the rapids on the Tembeling River. Rewarding though these activities may be, it's that swaying journey through the treetops that will be truly memorable!

**HOW:**
On foot
**WHEN TO GO:**
March to October
**TIME IT TAKES:**
Around half an hour to complete an aerial journey along the Canopy Walkway.
**HIGHLIGHTS:**
A night of animal watching from a hide – to give visitors the best chance of observing larger animals, there are a number of observation hides overlooking clearings and salt licks.
Visiting a settlement occupied by the semi-nomadic Batek people, who still practise their traditional way of life as hunter-gatherers within the Park.
The ear-shaped Gua Telingga Cave near the little town of Kuala Tahan.
**YOU SHOULD KNOW:**
Taman Negara was King George V National Park until the name was changed following independence – *taman negara* translating as (surprise!) 'national park'.

*Steady nerves are needed on this tree-top jungle walkway.*

# Cameron Highlands Road

**HOW:**
By car
**WHEN TO GO:**
Any time of year
**TIME IT TAKES:**
Around 90 minutes from Tapah
to Brinchang
**HIGHLIGHTS:**
The rushing Lata Iskandar Waterfall,
visible from the road – so don't
expect to have it to yourself!
The free-entry Highlands Apiary Farm
near Ringlet Lake, followed by a visit
to the Boh Tea Plantation, said to be
the largest in South-east Asia.
A poignant reminder of the British
colonial presence – Tudor-style inns
and stunning rose gardens
in Brinchang.
Brinchang night market for all the
fresh produce the Highlands can
offer – bag the bargains as midnight
closing time approaches!
**YOU SHOULD KNOW:**
The Cameron Highlands are over
twice the size of Singapore, from
whence many tourists visit.

After driving north from Kuala Lumpur for 90 minutes on the modern Expressway, take the turn-off for the town of Tapah and discover another world. For this is the gateway to the Cameron Highlands, named after a certain William Cameron who appreciated in the 1880s that these fertile mountains would be ideal for growing tea. The slopes were soon covered in plantations, and the British, who supervised humid lowland rubber plantations and tin mines, soon discovered that the cooler Highlands provided an ideal summer retreat.

Today, relaxing colonists have been replaced by holidaymaking city dwellers who also appreciate the cool, fresh climate. The journey up into the Highlands from Tapah is a drive to remember, as the old road (Route 59) is very narrow, twisting and turning sharply through beautiful scenery. The tea industry remains, but today all sorts of vegetables, fruit (especially strawberries) and flowers are grown on farms mixed in with tea plantations in the hilly green landscape. The route goes through Ringlet, Habu and Tanah Rata to Brinchang.

Until recently, this was the only way into the hills, though there is now access from the north and east, so it's possible to enter or leave the Highlands via Gunung Brinchang (to the west) or Tringkap (to the east). This improved access will be sure to increase tourist and commercial pressure. There is already some modern tourist development, but for now the Cameron Highlands preserve much of their original character, with many bungalows from the colonial era still standing in stunning hillside locations. But the Highlands are becoming so popular that (even with the new roads) traffic is often slow-moving or at a standstill. To dodge the busiest times, plan a journey that avoids local school holidays – especially the long Christmas break from mid-November through December.

*A tea estate in the Cameron Highlands*

# Penang Ferry

In the 1780s, the port of Penang was established on the tropical island of the same name by Captain Francis Light of the British East India Company. From small beginnings, this strategically located Malaysian port in the Malacca Straits has become a major Far Eastern commercial centre with Freeport status. The capital of Penang State – George Town – is on the island, along with extensive port facilities and numerous high-tech industries. Railway access is to Butterworth at the mouth of the Perai River, facing Penang across a 3-km (2-mi) channel.

From there, there's only one way for self-respecting travellers to proceed to Penang Island – by ferry (though in truth it is now possible to get there via a modern road bridge). The famous Penang vehicle and passenger ferry service is the oldest in Malaysia, having been established in 1920, and has long enjoyed iconic status. It connects the Sultan Abdul Halim ferry terminal near the station in Butterworth to the Raja Tun Uda terminal in George Town. The fleet of eight double-decker ferries constantly plies the waters of Penang's port from early morning until well after midnight. Once known as 'The Big Yellow Ferry', the boats have recently been repainted in an assortment of bright colours – oranges, yellows, reds, blues and greens – making them an even more distinctive feature of the busy waterway.

From the ferry's top deck there is an excellent view of the impressive 13.5-km (8-mi) Penang Bridge. The 21st-century skyline of George Town is not up to New York standards, though this is undoubtedly a work in progress. But still ferry voyagers enjoy one of the world's great 'must see from the water' sights – the historic town (yet another one known as 'The Pearl of the Orient') set against the timeless forested hills of the island's interior.

**HOW:**
By boat
**WHEN TO GO:**
November to March, June and July
**TIME IT TAKES:**
Around 15 minutes
**HIGHLIGHTS:**
Penang Bird Park (Taman Burung Perang) in Butterworth – for a fabulous display of over 300 bird species from South-east Asia.
In George Town – Beach Street and the streets leading off it, at the heart of the old colonial commercial quarter.
Fort Cornwallis – an old star-shaped fort on the north-eastern coast of Penang Island, rebuilt in 1804.
**YOU SHOULD KNOW:**
It's only necessary to pay on the outward ferry journey – the return trip from Penang Island is free.

*A hiker in Kinabalu National Park*

# Mount Kinabalu Trek

The two-day trek up Mount Kinabalu in the Malaysian state of Sabah on Borneo follows a well-trodden path, but this doesn't mean it's easy. The mountain is located in Kinabalu National Park, a World Heritage Site noted for extraordinary biodiversity. Kinabalu is South-east Asia's fourth-highest mountain at 4,095 m (13,345 ft). The freezing summit at Low's Peak may be reached by anyone who is physically fit, without mountaineering equipment. However, the climb may be attempted only with an experienced local guide. The journey begins with a stay at Park Headquarters, followed by a walk or minibus transfer to Timophon Gate at 1,800 m (5,900 ft). From there, the route continues up to the Laban Rata Guesthouse at 3,300 m (10,800 ft). Supplies to the hut are carried by porters, so that trekkers can enjoy a few basic home comforts like hot food, drinks and showers before attempting the final climb the next day. Some start to suffer altitude sickness at this height and should on no account continue the ascent.

The trek is quite often timed so climbers arrive at Laban Rata around dusk, to enjoy the fabulous sunsets and skyscapes, with an early start the following morning delivering a magnificent sunrise over the mountains, sometimes above the clouds. The final stretch to the summit is mainly over bare granite rock and – once there – panoramic views on a clear day are magnificent. The descent is steep and trekkers are more likely to suffer injury (happily usually minor) coming down than going up.

There is now an alternative route – the rugged Mesilau Trail – from the Mesilau resort some 15 km (9 mi) from Park HQ. This newer summit trail up the other side of Mount Kinabalu is much more challenging than the established route and thus appeals to those with a sense of adventure.

**HOW:**
On foot
**WHEN TO GO:**
March to October
**TIME IT TAKES:**
Four to six hours for the ascent to Timophon Gate, two to four hours from Laban Rata Guesthouse to the summit (spread over two days).
**HIGHLIGHTS:**
Plants galore – Kinabalu National Park is full of rare (often unique) plants.
A trip to Poring, 40 km (25 mi) to the southeast of Park HQ – for a great view of the mountain, hot springs, a butterfly farm, orchid centre and canopy walkway.
A side trip to nearby Tuaran Village to visit the crocodile farm – be there at feeding time for an impressive show of reptilian greed.
**YOU SHOULD KNOW:**
The trek is popular, so it is necessary to book accommodation at Park HQ and Laban Rata Guesthouse well in advance – no accommodation, no trek.

# Skrang River Safari

Sarawak is located in northwestern Borneo, and is one of two Malaysian states on the island (the other being Sabah). With large tracts of tropical rain forest, Sarawak is separated from the Indonesian part of Borneo by the central mountain range, where several rivers rise. These include the shallow, fast-flowing Skrang River, fiefdom of the fearsome Dayak Iban headhunters. They believed that freshly gathered heads led to an abundant rice harvest, and celebrated their headhunting in the form of elaborate tattoos. Women, too, often bore tattoos that celebrated their skills as weavers.

The Skrang Ibans still have a traditional way of life, but happily there are no fresh heads hanging in the rafters of their huge longhouses along the riverbanks – just a few ancient skulls. Instead, the Ibans now supplement their subsistence economy by welcoming a select number of guests. But first there's a five-hour drive from the state capital of Kuching to the river, from whence a motorised longboat takes over.

It is possible to make scenic river trip through longhouse country, enjoying the verdant rainforest. This a is a genuine jungle safari, sometimes beneath overhanging foliage, and it may be necessary to hop out if the boat grounds in the shallow water to help re-float it before continuing. There are also plenty of white-water rapids to add to the excitement.

However, most people prefer to arrange a stop at one of the riverside longhouses. Once there, visitors are shown around before being entertained by the residents, who put on a wonderful show of tribal music and dancing – not to mention a feast washed down with liberal helpings of tuak rice wine. You can sometimes stay in the longhouse itself, or in some places there may be a simple but comfortable guesthouse.

**HOW:**
By boat
**WHEN TO GO:**
March to August; October and November
**TIME IT TAKES:**
Up to four hours for the scenic journey along the Skrang River to see longhouses.
**HIGHLIGHTS:**
On the way from Kuching to the Skrang River – a stop at Serian to visit the bustling produce market.
An amazing display of deadly blowpipe skills by proficient Iban hunters.
Seeing the rich flora and fauna of the jungle that surrounds the longhouses, with the help of a local guide.
**YOU SHOULD KNOW:**
If you are visiting a longhouse it is customary to bring small presents for your Iban hosts.

*An Iban warrior travels up river on his pirogue.*

493

# AUSTRALASIA
# AND
# THE PACIFIC

# Great Ocean Road

The Great Ocean Road belongs in an élite group of classic coastal drives, which includes California's Pacific Highway and Italy's Amalfi Coast Road. It runs 285 km (180 mi) along Victoria's south coast, west of Melbourne between the towns of Torquay and Warrnambool. Constructed originally to open up a previously inaccessible coastline for commerce, the Great Ocean Road has now become a major tourist attraction in its own right. Started in 1919 with the labour of ex-servicemen and completed 13 years later, this engineering marvel clings precariously to sheer cliff faces, snakes around inlets, crosses narrow gorges and passes through tunnels blasted out of solid rock.

Leaving the lively seaside resort of Torquay with its world-famous surf break at Bells Beach, the road hugs the shoreline as it passes through the pretty little towns of Anglesea and Lorne. As you negotiate sharp corners and descend into protected bays you are presented time and again with stunning views of the Southern Ocean, endless expanses of virgin sands and rugged cliffs stretching off into the distance. After Apollo Bay the route bears inland and crosses Otway National Park, part of the Otway Ranges, an area of dense temperate rain forest which offers one of your best chances of seeing a koala in the wild. These shy creatures are notoriously hard to spot, thanks to their camouflage and inertia during the day.

Appropriately enough, the highlight of this trip comes towards the end. Just 70 km (45 mi) before Warrnambool the Twelve Apostles rise proudly from the sea, like giant sentinels guarding the coast. These majestic limestone stacks, up to 45 m (150 ft) high, are the result of coastal erosion and they provide a justly famous spectacle at sunrise and sunset.

*The Twelve Apostles near the
Great Ocean Road*

# Gibb River Road

Running straight across the heart of the Kimberley region in Australia's remote north-west, the Gibb River Road remains one of the country's great off-road driving adventures, although improvements in the road's condition has meant that there are many more travellers who take on the challenge than there used to be. Even so, there is still a real sense of achievement as you motor into the small towns of Derby at the western end or Kununurra at the eastern end, saddle-sore after 700 mostly bone-shaking kilometres (440 mi) and once you've cleared the last of the bulldust from your lungs.

'The Gibb', as the road is known locally, is serious 4x4 terrain. Apart from a short sealed stretch east of Derby, it is a red dirt and gravel track, fairly wide and smooth for the most part but badly corrugated in places from the effect of other vehicles and 'wash outs' from the wet season. All this might still be negotiated in a conventional car but what you really need the high clearance of a proper 4x4 vehicle for are the even rougher side tracks you must take in order to visit the main attractions along the route. Involving detours of up to 50 km (30 mi), places such as Bell, Adcock and the Manning Gorges showcase the natural features for which this ancient and rugged landscape is famed: narrow sandstone gorges, waterfalls, hidden creeks and tranquil pools.

Most travellers tackling the Gibb choose to camp along the way but there are accommodation options for those wanting more comfort. You can drive the road in either direction but as the majority of the big sights are in the western half you might prefer to start from the eastern end and save these delights for later.

**HOW:**
By 4x4
**WHEN TO GO:**
May to October
**TIME IT TAKES:**
At least five to six days if you want to make the most of being in this remarkable region.
**HIGHLIGHTS:**
Waterfalls in full flow in the gorges – but you need to go early in the season to see them (soon after the end of the 'wet').
Walking along beautiful Bell Creek and into the Gorge.
Swimming in a gorge pool (crocodile-free!).
The sunset over the Pentecost River and Cockburn Ranges from Home Valley Station.
**YOU SHOULD KNOW:**
Letting air out of your tyres before you set off will improve your journey considerably and reduce the likelihood of punctures. You must have a permit in advance to travel on any side tracks which cross Aboriginal land.

*The Pentecost River Crossing on the Gibb River Road*

# The Indian Pacific Railway

This classic long-distance rail journey crosses the Australian continent from the Pacific Ocean in the east to the Indian Ocean in the west. Running twice weekly in each direction, trains are hauled by huge diesel locomotives and can be up to a kilometre (over half a mile) in length. From Sydney the journey provides an inspiring overview of many of the country's most distinctive landscapes: the lush, heavily forested slopes of the Blue Mountains give way to the sprawling rural heartland of New South Wales which in turn is succeeded by the bleak outback scenery of the Broken Hill mining region. Crossing into South Australia gives you fine views of the Flinders Ranges with their dramatic ridges.

After an extended stop in Adelaide the Indian Pacific heads north west along the Spencer Gulf to Port Augusta before embarking on the most forbidding part of the journey, across the vast and featureless Nullarbor Plain (which means literally 'empty of trees') – 1,200 km (750 mi) of red earth, low scrub and nothing else, which includes the longest straight stretch of railway track in the world (478 km / 300 mi). The bustling gold-mining centre of Kalgoorlie returns you to human activity with a jolt before your last night on board conveys you the final 600 km (375 mi) for a morning arrival in the West Australian capital of Perth.

The Indian Pacific is run by the same company that operates the Ghan Railway, and it offers the same range of travelling options. If your budget allows, the most comfortable option is to travel Gold Kangaroo class – a definite recommendation for the en-suite accommodation, full on-board catering and the attentive but relaxed service throughout your journey.

*The legendary Indian Pacific*

# The Ghan

One of the world's great rail journeys, the Ghan takes two days to bisect the Australian continent from Adelaide on the Southern Ocean to Darwin, Australia's most northerly city and its gateway to Asia. Over its 3,000-km (1,900-mi) course it crosses three distinct climate zones, from the fertile coastal plains of South Australia through the vast dry desert of the Red Centre to the luxuriant vegetation of the tropical Top End. The Ghan takes its name from the Afghan camel drivers who with their animals opened up 19th-century trading routes into the interior. Constructed originally between Adelaide and Alice Springs in 1929, the line was only completed to the northern coast in 2004. The camel has not been forgotten, though – there are now more in Australia than on the Arabian Peninsula.

The company running the Ghan manages quite a trick spoiling you with all the benefits of modern rail travel in comfortable, air-conditioned carriages and the highest standards of on-board service, while at the same time imparting a real sense that you are blazing an adventurer's trail as you travel across one of the world's harshest, least hospitable terrains. As you gaze out from the window of your compartment over the endless expanses of red earth and spinifex grass, the flat horizon only rarely broken by sandstone outcrops, you have ample time to reflect on those early pioneers, as well as the indigenous peoples who have sustained themselves for centuries in this very environment. Then, as the vivid desert sun sets and the train continues its measured progress, you can give thanks you don't have to do the same, before you make your way to the restaurant car to dine on kangaroo steak or barramundi fish.

*Twin locomotives pull the Ghan away from Alice Springs.*

**HOW:**
By train
**WHEN TO GO:**
April to October
**TIME IT TAKES:**
Two days and two nights, including two extended stops for local excursions (optional), at Alice Springs and Katherine; two to three days longer if you break the journey at Alice Springs to visit Uluru (Ayers Rock)
**HIGHLIGHTS:**
The welcome and send-off by the train staff on the departure platform at Adelaide.
Waking up on your first morning to the reds and ochres of the vast central desert.
Absorbing the unique atmosphere of Alice Springs, a town that's an awfully long way from anywhere.
Dining on the train under the stars of the desert sky.
**YOU SHOULD KNOW:**
Trains run twice weekly between Adelaide and Darwin in each direction. Alice Springs is the mid-way point, where you will find the Ghan logo of a camel with rider in sculptural form on the station platform (a popular spot for photos).

*The steamer near Nildottie*

# Paddle Steamer on the Murray River

**HOW:**
By boat
**WHEN TO GO:**
All year
**TIME IT TAKES:**
Four nights for the round trip.
**HIGHLIGHTS:**
Watching the birds and animals as the riverbank comes to life in the early morning.
Taking a guided nocturnal tour to seek out the varied wildlife that emerges after dark.
The ancient rock carvings at Ngaut Ngaut Aboriginal Reserve.
**YOU SHOULD KNOW:**
If you want to be independent and fancy something a little more exclusive you can rent your own houseboat to take out on the river.

The presence of Australia's principal river, the Murray, has been a key factor in turning the south east of the country into its most productive and heavily populated area. The American writer Mark Twain hailed the Murray as Australia's Mississippi, although in a country where water has always been a limited resource it lacks the flow of its mighty American counterpart. Like the Mississippi the Murray offered a means of navigation for the early European settlers to reach the rich pastoral country inland; and for over fifty years from the 1860s it reigned unchallenged as the main transport artery for the region, carrying livestock and produce downriver to the coast and bringing supplies back to the sheep and cattle stations.

As in America the paddle steamer was the dominant means of river transport in these years. Where once they had a strictly commercial, utilitarian role these elegant vessels now ply their trade on the Murray as leisure boats. There is no better way to enjoy the varied sights of this riverscape – the mighty cliff-faces, the stands of towering red gums, the wetlands with their abundant wildlife – than from the deck of a paddle steamer as you glide by in sedate comfort. At the historic river port of Mannum, on the Murray's lower reaches and an hour's drive east of Adelaide, you board the *Murray Princess* for an extended cruise upriver to the first lock near Blanchetown and back again, sleeping on board in well-appointed cabins. The rewards for opting for this slower and gentler form of transport are many, not least the grandstand views it gives you of the river's spectacular birdlife – pelicans, black swans and egrets are all commonly seen here.

# The Ned Kelly Trail

The short and violent life of Ned Kelly, Australia's most famous outlaw, or 'bushranger', has long since gained iconic status. You can compare the legend with the more humdrum realities of a life spent in rural poverty in this driving tour around its key locations. By Australian standards it is a relatively compact affair – some 650 km (400 mi) in a round trip from Melbourne – since Kelly never strayed far from his roots in the 'high country' of Victoria's northeast.

The Hume Highway, the main Melbourne to Sydney road, conveniently connects many of the Kelly sites. Beveridge and Avenel, an hour's drive north of Melbourne, were two of Ned's childhood homes; his ex-convict father John 'Red' Kelly died when Ned was twelve and is buried in Avenel. Ned robbed the bank in nearby Euroa, while the town museum in Benalla has a number of interesting Kelly-related exhibits.

The next stop, Glenrowan, marks the heart of the Kelly story. Here Ned and his gang made their famous last stand in the local inn. While the other gang members all died in the police siege, Ned himself was wounded when trying to break out wearing a suit of homemade armour. A pleasant country drive brings you to Beechworth, the furthest point on the tour, where you can still see the gaol in which the fifteen-year old served his first sentence.

There are fine views of the King valley and mountains on the journey back to Mansfield, which takes you via Power's Lookout and Stringybark Creek; an atmospheric walk through blue gums and blackwoods leads you to the site where Ned achieved national notoriety when the gang shot three policemen dead; their graves and a memorial can be seen in Mansfield.

**HOW:**
By car
**WHEN TO GO:**
September to May
**TIME IT TAKES:**
Allow one week if you want to see all the sites properly.
**HIGHLIGHTS:**
The green silk sash in Benalla Museum given to the ten-year-old Ned as a reward after he had saved a boy from drowning; the sash bears the marks of his blood as he was wearing it when he was wounded and captured at Glenrowan.
Kate's Cottage and Ned Kelly Memorial in Glenrowan, an evocative replica of the Kelly home.
Ned Kelly's death mask and the beam from which he was hanged on 11 November 1880, both in Old Melbourne Gaol.
**YOU SHOULD KNOW:**
1. The trail takes you close to some of Victoria's premier wine-producing areas.
2. Ned Kelly's armour has survived and can be seen on display in the State Library of Victoria in Melbourne.

*The Ned Kelly statue at Glenrowan*

# Matilda Highway

The Matilda Highway is the main north-south route through the interior of the state of Queensland. Starting in Cunnamulla, the first town after the New South Wales border, it runs for 1,700 km (1,060 mi) in a north and north-westerly direction until reaching the Gulf of Carpentaria at Karumba. This is a classic drive through the great Australian outback, and if you like your roads straight and empty and your vistas boundless then you will enjoy this experience. But you should be warned that the landscape can be dauntingly unvarying: wide open expanses of grassland and low scrub, extending for kilometre after kilometre in every direction. Only as the highway approaches the Gulf in the north does it change somewhat to feature a coastal habitat of cracked saltpans – and to become, if anything, even flatter.

Many of the key towns of the Queensland outback line the route of the Matilda. Places such as Winton, Longreach and Charleville developed in the 19th century as supply and transportation centres for the vast and isolated sheep and cattle stations that cover much of the area. The towns themselves are not large and are relaxed and easy-going places in which to spend a day or two savouring the special atmosphere of the interior.

The Highway takes its name from the region's associations with 'Waltzing Matilda', Banjo Paterson's ballad which has become Australia's unofficial national anthem. You can visit the Combo Waterhole, the supposed setting for the story, outside Kynuna on the highway south of Cloncurry. The North Gregory Hotel in Winton is where 'Waltzing Matilda' is said to have had its first performance in April 1895 (although the hotel has since been rebuilt following a fire).

*The town of Winton along the Matilda Highway*

# Sydney to Melbourne Coast Road

The direct route linking Australia's two largest cities is the inland Hume Highway, but the coast road is unquestionably the more rewarding option, and the distance involved is not much greater. Known as the Princes Highway, this route follows the New South Wales coastline south from Sydney to the state border with Victoria, at roughly the halfway point on the 1,050-km (655-mi) journey. It then heads east across the Gippsland region towards Melbourne.

Leaving Sydney the Highway skirts Botany Bay, site of Captain Cook's famous first landing in 1770, before reaching the industrial city of Wollongong. The road then passes through a succession of small fishing villages and relaxed seaside resorts that stretch all the way down to the state border. Here you are rarely more than a few kilometres from the shoreline and there are regular opportunities to turn off for wonderfully secluded beaches. These, together with outstanding surfing and all manner of water sports, including diving and game-fishing, constitute the area's main attractions, but inland there are also easily accessible national parks, such as the Royal National (the second oldest national park in the world, after the USA's Yellowstone), Morton and Ben Boyd Reserves, which contain spectacular upland scenery and some of Australia's best-preserved temperate rainforests.

After the old whaling station of Eden, the Princes Highway strikes inland across southern Victoria and the fertile dairy-farming region of Gippsland. This is a land of gently rolling hills and forests of tall eucalypt. You brush the coastline once more briefly at Lakes Entrance, which as the name suggests is a good base for exploring the Gippsland Lakes, the country's most extensive network of inland waterways. And if you are after a bigger adrenalin rush, Ninety Mile Beach (which you can drive along!) is never far away.

*Ninety Mile Beach*

**HOW:**
By car or 4x4
**WHEN TO GO:**
Year-round
**TIME IT TAKES:**
Three to five days, if you allow time to explore the area's many natural beauties.
**HIGHLIGHTS:**
Mogo, site of a former gold mine where there is a reconstructed mid-19th century gold-rush town.
Take a trip out to sea to spot whales on their annual migration (June to November) at places like Jervis Bay, Narooma and Eden.
Croajingolong National Park in the far east of Victoria, over 100 km (62 mi) of isolated, unspoiled coastline with excellent bushwalking opportunities.
**YOU SHOULD KNOW:**
To get the most out of the many national parks along the route you will need a 4x4 vehicle and a good pair of walking boots.

*The Glass House Mountains*

# The Bruce Highway

Running between the state capital, Brisbane, and the bustling city of Cairns 1,720 km (1,075 mi) to the north, the Bruce Highway is Queensland's principal transport artery, connecting most of the main towns and cities of Australia's second-largest state. On this road you are rarely more than a few kilometres from the Pacific Ocean, so it is easy to relieve the tedium of highway driving with a short detour to chill out on a clean, deserted beach. Inland you are accompanied much of the way by views of the foothills, escarpments and plateaux of the Great Dividing Range.

On leaving Brisbane the Highway runs up the Sunshine Coast, more relaxed and less developed than its famous Gold Coast cousin. You cannot miss the striking profiles of the Glass House Mountains to your left, while to the north you will be hard put to resist the seductive seaside charms of Noosa. These coastal plains are rich agricultural country and intensive cultivation is evident throughout the journey: pineapples around Gympie, mangoes around Bowen, huge sugarcane fields in the Mackay region. At Rockhampton, self-styled 'beef capital' of Australia and a great place for a steak, you enter the Tropics and notice the vegetation becoming thicker and lusher as hills and rainforest edge ever closer to the coast.

A number of coastal towns north of Mackay provide excellent bases for exploring the Whitsunday Islands lying offshore and for longer trips to the Great Barrier Reef itself. Townsville is the region's main city; you certainly know you are in the Tropics wandering along its attractive promenade. And as you cover the final 300 km (190 mi) to Cairns you would be well advised to have some energy in reserve for the vast array of adventure activities offered by your destination city.

# Alice Springs to Coober Pedy

The vastness of the Australian continent is everywhere evident on this overland trip that takes you 700 km (440 mi) south from the centre. It follows the Stuart Highway, named after Scottish-born John McDouall Stuart, one of Australia's pioneering explorers who in 1862 finally succeeded, on his third attempt, in blazing a trail from south to north coast. This feat paved the way for the construction just ten years later of the Overland Telegraph Line linking Adelaide with Darwin; a further link to Java revolutionized communications between Britain and its far-flung colonies.

On leaving the lively town of Alice Springs you will not see another population centre until journey's end. Boundless stretches of flat highway extend to the horizon and are punctuated by occasional tiny roadside settlements like Kulgera and Marla, whose sole function is to service the needs of long-distance travellers. All the while you are surrounded by unbroken vistas of the great central Australian desert, one of the world's harshest, most arid environments. Amazingly, the earliest known evidence of animal life on the planet was found not far south from here, at Lake Torrens, while if you are lucky enough to be on the road following a desert rainstorm you will see the landscape transformed by a sudden profusion of wild flowers.

Coober Pedy, the self-styled 'opal capital of the world', is the place to come to gaze on this most beautiful and elusive of minerals. A huge range of stones are sold, but you can also try your luck at some 'fossicking' to find your own. The small town is not a lot to look at on the surface because much of it (including five churches) is built underground, where people have made their homes to escape the extreme summer heat.

**HOW:**
By car or 4x4
**WHEN TO GO:**
April to October
**TIME IT TAKES:**
You can do this trip in one day, although it is a long drive and you would be better advised to stay overnight at a roadhouse along the way.
**HIGHLIGHTS:**
Seeing the desert sun rise over the MacDonnell Ranges from a hot-air balloon above Alice Springs.
Shopping for Aboriginal art and crafts in Alice Springs' many galleries.
Staying in an underground hotel in Coober Pedy.
The Old Timers Mine in Coober Pedy for a historical perspective on opal mining.
**YOU SHOULD KNOW:**
Take care if you go hunting for opals yourself at Coober Pedy as there are many old disused shafts that are barely visible on the surface.

*The road to the opal town of Coober Pedy*

# Six Foot Track to the Blue Mountains

**HOW:**
On foot
**WHEN TO GO:**
March to May and September to November are the most pleasant times to do this walk.
**TIME IT TAKES:**
Three days, plus one to two days more for visiting the Jenolan Caves and the sights around Katoomba.
**HIGHLIGHTS:**
The views into the Jamison Valley from Echo Point at Katoomba.
Crossing Cox's River on the suspension footbridge, built by army engineers.
The spectacular limestone formations in the Jenolan Caves.
**YOU SHOULD KNOW:**
Take plenty of water on this hike, as well as warm clothing since spring and autumn nights can be quite chilly.

Easily accessible from Sydney, the Blue Mountains have been inspiring visitors since the early days of European settlement. This is a landscape of wooded slopes, dramatic escarpments and hidden valleys. The mountains really do look blue too, thanks to the mist given off by the ubiquitous eucalypt trees; it was this mist, indeed, which kick-started the tourism industry, when the first intrepid visitors came to savour the therapeutic benefits of the mountain air at the end of the 19th century.

The Six Foot Track, so named from the original specification for a track six feet wide, was created as a bridlepath back in the 1880s. Hiking its 42-km (26-mi) length from Katoomba to the Jenolan Caves remains one of the best ways to immerse yourself in the varied natural splendours of the area. There are several energetic climbs on a route that takes you up along high ridges and down into steep-sided valleys, dense with spreading ferns. The rewards for your efforts are panoramic views of distant canyon walls and sudden variations in habitat which increase your wildlife-spotting opportunities. Campsites at strategic locations along the way mean that you need not exert yourself to the extent of the doughty runners who compete every March in the Six Foot Track Marathon, billed as Australia's toughest off-road race.

Your best chances of seeing the local wildlife are at dawn and dusk when wallabies and kangaroos come out to graze, whilst many of the forest mammals – possums and gliders, for example – scavenge only at night. The birdlife is a different matter – you are unlikely to miss the brilliant hues of rosellas and lorikeets darting from tree to tree, and you may even be fortunate enough to come across the reclusive lyrebird foraging on the forest floor.

*The Blue Mountains in New South Wales*

# Kuranda Scenic Railway

Prolonged and torrential rains during the wet seasons in the early 1880s were making life very difficult for the tin miners of North Queensland. It became imperative to improve supply lines to their camps up on the Atherton Tablelands inland from Cairns, and so the line now known as the Kuranda Scenic Railway was born. There was fierce initial competition for the route up into the mountains, until the present one, which follows the course of the Barron River, prevailed. Opened in 1891, the line took five years to construct and is a remarkable feat of engineering. One thousand five hundred navvies, many of Irish and Italian extraction, used little more than hand tools, mules and dynamite to blast out fifteen tunnels and numerous cuttings, as well as to build bridges over the many steep-sided creeks.

You can begin your journey from the main station in central Cairns, or better still, join the train at Freshwater Station in the northern suburbs, where there are informative displays about the railway and its history as well as the chance to eat in a restored historic carriage. The line then winds for 30 km (19 mi) through the Barron Gorge, climbing all the while until it reaches Kuranda, an ascent of 330 m (1,100 ft). Each carriage is equipped with an audio-visual commentary on the route to enhance the unrivalled views of mountains, precipitous cliff-faces, waterfalls and a World Heritage rainforest. And if you are lucky your train might be drawn by the 1720 Class Diesel electric locomotive that has been painted to depict 'Buda-dji', the legendary carpet snake whose story from the Aboriginal Dreamtime you will hear during your journey.

**HOW:**
By train
**WHEN TO GO:**
Year-round, although the wet season (December to March) is best if you want to see the waterfalls in full flow.
**TIME IT TAKES:**
1.75 hours one-way
**HIGHLIGHTS:**
The Horseshoe Bend, a 180-degree curve which marks the start of the climb out of the coastal plain to Kuranda.
Stoney Creek Bridge on its three tall trestle piers.
The views of Barron Falls, especially during the 'wet'.
Getting away from the day-trippers and staying overnight in Kuranda, the 'village in the rainforest'.
**YOU SHOULD KNOW:**
The last train back from Kuranda leaves at 3.30 pm. For a different perspective on the landscape consider instead taking the Skyrail Rainforest Cableway down to Cairns.

*Kuranda Scenic Railway*

# Cape York Peninsula

The northernmost point of the Australian continent, lonely and remote, Cape York Peninsula has been described as one of the last great wild places on earth. The so-called 'Trip to the Tip' is a challenging one whichever mode of overland transport you choose. If you have the stamina and confidence, one of the best ways to encounter a landscape largely untouched by human hand is by mountain bike. Cairns is the place to organize your own transport or else sign up for an escorted tour. If you travel independently you should bear in mind that accommodation options are limited, so you need to take basic camping equipment as well as appropriate spares and supplies.

Most of the 1,000 km (625 mi) from Cairns to the Cape is on dirt tracks and unsealed roads. Whilst you have to be on constant alert for potholes and the heavy corrugations that form on many surfaces, you will find your progress is often not much slower than fellow travellers in motor vehicles. And your greater lightness and flexibility will give you the advantage when negotiating the many creek crossings with their swift-flowing streams and steep-sided banks.

The route from Cairns takes you up the coast through the Daintree Rainforest and on to Cape Tribulation and Cooktown, before heading inland across Lakefield National Park to join the main road running up the spine of the peninsula. The 160 km (100 mi) from the Wenlock River north to the Jardine River, which follows the route of the old Overland Telegraph Line, is a particularly exciting section. After a ferry crossing of the mighty Jardine River it is a relatively straightforward ride, via the small Torres Strait Islander town of Bamaga to Cape York itself, where a sign confirms you are at the tip of mainland Australia.

*Cycling through corrugations on Cape York.*

# Skyrail Rainforest Cableway

The World Heritage-listed tropical rainforests of north Queensland are the oldest continually surviving rainforests on earth. The opening of the Skyrail Rainforest Cableway outside Cairns in 1995 has given visitors an entirely new perspective on this dazzlingly lush environment. From the safety and comfort of your enclosed gondola cabin you gaze down on a previously inaccessible world as the cableway carries you silently over the dense, verdant rainforest canopy. And with much of the natural activity taking place in the heights of the trees, you have a good chance on your trip of seeing sights that are simply unavailable from the forest floor up to 60 m (200 ft) below.

Skyrail connects Smithfield, a northern suburb of the coastal city of Cairns, with the small inland town of Kuranda, 330 m (1,100 ft) up on the edge of the Atherton Tablelands. At 7.5 km (4.5 mi) it is one of the world's longest cableways and can carry up to 700 passengers per hour. Not only is it an enjoyable way to travel, it is also good for the planet; Skyrail's operators pride themselves on its low environmental impact which has been recognized in numerous ecotourism awards.

There are two stops on the route, at Red Peak and Barron Falls. Both give you the chance to get off and explore the rainforest at ground-floor level along boardwalks and with the help of knowledgeable local rangers. Here you may well see a brush turkey foraging on the forest floor, while from your gondola you should catch flashes of brightly-coloured parrots, lorikeets and cockatoos; and although you are unlikely to see them, you can listen out for the whip-crack call of the whipbird and the cooing of the Wompoo pigeon, among the most distinctive sounds of the rainforest.

*The Skyrail 'hangs' above Barron Gorge.*

**HOW:**
By cableway
**WHEN TO GO:**
Year-round
**TIME IT TAKES:**
1.5 hours one-way, including stops,
**HIGHLIGHTS:**
The panoramic views of the Cairns coastline and the Coral Sea during the initial ascent.
The Ulysses butterfly, a true Australian star with its electric blue wings.
Kuranda, with its laid-back atmosphere and huge array of arts and crafts stalls.
The Barron Falls in full flow (wet season only – December to March).
**YOU SHOULD KNOW:**
For a change of transport and scenery you can opt to make the return journey on the 100-year-old Kuranda Scenic Railway.

**509**

# Fraser Island Trek

Anyone for the world's largest sandcastle? Sand-based Fraser Island off the southern coast of Queensland extends to 123 km (76 mi) from north to south and is 26 km (16 mi) across at the widest point. Managed by the Queensland Parks and Wildlife Service as part of the Great Sandy National Park, this extraordinary place is a UNESCO World Heritage Site.

It has a variety of habitats – from pristine rivers to freshwater lakes, lush subtropical rainforest to eucalypt forests, mangroves to melaleuca swamps, heaths and – of course – endless beaches. All are inhabited by a wealth of wildlife, including over 200 species of bird and a variety of reptile life, with migrating whales frequently spotted off shore.

The easy way to explore this popular destination is by 4x4 vehicle – or is it? Even these powerful monsters get marooned in Fraser's soft sand and a surer (if slower) way of seeing this enchanting island is to make the Fraser Island Trek – a hike that follows the continuous beach up the eastern coast with possible detours into the interior, starting at Hook Point on the island's southern tip. The first stop is Dilli Village, where accommodation can be booked in advance. From there, the hike continues to the outpost of Eurong and on to the island's main settlement, Happy Valley, where the trekker can find accommodation and replenish stores.

The onward march runs north alongside imposing cliffs called The Cathedrals that are characterized by multi-coloured layers. After Cathedral Beach Resort the route passes through Dundubara before reaching the basalt promontory of Indian Head, with superb views from the top of the headland. Many walkers end their journey soon afterwards at Orchid Beach, though determined hikers continue through awkward soft sand and around impassable rocky outcrops to the Trek's official end at Sandy Cape Lighthouse.

**HOW:**
On foot
**WHEN TO GO:**
Any time of year
**TIME IT TAKES:**
Allow five days to include selected inland detours.
**HIGHLIGHTS:**
Seeing a large number of dingoes – the purest strain left in Australia is on Fraser Island, as there has been little inter-breeding with domestic dogs.
A long side trip from Dilli – the Southern Lakes Drive covering many of the interior's best features including Lakes Boomanjin, Benaroon, Birrabeen and McKenzie with its white sand and blue water.
The rusting remains of the ocean liner *Maheno*, driven ashore in 1935 whilst on the way to a Japanese scrapyard.
**YOU SHOULD KNOW:**
Even when the tide is out and the beach is up to 100 m (330 ft) wide, great care should be taken when crossing sometimes-treacherous creeks and rock bars.

*The Flinders Ranges*

# The Heysen Trail

**HOW:**
On foot
**WHEN TO GO:**
April to October (the Heysen Trail is
closed during fire-danger season).
**TIME IT TAKES:**
Around 60 days to hike the entire
Trail in one go.
**HIGHLIGHTS:**
The stunning Wilpena Pound in the
South Flinders Ranges, caused by
millions of years of erosion,
renowned for its unique geology and
Aboriginal cultural significance.
Walking through the world-famous
vineyards of the Barossa Valley in the
northern part of the Mount Lofty
Ranges (and managing the
occasional tasting).
The home of the artist after whom
the Trail is named – see Sir Hans
Heysen's The Cedars near Hahndorf
in the Adelaide Hills.
The sandy expanses of Tunkalilla
Beach on the Fleurieu Peninsula
facing the Southern Ocean.
**YOU SHOULD KNOW:**
Hikers should use special stations
along the Trail to cleanse footwear,
thus helping to inhibit the spread of
the introduced root-rot fungus
Phytophthora, which can devastate
native plants.

Any super-fit backpacker with two months to spare can achieve the ultimate prize – an end-to-end certificate and badge to prove that they've tackled and beaten one of Australia's toughest official long-distance hikes, also recognized as one of the world's great long-distance walks.

The Heysen Trail runs from Parachilna Gorge in the Northern Flinders Ranges down to Cape Jervis on the southern tip of the Fleurieu Peninsula, passing Adelaide along the way. It traverses some of South Australia's most breathtaking landscape, providing an incredible variety of stimulating sights to reward determined hikers who follow the distinctive red-and-white markers with their stylized representation of the Trail crossing hills and valleys.

The Heysen Trail takes in rugged gorges, native bushland, pine forests and scenic coastal areas, also passing through rich farmland, vineyards and historic towns. The northern part through the South Flinders Ranges offers rocky landscapes, ridges, gullies, pines and gum-lined creeks. The central section crosses rolling hills, farmland and grazing country with patches of bushland and forest. The southern part of the Trail offers fabulous coastal views, towering cliffs, gullies, sand dunes and dense bush.

Those who lack the time and/or energy to tackle the complete Heysen Trail can still enjoy many of its splendours. It is well-mapped and has been specifically designed to facilitate day walks along individual sections, though it is a linear trail – so those who wish to make the most of their walk should make arrangements to be picked up at the end of the day, to avoid wasting time by retracing their steps. The southern section from Spalding down to Cape Jervis follows the Mount Lofty Ranges and is most suitable for day walks, especially for families, as the northern section is more rugged and isolated.

# Port Phillip Bay

It's possible to be one among thousands, or do your own thing. Australia's passion for pedalling comes to a grand climax during October every year with 'Around the Bay in a Day' – the country's greatest mass cycling event, when up to 15,000 cyclists gather in Melbourne to ride around Port Phillip Bay, each choosing the route that best suits their capabilities – distances on offer are 50 km (31 mi), 100 km (62 mi), 210 km (130 mi) and 250 km (155 mi).

Port Phillip Bay, with Melbourne at the top, is almost land-locked – access to the Bass Strait is via the narrow Rip between Port Lonsdale and Point Nepean. The Bay has an irregular coastline of some 265 km (165 mi) and the full circumnavigation by road is somewhat shorter. It has many inlets and beaches, with the western shore being somewhat swampy and the eastern shore characterized by sandy beaches. For those planning their own ride there are numerous options, though there is increasing suburban development and consequent road traffic around the Bay, especially on the eastern shore. A full circumnavigation at a sensible pace to include recreational stop-offs and side trips could take a few days.

Clockwise from Melbourne, the route passes through the suburbs to Frankston and follows the water to Sorrento, where a ferry crosses the Rip to Queencliff. Then the road goes through Geelong before travelling back up the more sparsely populated western shore to Altona Beach and back to Melbourne.

In truth, it's best to get the buzz from being part of the amazing 'Around the Bay in a Day' mass ride. The event is beautifully staged by the Bicycle Victoria organization, with all sorts of support services offered. Advance registration is required (available on line) and is the key to an unforgettable cycling experience.

*St Kilda Beach, Port Phillip Bay*

**HOW:**
By bike
**WHEN TO GO:**
October for 'Around the Bay in a Day', any time for a solo spin.
**TIME IT TAKES:**
By definition, less than a day – a very long day of non-stop power cycling for the full circuit!
**HIGHLIGHTS:**
The high-rise skyline of downtown Melbourne viewed from Hobson's Bay. The revelling in Melbourne's Alexandra Gardens where the 'Around the Bay in a Day' event ends, including live music and entertainment.
**YOU SHOULD KNOW:**
Those stimulated by participating in 'Around the Bay in a Day' can go on to tackle another major event organized by Bicycle Victoria – the week-long 'Great Victorian Bike Ride'.

# Perth to Adelaide Road Trip

**HOW:**
By car
**WHEN TO GO:**
September to May to avoid the hottest desert conditions .
**TIME IT TAKES:**
Eight or nine days
**HIGHLIGHTS:**
Wave Rock near the small town of Hyden, and also nearby Aboriginal paintings on the walls of Mulka's Cave.
The Old Telegraph Station near Eucla, where encroaching sand serves as a reminder of the harshness of the Nullarbor Plain's unforgiving conditions.
A short side trip from the Eyre Highway to the Head of Bight for great views – and southern right whales disporting between June and October.
A refreshing side trip to the world-renowned Barossa Valley at journey's end, to toast that 'Ultimate Road Trip' in fine Aussie wine.
**YOU SHOULD KNOW:**
As recently as the late 1950s much of this route consisted of little more than hard-packed dirt roads (of which there are still plenty to be found off the main highway).

Billed as 'Australia's Ultimate Road Trip', the journey from Perth in Western Australia to Adelaide in South Australia lives up to its name. This epic route stretches for 3,200 km (1,900 mi) along Australia's southern coastline, delivering an ever-changing drama of striking landscapes, soaring cliffs, azure sea – and the mesmerizing desert that is the Nullarbor Plain. It's a largely empty land, with few significant towns along the way, but there's plenty to see. That emptiness also requires pre-planning, with a need to carry spare fuel and adequate emergency water supplies, just in case.

From Perth, the journey begins with a sortie down the coast along Highway 1, passing through Bunbury to the South Coast at Walpole, then along to Albany and the charming seaside settlement at Esperance, where the road turns north and runs up country to Norseman. Alternatively, it's possible to head inland from Perth along the Great Southern Highway, with a quick stop in the small town of York with its 19th-century buildings, before continuing through the small settlements of Aldersyde, Gorge Rock, Hyden and Forestania to Norseman.

From Norseman the long-distance Eyre Highway begins a long straight run parallel with the coast through the fearsome Nullarbor Plain to Eucla, the largest place on the Plain. Between the tiny settlement of Nullarbor and Eucla there are half a dozen lookout points that offer superb views of the impressive cliffs of the Great Australian Bight. After Eucla one of the longest stretches of tarmac road in Australia follows the coast through Nullarbor National Park to Ceduna, from whence the Flinders Highway continues through Streaky Bay, Elliston, Port Kenny, Port Lincoln and Port Augusta. The picturesque coastal towns of the Eyre Peninsula give way to the Clare Valley and the final run down into Adelaide. An awesome journey safely completed!

*The impressive cliffs of the Great Australian Bight*

# Pinnacles Desert Walk

*The Pinnacles in Nambung National Park*

Within the Nambung National Park in Western Australia may be found an extraordinary natural phenomenon – the Pinnacles. These surreal limestone monuments have become one of Australia's major attractions, and it's easy to see why. After driving up the coast from Perth, into the Park and along the unmade 27-km (17-mi) access track to the Pinnacles area, visitors have an opportunity to park and explore this extraordinary place on foot.

The Pinnacles were formed over millions of years to create a unique landscape that contains over four thousand sculpted monuments, scattered across a vast and arid desert landscape of rippled quartz sand dunes. They have been likened in appearance to fingers, termite mounds or even tombstones, but one thing is certain – Pinnacles come in all sizes and shapes and every single one is different, ranging from tiny spikes to sturdy monoliths that rise to over 4 m (13 ft) in height.

There's a loop track from the end of the access road that can be driven but is much better walked, as this allows for exploration of interesting groups of stones, with every twist and turn opening up new vistas. For those who prefer their excursions to be well organized in advance, it is possible to join guided walks through the Pinnacles, an approach with the advantage of guaranteeing that some of the most interesting formations will be visited. Even so, most people like to make their own discoveries.

To make the very most of the Pinnacles, it is sensible to arrive early in the morning or late in the day. Then, the desert becomes an eerie wonderland of contrasting colours and extended shadows when viewed in dawn light or at dusk against the purple and orange hues of a big sky. Photographers become ecstatic whilst the rest merely marvel.

**HOW:**
On foot
**WHEN TO GO:**
August to October
**TIME IT TAKES:**
Half a day gives ample opportunity for a fascinating walk, ideally starting/ending at dawn/dusk.
**HIGHLIGHTS:**
A sensational spring display of seasonal wild flowers around the desert area in the Park.
An encounter with the western grey kangaroos and emus that frequent Nambung National Park.
A spot of relaxation on the pristine white beach at nearby Cervantes.
**YOU SHOULD KNOW:**
If you have a hire car be sure that the insurance covers travel on unsealed roads – this is often specifically excluded in Australia.

*Spring Creek Track in Purnululu National Park*

# Purnululu National Park

**HOW:**
On foot and by 4x4
**WHEN TO GO:**
Only in the dry season – April to December
**TIME IT TAKES:**
Three hours for the Spring Creek Track.
**HIGHLIGHTS:**
Alongside Spring Creek Track – the strange bottle-shaped baobab trees that are a more common sight in Southern Africa and Madagascar. The short walk through the narrow Echidna Chasm, with its towering walls and tall palm trees – one of the most mysterious places in Australia. Piccaninny Creek on the southern edge of the Bungle Bungles, an impressive winding gorge contained by the high walls of the domes. Cathedral Gorge – well named, it is impossible to remain spiritually unmoved within this spacious cavern that soars to the sky.
**YOU SHOULD KNOW:**
The area is rich in Aboriginal art and Purnululu National Park contains many sacred burial sites.

Lots of Australia is pretty remote – and Purnululu National Park is more remote than most. This stunning place lies in Kimberley, the empty northeastern corner of Western Australia that is often described as 'Australia's last frontier'. The Park lies between Halls Creek – 110 km (68 mi) to the south – and Kununurra – 250 km (155 mi) to the north.

Although Aborigines lived in the area for countless generations, it only became generally known in 1982 when a TV crew 'discovered' the extraordinary landscape of orange-and-grey-striped beehive sandstone formations (called the Bungle Bungles), cliffs, tropical pools, plunging chasms and gorges with elegant fan palms adorning the rocks. Such was the impact of their revelation that Purnululu was officially declared a National Park just five years later and has now been designated as a UNESCO World Heritage Site.

Tourists being tourists, the usual way to tick off the incredible sights to be found in the Park is to view them from the air – regular flights by light aircraft are available from specialists in Halls Creek or Kununurra. There is also a helicopter service from the nearby Turkey Creek Roadhouse at Warmun on the Great Northern Highway.

But of course the best option is to get in amongst the real thing on foot, for a day hike or camping trip, though this requires more effort than merely turning up and tramping the terrain. It is possible to arrange a vehicle tour with the air carrier, who will land on the edge of the Park for a rendezvous with the ground crew. For hikers and campers, however, the only way in is along the unmade Spring Creek Track. This dusty 80-km (50-mi) route is only passable by 4x4 vehicle, with four-wheel drive engaged all the way to avoid damaging the dry road surface.

# Tasmania Coast Trek

After exploring the mainland, a trip across the Bass Strait to Tasmania seems like a visit to another country. This island is the most distinctive of Australia's states, with the relatively unspoiled environment that permits its self-proclaimed status as 'The Natural State'.

Those who wish to underline Tasmania's eco-credentials – and prove their own advanced self-sufficiency qualifications – should undertake the marathon hike along the connecting South Coast and Port Davey Tracks in the vast Southwest National Park. This is an epic wilderness adventure often described as 'the hardest trek in Australia', so it isn't for the faint of heart or weak of leg.

The easy part is getting there, with regular shuttles from Hobart servicing each end of the route. The heaviest part is the pack, which must contain everything needed for two unsupported weeks. That includes food and camping gear (there are basic campgrounds at regular intervals), plus a selection of all-weather clothing. It is essential to get a Backpacker Pass in advance and sign the registration book before starting (and after finishing).

Any hike in Tasmania involves battling against mud. The 84-km (52-mi) South Coast Track has plenty of it, plus two mountain ranges to cross where the coast is impassable and shoreline sections where the waves can be dangerous. The route is Cockle Creek, South Cape Rivulet, Granite Beach, New River Lagoon, Deadmans Bay, Louisa River, Cox Bight and Melaleuca. The demanding 80-km (50-mi) Port Davey Track begins at Melaleuca and goes inland via Spring River, Watershed Camp and Junction Creek to Scott's Peak, offering serious tests like bottomless mud and leech-infested swamps. Those who crack can be airlifted out from the mining camp at Melaleuca, but otherwise the only way out of the spectacular but dangerous wilderness is on two feet – or feet first!

*Louisa Bay on Tasmania's South Coast*

**HOW:**
On foot
**WHEN TO GO:**
December to March are the best months but can still produce cold winds and heavy rain – even snow flurries on the high tops!
**TIME IT TAKES:**
Eleven days if tramping the recommended daily sections.
**HIGHLIGHTS:**
Two rowboat crossings during the great trek – at New River Lagoon and Bathurst Narrows.
The beautiful Osmiridium Beach – check the map and look for a small path from the South Coast Track.
Staying in one of the hikers huts at Melaleuca – they may be primitive, but seem like the height of luxury after days of hard trekking.
A chance to see the rare and endangered orange-bellied parrot from the Deny King Memorial Hide near the airstrip at Melaleuca.
**YOU SHOULD KNOW:**
Some of the deadliest snakes on the planet lurk along the way – they tend to be shy but carry anti-venom in the First Aid kit, just in case!

# Helicopter Ride over Franz Josef Glacier

The Franz Josef Glacier and its near neighbour, the Fox Glacier, are extraordinary natural phenomena on the West Coast of the South Island. Descending from the Southern Alps, they terminate less than 300 m (985 ft) above sea level in verdant rainforest. Classification of both glaciers and the surrounding Westland National Park as a UNESCO World Heritage Site is well deserved. Due to heavy snowfall, Franz Josef is one of the few glaciers in New Zealand that is still growing. It is around 12 km (7.5 mi) long and terminates just 19 km (12 mi) from the Tasman Sea.

The glacier is one of the country's top attractions, with the former mining township of Franz Josef catering for visitors. It is some 5 km (3 mi) from the glacier's face and from there it is possible to hike up to the glacier, either solo or as part of a guided group (basic mountaineering equipment required). However, this is a fairly demanding walk that terminates at the first icefall – a frozen near-vertical slope.

By far the most popular way of experiencing this extraordinary place is to take a helicopter tour from the heliport in Franz Josef. It is possible to take a scenic ride that shows the glacier in all its glory from the comfort of a helicopter seat, or alternatively a longer trip that is extended to include the Fox Glacier.

But most able-bodied visitors prefer to set foot on the ice – the helicopter drops its passengers between the first and second icefalls on Franz Josef Glacier, where they have a guided tour of awe-inspiring glacial landscape – a wonderland of pinnacles and brilliant blue ice with sensational views of surrounding mountains. This is undoubtedly one of the world's most spectacular glacier experiences – or perhaps the most spectacular.

*A helicopter landing on the Franz Josef Glacier*

# Walking the Kauri Coast

For those who prefer to see their landscape from two feet rather than four wheels, and enjoy a bit of an adventure at the same time, walking the old Waoko Coach Road on the North Island is an ideal challenge.

*In the Kauri forest*

This historic route is an example of pioneering road building, dating back to the early years of colonial New Zealand. The Coach Road was once the only link between Hokianga and Kaipara Harbour on the sparsely populated West Coast, and remains isolated.

It extends to 22 km (13 mi) between Taheke and Tutamoe, with the northern entry at Waima and the southern entry at Tutamoe. It is certainly the shortest route between the two points – the distance between the two ends of the Coach Road by the modern State Highway is 90 km (56 mi).

Along the way the old road passes through the Waima and Mataraua forests, which are impressively preserved examples of the kauri forests that used to cover the coastal area hereabouts. Hikers will have the forest pretty much to themselves – the route is not well marked and little used, so it is essential to take good maps, food, water and wet-weather clothing...and wear stout boots. The journey goes up hill and down dale to a maximum height of 700 m (2,300 ft) but the gradients were chosen to allow horses to pull up fully laden wagons, so are never too steep.

The weather can be unpredictable and anyone who gets caught in one of the occasionally violent rainstorms on the high plateau can head for the public shelter halfway along the Coach Road. For anyone who likes their adventures organized, there are guided trips that offer accommodation and transport along with the scenic tramp.

**HOW:**
On foot
**WHEN TO GO:**
Any time of year (but be warned – this is a high-rainfall area).
**TIME IT TAKES:**
Though the distance is not long, the route is demanding and a full day (each way) is required.
**HIGHLIGHTS:**
Taking the interesting side leg to Wekaweka Valley near Weimamaku. Spotting remnants of the original construction, like a number of hand-cut stone culverts that still function today.
Starting very early to see kiwis in their natural habitat and hear the amazing dawn chorus.
**YOU SHOULD KNOW:**
Only one vehicle ever managed to drive the Coach Road without stopping or changing horses – it carried the then Prime Minister Sir Joseph Ward in 1912.

*Paihia - the 'Jewel of the Bay of Islands'*

# Twin Coast Discovery Highway

A stunning circular route provides a superb scenic drive through New Zealand's Northland, starting at Auckland, travelling up the North Island's East Coast before returning down the enchanting West Coast. This unforgettable journey goes through Warkworth, Wellsford, Mangawhai, Waipu, Marsden, Whangarei, Kawakawa, Waitangi/Russell, Paihia, Kerikeri, Kaitaia, Hokianga, Waipoua Forest, Dargaville and back from there to Auckland. The length of the Twin Coast Discovery Highway is around 925 km (575 mi).

The first stretch up the East Coast ends at the vibrant Northland centre of Whangarei, with its wealth of activities and strong cultural aspect. Then it's on to the famous Bay of Islands area, where hundreds of coves, beaches and islands are just waiting to be found. This is also the place to explore New Zealand's heritage, especially at Waitangi (where a treaty with the Maoris was signed in 1840) and Russell, a former whaling port once known as the 'Hell Hole of the South Pacific' and one of the first European settlements in New Zealand. Don't expect flames – happily it's now a charming waterside village full of historic sites. Another mandatory stop is at the seaside settlement of Paihia, known as the 'Jewel of the Bay of Islands'.

After crossing over the northern tip with its dense subtropical forests, the next stop is Kaitaia, gateway to the far north. From here, it's possible to take a side-trip along Ninety Mile Beach or go up to the tip of New Zealand at Cape Reinga. But the Highway heads south to the beautiful harbour at Hokianga and thence down the Kauri Coast – once heavily forested before being logged out it is now rolling pastureland. After the little farming town of Dargaville, on the north shore of Kaipara Harbour, the Highway crosses back to Wellsford on the east coast route south of Whangarei.

**HOW:**
By car

**WHEN TO GO:**
Any time of year

**TIME IT TAKES:**
Don't stint on this one – allow several days (or even a week) to explore the wonderful landscape as you go.

**HIGHLIGHTS:**
First stop – the impressive hot springs of the Waiwere Thermal Reserve, near the delightful seaside town of Orewa with its golden beaches.
Chartering a boat at Opua (with or without a skipper) to explore the beaches and coves of the offshore islands.
Gumfields Historic Reserve near Kaitaia – a ghost town that hasn't been occupied since the 19th century.
A visit to Waipoua Forest near Hokianga, home to the world's tallest kauri tree – known as Tane Mahuta (God of the Forest), it is over one thousand years old.

**YOU SHOULD KNOW:**
The Stone Store in Kerikeri is the oldest European building in New Zealand, dating back to 1836.

# Whanganui River Journey

Here's a novelty – a walk that's undertaken by canoe. That's because the Whanganui River Journey is officially classified as a 'Great Walk', underlining its status as one of New Zealand's great outdoor adventure trips. The mighty Whanganui River is situated in the southwestern part of the North Island, winding down in pristine splendour from the volcanic plateau near Mount Tongariro to the Tasman Sea.

The upper reaches run through dense rainforest. In the middle reaches its rocky banks are crowded by broadleaf woodland that forms the heart of Whanganui National Park, before it passes through rolling farmland on the last stretch to the sea. The whole area is rich in Maori tradition and from the 1890s to the 1950s a riverboat service used to support Europeans who had settled along the banks.

The 145-km (90-mi) canoe trip from Taumarunui to Pipiriki is well served with huts and camping grounds, allowing for leisurely paddling that gives ample time to enjoy the awe-inspiring river and its dramatic surroundings. The landscape is young in geological terms, formed a million years ago of soft sandstone and mudstone (*papa*) from the seabed and since eroded into dramatic ridges, deep gorges, sheer cliffs and plunging waterfalls. Broadleaf forest has evolved, and distinctive tree ferns cling to steep riverbanks.

The canoeing is easy – but exciting. There are numerous rapids along the way, but these are never more demanding than Level II, making for an exhilarating passage without much risk of dangerous capsize. The whole journey is special, but the three-day section from Whakahoro through the National Park to Pipiriki is wilderness canoeing at its best, traversing tranquil stretches and rushing water, through deep gorges and past towering bluffs where the local population of feral goats often stand to look down on passing canoes.

**HOW:**
By canoe
**WHEN TO GO:**
Any time (but New Zealand weather can change rapidly and be wet and/or cold in any season).
**TIME IT TAKES:**
Around five days of gentle paddling.
**HIGHLIGHTS:**
Meeting indigenous Tieke people beside the river at Tieka Kainga (if they're there!) and taking part in a traditional *powhiri* (Maori welcoming ceremony).
A side trip up the Mangapurua Gorge to see the haunting 'Bridge to Nowhere' – built in 1935 to open up the Mangapurua Valley to settlers, abandoned when the attempt failed.
Shooting the long Paparoa Rapid just before journey's end at Pipiriki.
**YOU SHOULD KNOW:**
Don't expect the journey to be all peace and quiet – you are likely to encounter an occasional jet ski speeding along the river.

*Canoeing on the Whanganui River*

*Lake Waikaremoana*

# Lake Waikaremoana

**HOW:**
On foot
**WHEN TO GO:**
September to June
**TIME IT TAKES:**
Three to four days
**HIGHLIGHTS:**
The view from the top of towering Panekire Bluff at the southern end of Lake Waikaremoana.
A side trip up to Korokoro Falls – a sight that is well worth the 30-minute walk.
The distinctive night calls of the protected – and slowly recovering – brown kiwi population of the Park.
A drive up from Aniwaniwa to nearby Lake Waikareiti after completing the Great Walk.
**YOU SHOULD KNOW:**
The deer, pigs and possums found in the Te Urewera National Park are quarry species, so hikers should keep a weather eye open for hunters.

A natural gem in the North Island's East Coast/Hawke's Bay Region is the remote and rugged Te Urewera National Park, which preserves some of the country's most magnificent scenery. Tucked away in the southwestern corner of the Park is the Lake Waikaremoana Great Walk – one of the nationally designated 'Great Walks' managed by the Department of Conservation, indicating that they are New Zealand's finest tramping tracks.

This 46-km (29-mi) hike loosely follows the lakeshore after which it is named, offering superb lake views when it strays from the water. The going is fairly easy and the Great Walk isn't that long, but the idea is to take it easy, stopping overnight and enjoying recreational opportunities such as swimming and fishing offered by Lake Waikaremoana as you go. There are five huts and campsites and prior booking is mandatory throughout the year – even in winter this is a popular trek, though the Great Walk is occasionally closed as a result of heavy snowfall that brings down overloaded tree branches to block the track.

Most hikers drive in to Aniwaniwa on the gravel-surfaced State Highway 38 that links the East Coast with Central North Island. From there, there are well-signed roads to both walk entrances, though most prefer to park securely at Aniwaniwa and take one of the regular shuttle buses or water taxis that service each end of the walk. They will also return hikers to their vehicles after completing the Great Walk.

It's possible to travel either way between Hopuruahine Suspension Bridge (north) and Onepoto (south). The route passes through a variety of terrain with varied vegetation, from the beech forest of Panekire Bluff to mixed broadleaf woodland, dense rainforest and open grassland. All harbour abundant birdlife, adding a colourful dimension to this unforgettable walk through varied and always stunning scenery.

# The Southern Scenic Route

This expedition in the South Island has a new boast – at last it's all on paved roads. But that doesn't mean travelling on tarmac all the way, as many essential sights and experiences involve exploring old-style New Zealand 'gravel tops'. Either way, the effort's worthwhile – the natural beauty of this wonderful country never ceases to amaze, but nowhere is it more impressive than along the aptly-named Southern Scenic Route.

The U-shaped journey takes you from Te Anau to Dunedin, skirting Fiordland National Park (part of the Te Wahipounamu World Heritage Site) and passing through Manapouri and Tuatapere to the coast at Te Waewae Bay, where the road swings east to Orepuki, Colac Bay and Riverton before turning south into Invercargill. Heading east again, the Route goes through Fortescue into the rugged Catlins, a sparsely populated area that contains New Zealand's southernmost tip, Slope Point. The next ports of call are Owaka and Balclutha. Here 4x4-drivers can take a detour along rough roads through Kaitangata, though the official course is along State Highway 1 to Milton and Lake Waihola. From there, the last leg crosses the Otago Coast Forest to Taieri Mouth before continuing through Brighton and Green Island to Dunedin.

The Southern Scenic Route extends to 440 km (273 mi)...and what kilometres! They connect a stunning combination of features found nowhere else in the country – rolling pastures, jagged mountains, lakes, native forest, bush rolling down to the water's edge, breathtaking ocean views, solitude and empty sandy beaches, spectacular fiords, bays and inlets, colourful fishing villages and Victorian towns. It all adds up to a scenic wonderland, but that's not all – quite apart from fabulous scenery, there are a host of interesting features and places to explore along the way, in an area famed for 'southern hospitality'.

**HOW:**
By car or 4x4
**WHEN TO GO:**
September through to May for the best weather.
**TIME IT TAKES:**
Although the Route can be driven non-stop in just ten hours, that's a criminal waste of opportunity – allow at least three days (five would be better).
**HIGHLIGHTS:**
Lake Te Anou – New Zealand's second-largest lake, mostly within the setting of Fiordland National Park.
Milford Sound – one of the natural wonders of the world.
A side trip from Invercargill to beguiling Stewart Island – a National Park where it's still possible to see kiwis in their natural habitat.
Purakaunui Falls near Owaka – a splendid multi-tiered display of cascading white water that is one of the best cataracts in New Zealand.
**YOU SHOULD KNOW:**
There are proposals to extend the Southern Scenic Route from Dunedin through Waitati to Oamaru.

*Milford Sound – one of the natural wonders of the world*

# The Classic New Zealand Wine Trail

**HOW:**
By car
**WHEN TO GO:**
Any time of year (the grape harvest takes place in March and April).
**TIME IT TAKES:**
A non-stop nine hours, or up to five leisurely days (stopping at Hastings, Martinborough, Wellington and Picton).
**HIGHLIGHTS:**
Pukaha Mount Bruce Wildlife Centre in Wairarapa – see many of New Zealand's most endangered wildlife species up close.
At least a day spent exploring the shops, restaurants and cultural delights of Wellington.

There's no respect left in the world when it comes to viticulture, as upstart newcomers come up with fine wines to compete with the great vintages produced by long-established European vineyards... and New Zealand's wine growers are high on the list of challengers. Anyone who doubts that merely has to drive the East Coast's well-signposted Classic New Zealand Wine Trail, choosing to stop at any number of wineries that welcome visitors with open arms (and opened bottles!), or finding organized collective tastings that offer the opportunity to sample wines from many different growers at the same time in the same place.

The Trail starts in Napier on the North Island and continues via Hastings, Waipukurau, Norsewood, Dannevirke, Woodville, Pahiatua, Eketahuna, Masterton and Martinborough to Wellington.

From there, the Cook Strait is crossed by ferry to Picton on the South Island, before the Trail goes on to end at Blenheim.

This 485-km (300-mi) road trip passes through 3 major wine-growing areas and five regions – Hawkes Bay, Tararua, Wairarapa, Wellington and Marlborough – that together offer the bonus of some great scenery. And many dozens of the vineyards to be visited along the way not only offer fine wines, but also excellent meals to go with them, so this can definitely be considered a self-indulgent gourmet experience.

The start of the Wine Trail takes in the Hawkes Bay wine-growing area, the heart of New Zealand's red wine country. Next comes Martinborough, the country's first great stronghold of the Pinot Noir grape. Then it's on to the sunny skies of Marlborough, where the claim to fame is undoubtedly superb Sauvignon Blanc that proves the point that – sometimes – the New World's winemakers can match or even exceed anything the Old World can put in a wine bottle. Bottoms up!

The 150-minute ferry crossing of the dramatic Cook Strait (if the weather's fine and the sea calm!).
A coastal side trip along the winding Queen Charlotte Drive from Picton to Havelock – it's like cruising the spectacular Marlborough Sounds without a boat!
**YOU SHOULD KNOW:**
Serious gastro tourists should know that there's more – specifically the Northland Food and Wine Trail, through New Zealand's fastest-growing wine region in the subtropical north.

*Black Bridge Vineyard near Hawkes Bay*

*The Tararua Mountains*

# Tararua Mountains Southern Crossing

The North Island has a mountainous spine that stretches from the East Cape to Wellington, parallel to the sea. The southernmost part is formed by the Tararua Range, spanning 80 km (50 mi) from Palmerston North to the Hutt Valley, which runs down to Wellington Harbour.

Within sight of Wellington is one of the country's best-known hiking routes – or tramping tracks, as New Zealanders prefer to say. The rugged Southern Crossing goes over the bare peaks of the southern Tararuas from Otaki Forks (reached by single-track unmade road – drive with care!), past Mount Hector and on to Kaitoke. It is no picnic stroll – New Zealand's unpredictable weather presents an ever-present and often-realized threat and there have been several fatalities over the years. But this is a challenge that will be relished – and met – by the well-prepared and experienced hiker, who will be rewarded with sensational panoramic views of mountains and sea.

There are huts along the route, providing both accommodation and bad-weather shelter. But there is only one hut – Kime Hut – on the exposed tops between the bush lines above Field and Alpha Huts, the latter pair being the usual places to overnight during the Crossing (nights one and two respectively). The climb to Field Hut is relatively short, so some hikers continue and stay at Kime Hut on their first night, though this is technically a bad-weather refuge. But the standard approach on Day One is a three-hour walk up to Field Hut, just below the bush-line, followed by a truly awe-inspiring eight-hour tramp along the tops to Alpha Hut on Day Two, with the Crossing being completed by a less dramatic eight-hour exit via the Marchant Ridge on Day Three.

A winter Southern Crossing in good snow conditions is one of the most exhilarating hikes in New Zealand (alpine equipment and crampons essential!).

**HOW:**
On foot
**WHEN TO GO:**
Any time (June to August for the possibility of a snow crossing).
**TIME IT TAKES:**
Three days
**HIGHLIGHTS:**
A magnificent panoramic view from Field Peak near Kime Hut – west to Otaki, north along the Tararua Range, east to Mount Hector and south to the Hutt Valley and Wellington.
The undulating ridge route over the humps and bumps of the aptly named Beehives.
A dramatically steep path down from Alpha Hut into the scarily named Hell's Gate.
A short side trip after fording the Tauherenikau River to see Cone Hut – one of the best examples of bush carpentry in New Zealand.
**YOU SHOULD KNOW:**
Kime Hut is named in memory of E.J. Kime, who lost his life attempting the Southern Crossing.

# Punakaiki Horseback Ride

Between the towns of Westport and Greymouth on the South Island's West Coast is Paparoa National Park, alongside State Highway 6. This is a land of extraordinary coastline, lush coastal forests, canyons and limestone cliffs, caves and underground streams.

One of the most notable features is the famous Pancake Rocks and accompanying blowholes of Dolomite Point near the small settlement of Punakaiki. The most invigorating way of appreciating these amazing natural phenomena is to see them from horseback after a ride through the heart of the scenic Punakaiki Valley. The local stables offers a variety of custom rides to suit individual requirements, but also run a popular standard short excursion that gives a wonderful flavour of Paparoa National Park's unique attractions. The horses are steady and it is possible to enjoy the trek without having previous riding experience (elementary tuition given).

It begins with an atmospheric ride into the Punakaiki Valley, fording the river and passing through native bush to view huge limestone bluffs topped with temperate rainforest. Abundant birdlife is a feature of the Park, and birds seem less cautious when the watchers are on horseback. Species to look out for are white-breasted native kereru (pigeons), the bright pukeko, inquisitive weka, paradise duck, spur-winged plover and harrier hawk.

There will be a short rest stop at a bush hut on the river flats, before returning to the coast and riding along Punakaiki Beach, with horses strolling through the seething white water at the water's edge. The climax of the ride is simply sitting and marvelling as the powerful sea crashes into the Pancake Rocks and erupts upwards through the blowholes. This expanse of water-sculpted grey rock resembles endless stacks of pancakes forming a fabulous tableau – can't be eaten, but never forgotten!

*A blowhole at Punakaiki*

**HOW:**
On horseback
**WHEN TO GO:**
Any time of year (just be sure to pick a fine day!)
**TIME IT TAKES:**
The standard ride takes around 2.5 hours.
**HIGHLIGHTS:**
Getting to (and going on from) Punakaiki along one of the most spectacular coastal highways in New Zealand, between the sea and Southern Alps.
The fascinating surge pool at Dolomite Point – known as the Devil's Cauldron, it can have a mesmeric effect.
With luck – spotting a pod of Hector's Dolphins disporting themselves just off Pancake Rocks.
**YOU SHOULD KNOW:**
The three blowholes at Dolomite Point put on their best show when there is a strong southwesterly swell at high tide.

# Abel Tasman Coast Track

*The Coast Track in Abel Tasman National Park*

The Abel Tasman National Park on the north shores of the South Island is in the Golden Bay area. It contains one of the country's 'Great Walks' – the Abel Tasman Coast Track. This 51-km (32-mi) hike is officially described as an 'easy tramping track', but the usual proviso about going equipped to deal with the weather's notorious mood swings holds good.

The Coast Track runs from Marahau to Wainui through wild and stunning coastal scenery, of which New Zealand has an almost indecent abundance. It crosses numerous watercourses and estuaries along the way. Rivers and streams are bridged, but some estuaries can only be crossed for an hour or two either side of low tide, and both bridges and estuaries can become impassable after heavy rain.

As the name suggests, the Coastal Track follows the sea, though often detouring inland to cross saddles that separate bays, sometimes losing sight of the sea altogether in dense forest. However, most climbs are rewarded with sensational sea and coastal views from those hard-earned vantage points. Down at sea level, there are many interesting coves to be found and estuaries to be explored, so it's best to proceed at a leisurely pace, planning an itinerary that involves overnight stops at the campsites and/or huts to be found at regular intervals (camp passes required).

The route goes from Marahau to Apple Tree Bay, Yellow Point, Torrent Bay, Anchorage Bay (hut and campsite), Bark Bay (hut and campsite), Tonga Quarry, Onetahuti Bay, Awaroa Inlet (hut and campsite), Waiharakeke Bay, Goat Bay, Skinner Point, Totaranui (major campsite complex), Anapai Bay, Mutton Cove, Whariwharangi Bay (campsite and hut – a restored farmstead) and finally on to Wanui Inlet, where transport out is available from the car park. Enjoy (and that's a promise)!

# Fiordland Long Distance Walk

In the southwestern corner of the South Island lies the country's largest National Park. Fiordland protects coastal landscape that typifies New Zealand's natural splendour. It is a wonderland of mountains, glaciers, beech forests and waterfalls that tumble into the sea – and of course the sculpted fiords that give the Park its name. It's possible to enjoy various outdoor recreational activities in Fiordland, but the best way to see the very best of the scenery is to undertake the 55-km (34-mi) waterside hike along the Milford Track from Glade Wharf to Sandfly Point (a permit is required from the visitor centre in Te Anau).

However, those experienced and super-fit individuals who look for a seriously demanding physical challenge will head straight for the Hollyford Track. They know they've got it right when they see the sign at the start of this 112-km (70-mi) return trip from the route's dead end at the sea. It reads: *'Warning: The Pyke Valley is a difficult track. It is subject to flooding and is suitable for fit, experienced trampers'*. Add to that the need to backpack camping equipment, survival gear and enough food rations for two weeks (just in case!) and the size of the task becomes apparent. After the Alabaster Hut on Lake Alabaster, this becomes a wilderness trip par excellence, travelling through wild, untamed landscape and meeting like-minded hikers along the way.

For utterly determined and super-fit adventurers who prefer not to retrace their steps and can take the pain, there is an additional 60-km (37-mi) route from the end of the Hollyford Track that returns to Alabaster Hut. The isolated and testing Pyke Route is badly marked, has only two huts and can be very dangerous if it rains hard. It's the ultimate test!

*Stunning scenery in Fiordland National Park*

**HOW:**
On foot
**WHEN TO GO:**
September to May (winter is best avoided).
**TIME IT TAKES:**
Around six days for the Hollyford Track – add an optimistic three days for the Pyke Loop.
**HIGHLIGHTS:**
Good company and tall tramping tales when over-nighting in one of the Trail's remote but welcoming huts.
The view of Mount Madeline reflected in the lake from Alabaster Hut at sunset.
Reaching the end of the Hollyford Track at beautiful Martins Bay with its glorious beach.
A hot shower after finally returning to civilization – tired but satisfied after completing this epic hike.
**YOU SHOULD KNOW:**
Pack plenty of insect repellent – sandflies are a persistent nuisance all the way along the Hollyford Track.

*The Canterbury Plains below Mount Hutt*

# The TranzAlpine Train

**HOW:**
By train
**WHEN TO GO:**
Any time of year
**TIME IT TAKES:**
4.5 hours
**HIGHLIGHTS:**
Riding a while in the open-sided viewing carriage that really lets you feel close to – and photograph – the beautiful surroundings.
Crossing the soaring Staircase Viaduct that is a dizzying 73 m (240 ft) above the River Waimakariri.
A delicious Devonshire cream tea from the onboard café bar during the journey.
Passing the old Brunner Mine near Greymouth, site of New Zealand's worst mining disaster in 1896 – spot the old suspension bridge across the River Waimakariri to the industrial area.
**YOU SHOULD KNOW:**
It doesn't have to end at Greymouth – a Scenic Rail Pass gives access to the entire Trans Scenic network on both islands and allows independent travellers to do their own thing at their own pace.

Yes, there are indeed trains in New Zealand – and given the country's outstanding natural attributes it is hardly surprising that one of the world's great scenic railway journeys may be found here. The sleek blue TranzAlpine runs for a distance of 224 km (140 mi) right across the South Island, westwards from Christchurch on the east coast to the small town of Greymouth (and vice versa). It runs once a day, starting at 08.15, and goes through sixteen tunnels and crosses five viaducts along the way, adding to the drama of a splendid journey.

Christchurch is the South Island's largest city, offering the cosmopolitan delights of urban living. However, the comfortable and relaxing TranzAlpine with its panoramic picture windows quickly leaves all that behind. Industrial outskirts and suburbs vanish and the lush pastures and farmland of the fertile Canterbury Plains start to slide by as the train hurries towards the distant mountains.

Before long, it leaves populated parts altogether – reaching the foothills and starting the long climb through the valleys and plunging gorges of the rushing Waimakiriri River. It then continues into the Southern Alps, crossing girder bridges and going through short tunnels amidst fabulous scenery. After crossing a grassy plateau dotted with hills the TranzAlpine stops at Arthurs Pass Station, with its backdrop of misty mountains, before going through the 8.6-km (5.3–mi) Otira Tunnel and starting the descent through a deep valley, criss-crossing the Grey River and passing waterfalls and lush beech rainforest before arriving at the old-fashioned wooden station at Greymouth, gateway to Punakaiki and the rugged splendours of the west coast.

Those who don't want to go on to explore by bus or hire car can actually return to Christchurch on the TranzAlpine that same day, after an hour's stopover in Greymouth.

# Haleakala Highway

Aloha – welcome to Maui, 'The Magic Isle'! And of course there's one journey you must take – the scenic drive from Kahului along the Haleakala Highway to the top of the massive shield volcano that forms more than three-quarters of the island's mass. The road is a modern two-lane highway, but it twists and turns alarmingly on the way to the 3,055-m (10,023-ft) summit with many blind bends, and is frequently close to sheer drops. To add to the risks, wildlife and cattle often stray onto the road, especially at night.

But the effort is well rewarded – there are great views over the island and surrounding sea during the drive and the sight that awaits at the summit is awesome – a vast crater that is around 11.25 km (7 mi) long, 3.2 km (2 mi) across and 800 m (2,600 ft) deep, with steep walls and a scattering of volcanic cones around the barren interior.

Actually, despite every appearance to the contrary, the summit crater of Haleakala is not volcanic in origin. It was formed when the walls of two erosional valleys merged at the volcano's summit and is technically a depression rather than a crater, but the distinction is too fine for all but vulcanologists, so crater it shall be. The volcano is active, but has not erupted since the 1600s and is considered dormant, soon to become extinct.

Haleakala National Park surrounds the crater, much of it is wilderness. Rainforest cloaks the windward slopes of the mountain, though the dry forest that once covered the leeward side has been drastically reduced. The Park contains Kipahula Valley, one of the most complete rainforest ecosystems in Hawaii. Visitors should look out for the rare silversword plant that only grows here, a strange member of the sunflower family.

**HOW:**
By car
**WHEN TO GO:**
Any time of year
**TIME IT TAKES:**
Up to three hours to drive the Highway, depending on traffic – allow a full day to include some exploration.
**HIGHLIGHTS:**
Getting to the summit at dawn to view one of the best sunrises you'll ever see.
The fabulous view into the crater from the Kalahaku Overview below the summit.
Science City at the summit – an astrophysical complex that takes advantage of the clear, dry atmosphere and absence of serious light pollution that makes this the perfect location for ground-based telescopes.
A strenuous 15-minute hike to the top of nearby Pa Ka'oao (White Hill) for a sensational panorama.
**YOU SHOULD KNOW:**
Thrill seekers travel to the top by bus before shooting back down the mountain at high speed on a rented bicycle.

*The volcano in Haleakala National Park*

# Exploring Viti Levu

Fiji's principal island of Viti Levu, the Pacific's third largest, contains most of the Republic's population. The majority live in the towns and villages that ring the coastline, as the centre of the island is forested and largely undeveloped. Main economic activities are sugar cane production, cattle ranching, gold mining and tourism – with holidaymakers attracted by resorts along the Coral Coast in the southwest and in the locally named 'Burning West'. These offer classic Pacific ingredients of offshore islands, white sand, reefs, emerald lagoons and palm trees. But there's more to Viti Levu than that, and those who stick to the beach are missing a great opportunity to explore a fascinating island.

Viti Levu is divided by a mountain range that makes it an island of two halves – with heavy rainfall and lush green vegetation on windward slopes to the east and drier brown landscape to the west. Most visitors who do explore Viti Levu hire a car and take the paved coast road that circumnavigates the island, with side-trips down tempting tracks. The working north coast has few tourist facilities and spectacular scenery whilst the soggy east coast is characterized by extensive mangrove swamps.

For adventurous souls who like to experience the culture of the places they visit, Viti Levu's busy Sunbeam Bus network offers endless possibilities. Express buses connect the major centres and stopping buses serve most villages. It's a great way of meeting the friendly locals and seeing the 'real' Fiji – a world away from the tourist resorts. One of the most interesting journeys is through the undeveloped interior from Nausori in the southeastern corner of the island through the highlands via Vunidawa up to Tavua on the north coast, crossing Viti Levu's mountainous spine and skirting the country's highest mountain – Mount Tomanivi (formerly Mount Victoria).

*The traditional village of Navala*

# Mount Koghi Rainforest Trek

'New Caledonia – now where exactly is that?' is a common reaction when this French overseas territory is mentioned, because the scenic island chain deep in the South Pacific is something of a secret in tourist terms. It is certainly less well known than destinations like French Polynesia or Fiji, though it has all the qualifications of a Pacific paradise – offshore coral islands, blue lagoons and white-sand beaches. To that may be added a certain *je ne sais quoi* – that indefinable element of stylish living that nobody does quite so well as the French.

The island of Grand Terre is at the centre of New Caledonian life, and the capital of Nouméa has a refined ambiance with fine colonial architecture, tree-lined squares, open-air cafés, casinos, boutique shopping and fine dining the norm. But wait! There is another Grand Terre – dismissed as *la brousse* ('The Bush') by sophisticated townies.

Much of the eastern end of the island is undeveloped and remains the domain of the indigenous Kanak people. This is a land of rainforest and fabulous scenery that includes imposing landscapes, bare mountains, unusual rock formations and dramatic cliffs that plunge into the sea. Every visitor to this magical island should venture into the ancient rainforest, which has survived untouched for millions of years – ever since New Caledonia was part of the lost continent of Gondwana.

Just 20 km (12 mi) from Nouméa is one of the most accessible yet rewarding options – a trek through the rainforest of Mount Koghi with its towering trees and lush foliage, alive with tropical birds. There are a number of recognized hikes of various lengths on offer, with or without guides. When the chosen trek is over, relax at the Mount Koghi station and enjoy the splendid views down over the spectacular Dumbéa Valley, Nouméa and the lagoon.

*A hiker walks through the rainforest of Mount Koghi.*

**HOW:**
On foot
**WHEN TO GO:**
Any time of year
**TIME IT TAKES:**
Allow one day for the longest marked rainforest trek at Mount Koghi.
**HIGHLIGHTS:**
Spotting a cagou – the white flightless bird with a large crest and strange barking call that is a national symbol of New Caledonia.
A guided botanical tour from Mount Koghi station for insight into the unique local flora.
The Museum of New Caledonia in Nouméa, for an overview of the ethnology of these fascinating islands – includes a magnificent collection of Melanesian artefacts.
**YOU SHOULD KNOW:**
The New Caledonia Lagoon on the west coast is the world's largest, encircled by a 1,600-km (1,000-mi) reef that is second only to Australia's Great Barrier Reef in length.

533

# Rapa Nui Tour

**HOW:**
By 4x4
**WHEN TO GO:**
Any time of year
**TIME IT TAKES:**
Two days to explore the island.
**HIGHLIGHTS:**
Two Windows Cave – accessed through a narrow passage that opens out into a cavern with two tunnel-like openings that run out to the cliff face above the sea.
Relaxing on Anakena Beach with its white sand and warm turquoise – plus the Ahu Nau Nau with its seven *moai*.
Ahu Tongariki, where 15 *moai* stand in line on their platform looking out to sea – the only ones to do so.
**YOU SHOULD KNOW:**
Countless horses roam unchecked all over the island – there are nearly as many horses as people!

There can be few more recognizable images in the world than the mysterious stone heads and torsos on Chile's overseas territory of Easter Island, carved by the Rapa nui people. These monumental statues are *moai* some of which are 10m (33 ft) tall. This remote Polynesian outpost is in the southeastern Pacific Ocean and it's one of the world's most isolated inhabited islands, so relatively few people have seen those famous stones at first hand.

Most of the island – a UNESCO World Heritage Site – is protected within the Rapa Nui National Park. There are unresolved arguments concerning the origins of the islanders and the history of the iconic *moai* – it is agreed that they were produced by a Stone Age culture, painstakingly carved with basalt chisels.

After flying in to the grandly named Mataveri International Airport, it is possible to rent a 4x4 and make a comprehensive tour of Rapa Nui. This small island was deforested long before the first

Europeans visited in the 18th century and is now mainly open grassland, but there is much to see. There is a single circular road from the only settlement, Hanga Roa in the southwest of the island, but there are also many dirt roads that allow a complete tour.

It is impossible not to be deeply moved by the sense of timeless history in this extraordinary place. Most of the *moai* are located around the outside of the island, looking inwards, many of them set on beautifully constructed *ahus* (ceremonial platforms), but hundreds at various stages of construction remain where they were abandoned in the quarry at Rano Raraku. There are also caves such as Ana Tai Tangata with red-and-white bird paintings. And it's all set in an atmospheric landscape dominated by three volcanic peaks.

# The Kokoda Track

**HOW:**
On foot
**WHEN TO GO:**
Dry (more accurately 'dryer')
season – April to September
**TIME IT TAKES:**
Three days is possible but the norm
at trekking pace is nine days.
**HIGHLIGHTS:**
Much evidence of surviving World
War II Japanese and Australian
defensive works at various points
along the Track.
Reaching one of the villages, where
friendly Koiari or Orokaiva peoples
will offer tempting seasonal fruits
and vegetables.
The memorial overlooking Kokoda
Valley – scene of a heroic battle
when Australians defied superior
enemy forces for four days, marking
the beginning of the end of the
Japanese presence in PNG.
**YOU SHOULD KNOW:**
If you're in a hurry it's possible to
join the annual Kokoda Challenge
Race where locals and incomers try
for the fastest time from end to end
of the Track (the running record is
currently just over 17 hours).

There's a little spat regarding the most famous hike in Papua New Guinea (PNG) – should it be called the Kokoda Track or the Kokoda Trail? Also in the mix are historic names such as 'The Buna Road' and 'The Overland Mail Route'. But whatever the name, the trek's the same – a demanding slog that runs in a straight line across isolated country for 60 km (37 mi). But don't assume that's just a long day's walk – the Track crosses terrain that can only be accessed on foot, demanding serious physical effort.

This single-file walking route runs from Ower's Corner in PNG's Central Province, 50 km (31 mi) east of capital Port Moresby, to Kokoda Village in Oro Province. The Track passes through rugged mountainous country of rainforest, fern jungles and streams tumbling into steep valleys, reaching the lung-testing height of 2,200 m (7,220 ft) as it skirts around the peak of Mount Bellamy. It can be hiked either way, with general agreement that Kokoda to Ower's Corner is the slightly easier direction. This is definitely the way to go for those who want a guide or porter, as there are plenty of experienced locals to choose from in Kokoda. There are rest houses along the route, some in villages and others at traditional staging points.

From Kokoda, the Track passes a number of unspoiled villages on the way to Ower's Corner – Kovolo, Hoi, Isurava, Alolo, Kagi, Efogi Creek, Menari and Naoro. Despite hostile terrain, burning days, freezing nights, intense humidity, capricious tropical rainfall and the ever-present risk of contracting endemic diseases such as malaria, the Track is a popular trekking challenge – especially for Australians. In 1942 Australian troops inflicted World War II's first military defeat on Japanese land forces along the Kokoda Track, which now has iconic status for Australians.

*One of the trail porters on the Kokoda Track*

# Aranui Cargo Boat

There's romance in the idea of island hopping in the Pacific aboard a freighter – especially when the journey begins in Tahiti and continues through the remote and unspoiled Marquesas, French Polynesia's most spectacular island group. And that's precisely what's on offer each time the sleek white Aranui 3 sails.

Actually, the 'Freighter to Paradise' offers rather more than the usual basic amenities – she's anything but any old freighter. Although Aranui 3 is a cargo ship, she also carries up to 200 passengers who are accommodated in air-conditioned cabins. There's also a pool, bar, dining salon and small theatre complete with resident lecturer to add culture to the proceedings, so this splendid adventure might be described as slumming it French style.

Better still, creature comforts are supplemented by the extraordinary thrill of a working boat being welcomed by excited islanders everywhere she calls – her regular visit is a highlight of life in the remote villages she serves. The route encompasses two ports of call in the Tuamotu Islands and fourteen on the six inhabited Marquesas, following this course – Tahiti, Fakarava, Ua Pou, Nuku Hiva, Hiva Oa, Fatu Hiva, Hiva Oa again, Tahuata, Ua Huka, Nuku Hiva again, Ua Pou again, Rangiroa and back to Tahiti.

As the ship can only dock at a limited number of places, cargo is mostly landed by barge, while passengers take the whaleboat to put in shore time. Despite the heat and humidity, the Marquesas are magical – with jagged coastlines and soaring volcanic peaks shrouded in mist, black sand beaches and emerald lagoons, coconut groves and lush forests, bougainvillea and frangipani. And luckily the locals no longer practise cannibalism, but are incredibly friendly. The phrase 'journey of a lifetime' is often used and not always warranted, but in the case of this unique cruise it certainly seems justified.

**HOW:**
By boat
**WHEN TO GO:**
Any time – Aranui 3 sails every third week, all year round.
**TIME IT TAKES:**
The round trip takes two weeks.
**HIGHLIGHTS:**
Hearing the Aranui 3's enthusiastic 6-piece crew band in action in the top deck bar on a sultry night, with Polynesian rhythms adding immeasurably to the atmosphere.
On Hiva Oa – visiting Paul Gauguin's grave and the House of Pleasure where he spent his last years.
On Nuku Hiva – the beautiful Notre Dame Cathedral in Taiohae Village, capital of the Marquesas.
A yummy Marquesan beach feast – roast suckling pig, *poisson cru*, curried goat, breadfruit *poi*, taro, guava, banana *po'e*, as well as coconut, in all its shapes and forms.
**YOU SHOULD KNOW:**
For those who feel freighter trips shouldn't be too comfortable (or expensive), there are two 12-bunk dormitories near the engine room!

*Sailing close to Fatu Hiva.*

# Cruising through the Antarctic

**HOW:**
By boat
**WHEN TO GO:**
November to January
**TIME IT TAKES:**
Each journey varies, but a typical
cruise lasts for three weeks.
**HIGHLIGHTS:**
Observing one of the penguin colonies
with tens of thousands of breeding
pairs that have no fear of man.
Visiting the Bay of Whales – the
closest point to the South Pole that
can be reached by ship.
The hut used by Captain R.F. Scott's ill-
fated polar expedition still stands on
the north shore of Cape Evans on
Ross Island, complete with well-
preserved contents, exactly as it was
left by the survivors in 1913.

Increasing affluence and awareness of global warming have led to the introduction – and considerable popularity – of cruises to the sixth continent and the world's last pristine wilderness. The Antarctic is undoubtedly suffering as the world warms and the great ice shelves start to disintegrate. So it may be a case of 'catch it while you can', but Antarctica remains an awe-inspiring destination.

Those who make this journey join the relatively tiny number of people who have ever visited this very special place, and are rewarded by a land of icebergs and soaring snow-covered peaks that rise from the sea, glaciers and ice shelves – a hostile land that nonetheless nurtures abundant wildlife that includes penguin colonies, giant albatrosses, six species of seals and different whales. And – perhaps best of all – no humans to spoil it!

Antarctic ships, mostly small by cruise standards, are designed to withstand severe conditions. Usually there are no more than a hundred

passengers (fewer for unusual trips). A wide variety of cruises is offered, allowing considerable personal choice for those lucky enough to be able to afford this unique (and expensive) journey. The grandest is a complete 9,650-km (6,000-mi) journey around the continent, from Argentina to New Zealand, but there are many less ambitious options, all fascinating in their own way.

Most of these specialist voyages commence in Argentina, with passengers flying in to Buenos Aires before transferring to the port of Ushuaia and joining the ship. From there, most cruises take in additional sights on the way to the Antarctic, such as Cape Horn, South Georgia, the Falkland Islands and South Shetland Islands. But the main attraction is always Antarctica, and almost all the visitors actually get to step ashore and gain first-hand experience of the white wonderland that is this magical continent first hand.

**YOU SHOULD KNOW:**
Every country that has any excuse whatsoever for claiming a piece of Antarctica has done so – all wanting their share, should the fragile consensus that this great wilderness should not be exploited by man ever be broken.

*Norwegian ships MS* Nordnorge *and MS* Nordkapp *in Paradise Bay*

PICTURE CREDITS

4Corners Images Limited/SIME/Belenos PS 189; /SIME/Spila Riccardo 257

Alamy//H. Abernathy/ClassicStock 52; /Peter Adams Photography 313; /AEP 309; /Amanda Ahn/dbimages 437; /Mark Alberhasky 414; /Walter G. Allgöwer/imagebroker 398; /AndyLim.com 488; /Roger Antrobus 314; /Arco Images GmbH 186 inset 1, 199, 327; /Arco Images/K Loos 247; /Jon Arnold Images Ltd. 7 picture 6, 190, 261, 356, 372, 455 top, 459, 473; /Atmotu Images 485; /Auscape International Pty Ltd 515; /Stefan Auth/imagebroker 413; /AWPhoto 510; /Bill Bachman 503, 513; /Andrew Bain 475, 508; /David Ball 357; /Romain Bayle 20; /Julia Bayne/Robert Harding Picture Library Ltd. 182; /Jason Baxter 506; /Banana Pancake 527; /Suzy Bennett 2 left, 10 inset 1, 114, 416; /Best View Stock 449; /Patricia Berwick/Grapheast 6 picture 4, 400 inset 3, 423; /Walter Bibikow/Jon Arnold Images Ltd. 35, 490; /Romero Blanco 471; /Tibor Bognar 385, 428, 457; /Peter Bowater 322; /Richard Bradley 489; /Bill Byrne/Natural Section/Design Pics Inc. 39; /Frank Blackburn 223; /blickwinkel/McPHOTO/ZAD 161, 162, 174; /G P Bowater 469; /Paul Carstairs 388; /Cephas Picture Library 286; /Nicolas Chan 505; /David Cherepuschak 241; /Carolyn Clarke 8 centre left; /Gary Cook 135, 156; /Alan Copson/Jon Arnold Images Ltd. 474; /Steve Corner/Gallo Images 144; /Dennis Cox 400 inset 2, 442; /Allan Cummins 376 inset 1, 378; /Shaun Cunningham 55; /Sue Cunningham Photographic 7 picture 5, 113; /John Daniels 504; /Sigrid Dauth Stock Photography 339; /Steve Davey Photography 183; /Cameron Davidson 44; /Michael deFreitas North America 29; /Danita Delimont 56; /Daniel Dempster Photography 62; /Deborah Dennis 154; /Adam Deschamps 145; /Deryck A Dillon 483; /Cora Edmonds/Danita Delimont 468; /Jeffery Drewitz/Cephas Picture Library 497; /Kevin Ebi 73; /Chad Ehlers 203; /Emil Enchev 365; /Javier Etcheverry 128; /eye35.com 296; /Peter Fakler 514; /Michele Falzone 478; /FAN travelstock 305; /Jose Pedro Fernandes 293; /Pavel Filatov 404; /Peter Erik Forsberg 353; /David R. Frazier Photolibrary, Inc. 22; /David Forster 270; /Danielle Gali/Jon Arnold Images Ltd. 9 bottom left; /Bertrand Gardel/Hemis.fr 28, 376 inset 2, 380; /Leslie Garland Picture Library 215; /Lyndon Giffard 517; /Gunter Gollnick/imagebroker 409; /Neil Grant 432; /Franck Guiziou/hemis.fr 429; /Darrell Gulin/Danita Delimont 111; /David W. Hamilton 9 top; /Nic Hamilton 528; /Robert Harding Picture Library Ltd. 226, 281, 292, 300, 361, 410; /Chris Harris/All Canada Photos 14; /Martin Harris 6 picture 5, 430; /Terry Harris Just Greece Photo Library 370; /Martin Harvey 146; /Jim Havey 31; /Gavin Hellier 358; /Gavin Hellier/Robert Harding Picture Library Ltd. 9 centre left above, 407, 408; /Hemis 204, 304, 349; /Brendan Hoffman 399; /Per-Andre Hoffman/LOOK Die Bildagentur der Fotografen GmbH 108; /Zach Holmes 68; /Horizon International Images Limited 530; /Peter Horree 254; /Friedrich von Horsten/Images of Africa Photobank 148; /ICSDB 288; /imagebroker 326, 334, 337, 340, 341; /imagebroker/Kurt Mobus 336; /Image Plan/Corbis Premium RF 461; /ImagesEurope 267; /Images&Stories 6 picture 2, 139 inset 1, 172, 376 inset 3, 382, 386; /ImageState 324; /IML Image Group Ltd. 366, 369, 371; /Ingolf Pompe 19 320; /INTERFOTO Pressebildagentur 76; /International Photobank 312; /Jirirezac.com 295; /Karl Johaentges/LOOK Die Bildagentur der Fotografen GmbH 446, 502; /JTB Photo Communications, Inc. 463, 464; /Jupiterimages/Agence Images 186, 276; /Michael Juno 287; /Bjanka Kadic 106; /Wolfgang Kaehler 5 picture 5, 78, 332, 405; /Rob Kavanagh 481; /Dorothy Keeler 74; /Paul Kingsley 171; /Christian Kober 484; /Art Kowalsky 479; /Hideo Kurihara 462; /Kuttig - Travel 115; /T. Lehne/Lotuseaters 451; /Gareth Leung 16; /Yadid Levy 441; /Barry Lewis 494 inset 3, 537; /Yan Liao 3 centre, 445; /Henrik Lindvall 200; /Eddie Linssen 338; /LOOK Die Bildagentur der Fotografen GmbH 238, 283, 308; /Sabine Lubenow/FAN Travelstock 329; /David Lyons 240; /Ciaran MacKechnie/Aliki Image Library 98; /Tom Mackie 222; /Jef Maion/Nomads'Land - www.maion.com 193, 205, 297; /Lois Mason 72; /Iain Masterton 406; /Pavlos Mastiki/Travel Ink 131, PCL 263, 375, 531; /Buddy Mays 7 picture 4, 11 inset 1, 65; /Neil McAllister 438; /Ross McArthur 436; /Gareth McCormack 10, 130, 248; /Roberto Meazza/IML Image Group 373; /mediacolor's 6 picture 6, 316, 318, 384; /Melba Photo Agency 285; /Mimotito/Digital Vision 51; /Brad Mitchell 53; /nagelestock.com 9 centre left below, 325, 343, 401 inset 1, 444;/Darren Niche Images 491; /David Noble Photography 265; /David Noton Photography 30, 125; /Kai-Uwe Och 198; /Ian Paterson 519; /David Pearson 400 inset 1, 434; /Doug Pearson/Jon Arnold Images Ltd. 8 top; /Bruce Percy 5 picture 1, 494, 496; /Brad Perks Lightscapes 6 picture 1, 36; /Photo Japan 458; /Photolibrary 501; /Picture Contact 291; /Javier Pierini/Photodisc 133; /Pies Specifics 118; /Nicholas Pitt 5 picture 2, 495 inset 1, 507; /Pixonnet.com 195; /Porky Pies Photography 121; /Tony Pleavin 54; /Robert Preston Photography 397; /Jürgen Priewe 450;/Neville Prosser 516; /R A Rayworth 367; /Dave Reede/All Canada Photos 18; /Magdalena Rehova 236; /Philippe Renault/Hemis.fr 21; /Bertrand Rieger/hemis.fr 401 inset 2, 493; /David Robertson 333; /Nigel Roberson 225 top; /Pep Roig 107; /Grant Rooney 427; /Galen Rowell/Mountain Light 123, 424; /Sybil Sassoon/Robert Harding Picture Library Ltd. 425; /George and Monserrate Schwartz 66; /Ian Shaw 348; /Sherab 431; /Juan Silva/Jupiter Images/Brand X 456; /Gordon Sinclair 81; /Skakanka 420; /Don Smith 526; /Don Smith/Robert Harding Picture Library Ltd. 7 picture 1, 419, 522; /Duncan Soar 470; /Joe Sohm/VisionsofAmerica/Digital Vision 37; /Joseph Sohm/Visions of America, LLC 69; /SPP Images 492; /Dave Stamboulis 418; /Will Steeley 122; /Nico Stengert/imagebroker 126; /James Sturcke 127; /Keren Su/China Span 5 picture 3, 448, 452; /Ulana Switucha 209; /tbkmedia.de 331, 352; /Tom Till 253; /Peter Titmuss 268; /Kubes Tomas/Isifa Image Service s.r.o. 173; /tompiodesign.com 354; /Peter Treanor 476; /Richard W Turner 482; /Tom Uhlman 43; /Upperhall Ltd./Robert Harding Picture Library Ltd. 422; /David Wall 494 inset 1, 494

inset 2, 500, 509, 512, 518, 524, 529; /Tony Waltham/Robert Harding Picture Library Ltd. 415, 532; /Richard Wareham Fotografie 206; /Richard Wareham/Sylvia Cordaiy Photo Library Ltd. 158; /Karl Weatherly/Digital Vision 34; /Maximilian Weinzierl 421; /Nigel Westwood 235; /Nik Wheeler 480; /Casey Williams 67; /Pete M. Wilson 110, 112; /Jochem Wijnands/Picture Contact 487; /Hans Winke 5 picture 4, 355; /Julian Worker/World Religions Photo Library 395; /WorldFoto 447; /Worldwide Picture Library 262; /Ron Yue 443, 465; /Ariadne Van Zandbergen 175; /Christian Ziegler/Danita Delimont 90; /Marek Zuk 351

Jon Arnold Images 310

Britain on View/Joe Cornish 186 inset 3, 216; /David Sellman  218

Camden Lock Market 227

John Carter 294

Corbis/Peter Adams 266; 377 inset 1, 391; /Peter Adams/JAI 186 inset 2, 350; /Peter Adams/zefa 225 bottom, 279; /O. Alamany & E. Vicens 290; /Arctic-Images 188; /Atlantide Phototravel 251, 259, 307, 393; /Dave Bartruff 377 inset 2, 396; /Tom Bean 38; /Remi Benali 169; /Niall Benvie 17; /Walter Bibikow/JAI 179, 196; /Jonathan Blair 298; /Christophe Boisvieux 178, 411; /Demetrio Carrasco/JAI 344; /Laurie Chamberlain 8 bottom; /Dean Conger 403; /Diane Cook & Len Jenshel 10 inset 2, 96; /Gary Cook/Robert Harding World Imagery 244; /Ashley Cooper 258; /Alan Copson/JAI 280; /Rob Cousins/Robert Harding World Imagery 224; /Richard Cummins 10 inset 3, 32; /Fridmar Damm/zefa 2 Centre, 328; /Daniel J. Cox 11 inset 2, 27; /Creasource 237; /Derek Croucher 231; /Fred Derwal/Hemis 439; /epa 208; /Michele Falzone/JAI 392, 472; /Natalie Fobes 15; /Frare/Davis Photography/Brand X 85; /Franz-Marc Frei 255; /Colin Garratt/Milepost 92 ? 233; /Walter Geiersperger 330, 342, 346; /Roland Gerth/zefa 321; /Franz Gingele/Handout/epa 538; /Philippe Giraud/Goodlook Pictures 94; /Franck Guiziou/Hemis 165, 264; /Blaine Harrington III 124, 374; /Martin Harvey 77, 129, 155; /Jason Hawkes 234; /Gavin Hellier/JAI 323, 359; /Gavin Hellier/Robert Harding World Imagery 284, 368; /Hemis 269, 271, 275; /Jon Hicks 9 centre, 48; /Dave G. Houser 71, 119; /Rob Howard 168; /George H. H. Huey 49, 59; /The Irish Image Collection 241, 242, 243, 246; /David Kadlubowski 50; /Wolfgang Kaehler 136, 212; /Catherine Karnow 363; /Mark Karrass 61; /Layne Kennedy 40; /Richard Klune 228, 272; /Bob Krist 6 picture 3, 82, 116, 412; /Frans Lanting 87; /Danny Lehman 498; /Michael S. Lewis 23; /Gunter Marx Photography 12; /Tim McGuire 302; /Mediolmages 191; /Wolfgang Meier/zefa 194; /Gideon Mendel for The Global Fund 138 inset 2, 157; /John Miller/Robert Harding World Imagery 260; /Christopher Morris 19; /David Muench 79; /Francesc Muntada 277; /Amos Nachoum 95; /Mike Nelson/epa 184; /Kazuyoshi Nomachi 109; /Richard T. Nowitz 33; /Pat O'Hara 387; /Charles O'Rear 137, 466; /Douglas Pearson 278, 306, 315; /Sergio Pitamitz 159; /Sergio Pitamitz/zefa 311; /Bryan Pickering/Eye Ubiquitous 319; /Jose Fuste Raga 7 picture 2, 99, 282, 454, 523; /Jose Fuste Raga/zefa 303; /Bertrand Rieger 192; /Galen Rowell 93; /Martin Ruetschi/Keystone 317; /Anders Ryman 197; /Bob Sacha 97; /Chico Sánchez/epa 103; /Skyscan 229, 232; /Paul A. Souders 7 picture 3, 24, 26, 139 inset 2, 160; /Kevin Schafer 86; /Alan Schein Photography 47; /Gregor M. Schmid 187 inset 2, 210; /Michael T. Sedam 41; /Paule Seux/Hemis 180; /Frédéric Soltan/Sygma 435; /Jon Sparks 394; /Hubert Stadler 117; /George Steinmetz 390; /Michael St. Maur Sheil 256; /Hans Strand 202; /Keren Su 252; /Emilio Suetone/Hemis 289; /Tim Tadder 299; /Tim Thompson 250; /Ivan Vdovin/JAI 213; /Pablo Corral Vega 104; /Ron Watts 64; /Tony Wilson-Bligh/Papilio 152; /Tim Wimborne/Reuters 499; /Winfried Wisniewski/zefa 150; /Adam Woolfitt 364; /Alison Wright 455 bottom, 495 inset 2, 534; /Pawel Wysocki/Hemis 335; /Michael S. Yamashita 389; /Bo Zaunders 45, 46; /Jim Zuckerman 301;

Crazy Horse Memorial Foundation 57

Halim Diker/Images&Stories 381

Renate Eichert 402

Eye Ubiquitous/Bryan Pickering/Hutchison 274; /Paul Thompson 520

Getty Images/AFP 143; /Jerry Alexander 214; /Michael Busselle 60; /Dennie Cody 70; /Connie Coleman 91; /Jason Edwards 440; /David Evans/National Geographic 101, 102; /Pio Figueroa 134; /Tim Fitzharris 63; /Michael & Patricia Fogden 138, 151; /Stuart D Franklin 3 right, 147; /Amanda Friedman 80; /Gallo Images-Lanz von Horsten 141; /Hans-Georg Gaul 142; /Gavin Hellier 170; /Paul Joynson Hicks 164; /Simeone Huber 2, 177; /Juan Mabromata/AFP 132; /Emil von Maltitz 149; /Hiroyuki Matsumoto 9 bottom right; /Natphotos 153; /Daniele Pellegrini 181; /Robert Postma 3; /Jim Richardson 219; /Whit Richardson 58; /Ellen Rooney 166; /Paul A. Zahl/National Geographic 92; /Ariadne Van Zandbergen 138 inset 3, 163

Joshua Gitlitz 129

Hedgehog House/Colin Monteath 400, 417; Andy Reisinger 521

Wendy Carlson 249

Phil Lawson 167

Jan Mariën 88

Municipality of Korsholm 207

National Geographic Society Image Collection/Otis Imboden 83

Noumea Discovery 533

James R. Page 75

Lonely Planet Images/Sune Wendelboe 176; /Woods Wheatcroft 105

Panos/Tim Dirven 362

Photolibrary Wales/Martin Barlow 221

Pictures of Britain/Dorothy Burrows 217; /Gary Hutchings 230; /John Tremaine 187 inset 1, 220;

Still Pictures/ullstein - CARO/Riedmiller 426

Alwyn Thomson 360

Travel Ink/Robin McKelvie 498

Peter Trubshaw 536

Eiki Yasuda/eyawlk60 460